Big Business and Economic Development

Around the world, conglomerates and economic groups have recently gone through a phase of rapid and impressive expansion and change. Global neo-liberal policy trends of large-scale privatisation, deregulation and economic and financial liberalisation have had major effects on these large business entities, while political relations and local circumstances also determine the outcome. Large transnational corporations from industrialised countries and the usually smaller and less transnational conglomerates that originated in a developing country or transition economy are all competing for making profits in the regions that were previously labelled as the Second and Third World.

The radical and ongoing economic concentration in the transnational-ising private sector of developing countries and transition economies is important. It not only affects economic and political relations, but social circumstances too. What explains the rise of conglomerates and economic groups in developing regions? Who are the winners and losers? What is the new role of the smaller state vis-à-vis the growing conglomerates and economic groups? And what are the consequences for (future) development? *Big Business and Economic Development* deals with these questions through a comprehensive introduction and 16 case-studies by an international and multidisciplinary group of experts who analyse the various causes and effects of the rise of 'big business' in a range of countries in Asia, Latin America, Africa and Eastern Europe.

Alex E. Fernández Jilberto is senior lecturer in International Relations at the University of Amsterdam, the Netherlands and **Barbara Hogenboom** is lecturer in Political Science at the Centre for Latin American Research and Documentation (CEDLA) in Amsterdam, the Netherlands.

Routledge Studies in International Business and the World Economy

Big Business and Economic Development

Conglomerates and economic groups in developing countries and transition economies under globalisation

Edited by
Alex E. Fernández Jilberto
and Barbara Hogenboom

Routledge
Taylor & Francis Group

LONDON AND NEW YORK

First published 2007
by Routledge
2 Park Square, Milton Park, Abingdon, Oxon OX14 4RN

Simultaneously published in the USA and Canada
by Routledge
270 Madison Ave, New York, NY 10016

Routledge is an imprint of the Taylor & Francis Group

Typeset in Baskerville by
Florence Production Ltd, Stoodleigh, Devon
Printed and bound in Great Britain by
TJI Digital, Padstow, Cornwall

British Library Cataloguing in Publication Data
A catalogue record for this book is available
from the British Library

Library of Congress Cataloging in Publication Data
Big business and economic development: conglomerates and
    economic groups in developing countries and transition economies
    under globalisation/edited by Alex E. Fernández Jilberto and
    Barbara Hogenboom.
        p. cm.
    Includes bibliographical references and index.
    1. International business enterprises – Developing countries – Case
    studies.   2. Investments, Foreign – Developing countries –   Case
    studies.   3. Developing countries – Economic policy – Case studies.
    I. Fernández Jilberto, A. E. (Alex E.)   II. Hogenboom, Barbara.
    HD2932.B54 2006
    338.8′881724 – dc22   2006020918

ISBN10: 0–415–41268–4 (hbk)
ISBN10: 0–203–96228–1 (ebk)

ISBN13: 978–0–415–41268–1 (hbk)
ISBN13: 978–0–203–96228–2 (ebk)

In loving memory of Raymond Feddema

Contents

Illustrations

Contributors

Stefan Andreasson is lecturer in Comparative Politics in the School of Politics and International Studies at Queen's University of Belfast. He received his Ph.D. from Arizona State University where he also taught Political Science. He has conducted field research on state–capital relations in South Africa, Botswana and Namibia, and worked as a research associate at the Institute for Global Dialogue in Johannesburg. He has published articles on the political economy of Southern Africa and related subjects in *Journal of World-systems Research*, *Global Dialogue*, *Journal of Contemporary African Studies* and *Political Studies*. Currently he is writing on post-development and socioeconomic transformation in Africa and the Global South.

Benedicte Bull is a political scientist and research fellow at the Centre for Development and the Environment (SUM), University of Oslo. Her main research interests include the politics of market reform and market governance in Latin America, regionalisation, and the politics of multilateral aid. She is currently also working on issues of development ethics in Latin America. She is the author of *Aid, Power and Privatization: The Politics of Telecommunication Reform in Central America* (Edward Elgar, 2005) and several articles published in journals, including *Third World Quarterly*, *New Political Economy*, *European Journal of Development Research* and *Journal of Developing Societies*.

Antonio Carmona Báez is guest lecturer at the Center for Advanced Studies on Puerto Rico and the Caribbean (CEA) in San Juan, Puerto Rico. He lectures at the College of General Studies and at the faculty of Social Sciences of the University of Puerto Rico in Rio Piedras, and is co-founder of the Puerto Rican Network for the World Social Forum. He has written various articles on Cuba's political economy, globalisation and the global justice movement. His most recent publications include *State Resistance to Globalisation in Cuba* (Pluto, 2004), 'Scholar Activism and the Global Movement for Socio-Economic Justice', in S. Thompson and S. John, *New Activism and the Corporate Response: Challenges for the 21st Century* (Palgrave Macmillan, 2003), and 'The Condition of Labour in the New

Cuban Economic Model', in A.E. Fernández Jilberto and M. Riethof, *Labour Relations in Development* (Routledge, 2002).

Alex E. Fernández Jilberto is senior lecturer in International Relations at the University of Amsterdam. He has published various articles and books on the political economy of Latin America and developing countries in general. His most recent publications include the edited volumes *Good Governance in the Era of Global Neoliberalism. Conflict and Depolitisation in Latin America, Eastern Europe, Asia and Africa* (with Jolle Demmers and Barbara Hogenboom, Routledge, 2004), *Labour Relations in Development* (with Marieke Riethof, Routledge, 2002), *Miraculous Metamorphoses: The Neoliberalization of Latin American Populism* (with Jolle Demmers and Barbara Hogenboom, Zed Books, 2001), *Regionalization and Globalization in the Modern World Economy: Perspectives on the Third World and Transitional Economies* (with André Mommen, Routledge, 1998), and 'The Political Economy of Open Regionalism in Latin America' (with Barbara Hogenboom, a special issue of the *International Journal of Political Economy*, 26 (3), 1997).

Serghei Golunov holds an MA in History from the Volgograd State University and a Ph.D. in Historical Sciences of the Institute of Oriental Studies, Russian Academy of Sciences. Currently, he works as associate professor at the Department of Regional Studies and International Relations. He is also director of the Centre for Regional and Transboundary Studies, specialising in border and security issues of the post-Soviet areas. Serghei Golunov is the author of a monograph and of numerous research papers and reports.

Barbara Hogenboom is lecturer in Political Science at CEDLA in Amsterdam. She writes on transnational politics, globalisation processes, and political and economic development in Mexico and Latin America. Among her recent publications are *Good Governance in the Era of Global Neoliberalism: Conflict and Depolitisation in Latin America, Eastern Europe, Asia and Africa* (edited with Jolle Demmers and Alex E. Fernández Jilberto, Routledge, 2004), *Miraculous Metamorphoses: The Neoliberalization of Latin American Populism* (edited with Jolle Demmers and Alex E. Fernández Jilberto, Zed Books, 2001), and *Mexico and the NAFTA Environment Debate: The Transnational Politics of Economic Integration* (International Books, 1998).

Momoko Kawakami is researcher at the Institute of Developing Economies (IDE-JETRO) in Chiba, Japan, and a Ph.D. candidate at the Department of Economics, University of Tokyo. She has published various articles on the development process of Taiwanese manufacturing industries, small and medium-sized enterprises, and globalisation of the Taiwanese economy. Her latest English publication is 'Changing Roles of Innovation and Imitation in Industrial Development: The Case of the Machine Tool Industry' (with Tetsushi Sonobe and Keijiro Otsuka, *Economic Development and Cultural Change*, 52 (1), 2003).

Piet Konings is senior researcher at the African Studies Centre, University of Leiden, The Netherlands. He has published widely on the political economy and labour in Africa, especially in Ghana and Cameroon. His most recent publications include *Negotiating Anglophone Identity: A Study in the Politics of Recognition and Representation in Cameroon* (Brill, 2003), *Trajectoires de Libération en Afrique Contemporaine* (Karthala, 2000) and *Unilever Estates in Crisis and the Power of Organizations in Cameroon* (LIT Verlag, 1998). He has also contributed to several volumes by the editors of this book.

Anna Laven is affiliated to the Amsterdam Institute for Metropolitan and International Development Studies (AMIDSt), University of Amsterdam, where she is conducting a Ph.D. research project on the interaction between local clusters and global chain governance among cocoa producers in Ghana. She studied Political Science and Environmental Management, and has participated in (fieldwork) research on international relations, environmental management and sustainable consumption and production.

J. Thomas Lindblad is Swedish-born but received his academic education in the United States and the Netherlands. He has been working as an economic historian at the University of Leiden since 1975 and currently holds a joint appointment at the Department of History and the Department of Southeast Asian Studies. His specialisation is the modern economic history of Indonesia, in particular since independence. In recent years, he has held positions as a guest researcher/lecturer at the Australian National University in Canberra, the Hankuk University of Foreign Studies in Seoul, and the Nagoya University in Japan. His recent publications include the co-authored textbook *The Emergence of a National Economy: An Economic History of Indonesia, 1800–2000* (Allen & Unwin, 2002), and the monograph *Foreign Investment in Southeast Asia in the Twentieth Century* (Macmillan, 1998).

André Mommen works at the Department of Political Science, University of Amsterdam. In the past, his research focused on neoliberal reforms in developing and transitional countries. Currently, he is writing on the effects of reforms in both developed and developing countries on the position of trade unions, and on Hungarian and Russian political and economic development. Among his recent publications is *Regionalization and Globalization in the Modern World Economy: Perspectives on the Third World and Transitional Economies* (edited with Alex E. Fernández Jilberto, Routledge, 1998).

Mariusz Niemiec holds MA degrees in Economics and in Law, and a Ph.D. in Economic Science. He is lecturer and research fellow in the International Economic Relations and European Integration Department, Institute of International Studies, University of Wrocław. His areas of expertise are international economic relations, international finance, European economic integration, foreign trade, foreign direct investment, and economic cooperation in Central and Eastern Europe. Currently his research is on foreign direct investment in Central and Eastern Europe, and economic cooperation between Poland and the European Union. He has published, among other things, the co-authored article 'European Union', in E. Stadtmuller's *Encyclopaedic Dictionary* (Wrocław, 2003).

Wioletta Niemiec has an MA in Economics and a Ph.D. in Economic Science. She is lecturer and research fellow in the International Economic Relations and European Integration Department, Institute of International Studies, University of Wrocław. Her areas of expertise are international economic relations, international finance, European economic integration, foreign trade and international economic organisation. Her current research is on economic cooperation between Poland and the European Union, and on the World Trade Organization. Her publications include the co-authored article 'European Union', in E. Stadtmuller's *Encyclopaedic Dictionary* (Wrocław, 2003).

Kwame Nimako holds degrees in Sociology and Economics from the University of Amsterdam, where he currently teaches International Relations at the Department of Political Science. He worked as a Tinbergen Fellow at the Department of Agricultural and Development Economics, and he was lecturer in Race and Ethnic Relations and Development Studies at the Centre for Race and Ethnic Studies, both at the University of Amsterdam. Among his books are *Beyond Multiculturalisation: Amsterdam Southeast as Strategic Location* (Amsterdam, 1998 – in Dutch) and *Economic Change and Political Conflict in Ghana, 1600–1990* (Amsterdam, 1991), and he contributed to *Liberalization in the Developing World: Institutional and Economic Changes in Latin America, Africa and Asia* (edited by Alex E. Fernández Jilberto and André Mommen, Routledge, 1996).

Kurt W. Radtke studied Economics, Sinology, Japanese and Russian, and obtained a Ph.D. in Chinese from the Australian National University Canberra. He worked at the Department of Japanese at Waikato University, the Centre for Contemporary China and the Japanese Department of Leiden University, where he was appointed professor of Japanese Studies in 1987. His current position is at the Institute of Asia-Pacific Studies at Waseda University, Tokyo. He has published widely on politics and security in East Asia in English, Japanese and Chinese. His main books are *China's Relations with Japan, 1945–83: The Role of Liao Chengzhi* (Manchester University Press, 1990) and *Poetry of the Yuan Dynasty* (ANU, Faculty of Asian Studies Monographs, 1984). He has edited a number of books, including *Competing for Integration: Japan, Europe, Latin America and Their Strategic Partners* (with Marianne Wiesebron, M.E. Sharpe, 2002) and *Comprehensive Security* (with Raymond Feddema, Brill, 2000).

Eva Rakel is assistant professor at the University of Amsterdam, where she teaches International Relations. She is currently writing a Ph.D. thesis on the Iranian Islamic political elite and their foreign relations, with special focus on the relations between Iran and the European Union. Her publications include 'Paradigms of Iranian Policy in Central Eurasia and Beyond', in Mehdi Parvizi Amineh and Henk Houweling's *Central Eurasia in Global Politics: Conflict, Security and Development* (Brill, 2004).

Roberto Rocco is a researcher at the Department of Urbanism, Delft University of Technology, the Netherlands. He has published various (translated) articles on urban policies, foreign direct investment and cities, and on Sao Paolo. Currently he is working on a comparative study of globalisation and the transformation of urban structures during the 1990s in Brazil and the Netherlands.

Miguel Teubal is professor of Economics at the University of Buenos Aires, Argentina, and researcher of the National Council for Scientific and Technological Research (CONICET). He has published widely on the political economy of food, agriculture and poverty in Latin America and Argentina. Recent articles and books are 'Tierra y reforma agraria en América Latina' (*Realidad Económica* 200, 2003), 'Soja transgénica y la crisis del modelo agroalimentario argentino' (*Realidad Económica* 196, 2003), *Agro y alimentos en la globalización: una perspectiva crítica* (with Javier Rodríguez, La Colmena, 2002), and *Globalización y expansión agroindustrial: Superación de la pobreza en América Latina?* (Ediciones Corregidor, 1995). He has also contributed chapters to previous volumes by the present editors.

Vasiliy Valuev is senior lecturer in International Relations at Nizhny Novgorod State University, Russia. He published various articles and books on the political economy of Russia's governance problems, and the role of big business in the industrial infrastructure of Nizhny Novgorod. His most recent publications include *Regional Defense and Security Structures: Corruptive and Anti-corruption Strategies* (Rus-Expert Transit Center, 2004), 'Russian Regions: Russia's foreign policy challenges' (*Nizhny Novgorod International Studies Journal* Fall 2002–Spring 2003), 'EU Enlargement and Kaliningrad: Bringing or Bridging Possible New Divisions', in Andreas Goldthau and Pavel Onokhine, *European Union – Russia: Interaction without Strategies?* (Ekaterinburg, 2003), and 'The Influence of Political and Economic Development of Nizhny Novgorod Oblast upon its Worldwide Positioning'(*NIC SENEX* October 2001–April 2002).

Hans van Zon is professor in Central and East European Studies at the University of Sunderland. Previously he worked for the Commission of the European Union, the University of Amsterdam, and the Institute of Work and Technology in Gelsenkirchen. He has published, among other things, *The Political Economy of Independent Ukraine* (Palgrave Macmillan, 2000) and *The Future of Industry in Central and Eastern Europe* (Avebury, 1996).

Preface

Nowadays it has become relatively common to claim the definite triumph of global markets over states. With this slogan apologists refer to the substitution of global Keynesianism and the end of economic nationalism of developing countries and centrally planned economies, which are a result of the neoliberal globalisation that took off in the early 1980s with the so-called debt crisis. In developing countries around the world policies of structural adjustment, privatisation and deregulation of the economies were implemented, ending most of the previous state intervention in economic activities and the model of the 'entrepreneurial state'. A similar process occurred in the so-called transition economies after the Berlin Wall fell in 1989. With their dreams of self-regulating markets and societies, the most fervent proponents of global markets have welcomed the dominance of neoliberal policies for bringing effective damage to their main enemy: the state.

The transfer of companies from the public sector to the private sector in developing countries and transition economies sooner or later involved a major transnational component. While foreign investors were among the first owners of privatised state firms, usually the technocratic elites carrying out the privatisation favoured the major local conglomerates and economic groups with access to transnational financial and investment capital. Shortly after, however, several of the former state companies acquired by local entrepreneurs were (partly) sold to transnational corporations. The various financial crises that have hit developing regions since the mid-1990s – the Mexican peso crisis, the East Asian crisis, the Russian debt moratorium, and Argentina's tumbling down – and the global effects of (fear of) contagion and international pressures for standardised national policies to prevent more crises have played a decisive role in the latter process of transnationalisation.

The process of economic concentration in the transnationalising private sector of developing regions is a relatively neglected issue in the debates on globalisation and neoliberal restructuring. Yet, as the contributions in this volume show, the radical denationalisation and privatisation of economic development, and the transformation of economic groups and conglomerates into the 'motors of economic growth' and the bearers of globalisation have deepened social inequalities and have turned economic concentration into a decisive political factor in the relations between economy, politics, the market and the state. A critical analysis of these profound changes and their many shapes in various countries in Asia, Latin America, Africa, and Central and Eastern Europe is the leading objective of this book, linking the studies of the role of conglomerates and economic groups to broader debates on global neoliberalism.

Evidently we would not have been able to achieve this profound and broad scholarly aim without the 18 knowledgeable country and region experts who have collaborated with us on this book. It has been an honour to edit the collection of their interesting, well-documented and thought-provoking analyses, and it has been a pleasure to work with these colleagues from different disciplines and all parts of the world, who committed themselves to working on this transnational project within the set limitations of theme and time. We dedicate this book to the memory of Dr Raymond Feddema out of gratitude for his support and for constantly reminding us of the social responsibility of all intellectual efforts.

Alex E. Fernández Jilberto
and Barbara Hogenboom

1 The new expansion of conglomerates and economic groups

An introduction to global neoliberalisation and local power shifts

Alex E. Fernández Jilberto and Barbara Hogenboom

In many parts of the world, conglomerates and economic groups have recently gone through a phase of rapid and impressive expansion and change. Global neoliberal policy trends of large-scale privatisation, deregulation and economic and financial liberalisation have had major effects on these large business entities. While allowing for more 'play room', financial resources and investment opportunities, these new circumstances have equally enlarged competition with other big corporate 'players'. Large transnational corporations from industrialised countries and the usually smaller and less transnational conglomerates that originated in developing countries or transition economies are competing with and among each other to make profits from or in those regions that were previously labelled as the Second and Third Worlds.

While the numeric side of the surge of foreign as well as home-grown direct investment flows in developing regions during the 1990s has been covered by international institutions, there is less knowledge of the changing nature and increasing economic importance of large economic groups and conglomerates in these regions. In general only in cases of a crisis or a scandal does one learn about the size and influence of these enterprises: many people heard for the first time about the *chaebols* of South Korea at the time of the Southeast Asian financial crisis; apart from Russians and energy specialists few knew about Yukos before the allegations of massive fraud in 2003; and India's largest industrial group, Reliance, only became international news when in 2004 the two leading Ambani brothers started a soap-opera-like row. Yet many more of these 'local' corporate giants control one or more domestic and/or regional (product) markets. This can result from historical dominance, buying privatised state firms, links with transnational capital, (ongoing or new) state protection or support, but often from a combination of several of these factors. The aim of presenting and comparing the contemporary role of conglomerates and economic groups in a range of developing countries and transition economies is to provide useful and much needed insight into the political economy of local development and global insertion of these parts of the world.

The transformation of the private sector into the predominant force for economic development in low income countries was the main objective of the international policies of liberalisation with a reduced role of the state in the economy. Competition would thus be enhanced and this 'survival of the fittest' would boost growth. The International Monetary Fund, for instance, claims that

> [a]mong many developing countries, the direct involvement of the state in economic activity is large and wide-spread, with state-owned enterprises having monopoly rights in a large number of sectors . . . Often state-owned enterprises are operated inefficiently, and despite the monopoly status they tend either to make low profits or to run persistent and large losses that burden government budgets . . . Market-oriented structural reforms . . . may be expected to boost growth by reducing distortions and encouraging greater private sector participation.
>
> (IMF 1997: 85–8)

The World Bank (1997: 61), states that

> in all too many countries . . . [p]rivate initiative is still held hostage to a legacy of antagonistic relations with the state. Rigid regulations inhibit private initiative. And state enterprises . . . dominate economic terrain that could more fruitfully be given over to competitive markets.

Although the Bank also stressed the importance of the role of the state and transparency (especially in the privatisation process), and over the years seems to have become less inclined to orthodox economic theory, it joined the IMF and other leading institutions in predominantly promoting 'free markets and sound money', which raised the expectations of this agenda to unrealistic heights (Krugman 1995).

Since the early 1980s, in almost all economies in development or transition, policies of opening the commercial and financial markets and privatisation have been key to economic restructuring. Large companies and economic groups in these countries often profited from privatisation, but they also had to adapt to the requirements of neoliberal restructuring. In the transition economies, the new entrepreneurial class is largely formed by the nomenclature (state bureaucracy) that inherited an important part of the state companies, but they have had great difficulty adapting to the neoliberal way of restoring capitalism (Ellman 2004). In general, the association of 'local' large companies with transnational capital became the crucial link to gain access to the international market and new technologies. Still, in many other cases transnational companies (TNCs) became the main new owners of the privatised firms, either immediately or when after some time the local private owner decided to sell it again. It is estimated that between 1988 and 1995 in a total of 88 developing countries and transition economies some 3,801 state companies were sold to TNCs; their assets, generally devalued for their privatisation, represented a value of \$135 billion (Suárez 1999). Simultaneously, large TNCs have turned into some of the principal agents of globalisation, which may be illustrated by the fact that the total sales of the five largest TNCs (General Motors, Ford, Toyota, Exxon and Royal Dutch Shell) are almost twice as much as the domestic product of all the countries in Southern Asia, and thrice that of sub-Saharan Africa (UNDP 1997).

What are the actual implications for developing regions of the global tendency for economic concentration in the private sector? First of all, economic concentration not only affects companies and the economy, but in many cases also political relations, social circumstances, and the prospects for future development of developing countries and transition economies. More profoundly, this trend signifies a process of restructuring of the relations between capital, labour and the state, which were previously shaped by Keynesianism and/or economic nationalism in developing economies, in the centrally planned economies of Eastern Europe, and the socialist economies of the Third World. In most developing countries it was the international crisis of foreign debt starting in Mexico in 1982 followed by structural adjustment policies that marked the start of the substitution of global Keynesianism by global neoliberalism (and neoliberal globalisation). In the case of the transition economies, the substitution of the model of centrally planned economies by neoliberalism was a process that followed the falling of the Berlin Wall (1989) and the collapse of the Soviet Union.

This volume aims to assess how privatisation, liberalisation and regional and global economic integration have affected the big players of the corporate sector in various developing countries and transition economies, as well as the wider economic, social and political implications of their recent expansion. Instead of commenting on theoretical debates with respect to the so-called pros and cons of neoliberal restructuring, the contributors have been asked to put forward empirically based analyses of the effects (including problems) of economic restructuring, foreign direct investment (FDI) and the enlarged role of the private sector in the country or region of their expert knowledge. Who currently owns the large enterprises in developing regions? To what extent have they been transnationalised? How do they operate under these new circumstances? Have they become more autonomous from politics? And are they really acting as the new motor for development? Evidently the answers to these questions not only enable a better understanding of the recent changes and current situation of conglomerates and economic groups, but may also help substantiate broader debates on the true nature of neoliberal globalisation for developing countries and transition economies, and possibly even contribute to a revision of theories and policies that have shaped many people's lives yet often in ways other than anticipated.

So far the extensive media attention for successes and scandals of conglomerates and economic groups has not been matched by similar academic attention to their development. And while several studies have been written on multinational companies from industrialised countries operating in industrialising and non-industrial countries,[1] the role and development of large 'local' economic groups in these parts of the world have hardly been analysed in a comparative setting. The economic groups and conglomerates that are currently on the rise in developing countries and transition economies are often a mix of old entities that have adapted well to new circumstances and new private sector giants that have emerged with the neoliberal tide. Next to shifts in the national economic model, and global economic and financial changes, the rise of conglomerates and economic groups is in many cases a result of specific political (elite) relations, links to foreign capital (in particular FDI) and local (historically evolved) circumstances.

In this book, the 16 case studies by country or region specialists present a fascinating insight in the development of conglomerates and economic groups in developing and transition economies at times of global neoliberalisation and neoliberal globalisation. The case studies include large and small countries (e.g. Russia and Puerto Rico), economies with advanced industries, economies with major oil and gas reserves as well as agricultural economies (e.g. Taiwan, Indonesia and Ghana), and countries with vastly differing current or historical regimes, including Southern Africa, Ukraine, Argentina, Cameroon and Iran. Together these analyses point both at several coinciding events and converging tendencies, and at the many different effects of economic concentration in the private sector resulting from specific local backgrounds and circumstances.

This introductory chapter discusses the main international developments that form the general context for all these country and regional case studies on the changing roles of economic groups and conglomerates. After clarifying the use of some definitions, the first section describes how a new economic model has conquered the world since the early 1980s, while the second section assesses how political and economic differences have influenced its specific shapes in various regions and countries. The third section provides an overview of the tendencies of change and growth of conglomerates and economic groups in developing countries and transition economies. In the fourth section, the experiences of low and middle income countries with the transnationalisation of investment capital are discussed. The fifth section, then, looks into the international attention on the issue of competitiveness, and the envisaged new role for the state in improving a country's position on the various global competitiveness indexes. Finally, in the concluding section, the prospects for the future of developing and transition economies after almost three decades of neoliberal restructuring are discussed. Which conglomerates and economic groups are likely to survive another few decades of global neoliberalism? And what may be the effects on the development of these regions?

In academic studies, economic groups and conglomerates are usually defined as an assembly of companies that function largely independently yet operate under some form of centralised control.[2] Their activities may be concentrated in one sector, they may consist of a chain of integrated production activities, but the very large ones are often made up of entities that operate in different sectors, usually including the financial sector. The structures of ownership, control and finance within economic groups vary greatly, and tend to be complex. The most straightforward organisation can be found in horizontally structured economic groups in which all units operate in one sector, performing the same activities, for example, a chain of hotels. Cases of a chain of integrated activities (e.g. production, assembly and distribution) are labelled vertical integration. The largest are generally diversified groups operating in various sectors with many companies, which can include horizontally and/or vertically integrated parts. The companies of a group may attract their 'own' external capital, for instance through bank loans or the issue of shares. However, within the group, capital flows may be channelled from one company or activity to another in the form of loans, bank guarantees or shares, possibly via a holding company of the group (Basave Kunhardt 2001: 10–15; Péres 1998). The complex and often far from transparent structures of ownership and finance of such large and diversified groups is a source of frustration to external suppliers of capital and tax departments – and of course to the scholars who want to study them.

When writing here about large economic groups and conglomerates, we sometimes use the adjective 'local' and 'foreign' to distinguish between, on the one hand, companies originating in the country or region under consideration, and on the other hand, companies of foreign origin, often multinational companies from industrialised countries in the West, but of course advanced Asian multinationals too. Yet many of the 'local' giants also have a presence in several countries (inside and some also outside their region) and are therefore not local in the narrow sense of the word. Moreover, large local conglomerates tend to also use foreign capital in one form or another (joint ventures, shares, credits, etc.). Finally, the terms multinational and transnational are both used when referring to companies that operate in several countries or regions.

Neoliberal globalisation and national policies

Ideologically, the triumph of global neoliberalism has been expressed in theoretical debates about globalisation, understood as the transnationalisation of neoliberalism, which in the case of developing countries put an end to the international strategy of the New International Economic Order

(NIEO), while, in countries of Eastern Europe, produced the collapse of the historic attempt to create an alternative system to global capitalism. The anti-state ideology that accompanied these processes was expressed in the idea of a 'refoundation of capitalism' for developing countries and the neo-liberal 'capitalist restoration' in transition economies. Both the substitution of global Keynesianism and the collapse of the socialist economies brought a definitive end to 'state capitalism' and the 'era of regulations' (1945–70), thus permitting transition from an entrepreneurial state that regulated the relations between capital and labour to a state taken hostage by international capital flows and an economy self-regulated by market actors (Chang 2004; Clark 1999; Strange 1996, 2002).

The neoliberal restructuring processes and the direct agents of globalisa-tion (particularly the IMF, World Bank and private foreign investors) intro-duced transformations driving towards the rise of the neoliberal state that searches for strategic alliances with other states and/or international organ-isations in order to jointly resolve the difficulties presented by globalisation. No longer is the nation-state the centre of everything, but it has turned into a node of a supranational network of states on the one hand, while on the other hand previous tasks and responsibilities of the nation-state have been decentralised to sub-national (local) state institutions and even non-governmental organisations, giving way to the rise of the nation-co-state (Castells 2003). In regional economic terms this is expressed in the active par-ticipation of states in the regionalisation of the global economy (regional eco-nomic integration in the cases of Mercado Común del Sur (Common Market of the South) (MERCOSUR), North American Free Trade Agreement (NAFTA), Association of South East Asian Nations (ASEAN) and Asia-Pacific Economic Cooperation (APEC) or in the strategy of open regionalism that aims to guarantee the multilateral economic participation in various forms of regional integration (Fernández Jilberto and Hogenboom 1997).

The global spreading of neoliberal ideology and policies during the last two decades of the twentieth century gave way to fundamental changes in national economies, governance and politics around the world. The triumph of capitalism that went with the end of the Cold War was largely captured by the neoliberal current, resulting in the reform of various capitalist and socialist models. This does not imply that the diversity of regional and national economic models has been fully erased, since national programmes of neoliberal restructuring have been partly shaped by the historical circum-stances (economic, political, social) and existing policies. Yet imbued with neoliberal thought, capitalist and socialist regimes have gradually taken the shape of neoliberal regimes, largely irrespective of the type of party or coalition in government.

It was the debt crisis of the early 1980s that drew a watershed between the era that combined capitalist models inspired by Keynes and socialist models inspired by Marx, Lenin and Mao, and the subsequent neoliberal revolution. Starting with Mexico's moratorium on its debt payments in

August 1982, the crisis rapidly spread through Latin America and then through the rest of the world. As a result, the cracks that had appeared in international Keynesianism during the 1970s, caused by the end of the system of fixed exchange rates, the first oil crisis, stagnating growth, mounting inflation rates and public budget deficits, could no longer be mended. The belief that the nation-state could operate as the determining force for balancing economic growth with the help of interest rates, public investment, state-owned companies and cheap state credit disappeared.

In this context, and under the leadership of Ronald Reagan and Margaret Thatcher, renewed (economic) liberal thought gained support. The fact that the New Right had gained control in the United States and the United Kingdom contributed to the expansion of neoliberalism throughout the rest of the world. A free market for capital, goods and services, with the state's role being largely limited to facilitating this market, was successfully declared the sole and indivisible solution to economic stagnation and budget deficits. But this was far from a voluntary process. The governments of developing countries had no other option than to go along with this current if they were to be accepted for new foreign loans and the renegotiation of debt payments, which were both indispensable for economic stabilisation and recovery. After years of (too) easy lending at the global capital markets the debt crisis forced developing countries to hand over their sovereignty de facto outlining in their national economic policies to the international financial organisations, particularly to the IMF and the World Bank, which also happen to be the gateways to the private capital markets. And at the time that countries came knocking on the doors of the Bretton Woods institutions, they had passed through a process of ideological reorientation that resulted in the policy of structural adjustment. Latin America's early experience with (authoritarian) liberalisation following the Chicago Boys' recipe was posed as an example to the new market democracies of Africa, Asia and later Central and Eastern Europe. The major influence of the United States in the IMF and the World Bank was crucial to the global spreading of the new neoliberal orientation. Around the globe, the economic policies of developing and post-socialist countries came to be heavily influenced by the transnational bureaucracies of the World Bank, the IMF and transnational forums such as the Group of 7, the World Economic Forum (WEF) (Davos) and the Trilateral Commission.

Apart from the general condition requiring a sound macroeconomic policy, the Bretton Woods institutions demanded many specific reforms directed at opening up the economies that were previously for some part sheltered against fierce foreign competition. Two main elements were the privatisation of state enterprises and the liberalisation of flows of goods, services and capital. In the 1990s, the countries in Central and Eastern Europe went through an accelerated process of liberalisation, while developing countries continued their programmes for liberalising their national markets. Developing and transition countries were told that opening up for transnational capital would

be beneficial for economic growth for it would, among other things, generate access to sources of cheaper private credit. For the state, liberalisation and
privatisation implied the loss of much of its previous economic steering capacity, either to the corporate sector or to international institutions. Partly as
a result of this development, the deregulation of national economies went
hand in hand with new initiatives for regional economic cooperation, that is,
integration in the global market via regionalisation (e.g. MERCOSUR,
NAFTA and ASEAN).

Socially and politically the rise and spread of neoliberal regimes have also
been very important. From a historical perspective the old bi-polar world
was a relatively stable system with steadily growing material wealth, particularly in the developed capitalist world, and manageable crises in both
camps. Economic growth was the key for political and military success for
all regimes. The breakdown of communism eliminated a competing model,
which had obliged most Western leaders to respect some kind of equilibrium between the worlds of capital and labour. In addition, the crisis and
fall of the Soviet Union gave way to rapid impoverishment of the countries
of the former socialist bloc and to disarray in most of the Third World.
The end of the Eastern bloc and the rapid liberalisation of certain parts of
the Chinese economy, in the early 1990s, further consolidated the globalisation of neoliberalism. The end of regimes based on welfare and import
substitution policies that embraced large parts of the working classes has
given way to further integration in the capitalist world system of practically
all countries, thereby contributing to a gradual denationalisation of politics.
The role and the functions of the state have become increasingly focused
on functionality of the global market and capital. Simultaneously, democratisation took place as authoritarian regimes of the Right and the Left
were defeated. Around the world, these developments had a similar impact
on different accumulation regimes and political systems. Economic liberalisation, denationalisation of policy-making, and formal democratisation
became the dominant elements of regime changes in Eastern and Southern
Europe, Latin America, Africa and Asia, with the Arab world as a notable
exception. While most citizens of these parts of the world thus gained with
respect to formal political rights, their economic and social rights did not
expand accordingly, as increasing socioeconomic inequality at a global (and
often also national) level, and ongoing massive poverty demonstrate.

Under these specific historical circumstances, neoliberalism and globalisation have been reinforcing each other, while the national context has
shaped the impact of these major forces, resulting in a variety of neoliberal
regimes. In the 1990s, thinking and acting in terms of economic globality
was strongly fed by the open market policies put in place in most countries,
while the other way around, globalisation strongly enhanced neoliberal
restructuring. The global process of neoliberalisation has not produced a
uniform output, but various neoliberal regimes, depending on the national
economic model and the political circumstances (Demmers, Fernández

Jilberto and Hogenboom 2004). The different points of departure and variety in content and timing of neoliberal restructuring is reflected, among other things, in an overview of the proceeds from privatisation (Table 1.1). National political elites played an important role: their views and interests, their relative autonomy in national politics and their relations with international actors (states, multilateral organisations and transnational banks and companies) substantially affected the specific contents and exceptions of neoliberal policies. Let us here briefly review some trends in Central and Eastern Europe (CEE), Africa, Latin America and Asia.

Regional perspectives

In CEE the restructuring of market–state relations has been the most sweeping. While the economic changes were more profound than anywhere else – moving from a socialist model to neoliberal capitalism – they also were implemented faster. Within less than a decade (the 1990s) the transition was a fact, and the region had opened up to global private capital. Most of the former socialist countries in Europe have decisively distanced themselves from the ex-Soviet Union and have been linking up to the European Union, either as new members (Hungary, Poland, Slovenia, Slovakia, the Czech Republic, Estonia, Latvia and Lithuania) or as candidate members (Bulgaria, Romania and Croatia). In effect, large flows of FDI have started to move into CEE countries, and the main conglomerates and economic groups are dominated by foreign capital, as can be read in the contribution of Wioletta and Mariusz Niemiec in this volume. There are of course also several local giants that have resulted from the large-scale privatisations in the region (see Table 1.1), such as the two steel and coal conglomerates System Capital Management and the Industrial Union of Donbass in the Donetsk region of Ukraine, which are analysed by Hans van Zon. At the same time, many new 'local' big businesses struggle hard to survive in the opening markets, such as in the case of the Polish 'rising star' telecom and power conglomerate Elektrim, which after some risky acquisitions and legal woes (following Elektrim's attempt to solve its cash flow problems by playing off the multinationals Vivendi Universal against Deutsche Telekom) had to file for bankruptcy (*The Economist* 21 October 2002).

In Russia, on the other hand, there has been less foreign capital, especially after the Russian moratorium in 1998, which leaves plenty of opportunity for Russian conglomerates to expand by investing in low-priced local companies. Capital earned by exporting raw materials such as oil, gas, steel and aluminium, is spent within their own country on holdings in manufacturing, defence and communication systems. Contrary to the tendency among TNCs from industrialised countries to focus on core businesses, Russians thus diversify their investments and operations. And this might be just the beginning of 'the conglomerate phase' in Russia (*Business Week* 16 July 2001). The internationally most well-known (and infamous) conglomerate is Yukos, which has had a major clash with the Russian state. In this volume, the rise of oligarchs in Russia and the regions Nizhny Novgorod and Volgograd is discussed by André Mommen with Vasiliy Valuev and Serghei Golunov.

In sub-Saharan Africa the structural adjustment programmes were the start of the region's neoliberalisation, but they did not create the 'promised' development. While state-mediated mechanisms of accumulation were ended, no viable alternatives were created, and the specific shortcomings of the domestic economies were not taken into account. For instance, in the industrial sector many incentives to promote (infant) industry were dismantled, giving occasion to a dramatic de-industrialisation. Akyüz and Gore (2001: 272) argue that sustained growth has not returned to the region because 'even where adjustment policies have been rigorously implemented, they have failed to establish a sustained accumulation process linking invest-ment with savings and export'. The chapter on Cameroon by Piet Konings and the chapter on Ghana by Anna Laven expand on these issues.

Other elements that help explain the relatively bad economic results of Africa are related to attitudes towards 'big business'. In sub-Saharan Africa, domestic capitalists tend to be regarded with suspicion. In particular modern large enterprises run by nationals of former colonial powers (e.g. 'British' in Zimbabwe) or by persons from an ethnic minority (including Asians) have a history of being seen as a negative. The colonial and post-colonial tendency to let political and ideological interests dominate over a pragmatic approach in Africa's economic policy-making continued with the introduction of the neoliberal model, when 'a bias against, and hostility towards, the nascent national entrepreneurial class' was replaced by 'a bias against state inter-

Table 1.1 Proceeds from privatisation by region, 1990–6 (US$ million)

	1990	1991	1992	1993	1994	1995	1996	1990–6
Latin America and the Caribbean	10,915	18,723	15,560	10,487	8,198	4,615	13,919	82,417
East Asia and the Pacific	376	835	5,161	7,155	5,507	5,411	2,679	27,123
Europe and Central Asia	1,262	2,551	3,626	3,988	3,956	9,641	5,466	30,491
Middle East and North Africa	2	17	70	417	782	746	1,477	3,510
South Asia	29	996	1,558	974	2,666	917	889	8,029
Sub-Saharan Africa	74	1,121	205	630	595	472	745	3,843
All developing countries	12,658	24,243	26,180	23,651	21,704	21,802	25,175	155,413

Sources: Lieberman and Kirkness (1998); Manzetti (1999).

vention per se' (Akyüz and Gore 2001: 283). Related to the latter tendency, some interesting contrasts show in Kwame Nimako's contribution to this volume on Africa's development strategies when compared with those of China. Also in post-apartheid South Africa the balance of power between the government and economic actors has clearly shifted in favour of the business community, foreign investors and international financial institutions, and African National Congress (ANC) economic thinking put a 'disproportionate emphasis on the significance of foreign capital' for growth (Habib and Padayachee 2000: 249). A comparative analysis of South Africa and Zimbabwe by Stefan Andreasson provides useful insights into the development and nature of their new capitalist elites.

Latin America's restructuring was particularly far-reaching with respect to privatisation, as Table 1.1 shows, involving a variety of support mechanisms for the new owners of former state firms. In the pre-neoliberal phase, national capital accumulation was particularly supported by policies of trade limitation and numerous state-owned companies (large and small) that were to enhance industrialisation based on import substitution. Conversely, neoliberal theories and policies have stressed the merits of open markets, corporate competition and an end to state regulation and support for certain sectors and groups of producers. In reality, however, the favourable arrangements for acquiring privatised state companies, and the special rescue efforts at times of crisis have served their new (local and foreign) private owners well (Fernández Jilberto and Hogenboom 2004).

Although investing through acquiring privatised companies was relatively cheap, there have been many cases in which the companies' risks were still transferred to the public sector, if not through national policies then through international policies. The case of Argentina has shown that a government that is unwilling to compensate some of the world's largest multinationals for losses caused by a financial and economic crisis (losses they can offset more easily than the public sector of Argentina) can be forced to do so under World Bank regulations. In this volume, the chapters on Latin America – on Argentina by Miguel Teubal, on Brazil by Roberto Rocco, on Central America by Benedicte Bull, on Puerto Rico by Antonio Carmona Báez, and on Chile and Mexico by Alex E. Fernández Jilberto and Barbara Hogenboom – affirm the importance of policies and politics at times of privatisation and crisis. In addition, they show that apart from economic concentration, transnationalisation is a strong tendency in Latin America's private sector, above all in the financial sector.

In the 1980s, contrary to crisis-struck countries in Africa, Latin America and CEE, things seemed to be moving in the right direction in Asia. Especially in East Asia's newly industrialising countries, which were in no need of a different model of development and integration in the world market. Since the 1960s, many economies in South and East Asia had experienced sustained high growth, together with a reduction of poverty and of income inequality. While private investment was high, public investment remained important and was countercyclical to the reduction in private investment in periods of economic contraction. This state support for the expansion of domestic business interests involved a long-term and intensive relationship (sometimes even typified as 'Korea, Inc.'). Since this model produced mainly positive economic and social results – the East Asian miracle – most East Asian governments were sceptical of neoliberal policies. In their view, '[a] major drawback of the neoliberal model was that it would entail a loss of national influence over resource allocation and strategies of industrial promotion and technological upgrading' (Whitehead 2000: 76).

However, in the early 1990s, policies of financial liberalisation ('sponsored' by the IMF and the World Bank) dismantled or weakened the functioning of several institutional arrangements for state guidance of private investment and for checks and balances on external borrowing. According to the United Nations Conference on Trade and Development (UNCTAD), this contributed to the massive flow of foreign capital to Asian corporations (largely via banks), and to the subsequent financial crisis (UNCTAD 2003: 85). Rather than acknowledging their responsibility and short-sightedness, the international financial institutions have used this crisis to further their aim of developing open markets in the crisis-hit countries. In this volume's section on Asia, Kurt W. Radtke contrasts this agenda to some specificities of East Asian notions of *public* and *private*, and the consequences of these contrasts for governance. Next to J. Thomas Lindblad's account of the power of conglomerates in Indonesia, and the chapter by Momoko Kawakami on the rise of economic groups in the telecommunications sector, this volume includes a piece by Eva Rakel on the case of Iran, where so-called Islamic Foundations (*bonyads*) are major economic entities, with the large ones actually operating as conglomerates.

Economic groups and conglomerates on the rise

How have conglomerates in developing countries and transition economies been affected by increasingly open markets? The replacement of international Keynesianism (and regional socialism) by global neoliberalism has had the general impact of less state control, and a transfer of power from the state to the private sector following from the transfer of assets, responsibilities, liberties, etc. The (official) purpose of this fundamental restructuring was to enhance the strength and vitality of the private sector in developing regions, and thereby the national economy. In this volume we see that in a few cases this goal is approached, at least partially, but in most cases it has not happened. Part of the explanation for this gap between theory and practice, according to Kurt W. Radtke in this volume, is that '[t]he distinction between public and private is not just a formal one, but is rooted in value concepts', which originated in the Western world and then were spread to non-Western parts of the world where these concepts are understood in a different way. Overall, the contributions on Asia, Latin America, Africa and

CEE point out that the main process has not simply been a transfer of economic power from the public sector to the private sector, but rather economic concentration in very large private companies, which are usually structured as conglomerates or economic groups. Although this global trend produces a range of outcomes, depending on the regional, national and local context, the case studies in this book coincide in that this economic concentration is problematic from a developmental perspective.

The case studies in this volume show that there is not a short answer to the question of what has recently happened to economic groups and conglomerates in developing regions. Economic liberalisation has been taking place around the world, but, as mentioned above, each country has its own point of departure, and its own timing and style of restructuring, resulting in a variety of neoliberal regimes. This diversity is clearly reflected in the experiences with economic groups and conglomerates of different regions, countries and regions within countries, as for instance becomes clear from the comparative analysis of three countries in Central America: Guatemala, Costa Rica and Honduras. In some cases ethnicity is also an important factor, such as in Indonesia, where many of the top conglomerates are owned by Indonesians of Chinese descent, or in Zimbabwe and South Africa, where black capitalists have been promoted by the government, however with very different effect. In addition, each economic sector has a modernisation and integration logic of its own, as one comes to understand from reading about the financial-industrial groups controlling the energy sector in Ukraine and Russia; pharmaceutical giants in Puerto Rico; telecommunications companies in Taiwan and Central America; and cocoa producers in Ghana. A final important factor is the history and governance structure of an economic group. Some of the currently giant corporations that originated in a developing region started as a family business that expanded over a longer period and then took advantage of the opportunities of economic restructuring. This pattern seems particularly strong in Asia and Latin America. Some still continue to be family-run, but conglomerates face the need to further modernise their management, often in order to attract more capital, but in some cases also because of family dynamics threatening to destroy the company's unity (see for instance Momoko Kawakami's chapter on two family business groups in Taiwan). There are also cases (especially in post-socialist countries) of new or small companies that rapidly turned into big businesses through acquiring privatised firms and/or using the increased access to international finance. And last, but definitely not least, TNCs from industrialised countries have over the past two decades acquired many more business stakes in developing regions (see the section on 'transnationalising capital' on p. 15 and Tables 1.2 and 1.3).

One of the greatest contradictions coming out of this volume's case studies is that although state control over the private sector and large companies has clearly declined, public sector support and/or protection for the large private sector actors is still strong, and so is the entanglement of politics and economic activity. Since this reality – of conglomerates and economic groups holding 'special relations' with important political actors and high state officials – is not according to the official 'rules of the game' of the neoliberal economic model, nor to those of the democratisation processes that are taking place in most of the developing regions, it tends to be hidden, concealed or camouflaged. Evidently, in any part of the world and under many economic and political systems, (owners of) conglomerates and economic groups have major political influence, based on their economic power and their social relevance (in particular as an employer). However, irrespective of which region, the majority of this book's contributions identify some perverse relations between big businesses and high-level politicians or state representatives. In Indonesia, most of the non-Chinese large conglomerates belonged to the children of President Suharto. In several Latin American countries, massive privatisations coincided with influential state technocrats becoming businessmen or investors in (or closely related to) the newly privatised companies. In post-apartheid South Africa businessmen connected to the ANC have received special treatment. And in Ukraine, initially economic liberalisation (under Gorbachev) especially favoured members of the communist youth league Komsomol as new capitalists, whereas more recently owners of (half-criminal) financial-industrial groups have tried to strengthen their economic position by becoming elected to a high political position.

Old and new perverse public–private practices – involving clientelism, nepotism, patronage, corruption and even extortion – often survive the (formal) democratisation processes in most countries, and international pressures for good governance (see below). These international pressures come from multilateral institutions concerned about the adverse effects of these practices on development as well as from (potential) foreign investors in developing regions. According to Young (2003: 249), in a political culture as in Latin America where 'know-who' is more important than 'know-how' local entrepreneurs of course have certain advantages over foreign investors.[3] Local and foreign companies may also work together, combining their economic and political capacities, as Mahon (1996: 179) argues:

> As trade integration proceeds, informal political access may prove to be more crucial as a competitive advantage of domestic capital. Foreign transnationals are likely to pressure for transparency, possibly supported by their home governments. But through alliances with local business they may also support these informal ties.

However, several contributors to this volume stress that this advantage for 'locals' is of little help when national policies of high interest rates, such as in Brazil, create a major handicap for local companies compared with foreign investors who can easily get access to (transnational) capital at much lower rates.

Moreover, with free market policies there has also been extensive public sector support for large conglomerates, including foreign ones. The pharmaceutical TNCs in Puerto Rico, for instance, are encouraged to stay by the use of low (corporate income) tax rates. In CEE, since the phase of massive privatisation has ended, countries have started to compete with one another in their efforts to attract new (green-field) investments, offering foreign investors, for example, financial incentives, tax exemptions and infra-structural changes. Next to these structural 'gifts' by the public sector of poor and middle income countries to the world's richest private companies, there have been the transfers of national public capital to private owner-ship with privatisations and at times of financial crisis. Both national and transnational conglomerates have benefited from the acquisition of *under-valued* state-owned companies and special financial arrangements, such as in Argentina. And when a financial crisis occurs, the public sector provides enormous sums for the recovery of the (recently privatised) banks and other (financial) companies, which then *overvalue* their assets to receive more support funding. Apart from the Argentine case, this can be seen in the chapters on Indonesia, and Chile and Mexico: while badly functioning or corrupt big banks were helped out, there were few support mechanisms for small companies, let alone a 'safety net' for the numerous citizens suffering from the crisis.

Transnationalising capital

Since the 1980s, the globally changing policies of states towards foreign invest-ment contributed to a growing role of FDI and international production (see Table 1.2) as well as increasing competition among developing countries for this foreign capital. In most countries a dismantling took place of legal arrangements that regulated, limited and selectively subordinated the partic-ipation of FDI to state-led development. Both the end of the Cold War and the rise of the Washington Consensus – inspired by the IMF and the World Bank, which had actively participated in the negotiations of the debt crisis – help to explain the consolidation of the deregulation policies of many states with respect to FDI. The end of socialist economies and import substitution strategies resulted in a rising number of countries that could serve as new mar-kets for production and distribution of goods. With globalisation and high indebtedness of developing countries foreign investment has become very important, and competition among these countries for this investment has significantly increased. While states in sub-Saharan Africa – through intense and frequent structural adjustment programmes – complied more profoundly with the conditions of international financial institutions (IFIs) than states in any other region (Akyüz and Gore 2001), several Asian states were far more reluctant to give up formal and informal practices supporting certain sectors and local companies. The transfers of state companies to private companies were particularly far-reaching in Central and Eastern Europe and in Latin America, partly benefiting local large enterprises and partly foreign multi-nationals (Fernández Jilberto and Hogenboom 2004).

Table 1.2 Selected indicators of FDI and international production, 1982–2003
(US$ billion)

	1982	1990	2003
FDI inflows	59	209	560
FDI outflows	28	242	612
FDI inward stock	796	1,950	8,245
FDI outward stock	590	1,758	8,197
Cross-border M&As	. . .	151	297
Sales of foreign affiliates	2,717	5,660	17,580
Gross product of foreign affiliates	636	1,454	3,706
Total assets of foreign affiliates	2,076	5,883	30,362
Export of foreign affiliates	717	1,194	3,077
Employment of foreign affiliates (thousands)	19,232	24,197	54,170
GDP (in current prices)	11,737	22,588	36,163
Gross fixed capital formation	2,285	4,815	7,294

Source: UNCTAD (2004b).

The policies of privatisation and market opening in developing countries were major attractions to foreign investors who, as Table 1.3 shows, from the mid-1990s became increasingly active in developing countries. By then, FDI and TNCs were considered by almost all governments as desirable and indispensable for economic growth, and an open economy was thought to be a guarantee for the presence of FDI. This new attitude explains the global trend of continuing liberalisation of FDI regimes through new laws and regulations, bilateral investment regimes and double taxation treaties, as well as the trends in investment flows, and the prospects for FDI. The foreign investments during the 1990s were mostly directed towards the sectors of services and production: the same sectors that many states had privatised.

Despite these worldwide shifts, overviews show that international production remains concentrated in two ways: among companies and among countries. It has been calculated that for 2003, the 100 largest TNCs represented less than 0.2 per cent of the world's transnationals, but 14 per cent of their total sales and 13 per cent of their employment. And the five largest recipients of FDI in the developing world attracted not less than 62 per cent of these total inflows in 2001. This figure is partly a reflection of the massive investment flows to China; in 2003 China became the world's largest FDI recipient, which traditionally was the position of the United States. At the other end of the spectrum is a large group of under-performers (combining low FDI performance with low potential); this group is largely made up of poor countries (UNCTAD 2002, 2004b).

Although most global capital flows are related to TNCs from industrialised countries, TNCs from developing regions are on the rise. While in the mid-1980s they still accounted for less than 6 per cent of global FDI

Table 1.3 Regional distribution of net inward FDI, 1991–2004 (US$ billions)

	1991–7[a]	1998	1999	2000	2001	2002	2003	2004[b]
Global total	275	713	1,113	1,530	800	721	537	612
Developed countries	170	474	837	1,229	553	517	366	321
Developing countries	87	186	220	238	203	144	132	255
Asia and the Pacific	50	96	102	134	99	85	76	166
Latin America and the Caribbean[c]	32	83	107	98	88	51	50	96
Central and Eastern Europe	8	24	26	28	25	31	26	36
Africa	5	8	11	7	16	7	6	20

Source: ECLAC (2005).

Notes:
a   Annual averages.
b   Preliminary figures.
c   The figures include financial centres.

flows, in 2003 their share of global outward FDI stock was some 10 per cent, representing $859 billion. The list of the top 25 (non-financial) TNCs from developing countries is traditionally led by Asian firms, but the list for 2002 also includes six companies from Latin America and four from South Africa. Interestingly, the top 50 developing-country TNCs are transnationalising even more rapidly than TNCs from developed countries, and the investment flows between developing countries grow faster than those between developed and developing countries (UNCTAD 2004b).

Although a strict division between large local and foreign companies may be of analytical use, in reality it is an overstatement that ignores the many similarities and relations between the two. Besides the already mentioned use of transnational capital by local economic groups, there have been several innovations in the relations between 'local' and foreign companies since the 1990s. Whereas FDI previously tended to be done through branches of multinationals that were directly controlled by their headquarters, many multinationals have started to operate in association or through joint ventures with local economic groups. These alliances appeared as a result of the privatisation process and/or on the basis of investment funds. There are also cases in which branches of TNCs have become associated with branches of other multinationals, to new or old local economic groups, or to foreign banks, in order to maximise their share in privatisations. These strategies enable corporate allies to combine the advantages of the new economic policies for foreign companies with the market knowledge and lobbying capacities of local economic groups, and with the financial participation –

often the acquisition of shares or bonds – of foreign banks (Kulfas *et al.* 2002). Nevertheless, such combinations can be very short-lived; changing company ownership, changing politics or the increasingly volatile international economic and financial markets have all been reasons for ending such a partnership.

The rapid growth of FDI of the late 1990s (especially 1997–2000), however, was not to last. In fact, in the years of 2001 and 2002 FDI to developing regions dropped rapidly and severly, although still remaining much higher than in the early 1990s. There are several reasons for this regional economic recession. The global contraction of FDI in 2001 was 51 per cent (the highest in three decades), and in 2002 another 27 per cent. TNCs were forced to reduce production costs as competition increased and markets slowed down. There has been a radical change in the global strategies of TNCs: instead of competing for a company's size and participation in many markets they have been bringing their costs and investments under strong control. Some multinationals have simply opted for relocating their installations to countries with lower labour costs, or to markets with higher growth potential. In Mexico, this happened in 2002 in the electronic sector with Canon moving its plant for photocopying machines from Tijuana to Thailand and Vietnam, and with Philips Electronics moving production to China. Other companies decided to reduce their Mexican personnel, such as Alps Electronic (1,700 employees), Casio Computer (700) and Sanyo (320) (ECLAC 2003).

The upward and downward moves have shown that contemporary FDI is far more volatile than expected, and not very different from portfolio capital. Disappointment about FDI flows and gross domestic product (GDP) growth in developing regions has, among other things, sparked a (renewed) debate about the advantages of foreign investment compared to local investment. Several recent studies claim that the positive effects of FDI for host economies have been overestimated. Contrary to conventional wisdom that the presence of multinationals gives way to a transfer of technology and organisational knowledge, Hanson (2001: vii) states that 'there is little evidence at the firm or plant level that FDI raises the productivity of domestic enterprises', which erases an often used legitimisation for offering multinationals special treatment. Besides, despite its expansion, foreign investment remains of limited importance in developing countries: of private gross fixed capital formation about three-quarters is still domestic (World Bank 2004: 2). Moreover, in figures of the shares of public investment, private domestic investment and foreign investment in developing countries, foreign investment is little more than a thin layer on top of the other two, only about half the size of public investment (UNCTAD 2003: 75).

UNCTAD's *Trade and Development Report 2003* convincingly shows that the important link between FDI and domestic capital accumulation differs greatly from one region (or country) to another. This partially explains why it is so difficult to establish the general impact of FDI on capital accumulation and economic growth, and why there is no consensus on this issue. A particularly large contrast can be found between Asian and Latin American countries. While in Asia the increase in inflows of FDI

> has been associated with a rising share of investment in GDP and increased investment in machinery and equipment, in Latin American countries, there has been little or no improvement in the level or the composition of investment. In fact, in most countries of that region, the investment ratio fell while FDI increased.
>
> (UNCTAD 2003: 84)

Roberto Rocco's analysis in this volume, for instance, shows the painful effects of Brazil's denationalisation of private investment in the 1990s on productivity: the local businessmen who sold their assets often did not invest (all of) this capital in other local companies while the new foreign owners have exported most of their profits. Together with indications of a rather permanent 'investment pause' in many developing countries, and a falling share of public investment in GDP, which failed to crowd in private investment, the UNCTAD report concludes that '[t]hese findings raise serious doubts about the strategies adopted in a number of developing countries for activating a dynamic process of capital accumulation and growth through a combination of increased FDI and reduced public investment and policy intervention' (UNCTAD 2003: 84).

Next to direct investments, both the states and the large economic groups of neoliberalised developing countries and transition economies have come to depend more on international capital markets, which has made them more vulnerable to international financial crises. After the debt crisis of the 1980s, and the Mexican peso crisis in 1994–5 – with its 'tequila effect' in Argentina – the primary proof of such vulnerability was the East Asian crisis that started in July 1997 with the devaluation of Thailand's baht and then gradually spread to the emerging economies of the region. This crisis affected very diverse economies: those with high levels of short-term debts (South Korea, Indonesia and Malaysia), those with solid international reserves and a significant surplus (Singapore and Hong Kong), and those with deficits in their current accounts (Malaysia). In 1998 the Russian crisis affected both transition economies and Latin American economies, especially Brazil (Palma 2004). Since the middle of 1998, with the flight of foreign investments from emerging economies and the negative re-evaluation of Latin American debtors by international creditors, Latin American governments had to implement several additional adjustment policies to resolve a serious disequilibrium in balance of payment. Nevertheless a second speculative attack against the Brazilian real in January 1999 was successful and caused a new regional crisis. The fact that the negative effects of the Asiatic crisis affected very different economies including those with a healthy financial situation has supported the idea that, in the neoliberal markets of global capital, 'contagion' and its massive economic and social impact has hardly any rational basis.

These financial crises of the 'last generation' have manifested the fragility of the current financial systems of developing countries and transition economies within the architecture of global capital markets. There are several causes for this: the negative effect of the liabilities of the external debt in foreign exchange; the increase of short-term debt in financial markets; the absence of or insufficient participation in secondary financial markets; and the small size of their financial markets, which cannot compensate for or resist the speculative pressures by large foreign investors and large local economic groups (Ocampo and Uthoff 2004). While most states no longer seem to posses the instruments necessary to influence the governability of financial globalisation, major conglomerates increasingly seem to have a decisive role in the expansion and explosion of financial bubbles. This is not simply a weakness of states from developing regions, it even happened in the United States during the 1990s, when financial institutions turned into giant conglomerates that contributed to the creation of a bubble. In the case of the telecom sector, large financial groups inflated investment, resulting in huge overcapacity and, finally, a bubble that burst (*Business Week* 9 October 2002).

The first global economic crisis of the third millennium has forced TNCs to focus on their 'core business' and to allow only cautious geographic expansion in contrast to the previous strategies of diversification and an almost worldwide *acte de présence*. Alongside this recent development there is a more long-term trend of the service sector becoming dominant, accounting for approximately 60 per cent of global FDI, or some $4 trillion (UNCTAD 2004b: 15). And with the privatisation of public services, rather than trade and finance, it is service industries such as electricity, water and telecommunications that have become big transnational business. In general, FDI flows to the more advanced sectors, and foreign investors have been more successful than local conglomerates in taking advantage of the new opportunities in the service sector (although the chapters on Taiwan and Central America also point to other experiences). Even in Latin America, where local economic groups were favoured in the privatisation process, in just a few years many transferred their stakes to foreign conglomerates. Meanwhile, the expected contribution to development of FDI in services (by means of the transfer of technology) so far has hardly been evidenced by data. UNCTAD (2004b: 24–5) therefore warns that foreign investment in services has to be managed carefully, and that 'free-market forces may not provide the desired outcomes', especially in basic utilities and socially or culturally sensitive areas. While this volume provides many examples of problematic privatisations and foreign investments in various sectors, it seems accurate that 'FDI in services through privatisation raises a special challenge in terms of regulation and governance' (UNCTAD 2004b: 36).

Competitiveness and governance

In the context of the expanding flows of transnational investment capital, and after the various (financial) crises of the mid- to late 1990s, the competitiveness of developing countries has become the topic of an international policy debate. In UNCTAD's *Trade and Development Report 2003* (2003: 63) this debate is directly linked to failure of neoliberal reforms:

> with the failure of a first generation of reforms to deliver on their promises, attention has recently turned to 'getting the investment climate right' through a marriage of macroeconomic stability with better business organisation, improved governance and measures to boost competition, not only as a way of generating an adequate level of investment, but also for ensuring its quality.

An early start of the competitiveness debate was made by the WEF, which has been publishing its *Global Competitiveness Reports* since 1979. This forum is an international corporate organisation whose members represent large multinational companies. Its yearly meetings in Davos have increasingly become major international events, where leading businessmen and policymakers meet to discuss the potential and terms of globalisation. Also, the coverage of the *Global Competitiveness Report* has been extended over the years, and currently includes over a hundred economies. Based on samples of mostly TNCs, the WEF's indexes point at the weak competitiveness of many developing countries. The Growth Competitiveness rankings analyse the potential for economies to attain sustained economic growth, taking into account the macroeconomic environment, the quality of public institutions and technology. As may be expected, the top 50 is made up of industrialised and/or resource-rich countries with a stable political system, whereas the bottom 30 consists of poor and/or politically unstable nations.[4]

Recently the World Bank has paid special attention to the matter in its *World Development Report 2005: A Better Investment Climate for Everyone*. It includes a section on measuring the investment climate, which is to complement the indices of the WEF and others by measuring various constraints faced by firms (e.g. regulation and tax administration, finance, access to electricity, and labour regulations) and relating them to measures of firm performance, growth and investment. These measures are linked to results of the World Bank's Doing Business Project, which collects country-level data on the details of relevant regulations such as the time it takes to start a business, enforce a contract, register property and resolve insolvency. In general, such procedures take about twice as much time in low and middle income countries as in high income countries (World Bank 2004: 244–9).

Yet the body of the World Bank report is about the links between investment climate and development, and its central message is that much more is required than the policy changes so far in order to achieve this *better investment climate* in low and middle income countries. Much of the message of the report could well be illustrated by the numerous negative experiences of developing countries and transition economies with large economic groups and conglomerates described by the contributors of this book. The report points at the general gap between paper (formal policies) and practice, and at the tension that lies at the heart of many policy failures: 'Societies benefit greatly from the activities of firms, but the preferences of firms don't fully match those of society' (World Bank 2004: 6). According to the Bank, this tension is related to four challenges for governments: restraining rent-seeking; establishing credibility; fostering public trust and legitimacy; and ensuring policy responses fit local conditions. Also phenomena such as patron-clientelism and capture of state agencies by firms are discussed in relation to the problem of rent-seeking. While the Bank's surveys confirm the general wisdom that the more influential companies face a more favourable policy environment than other companies, they also suggest that well-connected companies are likely to innovate less, probably because they spend more time and money on feeding these connections and less on innovation. Enhancing the transparency of government–firm dealings is presented as a common strategy to address all these problems and challenges (World Bank 2004).[5]

In the *Trade and Development Report 2003*, UNCTAD links the competitiveness issue to capital accumulation by the class of domestic entrepreneurs. It points out that after the first stages of industrialisation, 'capital accumulation is financed primarily by profits in the form of corporate retentions, rather than household savings', and that

> a high rate of corporate retention is almost always associated with a high rate of corporate investment and corporate dynamism. In its turn, such dynamism provides a social as well as economic justification for the concentration of an important part of national income as profits in the hands of a small minority of the population.
>
> (UNCTAD 2003: 63)

However, again the different development trajectories of East Asia and Latin America come to the fore: while in the late 1980s and early 1990s in East Asia there was a rapid rise of savings rates closely associated with a sharp rise of profit share and a rapidly increasing share of manufactures in GDP, Latin America's dropping savings rates were associated with a stagnant or falling share of manufactures. Based on a study by Amsden (2001) the report stresses that this strong investment drive of the East Asian economic elites resulting in sustained economic development did not happen by itself as

> market forces alone were not left to dictate either the pace or direction. Rather, the defining features of successful development strategies were the design of effective control mechanisms to both encourage and discipline private investors by raising profits above those generated by competitive market forces and active policies to ensure those profits

found outlets that would add to productive capacity, create jobs and help technological progress.

This was done through policies of low interest rates, controls on luxury consumption, and coordination of investment decisions 'to prevent "investment races" among large oligopolistic firms', and was supported by long-term ties between large corporations and banks (UNCTAD 2003: 64).

Still, a somewhat puzzling phenomenon of this attention to investment and competitiveness is that the competitiveness of not companies but of countries is an issue of debate. It is only one of many examples in which market-related concepts and issues – in this case competition for markets – are now attributed to the arena of politics and policy-making. In other words, the public sector has increasingly been burdened with the values, realities and interests of the private sector. This has also happened in the good governance debate, which stresses the (economic) importance of stable and responsible state policies and institutions, and democratisation. In the view of international organisations, restructured states and (new) democracies are primarily providers of attractive and open markets for capital, while the negative effects of neoliberal policies are easily explained as caused by bad governance (Demmers, Fernández Jilberto and Hogenboom 2004).

Will open markets and policies of national competitiveness and good governance eventually cause a unification of economic models, and is shareholder capitalism becoming the internationally dominant style – as has been happening in the two neoliberal frontrunners: the United States and the United Kingdom? Although there is definitely some truth in the statement by Cerny (1997: 181) that '[n]ational varieties of capitalism will be tolerated only so long as they do not undermine profits in international financial markets', this volume presents ample proof that despite worldwide neoliberalisation there still remains considerable variety in neoliberal regimes. Most countries (and in some cases even regions within countries) have their own history and culture of corporate governance, that is the way in which (large) companies are managed and legally and financially structured. Some authors also argue that a diversity of models is likely to remain as countries, just like companies, try to find their niche (cf. Kay 1993), and '[n]ations gain advantage because of differences, not similarities ... National differences are valuable and often essential to competitive advantage' (Porter 1990: 623). Similarly, economic studies on the mechanisms of various economic and corporate governance models show that expectations of (rapid) convergence of corporate governance models into one hybrid form of 'best practice' do have a point, but exaggerate with respect to the speed and depth of changes.[6]

Prospects for development

Developing countries and transition economies following the global trends of neoliberalisation and democratisation have experienced that conglomerates and economic groups have grown and transnationalised, and have thereby gained economic and often also political power. While this introductory chapter has analysed the general trend of economic concentration in and within the private sector, the other chapters study the variety of shapes this trend takes in developing regions, and the effects on politics and development. Both for politics and development, it is important to consider how the role of the state has changed with the rise of 'big business', and the implications for civil society. Generally, the price that the states with neoliberal developing and transition economies pay is their loss of sovereignty, motivating them to share power with other states via economic regionalisation so as to retain some influence on transnational investment flows.

In the 1990s the nation-state stopped being national, thereby separating the state and the nation, and creating a crisis of governability in developing and transition countries, expressed in the dissociation of the state towards civil society. Civil society largely continues to be linked to the parameters of the nation-state despite the neoliberal state's attempts at its relegitimation via decentralisation or regionalisation, and in the phase of privatisations via the introduction of popular capitalism (Saunders and Harris 1994). The new role of the state as an agent of the globalising capital flows weakens its relation with civil society: the state has lost its capacity to represent its citizens' social, economic and political demands, and the resurgence of ethnic, regional or religious (fundamentalist or moderate) identities can be seen as a social reaction to the crisis generated by the 'neoliberal co-state' (Castells 1998). In the meantime foreign investment deepens the social disarticulation in those countries in which the capacity of regulation of the market is insufficient to guarantee a minimum level of social cohesion, creating favourable conditions for the integration of socially marginalised segments in the global economy of criminality; the so-called perverse connection.

Parallel to this debilitation of the state in its relation to civil society, the economic concentration in the private sector also produces profound political shifts. As is pointed out by Huber *et al.* (1997: 335–6):

> Economic concentration, of course, means the concentration not only of wealth but also of power. The power of capital via-à-vis both labor and governments has been further enhanced by financial liberalisation and the internationalisation of production chains. These developments have made capital much more mobile, and thus the threat of exit more credible, which constrains governments in their policy options and induces labor to make concessions. This power shift has been felt even in advanced industrial democracies, and it is even more pronounced in new democracies.

The above assessment of recent trends in the expanding roles of large companies together with the case studies in this volume remind us of the general wisdom that any major concentration of power calls for checks and balances. In theory, liberal democracy is in favour of freedom and against the concentration of power in just a few hands, whether political (a strong state) or economic (monopolies or cartels). Since the financial crises of the late 1990s, international development policies have focused on issues of governance in developing regions, with better governance of the public sector as the main topic, whereas corporate governance is still primarily seen as a responsibility of companies and the private sector. Both the strict distinction between the public and the private sector and the focus on the public sector do not seem very logical in a time when the private sector has been taking over tasks of the public sector and has been expanding. Instead, it is important to put this distinction and focus in perspective. In the next chapter, Kurt W. Radtke stresses that 'individuals must surely be protected not only against "the state", but also against the non-transparent influence of other institutions'. From a very different angle, the chapter on Iran by Eva Rakel shows how semi-public institutions may act as uncontrolled giant monopolies, giving way to corruption and power abuse that are very similar to those by privatised uncontrolled giant conglomerates. And in his chapter on Africa, Kwame Nimako reminds us of André Gunder Frank's critique on the irrational and ideological differentiation between public and private enterprises.

Although this volume also includes some more positive experiences with the rise of conglomerates, the various accounts of irresponsible actions by both governments and large local and foreign companies serve as an illustration of the widespread failure to establish these important checks and balances to economic and political power in developing regions. Moreover, a simultaneous lack of responsibility in the public sector and the private sector is a specially damaging mix, as becomes clear from several of the case studies, in particular those on recent financial crises in Indonesia, Mexico and Argentina. Strengthening the checks and balances on concentrations of economic (and political) power is a politically and practically complicated objective. This is not only because market opening needs to be matched with social development, but also because the representation and the participation of citizens are often distrusted by local and foreign investors asa well as international financial markets. The contributions to this book provide valuable insights into the profound changes that the globalisation of free market policies has caused in the role of economic groups and conglomerates in developing countries and transition economies, but they also raise some pressing questions. Where does an 'enabling state' end and 'crony capitalism' start? What can be done about the inability of the (decreased) state in developing regions to control powerful conglomerates, let alone deal with criminal networks? And how is it possible to democratise the market in countries where the state and civil society have barely been democratised?

Notes

1 Interestingly, among these studies are several bestsellers, such as Naomi Klein's *No Logo* (1999) and William Greider's *One World, Ready or Not* (1997).

2   For the purpose of this volume no strict distinction is made between an economic group and a conglomerate because the use and definition of these two terms varies between countries and scholars, and the interest of this project is in all kinds of mega-size corporations. Since most of these large private companies are structured as economic group or conglomerate we may use either one of these nouns when writing about giant private sector actors in general.

3   Young (2003: 249) even claims that

> [t]he fact that foreign investment has been so heavily concentrated in a relatively small number of large-scale investments . . . suggests that patrimonial styles of governance have been a significant barrier to a more regularised, low-level penetration by foreign capital beyond self-contained, politically conditioned, enclave activities.

4   The first and last ten countries illustrate this contrast: Finland, the United States, Sweden, Taiwan, Denmark, Norway, Singapore, Switzerland, Japan and Iceland versus Nicaragua, Madagascar, Honduras, Bolivia, Zimbabwe, Paraguay, Ethiopia, Bangladesh, Angola and Chad. Meanwhile, the Business Competitiveness Index evaluates the business environment (the sophistication of company operations and strategy, and the quality of the national business environment). There is a similar split to that for growth competitiveness, although here the top 30 includes South Africa (no. 25) and India (no. 30) (World Economic Forum, 2004).

5   Since the late 1990s several issues of the *World Development Reports* (especially of 1997, 2000, 2001) indicate that the World Bank has become more aware of the importance of the state, and different local circumstances. The attempt to no longer be labelled as an institution of one-size-fits-all policies must be seen in the light of the criticism on previous Bretton Woods policies, in particular when the Asian crisis showed that worldwide blueprints for free markets could destabilise 'miracle economies' to the extent that it threatened the global economy.

6   For instance, Bratton and McCahery (1999) find that there has been a tendency of weak convergence of corporate governance, which may continue in the future.

Bibliography

Akyüz, Yilmaz and Charles Gore (2001) 'African economic development in a comparative perspective', *Cambridge Journal of Economics*, 25: 265–88.

Amsden, Alice H. (2001) *The Rise of 'the Rest'. Challenges to the West from Late-Industrializing Economies*, Oxford: Oxford University Press.

Basave Kunhardt, Jorge (2001) *Un siglo de grupos empresariales en México*, México, DF: UNAM-IIE & Miguel Ángel Porrúa.

Bratton, W.W. and J.A. McCahery (1999) 'Comparative corporate governance and the value of the firm: the case against global cross reference', *Columbia Journal of Transnational Law*, 38 (2): 213–97.

Castells, Manuel (1998) *El Poder de la Identidad*, Madrid: Alianza Editorial.

—— (2003) 'Panorama de la era de la información en América Latina: es sostenible la globalización?', in Fernando Calderón (Coordinador), *Es Sostenible la Globalización en América Latina? Debates con Manuel Castells*, Chile: Fondo de Cultura Económica.

Cerny, Philip G. (1997) 'International finance and the erosion of capital diversity', in Colin Crouch and Wolfgang Streeck (eds), *Political Economy of Modern Capitalism*, London: Sage.

Chang, Ha-Joon (2004) *Globalisation, Economic Development and the Role of the State*, London: Zed Books/Third World Network.

Clark, Ian (1999) *Globalisation and International Relations Theory*, Oxford: Oxford University Press.

Demmers, Jolle, Alex E. Fernández Jilberto and Barbara Hogenboom (eds) (2004) *Good Governance in the Era of Global Neoliberalism. Conflict and Depolitisation in Latin America, Eastern Europe, Asia and Africa*, London: Routledge.

ECLAC (2003) *Foreign Investment in Latin American and the Caribbean 2002*, Santiago: United Nations.

—— (2004) *Foreign Investment in Latin American and the Caribbean 2003*, Santiago: United Nations.

—— (2005) *Foreign Investment in Latin American and the Caribbean 2004*, Santiago: United Nations.

Ellman, Michael (2004) 'Transition economies', in Ha-Joon Chang (ed.), *Rethinking Development Economics*, London: Anthem Press, pp. 179–98.

Fernández Jilberto, Alex E. and Barbara Hogenboom (1997) 'The political economy of open regionalism in Latin America', special issue of the *International Journal of Political Economy*, 26 (4).

—— (2004) 'Conglomerates and economic groups in neoliberal Latin America', *Journal of Developing Societies*, 20 (3–4), Special Issue: 'Latin American Conglomerates and Economic Groups under Globalization', guest editors Alex E. Fernández Jilberto and Barbara Hogenboom: 149–71.

Garrido, C. and W. Péres (1998) 'Las grandes empresas y grupos industriales Latinoamericanos en los años noventa', in W. Péres (ed.), *Grandes Empresas y Grupos Industriales Latinoamericanos*, México: Siglo XXI.

Giarracca, Norma and Miguel Teubal (2004) '"Que se vayan todos". Neoliberal collapse and social protest in Argentina', in Jolle Demmers, Alex E. Fernández Jilberto and Barbara Hogenboom (eds), *Good Governance in the Era of Global Neoliberalism. Conflict and Depolitisation in Latin America, Eastern Europe, Asia and Africa*, London: Routledge, pp. 66–90.

Greider, William (1997) *One World, Ready or Not. The Manic Logic of Global Capitalism*, New York: Touchstone.

Habib, Adam and Vishnu Padayachee (2000) 'Economic policy and power relations in South Africa's transition to democracy', *World Development*, 28 (2): 245–63.

Hanson, Gordon H. (2001) *Should Countries Promote Foreign Direct Investment?*, G-24 Discussion Paper Series No. 9, Geneva: UNCTAD.

Huber, Evelyne, Dietrich Rueschemeyer and John D. Stephens (1997) 'The paradoxes of contemporary democracy: formal, participatory, and social dimensions', *Comparative Politics*, 29 (3): 323–42.

Kay, J. (1993) *Foundations of Corporate Success: How Business Strategies Add Value*, Oxford: Oxford University Press.

Klein, Naomi (1999) *No Logo*, New York: Picador.

Krugman, Paul (1995) 'Dutch tulips and emerging markets', *Foreign Affairs*, July/August: 28–44.

Kulfas, M., F. Porta and A. Ramos (2002) *Inversiones Extranjeras y Empresas Transnacionales in la Economía Argentinas*, Buenos Aires: CEPAL.

Lieberman, Ira and Christopher Kirkness (1998) *Privatisation and Emerging Equity Market*, Washington, DC: World Bank and Flemings Securities.

Mahon, James E. (1996) *Mobile Capital and Latin American Development*, Philadelphia, PA: Pennsylvania State University Press.

Manzetti, Luigi (1999) *Privatisation South American Style*, Oxford: Oxford University Press.

Ocampo, José and Andras Uthoff (eds) (2004) *Gobernabilidad e integración financiera: ámbito global y regional*, Santiago: ONU/Cepal.

Palma, Gabriel (2004) 'The "Three Routes" to financial crisis: Chile, Mexico and Argentina (1); Brazil (2); and Korea, Malaysia and Thailand (3)', in Ha-Joon Chang (ed.), *Rethinking Development Economic*, London: Anthem Press, pp. 347–76.

Péres, W. (ed.) (1998) *Grandes Empresas y Grupos Industriales Latinoamericanos*, México: Siglo XIX.

Phongpaichity, Pasuk and Chris Baker (1999) 'The political economy of the Thai crisis', *Journal of the Asia Pacific Economy*, 4 (1): 193–208.

Porter, M.E. (1990) *The Competitive Advantage of Nations*, New York: Free Press.

Saunders, Peter and Colin Harris (1994) *Privatisation and Popular Capitalism*, Buckingham: Open University Press.

Strange, Susan (1996) *The Retreat of the State. The Diffusion of Power in the World Economy*, Cambridge: Cambridge University Press.

—— (2002) 'The declining authority of states', in David Held and Anthony McGrew (eds), *The Global Transfomations Reader*, Cambridge: Polity Press.

Suárez, L. (1999) 'La globalización: fase superior y última del imperialismo?', *Análisis de Coyuntura*, No. 1, La Habana: AUNA.

UNCTAD (2002) *World Investment Report 2002. Transnational Corporations and Export Competitiveness*, New York: United Nations.

—— (2003) *Trade and Development Report 2003*, New York: United Nations.

—— (2004a) *Trade and Development Report 2004*, New York: United Nations.

—— (2004b) *World Investment Report 2004: The Shift Towards Services*, New York: United Nations.

UNDP (1997) *Human Development Report 1997. Human Development to Eradicate Poverty*, New York and Oxford: Oxford University Press.

Whitehead, Laurence (2000) 'Comparing East Asia and Latin America: stirrings of mutual recognition', *Journal of Democracy*, 11 (4): 65–79.

World Bank (1997) *World Development Report 1997. The State in a Changing World*, Washington, DC: The World Bank.

—— (2000) *World Development Report 2000–2001. Attacking Poverty (2000–2001)*, Washington, DC: The World Bank.

—— (2001) *World Development Report 2002. Building Institutions for Markets*, Washington, DC: The World Bank.

—— (2004) *World Development Report 2005. A Better Investment Climate for Everyone*, Washington, DC: The World Bank.

World Economic Forum (2003) *The Global Competitiveness Report 2003–2004*, Geneva: World Economic Forum, www.weforum.org.

—— (2004) *The Global Competitiveness Report 2004–2005*, Geneva: World Economic Forum, www.weforum.org.

Young, R. (2003) 'Foreign investment and democratic governance in Latin America', in Ana Margheritis (ed.), *Latin American Democracies in the New Global Economy*, Coral Gables: North-South Center Press, pp. 24–79.

Part I

Asia

2 Public versus private: governance in East Asia in the age of globalisation

Kurt W. Radtke

A basic issue in Western society has been the meaning and role of the division between public and private in the political, economic and social spheres. Lester Thurow (2000) has called globalisation a political revolution brought about by business. As a political project it is often identified with the project of spreading 'market democracy', one of the hallmarks also of the current administration of George W. Bush in the United States. 'Globalization means homogenization. Prices, products, wages, wealth, and rates of interest and profit tend to become the same all over the world . . . Under the protection of American military power, globalization proceeds relentlessly' (Waltz 1999).[1]

As a political project globalisation has so far failed to achieve global uniformity and conformity in the area of property and management rights – not surprisingly, since their shape is bound up with political, legal and other related concepts at the core of distinct traditions of civilisations, culture and political systems. Ideally, market democracy will not simply be imposed by the state – spontaneous actions by free individuals and their 'civil society' are meant to ensure a healthy balance between the state and society. The state is needed to provide a stable and secure environment for civil society and market democracy. To achieve good governance private and public interests must be clearly distinguished. Corruption will prevent this complex system from operating optimally, and if spreading unchecked may undermine political and social stability as well. The history of modernisation can be viewed from shifts in the concepts of governance: through changes in access to power and (financial) ownership by individuals and groups, and protection against the excessive use from the more powerful ones. In premodern times there have been basic differences in the relation between (political) power and ownership rights (both individual and collective ones) in Europe and East Asia. 'Globalisation' is also an attempt to unify the structure of these relationships. One of the means is to enforce acceptance of same rules for all societies. My hypothesis is that even as identical rules are accepted, their interpretation and implementation will differ as a result of a different heritage that took many centuries to develop, and cannot simply be nullified through signatures on treaties and agreements.[2]

The distinction between public and private is not just a formal one, but is rooted in value concepts. Modernisation that started with industrialisation in Europe has constantly exerted pressures on value systems in Europe itself, including shifting views on public and private. The relatively sudden spread of globalisation to the non-Western world poses enormous challenges for societies whose fabric often has a substantially different ancestry. The demarcation between the state, individuals and society in East Asia has traditionally been referred to in terms of divisions between the 'official sphere' (*guan* in Chinese, *kan* in Japanese) and the sphere of 'ordinary people' (*min* in Chinese and Japanese), concepts that continue to have a deep impact on the East Asian political economy. From the nineteenth century, China and Japan were affected by domestic instability, rebellions, reform, the onslaught of colonialism and foreign occupation. It is somewhat amazing that constants of society, such as the distinction between *guan* and *min* apparently survived long periods of thorough upheaval.

This chapter places 'privatisation' in the context of a long-lasting European (and later, American) search for rational management. This task was first entrusted to the state in France; in recent decades the company has taken over a new paradigmatic function to advance the search for a rational society. This deeply affects the substance and self-image of Western political, economic and social order that tended to be characterised in the desire to separate the private and the public realm. Rather than protecting individual freedom, privatisation in the global age may even become a threat to freedom. Attempts to create a 'new order' by totalitarian dictatorships failed, with enormous cost to human life.

Although concepts of private property and numerous political institutions were introduced first in Japan, subsequently to China (to some degree), their functioning in East Asia differs in various degrees. This chapter proposes that one of the major reasons lies in the fact that in East Asian societies the traditional division between officials and ordinary people, coupled with a symbiotic relationship between political and economic elites, continues to exert its influence even during processes of globalisation. The wide-ranging application of the principle of the selection of the fittest in market democracies, and global cooperation of domestic elites, has not (yet) been able to eradicate these features in East Asia. At stake is not a 'clash of civilisation' between 'East and West', since globalisation is also substantially affecting social, economic and political norms in the 'West'. Two case studies serve to illustrate my arguments: the complex moves surrounding the state-led privatisation of the postal system in Japan, and the role of the State Assets Supervision and Administration Commission (SASAC) in the reform of state-owned enterprises in China. Subsequently I suggest features of the franchise system as a useful way to conceptualise the implementation of models for globalisation in different societies. The conclusion takes up the changing relationship of individuals to their respective states, and changes in social norms within the life-world of individuals (micro-society).

In search of rational management: from state to company

Globalisation has often been viewed as the extension of the capitalist order to all parts of the world. The 'scientific' management by the state increasingly being applied to all aspects of society is part of a centuries-old project originating from Western Europe, and is not limited to 'capitalism'. In this sense the foundation of socialist dictatorships in Asia also signifies the introduction of basic European concepts – even if it did not take long before they assumed local characteristics ('socialism with Chinese characteristics'). In Leninist terms, globalisation appears to be the highest stage of the development of capitalism, advancing beyond traditional ideas of imperialism as the highest state of capitalism. However, *both* 'capitalism' and 'socialism' (Marxism, communism) are heirs to the European tradition. It is not by chance that both capitalism and socialism attach the greatest emphasis to the role of property and management rights. I suggest a conceptual approach that views major elements of globalisation as separate from the values of a 'Western' Christian-dominated tradition. Globalisation involves the application of scientific management to human society, but is also linked to the application of Darwinist ideas of selection of the fittest in concepts and models of competition in the economic and social order, including ideas of the fight for survival among states and civilisations. Demands for transparency in the fields of property and management rights are not merely an outcome of 'rational' capitalist management, but answer to the requirements of rational, scientifically formulated theories that range from management to state legislation. Profit performance is to be measured and judged through transparent statistics. The advent of statistics to grasp 'reality' numerically has not necessarily advanced the cause of truth (one of my first courses in elementary university economics focused on techniques to make balance sheets opaque).

The search for rationality first focused on the state as the creator of a rational order, symbolised in the utopian presentation by Leibniz and others of China as a model of a rational state that influenced ideas of the French revolution. In recent years, however, the rational 'company' has challenged and shaken the position of the state as the main creator of a rational order. Rational management has started to affect all walks of life. In my opinion rational management has already assumed the role of a paradigm for social order that has challenged the role of the family as the 'mother', the archetypal model of social organisations. In the eyes of many, the home of the nuclear family epitomises the walls enclosing and defending private space.

Around the globe political and cultural identities are changing under the impact of globalisation. In many countries the importance of the 'family' as the central paradigm of social, political and economic organisation was attacked not only in totalitarian systems, whose leaders nevertheless still love to be presented as 'patriarchal' arch fathers. 'Efficient' management along the lines of what is happening in companies has become a new paradigm that has affected social organisations as different as the family and universities. Changing views on health insurance and pension systems are just starting to impose new limits on the freedom of the individual to choose his or her lifestyle. This looks paradoxical in view of the fact that the individual is asked to accept greater risk taking with regard to job security and investing his or her savings in shares, rather than putting them in bank accounts.

These developments regularly clash with various traditions of value in Western civilisation. When the editor of a leading Japanese business journal, Ishibashi Tanzan, proclaimed in the mid-1930s that he regarded the state as an enterprise he elevated the enterprise (company) to the status of a new paradigm for the state (Radtke, 2003). In my view globalisation has extended the validity of this new paradigm, gradually replacing the traditional family paradigm as the main paradigm for economic, social and even political organisation. The company is on the way to become the new leading paradigm for the management of the state, and sometimes even the 'management' of the family as well. Related to this is the rise of 'production' as another basic paradigm for denoting all kinds of value-added creation that includes school and university education. Students are both 'products' of, and 'customers' within the education system. It is no accident that elements symbolising industrial production have deeply penetrated modern architecture. Public and private physical space has moved away from images of individuals protected in the cosy atmosphere of the family home. The individual becomes immersed as an element in the architectural space, rather than being protected by it.

The family continued to be the major paradigm of social and political organisation during the past three centuries of modernisation in Western Europe. The state was interpreted as having a contractual relationship with the assembly of autonomous individuals, but the family was usually considered the fundamental, 'organic' as it were, unit that assured socialisation of the individual and stability of society even during periods when the state had only reduced capacity to maintain order. Leaders in traditional states – including monarchs and totalitarian rulers in more recent times – tended to portray the state and themselves in terms of 'family organisation'. In the early and more advanced stages of industrialisation company organisation and leadership also often emulated relations within a family – a tradition that is still quite strong in some countries. However, in countries of the triad – the United States, the European Union and Japan – the family is no longer the main paradigm for industrial or even political organisation.

Private versus public

'Privatisation' is pushed in the name of 'efficiency'. It has been increasingly argued that the formerly presumed rationality of the state was a myth that interfered with rational production. On the contrary, now it is markets that should evaluate government policies. As one stockbroker put it to me: 'in a few years time it will be up to us to evaluate the state's performance, not parliament that is incompetent to do so'. He also argued that the economy had become so sophisticated that its running and supervision needed specialists: 'If a patient is sick you need to see a doctor – not a parliamentary committee'.

Emphasis on the market and civil society carried by spontaneous 'private' activities is said to put limits on the power of the state, even in a parliamentary democracy. Where once the rational state was upheld as the embodiment of progress, 'rational' (i.e. efficient) production carried by private companies functioning in a rational market place has now taken the place of the rational state. In an ironic twist, 'society' has come back with a vengeance, and we now also see a 'societalisation' of the state (cf. Bailey 2002). For Habermas (1989: 141) '[o]nly this dialectic of a progressive "societalization" of the state simultaneously with an increasing "stateification" of society gradually destroyed the basis of the bourgeois public sphere – the separation of state and society'.

The erosion of parliamentarian authority was also deepened by those who advocate the role of 'civil society' and non-governmental organisations (NGOs) in opposition to 'the state', thus throwing doubt on the level of the democratic content of parliamentary democracy. Since one of the major aims of democracy is the protection of the individual, individuals must surely be protected not only against 'the state', but also against the non-transparent influence of other institutions. There is no assurance that companies in a globalising world are better protectors of the freedom of the individuals than a freely elected government that retains a major say in the direction and execution of economic policies.

Once the 'public' domain (i.e. the state) is maligned as intrinsically 'inefficient' and given a bad name, 'private' becomes 'good' by default. The concentration of economic power in privately owned companies, holding companies and conglomerates is usually justified in terms of efficiency. Advocates of privatisation no longer need to prove that it leads to efficiency – the 'Washington Consensus' (who consented?) has acquired all the hallmarks of an ideology: it provides blanket value judgement. Should privatisation not work well then it must be the fault of those who do not implement its guidelines properly. Privatisation is thus no longer just a matter of economic efficiency, but a matter of assumptions, ethics and morals. It is freely admitted that markets are subject to malfunctioning. It is interesting to note that such malfunctioning is frequently related to issues of behaviour not subject to formal rules and norms. To give but one example: investor-driven markets are prone to causing wrong types of investment, and markets driven by 'private' consumers are preferred. It should not surprise us that behaviour of private consumers is given priority over investors – but it must not be forgotten that private behaviour is also subject to social norms and pressures. In a world of 'lifestyles' where identity boils down to 'I am what I buy', one may perhaps talk of 'driven consumers' in the market place.

Globalisation demands the separation of the public and private sectors, not just in the economy, but also in the political and social spheres. 'Privatisation' refers not so much to rights of individuals, but to the shift of ownership from public institutions (such as the state) to non-state investors. In liberalist thinking the protection of property is one way to protect the individual against the state, but in the age of globalisation the individual also needs protection against threats from other sources than the state. In the age of globalisation the actual financial 'voting' power of ordinary citizens is negligible compared to that of large institutional investors. It is no exaggeration to talk of an increasing 'anonymisation' of capital – where the actual 'owners' of capital often act behind the mask of institutional investors. Anonymisation has become a general feature of advancing globalisation – not just capital, but also the country of origin of products often remains concealed. Brand names suggest creation of products by 'personalities' even if the design of the product is the result of collective intelligence. Names of cars are invented to evoke associations with English (or Latin), even where the product has no relation with any English-speaking environment whatsoever.

Economic privatisation versus individual freedom

Compared with institutional investors the social 'voting power' of the vast majority of citizens is highly limited. As a result, 'privatisation' in the age of globalisation can no longer be equated with naive ideas about the protection of the individual against 'the state'. Freedom of the individual must not simply be defined in terms of macro-systems of political organisation. Free elections for parliament do not guarantee social and economic protection of the individual against threats against the private sphere and personal freedom. Long-term, structural unemployment not only prevents the individual from enjoying economic rights, but also severely restricts access to activities in society, let alone the effect on the people relying on a wage earner for support.

If democracy implies a better protection of the private individual than provided for in other systems, protection cannot simply be assured by focusing on the dynamics of market economics, formal parliamentary democracy and 'civil society'. Differing from images of society in the works of traditional European, Scottish and English social philosophers that placed the role of the natural person in society in a central position, modern 'civil society' is highly institutionalised. The voice of a single individual remains unheard, unless it becomes part of institutionalised civil society. Rather than being a neutral term for historic analysis, civil society is a value-loaded notion, apparent in concepts such as communitarianism American-style (Oren 2000).

Attempting to analyse globalisation in terms of market democracy and civil society reminds me of generals who all too often develop strategies to fight the past war, not future ones. In order to map out strategies for the future we first need to grasp the nature of underlying principles of global-isation, such as the division between public and private, which – far from being universal concepts – are closely linked to concepts prevalent in European and North American civilisation.[3] When belief systems collapse as they did in fascist countries (Italy, Spain, Germany and others), the Soviet Union or with Japan's defeat in 1945, individuals are challenged to re-examine the way they were bonded and linked to society and its past. At such turning points the relationship between the 'citizen', society and the state is likely to undergo important *qualitative* changes difficult to catch in simple, or quantitative, analysis. In this process historians play important roles as destroyers of past myths, at the same time creating new ones. Together with voices from the media, unofficial and official sources of opinion they create a new web of memories that seeks to fix the past in a static, manageable image (Minami 1984; Mizoguchi 1994), and at the same time moving society into the future.

In Asia, the collapse of the Japanese Emperor state with Japan's defeat in 1945 caused a latent belief crisis that resurfaced in recent years with the rise of neo-nationalism. China, Korea and other countries that were prevented from actively taking part in the occupation of Japan are showing increasing signs of anti-Japanese nationalism – perhaps partly due to this fact. The Cultural Revolution in China that ended in the 1970s led to general doubts about the legitimacy of the Maoist system even within the Communist Party. From a historical perspective one of the tasks of global-isation is to strengthen or re-establish forces for cohesion and stability in states that suffer from a collapse in the legitimacy of formally institution-alised ideology. Globalisation often appears to be truly transnational, not bound up with value systems of a particular civilisation.

The separation of moral precepts from demands of science-based devel-opment is a hallmark of globalising modernisation, constantly challenging and changing received values both in Western and non-Western civilisa-tions. Guehenno (1993) developed his model of globalisation on the basis of his understanding of Japan as a society that is based on rules rather than on moral standards internalised by individuals. Globalisation has brought about a significant change in relations between 'politics' and 'economics', 'private' and 'public', and their impact on society as a whole. The mean-ings of 'public' and 'private' have also often shifted in Europe, the United States and elsewhere. For most Western contemporaries 'public' should refer to some space that is, or should be easily accessible to all members of society, whereas 'private' denotes a space where individuals have (limited) rights to exclude others (including the state) from free access.

Although the Chinese, Japanese and Korean languages have terms for concepts akin to 'public' and 'private' in English and other European lan-guages, they never became concepts dividing the realm of 'state' and 'society'. In East Asia, the socialisation of the individual and social control was primarily a task not of the state, or any particular religious organisation, but of the family, clans and village communities whose composition displayed huge regional differences. Value education in merchant families could differ considerably from that of peasants, without leading to institutionalised opposition towards the existing 'political' order. The need to maintain political unity in order to create conditions for economic stability was an important factor preventing the emergence of open conflict between (local) economic elites and the existing centralised political order, and thus reduced the potential for functional differentiation and specialisation so characteristic of Europe. In East Asian history we observe a long-standing policy of governments to prevent religions and ideologies from becoming a focal point for opposition to government and mass mobilisation. This is not unknown in European history, either, but there religious splits forced rules to accept the simultaneous existence of opposing groups, creating mechanisms to cater for coexistence, and in the process creating 'neutral space' that could develop into 'public' space.

Guan versus *min*

In East Asia political ruling elites dominated the administration of territories as 'officials' (*guan* in Chinese, *kan* in Japanese), all others belonging to the sphere of 'ordinary people' (*min* in Chinese and Japanese). These spheres have characteristics opposite to those in Europe. 'Officials' have the authority to prevent general access to their realm while retaining the 'moral' right to interfere in all spheres of 'people's' lives, including property rights. To this must be added the fact that especially after the 9/11 attack Western governments have proceeded apace to put private activities under increasing surveillance.

China, Korea and Japan each differ considerably in the linkages that exist between officials and ordinary people. In China, the primary social environment of the individual was 'clans' (*zongzu*), with roles and functions at the social, economic and micro political and micro legal levels. Clans aspired to protect themselves against the state and others by having some of their members enter the exclusive club of *guan*, with officials continuing to have special obligations to their respective clans. In China, clans provided a kind of 'public' (*gong*) space for their members, akin to the function of the unit (*danwei*) or neighbourhood organisations since 1949. The term *gong* is usually translated as 'public', but in China is more akin to the notion of non-selfishness within one's group – reaching from the family and clan, and extending to the empire as a whole. As an ideal, personal loyalty to leaders was valued less than service to the Chinese empire. In Japan, the same term (read *koo* in Japanese) was arrogated first for the emperor more than one millennium ago, and was subsequently extended to officials operating in the name of personal leaders in general, be they the emperor himself, a *shogun*, or *daimyo* at the local level (Minami 1984). As in China, blood ties were important in shaping society in Korea and Japan as well, but in Japan after the medieval age personal loyalty could be extended to people in a quasi-blood or family relationship. This proved highly important in overcoming the limitations of a feudal-type society. Hereditary status and blood relations continued to influence status and class divisions. Conflicting with ideals embodied in the flood of statements produced by the pre-modern Japanese government local society in villages and small towns displayed far greater vitality and dynamics that prepared the ground for grassroots participation in the difficult period of early Japanese modernisation in the second half of the nineteenth century (Amino 2001).

In the past, at no stage was the 'private' given prevalence over the sphere of officialdom, either in its Japanese or Chinese meanings. In Japan social cohesion continued to be focused on personal social and political loyalties in the more immediate environment. In contrast, China saw important developments that started roughly one millennium ago, and sought to establish a direct relationship between the individual and the 'state', institutions of the empire and its officials. While this was an ideal, the actual pattern of relations between the individual, his or her direct political and social environment and the state continued to change until the present, leading to often quite contradictory comments by Chinese and foreign observers on relations between individuals and the state in pre-modern China. There is a common emphasis on the importance of individuals creating their own independent networks of social relations (Fei Xiaotong), while emphasising the importance of the family for the individual (Liang Suming) (both referred to in Liu Jianhui 2004). As an ideal, however, hereditary status was shunned from 'official' concepts of the Chinese imperial state and its bureaucracy. Numerous commentators pointed out that Chinese society as a whole lacked the cohesion characteristic of the modern nation-state: the founder of the Chinese Republic, Sun Yat-sen, was the most prominent critic. This points to a weakness of pre-modern China, with a sometimes amazing lack of loyalty by individuals to the Chinese state, often ascribed to its autocratic character. Kawajima Naniwa, who observed Chinese society in the early twentieth century, noted that the Chinese 'lack in social cohesion and [their] only motivation is profit: for this reason the downfall of China and its partition among the great powers will be inevitable' (Liu Jianhui 2004).

Chinese history since the Opium Wars was a mixture of reforms and failed attempts at revolution, the most famous the Taiping Revolution in the middle of the nineteenth century. Coupled with the impact of imperialist powers in China indigenous political and economic elites seldom had a chance to engage in gradual modernisation leading towards a stable and coherent system. The People's Republic of China marked the first occasion in more than a century when the state – or rather, the Chinese Communist Party (CCP) operating through the state – attempted to re-impose ethical values on individuals and society. 'Private' and 'individualism' were regarded with suspicion; 'public' and 'collective' were praised. It appears that this attempt built on previous traditions where freedom (*ziyou*) had usually been seen as detrimental to the positive value of unselfishness (*gong*) that had existed in pre-modern Chinese society. There is no denial that the imposition of such socialist ethics did for a considerable period have a deep impact on ethical thinking. The tragedies of the Great Leap Forward and the Cultural Revolution formed a basic attack on humane ethics. Not in theory, but in actual practice, political opportunism was elevated to the rank of highest 'value'.

Symbiosis of political and economic elites

Changes in China since 1978 and in particular since 1991 have caused considerable changes to values. It was not only that getting rich was 'officially' designated a positive value. The existence of newly rising economic elites became slowly legitimised, best expressed through the acceptance of business leaders as members of the CCP. Political elites and economic elites are looking for new forms of symbiotic coexistence, in tacit agreement to avoid deep political reforms. Neither political nor economic elites are willing to risk their relationship through reforms along the lines of transparent 'market democracy' or granting the private unfettered access to a larger public realm. Democracy started in South Korea from the 1990s with its first democratic presidents Kim Young Sam and Kim Daejong. They brought about changes to the political system, but did not put an end to the symbiotic relationship with economic elites. As in Japan, privatisation of enterprises has so far not undermined the symbiosis between political and economic elites. I assume that the weakness or absence of divisions between 'public' and 'private' along Western lines is at the root of the persistence of such patterns. This presents particular problems for the introduction of US-led globalisation and its ideology of market democracy.

In East Asia the 'public' realm remains very much under the impact of officials. Apart from relatively short phases in modern Japanese and Chinese history (Emperor state, and founding decades of the People's Republic of China) when ideology attempted to penetrate private ethics and micro-society, we now see a return to a pattern where the ethics of micro-society – at the workplace, in the neighbourhood – are of much greater relevance for individual ethical standards than 'official' ideology. It is the immediate social environment that tells the individual what his or her wrongdoings are, and in the case of transgressions enforces declarations of remorse. Officialdom may still require outward, 'public' conformity – but does not insist on thought control. This might contribute to the adoption of globalisation as a means to promote stability and cohesion by establishing a rational, efficient and transparent system irrespective of the cultural background of society and its civilisation. The lack of a clearly protected private sphere, coupled with a decreasing ability of the non-organised single individual to exert influence on economic, political and social decision-making in the public sphere appears to undermine confidence in the ability of globalisation to provide sufficient protection for the private individual. European historians and philosophers such as F. Braudel and Jean-Marie Guehenno also emphasised the decreasing ability of the individual to engage in free choice in the globalising world (Greider 1997; Guehenno 1993).

Freedom of the individual in the age of globalisation

Achieving transparency is not the only issue – increased passivity towards participation in parliamentary democracy seems indisputably related to the gap between the reality of the individual's life world and his or her inability to protect his or her freedom through participation in the orderly democratic process. This was one of the major reasons for recent protest votes against the EU constitution. The main concern of the individual appears to be his or her ability to compete in increasingly 'flexible' labour markets. The place of work, rather than the nation or nationalism, becomes a prime concern. This does not only involve jockeying for a good position within an enterprise or government office on the basis of job qualifications. As competition increases, demands on personal physical appearance, and conformity with fashion and rules confront the individual with enormous pressures also in his or her private life.

The beginning of this new age can roughly be put at the time of the suppression of organised labour in the United States since 1981, but it should not be forgotten that similar trends occurred in Japan during the 1960s, followed by Great Britain and other countries.[4] These trends were further pushed by the collapse of the Soviet colonial empire. To the contemporary historian globalisation presents the chance of a lifetime to grapple with the question whether history has meaning at all. The collapse of the Soviet Union stimulated debates by historians on 'globalisation', leading the American Francis Fukuyama (1992) to hail the end of history, while Frenchman Jean-Marie Guehenno (1993) announced the beginning of a new age, the 'imperial age', whose major features he discovers in contemporary Japanese society.

Common wisdom has it that those controlling power in all its aspects prefer to conceal the exercise of power, or exert power in indirect ways. This is partly motivated by the need to avoid or reduce blame for policy failures. Power prefers 'masks' from behind which to exercise power. Different 'national' cultures and civilisations use different kinds of masks. Globalisation has effectively created a plethora of ideological terms and institutions to conceal the fact that the only institution through which all citizens can exercise sovereign power, parliament, has seen the areas of its powers constantly being eroded. One example is the transfer of ever-larger parts of economic decision-making from parliament to institutions such as central banks (Michalet 2002). They in turn have become much less accountable to parliament or government, to which should be added the role of international financial institutions and, in the case of EU member countries, institutions of the EU as well. Moving further away from Central Europe it is obvious that the political economy of China and Russia cannot be captured in simple notions of transition from a (Western-style) socialist dictatorship with a planned economy to a market economy (Vinogradov 2003).

A deeper issue is the fact that globalisation is far from being culture-neutral. In fact, the global homogenisation of rules is also at loggerheads with major notions of the freedom of the individual at the grassroots level within the United States. American concepts of civil society, in particular its communitarianism, promise to protect the individual against the state even when the state takes the form of parliamentary democracy. One issue is the contradiction between received notions of values, justice and the demands of economic rationality, an issue also close to the heart of one of Japan's foremost liberal thinkers, Ishibashi Tanzan (Radtke 2003). Another, at least equally important factor is the cleavage between the domestic value system and US foreign policy. At home, communitarianism and its emphasis on self-help have a clearly anarchistic streak (in the sense of Kropotkin's anarchism), while the projection of US power abroad through the state and its military power risks to operate outside the principles of the domestic value system.

Selection of the fittest: principles of market democracy and the international order

The United States is realistically prepared to take part in a Darwinist struggle for survival against any potential rivals abroad. The protection of US companies by the state in the Darwinist fight for survival in the domestic and international market place also tends to undermine the logic of commonly shared globalist values. Market economics is advocated as the best mechanism to select those companies most suited to promote progress, in a manner evoking Darwinian thinking on the evolution of species, a game that simulates processes of natural evolution. Interpreting globalisation as the spread of 'market plus some democracy' seems an attractive proposition, since it is a form of democracy in which the selection of the fittest relies heavily on the market place, and in which political activities are frequently regarded as improper interference in market mechanisms. One may question whether the desires of individual or institutional consumers (or the 'driven consumer') are the optimal guiding principles to establish a humane society. From a different point of view, the theory and practice of market economics in the age of globalisation have gone beyond the concepts of a 'capitalist' society. The (quasi-)scientific management of human affairs is a much more fundamental, and revolutionary concept than the concept 'capitalism' itself. There is no room to argue in detail that 'capitalism', rather than being the outcome of objective, rational developments, is in fact linked to social and political values. Adam Smith, for one, argued that his 'system' would work only if Western moral values were respected.

Globalisation in its contemporary shape tends to be associated with the spread of 'market democracy', a term that unwittingly betrays a contradiction inherent in globalisation: the institution of the market provides a playing field where 'voting power' is proportionate to the amount of wealth, while parliamentary democracy equips all players with one and the same vote, irrespective of their financial or social status. Since there is no clear and/or formal separation between the competence of the market as an economic institution, and the parliamentary system as a political institution, decisions taken in the framework of economic and political institutions are likely to display rivalry. The structure of power in the market place is inextricably linked to the structure of economic power and authority. It is exercised through instruments such as (intellectual) property rights, or rights to exercise management and decision-making in various forms.

As I indicated above, there is an inherent conflict not only between globalisation and non-Western civilisation, but also a development that originated within Western civilisation that is revolutionising Western political and social morality from within. A proper understanding of globalisation also needs to address issues of the relationship between domestic and international, global order. Concepts of systemic maintenance of balance in the market have deeply influenced concepts of political order. The active spread of 'market democracy' goes beyond concepts of a static, or status quo 'balance'. The core states underwriting this globalising order are more or less identical with the Western 'great powers' of the nineteenth century, now including Japan in an (as yet) minor role. These core powers also pretend to represent the 'international community'. Suppose public opinion (i.e. by private individuals) in China, India, Indonesia, Japan, Nigeria and Brazil agrees on a particular issue, this obviously represents a major part of the global population – but unless sanctioned by the core states of the triad is unlikely to gain the status as representing the so-called international community. When the globalising order is seen as threatened, members of core alliances assume leadership to restore order, aided by more or less loose coalitions that include the largest possible number of countries. Coalitions have a remarkable similarity to united front tactics as applied by communist parties. In case the United Nations is unwilling to support policies of the core states, it is *their* international community, and not the members of the United Nations, that seek to re-establish the threatened order. This accounted for the refusal of the United States to use the United Nations as a forum to prepare for, and legitimise its intervention in Afghanistan.

Globalised order is based on a clear distribution of tasks, division of labour and leadership, rather than on global consensus. The hierarchical aspect is strengthened still further due to the need to speed up decision-making in all areas of military activities, as well as in the economy, visible in particular in financial markets. The question arises whether all these are inevitable historical developments. It usually is in the interest of authority to deny the possibility of alternatives, if for no other reason than the only alternative is 'anarchy'. The remainder of the globe attracts the attention of global leaders mainly when that core order is threatened. My use of the term 'core leaders' and 'core states' does not imply that the 'remainder' of the globe belongs to any kind of 'periphery' – it is hardy appropriate to call the overwhelming part of the world's population 'periphery'.

The strength of the United States is often taken as proof of the superiority of the system it advocates, and forcefully propagates. Historians are well aware that mono-causal explanations hardly ever provide fruitful explanations. What is appropriate to the physical environment of the United States may be highly unsuitable elsewhere. Becoming the world's uncontested hegemon is presented as being due to possessing advanced values, further used to legitimise the spread of globalisation as a political project.

Other countries have their own perspectives. China, for instance, is still prone to conceptualise the world in terms of a clash of civilisations, a concept introduced as a result of the introduction of ideas of social Darwinism to East Asia. The concept clash of civilisations (*wenhua chongtu* in Chinese) was an extremely popular topic in Japan, China, and Korea for about two decades beginning in the late nineteenth century (Chun 1992; Allen 2001). It also affected those who sought an escape from the seemingly unavoidable conflict, as in Okuma Shigenobu's (1923) *Toozai bunmei no choowa* (*Reconciling civilisation East and West*). Samuel Huntington merely rekindled memories of this earlier discussion through his popular writings on the 'clash of civilisations'. It also strengthened the position of those Chinese who conceptualise long-term US strategy in terms of Alfred Mahan and Mackinder, whose advocacy of overseas imperialism is linked to the visions of a global role for the United States in the thinking of Brzezinski, Kissinger and Nixon. Since the CCP decided to tone down public analyses of US imperialism, views related to the concept of a clash of civilisations have virtually replaced the analysis of the United States in terms of Marxist-Leninist 'class struggle'. This also facilitates the revival of concepts of a clash of civilisations between 'East and West', including assumptions of a final showdown between China and the United States that are structurally similar to ideas held in Japan during the 1930s. From there it is only a short step towards arguing that the US-led project of globalisation is simply a new name for traditional hegemonic goals. Apart from the extreme right and left, voicing anti-American sentiments remains restrained and muted in Japan on the assumption that cooperation with the United States serves Japanese ambitions best.

This is one of the reasons why perceptions of the United States in terms of 'neo-colonialism' are fairly popular in China and not so far removed from the portrayal of US expansionism across the Pacific popular in Japanese right wing thinking. Japanese nationalist feelings find their expression not only in domestic right wing nationalism, but also in an increasingly assertive policy towards Japan's neighbours, especially North Korea and China. The apparent support for a much larger Japanese military role serves to fan anti-American notions in Korea.

Globalised elites and local identity

From this point of view globalisation is threatening to the identity of states and civilisations in East Asia, especially if the history of the twenty-first century is seen as the history of globalisation that relegates the history of geographical regions and disparate civilisations to the realm of local history. Of course we are not yet able to evaluate the direction of global civilisation five decades from now, but I feel confident to assert that globalisation is unlikely to coincide with simple notions of 'Western civilisation' and its values. It seems much more likely that globalisation develops in the direction of imposing sets of rules on various countries and civilisations that leave considerable room for local self-determination, in a manner reminiscent of the way the Chinese empire was run. Features of the pre-modern Chinese empire such as the creation of a supra-regional officialdom with a common training and background in administration resembles globalised MBA training. Chinese elites shared a common language quite different from the spoken languages of the empire. Rather than directly setting out detailed blueprints for regional and local central government the empire was run along the lines of 'small government', coordinating, interfering where necessary, negotiating with regional and local powers, and adjusting taxation systems according to the greatly varying kinds of economies. Although there was a unified criminal code, this mainly pertained to exceptionally heavy misdemeanour, and civil and commercial law was largely implemented according to the requirements and customs of regions and localities.

The rise of globalised elites has advanced rapidly during the past decades, while attempts to construct an international space for domestic civil society have lagged behind. Globalised elites are members of an epistemic community that shares the experience of similar curricula of business and management schools worldwide. In a sense they resemble the political elites of the Chinese empire, a numerically fairly small number of officials who were systematically trained and socialised as supra-regional elites. Selected on the basis of knowledge of the Confucian canon through the examination system, they constituted an epistemic community engaged in the management of local and supra-local affairs. 'Western' countries have been the main powers pushing globalisation and in the course of doing so changing essential characteristics of their own culture and civilisation. If we look for paradigms of an evolving 'globalised' twenty-first century we would do well to study political and economic models of other societies – they may, in fact, provide paradigms that will make it easier to grasp the complexity of globalisation.

To be sure, the Chinese imperial system as a whole cannot become a useful model for future globalisation. The Chinese administration was not comprised of a federation of a small number of very strong and competing local entities of the kind that gave such dynamism to European and Japanese early modernisation. Rather it consisted of a large number of local elites who acted in concert with the remote central government but had very little interaction or interdependence among themselves. Such a system had little capacity for avoiding unrest by gradual adjustment and evolution. The Chinese empire did not impose one national language or uniform culture on the ordinary citizens of the empire, and adopted different forms of taxation according to the economic structure of regions. It accepted the widespread use of self-government both in the economy, moral education and even parts of the criminal law. In this sense, the organisation of the Chinese empire may present an early paradigm of 'globalised governance' that required only limited inputs to impose centralised political rule, but left precious little space for the development of a country-wide 'civil society', able and willing to supervise and, if necessary, confront the state. Cultural and ideological patterns were strong enough to keep alive the ideal of a universalistic central government even under adverse circumstances. Indeed, this concept of a unified system was maintained even during the many centuries when China was under the control of ethnic alien rule. A basic feature of globalisation is the willingness of parts of domestic elites to engage in transnational cooperation. In doing so they are frequently, if not continuously, opposed by other forces in society, as the following two case studies of privatisation will show.

State-led privatisation in Japan: the postal system

The implementation of the privatisation of state-owned enterprises (SOEs) in China through the SASAC, and the long-lasting fight by Japanese Prime Minister Junichiro Koizumi for the privatisation of the Japanese postal system, including the Postal Savings Bank and Pension Fund, illustrate the importance of such projects for systemic change. Affected are not only the enterprises concerned; at stake also are the structure of the financial system and the role of government in the banking system. The present system – both in China and Japan – allows officials, in the broad definition of the word that includes selected members of the ruling parties, to steer state money to institutions and (public) corporations beyond the control of the Ministry of Finance and the Central Bank. Privatisation will thus have a deep impact on the relationship of officials and political parties with society and state bureaucracy. Last, but not least, reforms are set to have a lasting impact on social norms, but it is far from clear yet whether this will lead to clear distinctions between 'public' and 'private', and better governance. The reforms have to be implemented by leaders whose power base may be negatively affected by the reforms. This explains a good deal of the difficulties in implementing reforms, leading to complex political manoeuvring and frequent changes in setting up new organs and institutions to oversee and implement the reform process.

By the end of the day most attempts at reform end in compromise that make it difficult to anticipate their lasting impact. China's state-led privatisation of SOEs is guided by SASAC, an organ functioning as part of the overall reform policy-making process at the same time as being the main manager of assets in competition with the Ministry of Finance. Lurking in the background are also interests from within political parties that are often difficult to gauge (Yomiuri 2005). Added to this must be the fact that in Japan the prime minister has only limited authority:

> Koizumi as leader of the ruling party is merely such. The real power is in Kasumigaseki, with the zokugiin [i.e., the parliamentary 'tribes']. What is interesting in the case of the post office is that Prime Minister Koizumi perceived that the General Affairs Ministry really did intend to privatise the Japan Post in the way that he envisioned, so he turned the task over to the Privatisation Preparatory Office of the Cabinet.
>
> (Inose 2005)

The Japanese postal savings system, including a pension and insurance system, has from the beginning of the Japanese modernisation process served to gather funds from individual depositors all over the country, and at the same time provided an affordable social safety net, mainly intended for those on relatively low incomes. It also served the purpose of providing many various officials with the means to exercise power in an informal, non-transparent way. The Fiscal Investment and Loan Program (FILP), for instance, funnelled funds to government corporations, 'including the Japan Development Bank (JDB, now known as the Development Bank of Japan or DBJ). The JDB, in turn, invested in projects to strengthen the nation's physical infrastructure' (Arai 2005). They are also part of Japan's long-standing policies to strengthen weaker economic regions that might otherwise not be able to compete effectively, causing social and political imbalances within Japan. One of the issues for reform is to remove the lower insurance and other costs for these semi-governmental corporations and institutions that are deemed to engage in unfair competition with companies in the free market economy (Inose 2005). These reforms affect 400,000 employees, and involve a huge capital.

The current reform plans anticipate a transitional period of ten years starting from 2007, resulting in the splitting up of various services into a holding company for the postal service, a public savings corporation, a public life and insurance company, and various other 'window services'.[5] The *Journal of the American Chamber of Commerce in Japan* (ACCJ 2004: 16) contains a rather apt description of past experience:

> In Japan, there is a tendency to convert a government agency into, first, a kosha, or public enterprise, and then to convert the kosha into a kabushiki kaisha [stock company], and to call that process privatisation. There have been very mixed results. In the debate over each individual case, the vested interests stake out their turf and the debate goes on around the extent to which their interests will be protected and preserved.

Maclachlan (2004: 45) has recently described in detail how postmasters of Japan's approximately 24,000 postal offices and their links with Liberal

Democrat Party (LDP) parliamentary members, especially those organised as the 'postal tribe' with close ties to the system play 'a big role in what types of reform measures could be considered in the Diet', the Japanese parliament. It is highly significant that the 'postal tribe' consists mainly of parliamentarians close to the thinking of former Prime Minister Tanaka Kakuei. He strongly advocated measures to maintain a safety net not only for weaker individuals, but also for weaker economic regions that would be badly hit in an unfettered market economy. In contrast, advocates of 'privatisation' also aim to force individuals and small and medium enterprises (SMEs) to accept far greater (personal) risk than has so far been the case, bringing about a lasting and deep effect on a broad range of social norms (Amyx *et al.* 2005). A factor complicating the reform process is that the legal system, especially the Commercial Code, also needs to be reformed at the same time (Companies Incorporated 2005). A very important purpose is to prevent the capital from the postal financial services being used to finance government budget deficits through the acquisition of government issued bonds – a practice that dates back to pre-war days (under Finance Minister Baba in 1936) and was taken up in the post-war period by circumventing laws from 1947 expressly forbidding this process.

State-led privatisation in China: SASAC

The Japanese reform process has surprising similarities with some of the features of the 'privatisation' process in China. SASAC was set up in 2003 to guide the reform of SOEs. As in Japan, SASAC competes with a host of other formal and informal institutions for power, management and ownership rights, including the Ministry of Finance (Slater 2004; Buckley 2005). One such organ was the State Economic and Trade Commission (SET), established as a component department of the State Council pursuant to the Chinese cabinet institutional restructuring scheme passed in March 1998 by the First Session of the Ninth National People's Congress of the People's Republic of China. In China the issue is further complicated by the fact that the privatisation of SOEs coincides with a major restructuring of the organisation for energy policy-making and the banking system (Cai and Yang 2005; Green 2004, 2005). SASAC is not merely a

> passive stakeholder in these assets; it has emerged as a massive conglomerate, engineering mergers and management transfers to achieve its goals, observers said. In September last year, the agency's chairman, Li Rongrong, told a conference in Beijing that China must nurture its own multinationals to challenge the dominance of foreign corporations. . . . 'To accelerate the strategic adjustment of China's economic structure', he said, 'we must vigorously pursue a strategy of creating major corporate conglomerates'.
>
> (Buckley 2005)

During the period from 1994 until 2004 there were 3,484 bankruptcies related to the execution of restructuring policies, including a massive amount of debt, and the relocation of 66.7 million workers. In the final phase from 2005 to 2008 SASAC is scheduled to deal with another 2,167 enterprises employing altogether 3.7 million workers. Beijing, Shanghai, Jiangsu, Zhejiang and Fujian have already stopped continuing policy-induced bankruptcies, and moved to bankruptcies according to legal procedures (Xinhua 2005). To date SASAC is directly entrusted with 180 large SOEs, quite a few of them profitable, including 10.2 million employees. Differently from Japan, the reform process is expressly designed to nurture efficient companies that are able to withstand global competition, but the reform process also involves strategic development goals in the energy sector, the banking sector and the development of China's Northeast, the Western provinces, and parts of Central China. In Japan the reform process intends to weaken the informal links between party politicians and the flow of state funds to the politicians' constituencies. In China, by contrast, leaders involved in the reform process take great care to stress maintaining, or increasing, the moral authority of the Party as a result of the reforms.

Proposals for market-oriented reform from the Organization for Economic Co-operation and Development (OECD) (and the World Bank) stress the importance of a systematic approach that includes references to a 'philosophical' framework commonly shared by countries involved in the globalisation process. A good description is found in the 'Principles of privatization: how global best practices should be used for effective privatization of public entities' (ACCJ 2004). Not so surprisingly, the reforms are supported by referring to the advantages China and Japan can derive from them. The arguments of fair play in a level playing field for markets in goods and financial instruments, facilitation of merger and acquisition, and equal access to building conglomerates are major reasons. Over the past three and a half decades a major force for reforms in Japan has also been the strong desire by '[m]any private financial institutions, domestic and foreign alike . . . to lure some of those [state-controlled] funds into other financial instruments, primarily in the private sector' (Amyx *et al.* 2005: 24).

In China this is also the case – but the rather shaky domestic banking system will soon be exposed to even much larger competition from foreign banks that will obtain major access to the Chinese market as part of China's accession to the World Trade Organization (WTO) (Yokota 2005). In addition, China needs to gain control over the – so far, illegal – widespread private financing operations that not only have beneficial effects, but are also held accountable for part of the housing bubble in major urban centres, a delicate topic with potential for social unrest (*China Daily* 20 June 2005). This chapter does not deal with management buyouts (MBOs), including foreign firms involved in buy out, and foreign takeovers of Chinese listed companies that also exert an important impact on the restructuring of ownership in the Chinese economy (Green 2004, 2005).

Even this short survey of state-led privatisation in Japan and China indicates major implications, and the width and depth of the reform process, that go far beyond technical, material issues of enterprise reform, and are likely to affect social and political norms that involve the ideological legitimisation of the current system. The ideological implications are easy to see in the case of socialist China. On the surface, privatisation does not face ideological obstacles in Japan – but there are serious implications for the status of officials and 'party officials' and their ability to steer significant amounts of capital. From the 1920s to the 1930s confidential committee meetings of the Upper House of Parliament debated the question whether the system of private property was incompatible with the Emperor system, and its claim for absolute authority over all other institutions. This ideological question could not seriously be debated in public. By the end of the war the occupying forces – especially the United States – held that Japan's peculiar structure of business conglomerates that cooperated with military leaders had been a major cause of Japan's 'aberration' from the path towards true parliamentary democracy. The attempts by the Occupation to change the Japanese 'system' permanently did not prevent the reappearance of a dense network of informal links crossing the lines of an ideal separation of 'public' and 'private.'

The franchise system as a paradigm for globalisation

If freedom of the individual is linked to the protection of the private sphere, and democracy to the maintenance of good governance, creating an appropriate international public space and good international governance is a pressing issue. I suggest the use of a business concept, the franchise system, as a paradigm for describing characteristics of a globalising order. It compares the main members of the triad to headquarters of a franchise system that provides models for economic, social and political order to other countries, thereby establishing networks with important implications for international relations.

The structure of the international order since the Second World War, dominated by alliance systems, resembled the rivalry between two franchise enterprises: the Soviet one, and the project later to be known as market democracy led by the United States. We may liken the export of forms of organisation in the political, cultural, social and economic sphere to the spread of a network of franchise enterprises, not 'owned' by company headquarters, but bound to it in a complex set of relationships. Its relative stability is among other things due to the fact that membership promises stable returns on investments. Withdrawal from the chain usually results in heavy losses of accumulated investments. A franchise enterprise 'thinks globally, and acts locally'. It markets its products in globally recognisable packages, but their contents are not always identical with those produced elsewhere (some people love to discuss the different taste of Coca Cola produced in Mexico compared with that of China). The language of debates on particular policy issues ('discourse') tends to be structured along the lines of the discourse prevalent at franchise headquarters, whatever the specific local conditions. Scholars affiliated with the culture of franchise headquarters carry greater weight than those in the so-called 'periphery', if for no other reason than that they can actually influence decision-making in Washington. The contents of 'good governance' reflect the codes set by franchise headquarters.

The international order is no place for the implementation of 'one state, one vote'. The core states of the triad underwrite globalising order. Global markets lead by definition to an international division of labour. Different structures of the economy, including military capabilities, coupled with differences in geopolitical circumstances result in a fairly clear distribution of tasks to maintain order (i.e. security). This, in turn, points to an increasingly hierarchical international order where 'sovereignty' has become thoroughly relativised. Some countries are more sovereign by a multiple factor. As a result, this evolving international order can no longer be adequately conceptualised in terms of the main schools in (US) international relations theory, in so far as they rely on balance of power theories where states can only choose between 'bandwagoning' and 'balancing'. The franchise paradigm emphasises a situation where states are willing (or forced) to accept domestic and international principles of order that promise to be more beneficial (profitable), even if this entails loss of freedom to select the nature of the domestic order. It also accounts for the semi-independent nature of most state actors (Armacost and Pyle 2001).[6]

The franchise paradigm seems particularly adequate in the analysis of East Asia. There is a remarkable coyness among Japanese security specialists to openly advance concepts that might challenge 'ruling' American concepts. True, China's Communist Party still presents its own brand of 'market socialism', but its accession to the WTO entails obligations of long-term, permanent changes to its social, political and economic systems. Since citizens of countries other than the core states have a lesser vote on the contents of the global order their impact on governance is by definition limited. The meaning of public space in the sense of allowing private citizens equal access to self-determination and government is therefore heavily circumscribed.

Societies outside the triad have few choices left: they either voluntarily accept modernisation and its concomitant separation of (traditional) values from the structure of modernising states, or attempt to construct rival orders. Attempts to create rival orders have so far failed, such as pre-war Japan's attempt to create its own Asian empire ('Co-Prosperity Zone'), the Soviet attempt at global revolution, or the Chinese attempt to construct a revolutionary global order based on cooperation among Third World countries. It is noticeable that among these countries only Japan succeeded in becoming part of the leading triad, even if its power to shape core elements of global order has so far been limited. This is also evident from its under-representation in major international institutions, including its failure to become a permanent member of the Security Council with full veto-rights.

A major achievement of globalisation is the creation of sets of orders that regulate relations between the individual, society and the state (civil society), the behaviour of companies (governance), and setting of standards for a global economic order symbolised in institutions such as the World Bank, the International Monetary Fund (IMF) and the WTO. Lest there be any misunderstanding: the order thus created rests on the shared acceptance of institutionalised forms of rivalry and conflict whose solution still requires the exercise of military, economic and political power. WTO dispute settlement mechanisms illustrate the point: in case a member state is said to have breached WTO rules a decision is handed down that *legitimises* punitive retaliation against the offender (Wiesebron and Radtke 2002). It does *not* preclude the possibility of a new Cold War between the United States and China. US alliances with European states (North Atlantic Treaty Organization (NATO)) and alliances such as the US–Japan alliance are core elements in maintaining a global security order led by the triad, while ad hoc coalitions created by the United States for the Gulf War, or the recent Afghanistan and Iraq wars, are merely temporary arrangements. Core alliances by far transcend tasks and functions described in balance of power theories. Going far beyond cooperation in military security they link member states in a semi-permanent fashion that recalls the organisation of a franchise enterprise. Certain features dominant in China and Japan seem to make China, and especially Japan even more susceptible to adopting a secularised, or largely de-ideologised concept of globalisation, to a greater extent than is the case in the United States or EU member countries. A brief glance at the history of these regions gives us clues to understanding the reasons for these differences. They also assist us in understanding how individuals and micro-society react differently to globalisation.

Imposing globalisation: from France to the United States

France's conquest of Europe at the turn of the eighteenth century speeded up the formation of common markets and nation-states in defence against any future similar aggression. This, however, did not prevent the rapid growth of trans-border markets in Europe. British expansion into Asia (India, the Opium Wars against China, to mention only a few) did not stimulate a similar growth of independent nation-states in reaction to British conquest and encroachment. Except for Japan (and, to some extent, Thailand) the traditional governments in East and South East Asia were either replaced by various colonial governments led by European countries and the United States, or forced into a semi-colonial dependent status (China).

The application of mathematical models not just in the natural sciences, but in all spheres of socialised human activities was first conceived and implemented in the mother of modern globalisation, France, with Prussia being an adept disciple of French ideas on modernisation. The French Revolution signalled the advent of a modernising state engaging in scientific management of its affairs, including large-scale social engineering, presenting itself as a model for the creation of other states. It also extended its reach by military conquest and the establishment of alliances to spread its model. The French-led 'Confederation of the Rhine' (Rheinbund) may thus be seen as the first beginnings of the globalisation process. The spread of a science-based model of governance distinguishes this from mere conquest or traditional-style colonisation, and is a daring feat no other civilisation attempted to achieve. The pretence of mathematical models as an adequate reflection of the laws of nature sets it apart from the use of numbers as in the Cabala, or other numerically based systems of interpretation of the world around us. Modern market economics has gone a step further. It has applied the lessons of biological Darwinism to economic development. It still needs to be shown that this attempt will also become the basis for modernised ethics and group loyalties that transcend the borders of cultures and civilisations.

Until the French Revolution wars created little 'national enthusiasm' – this concept was, ironically perhaps, prepared for by European enlightenment. Jean Jacques Rousseau summed this up by stating that fighting in war was an obligation, not a profession, and that every person must be a soldier to defend his freedom. The recent abolition of the draft in France (and in other developed countries) is not only a measure to rationalise the maintenance of the armed forces. The 'privatisation' of warfare (and the prison system) reached considerable proportions during the last US war and occupation of Iraq. Far from being mere policies to increase 'efficiency' they symbolise a deeper change in the relationship between the individual and the government of his or her state. Privatisation enables government to conduct war more easily. Both China and Japan experienced a multitude of different religious and political persuasions, but they were usually not organised on a nationwide scale ready to take on the state and government.

East Asia in historical perspective

Images of Chinese and Japanese 'civilisation' tend to be associated with values that remained consistent over longer periods of time. China was no exception when it came to the need to increase the legitimacy of the contemporary imperial system by emphasising its consistence with tradition, even when China was under foreign rule for several centuries in a row. Traditionally, the Chinese emperor stood at the apex of a society that was effectively governed under conditions of 'balance' and 'equilibrium'. Great pains were taken to prevent public expression of dissent towards the state, but society was far from being the 'just and harmonious' society of its

Confucian ideals. In actual fact, East Asian societies repeatedly underwent not only dramatic upheaval, but also systemic reconstruction and social engineering during their long medieval age. Modern-style 'social engineering' is a form of socialisation seeking change in the identity of its objects, the desires of consumers, akin to preachers wishing to alter the behaviour of believers, but social engineering as such is not a phenomenon unique to the modern age (Radtke 2004).

In its history China had suffered numerous conquests and division of the empire, as well as large-scale peasant uprisings. Japan had been lucky to escape occupation, but it had faced threats of (localised) invasion, and the Tokugawa government established in the seventeenth century had also been deeply concerned about attacks on Japan by the Manchus during that century (Kamiya 1997). Needless to say, this difference of exposure to foreign threats had a major impact on the domestic order, and the relation of individuals to rulers and state. In the thirteenth and fourteenth centuries the Mongols engaged in a thorough restructuring of Chinese society to fit their concepts of a multi-layered, hierarchically ordered society based on ethnic discrimination (Radtke 1984). More recently, '[t]he Manchus, warlords, foreign imperialists, Nationalists and communists (under Maoist and post-Mao regimes) tried to impose quite different conceptions of citizenship upon the populations living under their control' (Goldman and Perry 2002).

During the fifteenth and sixteenth centuries Japanese society underwent fundamental changes that made Japan very different from mainland Asia. Hereditary and blood relations continued to influence status and class divisions, but new patterns of cooperation among individuals and groups became important where no genuine blood ties were required (Yoda 1995). The Japanese system during the Edo period displayed features of increasing supra-regional trade accompanied by a highly complex arrangement between central (*Bakufu*) government and 'local' rule (the *Han*, domain). Local rulers displayed clear mercantilist policies versus rival domains – it is not mere coincidence that domains were called *kuni* (country) in common parlance, and domain interests were named *kokueki* (identical with the modern term signifying national interest). The pretence of political unification did not prevent Japanese villages from operating in semi-self-governing communities with aspects of a mini-state. Rather than opposing central political rule they were adept at negotiations that preserved the 'face' of unified rule, but left sufficient room for an informal 'public' space at the local level. Tanaka Keiichi describes how rising economic elites in the Edo period were partially co-opted by political elites, only to block off access to power by the following generation of rising economic elites. This process is a phenomenon that can also be observed in China. This is a vital key to understanding the vagueness of borders between politics and economics, private and public that continues to influence the present. Different from (early) modern Europe, economic elites, merchants and industrialists in Japan and China did not overthrow outdated political systems, although they clearly had an impact on politics. If globalisation can be seen as a political revolution brought about by business (Thurow 2000), judging from past behaviour business in Japan and China may not be as ready as European and US business to aspire for direct political power.

When we look at the countryside we notice another surprising parallel between in China and Japan. Government documents of the Tokugawa period (1600–1868) consistently portray Japanese society as being divided into the Confucian stereotypes 'gentry, peasants, artisans, tradesmen'. They pretend that society remained stable due to severe restrictions on the mobility between classes, and that also included the prohibition of land sales. In recent years some Japanese scholars have pointed out that reality was often at great variance from claims by the government (Amino 2001; Tanaka 2000). Using simple and widely available subterfuge land could actually be bought and sold, and attracting settlers from neighbouring and other domains in order to strengthening one's own domain economically did occur, in contravention of official ideology. The historical, political, social and economic conditions of eighteenth-century Japan and twentieth-century China can hardly be compared, but it is noticeable that in China, too, there is a lively market for land even as ideology prohibits sales. The ideological grounds for prohibition differ, of course, from those of pre-modern Japan. My point is that neither did the pre-modern Japanese nor the contemporary Chinese government insist hard-handedly on enforcing the ideology, nor did those in breach of ideology find it opportune to challenge government head on. This seems to underline that in the countryside, too, Japan and China shared a culture of modus vivendi, compromise and coexistence accompanied by tacit understandings. In the final analysis, this may be related to shared underlying visions where the state arrogates the realm of ideological unification but is wise enough not to provoke widespread popular resistance. The situation in contemporary Japan is of course quite different, with no restrictions on public opinion, or the imposition of a particular state ideology. Nevertheless, political elites remain very careful not to provoke widespread resistance to policies, preferring a long-term approach of gradually 'changing the atmosphere' to introduce change, so visible in the status of Japan's armed forces and Japan's defence relationship with the United States.

The role of 'officials' in the revival of East Asia

Nineteenth-century China incurred great expenses in military campaigns against internal and external enemies. The inability of the Chinese imperial central government to reorganise the tax system to obtain necessary revenue is merely one of the many indicators proving that the apparent cohesion of the Chinese empire had little to do with the integrative character of nineteenth-century European nation-states (Hazama *et al.* 1996). From the eighteenth century Europe rapidly speeded up the linking of local and regional markets beyond the borders of a highly scattered system of local and regional political entities. China, on the contrary, was politically united under a central government, even if the tax system, for instance, clearly indicated acknowledgement of the different economic structure of parts of the empire.

Chinese attempts to re-stabilise the country and regenerate it through modernisation movements repeatedly undertaken from the mid-nineteenth century failed. China first mistakenly assumed that the state itself was to create 'rational' forms of production (Yangwu movement in the 1860s). Stock companies were introduced towards the end of the nineteenth century, but there was far too little trust in society to induce investors to entrust their capital to companies unless they had personal relations with their owner/managers.

Japanese reforms were executed under heavy foreign pressure, and not just since the arrival of US Admiral Perry who noted in his diary that should Japan refuse to open its markets, he had a sufficient number of canons on board to persuade Japan to open its markets. The implications of China's defeat in the Opium Wars were obvious to Japan's leaders. Japan, too, subsequently suffered from unequal treaties impairing its sovereignty. Japan was lucky to avoid wholesale colonisation, and used the opportunities given to engage in reforms. Modernisation requires positive willingness to change moral values.

For better or worse, Japanese nationalists working for reform used the concept of a native 'Emperor system' to provide for legitimacy, but at the same time pushing for the introduction of concepts of private property and other elements of a capitalist order. Decades later there were lively discussions in the secret committee of the Upper House centring on the question whether the Emperor system and the capitalist order were compatible. From an intellectual viewpoint it was admitted that the two were incompatible. As a result, the discussions were kept secret, and care was taken not to cause widespread public dissent.

'Privatisation' of state assets has been a constant theme throughout Japanese and Chinese history since the latter part of the nineteenth century. The state was the only institution capable of gathering sufficiently large amounts of capital needed to set up companies essential for the initial early modernisation drive, in particular in the transport sector – shipping in Japan, railroads in China. The privatisation of such companies at fire sale prices to political friends was one factor in the ability of state elites to co-opt, or even create newly rising economic elites. The traditional symbiosis between 'political' and 'economic' elites reasserted itself. In China, however, privatisation of the railways involved admission of foreign business interests under the protection of China's foreign Manchu rulers – one of the factors that led the overthrow of the imperial state.

The successful construction of unified nation-states is usually followed by expansionism and foreign conquest, and Japan became another country to corroborate this point. One may argue that China was the proverbial exception to this rule, but in my view the initial support by China after 1949 for global socialist and communist revolution may be compared to the expansionism of other young nation-states. The establishment of the People's Republic of China in 1949 seemed to signify the definitive victory of secularised political and social concepts of European origin (i.e. communist ones) in China, with the addition of some 'Chinese characteristics'. The CCP claimed moral authority to change social relations in Chinese society, underpinned by its ideological monopoly. Mao's aim for *total* revolution included the destruction of traditional patterns of political culture, and support for total supremacy of the political realm. This was not meant to deny the economic imperative – but in Mao's eyes, China's successful economic build-up required revolution from above under the control of the political revolutionaries. It was obvious as early as the 1950s that in the eyes of many, communist officials were officials, and in the course of time not a few even used the term *guan* (official) to refer to themselves. Both the Great Leap Forward and the Great Proletarian Cultural Revolution also aimed to destroy and reconstruct patterns of China's political and economic culture, and prevent the rise of new economic elites ('bourgeois capitalists') from limiting the powers of its political leaders. Mao's revolution failed even before his death. The continuing dictatorship by the CCP posed the need to legitimise a situation where ordinary people (*min*) who were not Party members, were not only recognised as citizens (*gongmin*), but also allowed considerable room for economic initiatives as long as they did not challenge the Party or the state.

This is the background to the reform policies of the 1980s and 1990s. It does not surprise that the Party and the state continue to claim that the reforms of the 1980s were due to initiatives taken by the Party's leaders – but to some extent this should be seen as a face-saving measure. For the following decades the gradual acceptance of the rise of new economic elites made China return to older traditions of its political culture, where economic elites were co-opted by political ones. The separation of Party, state and economic institutions propagated in China since the early 1980s is a messy process, partly because it entails incessant challenges to the political monopoly of the Party. The introduction of a (socialist) market economy, and the formal acceptance of 'globalisation' symbolised in China's accession to the WTO provide some challenges to the ideological and moral monopoly of the CCP, but it is uncertain how this will change the position of the Party in future Chinese society. China's development can however not simply be judged by looking at the macro level. Indeed, it is developments at the micro level that tell us more about the effects of the 'marriage' between a one-party dictatorship and globalisation as a 'political' project.

In post-war Japan, opposition by business against excessive discretionary power of individual officials became an important force pushing for reform and privatisation. China's conditions are clearly quite different from those of Japan, but in China, too, excessive discretionary power of officialdom since the 1950s has been a leading factor for privatisation. In other words, 'privatisation' in both countries is not necessarily the result of foreign pressures to conform to the demands of US-led globalisation. Yet it cannot be overlooked that privatisation does undermine the assumed moral superiority of the state, and was often perceived in terms of 'corruption' of China's post-war model of government (Walder 1986; Lu 1993). Such views are also fostered by the fact that such 'privatisation' does not necessarily lead to the strengthening of the position of the individual citizen. More than anything else, it presages the resurrection of new forms of symbiosis between political and economic elites. It goes without saying that these developments are highly complex, and may differ widely from region to region:

> No independent economic elite has emerged from the market reforms. As in the Newly Industrialised Countries of East Asia, the state in China plays a crucial role in initiating and facilitating enterprise. There is, however, a crucial difference. In China, it is not the central state, but rather local governments and their cadres which have taken the lead.
>
> (Oi 1997)

Such developments do not merely affect industrialised urban areas (cf. Walder 1995; Hill 1996):

> Village cadres behave as business administrators rather than as government officials. Their personal connections are most important not only in township and village enterprises, but also in all other fields of management. . . . The recognition that at least the cohesive-type villages, with their well-defined administrative and economic boundaries, behave like competitive firms has important implications for the common preposition that Chinese enterprises tend to have fuzzy boundaries and soft budgetary constraints.
>
> (Pei 1997)

Micro-society in the age of globalisation

As mentioned earlier in this chapter, changes in micro-society are an essential part of globalisation. In Chinese companies, personnel management has shifted from Party control to specific business administration (Long 1999; Zhong 1996). The struggle for rights, and the survival of workers forms the subject of the novel *Union Chairman* (Yu *et al.* 1997). It discusses the position and protection of private property by the state, which recent legislation has strengthened. This is likely to weaken the foundations of socialist ideology. It is commonly believed that by now money decides nearly everything, and that includes the realm of human relations (Xu 1996). In a culture that traditionally looked down on sheer 'power' and 'personal gain' (*quan* and *si*) this must necessarily affect the status of 'public-spiritedness' (*gong*), and, equally important in the age of globalisation, a (gradual) transition towards predictable rule and order (expressed in the Chinese word for law, *fa*) (Zhang and Xin 1998). Long Zhiyi's (Long 1999) novel *Politicians* also deals with the change of values and norms (*jiazhi guilü*) as a result of the transition to a market economy, but this is not described as an 'automatic' process: human emotions do not change that simply (see also Qi 1998). There are far fewer references to positive new values arising from the change of the system, such as when it is argued that the new system introduces greater equality. The language of values is tenacious, however. Literature contains frequent references to the rule of the land (the traditional empire) such as 'the way of the kings' (*wangfa*) governing the empire/world (*tianxia*) (Zhong 1996; Xu 1996). These, and other events, raise the question to what extent globalisation will affect the ability of societies to maintain, and possibly increase, their social and political cohesion. There are signs of the rise of 'private' values. An individual ostracised by surrounding society (rightly or wrongly) may enjoy moral respect within the family that allows him or her to maintain moral self-respect as an individual (Zhang and Xin 1998). As in Japan, the nuclear family and its stable 'private' environment proves essential for contributing to social stability during the process of modernisation in general, and globalisation in particular.

In China, 'civic' responsibility is still a sensitive issue, since advocating individual responsibility invariably undermines the claim by the Party to set moral standards. The relation between private, public and social morality is usually not a static one, but changes in the course of history. During the 1920s there were numerous articles in China on *kokkashugi*, the idea of the state, such as by Li Huang. Li Huang argued that in Chinese history for thousands of years private, family and individual morality were at the centre, but not civic responsibility. Such views were fairly common during the pre-war period. Like others, Li Huang is fascinated by the idea that Jews too preserved their national identity even during long periods when they did not have a state.[7]

However, globalisation and economic privatisation are not coterminous with the retreat of the state. In an interesting analysis of Dutch colonial administration towards the end of the nineteenth century Romain Bertrand has shown that the privatisation of enterprises caused the colonial administration to shift its attention from direct control over enterprises, to an increasing 'snoopiness' of the government administration into the personal lives of workers in enterprises. Whether under the impact of 'terrorism' or other security threats the state has become increasingly intrusive on a global scale, and it needs little imagination to see parallels with the changing function of the state as described by Bertrand (Hibou 2004).

Conclusion

Neither the opening of Japan's markets by the United States in the nineteenth century, subsequent unequal treaties, the Meiji reforms (since 1868), nor the more than six years of US occupation and dissolution of the *zaibatsu* (economic conglomerates) were able to change basic features of the symbiotic relationship between economic and political elites. Although concepts such as 'private' and 'public' have gained greater attention and legitimacy, numerous features in actual political, economic and social life demonstrate a reluctance to restrain officials from using informal channels and pressure to achieve change in the 'private' sphere.

These changes were not merely the result of 'globalisation', or Japan's increasing shift towards becoming a 'member of the West'. During the 1960s it was the Japanese government that succeeded in breaking the power of trade unions before Thatcher and Reagan did in Great Britain and the United States, also preparing the groundwork for pushing back the leftist influence in teachers' unions. Changes in the Bretton Woods system, the global role of the dollar and the oil crises of the 1970s were other important factors leading to increased economic and security cooperation between Japan and the United States. Soviet expansionism contributed to an increasing legitimacy for Japan's armed forces, further weakening the ideological stance of the major opposition party, the Japan Socialist Party. It became publicly acceptable for Japan to portray itself as a member of the (political) West. Further pushed by Prime Minister Nakasone during the mid-1980s, and in particular by Prime Minister Koizumi, Japan seems set to become another core element in pushing the globalisation project. It remains remarkable, however, that despite continuous emphasis on such elements as privatisation, market dynamics and flexible labour markets (i.e. increased unemployment) the symbiotic relationship between economic and political elites has so far not been abolished.

Economic privatisation does not equal a greater emphasis of 'individualism'. As in the past, individuals find it difficult to transcend micro-society, and appeal directly to the state when their position in micro-society (the company, for instance) is threatened. The state itself does not propagate any particular compulsory 'ideology', but increasingly demands formal show of loyalty to national symbols, such as the singing of the national anthem in schools.

Changes in China since the 1980s have brought about tremendous change to micro-society, symbolised in the gradual retreat of the functions of the 'unit' (*danwei*) that used to encompass functions of not only state, politics, social pressure, but also the social welfare system. Attempts to resurrect the role of the state, such as emphasis on the 'reconstruction of the party', or the establishment of state-initiated urban 'neighbourhood communities' (*shequ*), are of doubtful consequence. As mentioned above, globalisation does not necessarily lead to global homogenisation of cultures, legal and political systems. Market democracy promises greater freedom for the individual. Increasing pressures on the individual by globalisation to put all his or her efforts into competition and survival in micro-society demonstrate that life as experienced through the individual's eyes may differ greatly from political and ideological pretence.

Notes

1   This essay is dedicated to the memory of my friend Raymond Feddema. The chapter is a summary of arguments on the topic of globalisation in Asia, which I published recently (Radtke 2000, 2001a, 2001b; these three articles are published in Chinese under the name of Li Deji, which is Kurt W. Radtke in Chinese; see also Radtke 2002). I do not claim originality for the concepts and ideas set forth in this chapter – the massive amounts of information to which researchers are exposed make it often extremely difficult to distinguish between creative eclecticism and 'originally' conceived ideas.

2   I do recognise that accessibility of government services and the law, corruption and taxation schemes favouring certain income groups and institutional property owners are also important issues greatly affecting good governance in the United States and Europe. One may – tongue in cheek – argue that Europe and the United States have developed advanced high-tech corruption. Globalising Europe and America have their own problems with good governance: siphoning off profits by management and/or stockholders, or faked bankruptcy to the detriment of the labour force threatens good governance in any economy, including the most advanced ones. Self-censorship by the media invoking state and national interest is another feature regularly preventing thorough exposure of corruption, both in the public and private spheres. While society influences the shape of the state, the reverse is often also true: states wishing to transform societies.

3   Needless to point out that there are also important differences between continental Europe, Great Britain and the United States in quite a few aspects relevant to globalisation, such as legislation on companies, stock trading and taxation – essential elements to be harmonised to achieve true globalisation.

4   I find it outright amazing that contemporary accounts of civil society usually do not include organised labour as part of civil society.

5   By the time this chapter was completed various drafts for reform existed within the ruling LDP (Inose 2005), and it is not yet clear what the final law will look like.

6   My forthcoming book on globalisation will deal in detail with the issue of 'autonomous' decision making by members of a franchise alliance. More specifically, what is required is a theoretical framework for describing the room for Japanese and RoK policy initiatives in the context of strategic and policy cooperation with the US. A more traditional approach is taken by Michael H. Armacost and Kenneth B. Pyle (2001).

7   Lack of space prevents me from citing examples from Japanese literature – which right from the beginnings of modernisation in the Meiji period developed new literary genres – the political and economical novels that depict the effects of modernisation on the lives of officials and ordinary people.

Bibliography

ACCJ (2004) *ACCJ Journal*, December: 14–25.
Allen, Michael J. (2001) 'Ambivalent social Darwinism in Korea', *International Journal of Korean History*, 2 (December), www.history.korea.ac.kr/journal/vol2/pdf/.pdf.
Amino, Yoshihiko (2001) *Nihon chusei toshi no sekai*, Tokyo: Chikuma.
Amyx, Jennifer, Harukata Takenaka and A. Maria Toyoda (2005) 'The politics of postal savings reform in Japan', *Asian Perspective*, 29 (1): 23–48.
Arai, Hiroyuki (2005) 'Bookoku no kaikakuan de wa nai no ka?', in Naoki Inose, *Kessen. Yuusei mineika*, Tokyo: PHP kenkyuujo.

Armacost, Michael H. and Kenneth B. Pyle (2001) 'Japan and the engagement of China: challenges for US policy coordination', *NBR Analysis*, 12 (5).

Bailey, Joe (2002) 'From public to private: the development of the concept of the "private", Part I: public/private', *Social Research* (internet edition), Spring.

Buckley, Chris (2005) 'Chinese writer tests the power of this press', *International Herald Tribune*, 1 June, p. 6.

Cai, Yungshun and Songcai Yang (2005) 'State power and unbalanced legal development in China', *Journal of Contemporary China*, 14 (42): 117–34.

Chun, Bok-Hee (1992) 'Die Funktion des Sozialdarwinismus in Korea in der Zeit vom Ende des 19. Jahrhunderts bis Anfang des 20. Jahrhunderts', Dissertation, Philipps-Universitaet Marburg.

Companies Incorporated (2005) 'Offshore firms face threat from change to Japan's commercial code', www.companiesinc.com/cinewsletter/story.asp?storyname= 20105 (June).

Fukuyama, Francis (1992) *The End of History and the Last Man*, New York: Free Press.

Goldman, Merle and Elizabeth J. Perry (eds) (2002) *Changing Meanings of Citizenship in Modern China*, Cambridge, MA: Harvard University Press.

Green, Stephen (2004) 'The privatization two-step at China's listed firms', China Project Working Paper No. 3, Chatham House, www.chathamhouse.org.uk.

—— (2005) *Exit the Dragon? Privatisation and State Control in China*, Oxford: Blackwell.

Greider, William (1997) *One World, Ready or Not: The Manic Logic of Global Capitalism*, New York: Touchstone.

Guehenno, Jean-Marie (1993) *La Fin de la démocratie*, Paris: Flammarion.

Habermas, J. (1989) *The Structural Transformation of the Public Sphere: An Inquiry into a Category of Bourgeois*, Cambridge, MA: MIT Press.

Hazama, Naoki *et al.* (1996) *Chuugoku gendaishi*, Yuuhikaku.

Hibou, Beatrice (ed.) (2004) *Privatizing the State*, London: Hurst.

Hill, Gates (1996) *China's Motor: A Thousand Years of Petty Capitalism*, Ithaca, NY: Cornell University Press.

IMF (1997) *Partnership for Sustainable Growth*, Washington, DC: International Monetary Fund.

Inose, Naoki (2005) *Kessen. Yuusei mineika*, Tokyo: PHP kenkyuujo.

Kamiya, Nobuyuki (1997) *Taikun gaikoo to higashiajia*, Tokyo: Yoshikawa Kobundo.

Kitashiro, Kakutaro (2005) *Yuusei min'eika koso nihon o kaeru*, Tokyo: PHP kenkyujo.

Liu' Jianhui (2004) *Zhongguo yu Riben de tazhe renshi. ZhongRi xuezhe de gongtong tantao*, ed. Zhongguo shehui kexue yanjiuhui, Beijing: Shehui kexue wenxian chubanshe [Dongying qiusuo, 2003 nian juan], pp. 83–104.

Long, Zhiyi (1999) *Zhengjie, Tianjin*, Tianjin: Baihua wenyi chubanshe.

Lu, Feng (1993) 'The origins and formation of the Unit (*Danwei*) system', *Chinese Sociology and Anthropology*, 25 (3): 87ff.

Maclachlan, Patricia L. (2004) 'Post office politics in modern Japan: the postmasters, iron triangles, and the limits of reform', *The Journal of Japanese Studies*, 30 (2): 281–313.

Michalet, Charles-Albert (2002) *Qu'est-ce que la mondialisation?*, Paris: La Découverte.

Minami, Hiroshi (1984) *Nihonjin no ningen kankei jiten*, Tokyo: Kodansha.

Mizoguchi, Yuzo (1994) 'Chuugoku to Nihon: Koo Shi kannen no hikaku', *21 seiki*, February.

Oi, Jean C. (1997) 'The Collective foundation for rapid rural industrialization', in Eduard B. Vermeer, Frank N. Pieke and Woei Lien Chong (eds), *Cooperative and*

Collective in China's Rural Development Between State and Private Interests, Armonk, NY and London: M.E. Sharpe.

Okuma, Shigenobu (1923) *Toozai bunmei no choowa*, Nihon: Bunmei Kyokai.

Oren, Ido (2000) 'Is culture independent of national security? How America's national security concerns shaped "political culture" research', *European Journal of International Relations*, 6 (4): 543–73.

Pei, Xiaolin (1997) 'Township-village enterprises, local governments, and rural communities: the Chinese village as a firm during economic transition', in Eduard B. Vermeer, Frank N. Pieke and Woei Lien Chong (eds), *Cooperative and Collective in China's Rural Development Between State and Private Interests*, Armonk, NY and London: M.E. Sharpe.

Qi, Shuyu (1998) *Shichang jingji xia de Zhongguo wenxue yishu*, Beijing: Daxue chubanshe.

Radtke, Kurt W. (1984) 'Poetry of the Yuan Dynasty', Dissertation, The Australian National University, Canberra.

—— (2000) 'Quanqiuhua zhi wai – 20 shiji zhongguo de geren yu shehui' (Beyond globalization – the individual and society in 20th century China), in *Jindai zhongguo – shehui, zhengzhi yu sichao*, Tianjin: Tianjin Renmin Publishers, pp. 151–66.

—— (2001a) 'Shilun jianli guangfan youxiaode guoji guanxi lilun – dongya guoji guanxi fenxi' (An attempt to establish a comprehensive effective theory of international relations – an analysis of international relations in East Asia), in Q.Y. Mi Qingyu, Z.Y. Song Zhiyong and P.H. Zang Peihong (eds), *Guoji guanxi yu dongya anquan* (*International Relations and Security in East Asia*), Tianjin: Tianjin Renmin Publishers, pp. 90–104.

—— (2001b) 'Quanqiuhua yu zhong, ri, ou, mei' (Globalization in China, Japan, Europe and the US), in Q. Zhang, K. Fang and J. Wang (eds), *Jingji quanqiuhua yu zhonghua wenhua zouxiang* (*Economic Globalization and the Future of Chinese Culture*), Beijing: Dongfanghong Shushe, pp. 857–71.

—— (2002) 'East Asia: systematic stability through alliance politics?', *Ajia taiheiyoo tookyuu* (Waseda University), No. 3, pp. 63–85.

—— (2003) 'Nationalism and internationalism in Japan's economic liberalism: the case of Ishibashi Tanzan', in Dick Stegewerns (ed.), *Nationalism and Internationalism in Imperial Japan: Autonomy, Asian Brotherhood, or World Citizenship?*, London: Routledge Curzon, pp. 168–94.

—— (2004) 'The construction of Chinese identities', *Tokyu* (Waseda University), 6: 99–121.

Rocca, Jean-Louis (2004) 'Is China becoming an ordinary state?', in Beatrice Hibou (ed.), *Privatizing the State*, London: Hurst.

Schaede, Ulrike and William Grimes (2003) *Japan's Managed Globalization: Adapting to the Twenty-first Century*, Armonk, NY: M.E. Sharpe.

Slater, Dan (2004) *Finance Asia*, 12 November.

Tanaka, Keiichi (2000) *Hyakushoo no Edo jidai*, Chikuma Shinsho 270.

Terasawa, Masaharu (2002) *Nihonjin no seishin koozoo, dentoo to genzai*, Tokyo: Iwanami Schoten.

Thurow, Lester (2000) *Yomiuri Shinbun*, 25 April.

Vinogradov, Konstantin (2003) 'The Russian Far East from the mid-1980s–1990s: power at the remote periphery in transition', Dissertation, Waseda University, Tokyo.

Walder Andrew G. (1986) *Communist Neo-Traditionalism*, Berkeley, CA: University of California Press.

—— (ed.) (1995) *The Waning of the Communist State: Economic Origins of Political Decline in China and Hungary*, Berkeley: University of California Press.

Waltz, Kenneth (1999) 'Globalization and governance', *Political Science and Politics*, **XXXII** (4): 693–700.

Wiesebron, M. and K.W. Radtke (eds) (2002) *Competing for Integration*, New York: M.E. Sharpe.

Xinhua (2005) www.finance.sina.com.cn/g/20050210/10251358036.shtml (February).

Xu, Jianbin (1996) *Xiangcun haomen*, Taiyan: Beiyue wenyi chubanshe.

Yoda, Yoshiie (1995) *The Foundations of Japan's Modernization – A Comparison with China's March Towards Modernization*, Leiden: Brill.

Yokota, Takaaki (2005) *Chuugoku ni okeru shijoo keizai ikoo no riron to jissen (The Theory and Practice of the Transition to Market Economy in China)*.

Yomiuri (2005) 'Yuusei shuuseian o soomukai teiji e, jimin shikkoobu ga oozume choosei,' *Yomiuri Shinbun*, 29 June.

Yu' Dezhe, Yang Rongxiang and Liu Ming (1997) *Gonghui zhuxi*, Beijing: Zuojia chubanshe.

Zhang, Ling and Xin Ruzhong (1998) *Guansi jingdong zhongnanhai*, Beijing: Falü chubanshe.

Zhong, Daoxin (1996) 'Weibi gongsi neimu gushi' in *Danshen guizu*, Tianjin: Baihua wenyi chubanshe.

3 Conglomerates in Indonesia
The road to power and beyond

J. Thomas Lindblad

Every Indonesian knows the *kretek* cigarette brand Djie Sam Soe of the Sampoerna Company, but few may realise that the country's second largest tobacco manufacturer is one of the oldest Indonesian conglomerates in existence, and that it recently was targeted for international takeover. In March 2005, Philip Morris purchased 40 per cent of Sampoerna's equity with the intention of bidding for additional shares in order to acquire majority ownership, leaving only a 5 per cent stake for the descendants of the founding father Liem Seng Tee. Fears were immediately voiced that Sampoerna would then 'go private', meaning that it would withdraw from trading and shareholder control at the Jakarta Stock Exchange (*Kompas* 15 March 2005). Sampoerna illustrates a number of features characteristic of conglomerates in Indonesia, including long-standing tradition, family ownership, economic power held by Indonesian businessmen of Chinese descent and, finally, being highly attractive for takeover once success in the domestic market has been demonstrated.

Conglomerates in Indonesia are invariably associated with the practices of corruption, collusion and nepotism that flourished during former President Suharto's long rule (1966–98). Highlighting the political economy aspects of conglomerates makes for drama, scandal and easy reading with arguments primarily being supported by circumstantial evidence (Backman 1999: 255–99). Far less attention has been given in the literature to the historical background of conglomerates and a rigorous statistical analysis has scarcely, if ever, been undertaken. This chapter aims at providing a fuller insight into conglomerates in Indonesia by surveying historical origins and identifying structural characteristics using both historical qualitative evidence and statistics. It thus forms a sequel to the existing discourse on political economy and big business in Indonesia (Robison 1986; MacIntyre 1990).[1]

The chapter consists of three parts. The first section offers a historical perspective extending from the late colonial period up to the early years of the Suharto regime with particular attention given to policies pursued by the Sukarno administration in order to further Indonesian entrepreneurship. The focus then shifts to the position of conglomerates in the Indonesian economy in the late 1980s and mid-1990s, that is after several decades of virtually uninterrupted rapid economic growth and shortly before financial crisis struck. The third, shorter section is by way of epilogue devoted to the fate of conglomerates in the aftermath of the crisis of the late 1990s.

What is a conglomerate? Diversification in terms of economic activity is clearly an important aspect that evokes associations with Japanese *zaibatsu* or Korean *chaebol*. Yet the main emphasis given by students of big business in Indonesia is on the tight link between management control and family ownership as is evident in the formal definition offered in one of the statistical sources used here. The definition runs as follows: 'a conglomerate is a group of companies under influence of a prominent businessman or group of businessmen who are either founders or owners of these companies' (Data Consult 1991: 3). Size is obviously of overriding importance here. Identifying the 200 largest business groups in the late 1980s or around 1990 was tantamount to selecting private enterprises with an annual turnover in excess of Rp. 50 to 70 billion or, at the then prevailing rate of exchange, the equivalent of $28 to $39 million (in 2005 $5.3 to $7.4 million) (CISI 1990; Data Consult 1991).

The historical perspective[2]

Sampoerna began as a home industry in Surabaya in 1913 and was incorporated as a trading company in 1928. Subsequent diversification has included transportation, printing, advertising, retailing and discount stores. By 1990 the group's payroll counted 20,000 workers and management was still in the hands of the founding Liem family. Around that time Sampoerna took two steps to enhance easy access to credit that have become highly characteristic of Indonesian conglomerates. One was to go public by offering shares for sale on the Jakarta Stock Exchange; the other to set up a bank of its own, Bank Sampoerna, catering specifically to the needs of the mother company. Next to Sampoerna, only one sizable conglomerate has survived from the early days of the twentieth century.[3] That is the Bumiputera group centred around a life insurance company set up in 1912 by three Javanese businessmen. In the late 1980s, Bumiputra 1912 was included among the 40 largest conglomerates in Indonesia (against rank 87 for Sampoerna). The long history of Bumiputera 1912 and Sampoerna illustrates that colonial rule did not altogether preclude successful large-scale business ventures undertaken by Indonesians, whether of Javanese or Chinese descent, even though numbers remained very small.

The 1930s – the final decade of effective Dutch colonial rule – saw several initiatives by enterprising businessmen in Indonesia. The Sekar group, established by indigenous Indonesians in Surabaya, concentrated on maritime food products whereas the Chinese-owned ABC group in Jakarta marketed syrups and beverages. In the late 1980s, the ABC group had become known as Indonesia's largest domestic producer of dry-cell batteries, ranking among the top 40 conglomerates (against rank 96 for Sekar). In Palembang, Agoes

Dasaad joined forces with other South Sumatran traders to take over some of the profitable textile trade from Chinese importers. In the 1950s, the Dasaad Musin concern operated Indonesia's largest textile factory, Kancil Mas, and enjoyed a host of sole agencies for vital imports, including automobiles, aircraft and aluminium. The ascent of Dasaad Musin was not in the least furthered by a close personal association of Agoes Dasaad with President Sukarno. In the 1970s, however, the monopoly agencies were lost and Dasaad's descent into oblivion began (Robison 1986: 51–3). Dasaad Musin forms an early example of the importance of political leverage in accelerating the build-up of a conglomerate in Indonesia.

The Japanese occupation (March 1942–August 1945) offered unique opportunities for new initiatives (Post 1997). Some of the firms set up at that time experienced a rapid expansion during the subsequent Sukarno period. One prominent example is Bakrie & Bros., established in 1942 as a trading firm in Lampung in southernmost Sumatra by Haji Achmad Bakrie. Steel pipe manufacturing eventually became the company's core business and a wide range of economic activities was added in the course of time, including agricultural estates, crude oil trading, livestock breeding and securities. Bakrie also set up its own bank, Nusa Bank, and expanded especially fast during the early 1990s. In 1994, this business group had assets worth Rp. 4,800 billion ($2.1 billion), good for a twelfth rank among the country's conglomerates, second among conglomerates owned by indigenous Indonesians.[1] In September 2004, former executive Aburizal Bakrie was appointed coordinating Minister for Economy and Finance in the cabinet headed by President Susilo Bambang Yudhoyono. Bakrie & Bros. has become a prototype for successful indigenous Indonesian entrepreneurship surviving successive changes in the political climate.

Some indigenous Indonesian contemporaries of Achmad Bakrie were highly successful during the Sukarno years but fell behind soon afterwards. Examples include Hasjim Ning from West Sumatra, a trader closely associated with Vice President Hatta, and Nitisemito, proprietor of the largest non-Chinese *kretek* cigarette factory in Java. Hasjim Ning passed into other ownership and by the late 1980s its rank among Indonesia's conglomerates was no higher than 61 whereas Nitisemito's Nojorono group did not figure at all among the top companies.

Conditions during the years 1945–9 were highly confusing with Dutch firms staying on in territories controlled by returning colonial forces and simultaneous efforts by the Sukarno administration to develop indigenous entrepreneurship in Republican-held regions. Only a few concerns have survived from these times, and all have remained small. The Merdeka group, founded in 1945 by Burhanuddin Muhamad Diah, still publishes the daily newspaper *Merdeka* ('Independence') and operates a five-star hotel, Hyatt Aryaduta, in downtown Jakarta. The Sukun group, owned by the Wartono family, ranks in the second tier of *kretek* cigarette producers in Central Java whereas the Wings group, known for soap and detergent, began in Surabaya in 1949. All three ranked below the 100 largest conglomerates in the late 1980s.

Dutch acknowledgement of Indonesian independence in 1949 was accompanied by the agreement that Dutch firms could retain their privileged position in Indonesia. This situation lasted until 1957–8 when remaining Dutch corporate assets were nationalised. The dramatic transition in the management and control of the nation's resources is best perceived as economic decolonisation, a topic in its own right to which I hope to return elsewhere. This transition was important for the rise of conglomerates in Indonesia in two ways. In the first place, the continued and conspicuous presence of leading Dutch firms in the newly independent nation prompted the Sukarno government to speed up the establishment and development of Indonesian business, in particular indigenous Indonesian business. Economic nationalism surfaced most explicitly in the execution of the so-called *Benteng* ('fortress') policy, essentially a form of positive discrimination giving priority to 'national traders' (Thee 1996: 317–23; Lindblad 2002: 54–6). In addition, the abrupt and seemingly unplanned appropriation of Dutch firms in late 1957 and early 1958 implied that management functions were at short notice entrusted to military authorities and well-placed business groups, which in turn accelerated the concentration of ownership and control in the Indonesian economy.

Julius Tahija originated from Ambon in East Indonesia. In 1955 he founded Bank Niaga and later he became one of Indonesia's most celebrated executives serving at one stage as Chairman of the board at both American-controlled Freeport, the world's largest copper mine, and the Indonesian subsidiary of Caltex. Bank Niaga became one the country's leading private banks and Tahija's Indrapura group counted as the first-ranking non-Chinese conglomerate in the late 1980s and early 1990s. With assets estimated at Rp. 6,600 billion ($2.9 billion) in 1994, the Indrapura group ranked ahead of Bakrie & Bros. among conglomerates owned and managed by indigenous Indonesians. Throughout the decades Tahija has cooperated closely with the Javanese businessman Soedarpo Sastrosatomo whose trading firm, established in 1952, developed into a major shipping line, Samudera Indonesia (Robison 1986: 337–9). The Soedarpo group is of comparable size to Indrapura and in 1993 these two conglomerates both ranked just below the 20 largest ones. The Indrapura–Soedarpo connection illustrates the synergy to be reaped from long-standing cooperation between leading indigenous businessmen.

A wide variety of business enterprises were set up by indigenous Indonesians in the 1950s as rivals to both Dutch corporations and firms led by Indonesians of Chinese descent. In Jakarta in 1954, Mohamad Saleh Kurnia started Indonesia's first supermarket chain, Hero, while H. Thayeb Mohamad Gobel began assembling transistor radios. The latter's firm, National Gobel, entered into a joint venture with Matsushita and became one of Indonesia's most successful electronics manufacturers. On occasion a strong local base and a radius of activities confined to the firm's own region facilitated success. One example is Pardedetex, founded in Medan (North Sumatra) in 1955, with textile factories and hotels still run by the Pardede family, another the Poleko group founded in the late 1950s by the then Governor of South Sulawesi, Arnold Baramuli (Robison 1986: 359–60). A third example, also in Sulawesi, is the highly diversified Haji Kalla group, established as a trading enterprise in Makassar (formerly Ujung Pandang) in 1952. The founder's son, Yusuf Kalla, was elected Vice President of Indonesia in 2004 on the ticket of Bambang Susilo Yudhoyono.

It was a hotly debated issue in the 1950s whether positive discrimination toward indigenous businessmen implied a discrimination against not only remaining Dutch firms but also Indonesian businessmen of Chinese descent. This matter was all the more complicated since the question of the dual citizenship of such Indonesians had not yet been resolved (Mackie and Coppel 1976: 9–12). Holders of Indonesian citizenship were sometimes, but not always, included among the favoured 'national traders' of the *Benteng* policy but the ban on alien traders in rural areas in 1959 was clearly directed against Indonesians holding Chinese citizenship. In the event, the 1950s saw a proliferation of enterprises established by Indonesians of Chinese descent that often formed the basis for subsequent spectacular growth during the Suharto period.

William Soeryadjaja (Tjia Kian Liong) has for decades played the role of one of the most public executives in Indonesia. The origin of his business group, Astra International, lay in a distribution centre for building materials in Jakarta and the business group was founded in 1957. Expansion was accelerated in the 1970s through joint ventures with Toyota, Honda and Komatsu in respectively the automobile, motorcycle and tractor businesses (Robison 1986: 277, 289–96). By 1990 the Astra concern consisted of more than 200 individual companies in the most varied of businesses. Total turnover was then estimated at Rp. 3,680 billion ($2,050 million). Among Indonesian conglomerates, Astra International has traditionally ranked second in size, surpassed only by the Salim group. Astra is renowned for its heavy reliance on indigenous Indonesian managers (Suryadinata 1997: 42–4).

Another major Chinese Indonesian conglomerate, Djarum, dates from 1950 and started with a large *kretek* factory in Kudus, Central Java. Eventually, electronics, garments and banking were all added as separate lines of production and, by the late 1980s, Djarum had become the sixth largest conglomerate in Indonesia. *Kretek* manufacturing also formed the starting-point for Bentoel, established in 1951 by Budhiwidjaja Kusumanegara (Tjioe Yan Hwie). Gajah Tunggal was founded in the same year by Sjamsul Nursalim (Liem Tek Siong) and developed into one of the three top tyre manufacturers in Indonesia, in the process acquiring a major private bank, Bank Dagang Nasional Indonesia (BDNI). Bentoel and Gajah Tunggal were of similar size, both counting among the 25 odd top business groups in the late 1980s. Slightly larger still were the trading concern Dharmala and the

Bira group, both dating from the mid-1950s. The latter one used to own the Bank Indonesia Raya and to cooperate closely with the Salim concern. A common feature of these six conglomerates – Astra, Djarum, Bentoel, Gajah Tunggal, Dharmala and Bira – is that they all established a solid basis for later expansion in a time of active discrimination against Indonesian businessmen of Chinese descent.

The sudden disappearance of Dutch private enterprise from Indonesian economic life in 1958 created a vacuum that, again, offered unique opportunities for new business ventures. Indigenous Indonesian newcomers appearing in 1958–9 included the Pioneer Trading group, distributing diesel engines, and the Perdata group in oil transportation. Chinese Indonesian business flourished, notwithstanding the overt anti-Chinese policies at the time. Mantrust in the food and beverage industry in Bandung (West Java) and the cosmetics concern Mugi both began operations in 1958 whereas the forestry-based Satya Djaya Raya and the amorphous Ometraco group started out in 1959. More widely known is the Rodamas group, founded in 1959 by Tan Siong Kie, which through its joint venture with Asahi Glass developed into Indonesia's largest glass producer. In the late 1980s, Rodamas ranked among Indonesia's top 20 firms, Mantrust and Ometraco were both among the top 40, whereas Satya Djaya Raya and Mugi were far smaller. They all bear testimony to the extraordinary situation in the Indonesian economy immediately after the departure of the Dutch in 1958.

More generally, however, the concluding years of the Sukarno era were marked by a shift in favour of state control of economic resources and activities. The leading Dutch trading houses, the so-called 'Big Five', as well as formerly Dutch-owned agricultural estates were henceforth run by the state, often through military administrative bodies. Private Indonesian firms, whether of indigenous or Chinese origin, grew increasingly dependent on government orders and relations with the political elite. Soedarpo Sastrosatomo has been described as the most successful indigenous Indonesian businessman of that time, benefiting from close links with the Sukarno cabinet (Robison 1986: 93). Nevertheless, rather few of today's conglomerates date from the final years of Sukarno rule. One of them is Maspion, a well-known producer of electrical and electronic goods, which was founded by Alim Husin (Go Kiem Moey) in 1962 and ranked among the largest 50 odd firms in the late 1980s.

Then came Suharto's New Order with ample space not only for resumed inflows of foreign investment but also for fresh investment by big business in Indonesia. The most well-known case is of course the Salim conglomerate of Liem Sioe Liong (Soedono Salim), which invariably ranks first of all Indonesian business groups. Total turnover in the mid-1990s exceeded Rp. 32,000 billion ($14 billion) and the concern reportedly employed some 135,000 Indonesians (Backman 1999: 113; Schwarz 1990: 110). Although Liem had founded his Bank of Central Asia (BCA) already in 1957, rapid expansion came only after Suharto's ascension to power and was aided by

Liem's personal friendship with Suharto dating from business dealings in the mid-1950s (Elson 2001: 64, 192). Liem built up a commercial empire that eventually comprised 450 individual companies distributed across a number of sub-conglomerates, such as BCA, Indocement, Indosteel and Kalamur, which each in its own right would rank among the country's top 40 conglomerates if they possessed an independent status. The story of how Liem became Indonesia's largest producer of instant noodles, flour and cement, and arguably also the richest man in Southeast Asia, has been told elsewhere and need not be repeated here (Backman 1999: 113–17; Robison 1986: 296–315; Suryadinata 1997: 38–40). It remains the most vivid illustration of the nexus between political power and private profit in Suharto's Indonesia.

Liem Sioe Liong had numerous business associates who are likely to have benefited in varying degrees from his direct access to the apex of political power in Indonesia. The three best known are Eka Tjipta Widjaja (Oei Ek Tjhong), Mochtar Riady (Li Wenzheng) and Ciputra (Tjie Tjin Hoan). The first one, often referred to as 'Mr EKW', had started as a copra trader in Sulawesi in the 1950s and his firm Sinar Mas underwent rapid expansion after Suharto had come to power. Trading, industrial chemicals, property management and banking (Bank Internasional Indonesia, BII) were added to the core business of producing cooking oil and eventually Sinar Mas comprised 150 individual firms employing more than 70,000 Indonesians (Suryadinata 1997: 44–5). By the late 1980s, Sinar Mas had reached third rank among Indonesia's top conglomerates, surpassed only by Salim and Astra, and in the mid-1990s its total assets were estimated at Rp. 24,500 billion ($10.6 billion), more than twice as much as those of fourth-ranking Gajah Tunggal. The cooperation between Sinar Mas and Salim was institutionalised in a jointly owned subsidiary, Sinar Mas Inti Perkasa, which developed into a conglomerate in its own right counting among the 20 largest business groups in Indonesia in the late 1980s.

Mochtar Riady was executive director of BCA while expanding his Panin Bank into the highly diversified Lippo group, which with more than 100 subsidiaries ranked fourth among Indonesia's conglomerates in the late 1980s and third by 1993. Ciputra, finally, had begun already in 1961 with the construction firm Pembangunan Jaya and later became well known for extensive real estate holdings, especially in Jakarta (Suryadinata 1997: 40–2). Two business groups under his command, Metropolitan and Ciputra, were taken together good for assets worth Rp. 3,900 billion ($1.7 billion) in 1994.

This section has demonstrated the importance of applying a long historical perspective when tracing the origins of today's conglomerates in Indonesia, a perspective ranging from the final decades of Dutch colonial rule to the early days of Suharto's New Order government. In the next section we turn to the situation as it had taken shape through two decades of virtually uninterrupted rapid economic growth at a time when few could foresee that crisis was pending.

At the time of consolidation

There is something evasive about conglomerates in Indonesia. Rumours circulate at all times about political connections, intertwined vested interests and Chinese tycoons (*cukong*) but hard facts are difficult to come by. At least one-half of the country's main private business firms are not listed on the Jakarta Stock Exchange and thus not under obligation to bring out annual reports. These are all family businesses little inclined to disclose information to outsiders. Summary statistics on major firms do on occasion turn up in the press. Most attention is then given to the predominance of Indonesians of Chinese descent and the business holdings of members of the presidential family, without doubt the most spectacular topics in relationship to big business in Indonesia. The intention here, however, is to examine the statistical evidence in greater depth in order to identify structural characteristics of the world of conglomerates in Indonesia.

In 1989 the Indonesian business magazine *Warta Ekonomi* published a list of the 40 largest private conglomerates in Indonesia ranked by sales volume in 1988 (reproduced in Widyahartono 1990: 70–1). Together, these firms accounted for a total turnover of Rp. 37,000 billion ($20.6 billion) or the equivalent of 26 per cent of gross domestic product (GDP), which was then by the Indonesian government estimated at Rp. 142,000 billion ($79 billion) (BPS 1992: 100).[5] Twenty-eight out of the 40 top conglomerates were majority-owned by Indonesians of Chinese descent and their combined share in total turnover amounted to 83 per cent. It is instructive to take a closer look at the composition of these two categories of conglomerates.

The Chinese Indonesian conglomerates embraced ten old-timers (i.e. firms dating from the Sukarno period or the very early years of the Suharto period), notably Salim, Astra, Sinar Mas, Lippo, Djarum, Rodamas, Bentoel, Gajah Tunggal and Mantrust. In addition, this category contained 19 conglomerates of which most had been established during the 1970s. Well-known examples include Gudang Garam in *kretek* cigarette manufacturing, the chemicals concern Pakarti Yoga led by Sofyan Wanandi (Liem Bian Koen), the real estate empire of Jan Darmadi (Fuk Jo Jau), the lumber concern Barito Pacific of Prajogo Pangestu (Phang Djun Phen) and, finally, the Bira (Bank Indonesia Raya) group of Atang Latief (Lauw Tjin Ho). Special mention must be made of one of Suharto's closest personal friends, Bob Hasan (The Kian Seng), who with his Pasopati group profited from privileged access to vast forest concessions.

Among the 12 conglomerates owned by indigenous Indonesians, the older generation was represented by public figures such as Julius Tahija, Soedarpo Sastrosatomo and Aburizal Bakrie while Bumiputera 1912 bore testimony to the force of tradition in indigenous Indonesian entrepreneurship. Several of the newcomers attributed their position to a special relationship with President Suharto. This applied of course in particular to Suharto's three sons. The second one, Bambang Trihatmodjo, set up his Bimantara group

in 1982 covering a wide range of economic activities such as chemicals manufacturing, trading and real estate. Bimantara soon developed into becoming
the nation's second-ranking non-Chinese conglomerate, surpassed only by
Tahija's Indrapura. The youngest son, Hutomo Mandala Putra (Tommy
Suharto), followed suit with his Humpuss group, which attained rank 22 in the
late 1980s, whereas the eldest son, Sigit Harjojudanto, entered into a joint venture with family friend Bob Hasan in controlling the Nusamba group, which
was at the time of similar size to Humpuss (see further Robison 1986: 343–7;
Backman 1999: 293–4; Schwarz 1999: 141–3; Friend 2003: 251).[6] Members
of the Suharto family have in fact conspicuously often figured as the foremost
minority shareholders in Chinese conglomerates (Schwarz 1999: 112–13).

Others too may have benefited in varying degrees from a proximity to
the apex of political power. Ibnu Sutowo enjoyed presidential protection
when heading the state oil company Pertamina and later built up his own
private conglomerate, Nugra Santana, which ranked 34 in the late 1980s
(Robison 1986: 350–8). It is likely that the president took a particular interest
also in the Hanurata group, owned by an array of army foundations. A
final example is Indoconsult, smallest of the 40 top conglomerates on the
1989 list, owned by renowned economist and former Cabinet Minister
Sumitro Djojohadikusumo, father-in-law of one of Suharto's daughters. Just
as the Chinese conglomerates, the indigenous Indonesian conglomerates at
this time testified to a juxtaposition of long-standing traditions in Indonesian
entrepreneurship with new arrivals conditioned by the specific political
economy that arose in Indonesia as Suharto rule was consolidated.

The 1989 list anticipated a larger survey covering the 200 top conglomerates that, however, only reached a limited circulation when published
(CISI 1990).[7] The full survey, already used above to provide qualitative
summary information on individual conglomerates, facilitates a statistical
analysis of the situation in the late 1980s as well as a systematic comparison with more recent sources.

The strong position of Chinese as opposed to indigenous Indonesian
conglomerates immediately strikes the eye when reviewing the structural
characteristics of the top business groups in the late 1980s (Table 3.1). The
top echelons counted 50 per cent more Chinese conglomerates than indigenous ones and the former accounted for three-quarters of total sales and
accumulated assets. Twice as many Chinese conglomerates had been established during the 1960s and 1970s whereas relatively more indigenous still
surviving groups dated from the Indonesian Revolution, or even before, and
the 1950s. This testifies to an investment climate during the early Suharto
period that was singularly conducive for undertakings by Indonesian businessmen of Chinese descent.[8] Chinese conglomerates did not only outnumber
indigenous ones according to the survey of the late 1980s. They were also
larger with more subsidiaries per business group and twice as large sales
volumes and asset values on average. Such statistics may be associated with
a more successful business performance.

Table 3.1 Characteristics of the top conglomerates in Indonesia in the late 1980s[b,c]

	Chinese Indonesian	Indigenous Indonesian	All
Aggregates:			
Conglomerates	116	77	193
Subsidiaries	2,928	1,376	4,304
Sales 1988 (Rp. trillion)[a]	47	15	61
Share (%)	77	23	100
Assets 1988 (Rp. trillion)	24	8	32
Share (%)	75	25	100
Founded:			
Before 1950	1	5	6
1950s	16	17	33
1960s	27	17	44
1970s	62	27	89
1980s	8	7	15
Main office:			
Jakarta	85	62	147
Outside Jakarta	31	15	46
Average/conglomerate:			
Subsidiaries	25	18	22
Sales 1988 (Rp. billion)	397	191	315
Assets 1988 (Rp. billion)	207	101	165

Source: CISI (1990).

Notes:
a   The list of the 200 largest business groups includes seven sub-conglomerates, for instance BCA in the Salim group and BII in Sinar Mas, where figures overlap with those of the 'mother' conglomerate. The total number of conglomerates covered is therefore 193, not 200. This also affects the aggregates and the identification of the foremost individual conglomerates (Table 3.3; see also Lindblad 2004: 248–9).
b   The date of establishment was not known in six cases.
c   Trillion stands for thousand billion. The rate of exchange at the time was Rp. 1800/US$.

The rise of conglomerates in Indonesia reinforced existing tendencies towards concentration of capital and control in the national economy. This applied, amongst others, also to the manufacturing sector, which has seen dramatic growth since the early 1980s (Hill 1990: 61). It also had a geographical dimension as three out of four leading conglomerates cited a Jakarta address for its main office. Surabaya was the second favoured location but did not accommodate more than 15 of the listed top conglomerates. Very few large conglomerates were found in other major Indonesian cities such as Semarang, Bandung or Medan.

In 1991, a new survey of the 200 largest business groups was brought out by another consulting firm in Jakarta, again with a limited circulation (Data Consult 1991). Total combined turnover of these conglomerates as recorded in 1990 reportedly corresponded to as much as 35 per cent of GDP, a figure that subsequently turned up time and again in the domestic discussion in Indonesia about the concentration of capital in few hands. In December 1993, B.J. Habibie, the later President, even stated in public that one-third of GDP was accounted for by only ten conglomerates, all controlled by Chinese Indonesians (Schwarz 1999: 122; Friend 2003: 233). Such a statement by a high-ranking government official – Habibie was then Minister of Research and Technology – was symptomatic for growing resentment among indigenous Indonesian business leaders about the strong position and privileges enjoyed by Indonesians of Chinese descent.

A comparison between the two rival surveys of the top 200 conglomerates around the same time gives rise to some interesting observations concerning continuity in big business in Indonesia. At first sight, rankings by turnover look much alike with Salim, Astra and Sinar Mas, in that order, occupying the first three positions. Closer scrutiny, however, reveals that only seven of the top ten appear in both lists.[9] More generally, only 130 conglomerates (i.e. 65 per cent of the total) figure in both surveys, which implies that 70 conglomerates (35 per cent) in the earlier survey were no longer large enough to be included in a similar ranking only two years later. This suggests a high degree of volatility among Indonesian conglomerates where business performance could vary considerably from one year to the next.

The susceptibility to short-run change is also borne out by the size distributions by sales volume that may be derived from the two elaborate surveys of the top 200 conglomerates. The category with firms registered for sales in excess of Rp. 1 trillion (Rp. 1,000 billion) more than doubled in size between the two years considered, 1988 and 1990 (Table 3.2). This reflects a rapid expansion in the scale of activities of the top conglomerates, not only in nominal but also in real terms since inflation over these two years amounted to only 15 per cent (BPS 1992: 115). Four indigenous Indonesian conglomerates (Bimantara, Bakrie, Humpuss and Pertamina-affiliated Krama Yudha) had now also entered this category. At the same time, however, numerous indigenous Indonesian conglomerates of moderate size, with annual sales less than Rp. 300 billion, had in the meantime been replaced

Table 3.2 Size of top Indonesian conglomerates, 1988 and 1990

Size category (Rp. billion)	1988 sales		1990 sales	
	Chinese	Indigenous	Chinese	Indigenous
> 2000	2	0	5	0
1001–2000	8	0	13	4
501–1000	13	5	22	5
301–500	13	8	20	7
151–300	30	19	44	15
< 150	50	45	51	14

Sources: CISI (1990); Data Consult (1991).

by Chinese Indonesian ones, which dramatically altered the ethnic composition of the population of top conglomerates. Measured by sales in 1990, 155 of the 200 largest were controlled by Chinese Indonesians, 30 more than according to sales in 1988.[10] A few well-placed indigenous groups, notably the two owned by the President's sons, thus surged forward while many smaller ones were surpassed by Chinese Indonesian conglomerates achieving faster growth.

Occasional listings of top conglomerates in the business press added fuel to the public discourse in Indonesia on conglomerates, political connections and Chinese predominance as it took shape during the 1990s.[11] Our analysis makes use of two listings published in different Indonesian business magazines in the mid-1990s. The first one lists the 25 largest conglomerates ranked by turnover in 1993 whereas the second one gives estimates of assets held by the top 100 conglomerates in 1994 (*Warta Ekonomi* 24 April 1994, reproduced in Hill 1996: 111; *Eksekutif* August 1995, reproduced in Suryadinata 1997: 67–74). Both lend themselves for a systematic comparison with the elaborate survey pertaining to the situation in the late 1980s.

Identifying the 25 leading conglomerates by sales and assets in the late 1980s and the mid-1990s brings out many familiar names (Table 3.3).[12] Eighteen conglomerates were included in this high-ranking category on account of sales in both 1988 and 1993 whereas the same held true for fourteen conglomerates ranked by assets in 1988 as well as 1994. There were four indigenous conglomerates in either ranking by sales, three of whom were the same. In the rankings by assets, the number of indigenous conglomerates rose from four to six between 1988 and 1994. The Suharto family, occasionally referred to as the Cendana group (after their street address in Central Jakarta), was represented here not only by two of the President's sons but also by his eldest daughter, Siti Hardijanti Rukmana ('Tutut') of toll-road construction concern Citra Lamtoro, Suharto's half-brother Probosutedjo of the Mercubuana group and his cousin Sudwikatmono who owned, amongst other things, the Golden Truly supermarket chain (Van Dijk 2001: 78–80). Newcomers in the 1990s included Tommy Winata, closely linked to the army and owner of Jakarta's largest wholesale textile market, as well as Marimutu Srinivasan, a textile baron of Indian origin who built up a friendship with the President.

The most conspicuous change with respect to Chinese Indonesian conglomerates was the decline of Astra, which had to be sold by the Soeryadjaja family at the time of the collapse of Bank Summa, Astra's chief sub-conglomerate, in 1992. The new owners, combined in the Prasetya Mulia group, were all Suharto (Lindblad 2004: 249–50). Otherwise much remained the same at the very apex of the conglomerate structure with Salim, Sinar Mas, Lippo and Gudang Garam ranking high on all accounts. Positions improved markedly not only for Bob Hasan but also for The Ning King and Prajogo Pangestu. A highly successful newcomer was Usman Admadjaja (Njau Jouw Woe) of the Bank Danamon who in 1994 possessed the eighth largest asset holdings among Indonesian business enterprises.

Table 3.3 Top 25 conglomerates in Indonesia, 1988 and 1993–4

Conglomerate	Sales		Assets		Owner
	1988	*1993*	*1988*	*1994*	
Salim	1	1	1	1	Soedono Salim
Astra	2	2	2	6	William Soeryadjaja
Sinar Mas	3	4	3	2	Eka Tjipta Widjaya
Lippo	4	3	20	5	Mochtar Riady
Gudang Garam	5	5	4	13	Rachman Halim
Djarum	6	11	6	36	Robert Budi Hartono
Pakarti Yoga	7	21	26	60	Sofyan Wanandi
Panin	8	13	18	11	Mu'min Ali Gunawan
Darmadi	9	16	9	30	Jan Darmadi
Arya Upaya	10	12	19	25	Kaharuddin Ongko
Indrapura	*11*	*25*	36	*9*	Julius Tahija
Bimantara	*12*	*8*	7	52	Bambang Trihatmodjo
Bob Hasan	13	6	8	4	Bob Hasan
Soedarpo	*14*	*24*	*16*		Soedarpo Sastrosatomo
Damatex	15	9	15	20	The Ning King
Dharmala	16	10	10	14	Soeh. Gondokoesoemo
Rodamas	17	14	12	53	Tan Siong Kie
Sinar Mas Inti Perkasa	18		13		Sinar Mas + Salim
Pendawa Sempurna	*19*		34	92	Muh. Jusuf
Bank Bali	20		17	10	Djaja Ramli
Metropolitan	21	23	14	29	Ciputra
Sinar Sahabat	22		35	54	Sukanta Tanudjaja
Bira	23		22	32	Atang Latief
Bentoel	24		39		Samsi
Batamtex	25		148		Karta Widjaja
Barito Pasific	29	7	32	7	Prajogo Pangestu
Surya Raya		15			Soeryadjaja family
Berca	39	17	52	43	Murdaya Widyawinarta
Humpuss	28	*18*	40	*17*	Hutomo Mandala Putra
Gajah Tunggal	27	19	31	3	Sjamsul Nursalim
Raja Garuda Mas	38	20	25	15	Sukanto Tanoto
Ciputra		22		39	Ciputra
Putra Surya Perkasa			5	23	Trijono Gondokusumo
Mercubuana	50		*11*	66	Probosutedjo
Nugra Santana	41		*21*	*18*	Ibnu Sutowo
Mantrust	32		23		Tegoeh Soetandyo
Sudarma	33		*24*		Joh. Purnama Sudarma
Bank Danamon				8	Usman Admadjaja
Bakrie & Bros.	30		38	*12*	Aburizal Bakrie
Ometraco	36		29	16	Ferry Teguh Santoso
Artha Graha				*19*	Tommy Winata
Texmaco	88		98	*21*	Marimutu Srinivasan
Jaya				22	Ciputra family
BHS				24	Hendra Rahardja

Sources: CISI (1990); *Warta Ekonomi*, 24 April 1994; *Eksekutif*, August 1995.

Continuous conglomerisation during the Suharto era resulted in a very high degree of concentration of the control over the country's economic resources. This is in particular highlighted by isolating the top 10, 25 and 100 conglomerates from the data in both the survey of the late 1980s and the two later listings in the mid-1990s (Table 3.4). Several observations can be made. First, the predominance of Chinese Indonesian conglomerates becomes more pronounced the further up that we move in the hierarchy. The share of indigenous Indonesian conglomerates was at most 5–6 per cent within the total held by the top ten and rose to approximately 10 and 25 per cent in respectively the top 25 and top 100 categories. Only two indigenous businessmen appeared among the top 10 on any of the rankings consulted here: Suharto's son Bambang Trihatmodjo among assets in 1988 and sales in 1993 and old-timer Julius Tahija among assets in 1994. Popular resentment against Chinese conglomerates stemmed from both their numbers and their size.

A second observation concerns the size distribution as such. The top 10 always accounted for a very substantial proportion of the total associated with the top 25, but this percentage moved in different directions over time depending on whether sales or assets serve as yardsticks. On the sales side, the share of the top 10 actually fell, from 67 per cent in 1988 to 54 per cent in 1993 (cf. Booth 1998: 320). On the asset side, however, it rose, from

Table 3.4 Concentration of sales and assets among top conglomerates in Indonesia, 1988 and 1993–4

	Chinese Indonesians	Indigenous Indonesians	All
Sales (Rp. billion)			
Top 10			
1988	21,045	0	21,045
1993	48,360	3,000	41,360
Top 25			
1988	28,065	3,435	31,500
1993	70,000	7,150	77,150
Assets (Rp. billion)			
Top 10			
1988	10,360	520	10,880
1994	124,400	6,600	131,000
Top 25			
1988	14,390	1,670	16,060
1994	160,100	25,000	185,100
Top 100			
1988	21,263	5,261	27,524
1994	217,200	46,300	263,500

Sources: CISI (1990); *Warta Ekonomi*, 24 April 1994; *Eksekutif*, August 1995.

67 per cent in 1988 to 71 per cent in 1994. The rising degree of concentration in asset holdings by large conglomerates is even more clearly reflected in the rising proportion of assets of the 100 largest conglomerates held by the top group of 10, from 39 per cent in 1988 to almost 50 per cent by 1994. This contrast between market performance and accumulation of wealth among Indonesia's leading conglomerates in the 1990s is worth noting and further research may be required to explain it.

A third and final observation refers to the magnitudes of aggregate sales and asset holdings associated with the top categories. Assuming an annual average rate of inflation of 8 per cent (Hill 1996: 6), nominal figures can be expected to rise by about 47 per cent for sales and 60 per cent for assets.[13] In the event, all increases were far larger, which testifies to a considerable expansion in real terms in the economic activities undertaken by leading conglomerates. The increase was especially steep on the asset side with the aggregate level in 1994 at least ten times as high as the one that had prevailed six years earlier. It is tempting to conclude that real estate and equity holdings of the large conglomerates were vastly overvalued by the mid-1990s.

This section has depicted the outcome of a long process of conglomerisation in the Indonesian economy. The main emphasis has been on individual business groups and clusters of conglomerates as ranked by sales or assets. Yet it should not be overlooked that networks and corporate alliances play a very important role in the world of big business in Indonesia, as indeed in most countries. One significant feature of conglomerates in Indonesia is a high degree of intertwined vested interests between on the one hand Chinese conglomerates and on the other hand indigenous enterprises with access to political power or connections with the armed forces (Robison 1986: 317–18). The participation by Suharto children in the shareholdings of Salim's BCA is just one case in point (Van Dijk 2001: 86). The complex cross-holdings and inter-company links have been mapped for 140 leading conglomerates of which 40 were identified as indigenous Indonesian ones, including 16 owned by members of the extended presidential family (Castle 1997). It was an impressive pictorial representation of a world of conglomerates where things were to change beyond any expectation in the late 1990s.

In the wake of crisis

In early August 1997, few leading Indonesian economists, let alone foreign observers, believed that Indonesia was going to be hit by the financial crisis that had just erupted in Thailand.[14] But by November 1997, the Indonesian rupiah had begun its steep descent, the International Monetary Fund (IMF) had stepped in and private foreign debt was estimated to be at least $65 billion, a figure later revised upwards to $73 billion (Van Dijk 2001: 73; Hill 1999: 57). Many of the country's leading conglomerates were in deep trouble, unable to meet even the most immediate obligations as short-run foreign loans had to be repaid with revenues from long-run investment projects materialising in a hugely depreciated rupiah. As events unfolded, the economic crisis translated into a social and political crisis culminating with Suharto's resignation in May 1998. The context in which the conglomerates operated thus changed dramatically. A climate of seemingly uninterrupted rapid growth gave way to slow and difficult recovery from the most severe economic crisis in Indonesia in decades. In addition, political protection that had been taken for granted for years vanished, first gradually under Suharto's immediate successor Habibie (May 1998–October 1999), then more radically under Wahid (October 1999–July 2001) and Megawati (July 2001–September 2004).

In June 1998, a very different type of ranking of conglomerates compared to pre-crisis listings saw the light in the Indonesian business press. These were the 50 most heavily indebted conglomerates, all with in excess of $50 million, some owing more than $1 billion to creditors abroad. The ranking looked familiar. The five top ones were: Sinar Mas ($4.6 billion), Salim ($3.2 billion), Astra ($2.5 billion), Bakrie ($2.3 billion) and the Tirtamas group of Hasjim Djojohadikusumo, son of the renowned economist ($1.8 billion). The list also included Bambang's Bimantara ($840 million), Bob Hasan ($700 million), Tutut's Citra Lamtoro ($490 million), The Ning King's Damatex ($350 million), Latief's Bira ($260 million) and Tommy Suharto's Humpuss ($160 million) (*Panji Masyarakat* 24 June 1998). It was not coincidental that several of the former President's children and personal friends counted among those who had borrowed most and worried least about the consequences.

A separate institution, Indonesian Debt Restructuring Agency (INDRA), was set up in July 1998 by the Habibie administration to facilitate settlement with foreign debtors on the basis of bankruptcies to be declared under a new law that was still forthcoming. INDRA proved a failure, possibly because of the weak legal underpinnings, and in September 1998 it was for all intents and purposes replaced by the so-called Jakarta Initiative, a scheme for debt renegotiations based on voluntary participation by firms that were operationally viable but short of cash. Nine months later, it was claimed that more than one-quarter of the foreign debts had been restructured under auspices of the Jakarta Initiative (*Forum Keadilan* 20 June 1999). A major problem was the evaluation of assets surrendered by debtors as security. Some shares fell to almost unbelievably low levels on the Jakarta Stock Exchange during the first year of crisis, 1997–8. The value of Astra, for instance, declined by 85 per cent, Bimantara by 95 per cent and Ban Bali by 97 per cent (Evans 1998: 21). Nevertheless, some debt repayment apparently did take place in the course of 1999 and 2000, albeit at a very slow pace.

Banking had been liberalised quickly in Indonesia in the 1970s and 1980s, just as in most other East Asian countries, and the proliferation of new banks was accelerated by the practice of conglomerates to set up their own banks. On the eve of the crisis, Indonesia counted 237 banks, more even than in Japan. There was a minimum of supervision of banks owned by and catering to the needs of conglomerates and a huge mass of dubious debts was accumulated. In 1997, non-performing loans in Indonesia corresponded to 12 per cent available assets (Hill 1999: 55). One of the first strong recommendations attached to the IMF rescue package was therefore to liquidate the 16 'worst' banks, effective on 1 November 1997. Yet this backfired as it gave rise to a massive capital flight rather than restoring confidence in the country's banking system. The group of sixteen included Bank Andromeda, owned by Bambang Trihatmodjo, who hastened to transfer assets to another bank, Alfa, which came under his command only weeks afterwards (Van Dijk 2001: 87–9).

In January 1998, a new body was erected to deal with the ailing banking system, Indonesian Bank Restructuring Agency (IBRA) or Badan Penyehatan Perbankan Nasional (BPPN).[15] Fifty banks were immediately placed under its supervision, and IBRA assumed responsibility for uncollectible debts and problematic loans requiring capital outlays over time of as much as Rp. 400,000 billion or $40 billion at the 1998 exchange rate (Pardede 1999: 27). In return, the banks' owners handed over assets that were to be sold in the open market by IBRA. The list of banks under IBRA's tutelage contained links to a large number of the country's leading conglomerates. Bank Danamon, Gajah Tunggal's BDNI, Bob Hasan's Bank Umum Nasional, Lippo Bank and Bank Niaga counted among those first audited and in May 1998 BCA too was brought under IBRA rule. In November 1999, IBRA published a list on internet of the 20 largest bank debts, together accounting for Rp. 72,000 billion. The first three names on the list were those of Prajogo Pangestu, Tommy Suharto and Bob Hasan (Van Dijk 2001: 489). This was an unprecedented and unambiguous demonstration of the link between reckless lending by conglomerates and access to political power of their owners.[16]

IBRA went through a tumultuous history with six consecutive directors in four years and repeated charges of favouritism and corruption. A major difficulty was how to prevent former bank owners from recovering their surrendered assets at fire sale prices using straw men. The Salim group, for instance, offered shares in more than 100 firms such as Indocement, Indofood and Indomobil to IBRA in lieu of repayment of BCA's debts. In mid-1999, however, it transpired that a majority equity holding in Indofood had been sold by IBRA at a very favourable price to First Pacific in Hong Kong, a subsidiary of Salim (Van Dijk 2001: 403). A similar episode was reported in early 2003 when the management of the Lippo Bank attempted to mislead the public by reporting far too low asset values in order to allow Mochtar Riady to buy back shares at a bargain price (*Kompas* 24 February 2003).

Ownership patterns often did change through intervention by IBRA. Its initial equity share in BCA, 30 per cent, was raised to a majority holding. The same also happened in BII where Sinar Mas had pledged Rp. 12,000 billion as collateral for government guarantees of repayment of outstanding loans (Dick 2001: 23). The opportunity even arose for the Soeryadjaja family to regain its hold over Astra. The Suharto cronies, owners since 1992, had surrendered almost half of the equity to IBRA, which in turn was looking for buyers. This equity was reported to be worth Rp. 4,000 billion ($400 million) and was widely considered to be IBRA's most attractive offer. In the event, more than $500 million was paid for one-quarter of Astra by an international consortium supported by the Singapore government even including a Soros fund in the background (Fane 2000: 41; Friend 2003: 469).

By the end of the year 2000, some of the targets had been met by IBRA. Nine private banks, including Bank Bali, BII, Lippo and Niaga, were being recapitalised at a cost of Rp. 21,300 billion ($2.1 billion) whereas 38 banks were to be closed. Conspicuous in the latter category were four banks (Alfa, Yama, Tata and Pesona Kriya Dana) with children of Suharto as chief owners (Van Dijk 2001: 408–9). Meanwhile IBRA had acquired assets worth $57.8 billion corresponding to a staggering Rp. 578,000 billion. However, only 7 per cent of the IBRA holdings had been sold (Friend 2003: 270). Difficulties in getting rid of the appropriated assets have plagued IBRA ever since and may be attributed to various factors. It is highly likely that many of the surrendered assets were overvalued in the first place, i.e. the companies in question were not as viable or profitable as they had appeared. Astra clearly forms an exception in this regard. To this must be added the general hesitancy to invest in Indonesia during the drawn-out recovery from the crisis when political stability still had to be restored. A final explanation lies in public resentment of sales to either former owners or foreign investors wishing to take advantage of the low price.

This brief section has highlighted the predicaments and changing alignments of the conglomerates as Indonesia was hit by financial and political crisis. The world of conglomerates then appeared far less stable than it had seemed in times of continuous rapid growth and political protection. It is still too early to assess how much of the inherited conglomerate business structure will remain intact into the future and how much will change.

Conclusion

Conglomerates in Indonesia are generally associated with corruption, collusion and nepotism – the acronym KKN (*korupsi, kolusi, nepotisme*) – became highly popular after the fall of Suharto in 1998. This chapter has placed the Indonesian conglomerates in a wider historical context and a more rigorous analytical framework using statistics on the leading business groups at various points in time. Some structural characteristics may be identified as follows.

The history of the rise of conglomerates in Indonesia reveals a juxtaposition of two types of entrepreneurship reflecting respectively a tradition of long standing, reaching back to the process of decolonisation in the 1940s or 1950s, and a newer version that gained strength during the era of rapid economic growth under Suharto. Both types contained an ethnic differentiation. Old entrepreneurship embraced indigenous beneficiaries of positive discrimination under Sukarno as well as Chinese Indonesians with a capability to survive and expand despite a climate of discrimination. New entrepreneurship has similarly combined and on occasion effectively aligned Chinese groups rising to prominence in the late 1960s and the 1970s with indigenous groups enjoying special protection from the presidential palace during the 1980s and 1990s. This testifies to a greater variety and more heterogeneity than is often appreciated in popularised impressions of conglomerates in Indonesia.

The statistics on conglomerates highlight a strikingly high degree of concentration of control over the country's economic resources. Predominance by Chinese Indonesian conglomerates is even more reinforced when focusing specifically on the very apex of the conglomerate hierarchy. There was, and still is, a considerable volatility and instability in the composition of the entire population of leading conglomerates but much less so at the top. Tendencies towards concentration in the 1990s were especially strong in terms of the accumulation of assets, far more so than with respect to growth based on market performance. This testifies to a complex structure with powerful vested interests safeguarding continuity but also containing a substantial for short-run change.

The combination of a high degree of concentration of control with a strong dependence on political privileges resulted in an extreme vulnerability to financial and political crisis as became manifest when the Indonesian rupiah collapsed and the Suharto regime came to disgraceful conclusion. The leading conglomerates paid the price, figuratively but not literally speaking.

Notes

1 This article offers an extended and improved version of the brief discussion of Indonesia's top 200 conglomerates given in Lindblad (2004: 248–9).
2 Unless otherwise stated, the firm-specific information derives from surveys of the leading mentioned conglomerates.
3 The foremost Chinese conglomerate of the late colonial period, the Oei Tiong Ham concern at Semarang (Central Java), stagnated after Indonesian independence and was nationalised in 1961 on charges of retaining links with Dutch business (Liem 1979; Yoshihara 1989).
4 The Bakrie family is of Arab origin but has always been considered fully indigenous Indonesian.
5 Caution is necessary when making such comparisons as GDP is based on value added whereas turnover of private firms is not. Nevertheless, the percentage is high by international comparison, albeit lower than in for instance the case of Korean *chaebol* (Kim 1997: 94). A lower figure, 15 per cent, was cited in an earlier reference to the 1989 list (Booth 1998: 320).
6 Strictly speaking, the 1989 list of the 40 top conglomerates therefore contained 28 fully Chinese-owned, 11 fully indigenous and 1 jointly owned business group.
7 Some processing was done by the editors of *Warta Ekonomi* when preparing the 1989 list from the raw data in the larger, then still unpublished survey. Nine

business groups were for unknown reasons left out so that the ranking (above position 17) differs in the 1989 list as compared to the original.

8 Most conglomerates dating from the 1960s were in fact established after 1966.

9 Ranks 4 to 10 in the later survey (Data Consult 1991) are occupied by the following business groups: Gudang Garam, Pakarti Yoga, Lippo, First Pacific, Barito, Bimantara and Djarum of which First Pacific, Barito and Bimantara did not appear among the top ten in the earlier survey. For the top ten ranks in the earlier survey (CISI 1990) see Table 3.3.

10 Seven sub-conglomerates are included in the 1990 size distribution but not in the 1988 one (see the notes of Table 3.1). Inclusion for purposes of comparison brings the total number of Chinese Indonesian conglomerates in the 1988 distribution to 124.

11 It is likely that the information for these lists derived from elaborate surveys prepared by the private consulting firm Data Consult in Jakarta. These surveys were prohibitively expensive and are generally not available in libraries.

12 Conglomerates controlled by indigenous Indonesians are given in italics in Table 3.3.

13 The rate of exchange of the Indonesian rupiah changed relatively little during this period, from Rp. 1,800/US$ in 1988 to Rp. 2,250/US$ in 1994.

14 The question why warning signals were so stubbornly neglected by virtually all observers is addressed elsewhere in the literature (Kenward 1999; Lindblad 2004).

15 Another, separate measure to resolve the crisis in banking was the establishment of Bank Mandiri in July 1999, which became the successor of the four most debt-ridden state banks.

16 Several of Suharto's children and personal friends were questioned on corruption charges and forced to withdraw from business. Bob Hasan was eventually imprisoned on Pulau Nusakambangan, an island south of Java, where he was later joined by Tommy Suharto who received a 15-year sentence for ordering the murder of the judge chairing the court that had sentenced him in the first place.

Bibliography

Backman, M. (1999) *Asian Eclipse: Exposing the Dark Side of Business in Asia*, Singapore: Wiley.

Booth, A. (1998) *The Indonesian Economy in the Nineteenth and Twentieth Centuries. A History of Missed Opportunities*, London: Macmillan.

BPS (1992) *Pendapatan Nasional Indonesia/National Income of Indonesia 1986–1991*, Jakarta: Biro Pusat Statistik.

Castle Group (1997) *Castle's Road Map to Indonesian Business Groups*, Jakarta: Java Consult.

CISI (1990) *A Study of Top-200 National Private Business Groups in Indonesia, 1989*, Jakarta: CISI Raya Utama.

Data Consult (1991) *Anatomy of Indonesian Conglomerates*, Jakarta: Data Consult.

Dick, H.W. (2001) 'Survey of recent developments', *Bulletin of Indonesian Economic Studies* 37 (1): 7–42.

Dijk, K. van (2001) *A Country in Despair: Indonesia between 1997 and 2000*, Leiden: KITLV Press.

Elson, R.E. (2001) *Suharto. A Political Biography*, Cambridge: Cambridge University Press.

Evans, K. (1998) 'Survey of recent developments', *Bulletin of Indonesian Economic Studies* 34 (3): 5–35.

Fane, G. (2000) 'Survey of recent developments', *Bulletin of Indonesian Economic Studies* 36 (1): 13–44.

Friend, Th. (2003) *Indonesian Destinies*, Cambridge, MA: Harvard University Press.

Hill, H. (1990) 'Ownership in Indonesia: who owns what and does it matter?', in H. Hill and T. Hull (eds), *Indonesia Assessment 1990. Political and Social Change*, Canberra: Australian National University, pp. 52–65.

—— (1996) *The Indonesian Economy since 1966: Southeast Asia's Emerging Giant*, Cambridge: Cambridge University Press.

—— (1999) *The Indonesian Economy in Crisis: Causes, Consequences and Lessons*, Singapore: Institute of Southeast Asian Studies.

Kenward, L.R. (1999) 'Assessing vulnerability to financial crisis: evidence from Indonesia', *Bulletin of Indonesian Economic Studies* 35 (3): 71–95.

Kim Kwan S. (1997) 'From neo-mercantilism to globalism: the changing role of the state and South Korea's economic prowess', in M.T. Berger and D.A. Borer (eds), *The Rise of East Asia: Critical Visions of the Pacific Century*, London: Routledge, pp. 82–105.

Liem Tjwan Ling (1979) *Raja Gula Oei Tiong Ham (Sugar King Oei Tiong Ham)*, Surabaya: Sinapura.

Lindblad, J.Th. (2002) 'The importance of *indonesianisasi* during the transition from the 1930s to the 1960s', *Itinerario. European Journal of Overseas History* 26 (3/4): 51–72.

—— (2004) 'The political economy of recovery in Indonesia', in J. Demmers, A.E. Fernández Jilberto and B. Hogenboom (eds), *Good Governance in the Era of Global Neoliberalism: Conflict and Depolitisation in Latin America, Eastern Europe, Asia and Africa*, London/New York: Routledge, pp. 246–64.

MacIntyre, A. (1990) *Business and Politics in Indonesia*, North Sydney: Allen & Unwin.

Mackie, J.A.C. and C.A. Coppel (1976) 'A preliminary survey', in J.A.C. Mackie (ed.), *The Chinese in Indonesia. Five Essays*, Melbourne: Nelson, pp. 1–18.

Pardede, R. (1999) 'Survey of recent developments', *Bulletin of Indonesian Economic Studies* 35 (2): 3–39.

Post, P. (1997) 'The formation of the pribumi business elite in Indonesia, 1930s–1940s', in P. Post and E. Touwen-Bouwsma (eds), *Japan, Indonesia and the War: Myths and Realities*, Leiden: KITLV Press, pp. 87–110.

Robison, R. (1986) *Indonesia: The Rise of Capital*, North Sydney: Allen & Unwin.

Schwarz, A. (1999) *A Nation in Waiting. Indonesia's Search for Stability*, St Leonards, NSW: Allen & Unwin.

Suryadinata, L. (1997) *The Culture of the Chinese Minority in Indonesia*, Singapore: Times Books International.

Thee Kian Wie (1996) 'Economic policies in Indonesia during the period 1950–1965, in particular with respect to foreign investment', in J.Th. Lindblad (ed.), *Historical Foundations of a National Economy in Indonesia, 1890s–1990s*, Amsterdam: North-Holland, pp. 331–48.

Widyahartono, B. (1990) 'Konglomerat: Antara teori dan realitas', in Kwik Kian Gie *et al.*, *Konglomerat Indonesia: Permasalahan dan Sepak Terjangnya (Conglomerates in Indonesia: Problems and Conduct)*, Jakarta: Sinar Harapan, pp. 53–72.

Yoshihara Kunio (1989) *Oei Tiong Ham Concern: The First Business Empire of Southeast Asia*, Kyoto: Centre for Southeast Asian Studies, Kyoto University.

4 The rise of Taiwanese family-owned business groups in the telecommunications industry

Momoko Kawakami

After three decades of impressive growth driven by export-oriented indus-trialisation, the Taiwanese economy encountered a turning point in the early 1990s. While a sharp appreciation of New Taiwan dollars (NTD) and an accelerated rise in wage rates triggered the relocation of labour-intensive manufacturing activities to Mainland China and elsewhere, the new capital-intensive service sectors expanded remarkably and began to support the economy of the island. In contrast to the former industries in which small and medium-sized enterprises played a central role as exporters, major investors in such growing service sectors as the financial and telecommuni-cations industries were family-owned and -managed conglomerates. These business groups made a move into the service sectors in response to the emergence of newly opened markets created by the deregulation policies of the Taiwanese government that started in the late 1980s. The policy changes induced a new form of competition among major economic groups, and eventually led to a new stage in their diversification.

This chapter explores the process through which Taiwanese family-owned and -managed business groups entered one of the most dynamic newly liber-alised service sectors, the mobile telecommunications industry, and examines the backgrounds that allowed the entry of the old business groups into the unfamiliar new market. The cases of two family business groups, the Far Eastern Group of the Hsu family and the Hohsin Group of the Koo family, are studied with a special focus on the following two points: first, the way the controlling families of the business groups mobilised resources from their affiliated public companies to enter the telecommunications industry; and, second, the way these groups acquired the skills and technology necessary to enter the unfamiliar service sector. What is argued here is that the family-owned business groups employed a unique combination of their conventional ownership structure with a policy of recruiting experienced professional managers from outside the group. This strategy allowed the business groups to mobilise capital from the affiliate publicly listed companies into the telecommunications industry and to acquire technology and know-how necessary for entry into the unfamiliar new sector, while it also enabled these groups to retain ownership control of the affiliate telecom operators.

This chapter is organised as follows. The first section studies the recent development of large Taiwanese family business groups, focusing on their investments in the newly liberalised service sector. The next section presents a brief history of the deregulation policy in the Taiwanese telecommunications industry, and the entry process of large conglomerates into the sector. This is followed by a brief history of the Far Eastern and Hohsin Groups, and an analysis of the ownership and management structures that underlie their investments in the mobile telecommunications industry. In the conclusion it is argued that the Taiwanese experience of old economic groups entering into the modern service sector of mobile telecommunications bears similarity to putting old wine into new bottles.

Taiwanese large family business groups in the 1990s

In most East Asian developing countries, the ultimate ownership of public companies rests in the hands of families (Claessens *et al.* 2000). Taiwan is by no means an exception. Based on data for 285 companies for 1994 and 1995, Yeh *et al.* (2001) estimate that more than 51 per cent of Taiwanese publicly listed companies are classified as family-controlled when the cut-off control level is set at 20 per cent. The same figure rises to an estimate of approximately 76 per cent when the critical control level is calculated separately for each firm.[1] Family members also keep a firm grip on their affiliate companies by taking part in management, primarily as chairmen, directors and general managers. In Taiwan, even among publicly listed large corporations, family control is still a dominant characteristic (SFI 2002: 5).[2]

One central apparatus that helps ensure the family control of public companies is the formation of business groups. Extensive cross-holding and pyramiding among member companies of these groups provide the owner-family with the solid control of the entire group and exploitation of the capital market simultaneously. With the rapid industrialisation of the economy, Taiwan has witnessed an emergence of a number of large diversified business groups. Table 4.1 shows the ten largest Taiwanese business groups in terms of net sales for 2003. Among them, eight are family-owned and -inherited groups, while one group is owned and managed by the founder, who is expected to be succeeded by his younger brother in the near future and by his daughter in the longer term. The table also reveals that most family-owned groups have their origins in the early 1950s to 1960s, and many have already been passed on to the second generation.

Traditionally, Taiwanese large business groups are characterised by the relatively specialised structure of their businesses. Compared to their Korean counterparts, Taiwanese large economic groups invest mainly in segments related to their core business and, as a result, their scale is substantially smaller than that of gigantic Korean *chaebols* (Abe and Kawakami 1997). However, in the early 1990s, Taiwanese large business groups began to

Table 4.1 Top ten business groups in Taiwan, 2003 (by net sales)

Rank-ings	Group	Year of establish-ment	Family-owned or not (owner-family, current generation)[a]	Core Businesses
1	Formosa Plastics	1954	F (Wang family, 1st – 2nd generation)	Petrochemical, synthetic fibre, plastic
2	Lin-Yuan	1962	F (Tsai family, 2nd generation)	Life insurance, banking, other financial services
3	Hon Hai	1974	F (Gou family, 1st generation) [b]	IT products
4	Lien Hwa Mitac	1955	F (Miao family, 2nd generation)	IT products, food
5	Quanta Computer	1988	NF IT products	
6	Shin Kong	1955	F (Wu family, 2nd generation)	Life insurance, banking, synthetic fibre
7	Yulon	1953	F (Yen family, 2nd generation)	Automobile manufacturing
8	Uni-President	1967	F (Kao & Wu family)	Food, retail
9	Far Eastern	1954	F (Hsu family, 2nd generation)	Synthetic fibre, telecom, petrochemicals, retail
10	Kinpo	1973	F (Hsu family, 2nd generation)	IT products

Source: China Credit Information (2004).

Notes:
a   F stands for family-owned groups and NF for non-family owned groups.
b   Hon Hai Group is owned and managed by the founder, Terry T.M. Gou. He is expected to be succeeded by his younger brother in the near future, and by his daughter in the longer term.

diversify vigorously, and their scale and scope of business expanded significantly. Table 4.2 shows the ratio of total sales and total employees of the approximately 100 large business groups to nominal gross domestic product (GDP) and total employment in Taiwan respectively. The increasingly wide coverage of consolidation of subsidiary firms across sample years makes a time–series comparison somewhat difficult, but it is apparent that large business groups have come to assume importance over the last ten years.

One important source of this remarkable diversification and expansion of the large business groups has been their aggressive investment in the newly deregulated service sectors, the lucrative markets created by the liberalisation policy of the Taiwanese government beginning in the late 1980s. Table 4.3 presents the basic profile of the six largest family-owned business groups in terms of assets as of 2003. From the right side of Table 4.3, we can see that large family-owned business groups rushed into such deregulated

Table 4.2 Predominance of large business groups in Taiwan (ratio of sales to GDP and share in total employment)

	Number of business groups counted	Ratio of total sales of business groups to GDP[a]	Ratio of employees of business groups to total employment
1979	100	31.9	4.9
1986	97	28.7	4.3
1990	101	38.3	
1996	113	44.8	6.4
2000	100	85.1	9.2
2003	100	98.7	12.5

Source: China Credit Information (2004).

Notes:
a There may be overestimation of total sales of business groups due to the possible double counting of foreign and domestic sales.

sectors as finance, telecommunications and public utilities after the 1990s. These markets were opened to entry by the private sector as a result of policy change in the late 1980s. The investments in the newly emerging service sectors revived the business structure of family-owned groups, and the scale and scope economies in the form of reputation and multiple-product marketing brought about the 'comeback' of big business groups (Amsden and Chu 2003: 124–5, 133). This has led to the expansion of these groups in the last ten years, especially in terms of asset value. In average, the real value of assets and revenues for all six groups presented in Table 4.3 increased by 18.2 per cent and 13.6 per cent respectively per year during 1993–2003.[3]

Two questions thus follow the successful entry of family-owned business groups into the services sectors, of which they had little experience prior to entry. First, what was the ownership structure of these groups that allowed the owner-family to make huge investments in this unfamiliar sector? Second, how did they acquire the technology and knowledge requisite for entry into this new market? In this chapter, we investigate these questions by focusing on the telecommunications industry, the most lucrative market among the newly deregulated service sectors.

Entry of large business groups into the telecommunications industry

The telecommunications market in Taiwan was long regulated and monopolised by the Directorate General of Telecommunications (DGT), an agency under the Ministry of Transportation and Communication (MOTC). Faced with international pressure, as well as growing local demand for telecommunications services, the Taiwanese government started to deregulate the industry in the early 1990s. In 1996, major law reforms, including a drastic

Table 4.3 Six largest family business groups in Taiwan, 2003 (by total assets in million NTD)

Group (owner-family)	Core business	Total assets (total ranking)	Net sales (total ranking)	Entry into newly deregulated sectors[a]				
				Banking	Bills finance	Power generation	Wireless telecom	Fixed telecom
Lin-yuan Group (Tsai family)	Financial services	2,380,470 1	534,883 2	1998				
China Trust Group[b] (Koo family)	Financial services	1,572,588 3	b 18	1992[c]	1996	1997	1997	
Shin Kong Group (Wu family)	Financial services, textiles	1,493,645 5	356,773 6	1992	1998			
Formosa Plastics Group (Wang family)	Petrochemical, plastics	1,437,914 7	938,713 1	1992	1995	1996		
Fubon Group (Tsai family)	Far Eastern	1,286,320 9	136,454 24	1992	1997			
Far Eastern Textile Group (Hsu family)	Textiles, telecoms, cement	783,559 11	256,103 9	1992		1996		2000

Notes:
a This overview includes the historical cases, where the business was later sold off or transferred to other groups as a result of restructuring of family business. For example, the entry of China Trust Group in power generation and wireless telecom stand for those investments the large Koo family made jointly, but later excluded from China Trust Group as a result of the split of the Koos' business. Also, the investment shares by the groups vary significantly across the cases.

b China Trust Group was formerly a part of the Hohsin Group, which split up into the China Trust and Hohsin Groups in 2003. Total assets and net sales of the new Hohsin Group were 198 billion NTD and 68 billion NTD respectively in 2003.

c China Securities and Investment Companies (CSIC) was established in 1966 and was transformed into Commercial Bank in 1992.

amendment of the Telecommunication Act, were promulgated, and the newly incorporated government-owned enterprise Chunghwa Telecom took over the role of providing telecommunications services from the DGT. In the same year, the wireless telecommunications service was liberalised to allow entry by the private sector. In 1999, integrated fixed-line telecommunications services (i.e. local, long-distance and international calls) were opened to private companies.

Of these telecommunications services, wireless mobile telecommunications was expected to be the most profitable market. The DGT had started the services in 1989, but soon growing local demand far outpaced the supply of cellular mobile services. On the eve of the entry of private providers, Chunghwa Telecom, the only wireless telecom operator at that time, had more than one million consumers waiting for subscription to its cellular phone services. In 1996, DGT announced it would grant eight licences, two island-wide GSM (Global System for Mobile Communications) 1,800MHz licences and six regional GSM 900MHz licenses, to new entrants. The growing expectation for enormous business opportunities and profitability in this sector had a strong attraction for a number of large business groups, resulting in a 'gold-rush' (Hung 1996a) swarming of prominent family-owned business groups into the application race for the new market. In 1996, a total of 42 applications competing for the eight licences from 17 consortia were sent to the Screening Committee.

The 17 applicant consortia had two common features. First, most of these consortia were alliances of multiple family-owned groups and foreign partners. To the eyes of local investors, possession of political connections seemed a requisite for winning the bid, and various combinations of influential family groups were formed to leverage their political power. Meanwhile, foreign telecom services providers were attracted by the lucrative market in Taiwan.

Second, it was the sons (or, in a few cases, daughters) of founders, the so-called second generation of family groups, who took the initiative to invest in this field. Among those applicants were the Wu brothers of Shin Kong Group, the Chiao brothers of Walsin Lihwa Group, the Tsai brothers of Lin-Yuan Group, and other younger members of distinguished business families. Based on interviews with these second-generation members, Hung (1996b) explains the motivations on the parts of these sons. First of all, the sons of great and celebrated founders were eager to show their abilities to their elders. As most of these second-generation members had studied abroad and were proficient in English, the telecom project, which involved international negotiation and alliance, was the best arena for these 'princes' to demonstrate their qualifications as capable successors to their families' businesses. Also, the personal ties among the second-generation members provided the backbone for business alliances. For example, the alliance among Pacific Electric Wire & Cable Group, Fubong Group and Continental Engineering Cec Group to establish Taiwan Cellular Corp. was based on the friendship among the second-generation members of these groups.

Early in 1997, MOTC awarded eight GSM licences to six applicants. As the six newly incorporated providers sparked a fierce competition to win customers, the long repressed demands for mobile telecommunications services exploded drastically, and the number of subscribers to cellular phone services jumped from 0.97 million in 1996 to 21.6 million in 2001 – approximately the entire population of the island.[4] Throughout the course of this market expansion, consolidation among the providers took place. The significant network externality in this industry, as well as the need for strategic alliances for mutual roaming, spurred active alliances and mergers. By 2000 the selection of service providers had expanded significantly. Besides the state-operated Chunghwa Telecom, three major private providers, Taiwan Cellular, Far EasTone Telecommunications, and KG Telecommunications came to share out the market.

It is noteworthy that all three of these private telecom companies are owned primarily by celebrated Taiwanese family business groups. Taiwan Cellular was established under the leadership of Jack T. Sun of Pacific Electric Wire & Cable Group, a business group collectively owned by multiple Mainlander families, and later changed hands to the Fubon Group in 2003, which is ultimately owned by the Tsai family. Far EasTone Telecommunications belongs to the Far Eastern Group of the Hsu family. KG Telecommunications was established by Taiwan Cement, a core company of the Koo family's Hohsin Group. These three private providers carried on a fierce competition with each other until the autumn of 2003, when Far EasTone announced a merger with the operations of KG Telecom.

It is interesting to analyse the process by which the family-owned business groups that had expanded mainly by investing in traditional manufacturing sectors emerged successfully as competitive providers of telecommunications services in a short period. We therefore explore the cases of two representative family-owned and -managed groups, the Far Eastern Group of the Hsu family and the Hohsin (Taiwan Cement) Group of the Koo family. Special attention will be paid to the strategy these business groups employed to enter this service sector, that is, their use of a unique combination of conventional ownership structure with the strategic acquisition of human resources required in the telecommunications industry.

History of the Far Eastern Group and the Hohsin Group

While both the Hsus of the Far Eastern Group and the Koos of the Hohsin Group are among the most influential business families in Taiwan, they are rather contrasting in several respects. First, the Hsu family represents one major type of leading entrepreneur of post-Second World War Taiwan, the Shanghai-origin capitalists, while the Koo family is a distinguished local Taiwanese family whose origin of capital accumulation dates back to the Japanese colonial period. Second, the Far Eastern Group has a concentrated structure of ownership and management control in the hands of Douglas Hsu, while the Hohsin Group is characterised by a relatively decentralised network-like structure of ownership and management. The latter group had been managed under a collective decision-making regime by the large Koo family, but in 2003 the group implemented a fundamental reorganisation and split into two sub-groups, the Hohsin (or Taiwan Cement) Group and the China Trust Group. Let us briefly go over the history of these two families and their businesses.

The Far Eastern Group

The origin of the Far Eastern Group dates back to the early 1940s, when the founder, Y.Z. Hsu (1912–2000), started a textile factory with his younger brother in Shanghai. With the relocation of the Republic of China (ROC) government to Taiwan, the Hsu brothers and their family moved to Taiwan, and resumed manufacturing knitwear on the island. Far Eastern Textile Ltd, the group's core company, was established in 1954. The company grew into one of the world's leading producers of polyester after the 1970s, while it continuously pursued integration of upstream and downstream production. In 1975, the group invested in the Oriental Union Chemical Corporation in order further to integrate manufacturing of synthetic-fibre raw material, ethylene glycol. Other main companies forming part of the group include Asia Cement Corporation, founded by the Hsu brothers in 1957 with joint investments from other Shanghai-origin capitalists, and Far Eastern Department Store, incorporated in 1967.

Until the late 1980s, the group steadily expanded its scale and scope of business under the leadership of Y.Z. Hsu. In the early 1990s, however, the founder's health started to decline, and the issue of succession came to the surface. Hsu had two wives who, between them, had given birth to five sons and four daughters. Among the nine children, Douglas Shiu-Tong, the oldest son of the second wife, and Shiu-Shi, the oldest son of the first wife, were the most likely candidates as successors. The two half-brothers were both born in 1942 and earned an MBA and a Ph.D. respectively from distinguished universities in the United States.

After years of intense rivalry between the half-siblings, the father finally picked Douglas Shiu-Tong as his successor. Unlike the common practice of Chinese family-owned business groups by which a father transfers to each son a piece of the business, Y.Z. Hsu decided to hand over the entire managerial responsibility of the whole group to only one son, Douglas Shiu-Tong, to avoid splitting the group.[5] In 1993, the disappointed Shiu-Shi sold off his stocks and left Taiwan, and in the same year Douglas assumed the position of chairman of the three major companies of the group and finally succeeded to his father's business. Ever since, the group has expanded under the strong leadership of Douglas Hsu, well-known as a 'tireless workaholic' (Wang 1995).

All through the 1990s, the Far Eastern Group made aggressive investments in the newly deregulated service sector under the strong leadership of Douglas. The group incorporated the Far Eastern International Bank in 1992 and power generator Chiahui Power Corporation in 1996, respectively. As for telecommunications, the group established the wireless-services provider Far EasTone Telecommunications in 1997, and invested in a fixed-network provider, New Century InfoComm, in 2000.

As of 2003, the Far Eastern Group ranked as the third, ninth and eleventh largest group in Taiwan in terms of net worth, net sales and total assets respectively. The conglomerate covers a wide range of business sectors, including textile and synthetic fibre, petrochemical, cement, transportation, construction, retailing, hotel business, financial services and telecommunications. The Far Eastern Group is one of the most diversified and successful economic groups in Taiwan. Among the Far Eastern Group's 130 affiliate companies, Far EasTone is the largest source of net sales, generating 40.3 billion NTD in 2004. Clearly, the central pillar of the group has shifted from mature manufacturing sectors such as textiles and cement, to modern services represented by telecommunications.

The Hohsin (Taiwan Cement) Group

The history of the Hohsin Group starts earlier than that of the Far Eastern Group. The capital accumulation of the Koo family originated in the early Japanese colonial period, when Koo Shien-Rong (1866–1937) became one of the earliest and most important cooperators with the Japanese colonial government, and amassed riches as a landlord and merchant. Koo Shien-Rong had six wives and twelve children, including three adopted sons. He passed away in 1937, and his son Chen-fu (1917–2005) took over his father's business. After the Second World War, Taiwan was returned to the ROC, and Koo Chen-fu entered into partnership with the Kuomintang government and assumed high positions in Kuomintang and business organisations. The Koo family has formed an intensive friendship and extensive marriage network with the most powerful Taiwanese and Mainlander families. Backed by these strong connections, as well as his own capabilities and charisma, Koo Chen-fu became one of the most influential figures in post-Second World War Taiwan, in both the business and political scenes.[6]

The Koos are a large family, and their Hohsin Group (otherwise known as 'Koo's Group') had been collectively owned and managed by two nuclear families, Chen-fu and his sons on one side, and Chen-fu's nephew, Koo Lien-sung (Jeffrey Koo), and his sons on the other side, until they split up into two groups in 2003. Koo Chen-fu is generally regarded as part of the second generation of the Koo family. It is true that Chen-fu's father laid the foundations of the family's prosperity, but this chapter regards Chen-fu as the first-generation leader of the Koo family business, for it was Chen-fu who established the basis for the post-war development of the Hohsin Group.

Chen-fu's nephew, Jeffrey Lien-sung Koo, is 16 years Chen-fu's junior. In 1966, he returned from the United States after receiving an MBA, and joined the newly founded China Securities and Investment Corporation (CSIC). He proved to be a very capable business partner for Chen-fu, and, based on his educational background and working experience in the American financial sector, he took a strong initiative to lead the company's growth. CSIC was reorganised into Chinatrust Investment Company in 1971 and transformed into Chinatrust Commercial Bank Co., Ltd in 1992. Under Lien-sung's strong leadership, Chinatrust Bank grew into one of Taiwan's most successful financial institutions, and became one of the group's mainstays. Beginning in the first years of the new century, Lien-sung's three sons started to assume high management positions in affiliated financial companies of the group.

Another core company of the Hohsin Group is Taiwan Cement Corporation (TCC), which has a long history. After the ROC restored Taiwan, the Kuomintang government nationalised three formerly Japanese cement plants and merged them into TCC. In 1954, the government implemented land reform, and the stocks of the TCC were dispersed to landlords as a part of the compensation for their land, thus privatising the company (for details, see TCC 1994). Koo Chen-fu was one of the largest shareholders of the company, and with the company's privatisation he assumed the position of executive director in 1954 and general manager in 1959. Keeping step with the government's protection policy for the sector and the economy's rapid industrialisation, the TCC enjoyed steady growth from the 1960s through the early 1980s. However, in the mid-1980s, the cement industry started to face a number of difficulties – a shortage of raw material, waves of anti-pollution movements accompanied by the rise of environmental consciousness, and increased competition from imports all eroded the profitability of the industry.

In the late 1980s, Koo Chen-fu's two sons, Chi-Yun (1953–2001) and Cheng-Yun (b. 1954), returned to Taiwan after receiving MBAs in the United States and started to participate in the management of the family business. These second-generation sons found that the business climate for their family's core business, the TCC, was deteriorating rapidly, and perceived the need for diversification. The elder son, Koo Chi-Yun, took a strong interest in the media business. During the 1990s, Chi-Yun invested boldly in the cable TV industry, broadband networks, media content and other multimedia sectors, but these projects failed dismally. Also in the late 1990s, Chi-Yun himself experienced personal financial trouble and serious health problems, and in 2001 he died at the age of 48. All these misfortunes exerted great pressure on the maintenance of joint ownership of the group by the two nuclear families. Until then, the Koo Chen-fu family and the Jeffrey Lien-sung Koo family had jointly owned and managed the large Koo family business. Each of the two sub-families managed manufacturing and financial companies respectively, and mutually invested in each other's main companies to maintain solidarity. They had also held a 'Hohsin Summit' regularly to make strategic decisions jointly. However, Chi-Yun's financial trouble and death made acute the need for a reorganisation of the family business.

In 2003, the family finally decided to split up into two separate groups, the Hohsin (Taiwan Cement) Group and the China Trust Group, in order to concentrate on their main businesses and enhance competitiveness. After the split, Koo Cheng-Yun took full charge of the businesses left to the Hohsin Group. He had entered TCC and had taken over the position of general manager from his father in 1991. It was he who took the initiative for TCC's investment in the mobile telecommunications industry.

Ownership and management structures

The swarming of family-owned and -managed business groups into the acquisition race for licences for mobile telecommunications operation was motivated by two major factors. First, most of those groups had come to face the pressure of upgrading their business structure by the early 1990s. In particular, those conglomerates with such core businesses as cement, cables and wires, and synthetic fibre manufacturing were confronted by the rapidly declining profitability of their main businesses, and were strongly motivated to diversify into the emerging sectors. Second, as mentioned earlier, the new generation of these families regarded the telecom project as an ideal chance to demonstrate their capabilities to their seniors. A prince needs an arena in which to display himself and his skills, and the telecommunications industry offered an ideal chance to second-generation family members. However, these factors explain only half of the story. Without effective measures to mobilise internal capital resources, these groups could not have made the huge investments required in the sector. Nor could they, without a channel to access the knowledge and skills required in the sector, have launched commercial operations.

The Far Eastern Group

The ownership structure of the Far Eastern Group as of 2004 is shown in Figure 4.1. The figure, though simplified substantially, illustrates the mechanism through which the Hsu family controls this huge and wide-ranging conglomerate. The family as a block holder invests rather a small share in each listed company, with the highest ownership share of approximately 7.8 per cent in the group's flagship company, Far Eastern Textile. Still, the apparatus shown in the figure and described below allows the Hsus to keep a firm grip on each member company in the group.

First, the Hsu family employs extensive pyramidal and mutual shareholding among group member companies to establish their ownership control. This tactic was originated by Y.Z. Hsu, who was called the 'inventor of mutual

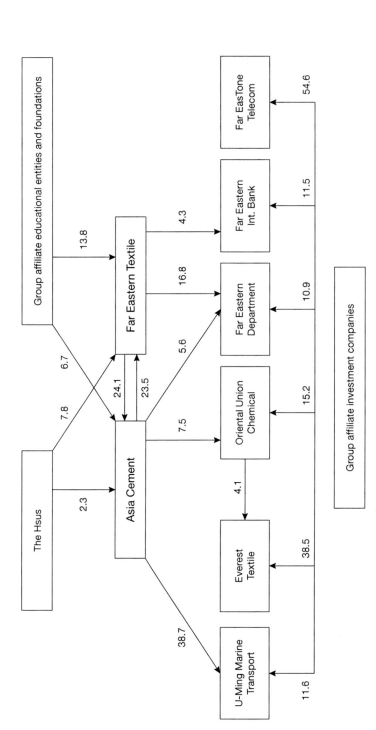

Figure 4.1 The ownership structure of the Far Eastern Group (2004)

Sources: Annual reports of group member companies; Hsu *et al.* (2004a).

Note: Group affiliate investment companies include Yuan Ding Investment, Bai Yang Investment, Der Ching Investment and numerous other investment companies established by member companies of the Far Eastern Group.

holding in Taiwan'. As of 2004, Far Eastern Textile and Asia Cement owned more than 20 per cent of each other's stocks, and these two pillar companies in turn invest in such affiliate publicly listed corporations as U-Ming Marine Transport Corporation and Far Eastern Department Store.[7]

Second, investment companies established by such core companies as Far Eastern Textile and Asia Cement occupy a critical place in the web of ownership. The largest shareholder of Everest Textile, Oriental Union Chemical Corporation, and Far EasTone Telecommunications is Yuan Ding Investment Corporation, which is almost wholly owned by Far Eastern Textile. These investment companies play a pivotal role in enhancing the ultimate control of the Hsu family. Yuan Ding and other investment companies function to pyramid the whole ownership structure of the group in such a way as to leverage the ownership control of the family with the investment of relatively little capital. At the same time, these investment companies are 'institutional shareholders' under the provision of the Company Law of Taiwan, and, as such, send family members or faithful managers of affiliate companies as their representatives to be elected as directors and supervisors (see directors/supervisors with 'R' in Table 4.4). This special arrangement is unique to Taiwan, where the Company Law states that 'where a government agency or a juristic person acts as a shareholder of a company', 'it may be elected as a director or supervisor of the company provided that it shall designate a natural person as its proxy to exercise, in its behalf, the duties of a shareholder' (Article 27 I), or 'its authorized representative may also be elected as director or supervisor of the company' (Article 27 II).

Third, such entities as educational institutions and foundations funded by the Hsu family act as another key block-holder of the group's core companies. The Hsu family's share, together with that of non-profit organisations, makes up 22 per cent and 9 per cent for Far Eastern Textile and Asia Cement respectively. As these institutions are exclusively controlled by the Hsus, the family can securely control the ownership of these core companies.

Supported by these arrangements, Douglas Shiu-Tong Hsu exercises strong management control over affiliated companies. From Table 4.4, we can see that among the eight listed companies affiliated with the group, Douglas Shiu-Tong occupies as many as seven chairman seats. The table also shows the participation of other family members. Douglas's brother, sister and brothers-in-law assume various positions in affiliate companies. In particular, the majority of the directors of Far Eastern Textile, the group's most crucial core company, are family members acting in their capacities as representatives of 'institutional shareholders' under the provision of Article 27 of the Company Law. Also, three non-family managers known as Douglas's 'three right-hand subordinates', Champion Lee, Shaw Y. Wang and C.S. Tu, hold directors' seats as representatives of institutional shareholders.[8] They are also the directors of the group's crucial investment company, Yuan Ding Investment.

All these arrangements underpin the effective mobilisation of the group's resources into its investment in the telecommunications industry. Far

Table 4.4 Board seats held by owner-family members and the 'three right-hands of Douglas Hsu' in major affiliate companies: the Far Eastern Group (2004)[a]

Name of listed companies	The Hsu family[b]					'Three right-hand subordinates'		
	Douglas Shiu-Tong Hsu	Johnny Shih	Peter Hsu	Alice Hsu	Laurence M. Yang	Champion Lee	Shaw Y. Wang	C.S. Tu
Far Eastern Textile	C	D as R	D as R	S as R	VC as R	D as R	D as R, VGM	D as R, VGM
Asia Cement	C	D as R	D			S as R	S as R	
Far Eastern International Bank	C as R	D as R					ED as R	
Far Eastern Department Store	C as R			D as R, GM	S as R			
U-Ming Marine Transport	C		S		VC	D as R		
Everest Textile	D as R	C as R						S as R
Oriental Union Chemical	C as R	D as R						
Far EasTone Telecom	C as R		D as R		VC as R	D as R		
(Reference: Yuan Ding Investment)		Far Eastern D as R				D	D	D as R

Sources: Annual reports of group member companies, various issues; China Credit Information (2004).

Notes:

a   C = chairman; VC = vice chairman; VC = vice chairman; D = director; ED = executive director; GM = general manager; VGM = vice general manager; S = super-visor; R refers to representative of an institutional shareholder (under the provision of Article 27 of the Company Law) whereas a position without R stands for the case in which the individual is elected as director/supervisor.

b   Johnny Shih and Laurence M. Yang are brothers-in-law, and Peter Hsu and Alice Hsu are the younger brother and sister of Douglas Shiu-Tong Hsu. In addition, four other family members assume positions as director/supervisor in group-affiliated companies.

EasTone Telecommunications was incorporated in 1997 and started commercial operation early the next year. Upon its establishment, Far Eastern Group invested in 62 per cent of the outstanding shares of Far EasTone, primarily channelling this through Far Eastern Textile's 100 per cent subsidiary company, Yuan Ding Investment Corp. Foreign partner AT&T Wireless invested 12 per cent. The ownership structure of the company changed over time, but Far Eastern Group has continuously held approximately 50 to 60 per cent of the company's shares through investment companies. The Hsu family has successfully exploited the ownership structure of the group discussed above to mobilise capital from the affiliate companies and pour it into the new sector, and at the same time establish a solid basis for control over the affiliate telecommunications providers.

Far EasTone became a GTSM (Gre-Tai Securities Market)-listed company in 2001. As of the end of 2003, just before its business merger with KG Telecom, the capital stock of Far EasTone amounted to 27.0 billion NTD ($794 million), with the percentage share of initial issuance of shares for cash, issuance of shares for cash and distribution of stock dividends of 33 per cent, 15 per cent and 51 per cent respectively, whereas total retained earnings were 10 billion NTD ($296 million). The company's long-term debt was 17.6 billion NTD ($517 million), with 13.3 billion NTD in bonds and 4.3 billion NTD in long-term bank loans and other loans. The operator plans to go public by the end of 2005.

The Hohsin Group

In contrast to the concentrated and solid ownership pattern of the Far Eastern Group, the Hohsin Group, especially those companies managed by the Koo Chen-fu family, is characterised by a rather decentralised ownership structure and shared management participation among family members. Figure 4.2 illustrates the ownership structure of the Hohsin Group just prior to their split in 2003. Table 4.5 shows the participation of family members as directors and supervisors in the major group companies.

A careful examination of Figure 4.2 reveals that there were two distinctive patterns of ownership observed in this group. In such financial corporations as Chinatrust Commercial Bank, China Life Insurance and KGI Securities, the Koo family establishes solid ultimate ownership mainly by channelling through the family's investment companies. For the Chinatrust Commercial Bank, the core company of the Jeffrey Koo family business, such family investment companies as Ho Hsin Investment, Chi Cheng Investment, Chung-kuan Investment and others serve as block-holders, each owning around 2 to 4 per cent of the corporation.

On the other hand, the companies in which Koo Chen-fu and his sons assume managerial positions show a different pattern. In the case of the TCC, the core company of the Chen-fu family's business, the Koos have a rather low profile as shareholders, with the shares of the family and their investment

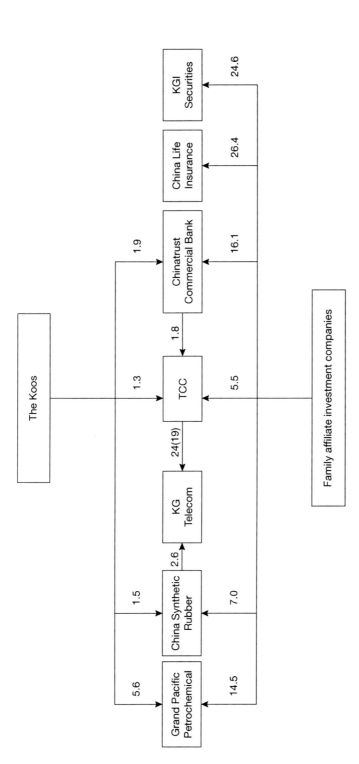

Figure 4.2 The ownership structure of the Hohsin Group before the split (2000–1)

Sources: Annual reports of group member companies; Hsu *et al.* (2004b).

Note: Family affiliate investment companies include Ho Hsin Investment, Chi Cheng Investment, Chung-kuan Investment and other investment companies funded by the Koo family.

Table 4.5 Board seats held by owner-family members in major affiliate companies: the Hohsin Group prior to the split (2001–2)[a]

	The Koo Chen-fu family[b]				The Jeffrey Lien-sung Koo family[c]			
	Koo Chen-fu	Koo Chi-yun	Koo Cheng-yun	Chiang An-ping	Jeffrey Lien-sung Koo	Lin Jui-hui	Jeffrey J.L.Koo, Jr.	Angelo J. Y. Koo
Taiwan Cement	C	D as R	D, GM					
China Synthetic Rubber Corp.		C						
KG Telecom		D as R						
Taiwan Polypropylene	C		D as R			D as R		
Wyse Technology Taiwan				C as R		D as R		
KGI Securities		D as R						D as R, GM
Chinatrust Commercial Bank					C as R		ED as R	
China Life Insurance	C as R	D, GM						

Sources: Annual reports of group member companies, various issues; China Credit Information (2004).

Notes:
a C = chairman; VC = vice chairman; D = director; ED = executive director; GM = general manager; VGM = vice general manager; S = supervisor; R refers to representative of an institutional shareholder (under the provision of Article 27 of the Company Law) whereas a position without R stands for the case in which the individual is elected as director/supervisor.
b Chiang An-ping is the brother-in-law of Chi-yun and Cheng-yun.
c Lin Jui-hui is the wife of Jeffrey Lien-sung Koo, who is the mother of Jeffrey J.L. Koo, Jr. and Angelo J.Y. Koo.

companies being 1.3 per cent and 5.5 per cent respectively. Compared with the case of the Far Eastern Group, where the ownership of the core companies is concentrated in the hands of the Hsus through extensive cross-holding and utilisation of investment companies, the Koos' position in the TCC is not very solid. This is partly because of the historical background of the company mentioned earlier. Still, the TCC and a number of other listed companies belong to the Koo family's business, the Hohsin Group.

How, then, could Koo Chen-fu and his sons ensure their management control without the solid backing of shareholding? In particular, how could the Koo family lead the huge investments of the TCC into the telecom-munications industry, and establish KG Telecom? Actually, the main source of the Koos' influence on the management of TCC was the prestige that Koo Chen-fu and his family have enjoyed as Taiwan's most distinguished and influential business family. In addition, the friendship and personal networks formed among successive directors and supervisors of TCC lever-aged the high profile of Koo Chen-fu and his son in the management of the company. The historical list of directors of the TCC includes Lins and Chens, both of whom were among the five most prestigious families in colo-nial Taiwan, as well as such business families as the Tsais of Lin-Yuan, the Wus of Shin Kong, and the Koos' relatives by marriage, the Chiangs of the Chia Hsin Cement Group.[9] The tight network of these celebrated business and political families, together with the fame of Koo Chen-fu, contributed to the Koos' initiative in the strategic decision-making of the TCC, thus leading, essentially, to 'control by prestige'.

KG telecom was incorporated in 1996 as a joint investment between the Hohsin Group (40 per cent) and Bell Canada International (10 per cent). Unlike the Hsus' investments in Far EasTone Telecom, the Koo family lacked the strong backup of ownership, and had to exploit its prestige and political resources as well as emphasise the potential of the telecom market in order to mobilise the capital of the TCC into the telecommunications industry.

Investing in technology and know-how

Prior to their entry, the Far Eastern and Hohsin Groups had no experience in the telecommunications industry. Thus, they needed to acquire technology and know-how from outside the group to compete in the market. According to the author's interviews with experienced experts in the Taiwanese tele-communications industry, the major means of acquiring technology and know-how for the new entrants included cooperation with foreign partners, technology transfer from multinational telecommunications equipment suppliers, recruiting of former employees of the Chunghwa Telecom Co., and attracting foreign experts who crossed borders in search of challenging job opportunities and higher compensation. Undoubtedly, all these factors contributed to the successful rise of the Taiwanese family-owned conglom-erates as providers of telecom services. From among them, we concentrate here on a discussion of human resource policy reflected in the composition of the management teams of each telecommunications operator.

Far EasTone Telecom

The global strategy of leading multinational telecommunications providers played an important role in the early stages of technology accumulation of Taiwanese local operators. AT&T Wireless had invested 12 per cent (later increased to 23 per cent) in Far EasTone until 2003, when it decided to withdraw from Asian markets and sold off all its shares to the Far Eastern Group. Upon its investment, AT&T Wireless chose the Far Eastern Group as a local partner with which to enter the Taiwanese market, counting on the rich and successful experience of the latter group in cooperating with foreign corporations. AT&T dispatched a large number of engineers to support the start-up of Far EasTone, and this, together with the recruitment of staff from Chunghua Telecom, resulted in a gain in technology and know-how that benefited the early growth of Far EasTone.

A review of annual reports of Far EasTone Telecom provides some interesting information on the profile of its directors/supervisors and top managers as of 2003–4, just before its business merger with KG Telecom. First, the board of directors was under the strict control of the Far Eastern Group with Douglas Shiu-Tong Hsu and his brother-in-law Lawrence M. Yang being chairman and vice chairman respectively.[10] The five directors are all representatives of institutional shareholders, and thereby under the ultimate control of the owner-family. Besides the younger brother of Douglas, they include the general manager of Far EasTone, Nilsson; the dean of the Engineering College of Yuan Ze University; and Douglas's right-hand subordinate, Champion Lee. These are the core figures of the management team of the Far Eastern Group.

Second, the profile of the management team reveals the human resource policy and preference of the Far Eastern Group for the management team. The company clearly prefers professional managers who have worked for prestigious foreign and local companies and have continuously risen up the ladder in the external labour market. The executive vice presidents have worked for various first-class corporations in the field. Also, it is worth noting that the successive presidents of the operator, O'Konek and Nilsson, are both foreigners rich in experience in management of telecom companies in emerging markets.

The preference for the recruitment of competent managers from external labour markets is not unique to Far EasTone. Rather, it is common to the newly established telecommunications providers in Taiwan generally. Comprehensive knowledge of the industry, clear market understanding and strong customer orientation were the keys to the success in this new sector, and business groups unfamiliar with the telecom business turned to the external market to acquire these managerial resources.

KG Telecom

The Hohsin Group invested in telecommunications through a joint venture with Bell Canada International. On the establishment of KG Telecom, Bell Canada invested in 10 per cent of the outstanding shares of KG Telecom. The company exited from the operation of KG Telecom in 2000, and in the same year NTT DoCoMo of Japan became the new partner and invested in approximately 20 per cent of the company.

In the early stages, KG Telecom relied on recruitment of professional managers experienced in the sector for its top management. Among them were former managers of foreign telecom operators and Chunghwa Telecom. However, compared with the Far Eastern Group, which through a series of diversifications has accumulated rich experiences in organising new investment projects, the 'project execution capability' (Amsden and Hikino 1994) of TCC was rather weak. The management team of KG Telecom lacked the systematic know-how and centripetal force to make long-range strategic decisions. A series of misjudgements eventually impaired its financial results. Among other things, the company made a misjudgement in choosing system equipment and had to pay a huge cost to replace the system. In addition, on the negotiation of the acquisition of a local mobile telecom provider, it overestimated the value of the target company. Major competitors all doubted the fruits of the deal, and eventually the acquisition imposed a heavy burden on KG Telecom. These poor strategic decisions are partly attributable to the lack of systematic know-how within KG Telecom, as well as its parent company, TCC.

From 2001 to 2002, Koo Cheng-Yun started a series of restructuring measures to tackle the difficulties facing the company. First, he himself assumed the position of general manager. Second, the company specially selected experienced managers trained in a highly competitive consumer market. Among five newly appointed vice-general managers, three were recruited from Citibank Taiwan, the famous 'cradle of professional managers'. Here again, we can see the strategy of the Taiwanese telecommunications providers to exploit the external labour market to acquire critical human resources.

In spite of these reorganisations, KG Telecom could not recover the lost confidence of customers in its services. The decision to exit from the auction for 3G telecommunications services in 2001 due to financial constraints also pressed the company to seek an alliance partner, and the company eventually agreed to combine its business with Far EasTone in 2003. As of December 2004, the total market share of Far EasTone and KG reached 30 per cent in terms of number of subscribers, second only to state-owned Chunghwa Telecom.

Conclusion: putting new wine into old bottles

Both the Far Eastern and Hohsin Groups are among the oldest family-owned business groups in Taiwan, with their origins of capital accumulation dating back to the pre-Second World War period. They were also among the most successful and influential groups in the early years of Taiwan's industrialisation. In the late 1980s, these old business groups came face to face with the challenge of the changing economic environment, and the so-called 'second-generation' leaders of the conglomerates, eager to demonstrate their capabilities, took the initiative on strategic investment in the emerging capital-intensive service sectors.

For these old groups, entering into the consumer-oriented, highly competitive service sectors posed a challenge similar to putting new wine into old bottles. To bottle the new wine successfully, these old business groups turned to the external labour market to acquire fresh blood in managerial resources. Professional managers with rich working experiences in excellent global companies were recruited to boost the competitive position of the operators in the market. Also, in the case of Far EasTone Telecom, foreign managers experienced in the telecommunications industry who make frequent cross-border job changes played an important role. The global strategy of the leading multinational telecommunications companies from the West offered the new Taiwanese entrants the chance to acquire the technology and know-how too. These factors all contributed to the rise of Taiwanese family-owned business groups as a central driving force in the rapid industrial upgrading and diversification that took place in Taiwan all through the 1990s.

However, their organisational efforts to emerge as a competitive provider of telecommunications services were backed by the conventional ownership structure that these groups had exploited for many years; the owner-families of these groups employed extensive cross-holding and pyramiding of ownership structure, as well as the establishment of nominal investment companies, to mobilise the resources of publicly listed companies for the purpose of investing in the telecommunications sector. This is exactly what Claessens *et al.* (1999, 2000) criticised as a measure to expropriate minor shareholders; as the resources of the affiliated publicly listed enterprises were injected into the new project, the interests of minor shareholders who owned shares in those publicly listed group companies under the family-owned conglomerates were exposed to risks. Thus, the entry of the Taiwanese family-owned business groups into the new service sectors was accommodated within the 'old bottles' of these groups through the long-standing artifice of their rather tricky ownership structures.

Notes

1 For the calculation of a firm's critical control level, see Yeh *et al.* (2001: 29), whose discussion is based on Cubbin and Leech (1983).
2 The same study by Yeh *et al.* (2001) reveals that for those Taiwanese firms in which the largest shareholder is a family, the average percentage of board seats held by the largest family shareholder was 53.1 as an average for 1994 and 1995. However, if we see the trend for appointments of general managers, the picture is somewhat different. Based on the analysis of the 50 largest private companies in 1983, 1993 and 2003, Sato (2005, forthcoming) finds a declining number of family members among general managers, and the growing importance of professional managers. In 2003, 41 out of 50 general managers of these largest corporations were non-family members.
3 Deflated by GDP deflator. The figures for the China Trust Group include the Hohsin (Taiwan Cement) Group for the convenience of comparison.
4 The cellular penetration rate as a percentage of total number of reported SIM cards to population grew from 52 per cent in 1999 to 105 per cent in March

2004. The penetration rate exceeds 100 per cent because there are users owing multiple SIM cards.
5 Meanwhile, Y.Z. Hsu distributed the shares of affiliate companies to sons and daughters quite equally.
6 He was also a key person in the Taiwan–China relationship, as he assumed chairmanship of the Straits Exchange Foundation, a semi-official institution for exchanges between Taiwan and China, which was established in 1990.
7 This practice is feasible in Taiwan because the Company Law of the ROC did not prohibit cross-shareholding between parent and subsidiary companies until the amendment of the law in 2001. Even after the revision, the regulation is rather loose; the amendment enacted that the subordinate company should not redeem or buy back any of the controlling company's shares (Article 167), but a loose definition of 'subordinate' company still allows controlling shareholders to exploit cross-shareholding and pyramiding structures to consolidate their control. Article 167 III states that where a majority of the total number of outstanding voting shares or of the total amount of the capital stock of a subordinate company is held by its holding company, the shares of the holding company shall not be purchased nor be accepted as a security in pledge by the said subordinate company.
8 These three managers were all employers of Far Eastern Textile, and were specially selected by Douglas as his trusted comrades during the period when he was competing with his half-brother for the succession to his father's business.
9 In the early 1990s, the Chens and other shareholders challenged the leadership of the Koos, but the Koos successfully defended their hegemony.
10 In the mid-1990s, a professor of Yuan-Ze University advised Lawrence M. Yang that the group should seize the opportunity to compete for the potential business chances of this lucrative market, and Yang's suggestion to Douglas Hsu became a starting-point for the project. Yang held the position of vice chairman of Far EasTone until his death in April 2005.

Bibliography

Abe, Makoto and Momoko Kawakami (1997) 'A distributive comparison of enterprise size in Korea and Taiwan', *The Developing Economies*, XXXV (4): 382–400.
Amsden, Alice H. and Takashi Hikino (1994) 'Project execution capability, organizational know-how and conglomerate corporate growth in late industrialization', *Industrial and Corporate Change*, 3 (1): 111–47.
Amsden, Alice H. and Wan-wen Chu (2003) *Beyond Late Development: Taiwan's Upgrading Policies*, Cambridge, MA: MIT Press.
Claessens, Stijn, Simeon Djankov and Larry H.P. Lang (1999) 'Who controls East Asian Corporation?', Policy Research Working Paper WPS2054, Washington, DC: World Bank.
—— (2000) 'The Separation of Ownership and Control in East Asian Corporations', *Journal of Financial Economics*, 58 (3): 81–112.
Chen Ping-Hun, 'The study of taiwan's cellular phone service industry: the analysis of its structure and concentration' (in Chinese), *Sun Yat-Sen Management Review*, 8 (3).
China Credit Information (2004) *2005 Business Groups in Taiwan*, Pekin: CCI.
Cubbin, J. and D. Leech (1983) 'The effect of shareholding dispersion on the degree of control in British companies: theory and measurement,' *Economic Journal*, 93 (June): 351–69.

Hsu Chung-yuan, Lin Wan-ying, Li Wan-chen and Cheng Wen-hsin (2004a) 'Fuza Jiaocha Kongku Xingtai(II) Yuandong Jituan (Futsa Chiaocha Kungku Hsingtai(II) Yuantung Chituan)' (in Chinese), *Huopi Kuantse yu Hsinyung Pingteng*, May.

Hsu Chung-yuan, Lin Wan-ying, Yu Chih-yuan and Tu Ying-Cheng (2004b) 'Fuza Jiaocha Kongku Xingtai(III) Hexin Jituan (Futsa Chiaocha Kungku Hsingtai(III) Hohsin Chituan)' (in Chinese), *Huopi Kuantse yu Hsinyung Pingteng*, July.

Hung, Mei-chuan (1996a) 'Qunxiong Jingzhu Dianxun Jinkuang (Chunhsiung Chingchu Tienhsun Chinkuang)' (in Chinese), *Common Wealth*, August.

—— (1996b) 'Dierdai Lianshou Zhengba Dianxun (Tierhtai Lienshou Chengpa Tienhsun)' (in Chinese), *Common Wealth*, October.

Sato, Yukihito (2005, forthcoming) 'Managers of Taiwanese large corporations: growing importance of salaried managers' (in Japanese) (book title undecided).

Securities & Futures Institute (SFI) (2002) 'Corporate Governance in Taiwan', Taiwan: SFI.

Taiwan Cement Corporation (1994) 'Forty years of Taiwan Cement Corporation: 1954–1994'.

Wang (1995) 'Xu Xudong Ningjing Geming Neimu (Hsu Hsutung Ningching Keming Neimu)' (in Chinese), *Wealth Magazine*, December.

Yeh, Yin-hua, Tsun-siou Lee and Tracie Woidtke (2001) 'Family control and corporate governance: evidence from Taiwan', *International Review of Finance*, 2 (1/2): 21–48.

5 Conglomerates in Iran

The political economy of Islamic Foundations

Eva Rakel

In the aftermath of the Iranian Islamic Revolution in 1979 the newly established Islamic state confiscated the assets of the 51 largest Iranian industrialists and their families, who were accused of having profited from 'illegitimate
ties' with the regime of the Shah, as well as the property of the Shah family.
These assets are now mainly under the control of para-governmental semi-
public Foundations, *bonyads*. Originally, these Foundations were established as
charities for the poor. In reality, however, they are operating as para-
governmental organisations, and they play a significant role in the economic
and political scene of the Islamic Republic of Iran (IRI). The Islamic
Foundations are estimated to account for 35 per cent of Iran's total gross
national product (GNP), controlling over 40 per cent of the non-oil sector of
the Iranian economy. All Foundations claim that they are welfare-oriented,
non-profit groups. For example, they are supposed to use the profits from their
enterprises for the poor, for the provision of inexpensive housing, health care
and other social services. In reality they make great profits and financially support members of the Iranian Islamic political elite (from now to be referred to
as the political elite). These tax-exempt organisations mainly focus on business,
production and banking, but also political propaganda, social services and art.
As Islamic charities, they are tax-exempt, receive favourable exchange rates,
and have a monopoly on import/export and all major industries.

The Foundations in Iran have a history of existence of more than 1,000
years. Since the Safavid Empire (1501–1772) with the legitimisation of *waqt*
(endowments, landed property belonging to the clergy) under their control,
the Foundations gained more economic independence from the state and
thereby could distance themselves from politics. The Foundations established
after the Iranian Islamic Revolution of 1979, however, are an integral
part of the Islamic political system. When Ayatollah Khomeini was consolidating his power in 1979–80 they played a significant role in the implementation of his populist economic policies and his Islamic ideology. The
Foundations are responsible to no one else but the *valy-e faqih* (Supreme
Leader, from 1979 to 1989 Ayatollah Ruhollah Khomeini and since 1989
Ayatollah Ali Khamenei) and his local representatives.

Apart from their responsibility to the Supreme Leader there is no control by the government of the Foundations' economic activities and expenses. The Foundations have no public accounts, and no concretely defined legal status. Despite their status as semi-public organisations they act as giant private monopolies rather than as charities. The Foundations have been a great financial burden to the Iranian economy and one of the main obstacles to economic reform in Iran. They have become pivotal actors in the power struggle among different factions of the political elite not only in terms of mass mobilisation, ideological indoctrination and repression, but also as financial resources. This makes them not only important economically but also significant actors in forming domestic policies in Iran. When Mohammad Khatami became president in 1997 the Foundations' activities came under great pressure from parts of the Iranian Islamic political elite who aimed to end the Foundations' exemption from taxes, and there have been attempts to privatise individual companies belonging to the Foundations. Yet, due to the low rate of capital accumulation in Iran, the government depends substantially on the Foundations for transfer of resources and domestic investment. Reforming the Foundations thus will be impossible without reforming the entire economic and political power structures in Iran.

To better understand the position of the Foundations in the current Iranian political system an overview of the formal and informal political power structure and the economic order in the IRI is given. Following that, the history of the Foundations in both pre- and post-revolutionary Iran will be discussed. After an introduction to the Foundations' activities within the political and economic system of Iran, three cases of Foundations in Iran will be looked at: the Bonyad-e Mostazafan va Janbazan (Foundation for the Oppressed and Disabled), the Bonyad-e Shahid (Martyrs' Foundation) and the Bonyad-e Astan-e Quds (Imam Reza Foundation). This chapter ends with a discussion of the future prospects of the IRI and the Foundations.

The nature of the politico-economic system in the Islamic Republic of Iran

The Iranian Islamic Revolution caused a fundamental change in the composition of the political elite whose secular oriented members were replaced by mainly traditionalist clergies and lay persons. Although it brought about a change in the mode of rule, it did not change the Iranian state–society relations as it reintroduced an authoritarian state, but one with a theocratic character (Amineh 2004: 25). The political system of the IRI is ambiguous. It is totalitarian, giving absolute supremacy over public life to an ideology – political Islam. It is authoritarian, but it permits a certain degree of pluralism and as in democracies the people may vote for the members of parliament and the president in elections (Chehabi 2001). Generally, it can be said that there is an ambiguity between the theocratic mode of rule and the rule of the people in Iran. On the one hand the post-revolutionary political elite has introduced a theocratic mode of rule in Iran based on the *velayat-e faqih*[1] (Governance of Jurisconsult) institutionalised according to the Con-stitution of 1979 by Ayatollah Khomeini. This principle grants the Supreme Leader the right of ultimate decision-making, which is the major obstacle to structural change in Iran. On the other hand the political insti-tutions of the IRI are based on a modern state, which finds its origins in the Constitution of 1906 (Abrahamian 1982). This ambiguity becomes most apparent in the structure of political institutions and the formal and informal power relations that cross political institutions in Iran.

The political power structure of the IRI is characterised by loosely connected as well as competitive formal and informal political power centres. The formal political power centres represent state institutions and offices. Alongside these, there also exists an informal power structure, which forms two distinct parts. First, there are the different factions of the political elite that cut across the state institutions and their aligned institutions such as the heads and members of state institutions, religious-political associations, the religious Foundations and paramilitary organisations. As there are no legal political parties in Iran it is the political factions that represent the different ideas on political, economic, foreign relations and cultural issues. Second, the informal power structure comprises those who directly or indi-rectly participate in the decision-making process in Iran and/or in the ideological discourse, and thus, includes not only members of the political elite but also those of the politically relevant elite (see p. 113).

The rivalry between the different political factions has a great impact on the process of political decision-making and is an obstacle to the formula-tion of a coherent foreign policy. Thus, while most state institutions in Iran are weak – due to the principle of the *velayat-e faqih* – personal networks are strong. As a consequence, the formal system for decision-making is often ignored or bypassed in favour of the informal, parallel system.

The formal political power structure of the IRI is composed of four main political institutions and three decision-making or advisory bodies. The polit-ical institutions consist of the Supreme Leader and the three governmental branches: executive, judiciary and legislative (*majlis*, parliament). The Supreme Leader is not only the ultimate decision-maker in Iran and the commander-in-chief of all armed forces,[2] he also has the power to declare war, to mobilise the troops and to dismiss the head of the judiciary, the head of state radio and television, the supreme commander of the Islamic Revolutionary Guard Corps (IRGC, *niruha-ye entezami*) with its paramilitary *basji* militia, and the supreme commander of the regular military and the security services, as well as the clerical jurists in the Council of the Guardian (Tellenbach 1990: 71).

The president is the head of government and the second most powerful member of the political elite behind the Supreme Leader.[3] He appoints and dismisses ministers (who have to be confirmed by parliament), controls the Planning and Budget Organisation, and he appoints the head of the Central Bank and chairs the National Security Council.[4] The president is responsible for economic, social and cultural policies but not foreign policy, and he has no control of the armed forces. The president can only be removed by a two-thirds majority in parliament (Milani 1993: 94). The parliament is elected every four years. Since the death of Khomeini its political importance has significantly increased. It drafts legislation, ratifies treaties, approves states of emergency, and approves loans and the annual budget (Bakhtiari 1996).

Additionally, another three political bodies have been established since the Iranian Islamic Revolution that are unique to Iran, thus cannot be compared to other political organs elsewhere in the world: the *shuray-e meghaban* (Council of the Guardian), the *majilis-e khobregan* (Assembly of Experts), and the *majma'-e tashkhis-e maslahat-e nezam* (Expediency Council) dominated by the clergy of the political elite. The Council of the Guardian consists of 12 members (six clerical and six non-clerical), all of them jurists. The six clerical members are selected among the ranks of the political elite and appointed by the Supreme Leader. The six non-clerical members are appointed by parliament at the recommendation of the head of the judiciary. The Council of the Guardian determines whether laws passed by parliament are compatible with the *shari'a* (Islamic law). It is controlled by the conservative faction of the political elite. The Council of the Guardian has supervises the elections for parliament, the Assembly of Experts, and the presidency. For example, it determines who may become parliamentary or presidential candidates (Schirazi 1997: 89). The Assembly of Experts is a council of 86 clerics elected by the Iranian people for an eight-year term. However, as said before, the Council of the Guardian first has to accept the candidates. The Assembly of Experts elects the Supreme Leader from its own ranks and dismisses him if he does not fulfil his duties (Schirazi 1997: 69–72). The Assembly of Experts comes together for two days once every year. The Expediency Council has 31 members who are appointed by the Supreme Leader among the ranks of the political elite. It was established in 1988 to act as a mediator between parliament and the Council of the Guardian and to advise the Supreme Leader. Its current head is former president Ayatollah Ali Akbar Hashemi Rafsanjani (Tellenbach 1990: 54).

Besides the formal power structure there exists also an informal power structure. As Iran has no formal party system, the current political elite can be divided into three main political factions within the Islamic regime consisting both of clerics and lay persons: the 'Conservative Faction' around Supreme Leader Ayatollah Ali Khamenei; the 'Pragmatist Faction', followers of the head of the Council of the Guardian Hashemi Rafsanjani; and the 'Reformist Faction' of former President Mohammad Khatami.[5] Although all three political factions fall within the pro-Islamic Republic sphere they differ in their respective positions on socio-cultural issues, economy and foreign policy. The Conservative Faction dominates the formal state institutions in the Islamic Republic of Iran (see Table 5.1). Despite their differences, what these factions have in common is their loyalty to the person and political teachings of Ayatollah Khomeini, especially the *velayat-e faqih* (Menashri 1990). Each faction has been able to recruit its members from both the modern and traditional sectors of society.

In addition, the informal power structure includes those who directly or indirectly participate in the decision-making process in Iran and/or in the ideological discourse. Following the approach of the study group 'Elite change in the Arab world' (Perthes 2004), I use the concept of the 'politically relevant elite'.[6] Based on Reissner (2002) the politically relevant elite can be categorised as follows: the clerical inner circle elite, the administrative elite and the discourse elite. The clerical inner circle elite in Iran consists of the highest clerics, most of whom belong to the Conservative Faction, and some of whom to the Pragmatist and Reformist Factions. Buchta (2002) calls those belonging to the inner circle the 'patriarchs'. The clerical inner circle elite determines the course of the IRI, but in contrast to the first years after the revolution – when Khomeini was still alive – they no longer determine the political discourse, they only react to it (Reissner 2002: 192).

The power of the clerical inner circle elite is legitimised by the constitution according to the principle of the *velayat-e faqih* as it was introduced by Ayatollah Khomeini after the Revolution. From this combination of religious and constitutional based legitimacy of rule it follows that the highest political positions within the system are occupied by this inner circle elite. The inner circle elite dominates those state institutions that, in contrast to the parliament and the president, are not elected by the people and are not responsible to them. These institutions are: the Assembly of Experts, the Council of the Guardian, the Expediency Council, the heads of those institutions that

Table 5.1 The structure of decision-making power of the political factions as of 2005

Conservative Faction	Pragmatist Faction	Reformist Faction
Supreme Leader	Central Bank	President
Council of ministers	Expediency Council	Council of Ministers
Judicial branch and revolutionary courts	Council of Ministers	Planning and Budget Organisation
Legislative branch		
Assembly of experts		
Council of the guardian		

Sources: Based on Akhavi-Pour and Azodanloo (1998) and Buchta (2000).

are installed by the Supreme Leader (i.e. the head of the judiciary branch, the commander of the regular military, the head of the IRGC), as well as the representatives of the Supreme Leader in all important state institutions and in the provinces, and the chairmen of the different Foundations also installed by the Supreme Leader (Iran Focus 2002). The clerical inner circle elite has, through the institutionalisation of the constitutionally legitimised religious institutions after the Revolution, gained for itself an independent position within the Iranian political system.[7]

The administrative elite is made up of those Iranians who participate in the political decision-making process, give advice or carry out political decisions. They belong to the second and/or third circle around the clerical inner circle elite. Most of them are civil servants. They are also mainly lay persons and have gained in significance in the political process since the revolution (Reissner 2002: 195). While the revolutionary background of the administrative elite still plays an important role in their political prestige, in contrast to the clerical inner circle elite, the administrative elite, is more diversified in their political-ideological ideas. Particularly among the reformist members of the administrative elite a change in political ideas can be noted. Many of those who now belong to the Reformist Faction of the Iranian Islamic political elite had been radical leaders in the movement of the Society of Forces Following the Line of the Imam[8] (*Khat-e Emami*, cf. Reissner 2002).

As well as men, women also play an important role in the administrative elite since the Iranian Islamic Revolution. Their biographies are strongly connected to the Revolution. For women to become members of the political elite, family ties seem to be even more important than for men, as with Zahra Khomeini, the daughter of Khomeini, who was member of parliament and active in the women's movement, and Fa'ezeh Hashemi Rafsanjani, the daughter of former President Hashemi Rafsanjani. Members of the administrative elite are viewed by the population as 'normal' politicians and are evaluated according to their political achievements, for which they compete with each other (Reissner 2002: 196).

The discourse elite are those members of the political elite who have a decisive impact on the diverse political and political-cultural discourse. To the discourse elite belong clerics, members of the administrative elite, and academics and journalists. For example, former President Khatami, who in his function as president belonged to the clerical inner circle elite, could also be counted as one of the discourse elite, or a journalist who gained political significance by writing a specific article (Reissner 2002: 197). The relation between clerics and intellectuals can be described as a kind of rivalry rather than a fundamental opposition. The essential point in this ideological dispute is the question how Islam can at best be realised in the IRI. Part of this dispute is also the problem of containment and arbitrary execution of power, and more recently, the secularisation problematic has gained in significance (Soroush 2000). The dispute between the clerical inner circle

elite and the discourse elite has led to a change of political culture[9] even in
the political state institutions. The clerical inner circle elite is no longer able
to distance itself from dispute (Reissner 2002: 198–9), which includes the
issue of reforming the Iranian economy.

Economic bases of the Iranian Islamic political elite

The three main factions of the Iranian political elite outlined above have different ideas on how the economy in Iran should be organised. While the
Conservative Faction opposes state intervention in the economy but favours
state control of the main economic sectors in Iran, the Pragmatist Faction supports less state intervention and privatisation, and the Reformist Faction a
combination of both. According to Akhavi-Pour and Heidar Azodanloo these
economic policies do not derive from the differing religious ideologies of the
three factions but from the different economic bases each faction depends on.
They argue that 'the decisions of Islamic political groups and government
factions are based on economic and political policies that are expected to
maximize their economic gains' (Akhavi-Pour and Azodanloo 1998: 69).

The economic strength of the different political factions is based on their
different financial sources (see Table 5.2). The most important source of
income in the IRI is its oil and gas resources. The rent from the oil and
gas exports gives the Iranian political elite a relative independence from
society. Economic relations between state and society are not regulated by
taxes but by a network of direct and indirect subventions (Maloney 2000).
The Pragmatist and the Reformist factions rely on official sources that stem
from fiscal tools (taxes, fees and borrowing) and oil and gas revenues (sources
of foreign currencies). They also control some main state economic enterprises in mining, manufacturing and services. The Conservative Faction
relies on fiscal revenues as well as non-official sources of income that lie
outside the fiscal tools. Three main economic sources of income of the
Conservative Faction are the mosques, the Shi'a holy shrines and sites, and
the religious Foundations (Akhavi-Pour and Azodanloo 1998: 75). Thus,

Table 5.2 The economic bases of the three main political factions in Iran

Sources	Conservative Faction	Pragmatist Faction	Reformist Faction
Oil and gas revenues	+	+	+
Taxes and fees	+	+	+
State enterprises	+	+	+
Municipalities' income	+	+	+
Mosques, holy shrines	+	–	–
Religious tax (*khums* and *zakat*)	+	–	–
Religious Foundations	+	–	–

Source: Based on Akhavi-Pour and Azodanloo (1998).

while the Pragmatist and the Reformist factions rely on official economic sources within the fiscal tools the Conservative Faction receives its major income from religious sources and the Foundations, outside the fiscal tools. Until now, the Conservative Faction has the political tools and fiscal means to maintain a dominant position both in political and economic life of the IRI. As long as the Pragmatists and Reformist factions are unable to success-fully consolidate their financial and economic resources the division between the factions on their economic sources will have its effect on overall polit-ical decisions as well as the control of the coercive forces.

From the early days in post-revolutionary Iran, the question of how to organise the Iranian economy became a central point among the various political groups who had supported the Revolution. Democratic secularists such as the National Front and the Islamic progressive *Nehzat-e Azadi-ye Iran* (Liberation Movement of Iran) of Mehdi Bazargan, the *bazaar* (merchants),[10] the industrial and agricultural bourgeoisie, and the conservative clerics promoted the protection of private-property rights and the limitation of nationalisation to those cases where national interest was involved or the original owners had fled the country (Behdad 1988: 111; Halliday 1983: 187; Ajami 1989: 155).

The dominant tendency among the political elite imposed far-reaching limitations on private-property rights, and promoted an interventionist state approach: Iran should become less dependent on the outside (especially the Western) world; the economy should be diversified in order to reduce the country's dependence on oil revenues; agriculture was seen as the 'pivot of development' in order to achieve self-sufficiency in food; non-oil exports should be increased and imports reduced (especially consumer-goods imports); rural migration was to be stopped; and military expenditure and foreign arms purchases should be cut down and instead the money invested to improve the living conditions of the poor (with better nutrition, housing, health care and cultural refinement) and to create a society that rejects materialism and consumerism and instead puts spiritual values on its agenda (Amuzegar 1993: 311–12).

However, as the economist Jahangir Amuzegar states:

> The post-revolution Iranian economy lacked a distinctive, home-grown, innovative, Islamic model. The anti-Shah opposition had an economic ideology that was neither totally Islamic, nor a matter of general consensus. The only common theme supported by all revolutionary factions was the allegation that the economy under the Pahlavis was unhealthy and non-viable. It was unhealthy because of: addiction to oil export revenues; highly inequitable income distribution among social strata and geographic regions; and subservience to superpower inter-ests. It was viable because of: perilous dependence on the external world for raw materials, semi-processed goods, management, and capital equip-ment; excessive military expenditure; and neglect of agriculture in favour

of rapid industrialisation. There was no consensus of opinion on an appropriate new economic model. In fact, there were profound differences in analysis and outlook between traditional bourgeois elements in and out of the bazaar on the one hand, and radical reformers in and out of religious circles on the other.

(Amuzegar 1993: 310)

The economic framework of Iran is laid down in several chapters of the 1979 Constitution, which is based on the concept of the *velayat-e faqih*. According to Article 44 in chapter IV the national economy comprises first a state, then a cooperative and finally a private sector. The state sector should include 'all the large-scale and major industries, foreign trade, major mineral resources, banking, insurance, energy'. The cooperative sector comprises cooperative companies and institutions that are involved in production and distribution. The private sector is limited to those economic activities that 'supplement the economic activities of the state and co-operative sectors'. Articles 47 and 49 define the right to own property based on their legitimacy or illegitimacy. According to Article 47 of the Constitution 'private ownership, legitimately acquired, is to be respected. The relevant criteria are determined by law' (*Constitution of the IRI* 1981: 44–7). In Article 49 illegitimate sources of ownership are defined. These include, in addition to usury, bribery, theft and illicit sources, the usurping and misuse of endowments.

The private sector has a subordinate status in the Iranian economy. Private entrepreneurs have often been named 'blood-sucking capitalists' in slogans plastered on walls or in semi-official papers. The private sector in Iran is presented by the Iran Chamber of Commerce, Industry and Mines, a semi-public agency representing the *bazaari* interests. The private entrepreneurs involved in major foreign trade have to be members of the Chamber of Commerce but the Chamber of Commerce has no say on economic decisions and so far has not been able to enhance the prestige of the private sector. The director of the Chamber is appointed by the Minister of Commerce and usually among the ranks of the *bazaaris* (Karbassian 2000: 626). In fact, the absence of real non-governmental institutions to represent the private sector is an important obstacle to the expansion of private sector activity in Iran (Khajehpour 2000).

The other important institutions that belong to the post-revolutionary public sector in Iran are the *bonyads*, the para-governmental Foundations that are usually led by religious figures. These Foundations own hundreds of nationalised companies, farms, hotels, theatres, newspapers and other property confiscated from wealthy Iranians who had supported the Shah. It is estimated that these Foundations account for 35 per cent of Iran's total GNP and have control over 40 per cent of the non-oil sector of the Iranian economy. When Khatami became president in 1997 the Foundations' activities came under great pressure from some parts of the political elite who aimed to end the Foundations' exemption from taxes. There have also been attempts at privatising individual companies that belong to the Foundations. At the same time, however, because of the low rate of capital accumulation in Iran the government depends heavily on the Foundations for transfer of resources and domestic investment.

The history of Foundations in Iran

Historically, charitable foundations have played a significant role in Islamic societies. They could be used as mechanisms for untaxed savings and investment and provided financial independence for the clergy from the state. Their origins derive from the teachings of the Koran. According to the Koran stronger people have to show solidarity with the weaker ones and in this concern the religious leaders have to serve as their guardians (Algar 1969: 18). To serve this purpose two taxes are drawn: a tax called *zakat*, normally translated as tax for the poor, or alms tax; and a tax called *khums*. The *khums* plays an important role for the Shi'ites (Halm 1997: 91). In Islamic jurisprudence these taxes are based on the mechanism of *taqlid* (emulation of another in matters of the law), according to which the *moqalled* (a believer who emulates) has the duty (*taklif*) to pay a tax to a *mojtahed* (jurisconsult) (Clarke 2001: 40).

During the Safavid rule, because of the security of endowments granted to the clergy by the Safavid rulers, the independence of the Foundations from the state became stronger providing the clergy with 'economic independence' and as a consequence non-involvement with politics (Keddie 1995: 12). During the Qajar Empire (1783–1925) the religious authority of the clergy developed with the collection and distribution of various kinds of taxes. The more taxes the clergy received the more it reflected their authority and importance. Additionally, the income from the endowments associated with shrines and mosques was one of the most significant sources of income for the clergy (Algar 1969: 14). The lands attached to the shrine of the Imam Reza in Mashad, in the province of Khorasan, probably were the largest single source of clerical income during the Qajar period (Curzon 1892: 163).

The security of the endowments has several times led to clashes between the Shah and the clergy. First during the Qajar period when the chief administrator of the endowments, who used to be selected from among the ranks of the clergy, became the most important figure next to the provincial governor (Algar 1969: 15). During the Pahlavi period (1921–78) when the Shahs (Reza Shah (1921–41) and Mohammad Reza Shah (1941–79)) attempted to control or restrict the endowments property; this led to unrest and riots in the provinces. The clergy saw these policies as a serious threat to their independence from the state (Saeidi 2004). At that time the resistance of the traditional sectors of the economy to these policies led to a coalition between the clergy and the merchant communities against the Shah (Vakili-Zad 1992: 22).

In contrast to the Foundations of the Safavid, Qajar and Pahlavi periods, the Foundations established after the Iranian Islamic Revolution have been part and parcel of the political system. After the Revolution the Islamic government gave to the Foundations the assets of the Shah, his ruling elite and other Iranians who had fled the country, including hundreds of companies in all sectors of the economy (Amirahmadi 1995). To the most important industrial families before the Revolution, which together owned about 390 large enterprises, belonged Farmanfarmaian (with 74 enterprises), Khosrow-Shaby (with 67), Lajevardi (61), Rezai (38), Sabet (33), Akhavan (22), Wahabzadeh (21), and Elqanian, Taymor Tash and Khayami (respectively 17, 16 and 10 enterprises) (Ravasani 1978).

The Shah and his family had been the greatest capitalist investors of the country. They owned more than 207 large trading companies, industrial enterprises and banks. The major part of the Shah's wealth was run by the Bonyad-e Pahlavi (Pahlavi Foundation) – after the Revolution replaced by the Bonyad-e Alavi (Alavi Foundation) – which had been established in 1958 by the Shah and was an important instrument for controlling the economy in Iran. Like all other Foundations the Pahlavi Foundation was a charity organisation. In reality, however, it was Iran's biggest industrial and trade organisation with interests in all major economic sectors in Iran (Amineh 1999). The Pahlavi Foundation and 51 other industrialists whose property was confiscated after the Revolution in 1979 together had owned 700 modern large and medium-sized enterprises (Abrahamian 1982: 432).

Endowments, private and public Foundations

Almost all Foundations are headed by clerics or other key figures among the political elite in Iran. They are also referred to as *moluk-e tavayef* (little kings). Despite the rivalry among them the heads of the Foundations are united in their desire to promote the ideology of the Iranian Islamic Revolution by all means, even by repression (Korooshy 1997: 10). All Foundations claim that they are welfare-oriented, non-profit groups. For example, they are supposed to use their profits from their enterprises for the poor people, and for the provision of inexpensive housing, health care and other social services. In reality they make great profits and financially support factions of the political elite (Amirahmadi 1996: 103). These tax-exempt organisations mainly focus on business, production and banking, but also political propaganda, social services and art.

The post-revolutionary Foundations can be divided into three main categories: public, private and endowments (Kazemi 1996: 141). The endowments Foundations, which were very fashionable in the pre-revolutionary period, have not grown very much in importance or number since 1979. One of the largest of Iran's endowments Foundations is the Bonyad-e Astan-e Quds (The Imam Reza Foundation) to be discussed later on pp. 126–7. Two other Foundations that belong to the endowments Foundations are the

Bonyad-e Panzah-e Khurdad (The Fifteenth Khordad Foundation) and the Mu'assasah-ye Nashr-e Asar-e Hazrat-e Imam Khomeini (Institute for Publication and Distribution of the Grand Imam Khomeini's Writings). Both Foundations were established after the Revolution: the first in memory of Khomeini's revolt in 1963;[11] the second after Khomeini's death (Amirahmadi 1995: 234–5). The Khordad Foundation has become famous because it promised to pay $2.8 million to the one who would kill Salman Rushdie after the Ayatollah Khomeini had declared a *fatwa* (legal statement issued by a religious lawyer) on him in 1988 (Akhavi-Pour and Azodanloo 1998).

Besides the endowments Foundations there are the public and private foundations that were created after the Revolution, and are not associated with the endowments Foundations. The distinction between public and private depends on the main source of their income: the public Foundations being supported and sponsored by the state and the private Foundations using private funds and donations (Amirahmadi 1995; Kazemi 1996). Many private Foundations have been established since the Revolution both by members of the political elite as well as those outside the political elite. Some of them have developed into great economic institutions; among others these include the Sazman-e Iqtisad-e Islami (Islamic Economic Organisation), Bonyad-e Javid (Eternal Foundation), Bonyad-e Raja (Foundation for Growth of Islamic Republic), Bonyad-e Rafah (Welfare Foundation), Bonyad-e Ta'avun (Cooperation Foundation). Other private Foundations control cultural activities such as cinemas, for instance the Bonyad-e Farabi (Farabi Foundation) and Sazman-e Tablighat-e Islami (Organisation for Islamic Propagation). Many of the private Foundations also support electoral candidates financially or with propaganda, such as the Bonyad-e Resalat (Foundation for Prophetic Mission) which supported the Conservative Nateq-Nuri in the presidential elections of 1997. It also publishes the daily newspaper *Resalat*. The public Foundations were established in the first years after the Revolution. To these Foundations belong, among others, the Bonyad Mostazafan va Janbazan (Foundation for the Oppressed and the Disabled) and the Bonyad-e Shahid (Martyrs' Foundation) to be discussed on pp. 123 and 124.

However, the borders between the financial resources of the Foundations are not well drawn, as all Foundations, including the endowments, profit from some sort of government support. At the same time, many of the public Foundations are not directly funded by the state, and the government has no control over their resources, spendings and activities (Maloney 2000: 150). Nevertheless, during the early years of the IRI the Foundations carried out functions that formally were assigned to the government. Some of them even merged with ministries or developed into independent government agencies. For example, the Bonyad-e Omur Mojaherin-e Tahmili became part of the Ministry of Labour, and the Islamic Propaganda Organisation, one of the cultural Foundations, came under the supervision of the government (Amirahmadi 1995: 235; Resalat 1996). Some of the public Foundations replaced other Foundations after the Revolution or were established in honour of certain individuals, such as the Alavi Foundation, which replaced the Pahlavi Foundation. Others have gradually been integrated into the structure of the political system: the IRGC and the Reconstruction Crusade have both become ministries; the Bonyad-e Omur-e Mojaherin-e Tahmili has been integrated into the Ministry of Labour; the Jihad-e Savad Amuzi (Mobilisation for Literacy) into the Ministry of Education; and the Komiteh-e Enqelab-e Islami (Islamic Revolution Committee) into the regular police force (Amirahmadi 1995: 235–6).

The Foundations as part of the politico-economic system

The post-revolutionary Foundations are an integral part of the politico-economic system of the IRI. They not only have control of large parts of the economy but they also have been involved in propagating the ideology of the IRI and the social security programmes. As Saeidi states:

> What is often not realized widely about these organizations is that they have been actively involved in Iranian polity by propagating the dominant ideology in a wide range of social and cultural activities. In fact, these organizations were established in order to assist institutionalization of the ideology of the ruling class by producing an ideological apparatus for new regime when the revolutionary forces could not trust the old regime's bureaucratic apparatus. They also increased the rate of social mobility among lower middle classes and supporters of revolutionary forces in order to extend the power of Islamic ideology. They assisted individuals from lower middle groups to move into new economic, social and occupational positions.
>
> (Saeidi 2004: 486)

Thus, the Foundations helped to restructure the state apparatus after the Revolution by controlling the access to higher education and public sector employment. In fact, the government of the IRI needed the resources of these organisations for the consolidation and expansion of the central state apparatus (Ashraf 1994: 118). It has also been mentioned that the Foundations mobilise tens of thousands of people from urban and rural lower classes for demonstrations that support the Islamic regime. They have supported the establishment of schools, universities and research centres, the publication of books and journals, the production of films, the organisation of art and book festivals, as well as the establishment of ideological museums. They thereby contribute to the indoctrination of a great number of young intellectuals into the Islamic political ideology (Mawlawi *et al.* 1987).

At the same time the Foundations claim to provide financial help to low-income groups, families of martyrs, former prisoners of war, rural dwellers, guardian-less households and the disabled. Foundations that are active in this regard are the Martyrs' Foundation, the Imam Khomeini Relief Aid Committee, the Oppressed and Disabled Foundation, the Housing Foundation, and the Fifteenth Khordad Foundation (Saeidi 2004: 488).

As mentioned earlier, although the official function of the Foundations is to serve the poor, in reality their economic activities can be compared to those of giant private monopolies. The Foundations have unlimited access to state funds and foreign currency at the official exchange rate, and are able to conduct their business free from government controls, often outside the country (Korooshy 1997: 10). They are allocated 58 per cent of the state budget (*Salam* 17 August 1994: 3) yet the government has no precise information regarding their economic activities or how many businesses they operate. As the state has no control of the Foundations' corruption, nepotism and abuse of power, have developed to a high level. According to Maloney (2000: 150),

> the foundations exemplify one of the core ideological innovations of the revolution's architect, Ayatollah Ruhollah Khomeini, the amalgamation of traditional religious imagery and modern organisational forms through a populist, class-rooted appeal that deliberately targeted a broad array of socio-economic groups. Hence, organisations which operate in the name of the 'deprived segments' of the population have, in practice, developed into conglomerates oriented toward capital accumulation, with their proclaimed ideological objectives distinctly subordinate, though never fully subsumed.

Between 1981 and 1988 the Foundations had the same privileges as state administrative and enterprises in the allocation of foreign currencies. After the Economic Adjustment Program (1988–93) had been introduced in the IRI the Foundations still could allocate foreign currencies below the market price (Bank-e Markazi 1994: 461–3, 469). As the Foundations and their many industrial enterprises depend on foreign exchange at subsidised rates for their economic survival they have been opposing all proposed economic reforms to apply exchange rate unification. Additionally, as the Foundations are in charge of supplying social security to the poor, it is difficult to realise an important element of economic reform: privatisation. The reason for this is that most state-owned and expropriated industries that are to be privatised are in the hands of Foundations, particularly the Foundation of the Oppressed and the Disabled and the Martyrs' Foundation (Saeidi 2004: 488).

When the new privatisation process started, some Foundations agreed to sell parts of their assets to the private sector, worth 62.2 billion rials (Amuzegar 1993: 100). During the fourth *majlis* (1992–6) the main figures within the Foundations put pressure on the conservative members of the political elite to change the implementation of the privatisation process by changing the privatisation of state enterprises from the private sector to the

Foundations. In 1994 parliament passed a law allowing the government to sell state enterprises to those people devoted to the war, the prisoners of war and the relatives and members of those who were killed in the war (*Ettela'at* 18 Mordad 1995). As these people did not have the financial resources to buy these enterprises and to run them, the law accepted the para-governmental Foundations as their representatives. The Martyrs' Foundation and the Foundation of the Oppressed and Disabled were the main para-governmental organisations that started to buy state enterprises.

The Foundation for the Oppressed and Disabled

The Foundation for the Oppressed and Disabled was established in March 1979, ostensibly to take over and manage the wealth of the Pahlavi family and those who had cooperated with them. The resources the Foundation has had under its control since then were to be used to improve the living conditions of those in need. It operates as a non-profit organisation using the revenues from its property and private contributions to finance its welfare activities. Despite being a semi-private organisation it is exempt from taxes and from public accountability.

According to reports in 1984, the Foundation owned or had interests in: 64 small and large mines; 5,000 small productive units; 20,000 real estate properties; nearly 150 industrial enterprises; 140 construction firms; 250 commercial and trading companies; and three of Teheran's leading newspapers, in addition to unspecified numbers of farms, parcels of land, houses, theatres and more than $280 million of personal property (see Table 5.3). By 1992, it employed more than 65,000 people and ran an annual budget of $10 billion, which was almost 10 per cent of the government's own budget (*Kayhan Havai* 22 January 1992; *Middle East Economic Digest* 24 April 1992). In the same year it made profits of US$400 million (*Economist* 25 September 1993: 58). The estimates of the Foundation's share of the national income range from 1.5 per cent of gross domestic product (GDP) (International Monetary Fund 1995: 46) to 8–10 per cent of GDP (Iran Research Group 1989), but there are no reliable data about its property and workforce, as its accounts are not publicly released and press reports vary in their estimates.[12] The Foundation owns thousands of hectares of confiscated land, tens of thousands of apartment buildings, other real estate property, and personal property, such as cars, carpets and jewels (Amuzegar 1993: 100–1).

The Foundation for the Oppressed and Disabled is the biggest economic entity in the Middle East. In 1994, the volume of transactions of this *bonyad* amounted to 6,000 billion rials. As a comparison the total tax revenue of the government in the same year was 5,500 billion rials. In the same year the Foundation had 400 companies that account for a major share of Iran's industrial and agricultural production: 70 per cent of the glass containers, 53 per cent of the motor oil, 43 per cent of the soft drinks, 27 per cent of the synthetic fibre, 26 per cent of the tyres, 20 per cent of the sugar, 20 per cent of

Table 5.3 The Foundations' (estimated) economic activities and property

	Foundation of the Disabled and Oppressed	Martyrs' Foundation	Imam Reza Foundation
Employees	Up to 700,000	30,000	15,000
Companies	600 and 5,000 small enterprises (in 1984)	150	65
Real estate and land	20,000 (in 1984)	6,000 items of real estate in Tehran, 140 orchards and plots of land	2,900 square miles or 90 per cent of arable land in Khorasan (worth $20 billion)
Annual budget	$10 billion or 10 per cent of government budget (in 1992)	n/a	n/a

the textiles, as well as 30 per cent of the dairy products. Additionally, it is the owner of 43 per cent of the hotel capacity of Iran and produced 2.4 million square metres of construction in 1994. It has also signed a contract for the building of a highway between Tehran and the Caspian Sea (*Payam-e Emruz* 4 February 1994: 23, December 1997/January 1998: 75; Waldmann 1992).

The Foundation is increasingly operating transnationally. It is engaged in trade and coordinates its activities with the government's regional ambitions, investing heavily in South and Central Asia, as well as in the Middle East. According to various press reports, the Foundation is negotiating investment or already is investing in Bosnia, Armenia, Turkmenistan, Kazakhstan, China, Pakistan, India, Bangladesh and Pakistan. In addition, it trades crude oil through a subsidiary in Britain, imports Japanese cars, runs joint venture shipping companies in Italy and England, and owns German holding companies (Maloney, 2000: 150, 156).

The Martyrs' Foundation

The Martyrs' Foundation was established in March 1980 to financially support disabled veterans and surviving relatives of the martyrs of the Revolution and later also started to support the families of martyrs of the war with Iraq. It supports the families of more than 188,000 people who have lost their lives during the war (Yarshater 1987: 360–1). It also provides in-kind transfers, educational support and housing services to widows, orphans and victims of the war. The Foundation does not support all victims but limits its help to those who are most affiliated with the government. The Foundation is subsidised by the government, receives private contributions, and has expropriated wealth at its disposal (Amuzegar 1993: 101). Mohammad-Hosein Rahimiyan has been the Foundation's chairman since

1992, appointed by the Supreme Leader Ayatollah Khamenei (see Figure 5.1). The resources allocated to it by the government increased between 1981 and 1990 annually by 29.3 per cent from 11.4 billion rials to 115 billion rials (Bank-e Markazi 1994: 817). In 1994, its total funding, composed of expropriated property and annual government subsidies, was 398.5 billion rials (IRNA 1994). It has 30,000 employees (Buchta 2000).

In 1992, the Martyrs' Foundation owned 150 enterprises active in industrial production, construction, agriculture, commerce and services. In 1995 it established the Shahid Investment Company, which is the largest of these enterprises, to mobilise and invest the savings of the families of the martyrs. The company controls about 50 firms with branches in Asian and Western countries. Nothing is known about the accounts of the company, information on which is withheld even from its shareholders (*Akhbar-e Eqtesad* 12 Isfand

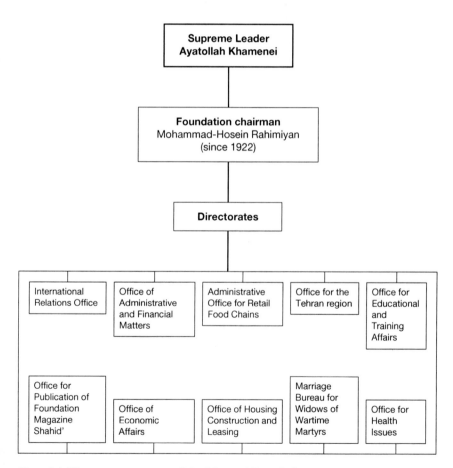

Figure 5.1 The power structure of the Martyrs' Foundation

Source: Buchta 2000

2000: 19). The charitable wing of the Foundation provides financial assistance, and grants special rights to those under its supervision, such as giving priority to university admission and employment. It also arranges marriages (Yarshater 1987: 360–1; Amrahmadi 1995: 236–7; Iran Research Group 1989: 10, 45–6). The Foundation owns about 6,000 items of real estate in Tehran such as: villas, apartments, shops, malls, schools, hospitals and hotels. Most of these buildings are used as housing for families of war dead. Additionally, it owns 140 orchards and plots of land (Yarshater 1987: 361).

The Imam Reza Foundation

The Imam Reza Foundation was established before the Revolution. It is located in Mashhad, and its centre is the Shrine of the Eighth Imam Ali Musa al-Reza and a destination for pilgrimage of eight million Shi'is annually from all over the world. Since 1979 the Foundation has been led by Abbas Vaez Tabasi. The holdings of the Imam Reza Foundation probably even exceed those of the Foundation for the Oppressed and Disabled, which is thought to be the biggest and wealthiest of the Foundations. Many believers have donated their property to the Foundation. In 1994 it owned more than 2,900 square miles or 90 per cent of the arable land in the Khorasan province, and therefore is the biggest landowner in Khorasan. The value of its land amounts to $20 billion. The Foundation owns 56 different companies and employs about 15,000 people in different fields: factories, construction firms, agricultural concerns, religious services, two universities, cultural institutions, social services and Iran's only Coca Cola plant. It makes US$130 million annually (Kocher 1995: 5).

In accordance with the economic interests of the Iranian government in Central Asia, Vaez Tabasi and his son Naser, who has many years of business experience in Central Asia, have the ambition to turn Mashhad into a gateway to Central Asia and a crossroad between Asia, the Persian Gulf and Europe. Abbas Vaez Tabasi has had a close friendship with Supreme Leader Khamenei for more than 40 years and their families are also linked through marriage: one of Tabasi's daughters is married to Khamenei's son, Sayyed Hasan, and Naser Vaez Tabasi is married to one of Khamenei's daughters. According to the *lajnat al-difa anhuquq al-marjaiya al-shiiya* (the Committee for the Defence of the Rights of the Shi'i *marjaiyat*, a London-based quietistic clerical opposition), Naser Vaez Tavasi is actively involved in obtaining the most modern weapons and nuclear technology in cooperation with firms from Austria and Switzerland (Buchta 2000: 76).

The Imam Reza Foundation also operates its own bank, several transportation firms and an airline. It has a monopoly in the exploitation of most gold and semi-precious metal mines in Khorasan, and a monopoly in the exploitation rights in the Sarakhs natural gas fields at the border with Turkmenistan. The Foundation is now believed to be the third largest economic organisation in Iran behind the National Iranian Oil Company

(NIOC) and the Foundation for the Oppressed and Disabled. And Abbas Vaez Tabasi can be considered a strong leader of an economically independent province who even at times can surpass governmental directions (*al-Sharq al-Awsat* 29 December 1998: 10).

Prospects: the future of the IRI and the *bonyads*

In this chapter I have analysed the role of the para-governmental Foundations as an integral part of the politico-economic system of the IRI. Many Foundations were established after the Revolution of 1979 following the confiscation and nationalisation of the property of the Pahlavi family and those rich families loyal to its regime. The Foundations not only control large parts of the economy, but they have also been involved in propagating the ideology of the IRI and the social security programmes. Officially they are meant to help the poor and other most disadvantaged people of the Iranian society. In reality, they have played an important role in the institutionalisation of the ideology of the IRI through the implementation of various differing social and cultural activities.

At the same time the *bonyads* have developed into conglomerates that are active in all different kinds of economic sectors. The Foundations make great profits and support parts of the Iranian political elite. The government has no control over their economic activities or their expenses, there are no public accounts, and the Foundations do not have a well-defined legal status. If there are any regular reports about the Foundations' economic activities they are probably only accessible to senior managers, members of the Conservative Faction of the political elite and the Supreme Leader. As their data are not made public, it is difficult to say anything about the Foundations' future activities. Should political and economic pressure on the Iranian Islamic political elite increase, this will also impact upon the Foundations.

The Iranians no longer have confidence in the IRI since Khomeini and his follower Khamenei have been unable to bring about prosperity and social justice as they promised. Although the average annual oil income in Iran has risen 100 per cent since the Revolution most economic indicators are very negative. Compared with the 1970s, average inflation has doubled, the unemployment rate has tripled, and economic growth has reduced by two-thirds. Per capita income has declined by at least 30 per cent since 1979 and according to private research 40 per cent of the population live below the absolute poverty line (15 per cent according to official statistics). According to a study carried out by the Iranian Interior Ministry 90 per cent of the population are dissatisfied with the government – 24 per cent of which demand fundamental changes, 66 per cent gradual reforms – and only 10 per cent are satisfied with the government. Both the bankruptcy of the Islamic ideology and the failed economic reforms challenge the legitimacy of the IRI, as both the public and the press openly question the role of the *velayat-e faqih* in the political system of Iran (Amuzegar 2003: 44–57).

So far, however, this criticism and reformist pressures have been suppressed. In 2004 the Council of the Guardian excluded more than 2,500 candidates for the parliamentary elections, including former President Khatami's own brother, several clerics and dozens of members of parliament. Most of the rejected candidates belonged to the reformist camp of the political factions. What followed were loud protests from the reformist camp, a sit-in in the *majlis* by a large group of members of parliament, the resignation of about 130 *majlis* deputies, several senior cabinet members, and all 27 provincial governors, a public condemnation by President Mohammad Khatami and the *majlis* Speaker Karroubi, and finally a request of the Supreme Leader Khamenei to the Council of the Guardian to reconsider their decision. Those reformists who were allowed to participate in the elections could put together a list of some 120 candidates with the confidence of receiving about 100 seats. The elections, however, turned out to be a disappointment for the reformists. Of the 290 seats the conservatives received over 150 and the reformists only some 60 seats. The parliamentary elections of 2004 again show that Iranian politics are under the control of a handful of hard-line clerics (Ehteshami 2004). In 2005 the Council of the Guardian excluded more than 1,000 candidates for the presidential elections held in June of the same year and all except one candidate of the Reformist Faction. Also the presidential elections were won by the Conservative Faction. The new President Mahmoud Ahmadinejad is one from the ranks of the Conservative Faction. The influence of the leaders of the Foundations on the process of political decision-making in Iran and their reluctance to accept any reform of the economic system will have profound implications for the future political and economic process in Iran as well as its regional and international relations.

Notes

1 On Khomeini's thought and his idea of the *velayat-e faqih* see Khomeini (1979), and also Amineh (1999).
2 The coercive forces are in the hands of the Conservative Faction and can be distinguished as two groups. The first group consists of the forces for domestic affairs including official and paramilitary forces. The official forces, or the Law Enforcement Forces, are composed of the gendarmerie, *komiteh*, police and the *basije* and *pasdaran* (revolutionary guards). The paramilitary forces are unofficial groups supported by the conservatives. They include groups such as Hezbollah and Ansar-e hezbollahis. The second group of the coercive forces are the military forces, primarily for foreign affairs.
3 Originally the 1979 Constitution divided the power over the executive between the president and the prime minister. Actual leadership over the executive branch was in the hands of the prime minister, who – in contrast to the president – was not elected by the Iranian people. The idea was that by this division of power a popular elected president could not undermine the authority of the Supreme Leader. With the revision of the Constitution in 1989 the office of prime minister was abolished and his tasks taken over by the president (cf. Milani 1993).
4 The National Security Council has 12 permanent members who coordinate governmental activities in defence, the intelligence services and foreign policy.

5 For detailed information on the different factions of the Iranian Islamic political elite see Rakel (2005) and Rakel (forthcoming).

6 The concept of the politically relevant elite comprises all those individuals that have the power or influence to: make decisions on the national and international level and or are involved in the decision-making process; participate in the decision-making process; participate in defining norms and values on what is the 'national interest'; and have a decisive influence on public debate on strategic subjects. The politically relevant elite comprises not only those people who have power according to their position in state institutions but also those individuals who influence or attempt to influence the political process, such as politicians in opposition, journalists, high bureaucrats, members of the security institutions, leading economists, non-establishment clerics, etc.

7 Clerics, who are not part of the political elite, but have reached the position as jurisconsult, are qualified to make judgements within the *shari'a* based on their own sources. It is interesting to note that most of these clerics have a higher position in the clerical hierarchy than those who belong to the political elite and that these either reject the principle of the *velayat-e faqih* or criticise its application as being in contradiction with the constitution. The most prominent figure among these clerics is Grand Ayatollah Montazeri who was to become Khomeini's successor but then fell into disgrace. Today, of about 300,000 clergy only 5 per cent are politically active and only 12 per cent of members of parliament are clergy (as many clergy retreat from politics). At the same time the majority of the Iranian population is disappointed with the clergy and very sceptical about the clergy's qualifications as politicians (Reissner 2002; Roy 1999; Bellaigue 2002).

8 With backing from the Revolutionary Council this group was responsible for taking hostage US diplomats and other staff at the US embassy in Tehran for 444 days, starting on 14 November 1979.

9 For example, what can be noted in Iran is the development of a kind of party-like political system, although officially political parties do not (yet) exist. The candidates who ran for presidency used to be affiliated with a faction, but they did not represent specific political groupings. Since Khatami was elected as president in 1997 this has changed. The candidate who was expected to win the 1997 presidential elections, Nateq-Nuri, had been chosen by the clerical conservative Jame'eh-ye Rowhaniyat-e Mobarez (JRM, The Militant Clergy Association). Khatami received political backing from several political groupings such as the Majma'e Rowhaniyun-e Mobarez (MRM, The Militant Clerics Society) and the non-clerical Sanzma-e Mojahedin-e Enqelab-e Islami (MIRO, the Mujahedin of the Islamic Revolution Organisation). Several of these groups acted like political parties during the electoral campaign, trying to mobilise support for their favoured candidate. Some of them have their own newspapers (Fairbanks 1998: 19–20).

10 The *bazaars* have a long history in Iran, dating back to the fifth century, and over the centuries they developed into large communities with shops, teahouses, restaurants, bathhouses, mosques, religious schools and *caravanserai*, and also into financial centres, with their own banking, credit and investment systems. The Grand Bazaar in Tehran is both a stock exchange and a commodities market, and market stalls on the *bazaar* (costing hundreds of thousands of dollars) hide the real activities of the *bazaaris*. Until a unified system of multiple exchange rates was introduced in Iran in March 2002 the *bazaaris* acted as moneylenders and bought currency at lower rates than the free market. There has always been a close relationship between the clerics and the *bazaaris* as the clerics needed the *bazaaris* to fund mosques and religious schools while the *bazaaris* needed the

clerics to keep their social position in Iranian society. Both their wealth and their links with the clerics give the *bazaaris* enormous political power. The *bazaaris* played an important role in overthrowing the Shah regime and bringing Khomeini to power in 1979. In recent times, the strong relationship between the *bazaaris* and the clerics has been receding due to the introduction of a unified system of multiple exchange rates, anti-profiteering campaigns against the *bazaaris*, and the overall crisis of the Iranian economy since the Revolution.

11 In June 1963 Khomeini led a revolt against the Shah, which was the climax of a political conflict between the different social forces, parts of the landowning class, the *bazaar*, the *ulama*, and parts of the modern middle class under the leadership of the National Front on the one hand and the Iranian government on the other (cf. Amineh 1999: 260).

12 Some number its subsidiaries as at least 800 (although figures of 1,500 are also regularly cited), and its workforce to up to 700,000 workers (or as much as 5 per cent of the male labour force) in Iran (*Financial Times* 17 July 1997: 4; *Economist* 18 January 1997: 7).

Bibliography

Abrahamian, E. (1982) *Iran Between Two Revolutions*, Princeton, NJ: Princeton University Press.

Ajami, F. (1989) 'The impossible revolution', *Foreign Affairs*, 67 (2): 135–76.

Akhavi-Pour, H. and H. Azodanloo (1998) 'Economic bases of political factions in Iran', *Critique*, Fall (13): 83–102.

Algar, H. (1969) *Religion and State in Iran 1785–1906: The Role of the Ulama in the Qajar Period*, Berkeley and Los Angeles, CA: University of California Press.

Amineh, M.P. (1999) *Die globale kapitalistische Expansion und Iran-Eine Studie der Iranischen Politischen Ökonomie 1500–1980*, Münster, Hamburg and London: Lit Verlag.

—— (2004) 'Demokratisierung und ihre Feinde', *Aus Politik und Zeitgeschichte* B9, 23 February: 25–8.

Amirahmadi, H. (1995) 'Bunyad', in J.L. Esposito (ed.), *The Oxford Encyclopaedia of the Modern Islamic World*, New York and Oxford: Oxford University Press, pp. 234–7.

—— (1996) 'Emerging civil society in Iran', *SAIS Review*, 16 (2): 87–102.

Amuzegar, J. (1993) *Iran's Economy under the Islamic Republic*, London and New York: I.B. Tauris.

—— (2003) 'Iran's crumbling revolution', *Foreign Affairs*, 82 (1): 44–57.

Ashraf, A. (1994) 'Charisma, theocracy, and men of power in post-revolutionary Iran', in A. Banuazizi and M. Weiner (eds), *The Politics of Social Transformation in Afghanistan, Iran and Pakistan*, Syracuse, NY: Syracuse University Press, pp. 101–55.

Bakhtiari, B. (1996) *Parliamentary Politics in Revolutionary Iran – The Institutionalisation of Factional Politics*. Gainesville, FL: Florida University Press.

Bank-e Markazi-ye Jomhuri-ye Islami-ye Iran (1994) *Barresi-ye Tahavvolat-e Eqtesadi-ye Keshvar Tey-ye Salba-ye 1361–1369 (Iran's Economic Development, 1982–1990)*. Tehran: Bank-e Markazi.

Behdad, S. (1988) 'The political economy of Islamic planning in Iran', in H. Amirahmadi and M. Parvin (eds), *Post-Revolutionary Iran*, Boulder, CO: Westview Press, pp. 107–25.

Bellaigue, C. de (2002) 'Who rules Iran?', *New York Review of Books*, 27 June: 17–20.

Buchta, W. (2000) *Who Rules Iran – The Structure of Power in the Islamic Republic*, Washington, DC: Washington Institute of Near East Policy.

Chehabi, H.E. (2001) 'The political regime of the Islamic Republic of Iran in comparative perspective' *Government and Opposition*, 36 (1): 48–70.

Clarke, L. (2001) 'The shi'i construction of Taqlid', *Journal of Islamic Studies* 12 (1): 40–64.

Constitution of the Islamic Republic of Iran (1981). Berkeley, CA: Mizan Press.

Curzon, G.N. (1892) *Persia and the Persian Question*, vol. 1, London: Longman, Green and Co.

Embassy of the Islamic Republic of Iran in Germany (1993) *Iran Yearbook*, Embassy of the Islamic republic of Iran.

Fairbanks, S.C. (1998) 'Theocracy versus democracy: Iran considers political parties', *Middle East Journal*, 52 (1): 17–31.

Halliday, F. (1983) 'The Iranian revolution: uneven development and religious populism', *Journal of International Affairs*, Winter: 187–209.

Halm, H. (1997) *Shi'a Islam: From Religion to Revolution*, Princeton, NJ: Princeton University Press.

International Monetary Fund (1995) *Islamic Republic of Iran – Recent Economic Developments*, IMF Staff Country Report no. 95/121, December, Washington, DC: IMF.

Iran Focus (2002) 'Upcoming elections concentrates the minds of Iran's factions', June.

Iran Research Group (1989) *Iran Yearbook 1989–1990*, Bonn: MB Medien & Buecher Gesellschaft GMBH, pp. 10, 45–6.

IRNA (1994) 'Details of subsidies amounting to more than 6,088 bn rials', 24 May, as translated in BBC Summary of World Broadcasts, 31 May 1994.

Karbassian, A. (2000) 'Islamic revolution and the management of the Iranian economy', *Social Research*, 67 (2): 621–40.

Kazemi, F. (1996) 'Civil society and Iranian politics', in A.R. Norton (ed.), *Civil Society in the Middle East*, vol. 2, Leiden and Boston, MA: Brill Academic Publishers, pp. 119–52.

Keddie, N.R. (1995) 'Can revolutions be predicted?', in N.R. Keddie (ed.), *Debating Revolutions*, New York: New York University Press.

Khajehpour, B. (2000) 'Domestic political reforms and private sector activity in Iran', *Social Research*, 67 (2): 577–98.

Khomeini, R. (1979) *The Leadership of the Jurists: The Islamic Government* (in Persian), Tehran: Panzdah-e Khordad.

Kocher, V. (1995) 'Das Imperium des Imam Reza von Meschhed', *Neue Zuericher Zeitung*, October, 7: 5.

Korooshy, J. (1997) 'Zur Veraenderung der sozialen Sturkuturen in Iran nach der Revolution von 1979 am Beispiel der Wirtschafts-und Industrieeliten', unpublished manuscript.

Maloney, S. (2000) 'Agents or obstacles? Parastatal foundations and challenges for Iranian development', in P. Alizadeh (ed.), *The Economy of Iran: Dilemmas of an Islamic State*, London and New York, Palgrave Macmillan, pp. 145–76.

Mawlawi, A. *et al.* (1987) 'Asan-e Qods-e Razawi', *Encyclopaedia Iranica*, London: Routledge & Kegan Paul, pp. 826–37.

Menashri, D. (1990) *Iran: A Decade of War and Revolution*, New York: Holmes and Meier.

Milani, M. (1993) 'The evolution of the Iranian presidency: from Bani-Sadr to Rafsanjani', *British Journal of Middle Eastern Studies*, 20 (1): 86–9.

Perthes, V. (2004) 'Politics and elite change in the Arab world', in V. Perthes (ed.), *Arab Elites – Negotiating the Politics of Change*, Boulder, CO and London: Lynne Rienner Publishers, pp. 1–32.

Rakel, E. (2005) 'Paradigms of Iranian policy in central Eurasia and beyond', in M.P. Amineh and H. Houweling (eds), *Central Eurasia in Global Politics: Conflict Security and Development*, Leiden and Boston, MA: Brill Academic Publishers, pp. 235–57.

——— (forthcoming 2007) 'The Iranian political elite, state, society, and international relations: the case of Iran–European Union relations', Ph.D. thesis, University of Amsterdam.

Ravasani (1978) *Staat und Gesellschaft in Iran* (in Persian), Tehran: Bina, pp. 109–17.

Reissner, J. (2002) 'Iran: vor dem Ende klerikaler Macht?', in V. Perthes (ed.), *Elitenwandel in der arabischen Welt*, Berlin: SWP-Studie.

Resalat (1996) 'Majiles Session: 30 Apr 96', in FBIS-NES-96–139-S, 1 May: 5, 13.

Roy, O. (1999) 'Crisis of religious legitimacy in Iran', *Middle East Journal* 53 (2): 201–17.

Saeidi, A.A. (2004) 'The accountability of para-governmental organizations (bonyads): the case of Iranian Foundations', *Iranian Studies*, 37 (3): 479–98.

Schirazi, A. (1997) *The Constitution of Iran. Politics and the State in the Islamic Republic*, London: Tauris Publishers.

Soroush, A. (2000) *Reason, Freedom, and Democracy in Islam*, Oxford: Oxford University Press.

Tellenbach, S. (1990) 'Zur Aenderung der Verfassung der Islamischen Republik vom 28. Juli 1989', *Orient*, 31 (1): 45–66.

Vakili-Zad, C. (1992) 'Continuity and change: the structure of power in Iran', in C. Vakili-Zad and H.Z. Bina, *Modern Capitalism and Islamic Ideology in Iran*, New York: St Martin's Press.

Waldmann, P. (1992) 'Clergy capitalism', *The Wall Street Journal*, 5 May.

Yarshater, E. (1987) (ed.) 'Bonyad-e Shahid', *Encyclopaedia Iranica*, vol. II, Costa Mesa, CA: Mazda Publishers, pp. 360–1.

Part II
Latin America

6 Latin American conglomerates in the neoliberal era

The politics of economic concentration in Chile and Mexico

Alex E. Fernández Jilberto and Barbara Hogenboom

Since the 1980s, Latin American conglomerates and economic groups have gone through a phase of rapid and impressive expansion and change. The privatisation of public enterprises together with policies of economic liberalisation and deregulation have given way to an enormous expansion of financial and industrial corporate groups. As a result, a process of economic concentration of unprecedented scale in the history of Latin American regional capitalism has taken place. Simultaneously, neoliberal policies have put an end to the development concept that supposed that industrialisation and economic groups were to have their basis within the nation-state. Parallel to sweeping liberalisation and privatisation, large private companies started denationalising and regionalising their investments (Fernández Jilberto and Hogenboom 2004).

Apart from this new economic model, the rise of Latin American conglomerates is a result of changing political circumstances. While in most of the region's countries neoliberalisation was initiated by the military dictatorships, the victory of neoliberalism involved a major turnabout in political power relations and their ideological embeddedness, coinciding with processes of democratisation. Like many other parts of the world, Latin America experienced what has been called the necessary de-ideologisation of the political-economic debate. During the 1980s democratic transition was thus accompanied by a de-radicalisation of politics and a loss of relevance of syndical organisations and parties that canalise popular demands. Simultaneously, the interests and influence of the private sector and especially those of the larger corporations became much more prominent in politics.

This chapter studies the rise of conglomerates in two countries located at the far ends of the region: Chile and Mexico. In this comparative exercise two important differences stand out. First, the neoliberal restructuring that forms the context of recent economic concentration in economic groups and conglomerates started about a decade earlier in Chile than in Mexico. Second, in Chile it was a military dictatorship implementing these new economic policies, whereas in Mexico this was done by the semi-authoritarian regime of the Institutional Revolutionary Party (PRI), but in both countries the neoliberal model has been consolidated during the subsequent democratisation process. Notwithstanding these and other differences, there are interesting parallels in the rise of conglomerates in Chile and Mexico, and in the access of the owners/executives of these conglomerates to the economic policy-making processes. According to Judith Teichman (2001: 199), they

> were in the best position to take advantage of the opportunities afforded by the new economic model, particularly in the areas of export promotion and the opportunity to purchase state companies. Moreover, as policy makers opened up channels of communication to the private sector, powerful private sector interests seized the opportunity to influence policy.

Chile was the first country in Latin America to restructure its economy along neoliberal lines, in 1973, right after Pinochet's *coup d'état*. In the first stage of privatisation, from 1974 until 1982, the intention was to lay the foundations of what the military called 'the re-foundation of Chilean capitalism': the privatisation of companies that had been nationalised during the Unidad Popular government of President Allende (1970–3). The aim was not only to restore capitalist mechanisms within the Chilean economy, but also to eliminate the domain of 'Social Property', which had been the guideline for the economic policy of the 'Chilean path to socialism'. This first stage particularly benefited local economic groups, but came to an end with Chile's foreign-debt crisis and economic recession from 1981 until 1983. The second stage of privatisation started after the economic recovery in 1985 and lasted until 1990. At this stage a massive transfer of the ownership of large state-owned companies to multinational conglomerates took place. In addition, the power-basis of new economic groups was consolidated, as they took advantage of the profound neoliberal convictions, and the unconditional support for multinational companies, which the government considered to be the materialisation of the globalisation of the Chilean economy. Many of the state's technocrats moved to the private sector as agents or strategic executives, associating with local economic groups and transnational conglomerates.

In Mexico the process of neoliberal restructuring started later on, in the mid-1980s. The hub of Mexican privatisation also came later than in Chile, in the early 1990s. Nevertheless, in Mexico 'conglomerisation' has advanced rapidly, and its economic groups are among the most powerful of Latin America. On the list of the top 50 developing country transnational companies, seven are Mexican, and Mexico's cement giant Cemex is the second largest. The transnational level of Mexican multinationals has even reached the same height as those from Hong Kong (UNCTAD 2002, 2003). Several of Mexico's largest local private companies are linked to the conglomerate of Carlos Slim, the richest person in Latin America. He has made his fortune in the aftermath of the crisis of 1982 and his corporate activities currently range from telecom to finance, and from electronics to trade. After privatisation he became the owner of a controlling share of Teléfonos de México (Telmex) with partners Southwestern Bell and Telecom France. In 2001, Slim started to expand his corporate dominance beyond Mexico, particularly through América Móvil, a giant and fast growing company in cellular phones. Slim's career is the ultimate example of the current regional power of Mexican conglomerates, illustrating their economic concentration and transnationalisation since the 1980s. Moreover, the expansion of Slim's conglomerate points at the use of good relations with politicians and state officials, and also shows how, for such large corporations, financial crises can be treated as opportunities rather than threats.

In this chapter the rapid rise of economic groups and conglomerates in Mexico and Chile is analysed in relation to policies of economic restructuring and regional integration, which substantially benefited old and new conglomerates and economic groups. The tendency of economic concentration in the private sector is important for, apart from economic relations, it also affects social and political relations. As this chapter shows there are many similarities in the rise of economic groups and conglomerates in Chile and Mexico since the introduction of the neoliberal economic model even though these two countries, situated at the far extremes of Latin America, differ greatly (in size of population and economy, in political and economic history, in social conditions, etc.). What explains these similar trends of economic concentration within large corporate entities in Mexico and Chile? Apart from the global economic and financial context, a key factor lies in the extensive and costly state support for large companies, economic groups and conglomerates, particularly favourable privatisation conditions, and massive assistance after financial crises. In both Chile and Mexico the economic model in which major companies are taken to be the new motor of growth was introduced in a context of close personal, political and economic relations between major entrepreneurs and the technocratic political elite, resulting in complex yet definite trends of 'conglomerisation' and transnationalisation.[1]

Economic concentration at times of crisis and restructuring

In most cases, economic concentration in Latin America's private sector started under military rule or under authoritarian neoliberal regimes that associated populism and import substitution industrialisation (ISI) with the communist peril. However, this political context changed radically in the 1980s, when Latin American regimes started to democratise. Interestingly, in this context of democratisation and processes of regionalisation of the Latin American economy, economic concentration increasingly became politically legitimised. The debates on development with equity (CEPAL 1990) and open regionalism (CEPAL 1994) referred to the need for a reconciliation between a concentration of economic power and the emerging democratic political regimes. The debates provided a local theoretical basis to the inevitable liberalisation of Latin American markets. In addition, these debates referred to the need to form Latin American economic blocs that would not inhibit economic association of countries with other regional blocs, combining three types of economic integration: agreements for sub-regional integration (e.g. MERCOSUR); bilateral accords for trade liberalisation; and agreements liberalising trade between groups of countries. This form of economic integration of radically neoliberalised economies became the new strategy for economic growth, and for the region's integration into the process of economic globalisation (Fernández Jilberto and Hogenboom 1997).

Economic groups and conglomerates in Chile

The first privatisations in Chile took place between 1974 and 1982. This stage of privatisation signified the subsidised transfer of government goods to economic groups, the control by these groups over the capital market and the financial system (national and foreign credit), and the start of repressive salary politics. The privatisation of state-controlled banks to local economic groups was considered necessary to resolve the shortage of financial capital that the Chilean economy had suffered between 1971 and 1977. In addition, from 1972 until 1977 Chile experienced high levels of inflation while the 1975–6 recession de-capitalised a large number of the companies in Chile (Table 6.1). On the other hand, the economic groups that purchased the state-owned companies could benefit from repressive salary reductions. This salary reduction was a direct result of the repression of the labour movement between 1973 and 1979 when all forms of collective bargaining were forbidden, as well as any form of union activities, while the right to strike was cancelled (Fernández Jilberto and Riethof 2003).

The lack of available capital and the fear of foreign investors created by the political instability of the military government forced the Pinochet dictatorship to perform debt-led privatisations. By doing so the dictatorship strongly favoured the large Chilean conglomerates and economic groups. The first round of privatisations included the return of 259 companies that had been nationalised by the Allende government, eventually rising to 325 re-privatised companies in 1982. The transfer of these companies to the private sector was done through an auction sale and resulted in the highest level of economic concentration (of productive and financial capital) in Chilean history. Between 1969 and 1978 the global assets of the 100 largest companies of the country, including Cruzat-Larrain, Javier Vial, Matte, Angelini, Luksic and Lepe, increased 52.4 per cent (Dhase 1979).

Table 6.1 Chile's macroeconomic indicators, 1974–84 (percentages)

	1974	1975	1976	1977	1978	1979	1980	1981	1982	1983	1984
GDP growth	1.0	-13.3	3.2	8.3	7.8	7.1	7.7	6.7	-13.4	-3.5	5.6
Unemployment[a]		18.8	19.3	17.5	17.7	18	16.1	16	28.2	22	20.2
Inflation	369.2	343.3	197.9	84.2	37.2	38.9	31.2	9.5	20.7	23.1	23
Salary change	-16.3	-3.2	2.9	10.3	6.4	8.2	8.6	9	0.3	-10.9	1.3

Source: Instituto Nacional de Estadísticas (1986).

Note: a Percentages include underemployed workers.

The major beneficiaries of privatisation were the traditional local economic groups. Most of these groups originated from the 1960s and were based on family structures under the legal umbrella of corporations or limited-liability companies, usually without a division between ownership, control and management of the company. The privatisations carried out by the military dictatorship converted these economic groups into conglomerates of numerous companies with multiple economic activities and highly diversified assets, which would indicate lower risks and stable profits. As examples of this concentration of property and activities we can think of the Matte group, controlling 46 companies in 1978, the Vial group (66 companies in 1978), the Cruzat-Larrain group (109), the Angelini group (21) and the Luksic group (31) (Sanfuentes 1984). The total number of companies controlled by these five largest groups rose from 41 in 1969 to 273 in 1978 (see Table 6.2). These expanding groups were formed by joining together a number of diverse companies that had been privatised at a rather fast pace and that originated from different economic sectors. Although the diverse assets of the expanding economic groups can be seen as a positive factor, the lack of efficient vertical integration among the individual companies constituting the groups formed one of the largest risks in the case of an economic recession. Eventually the 1981 debt crisis and its consequent economic recession showed that the collapse of a few of a conglomerate's companies could lead to the total collapse of the conglomerate, as happened with the Vial group and the Cruzat-Larrain group.

An important characteristic of the economic groups that benefited from the first stage of privatisation was the lack of competition between them, as they controlled almost all national production, and shared management and ownership over several companies (Dhase 1979). The strategy of the formation of holdings was the dominant mechanism applied by the main economic groups to exercise power over financial and industrial capital. Through the holdings the groups obtained control over a package of shares without having to perform economic activities in any of the related companies. In addition,

Table 6.2 Global assets of Chile's five main economic groups, 1969–78

Economic Group	Companies (no.)		Assets 1969 (US$ million)	Assets 1978 (US$ million)	Change in assets 1969–78 (%)
	1969	*1978*			
Angelini	6	21	43	140	224
Cruzat-Larrain	13	109	191	1,000	423
Matte	7	46	168	360	115
Vial	8	66	116	520	347
Luksic	7	31	90	150	67
Total	41	273	608	2,170	257

Sources: Dhase (1979); Sanfuentes (1984).

the creation of holdings enabled groups to evade direct scrutiny by third parties (including the government) over the real control they exercise over the assets of several companies. Another mechanism applied to obtain industrial and financial control in Chile was the interaction of dominant economic groups with allied groups or subgroups. With the help of these smaller groups the dominant groups managed to dominate the conglomerates of which they possessed significant share packages and in turn the smaller groups came to depend financially on the dominant groups. The overall management of these economic groups was realised through interlocking directories, which resulted in a secure presence of the groups' partners in strategic enterprises. With this strategy the five main economic groups managed to control two-thirds of the total assets of the 250 major private companies in Chile.

Another common feature among the economic groups that had taken advantage of the privatisations was a high level of indebtedness. Their initial indebtedness originated from preferential access to government credits for the subsidised acquisition of the public companies, in an economic landscape that between 1971 and 1977 was characterised by a profound lack of national as well as foreign credits. This lack of credit was a result of the forming of the Areas of Social Property (ASP) during the government of the Unidad Popular and the high levels of inflation in the 1972–7 period, which de-capitalised large numbers of the entrepreneurs during the 1975–6 period of inflation. The acquisition of the privatised state banks and their access to credits with preferential interest rates on the international financial markets enabled dominant economic groups to monopolise credits and finance themselves (see Table 6.3). The Vial and Cruzat groups, for instance, together were responsible for 51.9 per cent of Chile's total external banking debt in December 1981, 73.6 per cent of the pension funds and 81.8 per cent of the capture of mutual funds (Dhase 1983). Yet the 1981 international debt crisis and the subsequent anti-recessive economic politics applied in Chile turned the high levels of indebtedness of economic groups into the trigger that set off a prolonged economic crisis. The final solution to this crisis was sought in a second stage of privatisation this time directly favouring the inflow of foreign investment and transnational capital. Consequently, the economic groups that managed to survive the economic crisis were forced to either associate themselves with foreign companies, or simply subordinate themselves to foreign investment. This accelerated the process of globalisation of the Chilean economy.

Economic groups and conglomerates in Mexico

Over the past two decades economic power in Mexico has become increasingly concentrated in a small number of very large Mexican and foreign enterprises. In 1999, of a total of 2.7 million economic units, the overall majority was made up of micro enterprises (95.9 per cent), with 2.9 per cent being small companies, 0.9 per cent medium-sized companies and only 0.3

Table 6.3 Level of indebtedness of Chile's 15 main economic groups, 1978 (US$ billion)

Economic groups	Assets	Direct internal debt	Direct foreign debt	Brokers' credit	Debt with public sector (CORFO)	Debt with pension funds	Total indebtedness per group
Cruzat-Larrain	1,000	452.31	110.28	26.6	71	79	452.31
B.H.C. (Vial)	520	205.61	117.99	38.8	45	30	436.7
Matte	360	18.12	9.7				27.82
Angelini	140	16.5	1.5				18
Edwards	74	40.28	22.22	7.58			70
Luksic	150	31.53	17.55				49
Yarur Banna	100	61.96	26.7				88.66
Hochschild	70	2.33					2.33
Briones	55	13.24	5.44				18.68
Puig	40	26.61	15.9	9.16			51.67
Galmez	95	20.75	8.5		8		37
Lepe, Piquer and Lehman	70	13.43	1.5				14.94
Sumar	26	41.39	6.85				48.24
Abalos and Gonzalez		14.83	54.33				69.16
Mustakis	22	23.48	5.68				29.16

Source: Dhase (1979, 1983).

per cent (7,473 units) large companies (based on the number of employees, *El Mercado de Valores* 2002). Apart from a few giant state companies in the energy sector (petrol, gas and electricity), the group of large companies consists of so-called local companies (including 'multilatinas'), and foreign transnationals such as General Motors, Wal-Mart, Daimler-Chrysler, Delphi, Volkswagen, Nissan, Sony, IBM, Coca Cola and Nestlé. Between large Mexican enterprises and economic groups there is a strong relation, although figures on recent tendencies are hard to come by. In the period 1987–91, the 59 major economic groups were made up of almost 1,000 companies, 197 of which were on the list of Mexico's largest 500 companies. The share of the sales of these 197 even equalled 65 per cent of the top 500, showing that the main economic groups are at the heart of large private Mexican companies (Garrido 1998).

Financial crises and financial policies have proven to be important elements for the development of Mexican economic groups. A crisis shakes things up and may form an excellent opportunity for innovation and expansion. Moreover, apart from the evident pro-business bias of neoliberal policies, the governmental efforts to rescue financial capital from defaulting after the financial crises of 1982 and of 1994–5 were particularly beneficial to large Mexican investors. Evidently other changes have also affected their position, but it is striking that in analyses of the contemporary history of

Mexican economic groups much of the speed and nature of their development is linked to events in financial markets (currency and stock exchange) and changing government initiatives towards banking, financial services and exchange rates (Basave Kunhardt 2001; Concheiro Bórquez 1996; Garrido 2002; Morera Camacho 1998).

Most Mexican conglomerates already existed prior to the phase of economic restructuring policies, although Carlos Slim's empire forms an exception to this rule. In fact, policies of ISI (1940s to mid-1970s) created the basis for growth of Mexican economic groups as well as foreign companies in Mexico. Direct state participation in industrial production was not only a dynamising factor for economic growth (the 'Mexican miracle'), but also for economic concentration. This concentration took place both in large state companies and in large private companies and economic groups. The large state sector subsidised the (national and foreign) private sector, predominantly through price policies. The protectionist policies and the growth of both the Mexican and the US markets were very attractive to large companies of national as well as foreign origin, resulting in the start and expansion of numerous major companies, economic groups and conglomerates that became dominant in Mexico's economic structure. When, in the 1960s, centralisation occurred in the financial sector, many large companies were transformed into integrated economic groups (Basave Kunhardt 2001).

In the mid-1970s, with the crisis of the ISI-model, a concentration of capital in private companies, economic groups and conglomerates started. Major entrepreneurs diversified their activities and expanded them beyond borders. In addition, the banking reform of 1975 allowed banks to broaden their services and gave way to a process of mergers that entailed increasing ties between companies and banks, resulting in oligopolistic empires. This was also the time when holding companies were emerging: conglomerates with intra-group financial flows, decentralised decision-making on investment, growth and diversification, and minimal fiscal control by the government. Simultaneously, major entrepreneurs were involved in a perverse process of protecting their personal capital against a likely devaluation, while putting their companies in debt and speculating with pesos. Banks enabled these speculations and loans, which contributed to the depth of the crisis of 1982 and the post-1982 situation of 'poor enterprises and rich entrepreneurs' (Basave Kunhardt 2001; Concheiro Bórquez 1996). When, in 1982, the government announced that it could no longer pay its debt services, Mexico experienced a massive capital flight, followed by years of debt renegotiations, public rescue operations for 'poor' private enterprises, and economic restructuring.[2]

While, for most Mexicans and much of the economy, the 1980s were a lost decade, for Mexican economic groups it was the time of a miraculous centralisation. The nationalisation of the Mexican banking sector in 1982 resulted in former bankers creating new financial groups that invested in non-bank activities, including stock markets and insurance companies. The stock markets in fact turned into a parallel banking system, and a new group of giant firms emerged: *los bolsistas*[3] with, among others, Carlos Slim. Adjust-ments in their strategy of accumulation gave economic groups more than ever a financial capital character. The centralisation and 'financialisation' of these groups was supported by the creation of the FICORCA (Fideicomiso para la Cobertura de Riesgos Cambiarios) in 1983. This commission was to rescue large private enterprises from the effects of the debt crisis, many of whom otherwise would have defaulted. Through FICORCA $11.6 billion of public funding was transferred to the private sector. The bene-ficiaries of this state interference became strategic actors in mergers and centralisation through aggressive purchasing of shares of industrial com-panies. Yet these financial accumulation strategies came at the cost of productive investments, which decreased from 50 per cent in 1982 to 8 per cent in 1987. Within five years, these large companies had paid off their debts and were financially ready for more 'conglomerisation' and opening markets (Basave Kunhardt 2001: 75–81).

The presidency of Carlos Salinas de Gortari (1988–94) was a next crucial phase for the development of Mexican economic groups as he aimed to com-plete Mexico's restructuring process.[4] The economic reforms of Salinas expressed his special support for large enterprises, which Elvira Concheiro Bórquez (1996) has labelled *el gran acuerdo* (the great accord). Privatisation was a key element of economic restructuring policies, and it was central to the expansion of Mexican conglomerates under neoliberalism. While his prede-cessor had started to privatise some smaller and badly operating state com-panies, Salinas was responsible for the major transfers of larger and more productive parastatals to the economic sector. By transferring a considerable share of the state's economic power to large Mexican enterprises, the pri-vatisation process strengthened them as the new pioneers of growth and devel-opment (Table 6.4). Expansion in foreign and local markets, but especially the national bias in privatisations, allowed Mexican industrial companies to strengthen their position.[5]

The new private owners developed complex finance structures that allowed them to control these privatised companies with relatively limited invest-ment of their own. As companies were not sold on the open market but through a far from transparent state-controlled system of selection, the prices

Table 6.4 Mexico's GDP growth and inflation, 1980–2001 (percentages)

	1980–90 average	1991	1992	1993	1994	1995	1996	1997	1998	1999	2000	2001
GDP growth	1.9	4.2	3.5	1.9	4.5	–6.2	5.1	6.8	4.9	3.9	6.6	–0.2
Inflation	65.1	22.7	15.5	9.8	7.0	35.0	34.4	20.6	15.9	16.6	9.5	6.4

Source: OECD (2005).

and public revenues of these transfers remain unclear, but the total value is estimated around $20 billion. For prices (sometimes much) below their real value, 93 per cent of them were sold to large Mexican enterprises and economic groups (Guillen 1994: 32–3). Teléfonos de México (Telmex), for instance, was sold to the powerful Grupo Carso of Carlos Slim for $443 million, less than two-thirds of its estimated real value (*Proceso* 4 December 1995).[6] Through new financial strategies, such as strategies to obtain only the smallest number of shares necessary to dominate a firm, these 'new' important entrepreneurs took control over a large number of privatised companies. When banks were re-privatised from 1990 onwards, most of them were bought by economic groups that already owned stock markets. The result was further concentration of power into the hands of some 274 investors dominating the sector. Contrary to traditional family companies the new conglomerates of economic groups involved holdings, stock market quotation and international funding through credits, strategic alliances and joint ventures. With these new financial groups a powerful financial oligarchy, centralising the command over economic processes, came into being (Concheiro Bórquez 1996: 30–8, 98–100).

Of Salinas' efforts to improve Mexico's regional and global integration, the creation of the North American Free Trade Agreement (NAFTA) between Mexico, the United States and Canada was evidently the most effective result.[7] Next to free trade of goods, the agreement allows for free flows of services and capital. The liberalisation of flows from and towards the largest economy of the world (the United States) was especially for promising for Mexico. In addition, the agreement implied the regional locking in of Mexico's neoliberal economic policies. Together these implications of NAFTA added strongly to the attractiveness of investing in Mexico. This has been important for Mexican economic groups in that it eased, among other things, their access to strategic alliances with foreign capital, which has been a fundamental element of their competition in internal as well as external markets.

Mexican economic groups have become increasingly active in foreign investment, particularly in Central America, the United States and South America. Some of the success stories are Cemex in the Americas, Europe and Asia, Televisa in Latin America, Spain and the United States, and Telmex and América Móvil in Central and South American countries. This foreign expansion started in the late 1980s and was based on sophisticated financial operations, that is, complex equity and debt instruments including debt swaps. Apart from the crucial financial injection from the public sector mentioned above, the international stock market became a source of finance. 'They generally do not depend on their own internal financial resources to finance their expansion. Instead, they use sophisticated financial devices engineered by powerful transnational agents who have become a key link in the whole process of globalization' (Salas-Porras 1998: 151). By 1998, of the 60 largest non-financial Mexican economic groups over 60 per cent had become

Table 6.5 Sales of Mexico's ten largest private national groups or companies, 1992–2002 (US$ million)

1992		*1998*		*2002*	
Group	*Sales*	*Company (group)*	*Sales*	*Company*	*Sales*
1 Vitro	3,308.9	1 Telmex (Carso)	6,072.4	1 Telmex	10,944.0
2 Carso	2,554.4	2 Cemex (Cemex)	3,057.3	2 Cemex	6,543.0
3 Alfa	2,492.8	3 Visa (Visa-Femsa)	2,457.9	3 América Móvil	5,573.4
4 Cemex	2,213.2	4 Vitro (Vitro)	2,037.2	4 Grupo Alfa	5,170.0
5 Visa	2,100.1	5 Bimbo (Bimbo)	1,856.3	5 Fomento Económico	5,062.0
6 Desc	1,654.2	6 Modelo (Modelo)	1,552.3	6 Grupo Carso	5,031.3
7 Minera	937.4	7 Televisa (Televisa)	1,416.4	7 Telcel	4,224.2
8 Pulsar	921.6	8 Grupo Acerero (Grupo Acerero)	1,371.5	8 Grupo Bimbo	4,012.0
9 Peñoles	732.8	9 Alpek (Alfa)	1,314.5	9 Grupo Modelo	3,514.5
		10 AHMSA (Grupo Acerero)	1,212.4	10 Soriana	3,115.0

Sources: Garrido (1998); *Expansión* (12 August 1998); *América Economía* (4–31 July 2003).

global players by means of strategic alliances with foreign firms, and through expansion to stock markets. In short, the policies of economic restructuring allowed Mexico's large economic groups to rapidly expand (see Table 6.5) and be among the top of 'multilatinas' and of transnationals from developing countries. Inside Mexico, it was above all the process of privatisation that caused a centralisation of capital, resulting in a *nueva oligarquía* that was much more powerful and far more associated with transnational capital than the old oligarchy, as Morera Camacho (1998: 50) shows in his profound analysis of financial capital in Mexico under globalisation.

Economic groups and foreign capital

Foreign capital is another important explanatory factor for economic concentration in Latin America. In the 1980s and 1990s the position and policies of Latin American states towards the role of foreign direct investment (FDI) fundamentally changed. The neoliberal restructuring of the region's economies contributed considerably to the growing role of foreign investment. For this purpose a dismantling took place of almost all legal arrangements of the Keynesian era that regulated, limited and selectively subordinated the participation of FDI to state-led development. The processes of privatisation and market opening were the major attractions for foreign investors who, from the mid-1990s, became increasingly attracted to Latin America. By then, FDI and transnational companies were considered by almost all Latin American governments as desirable and indispensable for economic growth. As a result, at the end of the 1990s, Latin America received large amounts of FDI: in 1998 $74 billion and in 1999 $88 billion. But then the crisis of the beginning of the twenty-first century began. The contraction of net inward FDI in Latin America started in 2000 and continued until 2003, when FDI equalled only 42 per cent of inflows in 1999 (CEPAL 2004).

Foreign investment comes in many shapes and there have been several innovations in its relations with Latin American companies. The massive penetration of FDI in the 1990s involved new forms of channelling investment, linking foreign and local producers. Whereas most foreign investment had been previously done through branches of multinationals that were directly controlled by their headquarters, many multinationals started to operate in association or through joint ventures with local economic groups. These alliances appeared as a result of the privatisation process and/or on the basis of investment funds. There are also cases in which branches of transnational companies have become associated with other multinationals' branches, with new or old local economic groups, or with foreign banks, in order to maximise their share in privatisations. These strategies enable the advantages of the new economic policies towards foreign companies to be combined with the market knowledge and lobbying capacities of local economic groups and with the financial participation – often the acquisition of shares or bonds – by foreign banks (Kulfas *et al.* 2002).

Nevertheless, such combinations can be very temporary, as shown by the tendency of local economic groups to sell back their participation in foreign companies. Since the crisis started in 2000, new forms of foreign financial investment with limited risk in Latin America have become more popular. These new forms consist of involvement of limited duration (around five to ten years) and a combination of debt and equity features, such as the so-called mezzanine loans. An interesting feature of the rise of these and other forms of financial innovation in Latin America is that they are developed through the cooperation of foreign private financial companies (investment funds and banks) with (foreign) national and multilateral development institutions.

Most of the transnational companies newly entering the region in the 1990s by means of FDI based their corporate strategies on the penetration of the national and regional markets of manufacturing, services, infrastructure, primary materials and retailing. Major foreign companies active in the extraction of primary materials were Repsol España, Exxon, Broken Hill Proprietary and Royal Dutch Shell, and retailing companies included Royal Ahold, Groupe Casino Guichard, Wal-Mart and Carrefour. However, the major new area of interest for foreign investors was the service sector, particularly telecommunications, electricity supply and financial services. In telecom, companies such as Telefónica España, France Telecom and MCI WorldCom have become important players in Latin America; in electricity supply AES Corporation, Endesa España and Duke Energy are prominently present; and in the financial service sector Banco Bilbao Vizcaya Argentaria (BBVA) and Banco Santander Central Hispano (BSCH).

However, the contraction of FDI that started in 2000 demonstrated some of the problems for these transnational companies, which have been forced to reduce production costs as competition increased and markets slowed down. In fact, there has been a radical change in the global strategies of transnational companies: instead of competing for a company's size and for participation in many markets they have been bringing their costs and investments under strong control, and some multinationals have opted for relocating their installations to countries with lower labour costs, or to markets with higher growth potential. In addition, Latin America became a less attractive region for investment due to its political instability and/or economic crises. In Argentina, for instance, the economic crisis gave way to serious difficulties for Latin American conglomerates and transnational companies that had oriented their production towards MERCOSUR. Last, but not least, the severe fall of foreign investment was caused by the exhaustion of the privatisations, which during the 1990s had been the primary attraction of foreign investors.

The debt crisis and foreign capital in Chile

As a result of the debt crisis of the early 1980s, Chile experienced an economic and financial crisis that forced the military dictatorship to turn its economic policies towards temporary new state intervention, and to wait until 1985 before starting with a second phase of privatisation. The debt crisis threatened to result in an overall political crisis as it questioned the legitimacy of the most outspoken neoliberals in the Pinochet government. Furthermore, the formation of the Alianza Democrática (Democratic Alliance) in 1983 represented the first form of publicly outspoken opposition against the dictatorship in ten years. The crisis demonstrated that neoliberal restructuring had limited itself to a traditional scheme based on the principle that 'the political right privatises and the economic right buys'. However, the debt crisis was overcome through renewed state interventionism and through the entry of transnational companies attracted by a new wave of privatisation as a means to compensate for the lack of national and international credits due to the debt crisis. With a 13.4 per cent reduction of the gross domestic product (GDP) in 1982 as well as a 28.2 per cent unemployment rate, the dictatorship was forced to postpone a second stage of privatisation until 1985. After the debt crisis and the 1981–3 economic recession, Chile faced a collapse of its financial system and a total shut-off from the international financial markets. The national economic groups from the financial sector, with their banks nationalised or in bankruptcy, were in no condition to take advantage of the second stage of privatisation and were replaced by the transnational companies as buyers. The only economic groups that managed to survive were those that engaged in partnership with the foreign investors.

This state-interventionism towards economic groups and the redefinition of the property of the nationalised banks paved the path for a profound re-organisation of the country's financial capital and strengthened the concentration of economic power. The (re-)nationalisations were rooted in Chile's neoliberal principle of the socialisation of losses and the privatisation of profits. Based on this philosophy, the Chilean National Bank officially informed transnational banks in January 1983 that the Chilean government had decided to take over responsibility the total external debt of the nationalised banks, which had belonged to the economic groups in bankruptcy. At the same time, however, several transnational banks starting buying troubled Chilean banks. The Spanish Banco de Santander, for instance, bought 100 per cent of the Banco Español de Chile's assets, explicitly excluding expired assets and/or high-risk assets (expired portfolios), whose debts were assumed by the Chilean government. By doing this, the privatisation of financial institutions was subsidised in a similar way as in the 1974–82 period, when privatisation had been favouring the national economic groups. The state took responsibility for the debts of both industrial and financial enterprises as well as for the overall costs for the stabilisation of the Chilean economy. The Banco Español de Crédito (Banesto) took advantage of this mechanism as well, buying the Luksic group, the Banco O'Higgins and the Banco Talca in a combined operation. The operations of the Banco de Santander and Banesto show the conviction of the military dictatorship that the transnationalisation of the financial system was the only alternative to a total collapse of the entire Chilean financial system, which previously had been under control of the national economic groups. Another group of the financial institutions were sold and re-privatised under the idea of 'popular capitalism', in which shares were granted to the public with long-term credits without interest and credit for tributary investment. With the intention to de-concentrate property, maximum quotes of $5,000 were established and, in this setting, the sale of the Banco de Chile, the Banco de Santiago, the AFP Provida and Santa Maria – the main players in this sector – took place.

With the first signs of economic recovery in 1985, the government launched the second stage of privatisation. This second stage began with the sale of the companies in the so-called 'strange area' of the economy: companies that belonged to economic groups in which the government had intervened in prior years. Many of these companies were privatised for the second time, and international buyers took charge of these companies through the bidding on share packages prior to the verification of the economic reliability of the buyers. Because of the lack of national capital and credit most of these companies fell into the hands of transnational investors that were linked to the surviving Chilean economic groups, as happened with the Compañia de Petróleos de Chile (COPEC – oil) and the Compañia de Cervecerías Unidas (CCU – beer). The COPEC group was bought by the New Zealand company Carter Holt in association with the Angelini group, and in the case of the CCU a similar partnership was formed between the German consortium Paulaner and the Luksic group. Through this new form of association, transnational capital assumed power over Chilean conglomerates. Previously, transnational companies operating in Chile invested, by and large, through subsidiaries controlled by a head office, but during the second stage of privatisation transnational companies operated in association with or through joint ventures with the local entrepreneurial groups. New alliances were also established by means of investment funds in which both the local economic groups and the multinational companies participated. The intention was to combine the superior management of the foreign companies with the lobbying power in respect of government held by local economic groups and with the financial contribution of the international banks. However, the participation of the local economic groups often proved to be only temporary (or decreasing) as they often sold their shares to the associated transnational companies.

During the second stage, most of the largest public companies, representing a $1,200 million government income, were privatised. With the privatisation of these companies, four methods were applied simultaneously to sell share packages: popular capitalism, labour capitalism, institutional capitalism and traditional or patrimonial capitalism. The first involves the sale of share packages to the general public; the second to the employees of a company; the third consists of sales directed towards the pension funds, which not only benefited from the privatisation of the pension system but also from the subsidised acquisition of the large public companies; and the last method allows large-scale investors to obtain share packages in auction or by bidding on the Santiago stock exchange. The companies privatised by a combination of two or more of these methods were the Empresa Nacional de Electricidad (Endesa – electricity), the Compañia de Acero del Pacifico (CAP – steel), Linea Area Nacional (LAN – airlines), the Compañia Chilena de Electricidad Región Metropolitana (Chilectra R.M. – electricity), the Empresa Nacional de Teléfonos (ENTEL – telecom), Empresa Nacional de Petróleo (ENAP – oil) and the Sociedad Química y Minera de Chile (SOQUIMICH – chemistry and mining). The privatisation of companies such as CAP, Endesa and Enersis had significant effects on their respective economic sectors as a whole, as they were acquired by a company from the same sector, thereby monopolising important parts of the economic activities. Other companies such as the Compania de Teléfonos de Chile (CTC – telecom) fell directly in the hands of transnational companies. The magnitude of these major public companies that were privatised was enormous: halfway through the 1980s the largest six of these public companies had total assets of $4,239 million, which was more than twice the assets of the six largest private companies ($2,052 million). This comparison undermines the neoliberal argument regarding the inefficiency of the public companies, and shows the weakness of Chile's entrepreneurial class, which is more concerned with the flight of capital (of $5,500 million between 1976 and 1982) than it is interested in productive investment.

Many of the transnational companies that collectively entered the country during the second stage of privatisation – which led to the overall denationalisation and the globalisation of the Chilean economy – applied a strategy of investment diversification through the creation of groups of interrelated companies that were run centrally by investment corporations in the form of financial holdings (Carmona 2002). The so-called transnational economic groups (Rozas and Marín 1989) concentrated their activities in the financial service sector and in strategic industrial branches linked to the alimentary and forestry sectors. Transnational economic groups thereby played an important role in the recovery from the effects from the debt crisis, in the sense that they substituted the capital that was lacking because of the bankruptcy of the national financial groups, and consequently helped to restore and maintain the political stability of the neoliberal dictatorship. The government stimulated this participation of transnational companies by abandoning the fixed exchange rate. Of the 19 largest privatised companies, 13 came under the control of transnational economic groups, and in the case of 8 of these companies the transnationals' control in shares exceeded 50 per cent (Rozas and Marín 1989). In the CAP holding, for instance, the Swiss Schmidheiny group was a principal 18.7 per cent shareholder, sharing its power with an investment company made up out of the Menéndez group, the bankers Trust, the Angelini group and Carter Holt. Other examples include the Industria Azucarera Nacional Sociedad Anónima (IANSA – sugar) and in the pharmaceutical sector Laboratorio Chile, which came under control of the Continental Illinois Bank with a respective 38.8 and 12.1 per cent share.[8]

In the 1990s, during the first democratic government of Patricio Aylwin, the globalisation of the Chilean economy was consolidated in the sense that the hegemonic position of transnational groups was secured by companies such as Endesa España, Telefónica de España, BSCH and BBVA, the Australian Broken Hill Proprietary, the British Rio Tinto and Anglo American Plc, the electricity conglomerate AES Corporation, the Royal Dutch Shell, Telecom Italia (owners of ENTEL), ExxonMobil, Azucarera Ebro Agrícolas, Unilever, etc. (Table 6.6). When considering the 20 main conglomerates in Chile in the 1999–2000 period, 9 are in the hands of transnational conglomerates, 9 are local conglomerates, and 2 belong to the public sector. Out of these 20 largest conglomerates, 4 reached sales exceeding $1,000 million: Enersis (64 per cent owned by Endesa España) reached sales of $4,284 million; Endesa (38.4 per cent Endesa España) $1,622 million; Telefónica CTC de Chile (46 per cent Telefónica de España) $1,602 million; and Minera Escondida Ltda. (100 per cent Broken Hill Proprietary and Rio Tinto) achieved total sales of $1,174 million (Carmona 2002).

The absolute supremacy of the transnational conglomerates in the financial sector has been one of the main pillars of the globalisation of the Chilean economy. Today the transnational entities – controlling 17 of the 29 existing financial institutions – are in charge of 59 per cent of the financial system

Table 6.6 The 25 largest companies with foreign participation in Chile, 1999–2000 (US$ million)

Company	Sales	% foreign capital	Owner of the investment	Country of origin
Enersis	4,284	64	Endesa España	Spain
Endesa	1,622	38.4	Endesa España	Spain
Telefónica CTC	1,602	43.6	Telefónica de España	Spain
Minera Escondida	1,174	100	Broken Hill Propietary and Rio Tinto	Australia/ Great Britain
Gener	832	96.5	AES Corporation	USA
Shell Chile	768	100	Royal Dutch Shell Group	Great Britain/ Netherlands
ENTEL	710	54.2	Telecom Italia	Italy
Santa Isabel	695	74	Royal Ahold N.V.	Netherlands
Compañía Minera Doña Inés	680	100	Anglo American Pic (44%), Flaconbrigde Ltda. (44%) and Mitsoui Group (12%)	Netherlands/ Great Japan/ Japan
Esso Chile Petrolera Ltda.	651	100	ExxonMobil Corporation	USA
Nestlé Chile	650	100	Nestlé	Switzerland
Iansa	549	45	Azucarera Ebro Agrícolas	Spain
Chilectra	502	46.6	Endesa España	Spain
Lever Chile	425	100	Unilever	Great Britain
Chilquinta Energía	402	100	Sempra Energy	USA
Minera El Abra	401	51	Phelps Dogde Corporation	USA
General Motors Chile	370	100	General Motors	USA
Minera Disputada de Las Condes	368	100	ExxonMobil Corporation	USA
Coca Cola	344	44.4	The Coca-Cola Company	USA
Minera Candelaria	331	100	Phelps Dogde Corp. (80%) and Sumitomo Corp. (20%)	USA/ Great Britain
Soprole	311	50.5	New Zealand Dairy Board	New Zealand
Empresa Metropolitana de Electricidad	289	95.4	Pennsylvania Power and Light	USA
Johnson & Johnson Chile	260	100	Johnson & Johnson	USA
Minera Mantos Blancos	219	100	Anglo American Plc.	Great Britain
Methanex Chile	211	100	Methanex Corporation	Canada

Sources: ECLAC (2003); Carmona (2002).

in Chile. The BSCH has even become Chile's, Spain's and Latin America's largest financial group. Already in 1999 and 2000 foreign banks had raised their shares in Chile's financial sector from 14 to 45 per cent and the BSCH controlled as much as 28 per cent of this sector in 2002. In April of that same year the Central Bank of Chile sold the Banco de Santiago – into whose finances the government had intervened in 1983 and which belonged to the Cruzat-Larran group – for $680 million to the BSCH. Another Spanish bank, ranked second in the Chilean economy, is the BBVA, which with $350 million controls 55 per cent of the Banco Hipotecario de Fomento (BHIF), constituting the BBVA–BHIF, and in turn these control Chile's largest pension fund PROVIDA. On a less powerful level than their Spanish colleagues, there are other banks that operate in Chile's financial system, such as Citicorp, Bank of Boston, Bank of Nova Scotia – in control of 99 per cent of the Banco Sudamericano – the City Bank, ABN Amro Bank and the Deutsche Bank. They all operate in a captive financial market with an absolute freedom to establish interest rates. In 2001, for instance, the banking sector obtained profits of $874 million, 40 per cent higher than the year before and with a return rate of 18 per cent.

The peso crisis and foreign capital in Mexico

The development of Mexico's financial sector since the 1990s clearly demonstrates how liberalisation policies and crisis management can rapidly transform the composition of an economic sector. Between 1988 and 1994, initiatives for deregulation took the form of abolishing various previous restrictions. In particular, the end to the restriction on cross-sector participation gave way to the formation of vertically integrated financial groups including banks, insurance firms, stock markets and other financial entities. Several new regulations allowed banks to fully participate in the markets of state bonds, and to issue short-term bonds themselves (while some derivates were allowed too). Bonds of Mexican firms could also be issued abroad, and local markets were gradually opened to foreign investment (Guillén Romo 2002: 570). These liberalisation measures, together with the fixed parity of the peso, produced a strong increase in short-term transnational capital flows to Mexico as well as in financial speculation by Mexican capital. Subsequently, the NAFTA suggested opening Mexico's financial sector to US and Canadian investors and competition. In addition, the financial sector became gradually more open to foreign investment, finally (in 1998) resulting in a Foreign Investment Law allowing for majority foreign ownership.

Apart from these liberalisation policies, it was again a financial crisis and the state's response to it that contributed to the changing role of large Mexican companies in the financial sector. Like the impact of the debt crisis on the development of Mexican economic groups in the 1980s, the peso crisis of 1994–5 and its aftermath strongly affected Mexico's financial sector

and the economic role of Mexican conglomerates. The arrangements to
save Mexican banks from defaulting were made by the Fondo Bancario de
Protección al Ahorro (FOBAPROA), Fideicomiso de Cobertura de Riesgo
Cambiario (or Exchange Risk Coverage Fund, the Banking Fund for
Protection of Savings set up in 1990 – a follow-up of FICORCA), and later
on by the Institute of Protection of Bank Savings (IPAB, set up in 1999).
FOBAPROA was originally established as a fund for the sector of privatised Mexican banking, so that when in trouble banks would turn to this
fund rather than using public resources. However, FOBAPROA lacked the
resources necessary to solve the problems caused by the peso crisis, as devaluation and the strong rise of interest rates had left thousands of companies
unable to pay their debts. Therefore the government decided to help them
out. After the peso crisis, FOBAPROA bought unpaid loans from banks
(worth billions of dollars) while signing agreements that banks would be
receiving guarantee payments from 2005 onwards. Mexico's public sector
thus provided unprecedented support to private banks in the form of complex
structures of bonds to banks. The so-called *pagarés* FOBAPROA issued are
promissory notes (or IOUs) for the financial rehabilitation of the banks.
They were issued between 1995 and 1997 for a period of ten years, and
thus guaranteed interest paid by the government to the banks during these
years. Since 2000, IBAP has been issuing a new type of bond in an effort
to find funding to pay off the FOBAPROA bonds, but with limited success.[9]

This costly bank rescue illustrates the way Mexico's technocratic elite
governed the new relationship between the state and the envisioned motor
of neoliberal growth: large companies. Between 1995 and 1998 the public
resources spent on funding arrangements amounted to approximately $60
billion, which is five times the amount the government had previously earned
by the privatisation of these banks (Székely 1999: 14). This funding increased
from 5.5 per cent of GDP in 1995 to 14.3 per cent in 1999 (Guillén Romo
2002: 573), while the World Bank (2000: 59) even calculated that the fiscal
costs of the banking crisis is the equivalent 19.3 per cent of GDP. This
public money was also used to bail out investors who had been aware of
the weak supervision of the privatised financial sector, and who had will-
ingly taken great financial risks. Moreover there were major irregularities
involved in the process and both FOBAPROA and IPAB have been accused
of insufficient transparency, especially in the loans to the major banks. In
2003, for instance, Mexico's Federal Auditor ordered Banamex, Bancomer,
Bital and Banorte to return over $12 billion given to them as part of the
bank bailout. Even according to the president of the Mexican Association
of Banks (AMB), Héctor Rangel Domene, there have been frauds (*Expansión*
20 December 2001). In addition, the bonds were issued without the autho-
risation of the Mexican Congress.

Shortly after the rescue of Mexican banks, this sector transnationalised
due to numerous foreign takeovers. Both North American and European

banks started making large investments in Mexican banking, including Citicorp in 1994, BBVA in 1995, Bank of Montreal in 1996, and BSCH in 1997. Yet the hub of FDI in this sector came after 1999. In 2000, the large Spanish bank BSCH took control over the Mexican bank Serfin, and the Spanish BBVA came to control Bancomer. The next year, US transnational Citigroup purchased Banamex for $12.5 billion, which was the region's second largest acquisition ever, and the world's largest in financial services in that year. In 2002, the UK-based Hong Kong and Shanghai Banking Corporation (HSBC) paid $1.13 billion to acquire the fifth largest banking group of Mexico: Bital.

The foreign acquisitions of Mexican banks are a direct result of the peso crisis and subsequent state intervention. After the crisis Mexican banks were in great need of rapid capitalisation, yet the massive state support had the (perverse) result of attracting transnational capital to acquire these banks. The business of collecting these obligations turned into a major motivation for foreign banks to become interested in buying Mexican banks, and the *pagarés* make up a large share of banks' portfolios (ranging from 20 to 50 per cent in the largest five banks in March 2002). In addition, by providing many credits to a range of state agencies, 40 to 72 per cent of the portfolios of these banks consisted of funding to the government. Banks in Mexico have ended up depending strongly on a range of government-issued instruments, including those issued by FOBAPROA. In June 2000, 23 per cent of their total interests stemmed from bonds sold to FOBAPROA (World Bank 2000: 59–63).

The transnationalisation of the banking sector in Mexico is now (2006) almost complete since in 2002 foreign ownership was at 92 per cent (ECLAC 2003: 45). This transnationalisation of banking is related to that of other branches of the financial sector. For instance, it is also the dominant trend in the control over stock markets in Mexico, where the foreign share had risen to 54 per cent in March 2003. Together with large foreign acquisitions in telecommunications, this foreign investment in banking has turned the service sector into the largest recipient of FDI in Mexico: growing from 23 to 65 per cent in the period from 1994 to 2000. While the average share of financial services in FDI inflows in the period 1994–9 was 10 per cent, it rose to 32 per cent in 2000, and to 58 per cent in 2001, when Citicorp acquired Banamex (UNCTAD 2002: 66–7). Apart from Monterrey-based Banorte (part of the industrial-financial group related to Gruma-Maseca, the world's largest producers of corn products) all the large banks in Mexico – Banamex, BBVA Bancomer, Bital, Banco Santander Mexicano and Banca Serfin – had moved into the hands of external transnational companies, although control shows a tendency to shift among them.[10] One of the disadvantages of the banking sector being globalised is that it limits the information available in Mexico (on their Mexican operations); with their headquarters being located in the United States or Europe, they have fewer obligations to provide the Mexican government with extensive information.

Contrary to policy discourses, rescue arrangements and transnationalisation have barely contributed to a solid banking sector that serves the real economy better than before. The banks prefer to buy (relatively secure) state bonds instead of providing credits to companies, and therefore perform badly as providers of capital for productive activities. Credits that are made to the private sector are extremely concentrated in large enterprises whereas medium and small companies find that banks have little to offer them. Between December 1994 (when the peso crisis started) and June 2000, bank lending to the private sector fell 40 per cent, and direct commercial bank financing to the non-bank private sector also decreased 73 per cent (World Bank 2000: 59–64). In the end, the public sector's bailout for the banking sector was a transfer of public resources to the banks' previous Mexican owners and their current external owners. Since neither of these owners is making a particularly satisfactory contribution to the development of banking, the financial sector or the rest of Mexico's economy, the amount spent on rescue arrangements is perverse, especially when considering that this happened in a country where public resources are far from sufficient to cover even the most primary (economic and social) needs.

Implications of conglomerisation

As we have seen, in Chile and Mexico, as in the rest of Latin America, economic groups and conglomerates have grown bigger under neoliberal globalisation, due to both economic and political factors. Technocrats and large entrepreneurs established good relations and strong ties in their striving for economic restructuring. This not to say that their views coincided on all points: the first aimed for free, open markets, while the latter wanted privatisation and deregulated markets as well as arrangements that would protect their powerful position (Teichman 2001). The dependency of the technocratic elite on the support of 'big business' for economic restructuring, and the increasing personal interest of technocrats in becoming members of the entrepreneurial elite made them turn their pro-market agenda into a pro-conglomerates programme.

Economic concentration in conglomerates and economic groups went hand in hand with their transnationalisation. For the very large companies that have evolved in this process of conglomerisation, the adjectives 'local' and 'foreign' have lost much of their original connotation. Apart from some cultural and political importance, the regional origin of these companies hardly affects their operations: Latin American giants compete with transnational companies from other regions for local and increasingly global markets; 'multilatinas' increasingly use foreign capital in various complex arrangements, including forms of financial capital and foreign direct investment; and it has become a common feature that Latin American conglomerates buy companies in other regions, but even more so that parts of Latin American economic groups are sold to conglomerates originating from elsewhere.

Conglomerisation in Chile

A politically important characteristic of Chile's second stage of privatisation was the transformation of the neoliberal technocracy into an entrepreneurial class of emerging economic groups. In the democratic Chile of today, the majority of high-rank executives of local and transnational economic groups come from an entrepreneurial elite that started as (economic) government officials under the dictatorship. The so-called 'men of the privatisations' are made up out of former ministers, former sub-secretaries, former executives of the former public companies, former officers and generals of the armed forces, and, last but not least, relatives of the dictator himself, such as the entrepreneur Julio Ponce Lerou who is married to Verónica Pinochet and is in charge of the public company SOQUIMICH.

After the end of the Pinochet era many members of this elite organised themselves into the Independent Democratic Union (UDI) party, representing the civil heirs of the dictatorship. In their role as neoliberal ideologists, civil servants and entrepreneurs they arranged for the stabilisation and privatisation of the public companies, and many of them have become wealthy entrepreneurs. Ideologists saw neoliberalism and privatisation as fundamental to perpetuating their power, and to guaranteeing the irreversibility of a political system that unconditionally supports private enterprise and transnational capital. Others held positions at ministries, and designed and implemented the privatisation. A last category consists of actors from within the private sector who put pressure on the government to accelerate the privatisation process, and to create beneficial conditions for the 'new emerging owners' (Monckeberg 2001).

The transformation of members of the neoliberal technocracy and the military bureaucracy into entrepreneurs during the 1985–90 period was based on relations between former higher officials of the military dictatorship and local economic groups that were established in the first stage of privatisation. The Cruzat-Larrain group, for example, was the most influential economic group in the second half of the 1990s as it maintained a profound integration with the political rulers and with key government officials who in the first stage of privatisation had been presidents or managers of public companies. Yet there are many more examples of the close relations between the private and public sector: the Minister of Economy Pablo Barahona (1976–8), who became president of the major oil company COPEC; Sergio de Castro, minister of finance (1974–82), who became director at the Compañia Refinería de Azúcar Vina del Mar (CRAV) and would benefit from the privatisation of the state sugar refinery IANSA; and Alfonso Marquez de la Plata, a former agriculture and employment minister, who became the first president (1981–3) of the nationalised Banco de Santiago, when it served as source of finance for the Cruzat-Larrain group. Furthermore there are the cases of the former minister of employment and mining José Pinera, who had been chief of investigation at the National

Brokers Institution, and former finance minister Jorge Cauas, who also had been president at the Banco de Chile and of the AFP Provida until the debt crisis itself (Monckeberg 2001).

The increased political influence of the entrepreneurial class is often considered to be an effect of the political transition, resulting from the negotiations between the opposition and the military rulers after Pinochet's defeat in the 1988 plebiscite and the 1989 presidential elections (Portales 2000). The bargaining logics of the Reconciliation were based on the idea that the transition to democracy should be in accordance with the interests of the political right, the military and the entrepreneurial class. Evidently, both the military and the entrepreneurial class could provoke political tensions that would destabilise the new democracy as well as the neoliberal economy. Other scholars have stressed that the first Reconciliation government of President Particio Aylwin explicitly deserted the economic demands of the democratic opposition to the dictatorship (Fazio 1996). This desertion would be one of the factors that ended up strengthening the direct political influence of the entrepreneurial class and the organisations by which it is represented. For the Aylwin government, the decision to legitimise the economic politics of the dictatorship would have been taken with the conviction that this would make it possible to combine economic growth with greater social equity. As a result, the Reconciliation of Parties for Democracy applied a democratic strategy based on continuity (neoliberalism) and change (democratisation), which consolidated a democratic political system of civil administrators that would look after the retreat of the state from the economy; the deregulation of key markets; the functioning of the neoliberal model (finance, foreign credits and employment market); the self-adjustment of the economy as a natural mechanism of economic regulation; and the self-adjustment of a mechanism of internal savings based on massive tax-reductions for the economic sectors with the highest income. The democratic legitimisation of the Reconciliation granted neoliberalism the explicit recognition of the local conglomerates and transnationals as essential actors in the development process.

This neoliberal nature of Chile's democracy has been rejected by many citizens, in particular by the young. In 2004, 80 per cent of the electorate between 18 and 29 years old were not listed in the voters' registers (Valenzuela 2004). Consequently a debate has started about the depoliticisation of Chilean society as a result of the democratic consolidation of the neoliberal model. In Chile's two-party system the political parties give the impression that they are instruments for the access to the power of a political elite, which intends to reproduce itself independently from civil society (Moulian 1997). Another issue is the 'irrelevance' due to neoliberalisation of the political elite, such as Christian Democratic Party, which in the past has shared the principles of communitarian communism, or the Socialist Party, which in the name of democracy at the end of the Cold War adopted a pragmatic neoliberal ideology (Fernández Jilberto 2001). Depoliticisation, or the end of politics, which is expressed in civil apathy, is seen by many people as the result of the triumph of neoliberalism focused on the utopia of a society without a state. By replacing the focus on politics with a focus on market forces, such a neoliberalism is intended to create a self-regulated society, where social and political actors lack the ability to politicise the state. The key objective of such an entrepreneurial self-regulating society is economic growth – not the struggle against the inequalities generated from economic development itself.

Conglomerisation in Mexico

The close relations between the government and the top level of the corporate sector have had a strong impact on the outcome of Mexico's privatisation, regionalisation and other restructuring policies. Notwithstanding official claims that privatisation would enhance competition and efficiency, in the process several monopolistic groups were created that have also become large transnational players, especially in copper (Grupo México of the Larrea family) and in telecommunications (Slim's Telmex). Apart from a preferential status in privatisation procedures, close ties allowed businesses to put pressure on policy-making processes with respect to (foreign) competition (in the financial sector, telecommunications and airlines), as well as to effectively take over the conglomerates (the regulatory boards officially supposed to ensure fair competition).

Neoliberal restructuring has profoundly affected the operation and economic role of economic groups and conglomerates. Leading Mexican industrial groups used to dominate in products for mass consumption (particularly food and drink) and (intermediary) products for general use, including iron, cement and glass, and these sectors were the basis for the formation of economic groups. Until the 1990s, major Mexican industrial companies largely kept their traditional characteristics: they were owned as family property, they were leaders of the industries in Mexico, and they represented the heart of national industrial-financial groups. However, their leadership has grown significantly to the extent that these companies, and the conglomerates to which they belong, have started to compete for leadership with other large Latin American conglomerates. This internationalisation is the dominant tendency of the industrial activities of Mexican conglomerates, and has taken place at practically all levels: sales, finance, production, etc. Exports also increased strongly in food products. The manufacturing sector has witnessed profound change since the 1980s, with car (parts) production and chemistry increasing while traditional activities, such as textiles production, crumbled. The production from these conglomerates was also internationalised with the use of strategic associations and by co-investment with foreign firms (Garrido 1998).

The transnationalisation of Mexico's financial sector has caused major shifts in the funding for Mexican economic groups. The importance of bank credits has decreased whereas the importance of non-bank funding and foreign funds has increased. These groups balance their finance between capital providers, local and international banks and in other companies in the group (Garrido and Martínez Pérez 2004: 24–9). For instance, Grupo Carso owns Mexico's number one stock market, Inversora Bursátil (23 per cent of the sector), as well as the bank Inbursa. However, the selling of banks and stock markets to external transnationals implies that further expansion requires overcoming limitations in attracting financial resources. As they are losing participation in the banking and financial sector, while increasingly becoming regional multinationals, large companies search for possibilities in the foreign markets to finance their regional expansion. However, with foreign competition and/or a new financial crisis they may well become financially vulnerable, to the extent of losing control to foreign firms. In addition, with the sales and rentability of the conglomerates being weak, there is a high risk of bankruptcy, especially for a 'global winner' such as Cemex (Garrido 2002).[11]

While Mexico's entry into NAFTA is a major explanatory factor for the rise of Mexican economic groups, external transnational companies have also been growing strongly in Mexico, and the country's historical economic dependency on the United States has further increased.[12] After the Mexican recession following the peso crisis, the Mexican economy started to profit again from the booming US economy in the period between 1997 and 2000, and had average growth results of 5 per cent. The ongoing economic integration of Mexico in the United States has been most visible in manufacturing and services (food processing, chemicals, machinery, and electrical, electronic and transportation equipment), and is linked to the growth of export and *maquiladoras*. These predominantly (about 60 per cent) US-owned factories of assembly production for export have experienced spectacular growth rates since the middle of the 1980s, while Mexican exports tripled between 1991 and 1998 (Alba Vega 2000). Mexico has become an important export country for automotive products as a result of restructuring in the US automobile industry and NAFTA. In electronics, US, Asian and European transnational companies have expanded production in Mexico. In effect, almost two-thirds of Mexico's manufactured exports come from external companies (UNCTAD 2002: 173–6).

Despite some economic gains, overall liberalisation policies have not brought about sustained economic development in Mexico, as two economies have come into being: the economy of economic groups and the economy of the rest (Basave Kunhardt 2001: 97). In particular employment has become a sensitive issue: between 1988 and 2000 most sectors saw productivity growth, but they failed to generate employment since productivity was increased by dismissing staff (Ruiz Durán 2003: 8). The *maquiladora* sector is a substantial source of employment, but it cannot – by far – compensate for the loss of jobs in other sectors (e.g. agriculture) and the yearly need of about one million extra jobs for Mexico's growing younger population. Moreover, the *maquiladoras* are extremely dependent on the ups and downs of the US economy. In 2001, some 240,000 *maquiladora* jobs were lost, representing 18 per cent of this sector's employment (*Mexico & NAFTA Report* 16 April 2002).

As Mexico is increasingly struggling against foreign competition, especially from China, NAFTA-based growth may turn out to be a short-term success at best. In the last few years, there has been a radical change in the global strategies of transnational companies, and several transnationals have opted for relocating (part of) their installations to countries with lower labour costs, or to markets with higher growth potential. Of the *maquilas* closed in 2002, 60 per cent were relocated to Asia and 40 per cent to Central America. *Maquiladoras* do not provide a solution to the problems of the domestic economy, which represents about 70 per cent of total economic activity: they are highly dependent on imports, and are hardly integrated into the national economy, as less than 2 per cent of the assembled parts come from local providers (Alba Vega 2000).

Together, these trends have contributed to economic polarisation, which has profound social implications. Due to a policy focus on the macro level, the micro level has been harmed. A small group of large companies were encouraged by the state, but the majority of small and medium-sized firms have stayed behind. Mexico is thus facing multiple polarisation: economically, socially and also politically (Hogenboom 2004a). Its proximity and free trade with the world's largest national economy have allowed Mexico to have more extensive and prompt economic results of its liberalisation policies, but the pro-conglomerates bias of the governing technocratic team intensified the divide between a (small) modernised part of the economy and the large marginalised and underdeveloped segments. This economic polarisation is reflected in social relations, contributing to social inequality and major flows of migrant workers. While progress has been made in some important areas such as life expectancy, child mortality and extreme poverty, the number of Mexicans who are poor has grown and income inequality has increased. Important factors explaining these negative social trends are the dramatic fall of both real wages and minimum wages, and the new economic model's failure to create sufficient new jobs for the growing population.

Since the 1990s Mexico's political system has rapidly been democratising, ending the long state-party regime of the PRI. In 1997, the PRI has lost its majority in the chamber of deputies and in 2000 Vicente Fox, the candidate of the National Action Party (PAN), became president. Nonetheless the neoliberal model remains dominant even though the direction of Mexico's political transition is not very clear. Contrary to high hopes (especially within the PAN) that more businessmen in the government would improve its quality and effectiveness, the private sector background of President Fox (Coca-Cola Mexico) and many members of his cabinet has proved to be a hindrance for governance as their professional experience has not compensated for their lack of political experience. As in Chile, there is a strong dissatisfaction with politics in Mexico, and despite recent democratisation many people have lost their interest in politics, as was clearly shown by the unparalleled 58 per cent abstention during the mid-term elections of July 2003.

Conclusion

Key to the similarities in the processes of economic concentration and transnationalisation of conglomerates and economic groups in Chile and in Mexico (as in most other Latin American countries), is the nature of the support of the state. Contrary to policy discourses on the benefits of free markets and competition, state policies were directed at helping major private companies to take over the role of state companies as the motor for economic growth. The close relations between technocrats and important entrepreneurs 'personalised' the support of the public sector for big business.

As a result of these economic policies and the political elite relations of the neoliberal era, conglomerates and economic groups have turned into a new oligarchy in Chile and Mexico. As with the old Latin American oligarchies, the economic elite has strong bonds with the political elite while the political elite also strongly identifies with the economic elite, and its interests, notwithstanding the recent processes of democratisation. This is evidently a cause for tensions between state and society; especially as it has turned out that the assets and capital of both 'foreign' and 'local' conglomerates are globalised to the extent that the conglomerates have little interest in the development of the domestic economy. This may partly explain why recent economic growth has been more volatile, and has failed to create sufficient jobs and secure income in Latin America.

The political translation of a pro-market model into pro-conglomerates policies has been strongly criticised. Neoliberal policies did not bring an end to state interventionism; instead, the structural intervention *à la* Keynes has been replaced by non-transparent incidental (but massive) state intervention directed in support of an economic class that has little affinity with the domestic economy and its workers. Therefore, in Latin America the future of the remaining large state companies is an issue of fierce debate between proponents and opponents of privatisation. Those favouring a complete abolition of state-owned enterprises point at the increase of investment and growth that followed previous privatisation, and view recent developments as a threat to future economic integration and growth. Those who are more negative or sceptical stress the limited durability and doubtful socioeconomic results of the growth of domestic production and foreign investment based on privatisation and an open market. And, contrary to the heyday of neoliberal restructuring, when privatisation mostly met applause in governmental circles, nowadays there are both proponents and opponents of deepened restructuring present in Latin American governments.

Notes

1 This chapter is partly based on an analysis of the origin and formation of economic groups in neoliberal Chile (Fernández Jilberto 2004) and a study on economic concentration and conglomerates in Mexico (Hogenboom 2004b), in combination with some insights on general Latin American tendencies (Fernández Jilberto and Hogenboom 2004).

2 The primary causes for the crisis were Mexico's (public and private sector) lending behaviour in the 1970s and worldwide rising interest rates and falling oil prices during the early 1980s.

3 The term *bolsista* comes from *bolsa*: stock market.

4 Policies of privatisation and the liberalisation of trade, services and capital were widened and deepened, while fossil fuels and agriculture were no longer excluded. Salinas replaced de la Madrid's Pact of Economic Solidarity between the state, the business and agricultural sectors and labour by the Pact for Stability and Economic Growth, which aimed at growth through private investment, export of manufactured goods, and public investment in infrastructure. Legislative reforms served to strengthen financial intermediaries: commercial banking was re-privatised in 1990; foreign investment in banks, production and portfolio was liberalised; a new act encouraged the integration of financial groups, predominantly by allowing the establishment of financial holding companies; and Salinas' modernisation programme included a repeal of regulations restricting private investment, and the abolition of most price controls.

5 Their importance vis-à-vis foreign companies producing in Mexico increased notably between 1987 and 1992: in 1987, 73 per cent of the top 500 firms in Mexico were Mexican private companies, whereas in 1992 they made up 84 per cent of the list while simultaneously the share of transnationals dropped from 18 to 14 per cent (the rest consisted of state-owned enterprises). However, among the group of 60 largest non-financial companies in 1994 in Mexico, 19 (that is 32 per cent) are foreign (Garrido 1998: 403–6).

6 Another example of irregularities surrounding privatisation is the case of Carlos Cabal Peniche, who acquired control over the banks Unión and Cremi in 1991 and 1992 with hardly any capital of his own. Unión was bought for $240 million by a group headed by Cabal, however no members of the group had any experience in the banking sector. Contrary to federal banking regulations, major credits were obtained from related companies that were owned by shareholders of the bank: a dozen individuals led by Cabal took credits from this same bank. Although Cabal was accused of fraud involving $700 million and fled the country in 1994, he nevertheless tried to have the state compensate for his 'losses' in the peso crisis (*La Jornada* 26 May 2004).

7 Mexico also extended its international relations via new bilateral and regional trade agreements with Latin American countries (e.g. with Chile, Brazil, MERCOSUR and Central America), and membership of the Organisation for Economic Cooperation and Development (OECD) and the Asia Pacific Economic Cooperation (APEC).

8 The participation of the transnational companies in the privatisation that started in 1985 was based on a combination of subsidiaries already present in the Chilean economy and multinationals that for the first time entered in what was considered an emerging market. An example of this last concept would be the New Zealand consortium of Fletcher Challenger, which, under the name of Tasman Forestry Ltd, bought the companies Papeles (paper) and Bosques Bio Bio S.A. (forestry) from the Matte group. There is also the case of the Swiss transnational Nestlé, which acquired important companies from the alimentary sector, such as the Hacienda Rucamanqui (Chile's second largest agricultural and cattle extension), the Nacimiento de Papeles Sudamericana S.A. (paper), Forestal Colcura S.A. (forestry), the alimentary company PRODAL, and associations in different activities in the energy and mining sector with Shell and British American Tobacco.

9 Another recent creation in the transfer of obligations of IPAB to financial enterprises. Such companies buy IPAB bonds at a highly discounted rate (23 per cent of its original price) as a way of compensating for the high risk that these

bonds will not be recovered. These financial companies are usually part of large financial groups, mostly of foreign origin though some are Mexican (*Expansión* 21 August 2002).

10 In 2002, Citigroup paid $1,240 million to the Dutch transnational Aegon for 48 per cent of the insurance company Afore Banamex/Seguros Banamex. That same year BSCH started to merge its Mexican subsidiaries Serfin and Banco Santander Mexicano into a giant bank with $25 billion in assets, and the US financial transnational Bank of America bought 25 per cent of the Grupo Financiero Santander Serfin, paying $1.6 billion. In 2004, BBVA purchased another 38 per cent of Bancomer's shares for over $4 billion.

11 The stock market is only a limited source of finance to Mexican economic groups. In Mexico, about 70 per cent of the ownership of companies is with their bosses, and only 30 per cent is in the stock market. There are some companies that investors favour, including several local giants (e.g. Telmex and Cemex), and some subsidiaries of transnationals (e.g. Walmex and América Móvil). A number of Mexican conglomerates, including Cydsa (synthetic fibres) and Hylsa (subsidiary of steel company Hylsamex), have been forced to go through complicated negotiations on debt restructuring to arrange for extensions on the payments of millions of dollars in bonds (*Latin Trade* November 2003).

12 Between 1992 and 1999, the volume of trade between the two neighbours more than doubled, while between 1993 and 2002 the share of Mexican exports going to the United States increased from 83 per cent to 91 per cent (*Latin American Weekly Report* WR-2–40).

Bibliography

Alba Vega, Carlos (2000) 'México después del TLCAN. El impacto económico y sus consecuencias políticas y sociales', in Barbara Klauke (coord.), *México y sus perspectivas para el siglo XXI*, Münster: Westfälische-Wilhelms-Universität Münster.

Basave Kunhardt, Jorge (2001) *Un siglo de grupos empresariales en México*, México, DF: UNAM-IIE and Miguel Ángel Porrúa.

Carmona, Ernesto (2002) *Los Dueños de Chile*, Santiago: Ediciones La Huella.

—— (1999) *Chile Desclasificado*, Santiago: Carmona Ediciones.

CEPAL (1990) *Transformación Productiva con Equidad*, Santiago: CEPAL.

—— (1994) *El Regionalismo Abierto in América Latina y el Caribe. La integración económica al servicio de la transformación productiva con equidad*, Santiago: CEPAL.

—— (2001) *La Inversión Extranjera en América Latina y el Caribe*, Santiago: CEPAL/ONU.

—— (2004) *La Inversión Extranjera in América Latina y el Caribe 2003*, Santiago: CEPAL.

Concheiro Bórquez (1996) *El gran acuerdo. Gobierno y empresarios en la modernización salinista*, México, DF: Ediciones Era.

Dhase, Fernando (1979) *Mapa de la Extrema Riqueza*, Santiago: Editorial Aconcagua.

—— (1983) *El Poder de los Grandes Grupos Económicos Nacionales*, Santiago: FLACSO, documento No. 18.

ECLAC (2003) *Foreign Investment in Latin America and the Caribbean, 2002*, Santiago: ECLAC.

El Mercado de Valores (2002) 'Mexican statistics on micro, small, medium and large enterprises', 4 (July/August): 40–1.

Fazio, Hugo (1996) *El Programa Abandonado. Balance Económico Social del Gobierno de Aylwin*, Santiago: Arcis/Lom/Cenda.

—— (2000) *La transnacionalización de la economía chilena. Mapa de la Extrema Riqueza al año 2000*, Santiago: Lom.

Fernández Jilberto, Alex (2001) 'The neoliberal transformation of Chilean populism: the case of the Socialist Party', in Jolle Demmers, Alex E. Fernández Jilberto and Barbara Hogenboom (eds), *Miraculous Metamorphoses. The Neoliberalization of Latin American Populism*, London: Zed Books.

—— (2004) 'The origin and formation of economic groups in neoliberal Chile', *Journal of Developing Studies*, 20 (3–4), Special Issue: 'Latin American Conglomerates and Economic Groups under Globalization', guest editors: Alex E. Fernández Jilberto and Barbara Hogenboom: 189–206.

Fernández Jilberto, Alex E. and Barbara Hogenboom (1997) 'The political economy of open regionalism in Latin America', special issue of the *International Journal of Political Economy*, 26 (4).

—— (2004) 'Conglomerates and economic groups in neoliberal Latin America', *Journal of Developing Studies*, 20 (3–4), Special Issue: 'Latin American Conglomerates and Economic Groups under Globalization', guest editors: Alex E. Fernández Jilberto and Barbara Hogenboom: 149–71.

Fernández Jilberto, Alex E. and Marieke Riethof (eds) (2002) *Labour Relations in Development*, London: Routledge.

Garrido, Celso (1998) 'El liderazgo de las grandes empresas industriales mexicanas', in Wilson Peres (ed.), *Grandes empresas y grupos industriales latinoamericanos*, México, DF and Madrid: Siglo Veintiuno.

—— (2002) 'Economia, financiamiento y empresas en México. Evolución desde 1995, tendencias y desafios', trabajo presentado en el seminario internacional 'Coyuntura microeconómica en América Latina', 29–30 de agosto en CEPAL (Santiago).

Garrido, Celso and Juan Froilán Martínez Pérez (2004) 'El sistema financiero mexicano. Evolución reciente y perspectivas', *El Cotidiano*, 123: 19–29.

Guillen, Arturo (1994) 'El proceso de privatización en México', *Mondes en Developpement*, 22 (87): 29–39.

Guillén Romo, Hector (2002) 'Evolución del régimen macrofinanciero mexicano', *Comercio exterior*, 52 (7): 564–74.

Hogenboom, Barbara (2004a) 'Governing Mexico's market economy', in Jolle Demmers, Alex E. Fernández Jilberto and Barbara Hogenboom (eds), *Good Governance in the Era of Neoliberal Globalization – Conflict and Depolitization in Latin America, Eastern Europe, Asia and Africa*, London: Routledge.

—— (2004b) 'Economic concentration and conglomerates in Mexico', *Journal of Developing Studies*, 20 (3–4), Special Issue: 'Latin American Conglomerates and Economic Groups under Globalization', guest editors: Alex E. Fernández Jilberto and Barbara Hogenboom: 207–25.

Instituto Nacional de Estadísticas (1986) *Estadísticas Nacionales*, Santiago: INE.

Kulfas, M., F. Porta and A. Ramos (2002) *Inversiones Extranjeras y Empresas Transnacionales in la Economía Argentinas*, Buenos Aires: CEPAL.

Monckeberg, Maria, O. (2001) *El Saqueo de los Grupos Económicos al Estado Chileno*, Santiago: Ediciones B.

Morera Camacho, Carlos (1998) *El capital financiero en México y la globalización. Límites y contradicciones*, México, DF: Ediciones Era.

Moulian, Tomas (1997) *Chile Actual. Anatomía de un mito*, Santiago: Arcis/Lom.

OECD (2005) *OECD Economic Outlook No. 77*, Paris: Organization for Economic Co-operation and Development.

Portales, Felipe (2000) *Chile: Una Democracia Tutelada*, Santiago: Editorial Sudamericana.

Rozas, Patricio and Gustavo Marin (1989) *1988: El 'Mapa de la extrema riqueza' 10 anos despues*, Santiago: Centro de Estudios Sociales (CESOC) and PRIES-Cono Sur.

Ruiz Durán, Clemente (2003) 'The redimensioning of sector development', *El Mercado de Valores*, 1 (January/February): 3–10.

Salas-Porras, Alejandra (1998) 'The strategies pursued by Mexican firms in their efforts to become global players', *CEPAL Review*, 65 (August): 133–53.

Sanfuentes, Andres (1984) 'Los Grupos Económicos: Control y Políticas', *Colección de Estudios CIEPLAN*, 15: 131–70.

Székely, Gabriel (1999) 'Presentación' in Gabriel Székely (coord.), *FOBAPROA e IPAB: El acuerdo que no debío ser*, México, DF: Oceano

Teichman, Judith A. (2001) *The Politics of Freeing Markets in Latin America: Chile, Argentina, and Mexico*, Chapel Hill, NC: The University of North Carolina Press.

UNCTAD (2002) *World Investment Report 2002. Transnational Corporations and Export Competitiveness*, New York: United Nations.

—— (2003) *Trade and Development Report 2003*, New York: United Nations.

Valenzuela, Esteban, (2004) 'La democracia envejecida', *Revista Mensaje*, Santiago de Chile, 528: 39–41.

World Bank (2000) *Mexico. A Comprehensive Development Agenda for the New Era* (edited by Marcel M. Giugale, Olivier Lafourcade and Vinh H. Nguyen), Washington, DC: World Bank.

7 Economic groups and the rise and collapse of neoliberalism in Argentina

Miguel Teubal

The crisis that Argentina has recently been facing is one of the first major economic crises of the new millennium, and has been dubbed a crisis of neoliberalism (Giarracca and Teubal 2004). This crisis reflects the collapse of the neoliberal model drastically implemented in the 1990s. In many ways this sets aside the Argentine case from the Brazilian, Asian or Russian crises of the decade, all of which occurred in the wake of state-led 'developmentalist' and/or 'export-oriented' economic strategies.

The beginning of a new era in the political economy of Argentina was marked by two important events: the military coup of 1976 and the 'economic coup' of 1989. Both were instrumental in developing a new 'regime of accumulation' (RA) substantially different from that prevailing under the import substitution industrialisation (ISI) regimes of previous decades. These events were also important preludes to the Convertibility Plan and structural adjustments of the 1990s that fully consolidated the era of neoliberalism in Argentina.

Undoubtedly the military coup of 1976 was a major landmark as in the wake of the establishment of an extreme repressive 'bureaucratic authoritarian state' (O'Donnell 1979) a series of measures and institutions were adopted, particularly with respect to labour, financial and capital markets. It was during the military dictatorship (1976–83) that wage increases were frozen, in particular in the public sector, and a series of measures favouring financial interests and activities, and large conglomerates and economic groups were applied. It was in this period that foreign indebtedness increased substantially becoming one of the main factors that was to influence the policies and strategies of succeeding governments. The 'economic coup' of 1989 was motorised by the economic establishment when it induced wholesale capital flight, leading to an accelerating devaluation and hence the hyperinflationary spurts of the 1989–91 period. The so-called Convertibility Plan of 1991 and the implementation of a severe structural adjustment programme (SAP) by the Menem administration in the 1990s can be considered responses to this coup. Both events led to the consolidation of a new economic model in Argentine society that was to became an important showcase for international financial interests thereafter (Teubal 2000/1, 2001; Giarracca and Teubal 2004).

Various aspects of the policies adopted in the 1990s by the Argentine government as well as some of their consequences have been analysed elsewhere. Succinctly, some of the main aspects of the SAP included: an extreme privatisation programme; deregulations of all kinds, in particular with regard to the 'flexibilisation' of labour markets; and a new 'opening' to the world economy, especially concerning financial interests. As pointed out in this chapter the SAP was preceded in the 1970s and 1980s by policies and mechanisms enhancing international and local financial interests next to reducing wages and worsening income distribution, all of which were associated in one way or another with the increased foreign debt contracted mainly by the elite economic establishment and which thereafter was transferred to the state and society at large.

What has not always been sufficiently discussed is how since the mid-1970s and in particular in the 1990s this SAP and associated measures related to increased foreign indebtedness responded in many ways to elite economic interests, which has led to the consolidation of an economic and financial establishment based on a power block of large companies and the so-called *grupos económicos*, some of which are transnational (Azpiazu *et al.* 1989).[1] Thus, during the present crisis and especially after the default of part of the foreign debt in late 2001 and devaluation in early 2002, with the economy reaching rock-bottom levels, the role of economic groups was clearly brought to light. The anatomy of Argentine society was suddenly reflected in pressures exerted on the government by large companies and/or economic groups for the purpose of redressing their profitability, affected by post-devaluation measures, the run on the banks, capital flight, and the crisis itself (cf. Azpiazu and Schorr 2003).

In Argentina, large economic groups have traditionally had an important say in the development of the economy, but since the mid-1970s when a new RA began to be set in place they acquired an increased and renewed significance leading to a dominance they had not had up to then. Under the ISI strategies of the 1940s, 1950s and 1960s, their importance was circumscribed to some large banks, exporters and industries, for example, in the automobile, steel, petrochemical, and food and textile industries, apart from the traditional petroleum and cereal export conglomerates. Nevertheless, they operated in an environment characterised by the relative predominance of small and medium-sized business. Needless to say under ISI some of the largest companies were public services or producers of what were considered to be strategic goods (petroleum, steel or coal), all of which were public companies or entities that were state operated. In this context large conglomerates or economic groups did not have the hegemony they were to acquire later on under neoliberalism. Thus, since the mid-1970s large companies – forming economic groups and/or conglomerates – acquired an increased significance, but they sustained greater importance still in the 1990s when the SAP was implemented.

In the 1950s and 1960s the role of a national bourgeoisie was debated in Argentina, a debate that has recently been replicated. According to Basualdo, a national bourgeoisie refers to 'a fraction of the bourgeoisie associated with the domestic market . . . based on the consumption of mostly basic wage goods'. This category applies mainly to 'large oligopolistic industrial firms that . . . established agreements with salaried workers in an alliance that used to be expressed by *Peronism* in the period of import substitution industrialisation' (Basualdo 2004: 14–15). Galetti (2004) explains further:

> [W]hat was called a *national bourgeoisie* was mainly an industrial bourgeoisie that was developed in the era of ISI in particular during the Second World War. The government of General Peron was based on this sector developing a state that distributed income with greater equity and that implemented a series of social benefits. While at the time about 50 per cent of GDP was wage income at present this share represents no more than 20 per cent of GDP.

According to this author a paradigmatic expression of the national bourgeoisie was José Ber Gelbard, the Minister of the Economy of the Peronist government of the early 1970s, who emphasised the domestic market, a 'social pact' with the workers and increased trade with Cuba and the socialist block (Galetti 2004; cf. Teubal 2000/1: 484–5). It was this national bourgeoisie that in essence had conflicting interests vis-à-vis the traditional agro exporters, large landowners, as well as with foreign capital, that began investing in the automobile industry, petrochemicals and the like in the early 1960s. Needless to say the hegemony acquired by these large *grupos económicos* was parallel to the trend towards the disappearance of the national bourgeoisie.

On the whole policies having a special significance for the new elite establishment of large companies had to do with three major developments. First there is the foreign debt that increased significantly under the military dictatorship, and continued doing so thereafter, in particular in the 1990s after the Argentine government adhered to the Brady Plan. As a matter of fact it can be considered that the foreign debt and financial and speculative activities in general became the main activities characterising the new RA set in place since the mid-1970s. Second, the privatisation programme, deregulatory measures and an 'opening' to the world economy in the 1990s substantially favoured these new and old conglomerates, being thoroughly underpinned by state policies. Third, the overall dynamics of the Argentine economy in the 1990s led to a substantial concentration and centralisation of capital and to the consolidation of large firms excluding small and medium-sized businesses. While some measures favouring large companies and economic groups were begun in the 1970s under the military dictatorship it was notably under the Menem administrations of the 1990s that they consolidated their economic and political power. This process continued thereafter under the De la Rúa and succeeding administrations.

As Minsburg states, 'foreign indebtedness and (the associated) capital flight was the culmination of a long process for the purpose of strengthening the alliance between domestic economic groups, the (agrarian) oligarchy and transnational capital' (Minsburg 1987: 105). Policy measures adopted during the military dictatorship (1976–83), known as the *proceso*, were designed to favour financial and speculative activities associated in many ways with the foreign debt contracted in this period. The financial reforms of June 1977 'flexibilising' financial operations were instrumental to this effect. A new era of foreign indebtedness began and foreign debt increased from about $7 billion in 1976 to over $46 billion in 1983 at the conclusion of the dictatorship. The bulk of this indebtedness was contracted between 1978 and 1982. Foreign indebtedness also acquired a renewed significance in the 1990s under the fully fledged SAP of the Menem administration increasing from about $61.3 billion in 1991 to $145.3 billion in 1999. In these latter years foreign debt was combined with an important privatisation programme and became complementary to an intense process of concentration and centralisation of capital. These factors led to the emergence of new social actors among the economic establishment: local and foreign banks, new privatised firms, and concentrated conglomerates in industry and the services, all forming part of a new structure of the Argentine society.

In the era of ISI, large companies coexisted side by side with medium and small business, which represented an important part of the economy. However, under the new RA that began in the mid-1970s and in particular during the 1990s this situation changed substantially. Large companies, including the elite large companies and conglomerates, increased their share of the market in almost every sector of the economy, marginalising small and medium-sized business. In previous periods there was a conflict as between the two main business syndicates: the Unión Industrial Argentina (UIA), supported by the Sociedad Rural Argentina (SRA) and other organisations representing highly concentrated business; and the Confederación General Económica (CGE), supported by the Federación Agraria Argentina (FAA) and assorted cooperative organisations, representing a wide range of small and medium-sized firms, many from the interior of the country. Under the new RA the UIA gained substantial power, as did some new syndicates representing new participants of the business establishment, while the CGE and its allies lost out almost completely.[2]

The policies of the dictatorship and Alfonsín

In contrast with the country's current situation, in the early 1970s Argentina was one of the highest income per capita and industrialised countries of Latin America. It also had one of the more advanced scientific-technologic infrastructures; for example, Argentina's electronics industry at the time was said to be on the par with that of South Korea. In this context a more export-led industrialisation strategy was in the making, something that appeared to be similar to what was occurring with the newly industrialised countries (NICs) of Asia. As a matter of fact at the time it was considered that such a strategy could be much more employment generating than the traditional strategies based on the export of primary goods – agriculture and livestock commodities and petroleum. Nevertheless, this strategy was soon set aside. From the mid-1970s an important role was assigned to foreign indebtedness and to local and international financial interests, a strategy that increasingly diverged from the industrial exports strategy concocted in the early years of the decade. Why was this strategy adopted? Apparently a growth policy that implied increasing industrialisation would have favoured a national bourgeoisie and its alliance with labour, something that could have been confrontational with the traditional alliance of agrarian oligarchic interests with foreign capital (Minsburg 1987; Teubal 1983b).

A core aspect of the economic policies adopted during the military dictatorship was foreign indebtedness. Ninety per cent of this new indebtedness corresponded to finance activities, that is, operations not associated with imports or exports of commodities or capital goods. Thus, from the end of 1976 to the end of 1983 total foreign debt increased by almost $36 billion. While interest on foreign debt amounted to $515 million in 1976 it increased substantially to $5.4 billion in 1983. The mass of accumulated interest in this period amounted to $19 billion, most of which was paid while only a minor proportion was rolled over. 'This drastic increase in indebtedness had a clearly defined purpose ... to integrate Argentine finances into international financial markets, freeing exchange rates and establishing the full mobility of capital' (Minsburg 1987: 101).

There were several mechanisms used to enhance foreign indebtedness in this period. Government enterprises in certain public utilities were induced to finance themselves via foreign indebtedness; this indebtedness was considered more 'genuine' because, as was claimed, it tended to be less inflationary. In fact, during the crisis of 1981, state companies were not permitted to make use of the funds provided by their indebtedness for their own operational needs, or to carry out required investments. These funds were appropriated by central government and put to other speculative uses by transferring them to foreign exchange markets. In essence, this mechanism was used to provide the government with the necessary foreign exchange to finance capital flight, something that occurred notably during the crisis of 1981–2. Needless to say, funds that could have been used to increase investments in public services thus increasing their efficiency were lost. This aspect of public policy was also related to the political need to show that public companies were 'inefficient' and the main cause for fiscal deficits. Thus, the necessary scenario for the massive privatisation of the public services was deliberately created.

In this period most of private foreign indebtedness was endorsed or guaranteed by government, permitting local companies to have access to international loans at lower interest rates. This was one of the reasons for the substantial indebtedness in this period. The government eventually paid many of the private loans that were not honoured. However, a fully fledged investigation of this situation was never carried out. While many foreign loans were cancelled with funds provided by the national treasury, 'neither the Banco de la Nación Argentina nor the Banco Nacional de Desarrollo, as entities that had taken charge of these loans . . . initiated investigations tending to recuperate the sums paid by the state' (Cafiero and Llorens 2002: 134). Key measures tending to make foreign indebtedness profitable were related to the Financial Reforms of 1977 and 1979 when controls on finance activities and mobility of capital were eliminated, full liberalisation of financial transactions took place, and an absolute guarantee of the state for these operations was established. Furthermore the Central Bank established a mechanism whereby interest was to be paid on the funds immobilised by the banks by law, in accordance with declarations made by the banks, a factor that was thereafter subject to illegal claims.

In 1978 government established a pre-determined exchange rate system, a 'crawling peg' whose increase tended to be lower than the domestic rate of inflation, thus becoming a mechanism that contributed to a trend towards balance of payments deficits. Through this mechanism foreign debts were guaranteed: while government made sure that local interest rates in pesos transferred into dollars were higher than international interest rates, financiers were induced to invest in the local financial money markets. Exchange rates were managed so as to guarantee the profitability of these loans on the basis of the maintenance of differences in domestic and international interest rates. This guaranteed substantial profits for local and international money markets. Much of this foreign debt was fictional because funds provided were based on money deposited in international banks abroad by Argentinians – a consequence of previous capital flight. These funds also provided collateral to foreign banks for local indebtedness. These aspects of foreign indebtedness are what made Argentina's foreign debt essentially illegitimate (Basualdo 2001: 43).

This highly speculative scheme, however, was soon to end in disaster. By the early 1980s balance of payments deficits were increasing and funds began pouring out of the country. The government responded by obliging public utilities and state firms to increase their foreign debt and to transfer funds thus obtained to the foreign exchange market for the purpose of financing capital flight. Nevertheless, a run on the banks led to a series of bankruptcies, making this scheme untenable. In 1981 a 500 per cent devaluation was carried out. But the interests of the large economic groups were safeguarded by an exchange rate insurance, contracted after the fact. Private foreign debt was eventually transferred to government, that is, was wholly 'nationalised'. During the Alfonsín administration, the whole scheme was legitimised when a new stabilisation programme was signed with the International Monetary Fun (IMF). No critique concerning the legitimacy and legality of this enormous increase in foreign debt and its transference to government during the military dictatorship was made. The Plan Austral (of the Alfonsín administration), fully supported by the bankers, had as one of its implicit conditions that the foreign debt would not be investigated or questioned, which originated a famous debate in Congress (Cafiero and Llorens 2002: 97). Thus, the Alfonsín government did not heed numerous critiques made at the time concerning this foreign debt, nor did it question its legality, something that at the time was being contested in the judiciary.

It should be noticed that this enormous indebtedness had nothing to do with industrialisation or investments. On the contrary, it was contracted in a context of overall stagnation and de-industrialisation. It was used to finance military and repressive expenditures and operations; for the construction of several highways and a gas pipeline; and to finance the 1978 football World Cup played in Argentina; but the bulk of this indebtedness was used to finance speculative financial activities and capital flight. This period saw the beginning of a correspondence between the increase in foreign debt and deposits abroad of Argentine nationals that continues up to today (Basualdo 2000: 49, 2001: 37). The Morgan Guaranty Trust estimated that between 1976 and the end of 1982 capital flight in Argentina amounted to $28 billion (Minsburg 1987: 102). And World Bank estimates register a capital flight in 1978–81 of more than $31 billion (Basualdo 1994: 32).

The capital flight that has been usual in Argentina was significantly enhanced during the military dictatorship. This was related in part to indebtedness in dollars by the public enterprises that brought foreign exchange into the country with no restrictions and then sold it in the local money markets to people who were interested in withdrawing their speculative profits or the liquidity they obtained in financial operations from the local economy. In a second phase new external credits were obtained with the guarantees provided by government, as well as on a basis of funds deposited abroad that were taken as collateral (Basualdo 2000; Cafiero and Llorens 2002). What also made these operations profitable was the fact that they were based on a pre-ordained exchange rate, on the one hand, and higher than international local interest rates, on the other. These operations were dubbed the '*bicicleta financiera*' ('financial bicycle'). Thus, the 'perverse' Argentine debt (Calcagno 1986) became associated clearly with the economic strategy of the military dictatorship. Its main beneficiaries were government officials, the military and the elite economic establishment, via the enormous profitability guaranteed to local and international financial activities. Some of the names representing newcomers of the economic establishment were Pérez-Companc, Rocca, Macri, Soldati and Bulgheroni. Of course foreign creditors also acquired an enormous leverage over local policy measures, to a large extent via what were to become IMF conditionalities.

In this model of financial valorisation the state played a fundamental role. First, this was because local state loans of public utilities were instrumental in the maintenance of high local real interest rates relative to international rates. Second because foreign indebtedness was what provided foreign exchange that was to finance capital flight. And third, by assuming losses during devaluation, and by transferring to the state this foreign debt the elite private sector was substantially subsidised. Thus foreign debt transferred to the state, was thrust upon the shoulders of the population at large (Basualdo 2000: 29–31). As mentioned above the 'solution' to the crisis adopted by Domingo Cavallo, at the time President of the Central Bank, was to implement an exchange rate insurance to 'facilitate' local private debtors to pay their foreign debts. Thereafter this debt was transferred to the state, a process that continued throughout the 1980s. All this implied a transfer of public funds to the more concentrated segments of capital. It was estimated that only 28 local economic groups and 102 transnational corporations accumulated at the time 64 per cent of private foreign debt (Basualdo 1987; Kulfas and Schorr 2003: 23). According to Basualdo private debt representing more than $10 billion was transferred to the state in this period (Basualdo 2000: 24).

The subsidising of large economic groups and foreign capital during the 1980s by transferring their debt to the state also happened with the capitalisation of this debt via the redemption of foreign debt in the process of privatisation, when it was exchanged for net worth pertaining to the public services. In Argentina this 'capitalisation of foreign debt' was devised in 1985, though initially it was not associated with privatisations but with the transfer of private debt to the state, which had not been done before when the exchange insurance regime was applied. Added to this were other subsidising schemes of large companies, such as state overvaluation of purchases of goods and services, and other mechanisms. It is estimated that total state transfers to the more concentrated capital amounted to $105 billion in the period 1981–9, a magnitude similar to the total yearly gross national product (GNP) of Argentina. The main beneficiaries of these regimes were economic groups or conglomerates such as Pérez-Companc, Techint, Siemens and FIAT (Basualdo 2000: 24–5). During the Alfonsín administration the enormous foreign debt contracted during the military dictatorship and then transferred to the state was legitimised. The critique made by Olmos, the lawyer who initiated legal proceedings with regard to the foreign debt, declaring it illegitimate precisely because it was on the whole based on monies deposited abroad by Argentinians and because it was contracted during a military dictatorship (odious debt), was not considered.

The elite economic establishment thus acquired enormous power. This is reflected in the 'economic coup' of 1988–9, which appeared to have been a response to the Alfonsín administration, which had momentarily stopped servicing its foreign debt. Wholesale capital flight induced the hyperinflation of 1989 leading to a chaotic social situation and to Alfonsín's resignation, six months prior to the end of his term in office. According to some studies, this 'economic coup' also reflected conflicting interests of foreign creditors vis-à-vis local economic groups (Basualdo 2001: 54). In 1991 under the

Convertibility Plan of Cavallo, these diverse interests were finally reconciled. Thus, the 'economic coup' of 1989 induced by an economic establishment led to wholesale capital flight, to an accelerating devaluation and hence to the hyperinflationary spurts of the 1989–91 period. This then led to a need for new 'disciplinary' measures to be imposed on a large part of civil society in the 1990s.

The policies of Menem

The Menem years (1989–99) were in many ways emblematic with regard to the importance acquired by national and international economic groups, banks and financial interests in Argentina. In this period the interests of these groups were enhanced by the continuing indebtedness of government combined with a vast privatisation programme and widespread deregulatory measures that formed part of the severe structural adjustments adopted throughout the decade. While some privatisations began in 1990 the legitimacy of the SAP was based on the success of the so-called Convertibility Plan of 1991, which managed to bring down inflation and the inflationary expectations that had characterised the previous 1989–91 period. With the Argentine peso fixed on the par with the dollar devaluation expectations were controlled. This was combined with measures such as the full liberalisation of capital flows to and from the country. The new-found price stability and growth process of the early 1990s were instrumental in paving the way for the adoption and legitimation of a fully fledged SAP.

Under the Convertibility Plan a convertible peso pegged to the dollar on a one to one basis was established, and price indexing was prohibited by law (illegal exceptions were made with regard to certain public rates after the main public services had been privatised). All money creation not backed by foreign exchange reserves of the Central Bank or by the inflow of capital from abroad (mainly new indebtedness) was prohibited. Having been established by a Law of Congress, the Convertibility regime required the Central Bank to back 80 per cent of the monetary base with international reserves, thus reducing its ability to finance government and the financial system as a lender of last resort. This law also had the ostensible purpose of eliminating all government discretionality with regard to monetary and foreign exchange policies. Its effect was putting Argentina on a Gold or Dollar Standard scheme, limiting the functions of the Central Bank to that of an exchange broker.[3]

Minister of Economy Domingo Cavallo's main objective with the Convertibility Plan was to bring down inflation by drastically eliminating devaluation expectations. He also sought to establish a new and enduring monetary and foreign exchange regime that would permit him to apply a drastic SAP. A key element of this programme was the need to continuously increase foreign debt due to balance of payments deficits inherent in an overvalued exchange rate and increased servicing of foreign debt. On the whole, this

SAP was part of a 'shock therapy' strategy, whose application was due in large measure to political considerations: Menem needed to let it be known that he was *not* going to apply a typically Peronist (i.e. nationalistic and populist) economic strategy, despite his electoral promises (Teubal 2000/1).

Once in power, Menem thus implemented his extreme neoliberal programme. All prior industrial, regional and export promotion regimes were suspended and the advantages local manufacturers had in providing for state purchases were eliminated. Government finances were controlled; indirect taxes on consumption were increased, affecting mostly the middle and working classes. But some of the main measures that formed part of this SAP were related to the way new foreign indebtedness was combined with the privatisation programme. More than 30 state public enterprises, the bulk of the state enterprise system, were privatised. Observers noted the swiftness and thoroughness with which the Argentine government carried out this programme in the early 1990s. Privatisation reached such diverse areas as telephones and communications, airline companies, petrochemicals, petroleum, about 10,000 km of highways, railways and other transport systems, natural gas distribution, electricity, water, iron and steel industries, coal, a series of firms in the defence area, hydroelectric dams and other varied items such as television channels, hotels, port facilities, silos and horse-racing stadiums. By late 1994 privatisation had earned more than $27 billion for the government, though net worth transferred was much greater. About $15 billion corresponded to the capitalisation of public debt (domestic and foreign) on the basis of swaps of net worth for bonds valued at their face values (Azpiazu 2002).[4] However, the privatisation programme excluded the institutionalisation of efficient regulatory boards, which in the First World are an essential part of most privatisation programmes. It was also carried out in the wake of much corruption, and a judiciary, including the Supreme Court, operating according to the wishes of government, in implementing at all costs this privatisation programme even if many of the measures adopted were contrary to prevailing law.

Two laws, the Reforma del Estado (reform of the state) and Emergencia Económica (economic emergency), gave the Menem administration full rights to transfer state property in different forms, including the direct sale of net worth, share holdings, medium- and long-term concessions, and contracts of association with firms. Many of these measures tending to the wholesale auctioning of public enterprises sought to solve existing contradictions as between different local and international economic power groups (Azpiazu 2002: 10). Different consortia were established whereby local economic groups participated extensively with foreign firms in some of the main privatisations (see Table 7.1).

The law that established the Convertibility Plan of 1991 prohibited price indexation in all its forms due to increases of costs or other factors. Nevertheless, at the end of that year a decree of government permitted the privatised companies to index their rates in relation to the price indexes prevailing

Table 7.1 Participation of local economic groups in the privatisation of some state firms in Argentina

Firm privatised	Participating local economic groups	Main international partners
Empresa Nacional de Telecomunicaciones (ENTEL) (Área Telefónica) (telephones)	SCP (Grupo Soldati) Techint Banco Río (Pérez Companc)	Telefónica de España Citicorp
Empresa Nacional de Telecomunicaciones (ENTEL) (Área Telecom) (telephones)	Pérez Companc	Stet France Telecom JP Morgan
Servicios Eléctricos del Gran Buenos Aires (SEGBA) (Área Edesur) (electricity)	Astra	Electricité de France Endesa (Spain)
Servicios Eléctricos del Gran Buenos Aires (SEGBA) (Área Edesur) (electricity)	Pérez Companc	PSI Energy Chilectra
Gas del Estado (Área Metrogas) (gas)	Pérez Companc Astra	British Gas
Obras Sanitarias de la Nación (Área Aguas Argentina) (water)	SCP (Grupo Soldati)	Lyonnaise Des Eaux
Concesión Acceso Norte (roads)	Sideco (Grupo Macri)	Impregilo DYCASA

Source: Cámara de Diputados de la Nación (2005).

in the United States, and permitted them also to readjust them every six months. This implied a juridical transgression of enormous proportions. Not only because this decree permitted price indexation that had been prohibited by law, but also because this was based on indices prevailing in another country. As Azpiazu has noted, while the retail price index in Argentina fell from the beginning of 1995 to June 2001 by −1.1 per cent, this same index in the United States and in the same period increased 18.4 per cent; a similar situation occurred with regard to wholesale prices pertaining to both countries. This difference in indexation implied additional incomes for telephone, electricity and gas companies to the tune of $9 billion in detriment of the interests of the local consumers (Azpiazu 2002: 13).

Furthermore, prior to the transfer of state property to the private sector a series of increases in public rates were sustained. Some of these increases were based on new criteria concerning the calculation of costs, but in essence were related to the need to make these privatisations 'more attractive' (Azpiazu and Schorr 2003: 18). There were also cases where increases in rates were carried out *after* the privatisations had been already made, violating original contracts. Needless to say the same can be said with regard to investments compromised in the original contracts which, in most cases, were only minimally carried out.

With regard to the overall privatisation spree the privatisation of water is emblematic. The state-run National Sanitation Service (Obras Sanitarias de la Nación, OSN), created in the late nineteenth century, provided water services until it was privatised in 1993. OSN functioned relatively well throughout its history until in recent years it suffered technical deterioration and a lack of government funding, which caused a dramatic drop in the quality of its services in the mid-1970s. But prior to presenting the company to potential bidders, rates were increased several times: 25 per cent in February 1991; 29 per cent two months later; 18 per cent in April 1992; when the VAT was introduced another 21 per cent; and then, just prior to privatisation, another 8 per cent. The terms of the bidding process stipulated that the concession go to the bidder offering the lowest base rate along with an investment plan for improved and expanded services. The government had promised the population healthy and environmentally sound water and sewage services at the cheapest possible rates, something that was not sustained later on. The concession was won by Aguas Argentina, whose leading owners were Suez Lyonaise de Eaux-Dumez and Vivendi. Nevertheless, the new company solicited an 'extraordinary revision' of rates only eight months after the concession because of 'unforeseen operating costs'. Thereafter rates continued increasing much beyond contractual arrangements. Also the company did not implement expanded services and investments providing for additional potable water and sewage services to the extent promised in the contracts signed. The profitability of the company was shown to be much greater than those of equivalent firms in Europe and elsewhere.

The increases in public rates prior to the privatisation process also extended to other privatisations. A most ludicrous case concerned the privatisation of the telephone companies that was carried out in a record short time. Between February 1990 when the call for the privatisation of the state telephone company was made, and November of that same year when two private companies took charge, the value of the telephone pulse increased in dollar terms 711 per cent (from $0.47 per pulse to $3.81 per pulse). This rate increase can be compared with the wholesale price index increase of 450 per cent and an exchange devaluation of 235 per cent in the same period, as we are referring to the year prior to the Convertibility Plan when prices and exchange values were not yet fixed (Azpiazu and Schorr 2003: 20). This was a means whereby at the moment when the transfer of property was established the new price cap of the rate system was established. No wonder that telephone rates in Argentina tend to be among the highest in the world! A similar situation, though not as extensive, concerned the case of natural gas. In the period between March 1991 and January 1993 when the state firm Gas del Estado was transferred to the private sector public rates of gas increased 30 per cent. These rates affected mostly residential consumers, not so the largest entrepreneurial consumers, despite the fact that *subsidios cruzados* of different categories of consumers was prohibited.

On the whole, after privatisation contracts had been signed, renegotiation of their terms was continuously sought by the companies. Apart from rate increases, investments promised tended to be delayed, debts because of punitive measures were condoned, and the extension of concessions was in many cases substantially increased. In essence what emerged was a lack of a regulation that could minimally contribute to having the companies fulfil their contractual obligations with a view to public interest. More so, the national state actively contributed to the defence of the interests of these privatised companies.

The Brady Plan agreement on Argentina's foreign debt was reached in December 1992. Old bonds that had been issued by private banks were exchanged for new Brady bonds with a certain reduction of interest rates. But the gist of the matter was the fact that through this mechanism the foreign banks were divested of their exposure to Argentina's foreign debt that was now transferred to individual bond holders, thus atomising the foreign (and local) creditor universe. For this reason when default of foreign private debt was declared in early 2002, some of the main private creditors affected were the retired and pensioners mostly of Europe and Japan who had been (ill-)advised by the banks to purchase Argentine government bonds due to their very high profitability (their high risk was not always pointed out).

To favour the financial establishment of Argentina as well as international financial interests a substantial portion of the pension and retirement funds were privatised. In 1994 any person in Argentina had the option of choosing a private pension or retirement fund. This implied that a substantial portion of potential government income was transferred to the private administrators of pension and retirement funds. This contributed to the fiscal deficits of the late 1990s and to the subsequent increases in foreign indebtedness. Ironically, part of the fiscal deficits was in fact financed by new debt provided by these new private administrators of the funds. To the extent that in 2002 this debt was not *pesificado* it contributed to overall foreign debt.

In the period 1994–2003 an estimated $30 billion was transferred to these private pension and retirement funds. These companies associated with local and international banks charged $10 billion in commission. At the same time the payments that employers were required to make to the overall pension system were eliminated. These factors represented additional subsidies to local firms to the tune of $35 billion. Thus about $65 billion was the amount the government did not receive due to the creation of this private pension and retirement funds system. This was money transferred outright to finance interests and private firms (*Página 12* 31 August 2004).

In sum, the 'opening' of the economy not only contributed to de-industrialisation due to the persistence of an overvalued exchange rate but also led throughout the period to balance of trade deficits that required increased foreign indebtedness. It also was instrumental in causing a greater vulnerability of the economy to external shocks. Thus the Mexican *tequila* and Brazilian *caipirinha* crises, in particular, contributed substantially to capital flight and hence to deepening trends towards depression, as did the increase in international interest rates in the late 1990s.

Economic concentration

The SAPs in the 1990s gave leeway to both local and international large transnationals in controlling an increased portion of the market both in industry, agriculture and the services. These large economic groups, some of which participated in many privatisations, were also beneficiaries of an intense process of concentration and centralisation of capital in many branches of the services and manufacturing industries. Take the case of the agro-food system of Argentina: the production, processing and distribution of food and agricultural commodities. The 1990s were a period of great transformations in the agro-food system that contributes substantially global GNP, to employment, and that provides the bulk (about 60 per cent) of Argentina's exports (Teubal and Rodríguez 2002). One of the main agro industries of this period in terms of its contribution to exports (mainly soy) and production, though not necessarily in terms of its employment creation, was the vegetable oil industry. While the five most important oilseed industries exported 39 per cent of vegetable oils in 1990, this proportion increased to 58 per cent in 1998. In 2002 the five main exporters of soy exported 80 per cent of this item. A similar situation occurred in other agro industries. In the 1990s the seven largest milk industries were dominated mostly by two of them: SanCor and Mastellone managed to control 80 per cent of the market. As was to be expected the cereal exports in general are controlled by seven firms – Cargill, Bunge, Nidera, Vicentín, Dreyfus, Pecom-Agra and AGD – that managed to corner 60 per cent of the volume of these exports. Similarly, supermarkets increased substantially their share of the market, marginalising or even expelling numerous small and medium-sized businesses, a factor that contributed substantially to unemployment. On the whole supermarkets (both wholesale and retail) increased their share of the Greater Buenos Aires market from about 27 per cent in 1984 to over 50 per cent in 1997. The bulk of these sales was carried out by eight large supermarkets. This also occurred with different shopping centres.

Towards the end of the 1990s, this consolidation of the largest firms went along with the increased foreign control of key segments of the overall agro-food chain. Among the transnational firms that participated in these processes were Unilever, Nestlé, Nabisco, Suchard Kraft, Philip Morris, Danone, Heinz, Parmalat, Luksic, Brahma and Warsteiner. Many of the traditional firms of Argentina, such as Bagley, Terrabusi and Villavicencio, were bought by transnationals. An important development in Argentina in this period was the diffusion of soy and, since 1997, genetically modified soy. The seed industry has thus become dominated by Monsanto and its affiliates, which also was a licensee of the Glyphosate Round-up Ready, the herbicide whose sales expanded substantially due to the fact that the new seeds massively distributed were precisely resistant to it.

This concentration and foreign control extended to the banking system. In January 1995 there still were 205 banks in Argentina, of which 33 were publicly owned; by November 1998 this number had been reduced to 127, with only 17 publicly owned banks remaining. In 1994 foreign banks represented only 15 per cent of total assets of the banking system, but by December 1997 they controlled 40 per cent, and one year later even 53 per cent, a much higher percentage than in other countries (Teubal 2001: 52). On the whole, in the 1990s there was a marked trend towards the transnationalisation of the economy, with large transnationals acquiring an increased share of the assets of the largest companies of the Argentine economy. During the 1990s prior to the present crisis transnational groups bought 426 firms for a total of $29,000 million. With these acquisitions foreign companies managed to control more then half the assets of the thousand largest companies of Argentina, representing 30 per cent of gross domestic product (GDP) (Teubal 2001).

The economic and financial crisis

Argentina's economy stopped growing from 1998 onwards. This stagnation was looked upon as an omen that could easily lead to crisis. Despite an increase in social protest, and the change in the overall sociopolitical climate that had led to the defeat of the Peronist candidate Duhalde in the presidential election of 1999, the new government of De la Rúa proceeded to betray electoral promises and continued implementing strict adjustment policies. Increases in taxes, a reduction in wages and additional laws for the 'flexibilisation' of labour markets were some of the measures adopted, none of which were countercyclical in nature with regard to the impending crisis.

The economic stagnation led to a debate in Argentina about the persistence of convertibility and the presumed need to avoid a default at all costs in the servicing of foreign debt. Some, including the protracted hard line *Menemistas*, imbued with extreme orthodoxy, proposed advancing towards the full-fledged dollarisation of the economy, a measure that had been adopted quite unsuccessfully in Ecuador. Others insisted on the need to conclude convertibility, devalue and hence induce a required export strategy, a measure that nonetheless also implied enormous social costs for the bulk of the population if not complemented with an adequate redistribution of income. Once again the establishment was deeply divided by alternative projects that represented different interests. On the one hand, the owners of the privatised firms, local large banks and foreign creditors supported by the IMF and other international financial organisations defended at all costs convertibility and the fixed exchange rate. These were the groups that aimed at advancing towards dollarisation. On the other hand, part of the new elite establishment (related mainly to exports as well as having their deposits abroad after having sold out their firms to foreign capital in the late 1990s) supported devaluation. These conflicting interests of the elite establishment were once again brought to the fore. The background to these diverging interests was the deteriorating social situation affecting the bulk of the population. These increasing social protests eventually led to the massive rebellion of 19 and 20 December 2001.

The Ministers of Economy of the De la Rúa government (first José Luis Machinea and then Cavallo) called upon to 'save' Argentina from the impending crisis adopted new adjustments and schemes trying to generate 'confidence' in international financial organisations. But their actions only served to deepen the crisis: Machinea's '*blindaje financiero*' ('financial armour plate') of December 2000; the rapid pass through government of Lopez Murphy with his extremist adjustments; and then finally Cavallo supported by an 'amalgamation of banks and the media' (Cafiero and Llorens 2002: 126) only made things worse. Nothing was to stop the run on the banks and capital flight. Cavallo's expertise this time failed lamentably. Despite the great powers that were given to him by Congress (April 2001) and his *megacanje de deuda* (mega debt swap, June 2001) supported by his friend David Mulford of Credit Suisse and J.P. Morgan-Chase that implied restructuring foreign debt to the tune of $30 billion, the crisis could not be controlled. In this debt restructuring process 65 different types of bonds, most of them denominated in, for a total of $28 billion were rescued. They were exchanged for five new types of bonds for a value of $30 billion but with future interest rates that amounted to $85 billion dollars, and of course an enormous commission paid to Cavallo's banking friends. Argentina was to pay a yearly interest of 18 per cent, 13 per cent higher then interest on US Treasury bills.

None of this 'magic' was of use, and even a series of additional measures for the purpose of restructuring a rapidly increasing foreign debt could do nothing to stop the drainage of domestic funds, which largely pertained to the establishment. New funds available could not stop the irresistible drain of funds until in late November 2001 the so-called *corralito* was created, which restricted the withdrawal of deposits (mostly of small operators) from the banking system. From February 2001 to the end of November (when the *corralito* came into effect) deposits fell by 16.3 billion pesos (equivalent to the same amount in US dollars); from December 2001 to April 2002 despite the withdrawal restrictions the flight from deposits continued to the tune of 12.7 billion pesos. This flight from deposits, a total of more than 29 billion pesos, represented 34 per cent of total deposits prevailing in February of 2001. Measured in dollar terms, and considering the more than 300 per cent devaluation of the Argentine peso in early 2001, deposits fell from $87 billion in early 2001 to $19.4 billion in April 2002 (Alfredo Zaiat, *Página 12* 30 April 2002).

The Convertibility Plan implied that an important part of the Argentine economy had become dollarised. This had already been a trend due to inflation and hyperinflation characterising previous decades, but the Convertibility Plan legalised the partial dollarisation of the economy and certain dollar transactions became the norm (for example in the sale of property).

When inflation was brought down in the 1990s deposits in pesos were considered to be as good as deposits in dollars: convertibility created the illusion that a peso was as good as a dollar and that Argentina could also create dollars. Nevertheless, the new system had its flaws. At a certain juncture the share of dollar deposits in the banking system began to increase substantially. As uncertainty increased, depositors switched their pesos deposits into dollar ones. But then these deposits began to be withdrawn from the banking system and transferred, preferably abroad. The run on the banks rapidly became a run on the foreign exchange system. The vulnerability of convertibility was suddenly brought to the fore: the banking system on the whole did not have sufficient funds to underwrite deposits denominated in dollars. Argentina, despite convertibility, could not print dollars. The role of the Central Bank as lender of last resort could therefore not be assumed.

In 2001 capital flight reached astronomical levels. Throughout that year (prior the events of December when the system exploded) the reserves of the Central Bank fell about $19 billion. A recent publication of the research done by a special commission of the Chamber of Deputies on the flight of foreign exchange during 2001 (Cámara de Diputados 2005) shows that transfers abroad pertaining to the 'non-financial private sector' of the economy amounted to $29.9 billion, 87 per cent of which ($26.1 billion) corresponded to firms and the remaining 13 per cent ($3.8 billion) to private persons. This commission analysed the operations of 87 financial entities that transferred foreign exchange abroad (transfers related to foreign trade operations were excluded). The bulk of these transfer operations (62.3 per cent or $18.5 billion) were carried out through operations of four banks (Banco Galicia, HSBC, Rio and Citibank) and funds were sent mostly to the US and Uruguay. Local private banks transferred 16.6 per cent of these funds while foreign banks transferred 75 per cent. Most of the funds transferred by private persons were done so through the Banco Galicia and Citibank. Among the individuals who massively transferred funds are registered the names of traditional families, famous people and/or proprietors of some of the main local firms and economic groups.

As could be expected, the largest firms made the bulk of the transfers abroad. The 213 most important firms of Argentina (representing 3 per cent of the total number of firms considered by the commission of the Chamber of Deputies) made 70 per cent of total transfers carried out in 2001, for a total of more than $18 billion. Each of these firms transferred an average of $84.5 million (Cámara de Diputados 2005: 103). The ten firms that transferred most money to a total of more the $9 billion (35 per cent of total transfers by firms) were Pecom Energía, Telefónica de Argentina, YPF, Telecom Argentina-Stet France Telecom, Nidera, Shell Compañía Argentina de Petróleo, Telefónica Comunicaciones Personales, Esso Petrolera Argentina, Bunge Ceval, and Molinos de la Plata. About 50 per cent of these transfers are accounted for by the privatised public services (Telefónica de Argentina, Repsol-YPF, Telecom Argentina, Edesur, Central Puerto, Transportadora de

Gas del Sur, Aguas Argentina, Metrogas, and Transportadora de Gas del Norte). When considering the transfers of private persons, 27,828 persons transferred a total of $3.8 billion, an average of $138,000 each, but 409 persons transferred abroad more than a million dollars each. The ten persons who transferred the most together transferred $289 million, an average of about $29 million each (Cámara de Diputados 2005: 103). With all these funds transferred in 2001 the total capital flight of two decades amounted to over $115 billion (during the Convertibility Plan foreign debt had increased by $84 billion).

The financial crisis came at the worse moment for Argentina. The Secretary of the Treasury of the US had declared that no bailout for the crisis equivalent to that of Mexico (for $51.8 billion in 1995–6) or Brazil (for $41.5 billion in 1998) would be made, stating that funds provided by American carpenters or plumbers would not be used to bail out the banks. Thus, no US funds were available to underwrite the bankruptcy of the banking system, only local funds, which were also provided by local carpenters, plumbers, small business, professionals and the like. Nevertheless, the IMF provided $12.4 billion to support the policies of Machinea and Cavallo, contrary to the rules of the IMF itself.[5] Foreign banks themselves increased their debt with their home offices and privatised firms did similarly. New funds could not stop the irresistible drainage of funds. The *corralito* was the drop that overflowed the cup, increasing the band of protestors to important segments of Argentina's vast middle classes. The rebellion of 19 and 20 December 2001 precipitated the fall of Cavallo and De la Rúa. The latter had lasted only two years in office, but he will go down in history as one of the most inept of all presidents in Argentine history, and also as one responsible for the deaths of at least 40 people due to the repression of the rebellion.

During the short period with Rodríguez Saa as President the default on the foreign debt was declared; in reality this was a default on private foreign debt. Argentina continued servicing its financial obligations with the IMF and other international financial organisations. In early 2002 the peso was finally devalued and convertibility came to an end. At that moment pressures of all sorts began to be exerted on the government. Devaluation went along with the *pesificación* of deposits and loans. But this 'pesoification' was asymmetrical. Deposits were pesoified at a rate of 1.40 to the dollar but bank loans were considered at one peso per dollar. In reality banks had already withdrawn their funds from the country or had contracted debts with their home offices. Foreign banks did not honour local deposits, despite the fact that previous presidents of the Argentine Central Bank had declared that the financial system was 'solid' due basically to the fact that by then the bulk of the banking system was foreign owned, and that the head offices of these banks would surely honour local deposits. This of course did not occur, a factor that severely questioned the legitimacy of the banking system as a whole.

After devaluation the anatomy of Argentine society was suddenly brought to the fore. The newly formed privatised companies pressured the government for increases in public rates so as to redress their profitability in dollar terms, which had fallen due to devaluation. The banks did so too, because of the asymmetry in the pesoification process and because of their near bankruptcy. Foreign creditors lobbied against the default, this time supported by an atomisation of the creditor field in which pensioners and retirees were stuck with defaulted bonds.

In 2002 – after the default, the devaluation and rebellion of 19 and 20 December 2001 – new public debt was issued. Though not strictly foreign, this debt had enormous implications for Argentina's international financial relations. The state-issued bonds to return the 13 per cent discount the De la Rúa administration had applied on wages of public employees and retirees; to compensate the banks for the asymmetric pesoification of deposits new bonds were issued and given to depositors to rid the banks of the debt implied by these deposits in the wake of devaluation. Banks were also compensated for losses emerging as a consequence of lawsuits by depositors against the banks, and new bonds were used to finance the withdrawal of provincial quasi-monies. New debt also increased due to arrears of previous interest and debt, new debt to make viable opening the *corralito* in 2002. This new debt fully compensated debt lost by the previous pesoification process. Furthermore, despite defaulting on private foreign debt Argentina continued servicing her debt with the IMF and international organisations to the tune of $13 billion in the period 2002–5.

Due to the end of convertibility and the crisis, debt increased from about $144 billion in 2001 to over $191 billion in 2004 prior to the new agreement with private depositors. But debt also increased in relation to GDP as a consequence of devaluation: from 43.4 per cent of GDP in 2001 to 112 per cent of GDP in 2004 prior to the exchange of old bonds for new ones. After many of these bonds were exchanged for new bonds total debt fell to $126.6 billion or about 74 per cent of GDP. Nevertheless, at this time, after debt relations have apparently been on the whole 'normalised', every child that is born in Argentina begins his or her life with a debt of about $3,400 (instead of the $5,000 'owned' previously).

Final remarks

The crisis of 2001 and 2002 was one of the major crises of Argentine history. The partial default declared in the last days of 2001 and lasting until 2005 was also one of the major defaults in the recent history of the international monetary system. Needless to say despite this default Argentina continued servicing its debt with the IMF and international organisations. Nevertheless, by mid-2005 relations with the IMF had not yet been fully 'normalised'.

Much has been said concerning the crisis and who the main culprits for it were. According to some observers adjustments carried out were insufficient or policy measures such as devaluation should have been taken earlier. The management of the economy during the crisis itself has also been substantially criticised for numerous and varied reasons. The IMF and its conditionalities have also been singled out as one of the main culprits to be considered.[6] According to the report *Argentina's Economic Crisis: Causes and Cures* of the Joint Economic Committee of the US Congress:

> In 1998, Argentina entered what turned out to be a four-year depression, during which its economy shrank 28 percent. Argentina's experience has been cited as an example of the failure of free markets and fixed exchange rates, among other things. The evidence does not support those views. Rather, bad economic policies converted an ordinary recession into a depression. Three big tax increases in 2000–2001 discouraged growth, and meddling with the monetary system in mid 2001 created the fear of currency devaluation. As a result, confidence in Argentina's government finances evaporated. In a series of blunders that made matters even worse, from December 2001 to early 2002, succeeding governments undermined property rights by freezing bank deposits; defaulting on the government's foreign debt in a thoughtless manner; ending the Argentine peso's longstanding link to the dollar; forcibly converting dollar deposits and loans into Argentine pesos at unfavourable rates; and avoiding contracts. Achieving sustained long-term economic growth will involve re-establishing respect for property rights.[7]

In this chapter another perspective concerning the recent Argentine crisis has been presented. While much can be said concerning the mismanagement of the economy prior to and during the crisis, the report of the US Congress Joint Economic Committee does not delve into the more profound reasons for the crisis itself and some of its long-running socioeconomic consequences. The analysis of this chapter, however, ascribes the crisis precisely to the extreme structural adjustments applied in the 1990s, to the policies enhancing increased indebtedness from the 1970s onwards, and basically to the measures and policies tending to favour large economic groups and companies, in particular those pertaining to the financial system leading to wholesale capital flight. On the whole the system showed itself to be not only unequal and unjust but also highly unstable and vulnerable to international and local shocks precisely because it was based on policies enhancing speculative financial activities, leading inexorably to capital flight. In Keynesian terms the economy ended forming part of a huge speculative bubble.

Increased foreign indebtedness and capital flight – both intimately related to one another and to the overall model favouring large economic groups – were fundamental elements of the Argentine model. As was to be expected once recession began, when no countercyclical measures are adopted, the run on the banks and on the foreign exchange market led inexorably to crisis.

Since 2003, Argentina has sustained a very high growth rate, reversing previous trends. While GNP increased, a surplus in the balance of trade was attained, as well as a financial surplus amounting to more than 3 per cent of GDP. Certain industries grew, for example textiles, agriculture (due mostly to high soy international prices), and some of service sectors (e.g. tourism). Argentina in these years grew *without* access to international finances, and new foreign indebtedness. These favourable indicators of the economy may have come about precisely because the fully fledged neoliberal model was not continued, apart from the fact that servicing part of the foreign debt was not made. However, recent developments point towards increased pressures on behalf of the economic establishment and the IMF to return to the policies of the 1990s that led to the present crisis.[8]

Many problems remain. The living conditions of vast segments of the population are deplorable. Unemployment and poverty rates have fallen slightly, but still continue to be very high. Wages of the employed continued much below what, in real terms, they were 20 years ago. A substantial portion of the employed are non-registered employed (*empleo en negro*) and income distribution continues to be tremendously regressive. Despite low wages, the large companies including the privatised firms have increased their profits.

A system giving priority to large economic groups and conglomerates implied the wholesale transfer of income and wealth to these interests. The rest of society remained devastated, lacking food, health, education, security and adequate housing. This can be visualised as part of a vast process whereby the state adopted a series of transfer mechanisms of income and wealth in favour of these 'privileged' sectors. These measures not only did *not* serve to increase growth and accumulation – on the contrary, the performance of the economy leading to the recent crisis has *not* been notorious in any way – but also their social costs and economic consequences have created an enormous predicament for the future of Argentine society.

A vast number of people were the true losers of the crisis: unemployment reached 25 per cent, and if underemployment is considered this implied that over 50 per cent of the population was in some way unemployed. Poverty escalated to over 50 per cent of the population, 10 million of whom were extremely poor, that is, persons remaining below the indigence line. Devaluation also caused wages to fall drastically. One of the responses of government was the wholesale distribution of *Planes Trabajar*, a sort of unemployment subsidy that amounted to a bare 150 pesos per family (about $50 at the current foreign exchange rate).

The Argentine society has been substantially transformed in comparison to what it was 20 years ago. Income distribution worsened tremendously: in 1974 the gap between the richest 10 per cent income earning strata and lowest 10 per cent amounted to 12 times; in 1999 it had increased to 24 times; and in 2002 in the midst of the crisis to 34 times. In 2002 the lowest 10 per cent income earners received 1 per cent of national income; the highest 10 per cent income earning strata received 38 per cent (*Página 12* 25 August 2002). Access to food, employment, health, housing and security have all been trampled upon. All this can be construed to have been a consequence of the chaos created by what could be termed a system of legal but not necessarily legitimate *macroeconomic looting*, in the wake of the so-called process of financial valorisation.

In this context social protests of all sorts have increased and new forms of socioeconomic organisation have emerged. Over 120 firms have been taken over by their workers once their owners had abandoned them. *Piqueteros* have in many respects taken on the crisis in their own hands, and have begun to produce and develop a new social economy. Peasants, farm workers and indigenous communities are protesting and organising themselves in many ways and are therefore not only confronting the crisis but are also helping to transform society as well. Factories are being managed collectively, and communities have begun to take their destinies into their own hands, which shows that the crisis has also unleashed new energy, new ideas and new forms or organisation.[9]

Notes

1   Daniel Azpiazu, Eduardo Basualdo and the other members of the *Area de Economía y Tecnología* of the Facultad Latinoamericana de Ciencias Sociales (FLACSO) based in Buenos Aires are the main researchers studying the importance and significance of the *grupos económicos* in Argentina. The numerous reports and publications of the Institute de Estudios y Formación (IDEP) of the trade union Central de los Trabajadores Argentinos (CTA) directed by Claudio Lozano (2003, 2005a, 2005b) also contributed substantially to an understanding of these developments.
2   In the late 1990s and early years of the new millennium alternative approaches were presented in the UIA, some of which proposed devaluation and the support of a new export strategy.
3   For a critique of currency board systems adopted by countries such as Hong Kong, Bermuda, the Cayman Islands, Estonia and Argentina, see Eichengreen (1996: 139, 184).
4   The bonds that were used to purchase Telefónica Argentina were valued at $5 billion whereas their market value was 15 per cent of their face values (i.e. $754 million).
5   Article VI, section 1 of the Constitution of the IMF states that no member country can use Fund resources to confront a considerable and continuous capital flight and that the Fund can ask the member country to adopt control measures to avoid the use of these resources for such purposes (cf. Calcagno and Calcagno 2005).
6   For a discussion of the role of the IMF in not preventing the Argentine crisis see Stiglitz and Yusuf (2001) and several articles in Teunissen and Akkerman (2003).
7   The report was written by Kurt Schuler, Senior Economist to the Vice Chairman, but numerous economists in Argentina and elsewhere were consulted, see www.house.gov/jec/new-prdt.htm.

8   The latest demands of the IMF to the Argentine government include: increasing the fiscal surplus from 3.0 to 4.5 per cent of GDP; letting the dollar exchange rate fall (to facilitate debt payments and presumably dampen inflationary expectations); shelving demands to increase retirement and pension payments and wages; eliminating 'distortive' taxes such as taxes (retentions) on exports; renegotiating contracts of privatised companies and permitting increases in rates of public services; and offering a solution for the creditors who did not accept the previous debt agreement on the default of private debt.
9   For the analysis of a series of local projects taken on by peasants, ex-petroleum employees and indigenous communities, among others see Giarracca and Teubal (2005).

Bibliography

Azpiazu, Daniel (2002) 'Privatizaciones en la Argentina. La captura institucional del Estado', *Realidad Económica*, 189 (July–August).

Azpiazu, Daniel and Martín Schorr (2003) *Crónica de una sumisión anunciada. Las renegociaciones con las empresas privatizadas bajo la administración Duhalde*, Buenos Aires: IDEP, FLACSO and Siglo Veintiuno Editores Argentina.

Azpiazu, Daniel, Eduardo Basualdo and Miguel Khavisse (1989) *El nuevo poder económico en la Argentina de los años 80*, Buenos Aires: Legasa.

Basualdo, Eduardo (1987) *Deuda externa y poder económico en la Argentina*, Buenos Aires: Editorial Nueva América.

—— (1994) 'El impacto económico y social de las privatizaciones', *Realidad Económica*, 123 (abril–mayo).

—— (2000) *Acerca de la naturaleza de la deuda externa y la definición de una estrategia política*, Buenos Aires: Universidad Nacional de Quilmes, FLACSO, Página/12.

—— (2001) *Sistema político y modelo de acumulación en la Argentina*, Buenos Aires: Universidad Nacional de Quilmes, FLACSO, IDEP.

—— (2003) 'Las reformas estructurales y el Plan de Convertibilidad durante la década de los noventa. El auge y la crisis de la valorización financiera', *Realidad Económic*, 200 (noviembre–diciembre).

—— (2004) 'Notas sobre la burguesía nacional, el capital extranjero y la oligarquía pampeana', *Realidad Económica*, 201 (enero–febrero).

Cafiero, Mario and Javier Llorens (2002) *La argentina robada. El corralito, los bancos y el vaciamiento del sistema financiero argentino*, Buenos Aires: Ediciones Macchi.

Calcagno, Alfredo Eric (1986) *La perversa deuda argentina: radiografía de dos deudas perversas con víctimas muy diferentes: la de Eréndira con su abuela desalmada y la de Argentina con la Banca internacional*, Buenos Aires: Editorial Legasa.

Calcagno, Alfredo Eric and Eric Calcagno (2005) 'Finanzas al margen de la ley. Quiénes y cómo fugaron capitales', *Le Monde Diplomatique – Ediciones Cono Sur*, VI: 67, enero: 14–16.

Cámara de Diputados de la Nación (2005) *Comisión Especial Investigadora de la Cámara de Diputados sobre Fuga de Divisas de la Argentina durante el año 2001*, Buenos Aires: Cámara de Diputados de la Nación.

Carrera, Jorge (2002) 'Hard peg and monetary unions. Main lessons from the Argentine experience', paper. Unpublished paper.

Eichengreen, Barry (1996) *Globalizing Capital. A History of the International Monetary System*, Princeton, NJ: Princeton University Press.

Galetti, Pablo (2004) '¿Qué significa hoy "burguesía nacional"?', *Realidad Económica* 201 (enero–febrero).

Giarracca, Norma and Miguel Teubal (eds) (2005) *El campo argentino en la encrucijada. Tierra, estrategias, resistencias y sus ecos en la ciudad*, Buenos Aires: Alianza Editorial.

—— (2004) '"Que se vayan todos": Neoliberal collapse and social protest in Argentina', in Jolle Demmers, Alex, E. Fernández Jilberto and Barbara Hogenboom (eds), *Good Governance in the Era of Global Neoliberalism. Conflict and Depolitisation in Latin America, Eastern Europe, Asia and Africa*, London and New York: Routledge.

Hourest, Martín and Claudio Lozano (2001) *Recuperar la política contra la crisis de la violencia*, Buenos Aires: IDEF-CTA.

IDEP (Instituto de Estudios sobre Estado y Participación) (1992) *El Plan Brady. Economía y Política tras el Acuerdo Acreedor*, Buenos Aires: ATE.

Kulfas, Matías and Martín Schorr (2003) 'Deuda externa y valorización financiera en la Argentina actual. Factores explicativos del crecimiento del endeudamiento externo y perspectivas ante el proceso de renegociación', *Realidad Económica*, 96 (agosto–septiembre).

Lozano, Claudio (ed.) (2003) 'Acerca de la negociación del endeudamiento externo. Discurso y realidad. La economía contra la política', IFEF-CTA, unpublished document.

Lozano, Claudio, Ana Rameri and Tomás Raffo (eds) (2005) *La cúpula empresaria argentina: Estado de situación al 2003*, Buenos Aires: IDEF-CT.

—— (2005) *Boletín Estadístico: La situación a finales del 2004 en materia de pobreza e indigencia, distribución del ingreso, mercado laboral y proyecciones*, Buenos Aires: IDEF-CTA.

Minsburg, Naúm (1987) *Capitales extranjeros y grupos dominantes argentinos*, Vols 1 and 2, Buenos Aires: Centro Editor de América Latina.

O'Donnell, Guillermo (1979) 'Tensions in the bureaucratic-authoritarian state and the question of democracy', in David Collier (ed.), *The New Authoritarianism in Latin América*, Princeton, NJ: Princeton University Press.

Schorr, Martín (2004) *Industria y nación. Poder económico, neoliberalismo y alternativas de reindustrialización en la Argentina contemporánea*, Buenos Aires: Edhasa, IDAES.

Stiglitz, Joseph E. and Shahid Yusuf (eds) (2001) *Rethinking the East Asian Miracle*, Oxford: Oxford University Press.

Teubal, Miguel (1983a) 'Argentina: the crisis of ultramonetarism', *Monthly Review*, February.

—— (1983b) 'Argentina: fragile democracy', in Barry Gills, Joel Rocamora and Richard Wilson (eds), *Low Intensity Democracy. Political Power in the New World Order*, London and Boulder, CO: Pluto Press.

—— (2000/2001) 'Structural adjustment and social disarticulation: the case of Argentina', *Science & Society*, 64 (4): 11–20.

—— (2001) 'From import substitution industrialization to the "open" economy in Argentina: the role of Peronism', in Jolle Demmers, Alex, E. Fernández Jilberto and Barbara Hogenboom (eds), *Miraculous Metamorphoses. The Neoliberalization of Latin American Populism*, London and New York: Zed Books.

—— (2004) 'Rise and collapse of neoliberalism in Argentina. The role of economic groups', *Journal of Developing Societies*, 20 (3–4): 173–88.

Teubal, Miguel and Javier Rodríguez (2002) *Agro y alimentos en la globalización. Una perspectiva crítica*, Buenos Aires: La Colmena.

Teunissen, Jan Joost and Age Akkerman (eds) (2003) *The Crisis that Was Not Prevented. Lessons for Argentina, the IMF and Globalisation*, The Hague: FONDAD.

United States Congress (2003) *Argentina's Economic Crisis: Causes and Cures*, Joint Economic Committee (with Vice Chairman Jim Saxton), June.

8 Economic flexibilisation and denationalisation in Brazil

Roberto Rocco

Late capitalism, characterised by flexible and dispersed production, has dramatically changed and increased global exchanges of all sorts. Global economic integration has proceeded along two main lines: trade liberalisation (the increased circulation of goods) and financial liberalisation (the expanded circulation of capital). Increasing world economic integration has helped shape the phenomenon generally dubbed as 'globalisation'. In fact, in specifically economic contexts, globalisation is often understood to refer almost exclusively to the effects of trade, particularly economic liberalisation or free trade. For Krempel and Pluemper (1997), for instance, 'globalisation ... describes an economic process which results from the changes of the investment, production and distribution decisions made by individual firms'. For the World Bank (2005), globalisation is 'the growing integration of economies and societies around the world'. For the International Monetary Fund (IMF 2000), it refers to 'the increasing integration of economies around the world, particularly through trade and financial flows'. The IMF concedes that 'the term sometimes also refers to the movement of people (labour) and knowledge (technology) across international borders' and that 'there are also broader cultural, political and environmental dimensions of globalisation that are not covered here'.

However, globalisation understood as the increase and extension of all kinds of exchanges and flows to the global arena is a much further-reaching phenomenon that cannot be restricted to economic integration and liberalisation of markets. The failure to distinguish between globalisation and market liberalisation is blurry and ideologised, because it overlooks international division of labour and imbalances in access to financial and technology resources, suggesting that, if societies follow the path of economic liberalisation and free trade, all will benefit from globalisation evenly. The consequences of economic incorporation of societies into a 'global market economy' are extensive and unpredictable. A very clear pattern, however, emerges when we analyse the measures and actions taken by governments in developing countries in order to gain access to a 'globalised world'. The case of Brazil is paradigmatic.

During the 1990s, the Brazilian economy went through a deep and sudden process of flexibilisation of its former standards and regulations, largely perceived as obsolete, ineffective and obstructive to the country's ability to attract foreign investment, to grow and to modernise. Foreign investment was perceived as the only means through which the country could grow and develop, because of the huge external debt contracted in previous decades. This resulted in, among other things, the privatisation of economic assets, an unprecedented inflow of foreign direct investment (FDI) and an exceptional rise in the foreign presence in various sectors of the economy. It can be said that Brazilian industry suffered a marked process of denationalisation during the 1990s, when a part of Brazilian industrial bourgeoisie transferred its assets to international investors.

This chapter is concerned with the infrastructural scenario that in the 1990s made it possible and desirable for part of the industrial bourgeoisie to hand over their assets, and with the possible outcomes for Brazilian development in the future.

The way to economic dependency

In the 1990s, the main lines of contemporary economic liberalism and its political façade, the 'Third Way', were widely heralded by its most prominent advocates, in particular UK Prime Minister Tony Blair, French Prime Minister Lionel Jospin and American President Bill Clinton. They were followed eagerly by former Brazilian President Fernando Henrique Cardoso. Ideas about trade liberalisation and free market coupled with social development were also widely propagated and supported by international organisations such as the World Bank and the IMF. At the end of the 1980s, as Brazil slowly moved back to democracy after more than 20 years of military rule, the question of modernisation and development was reasserted. Cardoso was the first President to be able to implement an extensive and comprehensive economic programme. The aims of this programme were macroeconomic stabilisation and development.

Cardoso, an accomplished sociologist and political scientist, had theorised earlier on the 'inescapable' dependency of peripheral countries, like Brazil, whose bourgeoisie would never be able to carry out a successful programme of independent industrialisation and modernisation. Rocha *et al.* (2001: 1) point out that in his earlier days as a renowned academician, Cardoso had viewed the association of national capital in the periphery of capitalism with international capital as practically unavoidable. However, in his famous 'Theory of Dependency', Cardoso explicitly acknowledged that this association would not lead to economic convergence between the Third World and developed nations. It would, on the contrary, perpetuate deep social and economic inequalities and ultimately lead to loss of control over the direction of national development, along with the increase of vulnerability to external financial shocks. Cardoso was apparently right in his assessment, but as

President of Brazil between 1995 and 2003 (two consecutive mandates), economic dependency was greatly strengthened and vulnerability to worldwide financial shocks augmented.

As Brazilian philosopher Chauí (1999) points out, the 'Third Way', to which Cardoso whole-heartedly subscribed, had a deeply ideologised face. Most important of all, it attempted to abolish the concept of class struggle, a concept viewed as obsolete by mainstream political philosophy since before the fall of the former Soviet Union. According to Chauí, the 'Third Way' based itself on three main propositions in order to do so. First, '[t]he political polarity Left/Right would not make sense in a world scenario that is no longer bipolar, that is, in a world where the division between capitalism and socialism no longer makes sense'. Second, '[t]he division between Right and Left leaves the Left blind to the material benefits from capitalism, and the Right blind to the great humanistic values of socialism'. And third,

> [t]he coupling of those material benefits and high values has to be made in order to shape a new consensus. However, there are *sine qua non* conditions: to untangle the idea of social justice from the idea of social equality and to assert the priority of individual initiative as an instrument for collective progress against the obsolete postulate of collective property of the means of production.
>
> (Chauí 1999: 9)

These concepts formed the core of the first theorisations of the 'Third Way', whose basic assumption is

> the essential harmony between capitalism (the market society: pragmatic, innovative) and democracy ([with its] values of justice and individuality). [That is] because both are founded on the practice of competition and dislike the 'coward search for security at any price' (meaning, today's welfare state and tomorrow's collective property of the production means).
>
> (Chauí 1999: 9)

These formulations were not new, states Chauí. They have been used before in order to preserve the 'hard core of capitalist materiality' and to disguise it with socially biased discussion devoid of any real impact on the current exploitation of the working classes. Ideas like those propagated by the 'Third Way' have been used as a strategy for the renovation and perpetuation of the capitalist system at various moments of crisis. In its current form, it represents a deep intensifying of social contradictions and the assertion of the liberal option for the investment of public funds for the protection of capital, instead of the protection of labour.

In the Brazilian case, the idea of a fair insertion of developing countries in the world market brought with it the flexibilisation of the rules that had protected national industry within the framework of the 'import substitution' policy. This policy had been put into practice since the Revolution of 1930 and had encouraged rapid industrialisation of the country through high tariff barriers. Opposing voices to the import substitution policy advanced that Brazilian industry had become inefficient, outdated and poorly competitive because of excessive protectionism. Beginning with the short but frantic presidency of Fernando Collor de Mello (1990–2), who was impeached because of massive corruption, various channels of global exchange were opened at various levels. Deep changes took place as the labour market structure changed rapidly and the country had to adapt itself to global oriented production strategies. In consonance with an increasingly integrated world market, Brazilian economy became increasingly more exposed to global fluctuations.[1]

The new intensity of the connections between the domestic economy and the global market was illustrated by the importance given by the IMF to the crisis originated by the sudden fall of Brazil's currency, the real, in its report of May 1999. The abrupt but expected devaluation of the Brazilian currency had occurred in February of that year. It was in itself the consequence of a larger systemic crisis initiated with the speculative assault and later devaluation of the Thai currency, the baht, back in 1997, which opened the path for the greater crisis of East Asia. This particular crisis in financial markets took greater proportions as it swallowed the entire productive system of the 'emerging' countries of the region. It was the second great capitalist crisis in a period of 25 years and it unfolded as follows. In 1997, following the fall of the Thai baht, there was a general movement of currency devaluation in the so-called Asian Tigers (Korea, Taiwan and Singapore), as well as other newly industrialised countries of Southeast Asia (Indonesia and the Philippines). With the generalised fall in stock markets all over the world, the stock market exchange rate was heavily affected in Asia, Latin America and Eastern Europe. São Paulo's stock market exchange dropped by 15 per cent. In 1998, the Japanese economy slowed down, a phenomenon the IMF defined as dialectically cause and symptom of the crisis in Southeast Asia. Simultaneously, the Russian external debt crisis intensified. The country lost international credibility, but was supported by swift action taken by the IMF and the United States, who feared a stalemate in Russia's governance. The IMF offered Russia an extensive loan in order to normalise the payment of its international debt.

Then, in January 1999, a speculative assault took place against the real, the Brazilian currency. Foreign investors started to pull out from Brazilian stock exchange markets. They were afraid Brazilian authorities would promote a maxi-devaluation of the currency. In response, the Brazilian government promoted a considerable rise in domestic interest rates in order to keep international investment from leaving the country. At this time, Brazil lost even more international investors' credibility. There was a general feeling that Brazilian authorities would not be able to uphold the exchange rate of the currency. Internal debt increased enormously, due to the rise in interest rates. This made international investors even more apprehensive about Brazilian authorities' ability to tame the crisis. Once again, the IMF and the United States came to the rescue of an emerging country's economy. A huge loan was proposed. This was supposed to appease international investors and keep Cardoso's presidency protected until the following elections, for fear of a leftist rise. Hence, $70 billion was spent in order to keep investors' confidence and to secure the face value of the Brazilian national currency. The American Congress demanded explanations from its Central Bank on loans to Brazil. American authorities declared that Brazil was too big an economy to be left alone, and had to be rescued at all costs.

As a consequence of the success in securing Brazilian economic stability, President Cardoso was re-elected in November 1997 for another four years in office. He was inaugurated in January 1998. Soon afterwards, Brazilian authorities let the currency value 'float' within the limits of a pre-defined bandwidth. Brazilian stock markets fell dramatically. The government let currency rates 'float freely'. Within a few weeks, the Brazilian real lost 45 per cent of its face value in relation to the American dollar. In its report on the world economy of May 1999, the IMF observed, 'positive aspects in world economy recovery after the Asian Crisis of 1997 were overshadowed by some "steps backwards"' (IMF 1999). One of these steps back was the Brazilian crisis, which the IMF highlighted. Nevertheless, the report also stressed that the Brazilian economic turmoil had only limited effects, and its 'contagion' to other economies in the developing world could be prevented, with limited economic spillover. The notions of financial contagion and economic spillover are to be found throughout the analysis made by the IMF, which clearly corroborated the idea of the inevitable interconnectivity of world markets.

So-called emerging markets received rising amounts of FDI during the 1990s, increasing global interdependency. However, a great part of it was mostly volatile and speculative investment, which could be easily withdrawn in case of emergency. Brazilian economist Paulini (1996) states that

> when they are not merely speculative movements, such investments are nothing but simple merger and acquisition operations involving already existing companies. . . . [But] when they do create new productive capacity in Third World countries, it is the extremely low cost of labour that shapes investment.

Thus globalisation has a distinguished ideological character when it leads to the belief that its benefits are equally distributed among all countries. Yet as French sociologist Alain Touraine asserts in *Folha de São Paulo*, 'it sounds awfully more elegant to say that Coca-Cola, CNN and Microsoft are "global" enterprises, instead of American companies, which in reality they have never ceased to be' (*FSP* 14 July 1996: 5–6).[2]

On the one hand there has been a great expansion in the total amount of FDI, following the escalade of global business; on the other hand, of a total amount of $315 billion invested in 1995, approximately 68 per cent remained in developed countries. The investments in 'emerging countries' during that year were approximately $100 billion (32 per cent of the total investment). Until the mid-1990s, Brazil was the second largest receptor of FDI in Latin America, after Mexico. In the second half of the decade, and shortly before the Asian crisis, Brazil would regain the leadership of foreign investments. In 1996, $7.5 billion was invested in the country (*FSP* 25 September 1996: 2–14). However, fund remittances also soared higher. In December 1996, $5.4 billion was remitted overseas as a result of foreign companies' profits in the Brazilian domestic market (*OESP* 28 December 1996: B-8).

As regards flexibility and capital mobility, big transnational enterprises became even more 'flexible' than they had been before. In the case of a financial or political crisis, the withdrawal of investments should occur with the minimum possible losses and the reallocation of activities should be done in the shortest possible time. As for the productive units (factories), the flexibility in the connection of activities and plants should guarantee the possibility of a rapid interruption of activities and their transfer to other plants elsewhere in no time. In Brazil, investors were assured, by means of new legislation and special agreements, of the possibility for safe withdrawal of investments without major losses, whenever necessary. Finally, the growing tendency for the progressive reallocation of production resources to the tertiary sector and the outsourcing of activities contributed to the reduction in the costs of labour. This was accompanied by a reduction in the capacity of workers to organise themselves and a dilution of their common claims. Consequently, traditional labour unions have lost much of their importance in the last decade.

For instance, the Volkswagen truck factory, inaugurated in November 1996 in the city of Resende (Rio de Janeiro) was considered by labour unions a threat to the existing model of labour representation (*FSP* 2 January 1997). The plant included a 'modular consortium', that is, a new modality of partnership that took productive units of the various parts suppliers inside the plant. Each supplier unit (an independent company in itself) is located in a specific part of the plant and thus undertakes responsibility for its specific tasks in the automobile assembling process. The result is evidently the fragmentation of the labour force representation: in 1997, out of 1,000 workers in the factory, only 20 per cent belonged to Volkswagen itself. The new system represented a radicalisation in the process of production and labour segmentation and compelled workers to reformulate their strategies of action.[3]

Hindered accumulation and the Plano Real

For Déak (1986), 'Brazilian history so far is the history of the reproduction of the conditions of domination of a minute oligarchy, the origins of which go back to the colonial elite'. Peculiarities in Brazilian history explain why this old elite was never overthrown in favour of a modernising bourgeoisie. 'The most fundamental feature of the elite society is that . . . neither the commodity form is generalised, nor social relations are reified.' Déak, following Marx, affirms that the primacy of the commodity form (of exchange value over use value) and the reification of social relations are the very means of bourgeois domination. The excessive privileges enjoyed by the elite in Brazil are inconsistent with the full realisation of the commodity form and therefore capitalism has never been fully achieved. The Brazilian bourgeoisie is in fact unable to carry out reforms that would secure it at the head of the economic and political processes. The bourgeoisie is constrained by the excessive power of the old elites and therefore accumulation in Brazil is 'hindered', making alliances and dependency necessary for the survival of the bourgeoisie and the perpetuation of the elite domination. The pendulous and sometimes complementary relationship between regressive elites and modernising bourgeoisie was never resolved, but the import substitution policy had somehow protected the latter group, which thrived.

The 'opening' of the Brazilian market and the flexibilisation of economic regulations were initiated during the presidency of Collor de Mello (1990–2) and carried throughout the governments of Franco (1992–5) and Cardoso (1995–2003). Cardoso was its most enthusiastic advocate and the deviser of the Plano Real, the macroeconomic plan launched in 1993 in order to rescue Brazil from hyperinflation and chronic economic instability, while Cardoso was still Finance Minister. According to Rocha (2002: 7), the Plano Real was

> much more ambitious in conception than a mere scheme for stabilisation. . . . [I]ts central premise was that only by slashing inflation could an attractive investment climate be created for foreign investment by multinationals in Brazil, and only massive inflows of such productive capital from abroad could provide a new and sound basis for long-term domestic growth. . . . To this end, Cardoso recommended the elimination of barriers to foreign corporations in the exploitation of natural resources, and the consent for multinational corporations to take part in the privatisation of strategic state-owned enterprises in the infrastructure sector. In fact, a central section of the stabilisation plan advocated modernisation of the economy with the help of foreign capital.

The scenario raised by the Plano Real allowed the massive penetration of foreign capitals and products into the Brazilian market, resulting in denationalisation of Brazilian productive assets. The overvaluation of the currency resulted in a sudden and unprecedented rise in imports of all sorts, or 52.7 per cent in the first six months of the Plan alone (Rocha 2002). The consequences for local industry were immense. The insertion coefficient of imported manufactured and semi-manufactured goods increased from 4.8 per cent in 1989 to

20.3 per cent in 1998 (Castro 1999). This massive penetration of imports, in addition to the high interests practised by the Brazilian Central Bank in order to attract foreign investment, suppressed an incalculable number of small and medium-sized enterprises. However, some sectors gathered benefits with the possibility of buying machines and importing unfinished goods on the international market at low prices and comparatively low interest rates.

On the changes in the 1990s Castro (1999: 2) asserts:

> In order to evaluate the importance of what has happened in Brazil, we should consider two parallel phenomena. In the cases of Chile and Argentina, the opening of markets was accompanied by a flagrant recession of manufacturing activities. In Chile, some sectors have virtually disappeared; in Argentina, there was a shift from the actual production of goods to the mere assemblage of final products. Former East Germany and Russia are also examples of [industrial] regression. . . . It is essential to understand, however, that for the radical advocates of neo-liberalism . . ., the decline and even the death of industries that were formed during the import substitution period has never been regarded as a 'problem'. Nobody should cry for enterprises that, according to those radicals, were created by means of 'illicit association' between technocrats and industrialists. Rather on the contrary, the resources liberated after their disappearing would supposedly give place to other enterprises, not necessarily industrial ones. Nevertheless, these new enterprises would be free from the distortions created by public policies and would therefore be able to mirror the true comparative advantages of the country.

Although the import substitution policies might indeed have created some 'distortions', for many these policies constituted the very core of the rapid process of industrialisation that Brazil underwent from the 1950s until the mid-1970s (dubbed the 'Brazilian miracle'), when the national industrial bourgeoisie prospered. In a few words, the liberalisation of markets meant an accentuated change in the ownership structure of Brazilian productive assets.

Denationalisation and compromise of the national bourgeoisie

During the 1990s, numerous enterprises owned by Brazilian groups bent to foreign groups' merger proposals. Financial consultant Barrizzelli argues that the liberalisation of the Brazilian economy presented local businessmen with a dilemma: they could either 'reduce costs and acquiesce to a role of little prominence in the internal market', or else they could 'sell their enterprises to stronger groups'. Competition between enterprises has become even stronger with the rise of globalisation, and only enterprises that are able to obtain cheap loans and capital in order to invest and grow could survive. As money was scarce in Brazil because loans were granted at very high interest rates, 'the only exit is to sell your business'. Enterprises traditionally owned and managed by Brazilian families thus faced the situation that 'it would have been impossible to grow at the same pace as foreign enterprises, which had access to cheaper resources for investment', as they were subject to milder interest rates in their countries of origin (Barrizzelli 1999: 2–7).

Meanwhile, the Brazilian federal government

> offered investors not only one of the world's highest interest rates, but also the ability to move their funds out of the country at any time, through highly advantageous tax-exempt mechanisms known as CC5s: bank accounts for non-residents with free access to floating exchange rates. Investors were further lured with hedge mechanisms, such as exchange-indexed government treasury bonds, to insure that they would retain the value of their assets when they left.
>
> (Rocha 2002: 9)

In face of the huge advantages offered to international investors, the Brazilian bourgeoisie seems to have had to step aside.

A good example is Arno, a Brazilian electric appliances producer that shared the Brazilian market with Walita (of the Dutch group Philips). With a total budget of $305 million and a net profit of $32 million in 1996, Arno enjoyed a solid position. The enterprise, which had been operating in the Brazilian market for decades, had no financial reason to be sold or merged. In spite of this, the Arno family saw 'insurmountable obstacles' in continuing in business. The Arnos had arrived in Brazil after leaving Italy at the beginning of twentieth century. Italian immigrants constituted a large part of Brazil's very first industrial bourgeoisie concentrated in the city of São Paulo who benefited from capital accumulation issued from coffee exports and the introduction of waged labour after the abolition of slavery at the end of the nineteenth century. But in the 1990s, the Arnos claimed 'difficulty in getting access to new technology', among other factors, to justify their decision to sell their company. In March 1997, the enterprise was sold to the French group SEB, one of the largest producers of electric appliances and kitchen utensils worldwide. The value of the transaction remained well below the company's 1996 budget: $162 million (Nez 1997).

Data collected by consulting firm KPMG show that from 1990 to 2000 a total of 2,038 Brazilian enterprises were sold or merged with other enterprises, either national or foreign. Of all transactions 61 per cent involved foreign resources:

> The United States was the country that invested most in Brazil, followed by France, Portugal and Spain. The average growth in total transactions, including both domestic and cross border deals, totalled 13% per annum. The accumulated growth over the period reached 134%.
>
> (KPMG 2001: 3)

The KPMG study divides the 1990s into three distinct periods, defined by significant economic and political events. From 1990 to 1993 the Brazilian economy opened up to the world market. Those years were characterised by decentralisation, followed by privatisation, concentration and verticalisation of the market. 'Large mergers and acquisitions were registered in basic industries, such as chemical and petrochemical products (22 deals) and metal and steel (24 deals)' (KPMG 2001: 4). Between 1994 and 1997 the introduction of the Plano Real meant a change of emphasis on mergers from the basic sector to the financial sector (107 transactions over the period), electronics (53) and automobile parts industry (42). Increasingly, one could witness the effects of a globalised market, the concentration of investments and the government aid to banks in financial distress (via PROER[4]). The boom of mergers and acquisitions in Brazil occurred in 1997, when 372 transactions were carried out. Finally, between 1998 and 2000, the number of transactions dropped (especially in 1999), and there was a slow recovery after the aftermath of the Asian crises and the currency devaluation, in particular in more advanced industries such as telecommunications (104 transactions), information technology (93), advertising and publishing houses (59), following technological integration of the country thanks to investments in telecommunications.

During the 1990s international investors were particularly interested in Brazil's food sector. 'Large organisations such as Cargill, Arisco, Sadia and Parmalat filled their shopping cart with small and medium sized companies during the entire decade' (KPMG 2001: 5). As Table 8.1 shows, of the 269 transactions in that sector, 57 per cent were carried out with foreign capital, followed by financial institutions with 176 transactions of which 56 per cent were with foreign capital, and telecommunications enterprises with 136 transactions of which 70 per cent were with foreign capital. Despite the largest number of transactions being in the primary sector, the tertiary sector attracted more international investors; insurance (75 per cent),

Table 8.1 Merger and acquisition transactions by sector in Brazil, 1990–2000

Sector	Number of transactions	% of foreign capital
Food	269	57
Finance	176	56
Telecommunications	136	70
Information technology	127	69
Chemicals	110	60
Metals	98	63
Insurance	87	75
Automobile parts	81	68
Publishing houses/Advertising	78	58
Electronics	72	67

Source: KPMG (2001).

telecommunications (70 per cent), and information technology (69 per cent) had the largest foreign incursion.

Various analysts have claimed that there was an excess of capital in developed economies in the late 1990s. According to Morgan Guaranty Trust Bank Director Branco (in Nez 1997), the

> winding down of fast growing possibilities . . . in the already mature markets makes global enterprises interested in countries like Brazil. . . . The merger or acquisition of companies are just ways of burning steps in order to obtain a faster return of investments.

According to Barrizzelli's assessment, obstacles encountered by small Brazilian enterprises in order to grow and survive were 'annihilating the national industrial patrimony'. He viewed such a state of affairs as remarkably critical, since the acquisition of national enterprises by foreign groups would mean an even larger amount of profit remittances and repatriation of capital in the future, with modest advantages for Brazilian society. 'In the long term, we will have serious problems in the foreign exchange balance. If only the country had a solid national industrial policy, all those enterprises would not have had to be bought by foreign investors' (Barrizzelli 1999: 2–7).

Capital remittances by multinationals established in Brazil tripled during the second half of the 1990s, from $2.5 billion in 1994 to $7.2 billion in 1998 (see also Table 8.2). Brazilian businessman Jeha, the industrial policy co-ordinator at the mighty Industry Federation of the State of São Paulo (FIESP) asseverated: 'The indiscriminate internationalisation [of the economy] will strain the balance of payments and is putting the country in a position of total subordination' (*FSP* 3 October 1999: 1–10).

In an article published in 1999 by several Brazilian newspapers, journalist and political analyst Gaspari summarises the situation of the frantic rhythm of mergers and acquisitions in the 1990s:

> Since this 'feast' was instituted, profit remittances in the form of shares have tripled. Last year, they attained $7 billion. There are branches of multinational companies that complain to their headquarters because they are compelled to remit capital that, they ponder, would better be reinvested locally. As for a multinational company (or even a Brazilian

Table 8.2 Brazil profit remittances, 1980–99 (annual average in US$ million)

	1980–9	*1990–9*	*1990–4*	*1995–9*
Profit and dividend remittances	1.006	3.495	1.578	5.411

Source: Bacen, NEIT/UNICAMP (Laplane *et al.* 2000).

company with access to external credit) it is much more profitable to remit profits, which suffer a taxation of only 15%, and re-send the money to Brazil in the form of loans. The actual state of affairs implies that money gets out of the country because taxation is low and comes back in the form of loans because internal interest rates are high.

Gaspari ironically explains that these measures were taken 'in the name of the most advanced tributary cosmopolitanism'. Brazil is so 'advanced' in eliminating the barriers for the remittance of profits that in Brazil remittances are taxed only 15 per cent, compared to 51 per cent in the United States, 53 per cent in Japan, and 58 per cent in Germany. 'One may argue that these countries do not need to attract external investment; therefore they can tighten the rules. This is not the case for Argentina, who charges 33% for profit remittances to other countries' (Gaspari 1999: 1–13).

Effects of denationalisation

The intensive internationalisation of the Brazilian economy during the 1990s has not really represented any improvement in competitiveness and efficiency. A research among 120 merged or acquired enterprises in Brazil between 1990 and 1997 shows that there is no evidence of enterprises' profit increase until two years after the transactions, the market share has no significant increase, and there are no significant statistical differences in investment behaviour between foreign and national enterprises. In short, there was no significant increase in productivity and efficiency in Brazilian industry. Apparently, merger and acquisition operations in Brazil do not correspond to a traditional economic movement, such as in American or European cases. Mergers in Brazil 'occurred in the framework of the establishment of a new regulatory regime, a process marked by the priority given to macroeconomic stability and economic liberalisation' (Rocha *et al.* 2001: 5).

The main problem, according to economist Antonio Correa de Lacerda, then Vice-President of the Brazilian Society for the Study of Multinational Enterprises and Economic Globalisation (SOBEET), was that 'the best part of foreign industries that come to Brazil are not exportation companies. That is to say, they will send profits to their home countries without the necessary counterpart in dollars issued from exports'. As Lacerda highlights, the volume of production would not grow, since companies would be merely 'changing hands'. However, it would generate a great movement for labour and production reorganisation in the Brazilian territory. As a result, there would not be real gains, since new jobs would not be created and no real economic growth would occur (all quotes from *FSP* 3 October 1999: 1–10).

These trends, far from representing a defeat to the Brazilian bourgeoisie, actually meant an opportunity to accomplish massive financial accumulation. It allowed them to invest in the frenetic financial markets and the extremely lucrative pension funds. Such was the case of the Feijó family, former owners of supermarket chain Exxtra Econômico, in the state of Rio Grande do Sul. The selling of the supermarket chain allowed the family to invest their money in a banking share pool:

> Paulo Afonso Feijó ... says he could perfectly live on the profits from his investments in the financial market, since, apart from the capital he received from the selling of his supermarkets, the family also holds real estate property and car selling stores.
>
> (Barrizzelli 1999: 2–6)

Apparently, the Feijós had no intention of returning to the supermarket business, a sector almost completely taken over by large transnational companies in the 1990s.

A similar phenomenon occurred with some 'iconic' companies (for Brazilian consumers) that were sold in the second half of the 1990s. According to the business magazine *Exame*, the owners of Metal Leve (steel production), Estrela (toys), Lacta (chocolate production), Perdigão (food processing), Tupy and Arno (electric appliances), which were 'symbols of Brazilian capitalism', had not been 'cautious' enough when facing the new challenges presented by an open market and thus had had to sell their enterprises. This traditional market-oriented and liberal business magazine then poses itself the question 'does that mean that they made mistakes, as physical persons?', answering, 'not necessarily'(*Exame* 9 April 1997: 20–30).

An interesting issue is what happened to the Brazilian businessmen who sold their enterprises to foreign investors. Some families from the industrial elite chose to secure their standard of living by 'handling out' their enterprises to international investors either in exchange for commanding posts in the new organisations or in exchange for funds that could be invested in the highly lucrative financial market. This shift allowed those families to benefit from the high interest rates, instead of suffering the effects of a restraining economic policy caused by them. In some cases, the business was given up altogether. Economic consultants Lodi, who specialised in family enterprises, maintain that 'the great majority of businessmen who sell their companies eventually get back to business in less important enterprises connected to "supporting" activities', but also many Brazilian businessmen withdraw completely from the business world while continuing to enjoy an extremely high standard of living, thanks to investment of their new acquired cash in the financial markets (Barrizzelli 1999: 2–6).[5]

The very same businessmen who used to complain about the interest rates of the Brazilian banks thus made their profits out of these same high rates that made it impossible for them to continue doing business. Table 8.3 shows a list of selected big private Brazilian companies sold to foreign investors during the 1990s, as a result of the macroeconomic policies adopted by both federal and state governments during the 1990s. The importance of the enterprises listed in this table resides not only in their actual market

Table 8.3 Selected Brazilian families or individuals who sold their enterprises, 1993–2003

Family or individual	Company sold	Sector	Acquiring corporation (country of origin)	Year	Main activity of family or individual after transaction
Abraham Kasinski	Cofap Amortecedores	Car parts	Fiat (Italy)	1997	Various businesses, including a motorcycle factory in Manaus and a 75,000 ha cattle breeding farm in the State of Mato Grosso
Salvador & Carmelo Paoletti	Conservas Etti	Food processing	Parmalat (Italy)	1996	Founded Coniexpress SA, a food processing company
Cláudio di Marchi	Lacesa Laticínios	Dairy products	Parmalat (Italy)	1993	Mr Di Marchi became an executive at Parmalat Brazil
Cosette Alves	Mappin	Department stores	Grupo Ricardo Mansur (Brazil)	1996	Alves became President of the Brazilian Cinematheque
Dimitrios Markakis	Supermercados Cândia	Supermarket	Sonae Group (Portugal)	2003	Markakis applied most of the money in the financial market. He became a major partner at DiCicco building materials stores
Adhemar de Barros Filho and family	Chocolates Lacta	Food processing	Kraft Foods Inc. (USA)	?	The Barros family is a traditional dynasty of politicians
Brandalise family	Frigoríficos Perdigão	Food processing	Various pension funds (Brazil)	1994	?
Caloi family	Bicicletas Caloi	Bicycles	Edson Vaz Musa (Brazil)	1997	The Calois became minor partners in their own former family company
Conde family	Banco de Crédito Nacional	Banking	Bradesco (Brazil)	1998	The family declared 'We are not pressed by financial problems.' They invested in real estate companies and kept a company in order to manage investments in the financial market
Botton family/ André de Botton	Mesbla Lojas de Departamento	Department stores	Ricardo Mansur (Brazil)	1997	Retired from business
Demeterco family	Supermercados Mercadorama	Supermarket	Sonae Group (Portugal)	1998	The Demetercos started a logistics consultancy company
Feijó family	Supermercados Exxtra Econômico	Supermarket	Sonae Group (Portugal)	1999	Money applied in the financial market, web business, real estate and automobile sales
Pires, Lopes and Feria Families	Biscoitos Tostines	Food	Nestlé (Switzerland)	1994	?
Giaffone family/ Giuseppe Giaffone Jr.	Fogões Continental	Kitchenware	Bosch-Siemens (Germany)	1994	The Giaffones started a company specialising in armoured luxury cars. They also invested in racing cars and bought 80 fast-food 'Subway' franchise

Family/owner	Company	Sector	Buyer (country)	Year	Notes
Mindlin family/Sérgio Mindlin	Metal Leve	Metals	Mahle Group (Germany)	1996	Sergio Mindlin takes part in various NGOs. He was president of Abrinq and the Telefônica Foundation
Penteado family/Hélio Mattar	Fogões Dako	Kitchenware	General Eletric (USA)	1996	Mr Mattar along with other Penteado family members (Mattar is married to one of the Penteado heiresses) were kept on the company board of directors
Schmidt family	Fundição de Aço Tupy	Metals	Pension Fund Pool (Brazil)	1995	?
Varga family/Celso Varga	Freios Varga	Car parts	TRW Automotive (USA)	2000	Mr Varga started two medium-sized companies, including one specialised in catering
Villares family/Luis Dumont Villares	Villares (Elevadores Atlas)	Metals/elevators and rolling stairs	Acesita (Brazil)/Sul América	1995	The Villares became minor partners in the company
Arno family/Felippe Arno	Eletrodomésticos Arno	Kitchenware/house appliances	SEB Group (France)	1997	Retired from business life
João Gualberto Vasconcelos	Supermercados Petipreço	Supermarket	Bompreço Group (Brazil)	1999	At the time of this reseach, Mr Vasconcellos was looking forward to opening new businesses in other sectors
Luiz Macedo, Petrônio Corrêa and Luiz Mafuz	MPM Propaganda	Advertising	Interpublic (Lintas, USA)	1991	Mr Macedo spent his days at Rio de Janeiro Jockey Club, where he used to race 20 horses
Mário Adler	Estrela	Toys	Carlos Tilkian (Brazil)	1996	Became partner in a company that specialises in irrigation and sewage projects
Miguel H. Etchenique	Grupo Brasmotor	Kitchenware/house appliances	Whirlpool Corporation (USA)	1997	Mr Etchenique became a partner in the company. The family founded Synapsys Marketing & Media company and a car tracking and security company named Guard One
Prosdócimo family/Sérgio Prosdócimo	Refripar/Prosdocimo	House appliances (refrigerators)	Electrolux (Sweden)	1996	Sergio Prosdócimo became president of 'Instituto Brasileiro de Qualidade e Produtividade no Paraná' (Brazilian Institute for Quality and Productivity in the State of Parana), where he advocates greater protection for middle-sized national industries

Sources: various Brazilian journals and magazines.[6]

value, but also in their significance as emblems of the consolidation of a local bourgeoisie.

Merger and acquisition transactions involving foreign capital have allowed new corporative configuration and more specialisation in production, facilitating alliances between domestic and international capital, according to Miranda and Tavares (1999). However, the exceptionally high interest rates imposed by the Federal government and the preferential treatment dispensed to transnational companies (TNCs) willing to invest in Brazil seem to have created an insurmountable obstacle for national capital, with no real gains in productivity and labour creation, as Rocha *et al.* (2001) point out. The Federal government, backed by international organisations such as the IMF and the World Bank, claimed this was necessary in order to keep inflation under control, restrain the evasion of foreign investment and sustain the value of the Brazilian currency (until the end of 1998).

While Brazilian entrepreneurs found it increasingly difficult to finance their business, international corporations had access to much more favourable credit conditions. Even a public Brazilian financial institution such as the Bank for National Development (BNDES) gave preferential loans to foreign enterprises. In 1999, about 10 per cent of BNDES financing operations were destined to foreign enterprises. Between January and September 1999, the bank approved the concession of $667 million to finance companies with a majority of foreign shareholders, representing 10.7 per cent of the total $6.2 billion approved for the ensemble of Brazilian companies in the same period (these figures refer to loan authorisations and do not express actual loans made by the bank). The loans included financing for the acquiring of former state companies by foreign companies. There were three important cases: the privatisation of power and electricity companies from the states of São Paulo, Bahia and Rio Grande do Sul. The amount of the loans authorised in the previous year (1998) was comparable: $612 million (*FSP* 5 November 1999: 1–10).

This was a clear sign from the federal government to the Brazilian capitalist elite: financial stability was more important than economic growth and the creation of jobs. The country had taken massive loans from the IMF and the World Bank following the Asian crisis and would comply with these institutions' instructions on the direction of the economy. This did not go unnoticed by Brazilian industrialists. This policy was in fact rejected by some powerful names in the Brazilian economy, such as Antônio Ermínio de Moraes of the Votorantim Industrial Group (a producer of cement and steel) and Abílio Diniz of the Pão de Açúcar Group (a supermarket chain and financial institution). Both have chosen to continue operating their groups, which are in essence 'family businesses'.

The direction adopted by the Brazilian Federal government generated an intense debate inside the very core of the Federal government itself. In this debate, many criticised the *desenvovimentistas*, who believed the economy should continue to grow (thus contradicting the directions of IMF and the

World Bank and also the official position of the Brazilian presidential cabinet), and the *monetaristas*, who believed financial stability should be maintained at all costs. They pointed out that the wave of mergers and acquisitions that enveloped the whole economy during the 1990s was bound to management strategies that neglected labour and the creation of new jobs.

As a significant part of the means of production had been transferred to foreign hands, international economic groups sought to establish new production strategies, which should allow a rapid increase of profits. Deep changes in labour relations and the reorganisation of industrial production within the Brazilian territory reflected this fact. The new owners of Brazilian industry took some important measures. 'Modern' management techniques based on Japanese models were introduced, especially linked to management strategies of 'total quality', 'flexible production' and the tight control of stockpiles by means of 'just in time' production. 'Budget rationalisation' was used, in many cases meaning the withdrawal of investment in productive activities in favour of investments in the financial market. Another measure was the 'downsizing' or strategic cut in the payment roll. In the secondary sector 1.5 million jobs were cut between 1989 and 1997, representing 23.4 per cent of the total jobs in that sector (*FSP* 19 and 22 September 1999; Sabóia 1999). And a de-concentration of industrial plants took place. For example, Castro (1999) notes that the state of Rio de Janeiro lost 43 per cent of its industrial jobs between 1989 and 1997. On the other hand, the formerly little industrialised state of Ceará, in Northeastern Brazil, increased the number of industrial jobs in 9 per cent during the same period.

The flexibilisation of contracts is an essential component in the pursuit of the so-called comparative advantages in order to attract foreign investment.[7] The high level of organisation attained by labour unions in the region of São Paulo, for instance, went against the tendency of labour rights flexibilisation, as all fields of economic activity sought to establish flexible or temporary contracts in order to increase competitiveness. More frequently than not, the 'downsizing' formula adopted by buying corporations resulted in the elimination of jobs. The engagement of part of the funds generated by the selling of the family enterprises in the organisation of new ventures has not compensated for the losses in the labour market. This has happened especially because the newly created companies were of a non-industrial nature, and basically required a smaller numbers of workers, frequently higher qualified than industrial workers.

Conclusion

During the 1990s, Brazil's industrial elite withdrew without much conflict from areas attractive to international investors: industrialised food production and distribution, supermarket chains and automobile spare parts in the beginning of the decade and, later, telecommunications, advanced services and financial institutions. The industrial elite has either migrated to the tertiary sector or retreated from business altogether, investing their capital in the financial market, pension funds or real estate. Other possibilities were 'support activities' such as the building sector, packaging industry, car sales concessionaires, activities related to business and law consulting, business promotion, educational and cultural events, administrative and honorific positions in the 'third sector' (NGOs) and the administration of real estate.

Would it have been possible to resist this movement? Although difficult to assess, we may find an answer to this question in the macroeconomic policies adopted by the Federal government. They clearly indicated to the national industrial and financial bourgeoisie the path to be followed. In a report published by newspaper *Folha de São Paulo*, most businessmen complained about the 'lack of options' offered by the economic conjuncture created by the Federal government. Many declared they felt 'frustrated' by the fact they had to sell their 'life work'. If we subtract the rhetorical and demagogical aspects of these assertions, it is possible to assert that the compromise adopted by a large part of the Brazilian bourgeoisie was perceived by many as the *only way* to be followed. The *only way* (*la Voie Unique*) was fiercely criticised by many.[8]

There was neither resistance nor recovery by the Brazilian elite in face of the new challenges imposed by globalisation and market liberalisation. The above analysis indicates that there was a transference of industrial and financial activities to international groups. This granted Brazilian industrial and financial bourgeoisie some immediate financial benefits and the assurance of their position in the intricate balance of power established with the old elites, in exchange for their leadership in many dynamic sectors of national economy.

Notes

1   This was by no means an entirely new phenomenon, as demonstrated by the local effects of the many international crisis of capitalism during the twentieth century (like the New York Stock Exchange crash of 1929 that led many Brazilian farmers to bankruptcy).
2   For reference to newspaper articles, the following acronyms are used: *FSP* for *Folha de São Paulo* and *OESP* for *O Estado de São Paulo*.
3   In contrast with the new vulnerability of developing economies and their labour force, the IMF (1999: 1) observes that 'advanced economies in North America and Europe, as well as Australia, have proved resilient to the crisis in emerging markets', while also highlighting the 'surprising and continuous' growth of the American economy during the 1990s.
4   Programme of Stimulation to the Reorganisation and the National Financial System.
5   *Exame* (9 April 1997: 20–30) ironically declares:

> Don't cry for them: none of them is begging in the streets. Some have got away with a considerable amount of money and they will be freer now to enjoy the good things of life. José Mindlin, for instance, former owner of steel production factory Metal Leve, has much more time to dedicate himself

to his colossal personal book collection. But for all of them, the command of those capitalist icons is definitely gone.

6 The information in Table 8.3 roughly corresponds to what happened immediately after company sale; some companies were later on merged, sold or terminated, and individuals may have changed activities in the following years.

7 When Japanese car producers sought association with American enterprises in order to produce cars in American territory, they tried to locate their new plants in places where labour unions were less active or non-existent so as to be able to pay lower wages (Gorender 1996).

8 *La Voie Unique* is an expression created to challenge the fashionable political trend dubbed the 'Third Way' (cf. Ramonet 1997).

Bibliography

Barrizzelli, N. (1999) 'Falta política industrial, diz consultor', *Folha de São Paulo*, 5 December: 2–7.

Cardoso, F.H. and E. Faletto (1979) *Dependency and Development in Latin America*, Berkeley, CA: Berkeley University Press.

Castro, A.B. (1999) 'Vitória nas Trincheiras', *Folha de São Paulo*, 22 September: 2–19.

Chauí, M. (1999) 'Fantasias da Terceira Via', *Folha de São Paulo*, Caderno Mais, 19 December: 4–10.

Déak, C. (1986) *The Market and the State in the Spatial Organisation of Capitalist Production*, London: Bartlett School of Architecture and Planning.

—— (1988) *The Crisis of Hindered Accumulation in Brazil and Questions of Urban Policy*, London: Bartlett School of Architecture and Planning.

—— (1991) 'Acumulação entravada no Brasil e a crise dos anos 80', *Espaços & Debates*, 32: 32–46.

Gaspari, H. (1999) *Folha de São Paulo*, 1: August: 1–13.

Gorender, J. (1996) *Globalização, revolução tecnológica e relações de trabalho*, São Paulo: IEA-USP.

IMF (1999) *World Economy Outlook. International Financial Contagion*, Washington, DC: International Monetary Fund.

IMF (2000) 'Globalisation: threat or opportunity?', 12 April 2000 (corrected January 2002). Available from: www.imf.org/external/np/exr/ib/2000/041200.htm#II (accessed 5 September 2005).

KMPG (2001) *Mergers and Acquisitions in Brazil: Analysis of the 1990s*, Research report, Sao Paulo: KPMG Corporate Finance. Available from: www.kpmg.com.br (accessed 15 August 2005).

Krempel, L. and T. Pluemper (1997) 'International division of labour and global economic processes: an analysis of the international trade of cars with world trade data', in Working Group Netzwerkanalye (Netzkränzchen), MPIfG, World Congress of Sociology 10 July 1997, Cologne. Available from: www.mpi-fg-koeln.mpg.de/~lk/netvis/globale/ (accessed 25 July 2005).

Laplane, M. *et al.* (2000) *Empresas Transnacionais no Brasil nos anos 90: fatores de atração, estratégias e impactos*, Campinas: UNICAMP.

Miranda, Jose and Pedro Tavares (1999) *Antidumping, the Steel Industry and the FTAA*, Brasilia: Ministerio de Fazende.

New Zealand (2005) 'Trade matters', Ministry of Foreign Affairs and Trade. Available from: www.mfat.govt.nz/support/tplu/tradematters/glossary.html (accessed 10 August 2005).

Nez, C. (1997) 'As virtudes da paranóia', *Exame*, 633 (9 April): 20–30.

Paulini, L.M. (1996) *Jornal de Resenhas*, 8 November: 5.

Ramonet, I. (1997) 'Désarmer les marches', *Le Monde Diplomatique*, December: 1.

Rocha, C.F.L., M. Iotty and J. Ferraz (2001) 'Desempenho das Fusões e Aquisições na Década de 90: A Ótica das Empresas Adquiridas', *Revista de Economia Contemporânea* (Rio de Janeiro), 4: 20–7.

Rocha, G.M. (2002) 'Neo-dependency in Brazil', *New Left Review*, 16, (July–August): 24–32.

Sabóia, Joao (1997) *Produtividade na industria brasileira-questoes metadologricas e analise empírica*, Brasilia: IPEA.

United States (1999) 'Progressive governance in the 21st century', Presidential Summit, Florence, November, United States Embassy in Rome. Available from: www.usembassy.it/file9911/alia/9911210p5.htm (accessed 22 August 2005).

World Bank (2005) 'Development topics: globalisation'. Available from: www.worldbank.org/economicpolicy/globalisation/ (accessed 5 September 2005).

9 Transnationals, *grupos* and business associations in the privatisation of Central America's telecommunications

Benedicte Bull

Much of the literature on political and economic development in Central America has focused on the role of strong domestic producer groups and their relation to the state. The relative power of national agro-export and agro-industrialist oligarchies and the respective states and military apparatuses have been pointed out as keys to the differences between the five countries of the isthmus[1] in terms of peace, development and democracy.[2] Over the last 20 years, the Central American economies have been transformed towards market orientation, non-traditional exports, and closer integration into global production circuits. This has been accompanied by a shift in the structure of the local private sector: new economic groups have formed and linked up to transnational capital. Whether this really signifies a break with old patterns of domination or a continuation through new means is a disputed question.[3] What is clear is that the nature of interaction between the private sector and the state has changed; while during the period of state ownership of industry and infrastructure, private companies crowded around the large parastatals and developed close relationships with politicians in order to compete for contracts, in the 1980s a new form of relationship between politicians and the private sector emerged. Businessmen with significant personal interests in various economic sectors rose to political power and continued pursuing their interests from those positions.

The first part of this chapter discusses the general changes in the composition and organisation of the Central American private sectors. The second part provides a case study of one example of the encounter between old and new economic elites and their interaction with the state. This is the process of telecommunications reform, including deregulation and privatisation of former state-owned telecommunications companies (SOTs). The chapter focuses on Guatemala, Costa Rica and Honduras, and shows how alliances between local economic groups (*grupos*) and transnational corporations were crucial in pressuring for reforms. The story about the rise of market-oriented telecommunications policies in Central America is about local groups attempting to take advantage of the opportunities offered by the attention transnational companies paid to any unexploited market for telecommunications services – including small and poor ones – in the early 1990s. It is also about the regional strategies of a few telecommunications companies – primarily Telefónica de España and Telmex – with sufficient skills of culture and language to operate in highly non-transparent environments that characterised the telecommunications sectors at the beginning of the boom.

In recent literature on the private sector in Latin America, some mention has been made of possible tensions between *grupos*, transnational companies and business associations (Schneider 2004; Rettberg 2005). In several of the Central American countries – particularly Guatemala and El Salvador – encompassing business associations have played a significant role in politics. How the privatisation processes were influenced by, and contributed to the evolution of, this relationship is a secondary issue that will be explored in this chapter.

Economic actors in Central America

The relationship between the state and powerful groups related to productive activities has been a recurrent theme in much historical sociology, history and political science literature on Central America. In several studies, the term 'oligarchy' has been defined as strong private sector elites, knitted together through intermarriage and business relations (Dosal 1995; Casaus Arzú 1992a). Such national oligarchies were most likely to emerge related to sectors that were domestically controlled, particularly coffee and sugar production. In Honduras, where cattle, mining and later banana production dominated, foreign companies, and particularly US banana companies were more important (Flora and Torres-Rivas 1989; Schutlz and Sundloff Schultz 1994).

In the historical sociological literature a distinction is commonly made between agro-exporters and the agro-industrialists (Rueschemeyer *et al.* 1993). These are assumed to have fundamentally different interests regarding public investment[1] and export regime, and therefore also different political preferences. Dosal (1995) questions the fruitfulness of discussing such elites as separate. He argues that although the agro-exporters and agro-industrialists have different viewpoints in some debates, the connections between the sectors due to mutual investments and kinship have prevented a deep split. Similarly, Paige (1997) speaks of the *coffee elite* encompassing both agrarian and agro-industrial groups.

From the mid-twentieth century, business associations were established that encompassed various sectoral business associations in all the countries. They all had a unifying effect on the private sector, but varied significantly in strength and unity across Central America. The oldest and most powerful associations include the Guatemalan Coordinating Committee of Agrarian, Commercial, Industrial, and Financial Associations (CACIF) established in 1958. Also the El Salvadoran National Association for Private Enterprises (ANEP) and the Nicaraguan Superior Council for Private Enterprises (COSEP) have played important political roles (Johnson 1998; Spalding 1998). In Costa Rica, an umbrella organisation, the Union of Private Enterprise Chambers and Associations (UCCAEP) was established in 1975 by six influential private sector organisations. However, although its membership grew to 30 organisations in the following five years, its influence has been relatively limited due to its weak resource base and institutional rules (Ramírez-Arango 1985; Wilson 1998: 70–1). The Honduran private sector has been weakened by the strong presence of transnational companies and the split between the North-Coast business community (based in San Pedro Sula) and the Tegucigalpa-based businesses.[5] Nevertheless, in 1966, a private sector umbrella organisation, the Honduran Council for Private Enterprise (COHEP), was established, encompassing the various regional organisations, and it managed to bring a common vision to industry and commerce.

Of the three cases discussed here, it is particularly in the case of Guatemala that the capability of the peak organisation to undertake collective action has been emphasised. Several studies have pointed to how the unified private sector has prevented governments from implementing developmental policies and necessary tax adjustments (Martí 1994; Valdez and Palencia Prado 1998). However, some also emphasise CACIF's transformation in the 1980s, which led it to take a pro-democracy stand, and particularly to play a role in restoring democracy after the attempted self-coup by President Serrano in 1993 (McClearly 1999).

The phenomenon of creation of economic groups has been more prevalent in the northern part of Central America, particularly El Salvador and Guatemala. Some authors prefer to retain the Spanish term *grupos* in order to signal that this is a typically Latin American phenomenon that can be defined as 'networks of legally independent firms, affiliated with one another through mutual shareholding or by direct family ownership under a common group name' (Rettberg 2005: 38).[6] One reason for the differences between the north and the south may have been that the concentration of wealth was greater in the north. Another explanation is offered by later Costa Rican President Oscar Arias Sánchez in his study of Costa Rican pressure groups. He points to cultural factors and an individualist psychology in his explanation for lack of desire of Costa Rican business to form large investment groups, which he argues has also weakened business as a pressure group (Arias Sánchez 1971: 68).

The change of economic model in Central America brought deep changes to the Central American private sector, in terms of both relationships between different groups and organisational forms. These have been characterised by a transformation from traditional to non-traditional exports, and increased integration of Central American businesses into global production structures. Between 1990 and 2000 a complete turnaround in the production structure and particularly the export sector occurred. The role of the traditional 'desert-economy' declined (the export of coffee, sugar and bananas), and non-traditional agro-exports, manufactured goods and tourism increased (see Table 9.1). By 2004, tourism represented more than half of the services exported from all the Central American countries, except El Salvador. But even more important was the growth in manufactured goods, mostly meaning assembly industry, which in most of the region was synonymous with growth in the textile industry in the so-called *maquilas*. The exception was Costa Rica where electronics have also been important, partly due to the giant Intel investment in 1998.

Some of the export sector growth was based on foreign investments. In general, Costa Rica has been the most attractive for foreign investors. The

Table 9.1 Central America: total value of exports, 1993 and 2003 (US$ million)

		1993[a]	*2003*
Guatemala	Coffee[b]	267	262
	Sugar	153	227
	Manufactured goods	885	1,750
	Textiles (*maquila*)	684	1,709
	Tourism	212	582
Costa Rica	Coffee	202	165
	Bananas	560	478
	Manufactured goods	1,384	4,011
	Textiles (*maquila*)	755	745
	Tourism	681	1,190
Honduras	Bananas	225	171
	Coffee	125	175
	Manufactured goods	. . .	. . .
	Textiles (*maquila*)	265	959
	Tourism	57	192
El Salvador	Coffee	235	107
	Cotton	35	44
	Manufactured goods	309	1,073
	Textiles (*maquila*)	583	1,712
	Tourism	212	291
Nicaragua	Coffee	32	73
	Shrimp and lobster	27	76
	Manufactured goods	91	191
	Textiles (*maquila*)	74	446
	Tourism	50	113

Sources: World Bank (Country At a Glance); Taccone and Nogueira (2004).

Notes:
a   The numbers for the textile exports and tourism are from 1995 and 2002, not 1993 and 2003.
b   Since the coffee prices had dropped significantly between 1993 and 2003, this number does not reflect changes in export volume.

only exception was in 1998, when due to large privatisation receipts El Salvador and Guatemala received a great share (see Table 9.2).

However, there were also significant national investments in certain countries. A study of the *maquila* industry from 1997 showed that domestic ownership of the *maquila* industry ranged from 16 per cent in Nicaragua to 65 per cent in El Salvador (see Table 9.3). The United States was the most important investor in Costa Rica and Honduras, whereas the rest of the region has achieved more significant Asian investments (ILO 1997). This pattern may have changed towards the end of the decade, however. For example, by 2004, 66 per cent of the Guatemalan apparel sector was Korean owned (Agexpront 2005).

There is also a significant difference in terms of sources of foreign direct investment (FDI). Costa Rica receives most of its investments from the United States. For example, of the 119 companies that the Costa Rican Coalition for Development Initiatives (CINDE) attracted up to 101 were from the United States. In other countries, the surge of Asian (mostly Korean) and Mexican investments is more noticeable. By 2003, Central America had received 16 per cent of Mexican investments in Latin America and the Caribbean: $1,400 million had gone to Guatemala, $357 million to Costa Rica, $151 million to El Salvador, $131 million to Nicaragua and $25 million to Honduras (SICA/CEPAL 2004). The Mexican investments in Guatemala continued to increase and by 2005, 150 Mexican companies had invested $1,800 million in Guatemala (*AméricaEconomía* 8 April 2005).

Table 9.2 Central America: foreign direct investment, 1996–2003 (US$ million)

	1996	1997	1998	1999	2000	2001	2002	2003
Costar Rica	421	404	608	614	400	445	628	466
El Salvador	7	59	1,103	162	178	260	234	139
Guatemala	77	84	673	155	230	456	110	104
Honduras	91	128	99	237	282	195	143	216
Nicaragua	91	173	184	300	267	150	204	241
Central America	693	848	2,667	1,468	1,357	1,506	1,319	1,166

Source: CEPAL (2004).

Table 9.3 Ownership of the *maquila* industry in Central America, 1996 (%)

	Domestic	United States	Korea	Other Asian	Other
Costa Rica	21	60	2	2	16
El Salvador	65	11	8	6	10
Guatemala	43	9	44	2	2
Honduras	32	36	21	10	1
Nicaragua	16	32	16	32	1

Source: ILO (1997).

Few of the Mexican investments are 'greenfield investments'. Rather, large Mexican conglomerates have bought companies in their prime sectors in Central America. A prime example of this is the strategies of Teléfonos de Mexico (Telmex). As will be discussed later, since the early 1990s it was an active participant in the privatisation processes in Central America. In 2000, it separated out the mobile company América Movil, who aggressively sought concessions in the mobile market all over Latin America and became a major provider of services in Guatemala and El Salvador (CEPAL 2004).[7]

This trend has later been continued by investors originating in other parts of the world. Companies such as the cement company Cemex, the bread company Bimbo, the foodchain Grupo Maseca (Gruma) and the brewery Panamco became leaders in the isthmus through the takeover of smaller Central American companies. This process continued into the new millennium with other transnational partners, for example, the 2001 deal between La Fragua of Guatemala, Corporación de Supermercados Unidos de Costa Rica and the Dutch giant Royal Ahold that resulted in the establishment of the Central American Retail Holding, with more than 260 outlets throughout the region. Cementos Progreso of Guatemala entered as a strategic associated to Holcin, the world's largest cement company of Swiss origin (*AméricaEconomía* 12 July 2002).

This process has been most visible in the northern part of Central America, and partly as a result of this, the list of the 100 largest companies in Central America from 2002 is totally dominated by Costa Rican and Panamanian companies. In spite of the fact that Guatemala is the largest economy in the isthmus and that, as noted above, Guatemala and El Salvador traditionally have had the highest percentage of domestic industry ownership and generally the strongest private sectors, the largest Salvadoran company occupies the thirteenth place on the list, and the largest Guatemalan company is found in forty-fourth place (*AméricaEconomía* 12 July 2002).

The process of integration of Central American companies into transnational conglomerates or global production processes may be described as a transnationalisation of the Central American economy (Robinson 2003). This has involved the rise of transnational capitalist groups in Central America, encompassing both foreign investors and new economic groups that run businesses closely integrated in global production. As argued by Robinson (2003: 165), '[the] high proportion of local participation points to the emergence of a new Central American entrepreneurial class more thoroughly integrated into transnational production circuits than the old oligarchy, whose external linkage was strictly market-based'.

The process of transformation of the telecommunications sector provides one example of the changes that have taken place in Central America. In the following, I will discuss the role of different economic actors, including local economic groups, transnational companies and business associations.

The rise of state ownership in the telecommunications sector

The telecommunications sector has undergone deep transformations in the last 20 years. It has been at the crossroads between the old and the new economy in a quite particular way, and is therefore a good starting-point for studying changes in the Central American political economy. Telecommunications in Central America were originally in the hands of subsidiaries of US companies in alliance with local strongmen and dictators, but in ambivalent relationships with the local private sectors. Historically, the relationship between Central American dictators and the private sectors has been shifting and ambiguous, and the establishment of public infrastructure and state-owned companies was an important factor in the evolvement of it. For example, Guatemalan dictator Manuel Estrada Cabrera (1898–1920) opposed the autonomy of economic elites through concentrating wealth in his own hands and inviting foreign companies to invest in infrastructure (Ugarte 1999). His successor Jorge Ubico (1931–44), on the other hand, attempted to utilise public communications to extend his personal control over the hinterlands and extend his 'infrastructural power' (Mann 1993). Nevertheless, due to lack of funds for infrastructural development, he entered into a contract with Tropical Radio and Telegraph Company (TRT), a subsidiary of the United Fruit Company (UFCO) in order to develop telecommunications (Dosal 1993). TRT became the leading company operating telecommunications services throughout the region, along with the US Electric Bond and Share Company (ESBASCO).

From the late 1940s to the early 1970s, SOTs were established in all the countries. However, although having some traits in common, the political context in which the reforms were introduced ensured that the companies differed significantly with regard to their functioning and their main objectives. Costa Rica was the first country to establish an SOT. The junta that was in charge of writing a new constitution after the short 1948 civil war established the autonomous institution as an important feature of the new Costa Rican state, and the Costa Rican Electricity Institute (ICE) was the second autonomous institution to be created. It was originally only charged with the responsibility to develop electricity services, but telecommunications were added to it in 1963. The intention of placing the responsibility for both sectors in one company was to facilitate cross-subsidisation and to strengthen the social profile of communications. ICE evolved into one of the most efficient telecommunications companies in Latin America, and gained a highly symbolic position in Costa Rican society (Amador 2000).

As a contrast, the Guatemalan telecommunications company, Guatel, was established during the military regime of Colonel Carlos Arana Osorio (1970–4), on the recommendation of a World Bank mission in 1971. The establishment of Guatel was meant to improve coordination and planning of the telecommunications services, which were operated by three different state institutions. There were weak distinctions between military telecommunications services and public services. Over time, the military continued to be influential in the company throughout its lifetime and it was generally associated with bad services and high costs.

The same was true for the Honduran telecommunications company, Hondutel, which was established in 1978 as a part of the Honduran military's developmentalist project. However, Hondutel was even more intimately related to the military than Guatel was.[8] It was infamous for slow services and for being a conduit for patronage. But it was also, as most of the other telecommunications companies (and few of the remaining state-owned companies), a significant source of income for the government (often called *la caja chica*, the little cash box).

There were many reasons and justifications for establishing SOTs. First, the telecommunications sector was considered a natural monopoly, and thus the most efficient way of ensuring maximum network expansion for the lowest cost was to imitate a natural monopoly by only allowing one operator. Furthermore, telecommunications required large sunk capital investments with long-term amortisation. The existence of more than one company was therefore thought to be a waste of societal resources (Petrazzini 1995). Second, state ownership was a response to the problem of under-supply in areas not attractive for commercial operation. In Central America three more arguments were important. First, due to nationalist sentiments and previous experiences with transnational companies in the telecommunications sector that had failed to invest, particularly in poor and rural areas, there was a preference for domestic ownership. Second, the private sector in Central America was too weak, too dependent on the state and too risk aversive to be reliable investors. The general lack of capital was aggravated by the civil wars in Guatemala, Nicaragua and El Salvador in the 1970s and 1980s causing extensive capital flight. Third, the security situation increased the interest by the military and the military dominated states to control telecommunications.

The local private sector elites had conflicting interests towards the military dominated states and the telecommunications companies in particular. On the one hand, the most conservative parts of the private sector elites, often dominated by agro-export groups, supported a militarised state as a means to crush the left-wing insurgents.[9] Thus, they also supported the military domination of the SOTs. Schirmer argues for example that, in the case of Guatemala, there were close connections between conservative members of the National Agricultural Union (UNAGRO), and hard-line officers that dominated Guatel in the early 1990s (Schirmer 1998). On the other hand, particularly among industrialist groups, there was increasing dissatisfaction with the services provided by the state-owned companies. This differed significantly across the country. In Costa Rica, ICE gained a certain acceptance among the old elite, and contributed to the gradual establishment of legitimacy of the regime also in the eyes of the opposing forces (Paige 1997: 257).

There were also groups connected to the private sector that voiced ideological opposition to state ownership. Notably in Guatemala, the group connected to the Centre for Social Economy Studies (CEES), established in 1958, and later the Francisco Marroquín University, both led by businessman Manuel Ayau Cordón, promoted the ideas of a free market and a minimal state from the 1960s (Ayau Cordón 1992). Similarly, in Costa Rica, the National Association for Economic Growth (ANFE), also established in 1958, opposed the increasing Costa Rican state apparatus.

However, their influence was minimal until the 1980s when a series of developments deepened the opposition against the SOTs, added new arguments to those already existing, and made new groups call for change. The rapid technological development of the telecommunications sector that promised to lower the costs of services, as well as forge development of new services and improve the quality of existing, coincided with the fiscal crisis of the state that contributed to rapidly deteriorating public services. The decision by the World Bank and the Inter-American Development Bank (IDB) to stop funding SOTs investments added insult to injury. As a result of lack of funds for investment, not even ICE could keep up with its image as the symbol of modernisation and technological advancement in the country.[10] At the same time, local businessmen across the region understood that there was business in both ends of the telephone line. On the one hand, businesses were dependent on better services than the SOTs could offer. On the other hand, the telecommunications sector offered rare investment opportunities in the conflict-ridden countries. This set the stage for the first battle for the telecommunications sector, regarding the operation of mobile telephony.

The competition for cellular concessions

The first involvement of the private sector in the telecommunications sector in Central America after the nationalisation of communications was in mobile telephony. In the mid-1980s, mobile services were non-existent in the region, but pressure increased against the governments towards issuing concessions for developing such services.

The first country to give a cellular concession to a private enterprise was Costa Rica. Already in the 1970s, ICE had developed plans to establish a network of mobile telephony, and obtained funding for it under the Fifth Telecommunication Project of the World Bank. However, due to rapidly increasing demand for regular telecommunications services, ICE decided to increase the component of regular services of the project and postpone the mobile telephone service component. Thus, when demand started to increase for cellular services in Costa Rica in the early 1980s, ICE did not have its own funding for it, and the World Bank had by then adopted a strategy not to fund mobile telephony as it was considered eligible for commercial funding.

Faced with these financial limitations ICE attempted to establish a joint venture with the transnational company Millicom to develop cellular services.[11] It failed, however, to obtain the necessary permit from the Comptroller General, and ICE's attempt to develop mobile services on its own was stopped due to a new governmental policy that limited financing for the development of public services that could be exploited by private companies. Thus ICE was in a no-win situation: it was cut off from public funds due to the debt situation, and it did not get permission to use private capital.

By this time, a local company, Comcel, had already started to construct a private cellular network. In August 1987, the Office of Control of Radio gave a concession to Comcel to exploit approximately 10 per cent of the bandwidth. Some months later, President Oscar Arias Sánchez and Minister of Governance Rolando Ramírez ratified the concession, which was later transferred privately to Millicom in which both the President himself and a series of politicians were publicly known to have ownership interests.[12] With these permissions in hand Millicom started to develop its own cellular system and in April 1989 started to operate. However, Millicom's operations would not last long. In October 1993, the Union of ICE Engineers (SIICE) filed a complaint to the constitutional chamber of the Supreme Court (Sala IV), arguing that the concession given to Comcel was unconstitutional. In 1994, the Supreme Court approved the injunction filed by SIICE, and ruled Millicom's operations unconstitutional.

In Costa Rica it was local businessmen closely associated with politicians who jointly with transnational companies stood to gain from the first concessions, and this was also the case in Guatemala, although there the process was characterised by even less transparency. In Guatemala, the first concession to operate mobile telephony was given in 1989 to a joint venture between Millicom and local minority investors, also called Comcel. Among the minority investors were a series of persons close to the governing Christian Democratic Party, including Minister of Foreign Affairs and General Secretary of the Christian Democratic Party, Alfonso Cabrera, and President Vinicio Cerezo (1986–90) (McCleary 1999: 213). The concession to operate the B band was given for 20 years, and the conditions were that Comcel would have the monopoly on cellular services for the first five years, but had to pay 20 per cent of the profits to the government (CIEN 1999).[13]

Comcel's monopoly was soon challenged by possible competitors on the grounds that Article 130 of Guatemala's 1985 Constitution prohibits private monopolies. In 1991, a group of businessmen filed a complaint to the Constitutional Court against the monopoly, and after a series of attempts finally the court awarded the injunction. As a consequence, a local investment group (Grupo Londrina) led by former president of CACIF, Victor Suárez, applied to the new government of Jorge Serrano (1991–3) for a concession to operate the cellular band A. However, the application did not get resolved, and in May 1993 President Serrano was ousted as a result of his attempt to set aside the Constitution. Grupo Londrina continued the legal battle in order to be awarded the concession, but after two rounds of failed attempts to give a concession for the operation of the A band, it was left in custody of the Vice-President of the Republic awaiting a more comprehensive reform of the telecommunications sector.

In Honduras, a similar process occurred. As in the neighbouring countries, the first reform introduced to the old state-led model was the issuing of a bid for a concession to operate a cellular band (A). The process in which this happened was characterised by unclear concession criteria and corruption charges. Initially there were several contestants to the bid, but it was closed without conclusion, allegedly because the company that the government had promised the concession did not win through. The bid reopened and closed four times before finally Celtel, a consortium of Motorola, Millicom and local partners, gained the concession in 1995. At this point, all the other contestants had lost patience and faith in the government. Finally, Celtel managed to obtain a very favourable agreement with the government; it not only was to operate the A band, but the Congress committed to not concession the B band. Thus, Celtel operated in a monopoly situation and as such it was rewarded for having stayed put when other companies withdrew. According to the involved parties, the main reason was that they had partnered up with some of the most influential businessmen in the country, who knew both the formal and the informal routes necessary to reach a final agreement.

In sum, the mobile battle in Central America illustrates that in a political culture where 'know who' is more important than 'know-how', local entrepreneurs do have certain advantages over foreign investors (Young 2003). In this first phase of telecommunications reform, the main economic actors to participate were local investors – either individually or joined into groups – linked up with transnational companies. The policy shifts were limited and characterised by the lack of broader visions as well as transparency. The private sector was included primarily in order to get access to funds, as well as providing business opportunities for people close to the governments. This was a situation not only the unions were unhappy with. With completely different goals in mind than the unions, international agencies, primarily the US Agency for International Development (USAID), wanted to transform the local private sectors into more coherent policy advocates for market-oriented reforms.

External influence on business associations

Beginning in the early 1980s, there was a perception in USAID that the business associations in Central America represented a too narrow set of interests. Across the region, USAID attempted to create new organisations or support those that were pro-free market. In Guatemala, USAID proposed the creation of an alternative association to CACIF in order to promote policy reform. After having failed to get congressional approval for using funds from the Caribbean Basin Initiative (CBI) to create a new business organisation, a more modest project established the Cámara Empresarial de Guatemala (CAEM) in 1981 (Crosby 1985). However it never managed to become a real challenge to CACIF, and it was co-opted by it in 1985. This co-optation was part of a larger restructuring process of CACIF that began in 1983. The aim was to prepare it for the anticipated transition to procedural democracy that would demand a unified and flexible organisation. The stated objectives were to eliminate the practice of clientelism, to introduce fundamental market principles that would guide CACIF's activities, to promote industry as the priority of national economic policy, and to unify the private sector's voice for effectively lobbying government. The restructuring was essentially a result of the rise of a new generation of leaders influenced by liberal ideas (Dosal 1995; McCleary 1999). This, in turn was not only a result of the global turn towards neoliberalism, but equally of the consistent efforts of the Guatemalan liberals who over the years had educated a significant share of the local business leaders at the Francisco Marroquín University.

Therefore, USAID cannot be said to have been very successful in Guatemala in terms of creating a new pressure group, but its efforts were more successful in some of the neighbouring countries. Costa Rica had by the mid-1980s become the second-largest recipient of aid from the US government in Central America, receiving 27 per cent of the total aid, only exceeded by El Salvador (Salom Echeverría 1992). A major aim of USAID was to promote private sector development, and strengthen the private sector as a political actor (Sojo 1992). A centrepiece of this project was the creation of the Costa Rican Coalition for Development Initiatives (CINDE), which resulted from what Mary Clark (1997) has named a transnational alliance between USAID officials, Costa Rican private sector leaders and state technocrats. This alliance quickly assumed leadership in defining an export-led growth plan at the beginning of the Monge administration (1982–6).

CINDE was the main institutional legacy of this transnational alliance. It started in January 1983 and evolved into a centre for development and elaboration of political proposals for strengthening the private sector. The only direct impact of its work on the telecommunications sector in the early period was the attraction of Millicom, for which CINDE took much of the credit. However the establishment and strengthening of CINDE would later make a significant impact on the debate of telecommunications reforms, as will be discussed later. Thus, in Costa Rica, USAID did not create organisations in direct competition with the established business associations, but rather a complementary centre for developing business proposals, which contrasted with the strategy in Honduras.

The beginning of the end of the Central American conflicts in the late 1980s meant that Honduras lost its strategic location and thereby the protection from pressure to reform its economic policy. Increasing focus was placed on reform of the state, export orientation of the economy, and strengthening of the export-oriented segments of the private sector. In this context USAID worked to encourage the establishment of a Honduran free trade zone, development of the *maquila* industry, and export diversification. These strategies did not resonate well with the whole private sector. The private sector feared that encouraging growth in the export sector would require resources that in turn would have to be extracted from other sectors. Tension increased between the export sectors that potentially would benefit and those that feared they would have to pay for the party (Crosby 1985). Thus the traditional private sector organisations in Honduras were sceptical, and the only organisation that supported it was the North-Coast Chamber of Commerce and Industry of Cortés (CCIC).

In order to increase support for its policies, USAID supported both financially and organisationally the creation of a series of new organisations to serve functions presumed to be non-existent in the older organisations. Five new organisations were established in Honduras by USAID,[14] while only one of the traditional organisations (National Industrial Association – ANI) received more than token financing from USAID (Crosby 1985). The leaders of the new groups were younger and less well-connected members of the private sector, and although there was little outright hostility between the traditional and new private sector groups, their establishment contributed to 'something of a diluting effect on the capacity of the private sector organisations' (Crosby 1985: 18).

In short, by the early 1990s, USAID had altered the organisational structure of the Honduran business associations but it had the ironic effect of weakening it rather than strengthening it. The Guatemalan encompassing business association CACIF remained intact, and it transformed itself into a proponent of market-oriented reform (although not always consequent), but this was more thanks to the persistent efforts of the Guatemalan liberals than to USAID. In Costa Rica, a new organisation had been established that, although not a business association as such, was a main proponent for the interest of the private sector. These would in turn all have an important impact on the process of privatisation.

Business associations and *grupos* in telecommunications privatisation

By the mid-1990s, processes to deeply reform the telecommunications sectors were under way in all the Central American countries (Belt 1999; Raventós 2001). However, the kind of reform that they aimed for differed significantly across the countries. In Costa Rica, the experiences with Millicom, a general negative public attitude towards privatisation, and ICE's strong institutional integrity, together led to reform proposals that did not open for the outright privatisation of ICE. Rather a gradual opening for private sector participation together with a strengthening of ICE was considered the main route to a more efficient telecommunications sector. In Guatemala and El Salvador, on the other hand, radically liberal telecommunications legislations were adopted. These not only privatised the operation of services, but also the regulation of the sector and the radio spectrum. The SOT was to be auctioned, the sector opened for competition immediately, regulatory institutions with very limited powers were created to oversee the competition, and the radio waves that most often are considered state property were to be sold to private companies. This opened several opportunities for private participation. Finally, in Honduras and Nicaragua, new legislation opened for privatisation but within the framework of a strong state regulator, and a period of monopoly given to the incumbent carrier.

The private sector played many different roles in the discussions and implementation of privatisation of SOTs in Central America. Here I will differentiate between the role of organised business and that of individuals or groups of investors. Obviously there may be conflicting interests between the two, and a main 'test' of the business associations is the extent to which they are able to pursue coherent strategies in the face of differing investment interests of their individual members.

Guatemala

In Guatemala, starting with the Serrano government (1991–3), CACIF and several of its individual chambers started to elaborate policy for privatisation of the state-owned companies. In 1991, CAEM presented a study with a prioritised list of over 32 public enterprises that were recommended for privatisation or de-monopolisation, on which Guatel figured at the top (Cabrera 1997). Privatisation was also a main recommendation in the CACIF 'Yellow-Book' outlining desired economic and social policy for the Serrano government (1991–5).[15] CACIF further established a Private Sector Commission for the Sale of State Assets, which prepared a General Privatisation Law, and established sector commissions analysing possibilities for demonopolisation for each sector.

However, preparations were also made by individual investors and at the government level. Minister of Foreign Affairs of the Serrano government, Alvaro Arzú, discussed privatisation with the Mexican government related to a renegotiation of the debt that the Guatemalan government had with the Mexicans.[16] Moreover, the private sector had further formed a series of smaller companies operating a limited number of lines, mostly connecting businesses in Guatemala City. Various banks established their own telecommunications companies in order to take care of internal communications, as well as ATM services.[17] One of these small companies was Telered, which had been established in 1991, in which another investment group Luca, S.A. (hereafter Luca) invested.[18]

Ramiro de León Carpio, who entered power in 1993, hired the unquestioned leader of the Central American liberals, Manuel Ayau, as a governmental 'privatisor'. Ayau wanted to convert Guatel into a holding company of which 60 per cent of the stocks should be transferred to the Guatemalan people free of charge, using the election enrolment registers, 5 per cent should be transferred to the workers, 33 per cent should be sold in an international auction, and the remaining 2 per cent should be sold to workers on an optional basis. The proposition met resistance from various different actors, including the unions, military officers in the Guatel management and even parts of the government. However, what was more surprising was that although in essence in favour of privatisation, CACIF also failed to give him strong support. According to Ayau, the reason was that the prime interest of CACIF was to buy the companies.[19]

Privatisation did not take off until the private sector dominated Partido de Avanzada Nacional (PAN) entered power in 1996, under the presidency of Alvaro Arzú. Under Arzú, Guatel was prepared for sale parallel to the elaboration of the new telecommunications law. In order to bypass the constitutional requirement for a two-thirds majority in Congress for divestiture of autonomous institutions, Guatel was transformed into a hitherto unknown legal creature called a Unitary State Property, resembling a state stock holding company. Thereafter, 85 per cent of the stocks of Guatel were transferred into a new subsidiary, Telgua, leaving Guatel only with the rural infrastructure. Finally, the government announced its intention to sell up to 95 per cent of the stocks of Telgua to a strategic investor.

The main condition for presenting a bid was that the company should have more than 1.5 million telephone lines in operation, or annual sales worth $10 million in the telecommunications sector. This effectively excluded the participation of local groups. Five companies pre-qualified for the auction: MCI, Southwestern Bell, GTE, Telmex and France Telecom. Initially scheduled for September, the auction was postponed twice, and it finally took place on 17 December 1997. At auction day, only Telmex made a bid of $529 million, which was rejected by the government.

In January 1998, it was announced that a second attempt to sell the company would be made. Before this, the requirement that participants had to be international operators of telecommunications was removed. Now it was open for investment groups and banks to participate. This time around, six companies had pre-qualified, including two local groups: Telered and Luca. However, everyone but Luca and Datacom (a subsidiary of Deutsche Telecom) withdrew before the final auction. Only Luca finally made a bid of $700.1 million; a bid that was accepted by the government. To everybody's surprise, it was discovered that Luca was a local group registered with a capital of only 5,000 quetzals ($806 in value in 1998). Soon after the sale, it was revealed that Luca had made an agreement with the government for paying off Telgua in several phases. Of the first payment, $120 million would go to paying the debt that Telgua had acquired in order to pay the severance to laid-off workers. In sum, the difference between what Telmex offered in 1997 and the sum paid by Luca was preciously small.

Moreover, it turned out that it was not France Telecom, as initially announced, but Telmex that formed a strategic alliance with Luca in order to operate international telephony. Telmex gradually gained greater control over Telgua, and finally purchased 79 per cent of the stocks. Thus, after all it was Telmex that entered the market as the incumbent carrier in Guatemala. The Guatemalan government thus got the same operator as if it had accepted the 1997 offer, and approximately the same sum of money. Therefore, the main achievement of rejecting the offer by Telmex in 1997, but accepting Luca's offer in 1998, was to give a group of Guatemalan businessmen a piece of the pie.

Luca was a newcomer among the Guatemalan investment groups. However, among the investors in Luca were several established investment groups and banks.[20] Moreover, Luca also had connections to governments across Central America.[21] Furthermore, there were several traditional private sector actors that started to invest in companies competing with Telgua. Among them were the aforementioned Grupo Londrina, which later entered into partnership with Telefónica de España and started to offer cellular services as the first company competing with Telgua.

Costa Rica

The private sector in Costa Rica has never been able to match its Guatemalan counterpart in terms of economic strength and organisation. It also played a much less important role in the development of privatisation proposals. Indeed whereas the private sector in Guatemala pushed for privatisation of Guatel from the early 1980s, the Union of Private Enterprise Chambers and Associations (UCCAEP) and the Chamber of Commerce hardly knew about the first proposal for privatisation that was made already in 1988 in Costa Rica.[22]

In 1996, a new proposal to reform ICE and open the electricity and telecommunications sectors for competition (the Dobles project, named after then President of ICE Roberto Dobles) was presented to the Costa Rican Legislative Assembly. It would result in a model resembling the European style of liberalisation: keeping state ownership while opening for gradual liberalisation and allowing the state-owned company to make use of private capital. Although UCCAEP did not participate in the elaboration of the proposal, it was consulted, and it was highly critical of it, arguing that it left ICE in a too strong position, as a hybrid structure with no less monopoly power than it had had before.[23]

UCCAEP's lack of direct involvement in the elaboration of proposals to reform ICE does not reflect the fact that there were no private actors in Costa Rica that were interested in participating in the telecommunications sector, nor that the private sector was pleased with the manner in which ICE operated. From the late 1980s, also in Costa Rica, a series of small companies were formed, many aiming to compete with Millicom and also to exploit other markets assumed to be opened up.[24] Moreover, with a significantly higher degree of penetration of lines and higher income levels than its neighbouring countries, Costa Rica was home to the most attractive investment opportunity for transnational companies, particularly ICE's subsidiary Radiográfica Costarricense (RACSA), which was in charge of internet services.

However, the main private sector initiatives to reform the sector came, not from UCCAEP, but from CINDE. When the Dobles project was discussed in the Legislative Assembly in Costa Rica, the elaboration of new telecommunications law inspired by Berkeley Professor Pablo Spiller was already well under way in El Salvador and Guatemala. CINDE attempted to bring in experiences from the neighbouring countries to establish a liberal telecommunications framework also in Costa Rica.[25] However, the liberal ideas received little support in Costa Rica.

The Dobles project met strong opposition and, as elections were coming up, it was not even voted on in the Legislative Assembly. CINDE continued to work closely with the new government of Miguel Angel Rodríguez (1998–2002). CINDE's Ricardo Monge was appointed to lead the work of preparing a telecommunications law, and the plan that the government presented on 25 September 1998 to the national consensus process, which was to come to an agreement on, among other things, telecommunications reform, was basically the result of the work of CINDE.

The main effect of the new proposal was to alienate the ICE unions that also participated in the consensus process. A partial agreement had been found between the unions and the government in the consensus process. However, the proposal for a new general law of telecommunications that the government presented to the Legislative Assembly in January 1999 did not reflect this, but was rather a mix between this and the ideas of CINDE. This was later included in the so-called 'Combo' (combining three law-proposals to reform the telecommunications sector and the electricity sector as well as ICE as an institution), and provoked a massive public protest when debated in the Legislative Assembly in March 2000. The protests led to chaos across the country for two weeks, an unknown number of injured persons, and one person dead. The government was forced to back down, and on 19 April the Sala IV (the constitutional chamber of the Supreme Court) issued a resolution that found various aspects of the Combo proposal unconstitutional.

Thus, all private sector aspirations of a lucrative deal in the Costa Rican telecommunications sector were thwarted. This must be interpreted partly as a result of a weakly organised private sector, but also as a result of a strong public sector (the ICE) with capacity both to prepare proposals and to mobilise. Moreover, it showed the limits of the strategies to organise the private sector from outside; by significant groups of Costa Ricans, everything that came from CINDE was viewed as primarily serving transnational capital and thereby less legitimate. Combined, these factors contributed to closing off the space for the local private sector or the transnational companies to pursue their commercial interests in the telecommunications sector.

Honduras

In Honduras, as in Guatemala, it was the local private sector that first brought privatisation of Hondutel to the political agenda. With few other opportunities for investment, domestic groups were more openly interested in investing in telecommunications in Honduras than in Guatemala. However, the main proponent of privatisation of Hondutel among the private sector leaders, Jaime Rosenthal, did not have open commercial motives. Jaime Rosenthal was a liberal party politician (and former Vice-President candidate), but first and foremost a businessman with important ownership interests in banks, tourism, industry and media. He originally proposed privatisation of Hondutel in 1992 (Posas 1995). He wanted Hondutel to be sold to foreigners and that the transaction should happen in dollars for three reasons: to ensure that the state acquired foreign exchange, to ensure that foreign expertise would contribute to improvement of the communication systems, and to ensure that the process would be more transparent than had been the case with former privatisation processes.[26]

The private sector generally supported Rosenthal. However, beneath the consensus about the desire to privatise Hondutel there were significant differences between different groups with respect to motivation and means (Inforpress 12 September 1991). Some groups of private businessmen worried that the military and other groups close to the government would become the new proprietors of Hondutel. They feared that the military could make use of the clause of the law of liquidation of the National Investment Corporation (CONADI), which gave preferential treatment to social security foundations, including the Military Pension Fund, to acquire state institutions. In order to eliminate this possibility, the private sector wanted a law of privatisation that would prohibit such transactions (Posas 1995). Instead, in 1992, a new investment law was passed to ensure foreign participation in privatisation activities (Reporte Político 109/95). This reflected the viewpoints of Rosenthal and parts of the business community. However, there were still groups within Honduras that aimed to purchase Hondutel and that were less than pleased with the new legislation.

The legal framework for the telecommunications sector that was adopted in 1995 also emphasised attracting foreign investors. However, although a legal framework for the operation of the telecommunications sector was established, many problems occurred with regard to the creation of a framework to divest Hondutel. After a protracted legal process the government was finally ready to sell Hondutel to an international consortium with a guaranteed seven years monopoly period in 1998. However, in November 1998 Hurricane Mitch struck Honduras and cost approximately 6,000 people's lives, 70 per cent of the agricultural crop, and a large part of the country's infrastructure.[27] Mitch made the government change its development priorities in many respects. On 30 June 1999, a new decree was sent to Congress, aimed at making Hondutel a more attractive investment by increasing the percentage of the stocks to be sold to the private investor, by increasing the exclusivity rights, and by reducing the obligations to expand the rural network. In many respects, the emphasis of the proposal had shifted from efficiently regulating the telecommunications sector to achieving fiscal gains.

After the passage of the new decree in May 1999, the Minister of Finance Gabriela Núñez announced that the capitalisation would take place by the end of 1999. When finally the first phase of the qualification process was closed in February 2000, seven companies had pre-qualified for participating in the process of capitalising Hondutel (and thereby automatically also for gaining a concession to the cellular B band).[28] Telmex, Telefónica and France Telecom went on to the second round of pre-qualifications. Finally, on 16 October 2000 the auction of Hondutel took place. However, only Telmex made a bid and it was only $106 million, merely a third of the price expected, and it was rejected.

Secretary of the Privatisation Commission, Mario Agüero, pointed to three reasons for lack of offers for Hondutel. First, the number of interested companies had been exaggerated. Many of the companies had participated in the pre-qualification process in order to bid for the B band and not to participate in the capitalisation process. Second, the monopoly rights could no longer compensate for the many obligations placed on the new owners, both in terms of investments and in terms of obligations towards the labour unions. Third, taking into account the investment requirements, the minimum price was too high. [29] Less official sources argued that the government did not want Mexican investors. However, a comparison with the case of Guatemala may lead one to draw another conclusion, namely that by limiting the possibility for local groups to participate one also debilitated an important pressure group that could have speeded up the privatisation process and enticed foreign companies to participate. Without stable alliances with local groups that could provide the necessary 'know-how' and 'know who', investing in Honduras could be perceived as risky business by international companies. The partial exception was Telmex, which had solid experience in operating in those kinds of environments.

After the last failed attempt to sell Hondutel, the faith in the likelihood to find a buyer diminished. By 2000 the market for Latin American telecommunications companies had changed. Purchasing incumbent carriers with obsolete infrastructure was by then much less attractive than competing for concessions for operating international telephony or mobile lines. Thus, the government opted for concessioning the B band outside the privatisation package. This was obtained by Megatel, a consortium of local entrepreneurs and Swedish capital in 2003. In 2004, it was bought by América Móvil. Thus, in the end, whether it wanted it or not, Honduras was brought under the regional Mexican telecommunications hegemony.

Conclusion

Partly as a result of the different success of the activities of external actors, and partly as a result of the legacy of the national development model since independence, organised business played different roles in the discussions of telecommunications reform in the different countries. In Guatemala, CACIF developed several privatisation proposals and in any 'blue-ribbon' commission on privatisation there would be high-ranking CACIF members present. However, it is clear that during the process of privatisation, rivalry occurred between different investment groups that were members of CACIF and weakened CACIF as a collective actor. In Costa Rica, UCCAEP was also involved in the process to develop proposals in various ways. However, at the end of the day it was ICE itself that was the main agenda setter for telecommunications reforms. Of far more significance was the work by CINDE, which participated actively in the process of telecommunications reform. In Honduras, business associations were rendered to the back stage and it was rather individual businessmen who promoted privatisation. Moreover, in Honduras local investors never tried to hide their intentions to participate in the privatisation process as buyers. However, largely due to the World Bank influence in the development of the bidding documents, local investment groups were hindered from participating. Therefore, there was a lack of the necessary pressure group for making privatisation happen. In sum, private sector participation, whether through business associations or as local investment partners, varied significantly across the countries, and this had significant impact on the different outcomes of the privatisation processes.

In turn, the transnationalisation of telecommunications and other sectors of the economy in Latin America has forged major changes in the 'private sector landscape'. Most importantly, new local groups have emerged along with transnational companies, some of them truly global, and others that can be characterised as 'multilatinas'. The reform of the telecommunications sector may be interpreted as a process in which new and old members of the economic elite struggled to get a share of the lucrative new telecommunications market or at least a share in the process.

What may be the effect of this on the political economy in the region? More specifically, how will it affect the relationship between the private sector and the state? Based on the case of Colombia, Rettberg (2005) argues that the formation of *grupos* has led to a weakening of the political role of formal business associations, as the powerful economic groups have sufficient direct access to political authorities without having to coordinate with other businesses in associations. The development of extensive personal networks between politicians, high-level bureaucrats and business leaders has also been documented in the cases of Mexico, Argentina and Chile (Teichman 2001). To what extent will such personal networks replace business associations in Central America? Although much more research is needed to conclude, it seems as though influence through personal networks has coexisted comfortably with influence through formal associations in

Central America. What channel is used is rather a matter of the issue involved and whether friends or foes occupy the governmental offices. One could for example hypothesise that Guatemalan businesses had fewer personal relations with the administration of Alfonso Portillo (2000–4), during which the relationship between the government and the private sector reached a historical low, than during the governments of his predecessor (Alvaro Arzú 1996–2000) or successor (Oscar Berger 2004).

Another factor that may change the role of the private sector in the Central American political economy is the upsurge of foreign direct investment. Historically, foreign owners and managers of firms have not integrated into the domestic elite to any significant extent. The US businesses have been organised in American Chambers of Commerce, and have not been directly involved in local business associations. Moreover, with the important exception of the major US banana companies, foreign companies have played a modest political role. This may be about to change, particularly in Costa Rica, where major technology investments (first and foremost, of course, Intel's $600 million investment in 1998) have added potential important players in domestic politics. Anecdotal evidence suggests that this has weakened the role of UCCAEP in terms of influencing governmental policies.

The real consequences of the transnationalisation of the Central American economies remain to be seen. The pessimistic view is that the relational power of business associations and local economic groups has been exchanged for the structural power of transnational capital. In other words, businesses may no longer so successfully pressure the government to do what it otherwise would not, but the transformation of the links of the Central American economies with global capitalism makes them do it anyway. The more optimistic view is that when governments wrestle themselves out of the grip of the old oligarchies, there will be more space for alternative politics.

Notes

1 I here include Costa Rica, Guatemala, El Salvador, Honduras and Nicaragua in the term Central America. Although currently also Panama and Belize are considered as parts of Central America, for historical and cultural reasons they are set apart.

2 Consult, for instance, Rueschemeyer *et al.* (1992: ch. 6); Paige (1997); Lentner (1993); Dunkerley (1994); Booth and Walker (1989); Flora and Torres-Rivas (1989).

3 See, for example, Casaus Arzú (1992b).

4 The agro-exporters primarily need a transportation and communication system to connect their farms with the seaports and the capital city. Once this system has been built they need little more public investment. Therefore they should favour a minimal state. Industrialists, on the other hand, need a more sophisticated transportation and communication system as a prerequisite for the development of the domestic market. They often need substantial amounts of electric energy and a more complex education system, and should thus be more open to increased taxes and higher levels of public investment.

5 Historically, this split was aggravated by a third factor, namely the fact that immigrants from Palestine, Lebanon and Syria established much of the industry

in San Pedro Sula. These immigrants invested in various local industries and formed partnerships with the foreign-owned banana companies. But, whereas their wealth grew, they suffered from racism and political exclusion for many decades (Euraque 1996).

6 Interestingly, Rettberg bases her definition on William Zeile (1991) who uses it to define the Korean *chaebol*. Thus, it may not be such a specific Latin American phenomenon after all.

7 By 2004, it could count on a basis of more than 40 million clients in Mexico, Brazil, Argentina, Venezuela, Colombia, Ecuador, El Salvador and Guatemala.

8 To illustrate, whereas it was a general rule that military governments appointed military directors to Guatel in Guatemala, even civilian governments appointed military directors to Hondutel in Honduras.

9 William Stanley (1996) has used the term 'protection racket state' to describe the relationship between the militarised state in El Salvador and the economic elite. This can probably also be fruitfully applied at least to Guatemala also.

10 Much of ICE's success was explained by its autonomy from the central government. This was curbed already in 1970 by Law No. 4646 (Ley de 4/3), and by the Law of Executive Presidents of 1974, which both increased its dependence on the executive (Bull 2005). With the first structural adjustment loan resulting from the Costa Rican debt crisis, several limitations were placed on ICE's ability to invest and to hire people. As a result, waiting lists for getting a phone installed quadrupled and programmes to extend lines to new rural areas had to be cancelled (Monge 2000).

11 Millicom was the first international company to develop cellular services in Central America. It had various investors, but in its Central American investments was the private sector arm of the World Bank, the International Financial Corporation (IFC).

12 *La Nación* 11 May 1995, *La Nación* 22 May 1995.

13 In fact, they kept the monopoly until June 1999 (CIEN 1999).

14 FIDE (Foundation for Business Research and Development), Feproexah (Federation of Agricultural Producers and Exporters of Honduras), Gemah (Managers, Businessmen and Administrators of Honduras), the Honduran-American Chamber of Commerce, and a tiny organisation called Fudeh (National Development Association of Honduras). In addition, the Anexhon (Association of Honduran Exporters) benefited considerably from USAID encouragement and financing.

15 Serrano resigned two years before his term was up due to the aforementioned attempted self-coup.

16 The convention that was signed by Arzú said that the debt would be restructured 'in the context of a flexible scheme, that take into account mechanisms for debt reduction through programmes of interchange of this for state assets, in the frames of the policy of privatisation of public enterprises that the government of Guatemala adopts' (Inforpress 21 February 1991). Among the public enterprises mentioned was Guatel.

17 For example Totalcom, established by Bancared to operate their ATM machines, and Cablenet established in 1995 to give services to Banco de Construcción.

18 Telered was owned for 50 per cent by Banco Industrial, 25 per cent by Banco Granai & Towson and 25 per cent by Grupo de Cheppe Mirón.

19 Interview with Manuel Ayau, Guatemala City, 23 November 2000.

20 It included 22 Guatemalan and Honduran businessmen. The largest four stock holders were Grupo Banhcrecer (18.18 per cent), Centrans International (4.45 per cent), Grupo Optimal Investment, Co. (36.36 per cent) and Grupo Finsa-Banco Americano (40.91 per cent).

21 The manager of Luca was Ricardo Bueso Derás (originally of a Honduran family). He was not a well-established figure in Guatemalan business-life, but

he had been the Guatemalan ambassador to Belize during the government of Jorge Serrano. On the board of Luca was also Carlos Chaín Chaín, a Honduran businessman who had served as the Minister of Economy in the Callejas government in Honduras (1990–4) (*Prensa Libre* 11 December 1998).

22 Interviews with UCCAEP representatives, 20 and 29 November 2000. This contrasts with the union representatives who recalled the process very well.

23 Letter of 10 February 1997 by Samuel Yankelewitz, President of UCCAEP, to Ottón Sollís, with an analysis of the ICE.

24 A study conducted by one of the unions identified a list of companies providing services in which ICE did not have monopoly (e.g. beepers), but whose stated objectives were to provide various types of telecommunications services that were exclusively under ICE's authority. On the list both former members of the ICE management and governmental representatives figure prominently (Acta. No. 12, Comisión Especial (Exp. 11.444), Assamblea Legislativa, Costa Rica).

25 For example, in April 1997 CINDE arranged a seminar in cooperation with the Secretariat for Economic Integration in Central America (SIECA) funded by USAID and with the leaders of the processes in the neighbouring countries present (*La Nación* 6 April 1997).

26 This refers primarily to the process of privatising the companies of the CONADI.

27 The telecommunications sector was among the least affected. Although the official estimation of the losses in the telecommunications sector was $48 million (Gobierno de Honduras 1999), many contested this number. Conatel concluded that only a few of Hondutel's buildings had been affected and the basic infrastructure was intact (Conatel 2001).

28 These were Telmex, France Telecom, Videsh Snahcar Nigam Limited from India, Avantel from Mexico, Entel from Chile, Global Crossing Ltd from the United States, and Telefónica Internacional de España.

29 Interview, Mario Agüero, Tegucigalpa, 4 September 2001.

Bibliography

Agexpront (2005) 'Expectativa del Sector Vestuario y Textiles ante la aprobación del CAFTA', Guatemala: Comisión Cestex, Agexpront (Febrero).

Amador, José Luis (2000) 'El ICE: Un símbolo, 50 años después ¿Por qué los costarricenses siguen queriendo al ICE?', unpublished manuscript.

Arias Sánchez, Oscar (1971) *Quien Gobierna en Costa Rica?*, San José, Costa Rica: EDUCA.

Ayau Cordón, Manuel F. (1992) *No tenemos que seguir siendo pobres para siempre*, Guatemala: Editorial Centro de Estudios Económico-Sociales.

Belt, Juan A.B. (1999) 'Telecommunications reform to promote efficiency and private sector participation: the cases of El Salvador and Guatemala', *Economist Working Paper Series*, 10 (June).

Booth, John A. and Thomas Walker (1989) *Understanding Central America*, Boulder, CO, San Francisco, CA and London: Westview Press.

Brenes, Arnold and Kevin Casas (1998) *Soldiers as Businessmen. The Economic Activities of Central America's Militaries*, San José, Costa Rica: Fundación Arias Para la Paz y El Progreso Humano.

Bull, Benedicte (2005) *Aid, Power and Privatization: The Politics of Telecommunication Reform in Central America*, Cheltenham and Northampton, MA: Edward Elgar.

Casaus Arzú, Marta Elena (1992a) *Guatemala: Linaje y Racismo*, San José, Costa Rica: Flacso.

—— (1992b) 'El retorno al poder de las elites familiares centroamericanas, 1979–1990', *Polémica*, FLACSO, Costa Rica, Septiembre–Diciembre, 18: 51–62.

CEPAL (2004) *La inversión extranjera en América Latina y el Caribe*, Santiago de Chile: CEPAL.

CIEN (1999) Communications in Guatemala, *Infrastructure for the Third Millenium*, 1 (3), Guatemala: National Economics Research Center-CIEN.

Clark, Mary (1997) 'Transnational alliances and development policy in Latin America: Nontraditional export promotion in Costa Rica', *Latin America Research Review*, 32 (2): 71–97.

Conatel (2001) 'Comentarios al documento Honduras: Informe Marco Sobre la Infraestructura', unpublished note, Tegucigalpa, August.

CONSECA (1979) *Políticas de Gobierno. Documento Confidencial*, Guatemala: Consultoría en Economía y finanzas, Cta. Ltda.

Crosby, Benjamin L. (1985) *Divided We Stand, Divided We Fall: Public–Private Sector Relations in Central America*, Occasional Papers Series #10, Latin American and Caribbean Centre, Florida International University, Miami.

Dosal, Paul J. (1993) *Doing Business with the Dictators. A Political History of United Fruit in Guatemala, 1899–1944*, Wilmington, DE: Scholarly Resources.

—— (1995) *Power in Transition. The Rise of Guatemala's Industrial Oligarchy, 1971–1994*, Westport, CT: Praeger.

Dunkerley, James (1994) *The Pacification of Central America: Political Change in the Isthmus, 1987–1993*, London: Verso.

ESA Consultores (2001) *Honduras: Informe Marco Sobre la Infraestructura. Informe al Banco Mundial/PIAF*, Abril.

Euraque, Dario (1996) *Reinterpreting the Banana Republic: Region and State in Honduras, 1870–1972*, Chapel Hill, NC: University of North Carolina Press.

Flora, Jan L. and Edelberto Torres-Rivas (1989) *Sociology of 'Developing Societies': Central America*, New York: Monthly Review Press.

Gobierno de Honduras (1999) *Plan Maestro de la Reconstrucción y Tranformación Nacional: Estrategia para impulsar el desarrollo acelerado, equitativo, sostenible y participativo*, Versión ampliada, Reunión de Grupo Consultivo, Estocolmo, Suecia, Mayo: 25–9.

ILO (1997) *La Industria Maquiladora en Centroamérica*, Geneva, Switzerland: Internacional Labor Organization.

ITU (2000) *Americas Telecommunication Indicators 2000*, Geneva, Switzerland: International Telecommunication Union.

Lentner, Howard H. (1993) *State Formation in Central America: The Struggle for Autonomy, Development and Democracy*, Westport, CT: Greenwood Press.

McCleary, Rachel M. (1999) *Dictating Democracy: Guatemala and the End of the Violent Revolution*, Gainesville, FL: University Press of Florida.

Mann, Michael (1993) *The Sources of Social Power. Volume II, The Rise of Classes and Nation-States, 1760–1914*, Cambridge: Cambridge University Press.

Martì, Werner J. (1994) 'The Private Sector, the State, and Economic Development: The Guatemalan Experience', unpublished Ph.D. thesis, University of Texas at Austin.

Monge, Ricardo (2000) 'La economía política de un intento fallido de reforma en telecomunicaciones', in Ronulfo Jiménez (ed.), *Los retos políticos de la reforma económica en Costa Rica*, San José, Costa Rica: Academia de Centroamérica.

Paige, Jeffrey M. (1997) *Coffee and Power. Revolution and the Rise of Democracy in Central America*, Cambridge, MA and London: Harvard University Press.

Petrazzini, Ben A. (1995) *The Political Economy of Telecommunication Reform in Developing Countries. Privatization and Liberalization in Comparative Perspective*, Westport, CT and London: Praeger Publishers.

Posas, Mario (1995) *La privatización en Honduras*, Tegucigalpa: Fundación Friedrich Ebert.

Ramírez-Arango, Julio Sergio (1985) *The Political Role of the Private Sector Associations in Central America: The Cases of El Salvador, Nicaragua and Costa Rica*, unpublished Ph.D. Thesis, Harvard University.

Raventós, Pedro (2001) 'Deregulating Telecommunications in Central America', in Felipe Larraín B. (ed.), *Economic Development in Central America, Vol. II: Structural Reform*. Cambridge, MA: John F. Kennedy School of Government.

Rettberg, Angelica (2005) 'Business Versus Business? Grupos and Organized Business in Colombia', *Latin American Politics and Society*, 47 (1): 31–54.

Robinson, William (2003) *Transnational Conflicts: Central America, Social Change and Globalization*, London and New York: Verso.

Rueschemeyer, Dietrich, Evelyn H. Stephens and John D. Stephens (1992) *Capitalist Development & Democracy*, Cambridge, Polity Press.

Salom Echeverría, Roberto (1992) *Costa Rica: Deuda externa y Soberanía*, San José, Costa Rica: Editorial Porvenir.

Schirmer, Jennifer (1998) *The Guatemalan Military Project: A Violence Called Democracy*, Philadelphia, PA: Pennsylvania.

Schneider, Ben Ross (2004) *Business Politics and the State in Twentieth-Century Latin America*, Cambridge: Cambridge University Press.

Schulz, Donald and Deborah Sundloff Schulz (1994) *The United States, Honduras and the Crisis in Central America*, Boulder, CO, San Fransisco, CA and Oxford: Westview Press.

SICA/CEPAL (2004) *La Integración Centroamericana: Beneficios y costos*, Documento Sintesis, Mexico.

Sojo, Carlos (1992) *La mano visible del mercado: La asistencia de Estados Unidos al sector privado costarricense en la década de los ochenta*, Managua: Ediciones CRIES/CEPAS.

Spalding, Rose J. (1998) 'Revolution and the hyperpoliticized Business Peak Association: Nicaragua and el Consejo Superior de la Empresa Privada', in Francisco Durand and Eduardo Silva (eds), *Organized Business, Economic Change and Democracy*, Coral Gables, FL: North-South Center Press (University of Miami).

Stanley, William (1996) *The Protection Racket State: Elite Politics, Military Extortion, and Civil War in El Salvador*, Philadelphia, PA: Temple University Press.

Taccone, Juan José and Uziel Nogueira (eds) (2004), *Informe Centroamericano*, Buenos Aires: INTAL/SIECA.

Teichman, Judith A. (2001) *The Politics of Freeing Markets in Latin America: Chile, Argentina and Mexico*, Chapel Hill, NC and London: University of North Carolina Press.

Ugarte, Justo (1999) *La Venta de Telgua S.A. Una Lesiva Privatización*, Bancada de Diputados, Frente Democratico Nueva Guatemala (Mayo).

Valdez, J. Fernando and Mayra Palencia Prado (1998) *Los Dominios del Poder: la Encrucijada Tributaria*, Ciudad de Guatemala: FLACSO.

Wilson, Bruce M (1998) *Costa Rica: Politics, Economics, and Democracy*, Boulder, CO: Lynne Rienner Publishers.

World Bank, 'Country At a Glance', www.worldbank.org

Young, R. (2003) 'Foreign investment and democratic governance in Latin America', in Ana Margheritis (ed.), *Latin American Democracies in the New Global Economy*, Coral Gables, FL: North-South Center Press.

Zeile, William (1991) 'Industrial Policy and Organizational Efficiency: The Korean Chaebol Examined', in Gary G. Hamilton (ed.), *Business Networks and Economics Development in East and Southeast Asia*, Hong Kong: Center of Asian Studies.

10 The Viagra effect

Pharmaceutical giants and the Puerto Rican economy

Antonio Carmona Báez

Puerto Rico today is the Caribbean's only fully industrialised country. Dependent on pharmaceutical manufacturing, outbound shipment of products exceeded $31 billion in 2003. This represents approximately 42 per cent of the island's gross domestic product (GDP). To highlight the significance of these figures, 16 out of the top 20 pharmaceutical drugs consumed in the United States and Canada are manufactured in Puerto Rico, including the top five (or the so-called 'blockbuster drugs') such as Lipotor, Zoloft and Viagra.[1] Conducted at the island's 65 plants, production has increased in recent years as the country's largest corporations have taken to merging at monopolistic heights. For instance, in 2003 Viagra-maker Pfizer and Pharmacia Inc. merged to create the world's largest pharmaceutical conglomerate and closed the year with total annual revenues of $42.821 million. Although this represents only 12 per cent of the world's share of pharmaceutical production, it is considered to be of the highest valued percentages (Andreoli and Press 2004).

This chapter deals with corporate conglomerations in the pharmaceutical industry and their growth and impact on the Puerto Rican economy. In it, I will argue that industrial competition in the pharmaceutical sector, and Puerto Rico's dependence on the international market, is unsustainable and a detriment to both international health standards and the domestic and regional economy. Furthermore, the history of the Puerto Rican economy related to manufacturing for foreign economic conglomerates reflects a tendency similar to that of pharmaceutical drug use in individuals: as long as the drug is taken undesired symptoms disappear, leading patients and scientists alike to become erroneously more lax in their concerns about causes. As a result, pharmaceutical companies will profit; or they will lose if a 'safer' alternative in drug production is found. This chapter is entitled the Viagra effect because Puerto Rico's economy can be compared to the dilemma of erectile dysfunction. Males suffering from sexual impotency become dependent on this drug, but the symptoms return when the Viagra is no longer available. So too is the economic condition of the island; without the presence of pharmaceutical manufacturing (perhaps a soon-to-come reality), Puerto Rico can no longer be an industrial powerhouse of economic potency and macho prowess in capitalist production.

There are three areas concerning the Puerto Rican economy that need to be explored in order to assess the impact of pharmaceutical production and economic conglomerates in this country. These are: first, the economic-juridical factors related to corporate tax breaks on the island; second, the profile of Puerto Rican workers, which is essential to the case; and third, the volatility of the pharmaceutical market due to corporate competition and new findings in medicine. Here I will make mention of two comparable counties, Ireland and Singapore, as competing production sites. Finally, this chapter will also explore the future of pharmaceutical manufacturing and global trends in production. More specifically, the so-called 'China syndrome' will be explained and 'alternative' niche ideology exposed. But we will start with a brief historic and economic overview of the island, as most studies of the global economy and industrial production often ignore Puerto Rico.

Puerto Rico's exceptional political economy

After four hundred years of Spanish colonial rule, Puerto Rico was handed over to the United States as war booty at the end of the Cuban, Spanish and American War of 1898. In 1917, Puerto Ricans were granted US citizenship but not the right to have a voice or to vote in the US Congress nor participate in presidential elections. Since 1952, Puerto Rico's status has been considered to be a 'free associated state' in Spanish, and a US possession and non-incorporated 'commonwealth' territory in English, subordinated to US federal regulations and trade regimes. The now 4 million inhabitants of the island, the only fully industrialised country in the Caribbean, continue to live under US domination while maintaining their own national identity: a Spanish speaking majority; a Caribbean and Latin American culture; participation in international forums and events such as the Olympic Games; representation in the scientific community; and with their own flag and national anthem. Puerto Rico, however, is considered to be a separate nation in US global income reports, whereby Puerto Rico is counted as the largest economy for US investment, representing over 13 per cent of all US company income from their investments outside the 50 states. All commercial trade relations with other countries, however, are regulated by US federal law.

The bulk of federal money sent to the island annually is raised by the people of Puerto Rico. These sums include salaries, social security and disability benefits, retirement benefits for federal government employees and scientific researchers, veteran's benefits and Medicare. In this sense, Puerto Ricans have been non-dependent and responsible for their own welfare. The population's purchasing power, however, is due mostly to the lending-consumer habits fostered by local banks (Carmona Báez 2004; Odisheldzw 2004; Shapiro *et al.* 2003).

Between the 1950s and 1970s, especially in response to the Cuban Revolution of 1959, Puerto Rico's industrialisation process was portrayed by the United States as a successful economic showcase for developing societies, a model that the Asian Tigers and many countries in Africa, Latin America and the Caribbean would follow (Grosfoguel 2003). Even though this image has been intentionally erased from the memories of modernisation theorists and neoliberal economists, largely because of the unfavourable socioeconomic conditions on the island, manufacturing still represents 40 per cent of Puerto Rico's economy.[2] Currently, the general economy is highly dependent on pharmaceutical production and electronics, whereas, in contrast to neighbouring islands, tourism constitutes only 7 per cent of GDP (GDBPR 2001).

Out of the 64 pharmaceutical plants promoted by the Puerto Rico Industrial Development Company (PRIDCO), 44 are owned by conglomerates originating from the US mainland, 11 are owned by European and Canadian companies, and 9 medical equipment and supplies manufacturing sites are owned by small, local companies that are usually contracted by US and European corporations. Thirteen firms in this industry have more than one operation in Puerto Rico. Those with three or more plants are Pfizer, which recently merged with Pharmacia Corporation (five), Johnson & Johnson (five), Bristol-Myers Squibb (five) and Astra Zeneca (three). These are followed by companies such as Eli Lilly, Procter & Gamble, Merk & Co., Baxter International, Wyeth, Becton-Dickinson & Co., Cardinal Health, Schering-Plough Corp. and Warner-Lambert Co., all with two plants each, operating in Puerto Rico (PRIDCO 2004).

As Ramón Grosfoguel notes in his excellent account of Puerto Ricans and the global political economy, *Colonial Subjects* (2003), besides the United States having geopolitical interests in Puerto Rico, after the Second World War the island became a symbolic point of interest. This was manifested in two areas experiencing transformation: the political and the economic. First, the United States offered political concessions to elites, permitting them to create a semi-autonomous government extending democratic rights to citizens. Second was the process of industrial development through federal subsidies and incentives. During the 1950s the US State Department designated the island as the Point Four Programme international training ground for development in the Third World. During the Cold War, Puerto Rico became a showcase for capitalism and democracy. By the mid-1960s, Puerto Rico was the most important producer of textiles and apparel for the US market. Towards the end of the 1970s, however, it fell from capitalist grace as US federal regulations for a minimum wage were extended to the island:

> By 1980 the average salary per hour was $3.84 and the minimum salary was $3.10. A Dominican worker's wage per hour, for example, represented 34 per cent of a Puerto Rican manufacturing worker's at the end of the 1970s. . . . Thus, many labor intensive industries moved to the Dominican Republic, Haiti, Mexico, and Southeast Asia, which in turn increased unemployment in Puerto Rico from 11 per cent in 1970 to 20 per cent in 1977.
>
> (Grosfoguel 2003: 58)

Tax breaks and industrialisation

During the 1970s and 1980s the Cuban model was still adored by post-colonial countries, so if Puerto Rico were to experience long-term de-industrialisation the showcase would have collapsed and the Cuban experience would be favoured among most of the region's political elites. But by 1976 the key to maintaining Puerto Rico as industrial was already planned, with the introduction of Section 936 of the Internal Revenue Code (hereafter 936 IRC). The 936 IRC exempted from federal taxes the profit remittances of the industrial subsidiaries invited to Puerto Rico. Together with the new companies, investors from both the United States and abroad rushed to the island to render their services for building infrastructure. This experience resulted in Puerto Rico becoming a high-tech service and manufacturing powerhouse supporting such sectors as electronics, petrochemicals and finally pharmaceuticals.

These new capital-intensive industries did not generate the same number of jobs as did low-tech manufacturing, and unemployment continued to be a problem. Textile and apparel industries saw a dismissal of 22,000 jobs between 1970 and 1985, through electronics partially filled the gap by offering 20,000 jobs. Finally, the pharmaceutical industry increased jobs from 4,900 in 1970 to 16,000 in 1985. During the 1980s these three sectors accounted for 40,000 manufacturing jobs. Gradually, however, the country bade farewell to the last remaining low-tech manufacturing sites as well as many electronics and petrochemical plants.

In the period of industrialisation, from the 1950s to the 1980s, Puerto Rico also de-agriculturalised. Today Puerto Ricans import more than 90 per cent of the food that they consume from the United States and abroad. Additionally, agriculture represents less than 1 per cent of the GDP (GDBPR 2001). This means that any declining tendency in the industrial manufacturing sector or any other de-industrialisation scheme would spell disaster for a population that no longer knows how to wield a machete.

With the Cold War at its end, Puerto Rico lost its geopolitical-strategic significance. In addition, the United States found itself in an economic crisis caused by public debt. In this particular context it was decided to eliminate the 936 IRC for US corporations. In 1996, the federal government declared a ten-year sunset phase for the 936 IRC. This meant that newly arriving companies could not benefit from the tax incentives and those remaining corporations would have to find loopholes in order to avoid paying taxes similar to those found in the US mainland. In other words, the incentives are disappearing and the Puerto Rican economy is in danger of revealing its impotence.

Corporate income tax in Puerto Rico is similar to that of the United States, thus ranging from 22 to 39 per cent. The loopholes by which the pharmaceutical companies remain on the island, however, include the (maximum) 7 per cent tax rate offered to qualified industries and the 2 per cent tax rate for those conglomerates working on specific projects in the so-called life sciences sector such as biochemical research. The other option for corporations is to become a Controlled Foreign Corporation, whereby the subsidiaries will change their identities to foreign subsidiaries. In this case, US corporations can transfer research and development (R&D) offices to Puerto Rico and receive a 20 per cent tax credit for operating in US territory. The upcoming tax regime will be discussed further along.

Puerto Rico's workforce profile

As said, the pharmaceutical industry is currently the most significant business on the island. While tourism constitutes only a small percentage of the GDP, pharmaceuticals employ more than 11 per cent of the labour force and generate over 40 per cent of the GDP, currently at $72 billion. Directly, corporations such as Pfizer, Amgen, Eli Lilly, Merck and Abbot employ 30,000 people on the island. Indirectly, including subcontract workers, a full 90,000 are employed by these giants.[3] Average hourly earnings in the pharmaceutical and medicine industries in Puerto Rico are lower than wages paid in the United States: in this sector Puerto Rican workers earn on average $14.99 per hour, yet residents in the continental United States will earn $18.73 per hour (PRDLHR 2005).

The average salary in Puerto Rico is higher than in any other country in the region, but the island is still selected for a number of reasons. The Puerto Rican workforce is special, not only because of the nation's colonial relationship to the United States, but because of its high level of education, Spanish–English bilingualism and its *relative* physical healthiness in comparison to neighbouring islands. These conditions contribute to the making of a hard-working labour force. On average a Puerto Rican worker in the pharmaceutical and chemical industry gives 40 hours per week of actual labour. The term 'relative' healthiness, however, is an issue to be reckoned with as Puerto Ricans suffer from the many ills found in other rich societies. While on the one hand, hunger, protein deficiency and malaria are absent from Puerto Rico, obesity, diabetes, high cholesterol and blood pressure levels, heart attacks, narcotic (illicit) drug addiction, erectile dysfunction, depression and other mental illness related to modernity all have a high presence among the island's population. Since American corporations practically control the health care system, Puerto Ricans are consuming and are encouraged to consume the very drugs that they themselves produce, such as Zoloft, Xanax, Lipotor and Viagra. This reality bears some painful similarity to the British opium production and distribution in China during the nineteenth century.

Globally, there are only two other similar places for pharmaceutical production. These are Ireland and Singapore, which are also low-to-no-tax havens for corporate giants. What these semi-peripheral nations, including Puerto Rico, have in common are their proximity to the world's largest regional markets (North America, Europe and China/Japan), their relaxed environmental laws, a relatively stable (in the case of Singapore, authoritarian) government, and a skilled, healthy, labour force with centre or First World consumer desires.[4] More importantly, these countries are model (neoliberal) flexible labour regimes.

Pharmaceutical giants such as Pfizer and Bristol-Meyers boast that their employees at manufacturing plants are treated so well that they have no need for unions. Indeed, in comparison to compatriot workers in other sectors, those of the pharmaceutical industry usually enjoy a higher-than-average salary, a better and cleaner work environment, and more relaxed manager–worker relations. But as history has taught, keeping unions away creates the possibility that corporations might make their sly and easy exits to cheaper labour markets. And when the mud hits the fan for the corporate giants, layoffs will be undisputed. In this sense, pharmaceutical giants are no different than any other business conglomerate: they need 'optimal' labour relations for decentralised production, and countries such as Puerto Rico, Ireland and Singapore compete with each other in the game of 'how low can you go?'

Corporations and economists usually boast that the manufacturing of medicines represents the smallest amount of company costs, insinuating that these three countries should be thankful for their position and that workers at production plants are really insignificant. But at this lowest level of the pharmaceutical hierarchy is the essential 3 per cent of costs that create the industry's *raison d'etre*. It includes chemical engineers, microbiologists, technicians and chemical, industrial and mechanical engineers that might make up to $30 per hour (PRIDCO 2004). Even so, above the preparation of chemicals, manufacturing of pills, packaging and delivering, stands R&D, which is usually carried out in scientific laboratories in the United States and Europe. Also above manufacturing, at least in Puerto Rico, we find the *propagandistas médicos*, or drugs salesmen and marketing employees, who work for the pharmaceutical giants. Some of these Puerto Rican salesmen, dressed in Armani suits and earning minimally $60,000 per annum plus bonuses, visit physicians' offices and hospitals to spread the good news and wonders of new medicines. Others, usually subcontracted, dedicate their time to handing out sample pills, painkillers and cough suppressants at street parties, bars and popular festivals. They all earn much more money than the average production plant worker.

While Puerto Rico produces primarily for North America and Ireland produces for much of the rest of the world, Ireland is considered to be Puerto Rico's plant and labour competitor. This European semi-peripheral country, for instance, produces 70 per cent of Pfizer's Lipotor on a global scale and 50 per cent of those pills consumed in the United States, while Puerto Rico manufactures the other half. These two in turn compete with Singapore, which is now seen as the ideal place to move R&D sites, as this country does not even have a minimum wage, although salaries for professionals and scientists are comparable to Puerto Rico and Ireland (Heritage Foundation 2005).

Returning to the specific case of Puerto Rico, the Viagra effect of the pharmaceutical industry is multiplied for other sectors. Puerto Rican consumer habits, fostered by local banks, are directly related to the incomes of workers and scientists in this sector. Even though government and service jobs represent the largest point of employment, the total employees' compensation injected into the economy ($1.3 billion) by the foreign pharmaceutical conglomerates explains the First World-like material standard of living experienced by 12 per cent of the nation's workforce. The trickle-down effect is still debatable, especially when approximately 44 per cent of the population is still living below the poverty level.

Yet if the multiplier for this sector is taken seriously, then other sectors such as the underground economy and the work produced by undocumented immigrants should also be brought into consideration. There are approximately 30,000 undocumented Dominican workers on the island working mostly in the service industry, small-scale agriculture, and in the kitchens and homes of the rich and famous. One activist I interviewed stated that in contrast to years ago when Dominicans would come by boat to Puerto Rico as a way of getting to the continental United States, immigrants today are staying in Puerto Rico because of the wealth that the pharmaceutical industry produces. In turn, these immigrants send money transfers to their relatives in the Dominican Republic, probably the largest source of income for that country.[5]

The nature of the pharmaceutical market

Advanced technology and new discoveries in medicine and chemical R&D, and capitalist competition (including law suits) are the main causes of the volatility of the pharmaceutical industry. This makes the Puerto Rican economy extremely vulnerable. For instance, during the third quarter of 2004, pharmaceutical giant Merck was forced to remove the arthritis painkiller Vioxx from the market, as it was found to double the risk of heart attacks and strokes. The company is now under US federal investigation by the Justice Department and Securities and Exchange Commission into whether Merck failed to disclose knowledge it had held since 2000 concerning the risks of Vioxx usage. Merck has been named in more than 375 law suits and Merrill Lynch, the insurance company, estimates that Merck's liability from Vioxx could be as high as $12 billion. Since November 2004, the company's stock price has fallen by 40 per cent since the withdrawal of Vioxx, while shareholders are suing for the estimated $42 decline in the company's value (Martinez 2004).

The conglomerate Pfizer, which produces two arthritis treatments, benefited from the Merck scandal. While Celebrex's sales rose 14 per cent during the same quarter, to $797 million, Bextra sales rose 37 per cent to $324 million (Martinez 2004). Medical journalism, however, is already putting the brakes on Pfizer, as a study presented to a meeting of the American Heart Association demonstrated that Bextra could possibly be blamed for heart attacks and also for the Stevens-Johnson syndrome (causing blistering to mouth, skin and eyes) (AHA 2005a, 2005b).

Such volatile markets evidently affect local labour. Of Puerto Rico's workforce in this sector, more than 700 hundred people lost their jobs between December and March 2005 (PRDLHR 2005). Hence, the health risks that modern-day capitalism and business conglomerates in the pharmaceutical industry are fostering result in relatively high-earning job losses. In this light, the organisation of capitalist production and the architecture of economic conglomerate culture are unsustainable.

The tendency to merge is the other significant cause for unstable production relations in the pharmaceutical industry. For instance, while investors celebrated the making of the world's largest pharmaceutical conglomerate initiated by the merger of Pfizer and Pharmacia in 2003, 400 Puerto Rican employees in March 2005 went home jobless as a direct result of this $60 billion corporate act (Lama Bonilla 2005). Extremely flexible labour laws in Puerto Rico contribute to this problem. For instance, during the same merger process no layoffs were announced by Pfizer in Ireland. This is probably due to the fact that it is more difficult to fire a worker in the European Union than it is in the US colonial territory.

In 2004, Pfizer and Smith-Kline cut off shipments to selected Canadian pharmacies in an attempt to stop the flow of discount drugs from Canada to the United States. The federal Food and Drugs Administration (FDA) has for the last couple of years criminalised the importation of drugs and medicines from Canada for US patients. Today this criminalisation has resulted not only in losses for medium-sized local pharmacies in the neighbour to the north, but also in a threat to the lives of Canadians who might be faced with drug shortages, forcing patients to look to US distributors. Previously, the American poor, especially the elderly, were able to purchase life-saving medicines from Canadian distributors and pharmacies at 30–70 per cent savings in comparison to prices asked for in the United States.

Punishing Canadians in the name of sensible market strategies came hand in hand with a large-scale propaganda campaign to improve Pfizer's public image. The fairytale advertisements found in newspapers, the internet and corporate reports were used in the hope of quelling the public's sense of outrage at corporate voracity and to keep investors happy. These ads usually cover topics such as what the corporation is doing for the Aids problem in Africa, scholarships for young students in chemical engineering and pharmacy science in Puerto Rico, investments for research at university and other scientific centres, and price reductions or 'savings' on drugs for the poor, unemployed and those working poor without health insurance.[6]

In the United States, the pharmaceutical industry is also suffering from bad public image. According to the network lobby group Alliance for Human

Research Protection (AHRP), the American public is repelled by this industry's corrupt practices and unconscionable price gouging. The AHRP together with the American Association of Retired Persons (AARP) are finding that in public opinion polls the pharmaceutical companies' popularity is dropping. The main reason for this is that Americans are becoming increasingly aware that prices are cheaper in other countries. The cost of blockbuster drugs soared 28 per cent between 2000 and 2003. Popular heart medicines produced by Bristol-Meyers went up 35 per cent for the same period. Even the former chairman of Merck, Roy Vagelos, had condemned drug manufacturers for their exorbitant prices (*The New York Times* 8 July 2004; AHRP 2004). All of these factors contribute to the instability of the pharmaceutical sector.

The China syndrome and the search for alternative niches

During the 1990s, Western economic analysts foresaw that the future of manufacturing is in China. In 2006, the future is now and Puerto Rico cannot escape this reality. Just prior to the end of the twentieth century, China's manufacturing had been limited to low-end products and detailed plastics, but within the last few years it has expanded to such high-tech production as computer software and electronics, Puerto Rico's second industry. Even R&D laboratories are opening up in China, as this country is now a leader in stem-cell research against life-threatening illnesses. The focal point of the China syndrome can be found in the United States, where, since 2000, 2.7 million jobs have been lost in the manufacturing sector. In Puerto Rico, during the electronics boom of the late 1970s and the 1980s, companies such as Dell, Information Magnetics, Quantum, Digital and Wang Products were manufacturing on the island. Today only three remain, among them Hewlett-Packard, which may leave the island once it has completed its mission to open up factories in Asia. The cardinal issue is, unsurprisingly, that China is offering lower-cost labour; the average hourly wage for Puerto Ricans is $10–12, and $13.99 in pharmaceuticals, whereas the Chinese are earning 75 cents hourly. Additionally, storage and factory space in China is up to seven times cheaper than in Puerto Rico (Ocasia Teissonniere 2004).

The island's landscape has seen the closing of many factories and the direct move to the People's Republic. A prime example of this is Dual-Lite, an emergency light manufacturer whose two factories on the southeast side of the island closed down and relocated to China. Nypro, a giant plastics company operating in Puerto Rico, now has ten factories in China and, according to their sources, is planning to open ten more within the next two years, eventually employing 14,000 people. Even if Puerto Rico were to maintain good tax incentives for the foreign companies, in comparison to China, it has little to offer. The Puerto Rico Manufacturers Association is now warning political and economic leaders that the island's pharmaceutical industry is on the verge of collapse, as major companies are discovering the benefits of relocating to China.

The history of the low-tech manufacturing industries of the 1960s in Puerto Rico, mentioned above, should act as a precursor to what potentially might happen in the pharmaceutical era. The flight of the pharmaceutical giants will spell disaster for the island. Puerto Rican society has not only been industrialised, but also de-agriculturalised; the island produces only 10 per cent of the food it consumes. The social effects have already been disastrous, but what would happen to a Puerto Rico without Pfizer, Merck and Eli Lilly?

Now, as mentioned earlier above, Puerto Rico has already experienced a shift from low-tech labour-intensive manufacturing to a more advanced high-tech capital-intensive economy, both export orientated. The consequences, expressed mostly in job losses and a sudden jump in the unemployment rate, would have gravely affected Puerto Rico if it had not been for the 'plan B' of tax incentives for large corporations operating on the island, the 936 IRC. But these tax incentives have now gone and the loopholes are becoming less promising as China becomes more attractive. Also the additional 60,000 jobs that are indirectly related to the pharmaceutical industry are a concern here. This is not to mention the underground economy that is sustained by relatively high salaries, or the jobs that the strong economy creates for undocumented immigrants originating from the neighbouring Dominican Republic. What will these immigrants and their children do when opportunities start to dwindle when Puerto Ricans tighten their belts? The level of spending by Puerto Rican workers is also in danger. Seeing that Puerto Rican consumer habits are fostered by local banks, the financial sector is also feeling the vibrations of a doomsday scenario.

Puerto Rican business leaders and economists find themselves with a need to come up with alternatives. In response, financial gurus have fabricated an alternative niche ideology that aims at convincing the upcoming generation of professionals graduating from universities that, just as the island 'successfully' jumped from labour-intensive to capital-intensive production before, Puerto Rico can do it a second time. Throughout the past couple of years, an ideology of alternative niches has been disseminated in the local press, exhorting business leaders to find new sectors, especially in administration, delivery service and high-tech R&D laboratories. These alternative niches are supposedly to be found in the new life sciences of the biotechnology sector, whereby the Puerto Rican economy will be moved from major pharmaceutical manufacturing to R&D. However, the final result will be a reduction in the number of employees that spells nothing more than an increase in unemployment, which is already at 12 per cent.

While conservative economists continue to look optimistically at this second transformation of the Puerto Rican industrial economy, voices from the state apparatus are admitting concern. Department of Economic Development and Commerce Secretary Jorge Silva has already stated that, in a study provided by PRIDCO, 60 companies still operating under the 936 IRC, which ends on 31 December 2005, have more than a 60 per cent closure possibility without an incentive replacement. That is why he finds it important to lobby for the pharmaceutical industry in Washington DC.[7] The only response from those who contest this doomsday prediction is that the island's pharmaceutical companies will have to increase their production of blockbuster drugs. After having observed that these corporations are reducing the number of employees, one can conclude that a stepping up of production can only happen by exploiting the Puerto Rican working class.

Concluding remarks

The Puerto Rican economy is chronically impotent and its dependence on foreign conglomerates such as those found in the pharmaceutical industry provides only temporary and unsustainable relief. This is a problem for many semi-peripheral countries, as transnational corporations and conglomerates follow the trends of decentralised production and continue to find cheaper labour markets. Workers in the semi-periphery, however, are developing consumer habits and needs similar to those found in the post-industrial north and are demanding higher wages. Additionally, social movements that contest the process of neoliberal globalisation are making conditions less attractive for the movement of R&D laboratories and intelligence centres to those areas needing to find alternative niches.

But the case of Puerto Rico is exacerbated by the fact that global trends in pharmaceutical production, especially gigantic mergers leading to major layoffs and price wars between consumer countries such as the United States and Canada, are contributing to the sector's vulnerability.

Politically, no organisation, party or state figure has dared to touch upon the dangers the Puerto Rican economy is facing. Just as in old colonial times, the imperial powers are making the decisions; seemingly there is nothing that the native populations or colonial administrators can do. They simply adjust to what is available. At this point, a positive alternative for the Puerto Rican economy could only stem from radical transformation in the global economy.

Notes

1   Blockbuster drugs are those that sell at $500 million annually (Martinez 2005).
2   Over 44 per cent of the population currently lives below the poverty level; this includes a 12 per cent unemployment rate (GDBPR 2001; US Census Bureau 2003).
3   This figure was estimated along with the general multiplier index prepared by the Puerto Rico Planning Board in October 1999.
4   The terms centre, periphery and semi-periphery are borrowed from Wallerstein's world system theory, in an attempt to map out power and production in world capitalist development.

5 Interviews and conversations with Romalinda Gruñon of El Centro de la Mujer Dominicana and Saul Perez of El Comité Dominicano de Derechos Humanos, throughout April 2005 in San Juan, Puerto Rico. These two individuals work with the Dominican community and especially those undocumented immigrants that work in Puerto Rico's underground economy. Although no official number of undocumented residents is known, the estimate of 30,000 Dominican workers is based on the work conducted by the two above-mentioned institutes. This number of immigrants has sought help in accommodation services provided by the social work and human rights centres.
6 See Pfizer's annual reports of 2003 and 2004, and also 'Pfizer Will Offer Deep Discounts to Uninsured', www.consumeraffairs.com/news04/pfizer_pfriends. html (13 July 2004).
7 In 2005, Puerto Rico's Department of Economic Development and Commerce Secretary Jorge Silva presented five options to save the Commonwealth's economy to Washington Congressmen. These five options are: first, extend 936 IRC sections for one year until an economic report about Puerto Rico commissioned by the US Joint Tax Committee from the US General Accounting Office is published; second, implement an amendment to IRC sections so that the Controlled Foreign Corporations (CFCs) can be treated as domestic companies for tax purposes; third, extend a 20 per cent tax credit on research and development to CFCs and local corporations so stateside pharmaceutical companies will transfer their operations to the island, adding significant value to keep intellectual property in US territory; fourth, lobby for equal treatment under the American Job Creation Act Section 199 so manufacturing income from US firms in Puerto Rico will be taxed at 32 per cent, as opposed to the standard 35 per cent, in line with a tax revision made in 2004 by the federal government for incentives; fifth, use incentives to attract companies that establish their regional hubs in Puerto Rico. These five options were approved by the Puerto Rico's Manufacturing Association, the Puerto Rico Pharmaceutical Industry Association and the Office of the Governor of Puerto Rico (Martinez 2005).

Bibliography

AHA (American Heart Association) (2005a) 'Parecoxib, Valdecoxib and Cardio-vascular Risk' (editorial), *Circulation*, January.
—— (2005b) 'The use of non steroidal anti-inflammatory drugs' (Advisory from the AHA), *Circulation*, April.
AHRP (Alliance for Human Research Protection) (2004) 'Public tanks drug industry at bottom with oil, HMOS tobacco-Harris poll', www.ahrp.org/infomail/04/07/08.php (accessed 12 July 2004).
Andreoli, B.E. and D.M Press (2004) 'Puerto Rico remains strong', *World Trade Magazine*, 1 July, http://worldtrademag.com/CDA/ArticleInformation/coverstory/BNPCoverStoryItem/0,3481,127172,00.html (accessed 23 September 2004).
Caballero Mercado, J., L. Olmeda and G. Quiñones (1999) *Multiplicadores Interindustriales de Puerto Rico*, Gobierno de Puerto Rico: Oficina del Gobernador, Junta de Planificación, San Juan.
Carmona Báez, A. (2004) 'A Criollo financial conglomerate in the Caribbean: Banco Popular de Puerto Rico', in A.E. Fernández and B. Hogenboom (eds), 'Latin American conglomerates and economic groups under globalization', *Journal of Developing Societies* (Special issue), 20 (3–4): 247–58.

GDBPR (Government Development Bank of Puerto Rico) (2001) *A Glance at Puerto Rico's Economy*, San Juan, GDBPR.

Grosfoguel, R. (2003) *Colonial Subjects: Puerto Ricans in a Global Perspective*, Los Angeles, CA: University of California Press.

Heritage Foundation (2005) *Index of Economic Freedom-Singapore*, www.heritage.org/ research/features/index/country.cfm?id=Singapore (accessed 15 July 2005).

Lama Bonilla, R. (2005) 'Bristol: la pionera en el suelo Irlandés', *El Nuevo Día* (Edición Especial), *Negocios del Domingo en Irlanda*, 26 June, San Juan.

Martinez, M. (2004) 'Global sales of pharmaceutical drugs made in P.R. up 1.8%', *Puerto Rico Herald*, 18 November, 8 (47): 3.

—— (2005) 'Threat of more than 60 companies closing after Sections 936/30A phaseout takes Secretary Silva to Washington DC', *Caribbean Business*, 30 June.

Ocasio Teissonniere (2005) 'The China challenge', *Caribbean Business*, 3 February.

Odisheldzw, A. (2004) *Pay to the Order of Puerto Rico*, Fairfax, VA: Allegiance Press.

PRDLHR, Puerto Rico Department of Labor and Human Resources (2005), *Average Hourly Earnings*, Bureau of Labor Statistics, CES Program, San Juan.

PRIDCO, Puerto Rico Industrial Development Corporation (2004) *Pharmaceutical and Medicine Manufacturing*, Economic Analysis and Strategic Planning Project Analysis Division (NAICS Group) Report 3254, San Juan.

Shapiro, R. J. *et al.* (2003) *The Cost of Puerto Rico's Status to American Taxpayers*, American Alliance for Tax Equity, London.

US Census Bureau (2003) *Poverty Status in 1999 of Family and Non-family Households*, www.census.gov/prod/2003pubs/c2kbr-19.pdf (accessed 3 May 2005).

Part III
Africa

11 The neoliberalising African state and private capital accumulation

The case of Cameroon

Piet Konings

Faced with deep and prolonged economic and political crises, African governments have been compelled by international financial institutions and donors to adopt neoliberal reform packages. Some of the major tenets of neoliberalism are the call for less and better government, usually framed in terms of 'good governance', and the promotion of both domestic and foreign private enterprise, which should act as the motor of economic growth and development. Despite converging tendencies, the outcome of this neoliberal agenda appears not to have been uniform because of variations in the neoliberal policies of the different African regimes and the existing structures of economic and political power. This study focuses on Cameroon and explores the continuities and changes in the relations between state and private capital accumulation as a result of neoliberal globalisation.

Curiously, although there is a growing body of literature on neoliberal globalisation in Africa in general, and Cameroon in particular, its effects on private capital accumulation and state–capital relations appear not to have been widely studied (Pitcher 2002). This is surprising because, since the 1970s, there has been a lively debate on these issues in Africa, especially in Kenya, inspired by the dependencia theory (Leys 1994). The dependistas (the majority) sought to show that African private capital was weak economically and politically, and that the subsequent alliance between the African 'comprador' elite and foreign capital was responsible for the drain of capital from the periphery to the metropolis. The anti-dependistas, in contrast, argued that while private African capital was relatively weak, it had grown significantly and relatively quickly after independence thanks to close links with the state apparatus, and could be expected to become still stronger. Although the dependency-inspired literature suffered serious limitations in theoretical and empirical terms, it has had the merit of drawing the attention of researchers to the importance of state–capital relations in the process of capitalist development.

Of all the neoliberal policy prescriptions, two – namely privatisation and global open markets – appear to have had the greatest effect on relations between state and private capital accumulation in Cameroon and in many other parts of Africa. Privatisation called for a re-evaluation of relations between public and private sectors on the continent. Under pressure from international donors, African governments have been urged to reduce the scope of state ownership and enhance private-sector development. International donors tended to attribute the massive growth of state enterprises after independence and their generally poor performance to the 'bad governance' of African neo-patrimonial regimes. They claimed that statist conceptions of development resulted in the widespread politicisation of economic decision-making and the rent-seeking behaviour of the parasitic political elite.

Their criticism is undeniably justified to a certain extent but, as I have argued elsewhere (Konings 2004a), it tends to underestimate the importance of a series of other factors responsible for public-sector expansion. The view that the state should be the prime motor of development was widely shared in the 1960s, and ownership and intervention by the state were accepted as the dominant development paradigm. Public-sector expansion was also encouraged by the fact that, at independence, Africa's economies were characterised by a weak and subordinate domestic private sector and foreign control. Most post-colonial governments tried to forestall the development of a national bourgeoisie, which they regarded as a potential political threat, and to reduce foreign dominance. Attaining greater ownership and control of the 'commanding heights' of the economy would enable them to influence the broad direction of national development. Subsequently, the parastatal sector came to be viewed as 'national patrimony' and sales to foreigners were regarded negatively. And, last but not least, state expansion was an essential element in the maintenance and consolidation of power of African neo-patrimonial regimes. It created ample space for patronage politics that laid a solid foundation for co-opting the various ethno-regional factions into the 'hegemonic alliance' (Bayart 1979) and thus secured a considerable measure of political stability for the post-colonial state.

Paradoxically, as this study attempts to demonstrate, most of these factors continue to influence the privatisation process in Cameroon. Privatisation has been slow, not only because of numerous technical constraints but also because of the regime's neo-patrimonial logic. It has often been marked by a lack of transparency and accountability, enabling the parasitic political elite to engage in a variety of rent-seeking activities. It has also led to fierce conflict between ethno-regional factions within the hegemonic alliance about lucrative takeovers. In the absence of a well-developed domestic capitalist class and in an effort to discourage any takeovers by dominant ethnic entrepreneurial groups, the regime has sought an alliance with foreign capital, which it considered to be of mutual advantage. It has brought about a concentration of foreign capital in the most strategic sectors of the economy and minority participation of the Cameroonian state and private investors in foreign concerns. While there is growing resistance in Cameroonian society to what is called 'recolonisation', the government claims that such joint ventures will make a significant contribution to economic recovery, guarantee some measure of national control over the operations of transnational enterprises, and offer the political elite and allied entrepreneurial groups new opportunities for capital accumulation.

A second neoliberal prescription – global open markets – has had the unintended effect of stimulating transnational criminal activities in African countries that suffer from the nefarious effects of the economic crisis and economic liberalisation. Engagement in transnational criminal networks has become a new form of rapid private capital accumulation. Despite a lack of clear figures, it is becoming increasingly evident that Africa's share in transnational criminal activity has expanded on an unprecedented scale (Bayart *et al.* 1999; Shaw 2002; Bayart 2004), having conquered a substantial part of the most profitable markets of developed economies, such as those in drugs, diamonds, illegal immigration and high-value minerals. International donors have often blamed the predatory African political elite for the enormous increase in the parallel economy and criminal activities during the economic crisis and economic liberalisation. However, Bayart *et al.* (1999) allege that the African political elite itself has become increasingly involved in transnational criminal networks.

This study focuses on the emergence of transnational criminal networks outside the state, in particular among young, poorly educated Cameroonian men (and increasingly also women) who have been the major victims of neoliberal policies. Through involvement in such networks, they have succeeded in amassing fabulous wealth in a short space of time. Interestingly, they are inclined to re-invest their ill-gotten gains in a variety of legal entrepreneurial activities and even in the pursuit of political power. They form one of the exceptional examples of autonomous domestic private capital accumulation in Africa's post-colonial history. As Sklar (1979: 531–52) already pointed out many years ago, politics became the primary mechanism of class formation in Africa, as national accumulation was closely linked to political power. Little wonder then that the Cameroonian regime has devised several strategies to bring this autonomous mode of private capital accumulation under state control, including attempts to co-opt these young entrepreneurs into the hegemonic alliance.

The study is divided into three sections. The first section discusses the pattern of economic and political power prior to neoliberal globalisation. The second section analyses the continuities and changes in the structure of economic and political power as a result of privatisation, and the third section concentrates on transnational criminal networks as a new avenue to domestic private capital accumulation.

The post-colonial state and capital accumulation

At independence and reunification in 1961, Cameroon inherited an economy characterised by foreign control, especially French capital, and the almost complete absence of any domestic private capital (Hugon 1968). Given this situation, those now in positions of power, and headed by President Ahmadou Ahidjo (1961–82), soon launched a development strategy called planned liberalism (cf. Ndongko 1985; Fonge 2003), which championed both an intensification of state intervention, notably by establishing state-owned companies, and the encouragement of private investment. Similar development strategies were implemented in most other African states, albeit under different names. In this section, I intend to explore the socioeconomic groups that became the main beneficiaries of this planned liberalism and their relations with the state.

Like their counterparts elsewhere in Africa (Grosh and Makandala 1994; Tangri 1999), the Cameroonian authorities made a formidable effort to stimulate parastatal sector growth (Tedga 1990; Van de Walle 1994; Konings 2004a). From the handful of public enterprises inherited from the French and British Trusteeship Authorities, the Cameroonian parastatal sector grew to 219 enterprises by the mid-1980s, employing approximately 100,000 people. Generally, statist conceptions of development, together with economic nationalism and the need for political patronage, led to an excessive growth of state-owned enterprises (Tangri 1999: 19–22).

State expansion afforded prebendal and patronage possibilities and was, therefore, seen by the African political elite as a valuable mechanism in the consolidation and maintenance of political power. According to Van de Walle (1994: 155–6), public enterprise in Cameroon 'proved to be an ideal instrument to distribute state resources in the form of jobs, rents, power and prestige, enabling the president to reward allies and co-opt opponents, and thus secure his own power base'. A patrimonial logic existed in many African post-colonial states (Chabal and Daloz 1999), but was particularly forceful in Cameroon, a country with stark ethno-regional cleavages (Gabriel 1999; Nyamnjoh 1999). State resources could be used to forge the ethno-regional alliances among the various elite groups necessary for national unity and political stability and to obviate the need for coercion (Bayart 1979).

In his masterful study *Who Rules Cameroon?*, Ngayap (1983) notes that the managers of the largest parastatals were rarely chosen because of their technical competence; they were instead selected by virtue of their political ties. Thus, according to Ngayap, 79 per cent of managers were part of the bureaucratic-political elite, having previously served in top government positions as ministers, senior members of the president's staff, or secretaries-general (Ngayap 1983: 248; see also Tedga 1990). If public enterprises in Africa have recorded mediocre results, it is almost exclusively due to the fact that they have been systematically plundered for purposes of enrichment and the accumulation of power by members of the bureaucratic and political elite (Hibou 1999; Van de Walle 2001).

The political importance of state-owned enterprises is evident from the fact that the Cameroonian government used to subsidise parastatal-sector losses to the tune of FCFA 150 million a year prior to the start of the economic crisis in the mid-1980s. Though much of Cameroon's oil revenue continued to be kept in secret bank accounts, one of its major functions soon became the covering of parastatal deficits. In a 1987 review of the Cameroonian economy, the World Bank summarised its conclusion in uncharacteristically colourful terms: 'The good performance of the Cameroonian economy is badly eroded by the festering sore of the public-enterprise sector' (World Bank 1987: 3).

In addition to increased state intervention, Ahidjo was convinced of the vital importance of private initiative in his pursuit of rapid economic growth and development. Like most other African heads of state, he came to rely more on foreign than on domestic private capital for two main reasons. First, foreign investors were not considered to form an alternative centre of power to the incumbent political elite. And second, private foreign investment was seen as indispensable for Africa's development in terms of capital resources, technology, market access, employment, management and tax revenues. In his efforts to attract foreign private capital, Ahidjo designed an investment code that offered foreign entrepreneurs generous incentives to invest in Cameroon including preferential tax treatment, subsidies for recruiting and training any necessary manpower, government contracts, subsidised bank loans, enhanced access to imported and domestic raw materials, and easy repatriation of profits (Ndongko 1987; DeLancey 1989).

In many ways, a coincidence of interests developed between the African state and foreign investors. Indeed, some authors refer to the 'symbiotic relationship between multinationals and state' in Africa (Tangri 1999: 113). On the one hand, foreign capital enjoyed a considerable measure of autonomy and substantial benefits while conducting its operations in Africa. On the other hand, foreign investment tended to contribute to economic and social progress and enhance the political legitimacy of African regimes. In addition, foreign business has provided a variety of financial favours to the African political elite in exchange for political support. Some of the other benefits of foreign investment to the African elite include coveted directorships, partnerships and share holdings, all of which can be used for personal or political advancement.

From the late 1960s onwards, many African governments began to adopt a more critical stance towards foreign capital, claiming that it was antithetical to economic development and national sovereignty. Some countries, such as Uganda, Kenya, Tanzania, Zambia and Zaire, pursued policies of nationalisation that specifically targeted Middle Eastern and South Asian businesses (Van de Walle 2001: 113). In other African countries, such as Ghana and Nigeria, the governments initiated policies that required specific percentages of ownership of foreign concerns to be placed in indigenous hands (Biersteker 1987; Tangri 1999). In sharp contrast to this widespread resentment in Africa towards foreign domination and exploitation, the Cameroonian government continued to court foreign investment. Being one of the most prosperous and stable countries in Africa (Konings 1996), Cameroon was able to attract new foreign capital inflows in spite of the drastic decline in direct foreign investment rates in Africa since the 1970s. In 1960, some 17 per cent of total direct foreign investment to developing countries went to Africa but by the mid-1980s Africa's share had plummeted to less than 5 per cent (Tangri 1999: 116). It was not until the severe economic crisis started in the mid-1980s that a dramatic drop in direct foreign investment in Cameroon could be observed, and even a withdrawal of some foreign concerns from the country.

With a few exceptions, such as Botswana, Ivory Coast and Kenya, where local capitalists had achieved a stronghold in the state apparatus (Kennedy 1988; Rapley 1993; Berman and Leys 1994), African governments have failed to actively support domestic private initiatives. The main reason appears to be political. Nearly all African governments viewed the prospect of an autonomous domestic capitalist class with concern, seeing it as a potential threat to their positions of power. Possibilities for private domestic capital accumulation therefore remained largely restricted to those socioeconomic groups that maintained or developed close links with the state apparatus. Similar to most other African countries (Forrest 1994), there were two main groups in Cameroon that took advantage of state patronage to create or expand private enterprise.

The first group was made up of the parasitic bureaucratic and political elite who had used their position of power to pillage state resources. Most of them were inclined to either squander their newly acquired wealth in conspicuous consumption or to deposit it in foreign bank accounts (Joseph 1987; MacGaffey 1987). Only a small minority tended to invest in productive enterprise. Some tried to combine political office with entrepreneurial activities, while others resigned from office to devote themselves fully to private capital accumulation.

The career of Pierre Tchanque seems to be representative of this group. From modest origins, this bureaucrat from the Bamileke region in Francophone Cameroon rose to the pinnacles of state administration before starting his own business. Having been Secretary General at the Ministry of Finance from 1966 to 1969, Assistant-Director General in the state investment company La Société Nationale des Investissements (SNI) from 1969 to 1970, and Secretary General of the Union Douanière des États de l'Afrique Centrale (UDEAC) from 1971 to 1977, he left the public sector. In 1979, he launched a major new brewery, Nouvelles brasseries africaines (NOBRA), with the help of capital from the SNI and significant tax and tariff breaks. To reflect his new status, Tchanque was appointed to the Central Committee of the nation's single party, the Cameroon National Union (CNU) (Ngayap 1983; Van de Walle 1993).

The second group consists of a relatively small number of large domestic entrepreneurs. They initially started accumulating capital independently but eventually developed close links with the state and were able to expand their business activities when they were co-opted into the hegemonic alliance by the Ahidjo regime (Bayart 1979). Although Ahidjo constantly emphasised the need for an ethnic balance in the distribution of economic and political power, there is, nevertheless, sufficient evidence that entrepreneurs from two ethnic groups enjoyed a privileged position in opportunities for capital accumulation (Ngayap 1983; Konings 1996). These were, first of all, Fulbe entrepreneurs, especially those from Garoua, Ahidjo's hometown. And second there were the Bamileke entrepreneurs. The Bamileke territory was, until about 1970, one of the most important areas of the Union des Populations du Cameroun (UPC) rebellion against the regime (Joseph 1977). It is widely believed in Cameroon that Ahidjo was ready to grant the Bamileke entrepreneurs ample room for capital accumulation on condition that they supported his regime.

It is certain that Ahidjo's patronage politics have been of great help in allowing the Bamileke to become the leading force in Cameroonian business. The Bamileke ethnic group is known, and often feared, in Cameroon for its assumed dynamism and entrepreneurial spirit (Dongmo 1981; Warnier 1993). It values a disciplined and ascetic lifestyle, encouraging its members to re-invest any accumulated capital in expanded production rather than squander it in conspicuous consumption. The bibliographies of the older generation of Bamileke businessmen are as edifying as those of the great self-made American business magnates. Being poorly educated, they began their careers as petty traders and artisans during colonial rule. Through hard work and thrift they were able to save money in rotating credit associations, the so-called *tontines* (Henry *et al.* 1991). They used these savings for the gradual expansion of their businesses and by the end of the colonial period they had already succeeded in setting up their first large-scale enterprises. Following independence, they were able to diversify their entrepreneurial activities and to move into industrial production by establishing close links with the state, and foreign capital.

The life story of Victor Fotso, one of the biggest Cameroonian businessmen, is a good example of the kind of business careers the first generation of Bamileke entrepreneurs enjoyed. Born around 1936, Fotso entered the Catholic school in Baleng at the age of seven but a year later he was forced to leave to help his father grow manioc and bananas. As he recalled later in his autobiography (Fotso and Guyomard 1994), it was at the nearby market in Hiala that he was introduced to basic trading techniques. He soon migrated to the south where he became a travelling petty trader. He spent only a tiny part of his profits on food and clothing in order to save enough money to expand his business. In 1956 he opened a large store in the centre of Mbalmayo, a town near the capital Yaoundé, offering a variety of imported goods. His business prospered and, after independence, he began to diversify his activities, moving first into transport and later into the import of wine and alcoholic drinks after entering into a partnership with the Frenchman Pierre Castel, the owner of Brasseries et Glacières Internationales (BGI). A few years later he set up his first industrial enterprise with the assistance of another Frenchman, Jacques Lacombe, the director of La Société Industrielle et Forestière des Allumettes (SIFA). He now owns a large number of factories involved in the production of matches, note-books, batteries, packing materials, chemicals, food and agro-industrial commodities. He also owns real estate, a hotel (Ibis Douala) and the Commercial Bank of Cameroon (CBC), created with the technical assistance of Crédit Commercial de France (Ngayap 1983; Fotso and Guyomard 1994).

Fotso and other prominent Bamileke businessmen such as Kadji Defosso, Paul Monthé, André Souhaing and Pierre Monkam, were co-opted into either the Central Committee or the Political Bureau of the CNU during its fifth National Congress in 1980. Their close links with the state appa-ratus have given them similar opportunities for private capital accumulation as the bureaucratic and political elite, namely, privileged access to public loans and contracts, as well as ample space to engage in a variety of corrupt and illegal practices including the evasion of taxes and import duties. Since the 1970s, this older generation of Cameroonian businessmen has been joined by a younger generation of university-trained professionals.

A significant change in political power and chances for private capital accumulation occurred in 1982 when Ahidjo suddenly resigned from office. His successor, Paul Biya, encountered difficulties in consolidating power (Konings 1996; Takougang and Krieger 1998). As a consequence, he began to appoint an increasing number of the bureaucratic and political elite from his own ethnic group, the Beti, to pivotal positions in the administration, security organs and public enterprises (Takougang 1993). He also attempted to undermine the dominant position of Bamileke entrepreneurs and Fulbe wholesale traders by promoting a new class of businessmen from his own region. This was only partly successful since the Beti generally lack the busi-ness acumen of the Bamileke and Fulbe and tend to squander any accumu-lated capital (Tedga 1990; Rowlands 1993). Moreover, it would appear that the new regime's *barons* are much bolder in staking out claims to the state's resources than Ahidjo's supporters ever were. Corruption and rent-seeking had always been fundamental characteristics of the regime but after 1984 they increased to the point of being dysfunctional (Van de Walle 1993).

Economic liberalisation has thwarted further growth in the domestic private sector. With the removal of, or reduction in, trade restrictions and protection, African markets have been exposed to a flood of foreign exports. Competition from foreign manufacturers has undermined the fortunes of numerous domestic businesses, and many local manufacturing firms have experienced severe financial distress and have had to close down.

Privatisation and capital concentration

Privatisation has become a crucial issue on the neoliberal globalisation agenda. In 1988–9, the Bretton Woods institutions forced the neo-patrimonial regime in Cameroon to adopt a structural adjustment programme, making privatisation a cornerstone of their lending conditions. They claimed that divestiture would bring about a more efficient and productive economy on the grounds that it would depoliticise economic decisions and also end the mismanagement and corruption endemic in enterprises controlled by politicians. Moreover, it would solve the problem of rising budgetary deficits and in the process generate revenue that could be used to pay off government debt. And, above all, it would enhance the scope of the private sector, producing a desirable change in the balance of power between the state and the private sector. In this section, I explore whether privatisation has actually led to a decline in the political elite's neo-patrimonial and rent-seeking activities and a significant change in the chances for private capital accumulation. In other words, which of the existing socioeconomic groups has benefited most from privatisation?

There is considerable evidence that the Biya regime has been extremely reluctant to sell state-owned enterprises, which it looks upon as a threat to its patronage politics and the maintenance and consolidation of its power. Consequently, the initiation and execution of a privatisation programme has been slow in Cameroon. In 1991, a World Bank mission expressed its dissatisfaction with the government's performance, pointing to the delay in establishing effective government agencies to oversee the process, the government's reluctance to sell off anything but bankrupt and inconsequential enterprises, in-fighting over which firms would be the first to be sold or liquidated, and foot-dragging over issuing tenders and devising criteria against which bids could be assessed (Walker 1998: 4). Again, in its 1994 report *Adjustment in Africa: Reforms, Results and the Road Ahead*, the World Bank asserted that little progress had been made in Cameroon in the area of privatisation. The report rated Cameroon in the bottom range of economic policy and adjustment performance and pointed out that the International Monetary Fund (IMF) had signed and cancelled three successive stand-by agreements because of the government's failure to achieve its negotiated targets (World Bank 1994).

The slow progress of privatisation is clear in the number of privatisations that took place between 1989 and 2005. Out of the 219 state-owned enterprises at the start of the process, the government eventually decided to liquidate 87 and to privatise 30. Despite the limited number of enterprises on the divestiture list, no more than 20 had actually been sold by 2005 (see Table 11.1). Compared to some other African countries, such as Mozambique, Zambia, Tanzania, Uganda and Mali (Bennell 1997; Campbell White and Bhatia 1998; Tangri and Mwenda 2001; Pitcher 2002; Rakner 2003), this would seem to be a disappointing result both in number and implementation. However, one should not overlook the fact that privatisation in Cameroon, though limited, is a complex process for technical and political reasons. Many of the Cameroonian parastatals set for divestiture are large and strategic enterprises, notably in the agro-industrial sector, transport, communications and public utilities.

Although the neo-patrimonial logic of the regime tended to slow down the privatisation process in Cameroon, it soon became evident that privatisation

Table 11.1 Privatised state enterprises in Cameroon

Enterprise	Sector of activity	Buyer	Foreign participation (%)
OCB	Agro-industry	Compagnie Fruitière de Marseille (France) in 1991	70
SOCAMAC	Harbour handling	CCEI Bank (France) in 1991	51
CHOCOCAM	Cocoa industry	Barry SA (France) in 1991	70.7
SEPBC	Forest reserve	Delmas (France) in 1992	70
COCAM	Plywood	Khoury (Lebanon) in 1992	87.6
SCDM	Metallurgy	Hobum Afrika (Germany) in 1994	86.6
HEVECAM	Agro-industry	Golden Millennium Group (Malaysia/Indonesia) in 1994	90
REGIFERCAM	Railways	SAGA (France) and COMAZAR (South Africa) in 1994	77
ONDAPB	Agriculture and livestock	Fadil/Daniel Yok (Cameroon) in 1995	34
SOFIBEL	Forestry	Fadil (Cameroon) in 1995	45
SPFS-SRL	Agro-industry	SIPH (France) in 1995	92
CAMSHIP	Shipping	Several Cameroonian investors in 1997	48.2
CEPER	Printing	MUPEC Cooperative (Cameroon) in 1998	0
CAMSUCO	Agro-industry	Vilgrain (France) in 1998	98.1
BICIC	Banking	Banques Populaires (France) in 1998	52.5
SOCAPALM	Agro-industry	PALCAM/COGEPART (France) in 1999	60
CAMTEL	Mobile phones	MTN (South Africa) and Telecom (France) in 2000	100
SONEL	Electricity	AES-Sirocco (USA) in 2001	56
CDC	Agro-industry (tea sector)	Brobon Finex (South Africa) in 2002	65
Douala Port	Container terminals	MAERSK (Denmark) and Bolloré (France) in 2004	59

Sources: Tsafack-Nanfosso (2004); Bagui Kari (2001).

itself did not altogether foreclose rent-seeking opportunities for the parasitic bureaucratic and political elite. Indeed, some of its members have actually been benefiting from it. For politicians responsible for the privatisation process, privatisation measures have frequently been an opportunity for corrupt practices. Divestiture has mostly been a far from open and transparent process and, in return for the payment of substantial kickbacks, public enterprises have been sold at prices far below their true value. There are even reports of embezzlement of the proceeds from sales (Kangue Ejangue and Noubissié Ngankam 1995; Nguihé Kanté 2003; Tsafack-Nanfosso 2004). Moreover, privatisation has not necessarily excluded members of the bureaucratic and political elite from occupying top positions in former state-owned enterprises: some have been reappointed and others have been newly recruited.

The Biya government has regularly expressed its determination to promote the participation of private domestic capital in privatisations and even to give it priority in the process (Atangana Mebara 1997: 62). For example, in a press release on 1 November 1994, the inter-ministerial Commission for Privatisation stressed 'the need for creating instruments that could guarantee a consistent and balanced participation of nationals in the share capital of any enterprise set for divestiture' (Nguihé Kanté 2003: 235). A closer look at the privatised parastatals in Table 11.1, however, reveals that very few state enterprises have actually been taken over by domestic private capital.

One reason for this lack of takeovers by nationals is that the government continues to mistrust the development of a national bourgeoisie and is therefore reluctant to give potential national investors the necessary incentives. Entrepreneurs without sufficient capital resources face many constraints, including the absence of a well-established capital market, access to bank loans, and the high costs of credit. But even entrepreneurs with the necessary capital resources are often prevented by African regimes from taking over parastatals out of fear that this might strengthen the dominant economic position of ethnic rivals (Bennell 1997). The Beti-dominated government of Paul Biya has persistently tried to thwart a Bamileke takeover of state assets (Konings 1989; Hibou 1999). For example, when Bamileke entrepreneurs succeeded in obtaining a considerable proportion of the share capital in La Société Camerounaise de Manutention et d'Aconage (SOCAMAC) after its privatisation in 1991 (see Table 11.1), prominent Beti politicians declared: 'SOCAMAC has been a learning process for us and nothing similar will happen again in the field of privatisations' (Nguihé Kanté 2003: 234; Kangue Ejangue and Noubissié Ngankam 1995: 89). This proved not to be a mere threat. A few years later, in 1994, the government approved the takeover of La Société Camerounaise de Métallurgie (SCDM) by a German company, Hobum Afrika, even though a Bamileke group, Bachirou, had put in a higher bid (FCFA 7 billion against Hobum's FCFA 3 billion) (Bagui Kari 2001: 67). Discouragement of Bamileke investment was accompanied by attempts to promote Beti participation. In September 1998, the government approved the purchase of Le Centre d'Édition et de Production pour l'Enseignement et la Recherche (CEPER) for the sum of FCFA 5 billion by a former Beti Minister of National Education Charles Etoundi and a newly formed cooperative of Beti teachers (see Table 11.1).

Another reason for the striking lack of takeovers by nationals was the failure of the parasitic political elite to purchase strategic public enterprises as a result of conflicts between ethno-regional factions within the ruling class.

One example is the failed privatisation attempt of La Société de Développement du Coton (SODECOTON) in 1995, which some Cameroonian newspapers described as the year's greatest political scandal. SODECOTON is a huge agro-industrial parastatal in Northern Cameroon that has introduced a contract-farming scheme in which more than 250,000 peasants participate – a clear indication of the company's importance in regional development. A French company, La Compagnie Française pour le Développement des Fibres Textiles (CFDT), manages the company and owns 30 per cent of its share capital.

In January 1995, it was announced that the majority of the company's shares had been transferred to a new domestic enterprise, La Société Mobilière d'Investissement du Cameroun (SMIC), with Cameroon's treasury keeping its 22 per cent and CFDT its 30 per cent. The SMIC turned out to be a small group of politically well-connected elite, most of them originating from Northern Cameroon, who had bought the company at a give-away price (about 10 to 15 per cent of its market value). Prominent members included the *lamido* (chief) Rey Bouba, the President of the National Assembly Cavaye Yigue Djibril, the Vice Prime Minister Mustapha Amadou, the former Prime Minister and current National Director of the Banque des États de l'Afrique Centrale (BEAC) Sadou Hayatou, and the ruling party's Central Committee member Alhadji Baba Danpullo, who is an Anglophone businessman with close ethnic and religious ties to the Northern elite. The deal had been approved by the Anglophone Prime Minister Simon Achidi Achu and the Northern Minister of Industrial and Commercial Development Bella Bouba Maigari.

Unexpectedly, a few months later the deal was suddenly cancelled by the Southern Minister of Finance Justin Ndioro with the support of other Southern and mostly Beti cabinet members and President Biya himself. Two factors appear to be particularly relevant in explaining why the dominant faction in the Biya government declared the SMIC takeover 'null and void'. First, it wanted to protect the government's shaky standing with international financial institutions and France, which were both strongly opposed to the SMIC takeover. The World Bank immediately denounced the disregard for the guidelines about competitive bidding, the non-transparency of the exercise, and the ridiculously low price. France rejected the takeover in order to safeguard CFDT interests. The CFDT, which had not been previously consulted, was extremely hostile to privatisation due to its major economic stake in the Northern cotton industry in general, and in the company in particular. Its 30 per cent share capital in SODECOTON took 70 per cent of its earnings by controlling invoicing and sales abroad. Moreover, it was afraid that a takeover by politicians would lead to the collapse of the Northern cotton industry.

A second reason for the dominant faction's derailment of the SMIC was to maintain Southern dominance over the North and to avoid the emergence of ethno-regional lobbies for ownership of strategic national enterprises located in their region. If Northerners succeeded in seizing SODECOTON, Anglophones might demand ownership of another strategic agro-industrial enterprise located in their region, namely the Cameroon Development Corporation (CDC) (Takougang and Krieger 1998: 169–80).

The Northern elite protested vehemently against the government's decision to cancel its previously approved contract of sale. They instituted legal proceedings against the Cameroonian state that dragged on until 7 August 2001 when a settlement was reached and SMIC members were handsomely compensated for the loss of their shares. However, the final settlement could not conceal the fact that the SODECOTON privatisation scandal had resulted in domestic and foreign investors losing confidence in the transparency and even the credibility of privatisation procedures in Cameroon. Despite repeated pressure on the government from the Bretton Woods institutions to privatise the company, the government has so far failed to attract new investors.

Instead of promoting the development of the domestic private sector, privatisation has led to a renewed expansion of foreign private capital. The government has permitted a takeover of most parastatals by foreign investors for reasons similar to those in the period prior to economic liberalisation: investors such as these bring much needed capital resources, proven managerial capabilities, new technology and market access. Selling to a foreign investor is also often the only way to avoid accusations of clientelism or tribalism (Campbell White and Bhatia 1998: 32).

Table 11.1 shows that foreign participation in the new share capital of sold parastatals has increased dramatically. As elsewhere in Africa (Bennell 1997: 1794), foreign investment has been concentrated among the larger and strategic parastatals that have been sold. A further concentration of foreign capital in the commanding heights of the economy is to be expected since the remaining ten parastatals on the divestiture list belong to the same category of enterprises and serious negotiations between the Cameroonian government and foreign concerns about their eventual transfer are already under way. There also appears to be a concentration of investors from particular countries rather than a diversification of foreign investors. The table reveals that most parastatals in Cameroon have been taken over by French investors, which is hardly surprising when one takes into account the close links between Cameroon and France, and the existing dominance of French capital in the domestic formal sector. One French consortium, Bolloré, with its subsidiaries PALCAM/GOGEPART and SAGA, has made sizeable investments in the takeover of the Cameroonian railways, agro-industry and Douala port (see Table 11.1). What is also noteworthy is the substantial investment by South African private capital in the privatisation process, which reflects the increasing role of South African investors on the African continent since the abolition of apartheid.

Although privatisation has reinforced the dominant role of foreign capital in the domestic economy, both the government and foreign investors favour minority participation by the Cameroonian state and private capital in privatised parastatals. The government hopes that such joint ventures will guarantee some measure of national control over the policies and activities of multinationals in the domestic economy and stimulate capital accumulation by domestic entrepreneurs with close links to the state. Transnational companies, too, have a vested interest in such joint ventures. These companies have rapidly adapted themselves to the changing business environment and they are now actively seeking domestic alliances for vertically integrated partnerships that are more suited to their investment and production strategies (Pitcher 2002: 151).

This minority participation by the Cameroonian state and private capital in the privatisation process does not prevent the vast majority of Cameroonian intellectuals from severely criticising foreign dominance. Resurrecting many of the arguments made by the dependency theorists in the 1970s, they insist that the state has relinquished its sovereignty and is now dependent on the dictates of foreign investors and global markets. To the extent that Cameroonian nationals are the beneficiaries of privatisation, they are only the 'comprador' agents for foreign capital, providing a façade of domestic involvement when, in reality, foreign investors control the actual wealth and power (cf. Pitcher 2002: 142). Many Cameroonian critics have, therefore, referred to the current privatisation process as 'neo-colonialism' or a 'bargain-sale of the national patrimony' (Bagui Kari 2001; Nguiché Kanté 2003; Tsafack-Nanfosso 2004). Indeed, though generally in favour of privatisation policies, Nyom (2000: 66) maintains that 'it is unclear why the state is selling off in the process the national patrimony to foreign multinationals for a few dollars'.

It would even appear that resentment of the foreign takeover of strategic parastatals has become widespread in Cameroonian society, all the more so because a number of transnational enterprises have performed far below expectations. A few examples will suffice here.

Since its takeover of La Société Nationale d'Électricité (SONEL) in 2001 for $69 million, the American multinational, AES-Sirocco, has blatantly failed to keep to its promise of guaranteeing an uninterrupted supply of electricity. Various parts of the country have suffered from electricity rationing and regular power cuts, resulting in a reduction in economic output and hardship for consumers. This, together with excessive increases in the price for electricity and massive layoffs of workers, has led to several strikes and boycott actions by its workers and numerous demonstrations and court cases by consumers. Both workers and consumers have regularly demanded the departure of the Americans.

The privatisation of the CDC, a huge agro-industrial parastatal in Anglophone Cameroon, has been frequently postponed, as I have discussed elsewhere (Konings 2004a). This was mainly due to fierce resistance by the Anglophones who see its privatisation as an attempt by the Francophone-dominated post-colonial state to sell off one of the last-remaining Anglophone economic legacies, and by the Bakweri ethnic group in particular, which claims ownership of the CDC lands (Konings and Nyamnjoh 2003). To the consternation of Anglophones, it was announced in October 2002 that the CDC tea sector had been sold to a South African consortium, Brobon Finex PTY Limited, which would run it under the name of Cameroon Tea Estates (CTE).

As with SODECOTON, the privatisation of the CDC estates became a national scandal when it became known how the takeover by Brobon Finex had been affected and who was going to benefit from the transaction. On his own admission, it became clear that its privatisation had been masterminded by John Niba Ngu, a former CDC General Manager and Minister of Agriculture, who is generally known to be a close friend of President Biya. He used both his technical knowledge and his many connections in the highest echelons of the regime to arrange the privatisation of the CDC tea estates. While experts had conservatively estimated the estate's value at about FCFA 3.2 billion, Ngu managed to bring the price down to FCFA 1.5 billion. Less than three months later, the CTE sold tea worth FCFA 4.6 billion. In return for his excellent services, the CTE board allocated Ngu 5 per cent of the company's share capital and appointed him General Manager with a monthly salary and fringe benefits amounting to FCFA 4 million.

It also came to light that the major shareholder in the CTE was Alhadji Baba Danpullo, a well-known businessman with close links to the state apparatus who, like Ngu, comes originally from the North West Province of Anglophone Cameroon. He had previously been involved in the SODECOTON privatisation scandal (see above, pp. 262–3). Danpullo was the one who put Ngu in contact with Brobon Finex and it is alleged that he was able to launder a substantial sum of money by participating in Brobon Finex's takeover. Through this financial transaction he acquired a powerful position within the CTE. By becoming a member of its board of directors he was able to replace the former CDC managers with people from his other companies in Cameroon who were loyal to him but who lacked experience in tea production. He also fired Ngu when the latter dared to dismiss for incompetence 23 of the newly appointed managers. As a result of mismanagement and its inexperience in tea cultivation, the CTE is presently facing a variety of problems. On 15 January 2004, it laid off 585 workers 'in a bid to reduce the company's cost of production which has soared to an unbearable level' (CTE press release 15 January 2004). As a result of these developments, popular resistance to foreign takeovers has been strengthened both in the region and in the country as a whole.

Globalisation and new forms of domestic private capital accumulation

As elsewhere in post-colonial Africa, domestic private capital accumulation has tended to be associated with the possession of political power in Cameroon. During the process of neoliberal globalisation, a new form of domestic private capital accumulation has emerged that appears to be more or less independent of the state and is designated as *feymania*, a pidgin English expression meaning to 'fool' or 'cheat' someone (Malaquais 2001; Ndjio 2005). It came to refer to a specific mode of rapid capital accumulation as a result of involvement in transnational networks of criminal activities.

Remarkably, *feymania* emerged among a socioeconomic group that had been badly hit by the economic crisis and economic liberalisation, namely young men living in the slums of Cameroon's largest cities, notably New Bell in Douala and Madagascar in Yaoundé (Konings forthcoming). Initially, most of them belonged to the entrepreneurial Bamileke ethnic group. They tended to be poorly educated and they found it hard to get a job in the formal sector during the economic crisis and economic liberalisation. They mostly tried to eke out a livelihood by engaging in a variety of informal and criminal activities, such as petty trade and production, smuggling and theft, and some of them formed criminal gangs that terrorised the local population. Unsurprisingly, they were constantly on the lookout for ways to escape poverty.

The early 1990s was the heyday of political liberalisation when the newly created opposition parties still formed a serious challenge to the ruling party, the Cameroon People's Democratic Movement (CPDM), and the autocratic and corrupt Biya regime. Feeling, like other Bamileke, discriminated against by the Beti-dominated regime, the young slum residents saw the overthrow of the Biya regime and political change as avenues to socioeconomic advancement. They were, therefore, inclined to support the main opposition party, the Social Democratic Front (SDF) – a party based in the North West Province of Anglophone Cameroon where the population is ethnically related to the Bamileke (Konings 2004b). Many of them participated in the 1991–2 'ghost town' campaign. This was essentially a civil disobedience action organised by the political opposition to force the ruling regime to hold a sovereign national conference (Konings 1996; Takougang and Krieger 1998). The action aimed to bring the economy to a standstill by calling on the public to stay indoors, to boycott markets and offices (except at weekends), and not to pay taxes or their public-utilities bills. The 'ghost town' campaign was particularly successful in the opposition stronghold of New Bell in Douala where there were numerous violent confrontations between demonstrators and the forces of law and order, resulting in several deaths and numerous injuries (Konings forthcoming).

When the opposition eventually failed to overthrow the Biya regime and bring about political change, some of the marginalised youth switched to *feymania* as an avenue to rapid capital accumulation. Existing and newly formed criminal gangs of Bamileke youth joined or created transnational criminal networks stretching from the African continent to Western Europe, where Paris became the main centre of *feymania* activities, the Middle East and South East Asia (Malaquais 2001). For instance, one of the first and most powerful transnational criminal networks was created by the renowned *feyman* Donatien

Koagne, nicknamed the King of Cameroon, a young Bamileke man from New Bell in Douala. His group had at least 100 members, the vast majority of whom were Bamileke youth. Ndjio (2005) estimates the number of young Cameroonians involved in *feymania* to be about 2,000.

Feymen groups are involved in a variety of criminal activities. They persuade their victims that they are being offered fabulous bargains. They are adept at selling goods, which do not in fact exist, and propose non-existent projects to development and aid agencies so as to defraud foreign embassies. They claim to be able to multiply banknotes, which has become one of their most successful tricks to dupe leading politicians and wealthy businessmen in Africa and elsewhere. They are also engaged in the international trafficking of drugs, diamonds, arms, works of art, human organs, and young girls for organised prostitution. A number of national and international newspapers connect Cameroonian *feymen* with Nigerian drug traffickers and Congolese and Liberian diamond smugglers who are increasingly active in Western Europe and South Africa (Bayart *et al.* 1999). In addition, they are involved in counterfeiting not only banknotes but also credit cards and passports, money laundering, smuggling, usury, speculation, embezzlement, and the theft of luxury cars and other valuable items.

As a result of these and other criminal activities, they have been able to amass fabulous wealth in a short space of time and, unlike the older generation of Bamileke entrepreneurs, they are not ashamed of displaying their newly acquired wealth. The attitude of the Cameroonian population towards this new mode of capital accumulation would seem to be ambivalent. The older generation is inclined to question the supposedly mysterious origins of the *feymen*'s sudden wealth, often associating it with sorcery and witchcraft. In sharp contrast, the younger generation tends to admire their achievements, seeing the *feymen* as role models and national heroes (Malequais 2001; Ndjio 2005).

However, it would be wrong to assume that *feymen*, as the parasitic political elite, are inclined to merely squander their accumulated capital. While they tend to maintain a lavish lifestyle, most of them do reinvest some of their wealth in productive enterprises. Curiously, an increasing number of *feymen* are tending to invest their ill-gotten gains in a variety of legal entrepreneurial activities, albeit without abandoning their criminal activities altogether. In fact, they have come to occupy a dominant position in certain sectors of the national economy, taking advantage in some cases of the government's liberalisation policies.

Without doubt, the current boom in the gambling industry in Cameroon has to be attributed to a large extent to the initiatives of *feymen*. After the legalisation in the early 1990s of what are known in Cameroon as 'games of chance and hazard', a large number of *feymen* invested their illegally acquired wealth in the gambling industry. This form of investment has proved to be of mutual benefit to the new investors themselves and to the state: it has become a major source of private capital accumulation for *feymen* and of tax revenue for the state. One of the largest investors in the gambling industry is Claude Feutheu, alias Claude le Parisien (he owes this nickname to his *feymania* activities in Paris) who is known in Cameroon as the 'King of Bally-Bally'. This notorious Bamileke *feyman* owns several casinos and gambling houses in the country. His company, Fortuna Cameroon, is the largest enterprise in the country's gambling industry, employing over 100 nationals and about 20 Europeans. His associations with a Dutch company, Holland Casino, have enabled him to broaden his activities and to do business in the neighbouring countries of Gabon, Chad, Congo-Brazzaville and Equatorial Guinea (Ndjio 2005).

Some *feymen* have set up large companies that are involved in the import and selling of new and second-hand clothes and cars, mostly in partnership with foreign entrepreneurs. Selling second-hand clothes has become another booming business following the legalisation of such imports in December 1990 and the sharp fall in the purchasing power of a large section of the population since drastic reductions in wages and salaries in 1993 (Konings 1996). The expanding second-hand clothes market has even threatened local textile manufacturing. *Feymen* who are involved in the car business usually sell second-hand cars, but a few import new luxury cars to sell to the Cameroonian upper classes and to other *feymen*. In addition, almost all *feymen* have invested in real estate in the large cities. Some, like Claude le Parisien, have also set up big construction companies and a few who are based in Paris have moved into music production and catering.

Interestingly, a growing number of *feymen* have begun to use their economic power for the pursuit of political power, standing as candidates in municipal and parliamentary elections. No fewer than 30 prominent *feymen* – accounting for one-sixth of all seats in the National Assembly – were elected in the 1997 parliamentary elections.

Confronted with this new and autonomous mode of domestic private capital accumulation, the regime has devised a number of strategies to bring it under state control. Initially, *feymen* were presented as professional swindlers and crooks involved in transnational criminal networks. Some leading Beti politicians were even convinced that *feymania* was a new Bamileke scheme to assert their economic dominance over other ethnic groups and to discredit the country's international reputation, claiming that Cameroon was now seen as a country of swindlers and criminals (Ndjio 2005). Some *feymen* were arrested and jailed but repression proved unsuccessful, all the more so because some powerful members of the government, including the former Chief of Security Services Jean Fochivé and the former Vice Prime Minister in charge of Territorial Administration Gilbert Andzé Tchoungui, tended to protect the most renowned *feymen* such as Donatien Koagne and Claude le Parisien to ensure personal gains.

In reaction to the rapid expansion of *feymania* and the growing economic and political power of *feymen*, a shift in government strategies can be observed from the mid-1990s onwards. The first tactic was to make the safety of *feymen* and their success in legal and illegal activities dependent on their allegiance to the regime in power. Consequently, *feymen* who joined the ruling CPDM party were not only assured of state protection and the legitimisation of their ill-gotten wealth but also given similar rent-seeking opportunities to other businessmen with close ties to the state. These *feymen* were now presented in public discourse as young, dynamic Cameroonian entrepreneurs who were making a significant contribution to economic revival, and as role models for the youth. The regime even started actively promoting the emergence of a group of *feymen* among the better-educated youth with close ethnic or family ties to the ruling class. These new *feymen*, mostly of Beti origin, were regularly given lucrative state contracts or import licences. They became derisively dubbed as 'fake' *feymen* or *feymen du Renouveau* ('*renouveau*' or renewal being the regime's ideological label). Conversely, *feymen* who refused to join the ruling party or were active in opposition continued to be presented as criminals and to be exposed to arbitrary arrest.

A second tactic was to co-opt the most prominent *feymen* into the hegemonic alliance. Some became members of either the Central Committee of the CPDM or were prominent among the leadership of one of the ruling party's satellite organisations. Others were offered the opportunity to be elected as a member of parliament, mayor or local councillor on a CPDM ticket, even at the expense of former politicians. The co-optation of *feymen* has evidently been of benefit to both the ruling party and the regime: they have been of great help in financing party activities and have acted as vote-banks during elections. Nevertheless, it would appear that the regime is trying to keep them away from the centre of power so as not to enhance their political influence. None of the co-opted *feymen* has yet been appointed to a top position in the party or government.

Conclusion

In this chapter I have attempted to analyse the effects of two key policy prescriptions of the neoliberal reform package, namely privatisation and global open markets, on the existing structures of economic and political power in Cameroon. It has shown the continuities and changes in relations between the Cameroonian state and private capital accumulation.

While privatisation has been one of the cornerstones of the neoliberal agenda, linking good governance to private-sector development, it is evident from this study that it has not presented as big a break with the previous dynamic of the post-colonial state as the Bretton Woods institutions and international financiers would have expected. Most African governments have only reluctantly accepted the privatisation of state-owned enterprises and their calculations as to how their political concerns can best be served have shaped the outcome of the privatisation process in a decisive manner.

There is ample evidence to show that privatisation has failed to free the Cameroonian parastatal sector from 'politics', in particular from the government's neo-patrimonial logic, which is seen as the basic reason for its malfunctioning. State enterprises continue to form an essential element in government patronage politics, which has not only helped to maintain political stability in the country's vulnerable political system but has also been attractive to the political class that has selfishly used it as a clear avenue to capital accumulation.

Privatisation has failed to introduce transparency, accountability and the rule of law in policy-making and the implementation needed for the efficient operation of market forces. Lack of transparency in transactions surrounding the sale of state-owned enterprises has been a major concern among prospective investors. In part, this can be attributed to weaknesses in the management capabilities of those who have been entrusted to implement privatisation programmes. To a large extent, however, poor transparency has been the direct consequence of the parasitic behaviour of politicians and bureaucrats eager to cream off, perhaps for the last time, sizable rents. Pre-emptive divestitures are particularly susceptible to the undervaluation of assets and the preferential treatment of a particular bidder in return for kickbacks for leading politicians and bureaucrats (Bennell 1997).

Privatisation has equally failed to stimulate domestic private capital. The weakness of domestic private capital and the persistent fear of the Cameroonian post-colonial state of the emergence of a vigorous and autonomous national capitalist class are undeniably the major reasons for the blatant under-representation of nationals in the divesture exercise. The Cameroonian government has particularly discouraged any takeovers by Bamileke entrepreneurs, the dominant economic group among domestic private capital, and ethno-regional elite groups, which it perceives as a severe threat to Beti political power and the nation-state. Privatisation has instead strengthened the role of foreign capital to such an extent that it now dominates the most strategic sectors of the economy. The economic and political benefits to be gained from foreign investment have caused the regime to welcome it and to push aside any negative comments. Foreign capital was expected to contribute to an economic recovery and thus enhance the regime's legitimacy. In addition, through profitable joint ventures foreign investors would promote the business interests of a number of high-ranking politicians and bureaucrats as well as entrepreneurs with close links to the regime. This chapter, however, has shown that the transfer of the 'national patrimony' to foreign capital and the poor performance of some foreign concerns have led to further erosion of the regime's legitimacy among the local population.

In sharp contrast to privatisation, global open markets have had the unintended effect of offering chances of private capital accumulation to Cameroon's marginalised youth. By engaging in transnational criminal networks and re-investing part of their newly found wealth in legitimate entrepreneurial activities, these young men laid the foundations for their current economic and political power. This new and autonomous form of private capital accumulation has posed a serious challenge to the existing power structures that are based on close ties between political and economic power. As a result, the government has tried to submit *feymen* to state control by co-opting them into the hegemonic alliance, albeit in a subordinate position.

Bibliography

Atangana Mebara, M.J.M. (ed.) (1997) *La Privatisation des Monopoles de Service Public au Cameroun: Évolution et Enjeux*, Yaoundé: Fondation Friedrich Ebert.

Bagui Kari, A. (2001) *Regard sur les Privatisations au Cameroun: Suivi d'un Recueil de Textes*, Yaoundé: IPAN.

Bayart, J.-F. (1979) *L'État au Cameroun*, Paris: Presses de la Fondation Nationale des Sciences Politiques.

—— (2004) 'Le crime transnational et la formation de l'État', *Politique Africaine*, 93: 93–104.

Bayart, J.-F., S. Ellis and B. Hibou (eds) (1999) *The Criminalization of the State in Africa*, Oxford: James Currey.

Bennell, P. (1997) 'Privatization in sub-Saharan Africa: progress and prospects during the 1990s', *World Development*, 25 (11): 1785–803.

Berman, B.J. and C. Leys (eds) (1994) *African Capitalists in African Development*, Boulder, CO: Lynne Rienner Publishers.

Biersteker, Th.J. (1987) *Multinationals, the State, and Control of the Nigerian Economy*, Princeton, NJ: Princeton University Press.

Campbell White, O. and A. Bhatia (1998) *Privatization in Africa*, Washington, DC: World Bank.

Chabal, P. and J.-P. Daloz (1999) *Africa Works: Disorder as Political Instrument*, Oxford: James Currey.

DeLancey, M.W. (1989) *Cameroon: Dependence and Independence*, Boulder, CO: Westview Press.

Dongmo, J.-L. (1981) *Le Dynamisme Bamiléké (Cameroun)*, Yaoundé: CEPER (2 vols).

Fonge, F.P. (2003) 'Cultivating an economic crisis in Cameroon: the rhetoric versus the reality of planned liberalism', in J.M. Mbaku and J. Takougang (eds), *The Leadership Challenge in Africa: Cameroon under Paul Biya*, Trenton, NJ: Africa World Press.

Forrest, T.G. (1994) *The Advance of African Capital: The Growth of Nigerian Private Enterprise*, Edinburgh: Edinburgh University Press.

Fotso, V. and J.-P. Guyomard (1994) *Le Chemin de Hiala*, Paris: Édition Septembre.

Gabriel, J.M. (1999) 'Cameroon's neopatrimonial dilemma', *Journal of Contemporary African Studies*, 17 (2): 173–96.

Grosh, B. and R.S. Makandala (eds) (1994) *State-Owned Enterprises in Africa*, Boulder, CO: Lynne Rienner Publishers.

Henry, A., G.H. Tchenkand and Ph. Guillerme-Dieumegard (1991) *Tontines et Banques au Cameroun*, Paris: Karthala.

Hibou, B. (1999) 'The "social capital" of the state as an agent of deception', in J.-F. Bayart, S. Ellis and B. Hibou (eds), *The Criminalization of the State in Africa*, Oxford: James Currey.

Hugon, Ph. (1968) *Analyse du Sous-Développement en Afrique Noire: L'Exemple de l'Économie du Cameroun*, Paris: Presses Universitaires de France.

Joseph, R.A. (1977) *Radical Nationalism in Cameroon: Social Origins of the UPC Rebellion*, Oxford: Oxford University Press.

—— (1987) *Democracy and Prebendal Politics in Nigeria: The Rise and Fall of the Second Republic*, Cambridge: Cambridge University Press.

Kangue Ejangue, T. and E. Noubissié Ngankam (1995) *Les Privatisations au Cameroun: Bilan et Perspectives*, Yaoundé: Fondation Friedrich Ebert.

Kennedy, P.T. (1988) *African Capitalism: The Struggle for Ascendancy*, Cambridge: Cambridge University Press.

Konings, P. (1989) 'La liquidation des plantations Unilever et les conflits intra-élite dans le Cameroun Anglophone', *Politique Africaine*, 35: 132–7.

—— (1996) 'The Post-colonial state and economic and political reforms in Cameroun', in A.E. Fernández Jilberto and A. Mommen (eds), *Liberalization in the Developing World: Institutional and Economic Changes in Latin America, Africa and Asia*, London/New York: Routledge, pp. 244–65.

—— (2004a) 'Good governance, privatisation and ethno-regional conflict in Cameroon', in J. Demmers, A.E. Fernández Jilberto and B. Hogenboom (eds), *Good Governance in the Era of Global Neoliberalism: Conflict and Depolitisation in Latin America, Eastern Europe, Asia and Africa*, London/New York: Routledge.

—— (2004b) 'Opposition and social-democratic change in Africa: the Social Democratic Front in Cameroon', *Commonwealth & Comparative Politics*, 42 (3): 1–23.

—— (forthcoming) '"Bendskin" drivers in Douala's New Bell neighbourhood: masters of the road and the city', Leiden: Afrika-Studiecentrum.

Konings, P. and F.B. Nyamnjoh (2003) *Negotiating an Anglophone Identity: A Study of the Politics of Recognition and Representation in Cameroon*, Leiden: Brill.

Leys, C. (1994) 'African capitalists and development: theoretical questions', in B.J. Berman and C. Leys (eds), *African Capitalists in African Development*, Boulder, CO: Lynne Rienner Publishers.

MacGaffey, J. (1987) *Entrepreneurs and Parasites: The Struggle for Indigenous Capitalism in Zaïre*, Cambridge: Cambridge University Press.

Malaquais, D. (2001) 'Arts de Feyre au Cameroun', *Politique Africaine*, 82: 101–18.

Ndjio, B. (2005) 'Sorcery and new forms of enrichment in Cameroon: Feymen's case', Ph.D. project, University of Amsterdam.

Ndongko, W.A. (1985) *Reflexions on the Economic Policies and Development of Cameroon*, Yaoundé: MESRES/ISH.

—— (1987) *Economic Management in Cameroon: Policies and Performance*, Yaoundé: ISH/Friedrich-Ebert-Stiftung.

Ngayap, P.F. (1983) *Cameroun: Qui Gouverne?*, Paris: L'Harmattan.

Nguihé Kanté, P. (2003) 'Les contraintes de la privatisation des entreprises publiques et parapubliques au Cameroun', *Revue Juridique et Politique*, 2: 212–37.

Nyamnjoh, F.B. (1999) 'Cameroon: a country united by ethnic ambition and difference', *African Affairs*, 98 (390): 101–18.

Nyom, R. (2000) *La Crise Économique du Cameroun: Essai d'Analyse Socio-Politique*, Paris: Édition Montparnasse.

Pitcher, M.A. (2002) *Transforming Mozambique: The Politics of Privatization, 1975–2000*, Cambridge: Cambridge University Press.

Rakner, R. (2003) *Political and Economic Liberalisation in Zambia 1991–2001*, Uppsala: Nordic Africa Institute.

Rapley, J. (1993) *Ivoirien Capitalism: African Entrepreneurs in Côte d'Ivoire*, Boulder, CO: Lynne Rienner Publishers.

Rowlands, M. (1993) 'Accumulation and the cultural politics of identity in the grass-fields', in P. Geschiere and P. Konings (eds), *Itinéraires d'Accumulation au Cameroun*, Paris: Karthala.

Shaw, M. (2002) 'West African criminal networks in South and Southern Africa', *African Affairs*, 101 (404): 291–316.

Sklar, R. (1979) 'The nature of class domination in Africa', *The Journal of Modern African Studies*, 17: 531–52.

Takougang, J. (1993) 'The demise of Biya's new deal in Cameroon, 1982–1992', *Africa Insight*, 23, 2: 91–101.

Takougang, J. and M. Krieger (1998) *African State and Society in the 1990s: Cameroon's Political Crossroads*, Boulder, CO: Westview Press.

Tangri, R. (1999) *The Politics of Patronage in Africa: Parastatals, Privatisation and Private Enterprise*, Oxford: James Currey.

Tangri, R. and A. Mwenda (2001) 'Corruption and cronyism in Uganda's privatization in the 1990s', *African Affairs*, 100 (398): 117–33.

Tedga, P.J.M. (1990) *Enterprises Publiques, État et Crise au Cameroun*, Paris: L'Harmattan.

Tsafack-Nanfosso, R.A. (2004) 'The process of privatisation in Cameroon', in K. Wohlmuth, A. Gutowski, T. Knedlick, M. Meyn and S. Ngogang (eds), *Private and Public Sectors: Towards a Balance*, Münster: LIT Verlag.

Van de Walle, N. (1993) 'The politics of nonreform in Cameroon', in T.M. Callaghy and J. Ravenhill (eds), *Hemmed In: Responses to Africa's Economic Decline*, New York: Columbia University Press.

—— (1994) 'The politics of public enterprise reform in Cameroon', in B. Grosh and R.S. Makandala (eds), *State-Owned Enterprises in Africa*, Boulder, CO: Lynne Rienner Publishers, pp. 151–74.

—— (2001) *African Economies and the Politics of Permanent Crisis, 1979–1999*, Cambridge: Cambridge University Press.

Walker, S.T. (1998) 'Both pretense and promise: the political economy of privatization in Africa', unpublished Ph.D. thesis, Indiana University.

Warnier, J.-P. (1993) *L'Esprit d'Entreprise au Cameroun*, Paris: Karthala.

World Bank (1987) *Cameroon Country Economic Memorandum*, Washington, DC: World Bank.

—— (1994) *Adjustment in Africa: Reforms, Results and the Road Ahead*, New York: Oxford University Press.

12 The resilience of comprador capitalism

'New' economic groups in Southern Africa

Stefan Andreasson

Former liberation movements control dominant party governments in several Southern African countries and are aiming at transforming the region's political and economic landscapes. How to transform the legacy of extremely uneven capitalist development remains a salient and volatile issue following political transitions to majority rule. New capitalist elites have emerged across Southern Africa, promoted by government policy and taking advantage of the removal of laws barring black Africans from the (economic) 'commanding heights'. Old capital, prospering under colonial and apartheid rule, has accommodated itself to new realities and in many cases played key roles in moderating, and arguably 'subverting', political transitions across the region.[1] However recent changes are interpreted, immense poverty and marginalisation remains a fact of life for a majority of Southern Africans.[2]

In regions like Southern Africa, where economic restructuring is intensely political and partly a result of shifting societal power (from white minority towards black majority), the 'economic groups' of primary importance are (capitalist) elites themselves, not merely the specific corporations and other agglomerations that they control. More specifically, economic groups are those business leaders and other (organised) economic interests that play a significant part in shaping the region's economies. In terms of economic and sociocultural identity, emerging economic groups in the region may be 'new' in a demographic sense (i.e. black capitalists) but not necessarily new in the sense that their motivation, or 'intent', differs from that of established economic groups. These 'new' economic groups are likely to represent 'old' economic interests – that is, profit and their own empowerment, rather than deep and broad societal transformation that governments in the region wish a national, or 'patriotic', bourgeoisie would champion (cf. Friedman and Chipkin 2001: 26; Peet 2002). In addition, the interests and actions of domestic 'power brokers' cannot be detangled from the interests of major multinationals and international financial institutions (IFIs) that, along with key officials shaping government economic policy, also play an important role in the region.

As relations mature, old and new economic groups may see their interests coalesce while at the same time also clash with government attempts to (ostensibly) promote socioeconomic transformation and broad-based development. Moreover, relations between economic groups and governments in the region are becoming increasingly complex, the imperative of 'profit over people' becoming influential in key government circles as well (cf. Chomsky 1999). Already in 1996, the same year South Africa's President Thabo Mbeki and Minister of Finance Trevor Manuel introduced as 'non-negotiable' the neoliberal Growth, Employment and Redistribution (GEAR) macroeconomic framework, South Africa's then Deputy Trade and Industry Minister and former trade unionist (now Minerals and Energy Minister) Phumzile Mlabo-Ngcuka exhorted the country's newly emergent black bourgeoisie to become 'filthy rich' (quoted in Adam *et al.* 1998: 201). Whereas African elites in the 1970s were inspired by Amilcar Cabral's injunction to commit 'class suicide', becoming a 'petty bourgeois class with proletarian/peasant aspirations', they turned by the 1990s into a 'petty bourgeoisie with bourgeois aspirations' (Adesina 2004: 137). While Southern Africans are not passive bystanders in transformations occurring across the region, their fortunes are nevertheless greatly influenced by the directions in which relations between old and new economic groups, and between economic groups and governments, evolve.[3]

Recent studies of the political economy of Southern Africa emphasise both regional and global aspects of the region's push for (economic) integration and (social) transformation in the post-Cold War era. According to Thompson (2000: 41), 'Southern Africa has been engaged in formulating "new regionalism" for over a decade'. Pallotti (2004) examines the implementation of the Southern African Development Community's (SADC) Trade Protocol and the emergence of a regional inter-state cooperation, based primarily on trade liberalisation that has replaced earlier emphases on self-reliance and pan-African solidarity. Bond (2001, 2004) charts South Africa's role as the region's key representative at the seats of global economic power; among the G7 and the IFIs, government's political rhetoric about structural transformation and an 'African renaissance', based (in its economic guise) on domestic reforms and international cooperation anchored in the New Partnership for Africa's Development (NEPAD), is often supplanted by 'sub-imperial' practices vis-à-vis other states in the region and beyond. Hammar *et al.* (2003) and Phimister and Raftopolous (2004) analyse the ongoing crisis in Zimbabwe in the context of a wider 'anti-imperial' (economic, political and cultural) struggle. It is in this global context that the political economy of Southern Africa, and the old and new economic groups that play an important part shaping it, ought to be understood.[4]

Two overlapping historical trajectories shape state–market relations in contemporary Southern Africa. The first trajectory is the attempt by governments in the region to manage as smoothly as possible further integration into an essentially neoliberal global economy. This entails balancing global market pressures for liberalisation on one hand with domestic (populist) pressures for economic redistribution and mitigation of dire living conditions on the other: 'the challenge of simultaneous democratisation and economic adjustment or recovery, amid high expectations' (Bradshaw and Ndegwa 2000: 4). While the balancing of pressures for reform and demands for redistribution does not inevitably constitute a zero-sum game, it is nevertheless appropriate to assume that such a balancing of policy priorities will necessarily entail some trade-offs and conflict in societies characterised by high socioeconomic inequalities. The second trajectory is the pursuit by governments of a structural transformation of the region's post-colonial, post-apartheid economies that are characterised foremost by generations of uneven development that has created dual economies, making conversion of aggregate growth into broad-based development very difficult to achieve.[5] Such transformation aims at a more fundamental reordering of the region's economic and political realities than does the task of integration. In order to understand the nature of state–market relations and the emergence of new economic groups in contemporary Southern Africa, we must examine in detail how the political and economic processes associated with each of these historical trajectories interact with each other.

This chapter examines the emergence of new economic groups in South Africa and Zimbabwe in the context of 'paternalistic trusteeship' by governments themselves or by old economic groups managing to retain economic and political influence and aiming to forge stable and mutually profitable relations with new economic elites. New economic actors emerge when political and economic liberalisation increases 'points of entry' to economic (and political) activity for those previously marginalised or barred from entry (cf. Habib and Padayachee 2000: 245–6). A key point of contention in the debate on the aims and roles of these groups is whether old, entrenched economic groups are simply in the business of 'grooming' a new comprador class to serve (or at least not actively oppose) their interests, or if they are indeed making an effort to facilitate empowerment by engaging with and supporting the new economic groups emerging as a result of political and economic liberalisation.

What sort of capitalism for Southern Africa?

Liberal theories expect that neoliberal economic reforms will result in increasing competitiveness and, somewhere along the line, enhanced possibilities for development via a 'trickle down' process (e.g. World Bank 2000; cf. Broad and Cavanagh 1999: 79–88; Chan 2002: 16–17). This is generally African National Congress (ANC) policy at the leadership level in South Africa and has been, for at least part of the 1990s, Zanu-PF policy in Zimbabwe as well. Neo-Marxists and other market-critics see neoliberal reorientation of countries in transition as a recipe for new and old elites to collude with each other and hijack new economic opportunities resulting from the privatisation of state-owned assets, deregulation of finance and trade and so on (e.g. Gray 2002; Rapley 2004). The case for privatisation is often shrouded in the 'progressive' language of indigenisation, suggesting that privatisation promotes the emergence of a broader, local entrepreneurial class, whereas it usually entails a limited transfer of assets from public elites to private elites, delimiting the state's future ability to guide development-related economic policy (Bracking 2004: 893–4). From this perspective, benefits and opportunities will not 'trickle down' – increasing profit generation will largely benefit domestic luxury consumption or be routed abroad for the benefit of domestic elites and their international compatriots (Bond 1998: 390–3; Moore 2001: 915; Bracking 2004: 892).

Fundamentally this debate concerns what sort of capitalism may be expected to develop in peripheral regions of the world economy.[6] Marxist theories of imperialism, originating in the works of Lenin and Hilferding, see few prospects for the emergence of genuine, independent capitalists in Third World countries transitioning to formal independence. Rather than seeking to promote national development, emerging 'comprador capitalists' serve the interests of an international capitalist class (Sklair and Robbins 2002: 81–2).[7] The notion of comprador capitalism underpins the powerful metaphor about South Africa's present leaders 'shining', rather than breaking, the 'chains of 21st-century global Apartheid' (Bond 2001: xi).[8]

Crucially, the comprador capitalist (class) is one that cannot function *on its own* (hence 'servitors'), but is dependent on the resources of established capitalists. Southall's characterisation of the new 'black bourgeoisie' in South Africa resembles earlier understandings of the concept of a comprador capitalist class: their 'basic dilemma ... remains the quandary of how black aspirant *capitalists without capital* can be capitalised. The answer is that *they either have to be given it or they have to borrow it*' (Southall 2004: 319; cf. Randall 1996). Hence they are dependent on the old, established capitalists in the region and beyond. This dependency makes new economic groups vulnerable both economically and politically, and therefore less likely to drive any independent, transformative, agenda.

Similarly, Dansereau and Zamponi (2005) understand the emergence of new, 'indigenous' capitalist interests in post-independence Zimbabwe as first emerging slowly under the oversight of an elite consensus between government and the old (white) industrial and financial interests. With the fracturing of this consensus, indigenous capitalism becomes promoted as a more explicitly crony project via the patronage of the ruling Zanu-PF party, as in the notorious case of forced transfer of land ownership from white commercial farmers to black Zimbabweans in which many of the beneficiaries are politically connected elites rather than the landless peasants that land resettlement policy is intended to benefit (Moore 2003; Sachikonye 2003).

Comparing new (and old) economic groups in South Africa and Zimbabwe uncovers both similar and distinct trajectories. Both countries liberalised their economies in the 1990s, albeit the process was a steady one in South Africa and characterised by sharp reversals in Zimbabwe; both countries attempted to apply market-driven solutions to the societal pressures created by their historically very uneven development. Clearly processes of transition (democratisation) and transformation (liberalisation) have in recent years been more volatile in Zimbabwe than in South Africa. The crisis in Zimbabwe is interpreted by international and local commentators alike as an indicator of what 'irresponsible' economic and political decisions (defying the logic of the global capitalist economy) by South African policy-makers would produce. Taken together, experiences in these two countries provide a nuanced picture of the opportunities and difficulties governments face when attempting to manage oftentimes cross-cutting pressures from businesses and civil society. The two 'case studies' in this chapter examine interactions between key economic and political actors in each country and their preferences with regard to policies governing economic and sociopolitical transformation. Both economic groups and governments have inevitably become transformed (in terms of policy preferences and strategies) by the many changes sweeping across the region in recent decades.

South Africa: continuity rather than transformation

A recent report published by South Africa's leading corporate lobby organisation, the South Africa Foundation (SAF), notes that

> South Africa is not a society in which business corporations can define their roles in purely economic terms and play a backstage role in public affairs. Throughout its modern history, but particularly over the last four decades, large corporations have found it impossible not to become enmeshed in the major political and developmental challenges facing our society.
>
> (Schlemmer 2004: 3)

According to Schlemmer and the SAF, this involvement is one of a constructive engagement with developmental goals of the country as a whole. Good relations with government have, according to the SAF's Executive Director Neil van Heerden, been possible given the emergence of a new 'legitimacy of government' stemming from its willingness to break away from 'old thinking' and attracting 'clever people in departments dealing with the economy'.[9]

The historical trajectory of state–capital relations in post-apartheid South Africa is complex and fraught with contradictions. The legacy of racial oppression cannot be disentangled from contemporary debates, and a wish to transform society coexists, perhaps somewhat uncomfortably, with a desire to 'buy into' existing economic structures that offer potentially great rewards for those relatively few able to take advantage thereof. Lewis *et al.* (2004) suggest a significant transformation of state–business relations during the South African transition: in the early 1990s, when the ANC began engaging with white business interests, 'there was no business lobby capable of restraining the ANC's desire to discipline White capital. At the end of the 20th Century, the only permissible discipline was that of the market'.

According to Szeftel (2004: 194–5), the ANC could choose between three broad options when coming to power in 1994. First, it could embark on a 'revolutionary path', expropriating the commanding heights of the economy and engage in comprehensive and compulsive redistribution by directly confronting domestic and capital interests, thus forcing the ANC to 'become what it had never been, a revolutionary party'. Second, it could embark on a 'radical reforming path', combining liberal political institutions with high taxation and spending, along with some nationalisation as envisaged by the 1955 Freedom Charter and (to a lesser extent) the 1994 Reconstruction and Development Programme (RDP). Or third, it could choose the 'neoliberal option' symbolised by the 1996 GEAR macroeconomic framework and a reliance on improving competitiveness to integrate with the global economy and thus fund development with growth that ought to eventually trickle down. The government has since the 1994 elections 'moved progressively away from the second option towards the third' (Szeftel 2004: 195).

Consequently, the South African government has since the early 1990s political transition worked closely and consistently with business leaders such as the Brenthurst group and IFIs to ensure international and domestic approval of its market credentials (cf. Peet 2002: 73).[10] In December 1993, the Transitional Executive Committee (a 'government-in-waiting' comprising both ANC and National Party leaders) signed an $850 million balance of payments loan with the International Monetary Fund (IMF), ostensibly for drought relief but arguably to be able to repay the accumulated multi-billion dollar apartheid-era debt. Conditions of the loan were leaked to *Business Day* in March 1994, perhaps to convince international markets, one month before South Africa's first democratic elections, that with IMF conditionalities imposed from the outset on an incoming ANC government it would be forced to conduct 'responsible' (i.e. neoliberal) economic policy-making (Bond 2001: 68; Ashley 2003). The ANC leadership has been able to work closely with established economic groups and IFIs as the party 'enjoys the comfort of being removed from its constituencies in ways of which European party-élites could only dream and can afford to strike bargains with the industrial elites in ways inconceivable in other democratic settings' (Koelble 2004: 66).

According to Habib and Padayachee (2000: 246), the ANC 'gave priority and prominence to the international financial and investor community' as a result of its 'perception and interpretation of the balance of economic and political power', both locally and globally; that is, appeasing financial and business interests had to come first, with attention to the plight of im-poverished South Africans hopefully following. President Mbeki has a long-standing practice of hosting *indabas* (gatherings) with business 'working groups', representing key domestic and international corporate interests as part of a larger lobbying network. A big business working group, consisting of senior government representatives including the President, key ministers and executives of the major multinationals and local corporations, meets biannually. The Business Trust, established in 1999 to 'create jobs and build capacity while enhancing trust and building co-operative relationships between business and government', argues that while it addresses issues 'from a business perspective, [it] aims to present those views in what it believes to be the national interest'.[11]

Thus several powerful interest groups vie for influence with government policy-makers. Prominent corporate lobbies, representing primarily the interests of South Africa's export-oriented businesses, are the Centre for Development and Enterprise (CDE) and the SAF. They actively promote interests of their members via policy advocacy in research, conference and media settings, as well as via their connections with government officials. These organisations represent leading banks and insurance houses (e.g. Standard Bank, ABSA, Nedcor, Old Mutual, SANLAM), mining companies (e.g. Anglo American, de Beers, African Rainbow Minerals, ISCOR), oil companies (e.g. Shell, BP, Sasol) and export-oriented firms (e.g. South African Breweries, Sappi, African Harvest, Unilever, BMW) (Koelble 2004: 63). Notably, all the companies represented by the SAF and the CDE are 'either large multinational[s] . . . or have significant interests in establishing and maintaining international market opportunities'; these companies promoted the 1996 SAF document *Growth for All*, which became the 'ideological and rhetorical foundation' for GEAR (Koelble 2004: 64).

A pro-business government?

GEAR is usually identified as the key manifestation of government's decision to pursue a neoliberal economic path, relying on fiscal stringency and private sector growth to resolve the historical legacy of uneven development.[12] However, Michie and Padayachee (1998: 625–6) identify five key components of the government's pre-GEAR (1994–6) agenda that suggest a neoliberal strategy from the very outset: maintenance of an orthodox economic stabilisation package; rapid trade liberalisation; restoring 'industrial peace' and labour market stability; competition policy; and privatisation. That the constraints on policy imposed by GEAR 'coincided' with interests of powerful local export-oriented industry, and that the ANC leadership 'followed the advice of . . . powerful banks, export-oriented manufacturers, and mining houses' (Koelble 2004: 59) – as opposed to the wishes of its Alliance partners, the South African Communist Party (SACP) and the Congress of South African Trade Unions (COSATU) – suggests a continued powerful influence exercised by economic groups, especially older, established ones (cf. Lewis *et al.* 2004).[13]

Where criticism is voiced regarding government's pro-market credentials, it tends to come from 'hard-line' sections of the (smaller) business community and financial press demanding that every last vestige of government intervention in the market is further relaxed or completely eliminated, such as the retention of some 'restrictive' labour legislation (what unions would consider minimal job security and a 'living wage') and the pursuit of Black Economic Empowerment (BEE). In December 2004, President Mbeki's Joint Economic Working Group (including key representatives from government, business and labour) met in the wake of IMF criticism of continued 'rigidities' and 'high costs' in the labour market that are hampering job creation efforts (modest GEAR-led growth has coincided with the shedding rather than creation of formal sector jobs). Essentially the IMF suggested that South Africa further relax its labour legislation by decentralising the collective bargaining system so that small and medium-sized businesses have more 'autonomy' in setting (i.e. lowering) wages. According to Business Unity South Africa (BUSA) President Patrice Motsepe, who represents the country's major business chambers, the government would give serious consideration to South Africa's 'overregulated business environment, particularly for entrepreneurs' (quoted in *Business Day* 15 December 2004). As when responding to criticism by capital interests in the past, government is keen to send 'the right signals' to the international and domestic business communities (cf. Andreasson 2003: 391). In any case, that the ANC leadership is aligned with capital interests, whether in a genuine quest for transformation or a cynical play for power, is not seriously disputed.

Government is undoubtedly sensitive about business responses to its policies, and especially responses from old, established economic groups. This 'business first' approach has caused frustrations within the ANC itself, as made clear by one internal ANC discussion document:

> While on one hand [developing states] are called upon to starve and prettify themselves to compete on the 'catwalk' of attracting the limited amounts of foreign direct investment ... they are on the other hand reduced to bulimia by the vagaries of an extremely impetuous and whimsical market suitor!
>
> (African National Congress 1998)

This 'pandering' to the markets has, however, yielded some positive response. The World Economic Forum's (WEF) *Global Competitiveness Rankings*, reflecting the viewpoints of business leaders around the world, rank South Africa as the most competitive economy in Sub-Saharan Africa in 2004 (ranked forty-first out of 104 countries surveyed), replacing Botswana at the top for the first time (*Business Day* 18 October 2004).

While the success of GEAR was to be reliant on market-friendly policies attracting significant amounts of foreign direct investment (FDI) to the country, fuelling economic growth and thus providing means to finance development, FDI inflows since 1996 have been disappointing. In fact, GEAR initially failed to deliver on its optimistic projections in all areas except lowered inflation, budget deficit reduction, and export targets (Bond

2000: 78–82; Pillay 2000: 4–5; Mhone 2004: 49–62), and none of these 'successes' has triggered job creation or broad-based development. Despite the disappointing results, international commentators such as the arch-conservative American Enterprise Institute proclaim that 'to its great credit, the ANC in office could not have proved the naysayers more wrong as it became the very model of fiscal and monetary policy rectitude' (Lachman 2004), noting further that increasing market orientation will, of course, be necessary. Streak's (2004) evaluation of GEAR is more ambivalent; she echoes the concerns of the GEAR 'sceptics', but also suggests that GEAR's partial 'success' (fiscal stringency) has now produced a space for government to move in a more 'pro-active' macroeconomic direction, into what may become a post-GEAR phase, as it is on a more solid economic footing.

In the end, however, it seems that both international and domestic investors have taken a very cautious approach to investing in post-apartheid South Africa. When Anglo American CEO Tony Trahar, arguably South Africa's most powerful businessman, voiced concerns in an interview with the *Financial Times* (12 September 2004) about lingering 'political risk' in South Africa (discussing 'hypothetically' a move of Anglo American's head-quarters from Johannesburg to London) he drew an angry public response from a frustrated President Mbeki. Mbeki suggested that despite the many concessions government makes to business policy demands these efforts are not being properly recognised by the business community, the implication, according to Mbeki, being that a black government will necessarily be considered 'unsafe' for (white) businesses (Mbeki 2004). Alluding to racially motivated prejudices, the President asked:

> [I]s it moral and fair that [South Africans], who daily bear the scars of poverty, should suffer from the guilt of their masters, who are fixated by the nightmare of a risky future for our country, which derives not from what the poor have done and will do, but from what the rich fear those they impoverished will do, imagining what they themselves would have done, if they had been the impoverished?
>
> (Mbeki 2004)

In the aftermath of the Trahar–Mbeki exchange, Deputy Minister of Mining, Lulu Xingwana, went so far as to publicly accuse 'rich white cartels . . . continuing even today to loot our diamonds' (*Business Report* 20 September 2004). Despite disagreements like these, both Anglo American and de Beers, mining giants with great sunken costs that make them dependent on long-term stability to a degree that smaller businesses more easily able to relocate are not, have adopted rather conciliatory stances vis-à-vis government. Anglo American, which recently appointed Lazarus Zim as its first black CEO of Anglo American South Africa, issued a public statement assuring it was committed to South Africa, its political leadership and transformation, noting its plans to invest some 26 billion rand in the economy. De Beers stated it was 'fully committed to the transformational objectives of government' (*Business Report* 20 September 2004).

Businesses would like to see even further liberalisation of the South African economy and are wary of the long-term implications of the government's Mining Charter and similar policies that restrict private property rights. Consequently they are 'holding the economy ransom' contingent upon further reforms, which, according to Edigheji (2004: 82), is tantamount to a business sector 'investment strike'. However, given the government-enacted charters for achieving major structural transformation in the country's financial, mining and liquid fuel sectors (*Business Day* 1 April 2005) – that is, moving assets from white to black ownership, and reducing the over-representation of whites at all levels of employment – responses by (old) business groups have perhaps been surprisingly restrained.

Black economic empowerment

Randall (1996: 675–84) identifies four major factors providing black capitalists in South Africa a more effective means of projecting influence than has been the case elsewhere on the continent, where local capitalist development has often been slow to emerge. First, the political insecurity of white capital means that entrenched economic groups are more willing to cooperate with new ones so as to secure their own privileged position within the South African economy.[14] Second, there is the promotion of black business by a competent policy-making regime, such as Mbeki's government, that presides over macroeconomic management that is 'among the best in the developing world ... [outperforming] European Union members on their own Maastricht Treaty's convergence criteria for European Monetary Union' (*Financial Times* 19 March 2005). A third factor is the mobilisation of opinion against 'fronting' and politician-capitalists, although this is precisely what critics of BEE in South Africa suggest is taking place. And finally, the fourth factor is the relative sophistication of an economy that is, despite its dualistic nature, unrivalled on the African continent.

Several studies show that the governments of Presidents Mandela and, especially, Mbeki have not only been eager to accommodate business demands for neoliberal economic reforms, but have also actively promoted the rise of party-connected individuals into elite circles of South African corporate life (Adam *et al.* 1998; Bond 2000, 2004; Saul 2001; Andreasson 2003). This is the process of 'embourgeoisement of key cadres from the anti-apartheid struggle' (Randall's 'activist capitalists'), among them Saki Macozoma, Popo Molefe, Jayendra Naidoo, Cyril Ramaphosa and Tokyo Sexwale, who have emerged into 'key political and (then) corporate positions in the post-apartheid era' (Andreasson 2004: 2). That relatively few individuals are the main beneficiaries of major BEE deals has now been recognised as a problem even within high ranks of the ANC. Because BEE has often-times entailed 'transfer rather than transformation', it has, according to ANC

General Secretary Kgalema Mothlante, failed to create 'new markets and new drivers of domestic demand in the economy' (*Business Day* 1 October 2004).

BEE is the key government strategy for long-term socioeconomic transformation by promotion of a black capitalist class in all spheres of the national economy. To comply with BEE legislation, companies in South Africa must ensure that they act to promote appropriate black ownership and black representation at all levels of operation, from entry-level employees to highest level executives (Andreasson 2004; Lewis *et al.* 2004; Southall 2004).[15] The BEE Commission, created in 1998 by the government to evaluate empowerment progress, is chaired by Cyril Ramaphosa, the former National Union of Mineworkers and ANC leader who is now one of South Africa's foremost black businessmen (or 'BEE gentlemen', as the sceptics would have it).[16] While new (black) economic groups have supported BEE and old (white) ones have taken a more cautious approach – big businesses being more receptive to the arguments for BEE than small ones, the latter more concerned about short-term costs of compliance with BEE legislation – it has not been considered politically expedient for any economic actors to come out very strongly against the fundamental idea underlying BEE, namely that both private and public sectors have a responsibility ensuring that previously marginalised South Africans are integrated at all levels of the economy, and that such integration is in the long-term interest of all parties involved. According to Colin Reddy of BusinessMap, which monitors BEE compliance by companies in South Africa, 'business people are talking largely about the details of implementation [of BEE policies], rather than expressing total opposition to the very notion [of BEE]' (*Business Day* 1 April 2005).

According to a recent study of how BEE has transformed the South African economy since 1994, progress has been 'uneven and difficult to quantify'; the initial drive to transfer (primarily financial) assets into black hands flagged at the end of the 1990s when black ownership of the Johannesburg Stock Exchange fell to below 4 per cent from a peak of about 10 per cent in the mid-1990s. Moreover,

> the private sector remains overwhelmingly in white hands: 98% of executive director positions of JSE-listed companies in 2002 were white ... by far the most important point is that blacks have made extremely limited inroads into the ownership, control and senior management of the private corporate sector.
>
> (Southall 2004: 318–19)

In this case, then, acquiring the political kingdom has not delivered the economic one. While South African transformation has not progressed in the spirit of the Freedom Charter and the National Democratic Revolution that ANC grassroots, unions and anti-apartheid activists have hoped for, the country has not experienced the violent reversal of neoliberal policies as did Zimbabwe at the end of the twentieth century.

Zimbabwe: collaboration and confrontation

With independence in 1980, corporatist arrangements surviving the Rhodesian era now linked the incoming Zanu government with (white) local and multinational companies, an assortment of emerging black interest groups, IFIs and other external agencies. Organisations representing mainly white capital, e.g., the Commercial Farmers' Union (CFU), the Confederation of Zimbabwe Industries (CZI) and the Chamber of Mines were 'in continuous contact-cum-dialogue with government ministries and parastatals' on economic policy matters (Shaw 1989: 153). Old economic groups, captains of industry and commercial farmers, retained sufficient economic resources in the post-independence era to constitute a powerful bargaining block vis-à-vis the new black political elite. Anticipating on the eve of the neoliberal Economic Structural Adjustment Programme (ESAP) the oncoming crisis in contemporary Zimbabwe, Shaw questioned the continued viability of maintaining corporatist structures inherited from settler rule in a post-independence era where government is expected to deliver on promises of broad-based development: 'The established patterns of settler agriculture and industry now coexist sometimes uncomfortably with new institutions of government and administration: how long can the super-imposed non-racial superstructure articulate with the inherited racist substructure?' (Shaw 1989: 151).

That 'a close alliance between government and the private sector must be developed' – ignoring the fact that it already existed? – was the World Bank's express wish (dictate) on the eve of Zanu's decision to adopt ESAP in 1990 (Hinds 1990, quoted in Bond and Manyanya 2003: 23). While ESAP constituted an unambiguous commitment by the Zimbabwean government to a neoliberal development strategy, its adoption was no more a 'watershed moment' than was the shift in South Africa, some six years later, from the RDP to GEAR. The adoption of ESAP can be understood as a culmination of pressures by international and domestic economic groups (private finance and the IFIs) that had been building throughout the 1980s. Among the old economic groups, industry (represented by the former CZI leader Eddie Cross who was appointed economic secretary for the opposition Movement for Democratic Change (MDC) in 2000) and agriculture (represented by the CFU) led, together with transnational capital, the push for liberal restructuring (Carmody and Taylor 2003).

The drive to adopt ESAP was led in government circles by Finance Minister Bernard Chidzero, supported by heavy agitation from IFIs and the business community who 'hammered' influential local media such as the *Financial Gazette* with the need for restructuring.[17] However, already in the years immediately following independence the Zanu government decided it could not afford to break with entrenched economic groups and their international compatriots. Thus, according to a leading US banker (in Bond and Manyanya 2003: 27), 'the management of the more sophisticated larger companies . . . seem to be impressed by and satisfied with Mugabe's management and the increased level of understanding in government of commercial considerations'.

As in South Africa, big business generally manages better relations with government than do smaller businesses. Already in May 1980, the newly elected Prime Minister (now President) Mugabe felt compelled to cooperate with Harry Oppenheimer, deploying both police and military in crushing strikes at Anglo American's coal mines and sugar estates (Bond 1998: 153). This conciliatory government stance had its early origins in the policy of 'Reconciliation', introduced with independence in 1980, whereby government 'sought a peaceful co-existence with white capital which continued to dominate the private sector'. Consequently, the government's 1981 *Growth with Equity* policy largely excluded any significant role for the existing black entrepreneurial class (Raftopolous 1996).

Piecemeal 'indigenisation'

Zimbabwean state–business relations have despite periodic collaboration always been more complicated and volatile than in South Africa, recently 'cascading into a high congestion grid of irreconcilable demands' (Zwizwai *et al.* 2004). This is partly due to a more 'militant' history of liberation struggle in Zimbabwe; Zanu did not, like the ANC, have a bourgeois leadership core and never really demobilised to become a 'normal' political party. Moreover, Zimbabwe's entrenched white business community was smaller and, following the 1965 Unilateral Declaration of Independence from Britain and greater reliance on import substitution strategies, less well linked with international capital than was Apartheid South Africa (cf. Bond 1998). The Zanu government had also less success with fostering a new 'indigenous' business elite. Indeed, the pace of indigenisation of the Zimbabwean economy was tempered during most of the 1980s and 1990s due to government's unwillingness to promote autonomous bases of power in society (Raftopolous 1996), which a new black business class would likely represent.

Where indigenisation occurred, it often involved high-level officials in Zanu acquiring commercial farms and entering into a variety of ventures; the proliferation of parastatals in the 1980s created a 'state dependent petty-bourgeoisie' of well-connected black Zimbabweans. Given the lack of structural transformation during the 1980s, demands grew for greater involvement of black Zimbabweans in the economy (Bond and Manyanya 2003: 23–7). An Indigenous Business Development Centre (IBDC) was formed in 1990 to promote black entrepreneurship under ESAP by allocating state assets to black Zimbabweans on preferential terms; by 1995 IBDC members held two Deputy Ministerial positions. A Select Committee on the Indigenisation of the National Economy was established in 1991. A more stridently nationalist lobbying group for emerging black business interests, the Affirmative Action Group (AAG) was established in 1994 to pressure harder for transformation of the economy where, it felt, the IBDC and other lobbies had failed (Raftopolous 1996; cf. Moore 2003). As with GEAR in South Africa, a major policy of economic liberalisation (ESAP) created opportunities for well-connected individuals representing new economic groups to establish themselves as serious actors in the national economy. That such opportunities are not likely to produce the deep structural transformations of society that leaders of the region have envisioned continues to be a major source of societal tension.

To the degree that new economic groups, with some independence from the state, have emerged following independence in Zimbabwe they have not enjoyed the same prolific rise to positions of influence, nor have they been as smoothly integrated with the old establishment and its international compatriots as have new economic groups in South Africa. Essentially Zimbabwe lacks the 'star cast' of new black businessmen, accepted as bona fide businessmen in international financial circles, that has developed in South Africa (such as Randall's 'activist capitalists'). Even in the case of the government's infamous and very costly foray into the Democratic Republic of Congo civil war, deploying troops in support of then President Laurent Kabila (reportedly spending more than $200 million between 1998 and 2000) in return for access to the country's rich mineral resources, it seems that the leadership preferred working via tarnished representatives of the white business community, such as Billy Rautenbach (now wanted on criminal charges in South Africa, where his assets are frozen), following government troops north (MacLean 2002). Nevertheless, there is as in South Africa an implicit assumption that playing an important role in the liberation struggle ought to pay off in the post-transition era, not only in political terms. In the words of Solomon Mujuru, the wealthy farmer and husband of Zimbabwe's recently appointed Vice-President Joyce Mujuru (a potential successor to President Mugabe), 'I didn't fight the liberation war to end up a poor man' (in *Scotsman on Sunday* 5 December 2004).

With the beginning of full-scale land occupation and resettlement in spring 2000, white commercial farmers have been effectively swept aside and no longer constitute a powerful economic group (Andreasson 2006). In this case the war veterans who organised and led the farm invasions have managed to ruthlessly capitalise on the indigenisation agenda. However, the industrial sector is 'still white' (Carmody and Taylor 2003), and therefore presumably a future target for those who, in the name of a third *Chimurenga* (liberation struggle], seek to remove all remaining 'colonial elements' in the nation's economy. In 2000, statements by Zanu-PF Politburo members and President Mugabe promised that national mines would be facing complete takeover or 'aggressive indigenisation' after the land distribution issue was resolved (*The Mail & Guardian* 14 May 2002). While violent incidents involving people associated with the war veterans' pursuit of 'indigenisation' have in some instances spilled over from farming areas into urban business premises, an uneasy truce seems to exist between government and the (urban) private sector.

The MDC is at present the only viable political opposition, despite electoral losses under un-free and unfair conditions in 2000, 2002 and 2005. It is, however, not clear what interests would dominate policy within a future ruling MDC. Would business interests, represented within the party by the preferences of Eddie Cross and white capital backers, or the labour movement in which the MDC originated prevail in a battle for the 'ideological soul' of the party? If neoliberal interests emerge victorious in the end, the MDC will likely pursue black empowerment along the lines of the South African ANC model.

Culprits of the crisis?

Who, then, are the main culprits behind post-independence Zimbabwe's departure, from the early or mid-1980s onward, from initially hopeful projections regarding the country's development potential? What are the driving forces behind the 1990s crisis, leading to the contemporary political impasse and its attendant economic collapse? At a superficial level, competing explanations for Zimbabwe's ongoing crisis seem to neatly follow opposing ideological/theoretical frameworks.

IFIs and representatives of Zimbabwe's powerful commercial interests have laid blame squarely at the feet of a government intent on defying market laws by irresponsible spending, political cronyism and a lack of transparency and commitment to market reforms. According to Raftopolous (1996), the World Bank 'challenged virtually all the key assumptions and demands' of those promoting socioeconomic transformation (i.e. 'indigenisation') in Zimbabwe. By 1995, the Bank called for 'restraint' on government intervention for the purposes of indigenisation, warning that such policies would lead to 'individuals with privileged access to decision makers being favoured' (World Bank quoted in Raftopolous 1996), preferring instead, as did Zimbabwe's white businesses, to promote 'racial harmony' – meaning that any opportunities for transformation would be left to the workings of the private sector and be 'totally subordinate to [the goal of] market driven growth'. From this perspective, old economic groups are perceived as weakened and too alienated from government to exercise effective influence whereas new groups are also weak or simply products of government cronyism, in which case they are too dependent on government favours to act independently.

In 2004, a tersely worded IMF report identified 'inadequate' macroeconomic and structural policies, lack of liberalisation and fiscal and monetary discipline as reasons for the current economic collapse that is having 'dire consequences' for the country's population (IMF 2004: 2–4). Leading mining interests (representing the largest sector for FDI) accuse government of 'strangling' their business activities by preventing mining groups from holding proceeds in offshore accounts protected from the extreme decline and volatility of the local currency, sweeping aside an international agreement signed by both the South African and Zimbabwean governments granting mining groups direct control of their earnings. Zimplats, the leading platinum mining company (controlled by South African Impala Platinum), considers the new government proposal 'unacceptable' and wholly counterproductive for the ability to invest further in one of the country's few prospering industries (*The Financial Gazette* 3 March 2005; *The Mail & Guardian* 7 March 2005). Kenneth Schofield of Radar Holdings, representing general business sentiments, describes current government policy as producing 'continued wanton destruction in absolute terms of the social, economic and structural fabric of this country' (*The Standard* 5 October 2003). If there is wariness about government intentions on the part of businesses in South Africa, there is near-panic in Zimbabwe.

Critics of neoliberalism see Zimbabwe's decline as a result of government collusion with businesses and IFIs in pursuing draconian, liberal market reforms that undermine domestic economic and social capacity while at the same time underwriting the already rich at the expense of Zimbabwe's continually suffering people (Bond 1998; Bond and Manyanya 2003; Moore 2003). From this point of view, government's eagerness to appease business demands for liberalisation, at whatever cost to population and economy, creates the volatile situation from which stems the recent collapse originating in the 2000 referendum defeat of the government's proposed new constitution and the following land invasions. While these critics do acknowledge the need for democratic and accountable government as a prerequisite for broad-based socioeconomic development and do not ignore the increasing authoritarianism and blatant use of violence by the government in its quest to retain power, they perceive the influence of entrenched economic interests as a primary cause of the crisis.

Both sets of explanations are complicated by internal contradictions and oversimplification. While liberal theorists have been continually critical of market hostile policies, they have also praised the government's commitment to market reforms. As late as October 1997, *The Economist* lauded Zimbabwe for its commitment to market reform: 'Africa is a bit short of economic stars, so countries that do well tend to get noticed. Hence the enthusiasm for Zimbabwe.' A few years later Zimbabwe is the global 'poster child' (for IFIs and governments, if not for speculators still able to extract profit from Zimbabwe's increasingly chaotic political-economic environment) of how an entire economy can be ruined by reckless, anti-market policies. On the other hand, when neoliberal market policies and commercial interests are identified as the main culprits in Zimbabwe's decline, government's profligate spending in the 1980s, its corruption and waste, and, later on, its oftentimes hollow commitments to much-publicised market reforms are important factors that become marginalised, or at least downplayed, in explanations for the crisis.

Rather than attempting to dichotomise and choose between these explanations, it is more useful to understand the evolving crisis as a result of dual processes of accommodating capital demands for liberalisation and responding to popular pressures for socioeconomic transformation. From enacting structural adjustment policies (appeasing local and international financial interests) to providing unbudgeted pension payouts for war veterans (appeasing a powerful crony constituency) and embarking on violent land redistribution (also appeasing powerful cronies, but some landless peasants and small-scale farmers as well), the government is playing at a complex game of appeasement. A government attempting to navigate complex sets of demands and pressures, in a situation where politics becomes crisis management, will attempt to forge close relations with capital actors that are able to continue profiting from such crony relations, even in a situation of extreme political and economic uncertainty. These actors are primarily short-term (financial) speculators that can, if necessary, easily extract their investments. At the same time, the government will respond with populist, 'anti-market' moves whenever domestic pressures increase and the (neoliberal) policy straitjacket becomes perceived as too inhibiting/untenable (a policy straitjacket that arguably was forced on Zanu already in 1979 by the Lancaster House agreement with Britain). If successful, this game may represent President Mugabe's machiavellian ability to ruthlessly divide and rule among his many competing 'constituencies'.

'New' economic groups: compradors or agents of transformation?

What are the prospects for the emergence of a 'patriotic' bourgeoisie, socioeconomic transformation and broad-based development in Southern Africa? Despite their various attempts at delivering transformation and development, leaders across the region clearly feel that greater efforts are necessary. Addressing the Johannesburg branch of the Black Management Forum on September 30 2004, ANC Secretary General Mothlante (2004) exhorted attendees representing the new black bourgeoisie to create

> a social consciousness that goes beyond self-enrichment. Many of us, upon acquiring wealth, pay little attention to our social responsibilities. [We] must create new value systems which are able to root the beneficiaries of black economic empowerment in the communities from which they emerged. These communities are still struggling for a better life.

Speaking at the fifty-seventh session of the Zanu-PF Central Committee in Harare on 2 April 2004, Zimbabwe's President Mugabe (2004) berated those who use political connections and the rhetoric of transformation to enrich themselves:

[Zimbabweans] have seen the effects of corruption and how it erodes and collapsed their welfare because of ill-gotten affluence. We have all seen how riches that come easily through devious ways translate into arrogant flamboyance and wastefulness ... [W]e thought these men were leading business luminaries of our country! They have cheated us and deserve their punishment ... Some have sought to defeat [the government's anti-corruption] campaign by pleading the cause of indigenisation. Let them remember that indigenisation does not, and shall never, mean empowering crooks who cut business corners and thrive on dirty deals. Certainly, it does not mean putting your shameless indigenous finger into the national till.

Whether these comments ought to be taken seriously, both South African and Zimbabwean leaders acknowledge the persistent danger of crony capitalism and the potential for new economic elites to abuse policies aiming at 'indigenisation'. Such acknowledgments do not, however, provide any answers to the question whether introducing 'new' economic groups (in this case a 'black bourgeoisie') into the higher ranks of the regions' economies will produce a capitalism capable of generating broad-based development, or whether it will merely make maintenance of a deeply unequal and exploitative status quo more palatable. In this case of a region historically characterised by racially defined inequality, 'more palatable' might merely mean ensuring that the skin complexion of the exploiters more closely resembles that of the exploited.

As this debate continues to rage in Southern Africa, several potential outcomes can be envisioned. A first possibility is maintenance of the status quo, in which new economic groups are co-opted by old groups. This is essentially the generic liberal preference, where 'trickle down' development is held out as a longer-term possibility, thus keeping a lid on any outbursts of popular demands for improvements in living conditions. A second possibility is that of the government being successful in sponsoring the emergence of a 'patriotic' bourgeoisie that in turn contributes to structural transformation: the ideal preference (?) of an ANC leadership committed to a liberal market economy, but also, if such a market can deliver as promised, (state-promoted) transformation and broad-based development along a 'third way' economic model. A third potential outcome is a regional collapse (the 'Zimbabwe scenario') in the case where it proves impossible to forge lasting collaboration between old and new economic groups and governments. Deterioration in state–business relations would trigger capital flight, political conflict and societal breakdown. Finally, there is the possibility of anti-capitalist/liberal solutions found to the region's developmental dilemma that are based on some form of (rejuvenation, or retrieval, of) traditionalist/ socialist/anti-capitalist policies. Such solutions are certainly not the ones key South African actors are seriously considering, nor will they likely be sought by a post-crisis Zimbabwean leadership that will instead be interested in seeking speedy reconciliation with global and domestic capital, as already indicated in recent policy statements by, among others, Zimbabwe's newly appointed Reserve Bank Governor Gideon Gono. In any case, the nature of interaction between governments, old and new economic groups and IFIs (i.e. state–capital relations) will continue playing a crucial role in shaping the political economy of Southern Africa.

Notes

1 See Haggard and Kaufman (1995) on the 'political economy of democratic transitions'. On transition in South Africa, see Marais (1998), Bond (2000) and Mhone (2004); in Zimbabwe, see Bond (1998) and Bond and Manyanya (2003).
2 For them, what Karl Marx observed regarding bourgeois excesses in Europe then is confirmed by their own experiences today: 'Bourgeois society, freed from political cares, attained a development unexpected even by itself . . . Financial swindling celebrated cosmopolitan orgies; the misery of the masses was set off by a shameless display of gorgeous, meretricious, and debased luxury' (Marx in McLellan 2004: 586).
3 On how contemporary civil society engages with the challenges of transformation in South Africa and Zimbabwe, see Mhone and Edigheji (2004) and Hammar *et al.* (2003) respectively.
4 Following Sklair and Robbins (2002: 83), the most useful way of understanding the emergence of new economic groups in Southern Africa would be to go beyond state-centric perspectives that emphasise the important role of the state in creating new economic elites by also focusing on 'the global capitalist system and the transnational capitalist class, both locally and globally'. This transnational capitalist class is a major factor in shaping the political economy in Southern Africa and other regions of the world as it seeks to 'exert economic control in the workplace, political control in domestic and international politics, and culture-ideology control in everyday life' (Sklair and Robbins 2002: 84).
5 See Mhone (2000) on 'enclave' (dual) economies in Southern Africa.
6 On South Africa as a semi-peripheral anchor in the overall peripheral Southern African political economy, see Andreasson (2001).
7 The Sixth Congress of the Communist International defined comprador capitalists as 'servitors of foreign imperialism concerned mainly with trade operations connected with the export of indigenous raw materials and the import of manufactured goods from imperialist countries' (quoted in Karat 2000) and Mao Zedong used the term comprador capitalism to characterise capitalist activity in pre-revolution China. Karat (2000) disagrees with those who wish to extend the concept 'comprador' to capitalist activity in the post-colonial, post-imperial era. However, given current debates about the prevalence of neo-colonial, neo-imperial relations between North and South, Karat's suggestion for a very limited use of the term 'comprador' is unjustifiably narrow.
8 This metaphor originates with South African Archbishop Desmond Tutu accusing the American Reverend Leon Sullivan in 1986 of 'shining the chains of Apartheid' when arguing that multinationals should invest 'responsibly' in apartheid South Africa, rather than divest from the country completely as the global anti-apartheid movement was calling for (Bond 2001: x–xi).
9 Interview with the author, Johannesburg, 19 October 2001.
10 Some leading capitalists, such as the Oppenheimer family and other mining and industrial magnates, felt already by the early 1980s that South Africa's apartheid policies were becoming an impediment for the continued prospering, and even survival, of the South African economy (Lipton 1986: 231).

11 Business Trust website, www.btrust.org.za/about/bbwg/.
12 On the move from the RDP to GEAR, see Marais (1998: 146–76) and Mhone (2004: 20–4).
13 Southall (2004: 326) dislikes the neoliberal label, suggesting that the South African state under ANC governance has become 'procapitalist' and 'interventionist' in using its political power to create a black capitalist class, rather than 'minimalist' and (almost exclusively) relying on market forces as would be the prescription under a neoliberal regime. Southall's emphasis on the 'minimalist state' is somewhat misguided; it is the overall ANC economic policy package – especially fiscal stringency, FDI, further integration into global markets and market solutions to problems of uneven development – that makes ANC policies essentially neoliberal in orientation (Andreasson 2004).
14 See Katzenstein (1985) and Maxfield and Schneider (1997: 25–30) for theoretical accounts of business cooperation due to (political) threat.
15 The Broad-Based Black Economic Empowerment Act of 2003 defines 'black people' as a generic term including 'Africans, Coloureds and Indians'. Broad-based black economic empowerment refers to the economic empowerment of all 'black' people, generously including women, workers, youth, people with disabilities and people living in rural areas (Republic of South Africa 2004).
16 Ramaphosa is one of South Africa's most well-connected corporate leaders. He is Chairman of Bidvest Group, Johnic Holdings, Capital Property Fund and Molope Group, and he represents other major corporations as Chairman and in various other positions. Recently he also secured lucrative BEE deals with Standard Bank and Liberty Life.
17 Mhone, interview with the author, Johannesburg, 13 November 2001; see also Andreasson (2003: 393).

Bibliography

Adam, H, F. van Zyl Slabbert and K. Moodley (1998) *Comrades in Business: Post-Liberation Politics in South Africa*, Utrecht: International Books.
Adesina, J.O. (2004) 'NEPAD and the challenge of Africa's development: towards the political economy of a discourse', *Society in Transition*, 35, 1: 125–44.
African National Congress (1998) 'The state, property relations, and social transformation: a discussion paper towards the alliance summit', *Umrabulo* 5, www.anc.org.za/ancdocs/pubs/umrabulo/articles/sprst.html.
Andreasson, S. (2001) 'Divergent paths of development: the modern world-system and democratization in South Africa and Zambia', *Journal of World-Systems Research*, 7, 2: 175–223.
—— (2003) 'Economic reforms and "virtual democracy" in South Africa and Zimbabwe: the incompatibility of liberalisation, inclusion and development', *Journal of Contemporary African Studies*, 21, 3: 383–406.
—— (2004) 'The ANC confronts a new "rooi gevaar": predatory liberalism and cadre embourgeoisement in post-apartheid South Africa', paper presented at the European Consortium for Political Research Standing Group on International Relations Fifth Pan-European Conference, The Hague, 9–11 September 2004.
—— (2006) 'Stand and deliver: private property and the politics of global dispossession', *Political Studies*, 54, 1: 3–22.
Ashley, B. (2003) 'Apartheid South Africa as a case study for cancellation of illegitimate debt', Jubilee South Africa, 1 March, www.odiousdebts.org/odiousdebts/index.cfm?DSP=content&ContentID=8004.

Bond, P. (1998) *Uneven Zimbabwe: A Study of Finance, Development, and Underdevelopment*, Trenton: Africa World Press.

—— (2000) *Elite Transition: From Apartheid to Neoliberalism in South Africa*, London: Pluto Press.

—— (2001) *Against Global Apartheid: South Africa Meets the World Bank, IMF and International Finance*, Lansdowne: University of Cape Town Press.

—— (2004) 'The ANC's 'left turn' & South African sub-imperialism', *Review of African Political Economy*, 31, 102: 599–616.

Bond, P. and M. Manyanya (2003) *Zimbabwe's Plunge: Exhausted Nationalism, Neoliberalism and the Search for Social Justice* (second edn), London: Merlin Press.

Bracking, S. (2004) 'Neoclassical and structural analysis of poverty: winning the "economic kingdom" for the poor in southern Africa', *Third World Quarterly*, 25, 5: 887–901.

Bradshaw, Y. and S.N. Ndegwa (eds) (2000) *The Uncertain Promise of Southern Africa*, Bloomington, IN: Indiana University Press.

Broad, R. and J. Cavanagh (1999) 'The death of the Washington consensus?', *World Policy Journal*, Fall: 79–88.

Carmody, P. and S. Taylor (2003) 'Industry and the urban sector in Zimbabwe's political economy', *African Studies Quarterly*, 7, 2 and3, www.africa.ufl.edu/asq/v7/v7i2a3.htm.

Chan, S. (2002) *Liberalism, Democracy and Development*, Cambridge: Cambridge University Press.

Chomsky, N. (1999) *Profit Over People: Neoliberalism and Global Order*, New York: Seven Stories Press.

Dansereau, S. and M. Zamponi (2005) *Zimbabwe – The Political Economy of Decline* (compiled by H. Melber), Discussion Paper 27, Uppsala: Nordiska Afrikainstitutet.

Friedman, S. and I. Chipkin (2001) 'A poor voice? The politics of inequality in South Africa', Research Report no 87, Johannesburg: Centre for Policy Studies.

Gray, J. (2002) *False Dawn: The Delusions of Global Capitalism*, London: Granta.

Habib, A. and V. Padayachee (2000) 'Economic policy and power relations in South Africa's transition to democracy', *World Development*, 28, 2: 245–63.

Haggard, S. and R.R. Kaufman (1995) *The Political Economy of Democratic Transitions*, Princeton, NJ: Princeton University Press.

Hammar, A., B. Raftopolous and S. Jensen (eds) (2003) *Zimbabwe's Unfinished Business: Rethinking Land, State and Nation in the Context of Crisis*, Harare: Weaver Press.

Hinds, M. (1990) *Outwards vs. Inwards Development Strategy*, Washington, DC: World Bank.

IMF (2004) 'IMF concludes Article IV consultation with Zimbabwe', Public Information Notice No. 04/104, 17 September, www.imf.org/external/pubs/ft/scr/2004/cr04297.pdf.

Karat, P. (2000) 'CPI(M) programme: basic strategy reiterated', *The Communist* (New Delhi), 16, 3 (July–December), www.cpim.org/marxist/200003_marxist_progrm_pk.htm.

Katzenstein, P.J. (1985) *Small States in World Markets*, Ithaca, NY: Cornell University Press.

Koelble, T. (2004) 'Economic policy in the post-colony: South Africa between Keynesian remedies and neoliberal pain', *New Political Economy*, 9, 1: 57–78.

Lachman, D. (2004) 'ANC faces mountain of expectations', American Enterprise Institute, 7 April, www.aei.org/include/news_print.asp?newsID=20246.

Lewis, D., K. Reed and E. Teljeur (2004) 'South Africa: economic policy-making and implementation in Africa: a study of strategic trade and selective industrial policies', in C. Soludo, O. Ogbu and H.-J. Chang (eds), *The Politics of Trade and Industrial Policy in Africa: Forced Consensus?*, Lawrenceville: Africa World Press.

Lipton, M. (1986) *Capitalism and Apartheid: South Africa, 1910–86*, Aldershot: Wildwood House.

MacLean, S. (2002) 'Mugabe at war: the political economy of conflict in Zimbabwe', *Third World Quarterly*, 23, 3: 513–28.

McLellan, D. (ed.) (2004) *Marx: Selected Writings* (second edn), Oxford: Oxford University Press.

Marais, H. (1998) *South Africa – Limits to Change: The Political Economy of Transformation*, Cape Town: University of Cape Town Press.

Maxfield, S. and B.R. Schneider (eds) (1997) *Business and the State in Developing Countries*, Ithaca, NY: Cornell University Press.

Mbeki, T. (2004) 'Letter from the President: questions that demand answers', *ANC Today*, 4, 36, 10–16 September, www.anc.org.za/ancdocs/anctoday/2004/text/at36.txt.

Mhone, G. (2000) 'Enclavity and constrained labour absorptive capacity in Southern African economies', International Labour Office/Southern Africa Multidisciplinary Advisory Team Discussion Paper No. 12.

—— (2004) 'Democratisation, economic liberalisation and the quest for sustainable development in South Africa', in G. Mhone and O. Edigheji (eds), *Governance in the New South Africa: The Challenges of Globalisation*, Lansdowne: University of Cape Town Press.

Mhone, G. and O. Edigheji (eds) (2004) *Governance in the New South Africa: The Challenges of Globalisation*, Lansdowne: University of Cape Town Press.

Michie, J. and V. Padayachee (1998) 'Three years after apartheid: growth, employment and redistribution?', *Cambridge Journal of Economics*, 22: 623–35.

Moore, D. (2001) 'Neoliberal globalisation and the triple crisis of "modernisation" in Africa: Zimbabwe, the Democratic Republic of the Congo and South Africa', *Third World Quarterly*, 22, 6: 909–29.

—— (2003) 'Zimbabwe's triple crisis: primitive accumulation, nation-state formation and democratization in the age of neo-liberal globalization', *African Studies Quarterly*, 7, 2 and 3, www.africa.ufl.edu/asq/v7/v7i2a2.htm.

Mothlante, K. (2004) 'Address to the Johannesburg branch of the Black Management Forum', 30 September, www.anc.org.za/ancdocs/speeches/2004/sp0930.html.

Mugabe, R. (2004) 'Address by His Excellency, the President and First Secretary of ZANU PF, Cde Robert Mugabe, on the occasion of the 57th Session of the Central Committee', Harare, 2 April, www.zanupfpub.co.zw/address.htm.

Pallotti, A. (2004) 'SADC: a development community without a development policy?', *Review of African Political Economy*, 31, 101: 515–31.

Peet, R. (2002) 'Ideology, discourse, and the geography of hegemony: from socialist to neoliberal development in postapartheid South Africa', *Antipode*, 34: 54–84.

Phimister, I. and B. Raftopolous (2004) 'Mugabe, Mbeki and the politics of anti-imperialism', *Review of African Political Economy*, 31, 101: 385–400.

Pillay, P. (2000) 'South Africa in the 21st century: key socio-economic challenges', December, Johannesburg: Friedrich Ebert Stiftung.

Raftopolous, B. (1996) 'Fighting for control: the indigenization debate in Zimbabwe', *Southern Africa Report*, 11, 4, www.africafiles.org/article.asp?ID=3875.

Randall, D.J. (1996) 'Prospects for the development of a black business class in South Africa', *Journal of Modern African Studies*, 34, 4: 661–86.

Rapley, J. (2004) *Globalization and Inequality: Neoliberalism's Downward Spiral*, Boulder, CO: Lynne Rienner.

Republic of South Africa (2004) *Broad-Based Black Economic Empowerment Act*, No. 53, 2003 *Government Gazette*, 9 January, www.polity.org.za/pdf/BroBasBlaEcoEmpA53. pdf.

Sachikonye, L.M. (2003) 'From "growth with equity" to "fast-track" reform: Zimbabwe's land question', *Review of African Political Economy*, 30, 96: 227–40.

Saul, J. (2001) 'Cry for the beloved country: the post-apartheid denouement', *Review of African Political Economy*, 28, 89: 429–60.

Schlemmer, L. (2004) *Business in Change: Corporate Citizenship in South Africa*, South Africa Foundation, Occasional Paper 2 (June), www.safoundation.org.za/documents/ Business_In_Change.pdf (accessed 3 March 2005).

Shaw, T.M. (1989) 'Corporatism in Zimbabwe: revolution restrained', in J.E. Nyang'oro and T.J. Shaw (eds), *Corporatism in Africa: Comparative Analysis and Practice*, Boulder, CO: Westview Press.

Sklair, L. and P.T. Robbins (2002) 'Global capitalism and major corporations from the Third World', *Third World Quarterly*, 23, 1: 81–100.

Southall, R. (2004) 'The ANC & black capitalism in South Africa', *Review of African Political Economy*, 31, 100: 313–28.

Streak, J.C. (2004) 'The Gear legacy: did Gear fail or move South Africa forward in development?', *Development Southern Africa*, 21, 2: 271–88.

Szeftel, M. (2004) 'Two cheers? South African democracy's first decade', *Review of African Political Economy*, 31, 100: 193–202.

Thompson, C.B. (2000) 'Regional challenges to globalisation: perspectives from Southern Africa', *New Political Economy*, 5, 1: 41–57.

World Bank (2000) *Can Africa Claim the 21st Century?*, Washington, DC: The World Bank.

Zwizwai, B., A. Kambudzi and B. Mauwa (2004) 'Zimbabwe: economic policy-making and implementation: a study of strategic trade and selective industrial policies', in C. Soludo, O. Ogbu and H.-J. Chang (eds), *The Politics of Trade and Industrial Policy in Africa: Forced Consensus?*, Lawrenceville: Africa World Press.

13 African regional groupings and emerging Chinese conglomerates

Kwame Nimako

China's economic growth in the past two decades is in sharp contrast to the economic decline and political implosion in much of Africa in the 1980s and 1990s. On the one hand, not only has China's economic growth been reinforced by foreign direct investment (FDI) and accumulation of foreign exchange but also it has transformed some Chinese state corporations into emerging conglomerates on the international scene. In turn, China's economic growth has given rise to a greater demand for natural resources. On the other hand, Africa's economic decline and political implosion has led to the designation of many African countries as heavily indebted poor countries (HIPC), which in turn has placed most of them on a 'HIPC diet' by international financial institutions (IFIs) and 'Western' donors. However the availability of natural resources in Africa implies that some African countries fare well, positioned to form effective partnerships with Chinese conglomerates for infrastructure development in Africa and to export natural resources from Africa to China.

This chapter will examine a Chinese international investment conglomerate in relation to the Chinese construction/engineering sector and the prospects of their positive impact on Africa's economy and politics. It will be argued that world economic forces in the twenty-first century are shifting in favour of China. On the positive side, if properly managed by African governments, the emergence of China as a major economic force and emergence of its conglomerates could relieve Africa from its debt burden and dependence on IFIs and EU and US donors. On the negative side, if poorly managed by African governments, China's demand for natural resources could make Africa a battle ground reminiscent of the 'scramble for Africa' in the late nineteenth century.[1]

The global context

The ascendancy of China as a major player in the world economy constitutes a crack in the international political economy. Specifically, in the short run, the rise of China and the subsequent fissure in the international political economy challenges the dominance of the G3, namely, the United States,

Germany and Japan, of the world economy. According to Hinloopen and van Marrewijk, China's gross domestic product (GDP) moved from fifth place in the world ranking of 1980 (behind the United States, the Soviet Union, Japan and Germany) to second place (behind the United States) in 2004. It is also worth noting that relative to the GDP of the United States, Chinese GDP rose from about 25 per cent in 1980 to about 62 per cent in 2004. This growth went hand in hand with external trade; China's exports and imports increased from about 2 per cent of GDP in the 1970s to about 24 per cent in 2004 (Hinloopen and van Marrewijk 2004). In a separate account, but in affirmation of the above trend, Robert J. Samuelson, citing the study of Andy Xie, noted that in the past 25 years, China's economy has expanded by a factor of almost 9, but exports have grown 45 times (Samuelson 2004).

The ascendancy of China as an important player in the world economy is a consequence of consistent economic growth in China during the past two decades. According to Hinloopen and van Marrewijk (2004) the Chinese economic growth (after correcting for international price differences) was about 7.25 per cent per year in real terms in the period 1980–2001, implying a doubling of output every ten years. There are even those who think official China conceals part of its economic data. James Kynge, for instance, claims that 'although officially its gross domestic product grew by 9.1 per cent in 2003, independent economists suggest that the real figure was nearer 11 or 12 per cent' (*Financial Times* 24 March 2004). Not only does the repositioning of China imply that various countries and regions have to reposition themselves in the world economy, but also it can be advantageous or disadvantageous to Africa as a region in the world economy depending on the responses of different African states and their regional groupings.

By all accounts and observations China's economic growth in the past two decades is in sharp contrast to the economic decline and political implosion in much of Africa during the same period. According to African Development Bank (ADB) sources, between 1961 and 1997, the median real GDP growth rate of 35 African countries was 3.7 per cent. But this was better than the growth rates between 1980 and 2000. Of the 49 African countries surveyed by the ADB for the period between 1980 and 1990, only 6 countries (Botswana, Cape Verde, Congo, Egypt, Swaziland and Zimbabwe) recorded GDP growth rates of more than 5 per cent; 15 countries experienced GDP growth rates of 3 to 5 per cent; 27 countries less than 3 per cent, whereas one (Côte d'Ivoire) slipped into negative growth.[2]

It is important to note that of the countries that recorded GDP growth rates above 5 per cent between 1980 and 1990, only Botswana continues to report GDP growth rates above 5 per cent in the 1990s. Not only is Africa's economic decline in contrast to economic growth in China but also it is in contrast to Africa's own recent history. For instance, between 1960 and 1980 almost all African countries experienced some form of economic growth. Of the 35 African countries from which data is available, between 1960 and 1970, 12 countries recorded GDP growth rates of more than

5 per cent; 12 countries experienced GDP growth rates of between 3 to 5 per cent, and 11 countries less than 3 per cent (ADB 2000).

Recent data on Africa suggest that compared with the previous decade, the year 2003 saw a record rise of the number of high growth countries. Of the 53 African countries surveyed by the ADB (2004), 18 recorded GDP growth rates of more than 5 per cent (including the oil producing countries: Algeria, Chad, Equatorial Guinea, Libya and Nigeria); 16 countries experienced GDP growth rates of between 3 to 5 per cent and 11 countries less than 3 per cent; however 6 countries slipped into negative growth, namely, Central African Republic, Burundi, Côte d'Ivoire, Ethiopia, Seychelles and Zimbabwe. However, during the past four decades, only three African countries have recorded GDP growth rates of more than 5 per cent for two decades or more without leading to transformations comparable to that of China or the Asian Tigers. These three countries are Botswana (1960–2000), Egypt (1960–90) and Côte d'Ivoire (1960–80). This of course raises the question as to how African states understood, interpreted and explained their economic fortune. We shall return to this later in the chapter.

Regarding the underpinning of China's economic growth, Hinloopen and van Marrewijk (2004) identify two moments of structural change. The first was 1980, when China started to open up to international trade flows. The second was 1985, when the start of FDIs initiated the rise in technology-intensive exports. During this period the composition of Chinese exports changed structurally towards more unskilled labour-intensive and technology-intensive exports, while there was a drastic decline in the export of primary products. Of course these structural changes in China in the 1980s did not take place in isolation. They formed part of changes in the international political economy in response to the 1979–82 world economic recession, which formed part of the worldwide reaction to inflation and crisis in the world economy in the 1970s. In turn these developments manifested themselves in several forms in different countries in the 1980s and 1990s, ranging from French President Mitterand's U-turn in 1981 through Thatcherism, Reaganomics and neoliberalism to Gorbachev's economic *perestroika* and political *glasnost* and the subsequent collapse of the Soviet Union.

Clearly a crisis is a decisive turning point, which is filled with danger and anxiety and requires adaptation, and on this score China adapted better than several African countries and the Soviet Union. As will be argued here, one of the keys to this adaptation was the role of state-owned enterprises (SOEs). For the moment it suffices to say that by the end of the twentieth century, 70 per cent of the FDI in the world outside the United States, the European Union and Japan was going to China whereas only 2 per cent went to Africa. Of this FDI in Africa, 80 per cent went to four countries: Egypt, Morocco, Nigeria (in the oil sector) and South Africa.

These economic differences between Africa and China evidently cause social differences too. The structural changes and economic growth in China were accompanied by social gains:

[F]rom 1978 to 2002, the average annual per person income rose from $190 to $960. Life expectancy increased from 61.7 years in 1970 to 71 in 2002; adult illiteracy fell from 37 per cent in 1978 to less than 17 per cent in 1999; infant mortality dropped from 41 per 1,000 live births in 1978 to 30 in 1999.

(Samuelson 2004: 47)

In contrast, many African countries could not recover from the 1979–82 world economic recession. The resulting foreign exchange shortages, aggravated by drought, made it impossible for many African governments to import sufficient food to bolster the resulting shortages. This obliged several African governments to seek foreign aid to ease the food crisis and foreign loans to revive their economies.

Not only did the crisis in Africa lead to the accumulation of foreign debt in much of Africa but also hitherto African state elites and the IFIs, such as the World Bank and the International Monetary Fund (IMF), used different units of analysis to explain the region's economic performance. This in turn gave rise to different perspectives on Africa's economic decline. At the broader level, African states attributed the crisis that preceded Africa's economic decline to the 'oil crisis' and unfavourable terms of international trade for primary commodities, and instability of the international commodity markets. Apparently African states were accustomed to commodity price fluctuations on the world market. Not only was it assumed by African state elites that the world market is controlled by the so-called Western world but also it was assumed that commodity prices would bounce back, perhaps within three years, which in turn would lead to economic recovery. The perspectives of African states found their expression in the numerous five-year development plans of the United Nations Economic Commission for Africa (UNECA), such as the *Lagos Plan of Action for the Economic Development of Africa 1980–2000* (1981) and the *African Alternative Framework to Structural Adjustment Programmes for Socio-economic Recovery and Transformation, AAF-SAP* (1989). The IFIs, however, attributed the same crisis to economic mismanagement and assumed they could fix the economies of these 'people without history' within one year based on IMF monetary policy. The perspectives of the IFIs were expressed in the Berg Report (1981), also known at the World Bank (1989) as *Accelerated Development in Sub-Saharan Africa: An Agenda for Action* and *Sub-Saharan Africa: From Crisis to Sustainable Growth*.

Like China, African elites considered the state as the prime agent of change and development whereas the IFIs viewed the magic of the market as the agent of the same. It was against this backdrop that several African states resorted to the sale of SOEs for public finance. However, whereas African elites considered privatisation as de-industrialisation and loss of sovereignty, the IFIs viewed this as part of globalisation. Nevertheless African states and IFIs agreed that borrowing from these institutions, as an instrument of public finance, was necessary. By the mid-1990s, not only had African states accumulated foreign debt but also one of the ways for the leadership of an African country to demonstrate that it was not corrupt was to subject itself to the status of HIPC, which in turn has placed most of them on an 'HIPC diet' by the IFIs and 'Western' donors. In plain language, the HIPC diet implies that African economies have to be monitored and controlled by IFIs through conditionality in exchange for less stringent debt collection, considered as development aid by their creditors, also referred to as 'donors'.

By the end of the twentieth century African states had accepted the IFIs' version of the interpretation and explanation of Africa's economic decline, namely, bad governance and economic mismanagement. This is clearly expressed in the publication of the document *New Partnership for Africa's Development*, or *NEPAD* (UNECA 2001). Not only does *NEPAD* serve as an umbrella for the five sub-regional groupings in Africa, but also it was designed ostensibly to rebuild Africa through the consolidation of democracy and sound economic management (UNECA 2001: nr. 204). Regionalism became one the main pillars for Africa's economic recovery.

According to *NEPAD*, the ADB 'must play a leading role in financing regional studies, programmes and projects' (UNECA 2001: nr. 96). *NEPAD*'s rationale for sub-regional and regional approaches to development is as follows:

> Most African countries are small, both in terms of population and per capita incomes. As a consequence of limited markets, they do not offer attractive returns to potential investors, while progress in diversifying production and exports is retarded. This limits investment in essential infrastructure that depends on economies of scale for viability. . . . These economic conditions point to the need for African countries to pool their resources and enhance regional development and economic integration on the continent, in order to improve international competitiveness. The five sub-regional economic groupings of the continent must, therefore, be strengthened.
> (UNECA 2001: nr. 93, 94)

Indeed most African countries are small in terms of population, but evidence available from the ADB does not support part of the rationale of *NEPAD* for regionalism because African countries with small populations tend to have per capita income above African average. In fact, a study by the ADB (2000) demonstrates that of the 53 African countries, six (Cape Verde, Equatorial Guinea, Seychelles, Djibouti, Comoros and Sao Tome and Principe) had populations of less than one million, and two of these (Comoros and Sao Tome and Principe) had GDP per capita below African average. In other words 50 per cent of the smallest African countries had more than average income per capita. Of the seven African countries with populations of between one and two million (Botswana, Gabon, Gambia, Guinea Bissau, Mauritius, Namibia and Swaziland), only two (Gambia and Guinea Bissau) had GDP per capita below Africa's average. This means that 70 per cent of the very small African countries have income per capita above Africa's average.

This is in contrast to the countries with large populations. Of the nine African countries with populations of more than 30 million (i.e. nearly 40 per cent of African population), six had GDP per capita below African average (Democratic Republic of Congo, Ethiopia, Kenya, Nigeria, Sudan and Tanzania), which means that nearly 70 per cent of African countries with large populations have income per capita below Africa's average. The implications are that positive economic development in these six countries will have a very positive impact on Africa. Not only do the three other countries, South Africa, Egypt and Algeria, have income per capita above African average, but also each has GDP per capita above that of China. Besides, Egypt and South Africa have the scientific and technological infrastructure to achieve economic growth and socioeconomic transformation. The poverty in South Africa, Egypt and Algeria thus has more to do with historical injustices and current race, ethnic, political and social relations rather than with a lack of foreign investment, inadequate infrastructure and lack of economies of scale. The question is whether the quest for regional groupings and economies of scale constitutes a quest for conglomerates in Africa.

SOEs and privatisation in Africa and China

As noted above, as in China it was taken for granted within African states that the state should be the agent of change and development. As a result many SOEs were called into being. However the IFIs considered the magic of the market as the agent of change and development. It was against this background that structural adjustment programmes (SAPs) became a major theme of public policy in the 1980s. It was also against this backdrop that at the height of the SAPs in the 1980s Andre Gunder Frank noted that the then privatisation craze was just as economically irrational and politically ideological as the earlier nationalisation craze. This is all the more so since in and to the market

> it makes very little difference whether an enterprise is owned privately or publicly; for they all have to compete with each other equally in the same world market. The only exceptions are public enterprises that are subsidised by the state budget and private enterprises that are also subsidized from state budget and/or otherwise bailed out in the public interest. . . . Moreover, public and private enterprises can make equally good or bad investment and other management decisions in the market. . . . In the 1970s, (public) British Steel overinvested badly, and (private)

US Steel underinvested badly. In the 1980s, both closed steel mills over the public objections of labor. So did simultaneously the private steel industry in Germany under a Christian Democratic government and the public steel industry in France under a socialist government.

(Frank 1990: 10–11)

It was not only the ideology of privatisation that was questioned but also the praxis of privatisation. Frank thus argues

> that privatizing public enterprises now at bargain-basement-share prices that doubled next week on the national stock exchange is just as fraudulent a practice as nationalizing loss-making enterprises and paying for them above market value, or nationalizing profitable enterprises with little or no indemnification. This 'now you see it, now you don't' game is all the more egregious for enterprises in the East and the South that are now privatized and bought up with devalued domestic currency purchased (or swapped for debt) by foreign companies or joint ventures with foreign exchange from abroad. In sum, the privatization debate is a sham; it is far less about productive efficiency than about distributive (in)justice.

(Frank 1990: 11)

Back in 1991, as an extension of Frank's observations, I argued with reference to the privatisation drive in Ghana that one of the main problems with most of the SOEs (in Ghana) was that they were established as import substitution industries, and continued to be viewed as such. As a result of this SOEs have become foreign exchange consumers, rather than foreign exchange earners. If a turn-around was required, it was not through a transfer of ownership from public to private, but should rather have been through a turn-around from satisfying only local consumers or import substitution, to exports and foreign exchange earnings. The success of such a turn-around would require an effective international marketing strategy and the re-organisation of the country's Ministries of Trade and Foreign Affairs (Nimako 1991: 212). Recent political and economic developments in China and Africa have confirmed Frank's thesis and my observations on Ghana. Like China, most African countries had SOEs before the neoliberal onslaught in the 1980s, which found its expression in the implementation of SAPs. Unlike China, however, African countries have not been able to transform their SOEs into conglomerates. This is partly because China's SOEs were granted more autonomy to operate effectively and efficiently.

A case in point is the China International Trust and Investment Corporation (CITIC). A state-owned corporation established in 1979 to serve as window on China's opening to the outside world, CITIC has grown into a large translational conglomerate with 44 subsidiaries in and outside China including Hong Kong, the United States, Canada, Australia and New

Zealand. One such subsidiary is CITIC International Contracting Inc. (CICI), jointly established by CITIC and the Ministry of Railway. According to its 1998 annual report, CICI 'is guided by the Ministry of Foreign Trade and Economic Cooperation. It's a large-scale state-owned combined enterprise with the principles of autonomous business operation, sole responsibility for its profits or losses, self-restraint and self-development.' Besides, CICI 'has a qualification certificate of Class A ratified by the Ministry of Construction, for general contracting of construction works'.[3] This company has become 'a big complex with its multi-function in the field of scientific research, survey and design, construction, manufacture and processing in one entity'. It has developed a

> technical force of more than 30,000 senior and regular engineers and technicians for design, scientific research, construction and manufacturing as well as a large well-trained, multitrade work force with 300,000 workers engaged in construction and installation. . . . Over the past 10 years, the member units of CICI have built over 5,000 km railroad mainlines, 1,000 km highway, 200 bridges, 500 million cubic meters of earth and stone, 5,000 km electric railway, and have constructed many five-star hotels, civil and industrial buildings, channels, tunnels, dams and airports in and outside China.

Besides its core business, 'the labor service business of the company has been progressively expanded since its set-up'. CICI has sent a large number of workers and technical people to many countries and areas such as the Republic of Korea, Japan, Singapore, Malaysia, Indonesia, Thailand, Sri Lanka, Iraq, Georgia, Kazakhstan, Mexico and Hong Kong (CICI 1998).

Unlike China, however, in much of Africa, due to foreign exchange shortages, on the conditions of the IMF and the World Bank most African governments resorted to privatisation as one of the means of earning foreign exchange and, flowing from this, attracting FDI, resolving debt crisis and stimulating economic growth. Bhinda *et al.* have noted that

> privatisation revenue as a source of FDI to sub-Saharan Africa (SSA) is important relative to other developing areas. It comprised 20% of total FDI in 1988–95. This indicates high dependence on privatisation as a source of FDI: one third of Tanzanian and Ugandan recorded FDI since 1992–93 has come from privatisations (though this is well above the SSA average). World Bank data show that FDI was 42% of total gross privatisation revenue for SSA in 1988–95, with the bulk going to Ghana, Nigeria and Zimbabwe. For our project countries except South Africa this is even higher. They state that privatisation programmes have often been an entry point for FDI to a country or sector, and are perceived by investors to have had positive effects in Tanzania, Uganda, Zambia, Zimbabwe and South Africa.

In sub-Saharan Africa (i.e. excluding North Africa)

> sales of state owned enterprises (SOEs) were below the developing world average until 1995, with some notable exceptions such as Ghana's Ashanti Goldfields (1994), which brought large net inflows of foreign exchange. However, 1995 saw a broadening of the countries in which sales were occurring, and 1996 a dramatic increase in gross privatisation revenue (though most of this reflected three large scale sales in Ghana, Kenya and South Africa).
>
> (Bhinda *et al.* 1999: 57)[4]

It is important to reiterate that whereas some African governments have viewed privatisation as a means of saving and/or raising foreign exchange, the IFIs view it as one of the prime objectives of their intervention. In IFI circles privatisation is an end in itself because 'private enterprise is considered to be better able to respond to the stick and carrot of competition, which is seen as a criterion of improved efficiency'. In Ghana, in the history of economic programming with regard to the private sector and the public sector, 'pragmatism rather than ideology underpinned the rebalancing process' (Akuoko-Frimpong quoted in Nimako 1991: 33).

Privatisation in Africa did not give rise to African conglomerates. Some SOEs were left to rot or liquidated, much of the investment in SOEs was wasted, and the few that were privatised fell into foreign hands. According to Bhinda *et al.* (1999: 57), most privatisation programmes have begun with large utilities (telecoms, water, electricity, transport), or small guaranteed profit-makers such as cigarettes (Tanzania selling to RJ Reynolds (US)), breweries (Tanzania to South Africa Breweries) or cement (Zambia's sale to Chilanga). They also note that Tanzania and Zambia 'have liquidated or sold for virtually nothing a large number of companies, particularly manufacturing and agriculture'. In Zambia,

> privatisation has been delayed by the absence of functioning stock markets, political opposition to foreign purchasers, technical issues of valuing assets, and complex bidding procedures (which potential foreign investors nevertheless see as non-transparent). After delay has degraded their assets and forced them to be revalued downwards, many companies find few interested buyers, and in final negotiations governments have to take over large amounts of debt, often turning the privatisation into a net foreign exchange loss! Even Zambia Consolidated Copper Mines risks earning less than 30% of its original valuation. While a few prime companies remain to be sold in each country, it is vital to capitalise on these sales with strong positive publicity about wider policies, to mobilise FDI additional to privatisation.
>
> (Bhinda *et al.* 1999: 59)

In Ghana, however, privatisation began with the profit-making sectors. Initially, out of about 235 public enterprises in the country, 37 were considered marketable and were earmarked for privatisation by May 1989. The government did not intend to privatise 21 core SOEs (including public utilities) by virtue of their strategic importance to the economy. In between the two categories (core–marketable) were about 177 SOEs that remained undecided upon by the government by the end of 1989. By 1990 only the Continental Hotel (Accra), the most profit-making hotel among the SOEs, had been privatised and purchased by a Libyan company for $3.6 million; six other SOEs had been liquidated. The sale of the most profit-making hotel contradicted the government's claim that 'considering that (public enterprises) continue to constitute a drain on national budget, it should be prudent for their ownership to change from public to private, where the private sector can bring a turn-around in these enterprises' (Nimako 1991).

Thus, unlike Africa where mass privatisation became the order of the 1980s and the 1990s, China decided to improve the management of their SOEs rather than sell them. Besides, not only has China's economic growth been reinforced by FDI and accumulation of foreign exchange reserves, but also it has transformed some Chinese state corporations into emerging conglomerates on the international scene. As mentioned above, in and to the market it makes very little difference whether an enterprise is owned privately or publicly; they all have to compete with each other equally in the same world market. Whereas the structural changes in China gave rise to FDI, structural changes led to debt accumulation in Africa. The end result is that African states neither have a vibrant private sector nor a strong state. It is against this backdrop that African states want to strengthen their regional groupings.

African regional groupings: from Rome to Abuja

Africa's regional groupings currently find their expression in the Africa Union (AU) and the *NEPAD* programme. As noted above, the *NEPAD*, which serves as an umbrella for the five sub-regional groupings in Africa, was published in October 2001 in Abuja (Nigeria) by African Heads of State ostensibly to rebuild Africa through the consolidation of democracy and sound economic management, and to renegotiate relations with developed countries through 'development aid'. Apparently the former (i.e. democracy and sound economic management, also referred to as good governance) is supposed to serve as precondition to the latter (i.e. aid or development assistance). The authors of *NEPAD* hoped that the launching of the programme would 'mark the beginning of a new phase in the partnership and co-operation between Africa and the developed world' (UNECA 2001: nr. 206); this in turn would enable Africa to catch up or bridge the development gap between Africa and the developed countries, also referred to in official jargon as 'donors'.

The *NEPAD* document also noted that:

> *The various partnerships between Africa and the industrialized countries on the one hand, and multilateral institutions on the other, will be maintained.* The partnerships in question include, among others: the United Nations New Agenda for the Development of Africa in the 1990s; the Africa-Europe Summit's Cairo Plan of Action; the World Bank-led Poverty Reduction Strategy Papers; the Japan-led Tokyo Agenda for Action; the Africa Growth and Opportunity Act of the United States; and the Economic Commission on Africa-led Global Compact with Africa. The objective will be to *rationalize these partnerships* and to ensure that real benefits to Africa flow from them.
>
> (UNECA 2001: nr. 187, emphasis added)

The 'development' journey to Abuja started in Rome over four decades ago. Articles 131–6 of the European Economic Community (EEC) Treaty of 1957, also referred to as the Treaty of Rome, provided for *association* of non-European countries and territories with which EEC member states had special relations (i.e. colonies). According to the Treaty of Rome, the purpose of such an *association* was to 'promote the economic and social development of the countries and territories and to establish close economic relations between and the Community as a whole' (Article 131). Furthermore, the Treaty stated that the 'association shall serve primarily to further the interests and prosperity of the inhabitants of these countries and territories (i.e. colonies) in order to lead them to the economic, social and cultural development to which they aspire'. In other words, formally, the *association* was designed for the good of the colonies.

However, decolonisation challenged these EEC arrangements and called for a new relationship. On this score, at the broader level of generalisation, Africa's international political and economic relations, and for that matter, the foreign policy of African countries, have been shaped by two historical forces; colonialism/neo-colonialism, and self-determination/pan-Africanism. The former called for a closer association and asymmetry relations with – or vertical integration towards – Europe and found its expression in the Treaty of Rome. The latter called for greater autonomy from Europe and closer cooperation among African countries – or horizontal integration.

Charles De Gaulle of France represented vertical integration whereas Kwame Nkrumah of Ghana represented horizontal integration. As extension of the Treaty of Rome, De Gaulle's brand of Africa's foreign policy was institutionalised through the Yaoundé I Convention (1963), Yaoundé II (1969), Lomé 1 (1975), Lomé II (1980), Lomé III (1985), Lomé IV (1990–5), Cotonou (2000) and related regional arrangements such as the West African Economic and Monetary Union (UEMOA). Nkrumah's brand of Africa's foreign policy was institutionalised through the Organisation for African Unity (OAU 1963), the AU, and related regional integration arrangements such as the Economic Community of West African States (ECOWAS) and Southern African Development Community (SADC).

NEPAD is designed to navigate between the vertical and horizontal integration, but it has its doses of illusions, especially its desired 7 per cent economic growth – to be determined by domestic policy or mobilisation of local resources – and the $64 billion investment – to be determined by foreign policy or development assistance. In plain language, *NEPAD* envisaged to keep what they have, namely 'development aid', and add new things to it, namely 'development aid'. The origins of *NEPAD* and the idea to renegotiate relations between African and developed countries go further as *NEPAD* is not the first new partnership with the developed countries. In fact, already the Lomé I Convention signed on 28 February 1975 in Lomé (Togo) between 46 Africa, Caribbean and Pacific (ACP) countries (37 African, six Caribbean and three Pacific) and nine EEC member states, 'resolved to establish a *new model* for relations between developed and developing States, compatible with the aspirations of the international community towards a more just and balanced economic order' (emphasis added).

In turn the Lomé I Convention was preceded by Yaoundé Convention, which was again preceded by the Treaty of Rome. With regard to the Treaty of Rome, not only were the associated states to define and determine their aspirations, but Section 4 of Article 132 is also explicit on the issue of equality among the EEC member states.[5] Apart from Somalia, all the associated countries were former colonies of France and Belgium. Yaoundé I was followed by the Yaoundé II Convention, signed between the 18 Associated African States and Madagascar (AASM) member states and the 6 EEC member states on 29 July 1969 to reaffirm and renew their association on the basis of the objectives enshrined in Yaoundé I. Meanwhile a new form of relationship and agreement had been reached between the EEC and the three member states that formed the East African Community (EAC 1968), Kenya, Tanzania and Uganda. Although the objectives of this agreement were the same as those governing the EEC–AASM relationship, the EAC states became known as *partner states*, rather than *associated states*.

Yaoundé II was replaced by the Lomé I Convention, representing a transformation, extension and expansion of the provisions of Yaoundé II. Not only was it established on the basis of *partnership* instead of *association*, but also it 'resolved to establish a *new model* for relations between developed and developing States, compatible with the aspirations of the international community towards a more just and balanced economic order'. While Yaoundé I was formally intended to respond to the aspirations of the Associated States, the Lomé I Convention was designed to respond to the aspirations of the 'international community'. Lomé I extended the provisions of Yaoundé II in that the *partners* were 'anxious to establish, on the basis of complete equally between partners, close and continuing co-operation, in a spirit of international solidarity'. The Lomé I Convention had the following objectives:

To establish, on the basis of complete equality between partners, close and continuing cooperation, in a spirit of international solidarity . . . for the economic development and social progress of ACP States; to promote, having regard to their respective levels of development, trade and cooperation between the ACP States and the Community and to provide a sound basis therefore in conformity with their international obligation; to promote the industrial development of the ACP States by wider cooperation between these States and the Member States of the [European] Community.

By the end of 1995, the ACP states numbered 70 and the EU states 15, making the Lomé IV Convention the largest development partnership in the world outside the United Nations. Against this backdrop *NEPAD* was launched, with objectives similar to Lomé but within a different world political context. Whereas the Lomé I Convention was constructed against the backdrop of the Cold War, *NEPAD* is constructed to reflect what is now known as globalisation. Besides, whereas the Treaty of Rome, Yaoundé and Lomé Conventions were proposed by the European countries, *NEPAD* was proposed by the AU. According to the initiators of *NEPAD*,

[i]n proposing the partnership, Africa recognizes that it holds the key to its own development. We affirm that the NEPAD offers an historic opportunity for the developed countries of the world to enter into a genuine partnership with Africa, based on mutual interest, shared commitments and binding agreements.

(UNECA 2001: nr. 205)

On this score, *NEPAD* is built on moral persuasion rather than economic arguments. First, *NEPAD* assumes that the developed world – or the imagined international community – has a responsibility for Africa's development. The second problem is how to enforce an agreement between Africa and its 'development partners'; even if the developed countries agree to assist Africa, they are not obliged to do so under law; they may not know how to assist Africa; and they may also not have the capacity, ways and means to assist Africa.

NEPAD is thus designed to navigate between vertical and horizontal integration. However, viewed in the context of Africa's relation to the EU, what *NEPAD* did (new) was to ask the United States, Canada and Japan to behave like the EU, thereby expressing the need to *rationalise these partnerships*. On the one hand the need to rationalise these partnerships is a reflection of dependency ('a critical dimension of Africans taking responsibility for the continent's destiny is the need to negotiate a new relationship with their development partners'). On the other hand the need to rationalise these partnerships made 'development aid' or assistance, the agency of Africa's development:

The manner in which development assistance is delivered in itself creates serious problems for developing countries. The need to negotiate and account separately to donors supporting the same sector or programme is both cumbersome and inefficient. Also, the tying of development assistance generates further inefficiencies. The appeal is for a new relationship that takes the country programmes as a point of departure. The new relationship should set out mutually agreed performance targets and standards for both donor and recipient. There are many cases that clearly show that failure of projects is not caused only by the poor performance of recipients, but also by bad advice given by donors.

(UNECA 2001: nr. 186)

Yet as we will see, the problem of maintaining the various partnerships between Africa and the industrialised countries and multilateral institutions is that the old partnerships may serve as an obstacle to fostering new partnerships to cope with the cracks in the new international political economy.

NEPAD and emerging Chinese conglomerates

The *NEPAD* idea of 'rebuilding a continent' is based on economic decline in the 1980s and political implosion in the 1990s, while recognising that Africa experienced economic growth before. However, from the point of view of world system analysis, international political economy, and public finance, the economic analysis underpinning the *NEPAD* document was (and is) weak at best and disappointing at worst. First, its weakness is the not explicitly stated assumption that the world market is controlled by the developed countries. In reality, the world market is beyond the control of every country. The last sentence of the *NEPAD* document says that '[i]n fulfilling its promise, this agenda must give hope to the emaciated African child that the 21st century is indeed Africa's century' (UNECA 2001: nr. 207). From a world system perspective, it is an illusion; at the time of the drafting and launching of *NEPAD*, there was every indication that this century was becoming an Asian century. A recent *Newsweek* (2004) report indicates that of the world's $2.5 trillion foreign reserves, four Asian countries, namely, China, Japan, South Korea and Taiwan, own $1.5 trillion or 60 per cent. If the nineteenth century was Britain's century, and the twentieth century was America's century, the twenty-first century will be China's century.

A second weakness of *NEPAD*, from an international political economy point of view, is the economic analysis underpinning the programme as there is no connection between economic development on the one hand, and infrastructure development on the other. Not only do the authors assume that 'the international community' has responsibility towards Africa's economic development, but also they assume that infrastructure development has to take place before economic growth can take off (à la Rostow?).[6] This disconnection between infrastructure development and economic growth is contrasting with indications that economies grow faster when infra-structure and other economic activities are growing simultaneously. At least in China, economic growth in the past two decades went hand in hand with infrastructure development. On this score the role of China's conglomerates should not be overlooked as the above CICI case with its many investments in infrastructure showed.[7]

A third weakness of *NEPAD*, from the point of view of public finance, is that it heavily depends on private foreign finance and lacks a Plan B. '[I]f infrastructure is to improve in Africa, private foreign finance is essential to complement the two major funding methods, namely, credit and aid' (UNECA 2001: nr. 103). This of course raises the question which private capital will develop Africa's infrastructure? The assumption that foreign will, foreign credit and foreign capital are instrumental in infrastructure devel-opment may explain why the West Africa Gas Pipeline, which ECOWAS agreed to build in 1975, is still on the drawing board: African regional groupings expect too much from their 'development partners' with respect to infrastructure development. This is contrary to the development of the infrastructure in China. When negotiations between Petrochina, a state-owned behemoth and overseas participants (Royal Dutch Shell, ExxonMobil and Russia's Gazprom) broke down regarding a $18 billion west to east gas pipeline, the Chinese government decided to go ahead and build it anyway. Peter Flowerday of Gas Strategies, a consulting firm, said it was not surprising that negotiations broke down. 'It is a bad sign for international companies wanting to invest in China; this appears to be part of a wave of China investing for itself', he said. 'I don't understand why the west–east pipeline needed foreign investment as the Chinese have already gone ahead and built it without foreign help' (*Financial Times* 4 August 2004).

From the point of view of public finance, multilateral institutions' funding for infrastructure development is a dead-end for two reasons. First, different African countries have reached different levels of economic and political development. Political instability in one country can cause a delay in a regional project and thus requires a Plan B to take such factors into account. Second, developed countries compete among themselves within multilateral agencies for contracts. This implies that developed countries tend to 'sabo-tage' each other in the process of competition, even if they give an appearance of unity.

However, from the point of view of international politics and international relations, *NEPAD* is a useful tool because it can be used as an instrument of international diplomacy at several levels. Indeed earlier initiatives from the EU constructed in the context of the Treaty of Rome, such as Yaoundé and Lomé, led to nothing; earlier initiatives from Africa such as the Lagos Plan of Action also led to nothing, and so the circle is complete. *NEPAD* could be used to challenge the developed countries' treatment of Africa as three entities, namely North Africa, Sub-Saharan Africa and South Africa. This in turn can enhance Africa's negotiation capacity within multilateral agencies even though any concession by the developed countries may stem from world economic forces rather than from agreements that cannot be enforced or from moral persuasion. On this score, the economic growth of China and India, and China's integration into the World Trade Organization (WTO) have transformed the old 'Third World' politics of resistance into economics of resistance. In April 1955, the politics of resistance found an early expression in the Bandung Conference (Indonesia), and in the early twenty-first century, led by Brazil, India and South Africa, the economics of resistance gathered momentum at the World Trade Summit in Doha (Qatar) in November 2001, culminating in the collapse of the WTO Conference in Cancun (Mexico) in September 2003.

China's economic expansion has given rise to a major demand for natural resources: China's steel production capacity has eclipsed those of the United States and Japan combined, and it is expanding feverishly. In 2003, China consumed 40 per cent of the world's cement; its demand for metal ores and grain have turned it into a price-setter in international commodity markets; in 2004 China surpassed Japan as the world's second largest importer of oil, after the United States; and China is expected to soon overtake Japan to become the world's second biggest automobile market (*Financial Times* 24 March 2004, 2 June 2004). While China's increasing demand for natural resources could be bad for 'mother earth', to Africa it could be advantageous in the short and medium terms since the comparative and competitive advantage of Africa is natural resources. This is not because Africa is more endowed with natural resources than other continents, but because in Africa it would be comparatively easy to negotiate and cheaper to exploit.

Still, the comparative and competitive disadvantage of Africa is infrastructure. There is thus a mismatch between natural resources and infrastructure development, which in turn has given rise to a disconnection between infrastructure development and economic growth in the economic analysis underpinning of the *NEPAD* programme. This is not surprising because in the past natural resources, as an instrument of international trade for Africa, were (justifiably) also viewed in the context of exploitation, neocolonialism and underdevelopment, and in order to overcome these, the anti-neocolonialism school of thought proposed regional integration and diversification (Rodney 1972). In recent years the issue has been discussed in the context of the 'resource curse' (Ross 1999) and 'enclave production' (Leonard and Strauss 2003). Many conventional and civil wars have been fought and continue to be fought over natural resources, and natural resources and conflict in Africa have become inseparable. Also the scramble for Africa and for that matter the making of modern African nation-states through European-led colonialism was part of the natural resources conflict (Nimako and Willemsen 2004).[8]

Despite its weaknesses *NEPAD* could still be used as instrument to negotiate a natural resource-based international trade regime in exchange for infrastructure development. As China's growth has given way to a large demand for natural resources, for Africa the advantages of trading natural resources for infrastructure with China are twofold: the availability of foreign exchange in China, and the transitional nature of China's conglomerates. There is thus an opportunity to deal with China in the context of South–South cooperation. As time goes on, Chinese conglomerates will develop inter-locking shares with global capital and finance, which will consolidate China's conglomerates on the global capital market and raise the entry cost, eventually blocking Africa from entry and deepening its marginalisation. In 2004, over 170 Chinese (mainland) companies operated in Britain against barely 50 in 2001 (*Financial Times* 25 August 2004). The transitional nature of China's rise means that it is still open to negotiations. Contrary to dealing with Europe, the United States and IFIs, African governments do not need to renegotiate a 'new partnership' with China; African governments can therefore choose to engage with China bilaterally or collectively. However, to engage China in the context of regionalism, *NEPAD* will need to reassess its economic analysis underpinning its programmes on natural resources, infrastructure, and capacity building.

Concluding remarks: beyond *NEPAD*

Clearly, China's economic growth in the past two decades is in sharp contrast to the economic decline and political implosion in much of Africa in the 1980s and 1990s. The ascendancy of China as a major player in the world economy constitutes a crack in the international political economy. Not only does this imply that various countries and regions have to reposition themselves in the world economy, but also the repositioning of China can be advantageous or disadvantageous to Africa, depending on the responses of different African states and their regional groupings.

Like China, most African countries had SOEs before the neoliberal onslaught in the 1980s, but unlike China, African countries have not been able to transform their SOEs into conglomerates. This is partly because China's SOEs were granted more autonomy to operate effectively and efficiently whereas African states resorted to privatisation. Whereas the structural changes in China gave rise to FDI, in Africa they led to debt accumulation. The end result is that African states have neither a vibrant private sector nor a strong state.

In response African states have attempted to intensify regional integration through the launching of *NEPAD*. This programme raises the question as to whether 'you can manage big things if you can't manage small things'; that is, if African elites have failed to manage small national economies, how can they manage large regional entities? Not only did Africa's 'development journey' to Abuja (i.e. *NEPAD*) start in Rome (i.e. the Treaty of Rome) over four decades ago, but also when viewed in the context of world system analysis, international political economy, and public finance, the economic analysis underpinning the *NEPAD* document is weak and disappointing, partly because *NEPAD* was built on moral persuasion rather than economic arguments. The implications are that through *NEPAD* Africa is increasingly tying itself to the traditional dominant economic forces in the world (the United States, the EU and Japan), at a time when these traditional dominant economic powers are becoming less dominant due to the rise of China.

Nevertheless, viewed in the context of international politics and international relations, *NEPAD* is a useful tool because it can be used for international diplomacy at several levels. In particular, *NEPAD* could be used as an instrument to negotiate a natural resource-based international trade regime in exchange for infrastructure development. For Africa, the advantages of trading natural resources for infrastructure with China are twofold. The first is that China now controls a large share of world foreign exchange reserves. The second is the transitional nature of China's conglomerates. In sum, there is still an opportunity for Africa to deal with China in the context of South–South cooperation. If properly managed by African governments, the emergence of China as a major economic force and the rise of its conglomerates could relieve Africa from its debt burden and dependence on IFIs and EU and US donors. If poorly managed by African governments, however, China's demand for natural resources could make Africa a battle ground reminiscent of the 'scramble for Africa' in the late nineteenth century.

Notes

1   This article is dedicated to Andre Gunder Frank (1929–2005), my teacher, colleague and friend.
2   Of the 53 African countries surveyed for 1990 and 1997, six (Botswana, Equatorial Guinea, Lesotho, Mauritius, Sudan and Uganda) recorded GDP growth rates of more than 5 per cent; 19 experienced growth rates of between 3 to 5 per cent; and 23 less than 3 per cent, whereas five (Burundi, Cameroon, Democratic Republic of Congo, Djibouti and Sierra Leone) slipped into negative growth (ADB 2000).
3   The core business of CICI is the

> contracting engineering projects at home and abroad including design, construction, supervision and equipment installation as well as international and domestic trade, providing technical services and manpower of various occupational categories for foreign firms all over the world, investment and industrial development, technical importation and consultancy service and other forms of foreign economic and technical cooperation.
>
> (CICI 1998)

4   It should be mentioned that in the case of Ghana, state ownership was undermined a decade before Ashanti Goldfields was sold. On 8 May, 1985, the International Finance Corporation (IFC) announced that it was providing loans of $55 million to Ashanti Goldfields Corporation (Ghana) Ltd (AGC), a joint venture between Ghana state and the British firm Lonhro. The loan formed part of a project to co-finance a $158 million, five-and-a-half-year rehabilitation programme of the gold industry. This has been the single biggest investment and privatisation project.

5 The article notes that '[f]or investments financed by the [European Economic] Community, participation in tender and supplies shall be open on equal terms to all natural and legal person who are nationals of a Member State or of one of the countries and territories' (Treaty of Rome, Article 132). It was against this backdrop that the Yaoundé I Convention was signed (two months after the Organisation of African Unity was launched) on 20 July 1963 between 18 African states (AASM) and six EEC member states and Overseas Departments and Territories (ODTs), namely the Dutch Antilles and Suriname, and the French overseas territories and departments.

6 On this issue *NEPAD* mentions two important things.

> The view of the initiating Presidents is that, unless the issue of infrastructure development is addressed on a planned basis – that is, linked to regional integration development – the renewal process of the continent will not take off. Therefore, the international community is urged to support Africa in accelerating the development of infrastructure. [. . .] If Africa had the same infrastructure as developed countries, it would be in a more favourable position to focus on production and improving productivity for international competition. The structural gap in infrastructure constitutes a very serious handicap to economic growth and poverty reduction. Improved infrastructure, including the cost and reliability of services, would benefit both Africa and the international community, which would be able to obtain African goods and services more cheaply.
>
> (UNECA 2001: nr. 197, 101)

7 According to its annual report, CICI has contracted numerous infrastructure development projects, which obviously play an important role in stimulating and facilitating economic growth (e.g. major railroads and railway stations, bridges over the Yangtse River and the Yellow River, cross-sea bridges, tunnels, subways, expressways, city roads, five-star hotels, airport terminal buildings, super-high buildings, embassies, dams, stadiums and electrical and machinery installations).

8 This is partly because the need to secure natural resources (e.g. the need to protect oil fields and maritime trade routes) is at times achieved through military force, but these historical facts do not explain why and how some countries and regions have more military capability to subjugate other regions or countries.

Bibliography

ADB (African Development Bank) (2000) *Regional Integration in Africa*, Oxford: Oxford University Press.
—— (2004) *Africa in the World Economy*, Oxford: Oxford University Press.
Bhinda, Nils, Stephany Griffith-Jones and Matthew Martin (1999) 'Foreign direct investment', in Nils Bhinda, Stephany Griffith-Jones, Jonathan Leape and Matthew Martin (eds), *Private Capital Flows to Africa: Perception and Reality*, The Hague: FONDAD.
CICI (CITIC International Contracting Inc.) (1998) *Annual Report*.
Cooper, Neil (2002) 'State collapse as business: the role of conflict trade and the emerging control agenda', *Development and Change*, 33 (5): 935–55.
Frank, A.G. (1990) 'No end to history! History to no end?', *Social Justice*, 17 (4), San Francisco.
Hinloopen, Jeroen and Charles van Marrewijk (2004) *Dynamics of Chinese Comparative Advantage*, Tinbergen Institute Discussion Paper (TI04–034/2).

Klare, Michael T. (2001) *Resource Wars: The New Landscape of Global Conflict*, New York: Metropolitan Books.

Leonard, David K. and Scott Strauss (2003) *Africa's Stalled Development: International Causes and Cures*, Boulder, CO: Lynne Rienner.

Mullard, C., K. Nimako and N. Murray (1997) *Demographic and Legal Status of ACP Migrants in Europe: ACP General Guide Book*, Vol. 1, Wiltshire: Focus Consultancy.

Nimako, K (1991) *Economic Change and Political Conflict in Ghana, 1600–1990*, Amsterdam: Thesis Publishers.

—— (1996) 'Power struggle and economic liberalization in Ghana', in Alex E. Fernández Jilberto and André Mommen (eds), *Liberalization in the Developing World: Institutional and Economic Changes in Latin America, Africa and Asia*, London: Routledge.

—— (2002) 'Labour and Ghana's debt burden: the democratisation of dependency', in Alex E. Fernández Jilberto and Marieke Riethof (eds), *Labour Relations in Development*, London: Routledge.

Nimako, K. and G. Willemsen (2004) 'Suriname en de banvloek van haar natuurlijke hulpbronnen' (The resource curse of Surinam), in H.W. Campbell and F.E.R Derveld (eds), *Wegen van verandering: In dicaties en effecten van politieke, economische en sociale ontwikkelingen in Suriname*, Beuningen: Studia Interetnica.

Robinson, Peter B. (1996) 'Potential gains from infrastructural and natural resource investment coordination in Africa', in Jan Joost Teunissen (ed.), *Regionalism and the Global Economy: The Case of Africa*, The Hague: FONDAD.

Rodney, Walter (1972) *How Europe Underdeveloped Africa*, Dar es Salaam: Tanzania Publishing House.

Ross, Micheal L. (1999) 'The political economy of the resource curse', *World Politics*, 51: 297–322.

Samuelson, Robert J. (2004) 'China, trade and progress', *Newsweek*, 5 April: 47.

South Centre (1993) *Facing the Challenge: Responses to the Report of the South Commission*, London: Zed Books.

UNECA (1981) *Lagos Plan of Action for the Economic Development of Africa 1980–2000*, Addis Ababa: UNECA.

—— (1989) *African Alternative Framework to Structural Adjustment Programmes for Socio-Economic Recovery and Transformation, AAFF-SAP*, Addis Ababa: UNECA.

—— (2001) *New Partnership for Africa's Development (NEPAD)*, www.uneca.org/eca_resources/Conference_Reports_and_Other_Documents/nepadNEPAD.htm. Addis Ababa: UNECA.

United Nations Security Council (2002) *Plundering of DR Congo Natural Resources: Final Report of the Panel of Experts on the Illegal Exploitation of Natural Resources and Other Forms of Wealth of DR Congo*, www.reliefweb.int/w/rwb.nsf/vID/706B89B947E5993DC1256C590052B353.

World Bank (1989) *Accelerated Development in Sub-Saharan Africa: An Agenda for Action* and *Sub-Saharan Africa: From Crisis to Sustainable Growth*, Washington, DC: World Bank.

14 The risky business of cocoa in Ghana

Local entrepreneurs in a buyer-driven chain

Anna Laven

With the beginning of the new millennium an issue of the 'old millennium' has returned to the international agenda, namely the dependence of developing countries on agricultural value (or commodity) chains and its link to poverty (CEC 2004; Oxfam 2004; UNCTAD 2003). There are approximately 50 countries in which three or fewer agricultural export commodities constitute the bulk of export revenue (CEC 2004: 4). From 1980 to 2002 the prices of 12 tropical agricultural commodities declined between 50 and 86 per cent, and these price-falls were relatively highest in countries in Africa (Oxfam 2004: 3). This has resulted in high losses in export earnings for most African countries.

The economic crisis in countries that are highly dependent on the export of a few agricultural export commodities does not only reflect the imbalance between industrialised countries and so-called developing countries but also the imbalance between suppliers of agricultural export commodities and international buyers. Poor small-scale farmers who, together with their caretakers and workers, form the majority of suppliers of agricultural export commodities in developing countries, are part of the same value chain as large international buying companies (e.g. Nestlé) that continue to reap enormous profits.

While the price-falls in agricultural export commodities had rather disastrous results for the position of producers of these commodities in agricultural value chains, international buyers have become stronger entities due to takeovers that have taken place and increase in scale of their operations. Furthermore, the introduction of the structural adjustment programmes (SAPs) by the World Bank in the 1980s increased the control that these buyers exercise on (parts of) the chain, even in the absence of ownership, which makes these chains increasingly 'buyer-driven' (Fold 2002; Humphrey and Schmitz 2000). The introduced reforms stipulate a reduction of state's involvement in the provision of well-organised marketing channels and services and the opening of these markets to competition (Akiyama *et al.* 2001). The entrance of new (private) actors in agricultural sectors affected the composition of agricultural value chains and the way these chains are being governed.

Focusing on the cocoa sector of Ghana, this chapter will discuss how the position of small-scale cocoa farmers develops in a chain where buyers have not only become the main drivers, but have also become more powerful due to the concentration of their operations. Another interesting issue is how other local entrepreneurs behave in such a chain and what kind of role they fulfil. Ghana is presented as an exceptional case because 'unlike other cocoa producing countries, Ghana has systematically tried to protect its effective system of parastatal-based governance' (Kaplinsky 2004: 25). However, in Ghana reforms have also taken place, be it on a more gradual scale compared to other cocoa-producing countries in the region. The result is that the Ghanaian state continues to play a role in a sector where a growing imbalance between suppliers and buyers occurs and new relations, between buyers and suppliers as well as between other actors, develop.

Whether the ongoing involvement of the Ghanaian state reinforces the imbalance or rather opposes it is not immediately clear. In order to explore whether farmers and other local entrepreneurs in Ghana are really better off than their 'colleagues' in fully liberalised economies this chapter will look at the reforms that have taken place in other cocoa-growing countries in West Africa, where cocoa production is concentrated. After that I will discuss the reforms that have taken place in Ghana, and their impact on the position of local entrepreneurs. But first, in order to understand the concept of value chains and the way these are governed, I will elaborate more generally on buyer-driven agricultural value chains, with a focus on coffee and cocoa, and the (new) risks that buyers and suppliers of these commodities perceive.[1]

Shifts in governance in agricultural value chains

Looking closely at the impact that the price-falls in agricultural export commodities have had on the position of their suppliers, some rather disastrous results become evident. Coffee, which worldwide has the largest market and is produced in more than 70 developing countries, has experienced the greatest fall in price. The coffee price in 2002, adjusted for inflation, was just 14.2 per cent of that of 1980 (Oxfam 2004: 3). This has forced coffee farmers to leave the coffee business or to sell their coffee beans for less than they cost to produce. Market forces have not been able to solve this problem. In some countries, reforms in the coffee sector have resulted in an increase in the producer price paid to farmers. However, it has been argued that the positive effects of liberalisation are often exaggerated because of the prominent place this policy has on the international agenda. According to Kaplinsky (2004: 12) even though in several countries farmers have started to receive a greater share of the profits that accumulate within the producing countries, their share of total profits in the chain as a whole has fallen.

In the case of cocoa, which is more important than coffee in sub-Saharan Africa in terms of export value, one can also see an overall decline in prices:

in 2000 the world cocoa price was only a third of that of 1980, but recently it has recovered up to 70 per cent (ICCO 2004). The structural adjustment policies have exacerbated the economic problems of cocoa farmers. Although the reforms, as intended, did increase the share of the freight on board (FoB) price paid to the farmers, their absolute incomes declined and the fluctuating prices posed new risks to them. The SAPs reduced the participation of the state in the provision of services such as extension services and put an end to subsidies on chemicals that were used to combat pests and diseases (from now on called *input*). This has resulted in a fragmentation of the institutional support for cocoa farmers as well as in higher production costs. The imposed reforms forced farmers to consider farming not simply as a way of life but as a profitable occupation.[2] Liberalisation, however, did not go hand in hand with institutional reforms that could have enabled the farmer to participate as a real entrepreneur in the chain. Tiffen (n.d.) confirms this for cocoa farmers in Ghana and claims that farmers are likely to be 'losers' in the process of liberalisation. 'Winners' on the other hand are to be found among large buying companies, who have become stronger entities in agricultural value chains.

Both the coffee and the cocoa sectors have experienced a worldwide concentration of their processing industries and manufacturers. In the coffee sector, trading is concentrated with just three firms dominating (Volcafé Holding Ltd, Neumann Kaffee Gruppe and ECOM Agroindustrial Corporation) (Kaplinsky 2004), while Philip Morris and Nestlé together hold almost 50 per cent of the market share of manufacturing. In the Netherlands, Douwe Egberts (a subsidiary of US food conglomerate Sara Lee) covers 69 per cent of the entire consumer market (Oxfam 2004: 11). In the cocoa sector, we see similar high levels of concentration among both cocoa processors and chocolate manufacturers. Between 1970 and 1990 some 200 mergers and acquisitions took place, and, as a result, by the mid-1990s about 70 per cent of all cocoa grindings were conducted by the top ten corporations, with the three largest accounting for 50 per cent. Archer Daniels Midland (ADM) became the world's largest cocoa processor with the takeover of Grace Cocoa and the buying of the cocoa processing units of E.D. & F. Man in 1997, followed by Cargill. Barry Callebaut became the world's third largest processor in 1996, with the takeover of Callebaut by 'Cocoa Barry'. The Netherlands is the leading cocoa-processing country and Amsterdam is the world's leading cocoa import and distribution point. Among chocolate manufacturers the six largest constitute 60 to 70 per cent of the world market, with Mars being the world's number one, followed by Nestlé, Cadbury Schweppes and Ferrero SpA (ICCO 2003; Vingerhoets 1997).

These concentrated multinational corporations have a growing potential to limit competition and force down prices (Gilbert 2000). Like other commodities, annual fluctuations in cocoa bean prices are caused by changes in the world markets' supply and demand for the product. Historically, cocoa bean prices have fluctuated in tandem with the availability of stocks of cocoa beans in relation to the annual world grindings (which measure the world demand for cocoa beans); when the 'stocks-to-grindings' decline, the price of cocoa beans rises. Stabilisation of the cocoa stocks used to be regulated by the International Cocoa Agreement, but this system was abandoned in 1994 due to a shortage of funds to finance the buffer stocks. The private sector, however, has no shortage of funds and owns a giant stock of cocoa, equalling two-thirds of total demand. The main owners of these stocks are cocoa-processing companies and traders who hold cocoa in stock for the futures market,[3] which allows them to determine the price levels. Kaplinsky (2004: 28) therefore warns for a growing asymmetry of incomes in both coffee and cocoa chains.

The imbalance between international buyers and local suppliers in agricultural value chains is aggravated by the trend that these chains become increasingly 'buyer-driven'. The increased control of international buyers over the chain partly resulted from the need to take over tasks that prior to liberalisation were the responsibilities of the state. The reduced involvement of the state in marketing and the provision of services made buyers more vulnerable to possible flaws in the performance of their suppliers in developing countries (Fold 2002; Humphrey and Schmitz 2000, 2002). This explains why buyers have become more concerned with specifications of both products and processes further back along the value chain. The level of 'buyer-driven-ness' has also increased due to the (new) risks perceived by buyers related to changes in consumer demand.

The growing importance that consumers give to non-price factors, such as product quality, and the increasing concerns about health and safety, and environmental and labour standards have increased the risks for supplier failure, as it is expected producers in developing countries will have difficulty meeting these changing requirements because usually these do not (yet) apply to their domestic markets and/or because they require high investments (Keesing and Lall 1992 in Humphrey and Schmitz 2000: 16). This development also entails risks for suppliers. In some cases, farmers are obliged to bear the costs of compliance to new standards, and moreover run the risk of being excluded from the market if they fail to meet these new requirements. In other cases buyers will actively look for partnerships with suppliers and support them in meeting the new demands, which can benefit producers of agricultural commodities. A pre-condition is that these producers are to some extent organised, as they are large in number and in general small in scope, which makes it difficult for buyers to reach them.

The increasing risk of supplier failure has made international buyers actively search for new alliances with local suppliers. These shifts are captured by the distinction that Humphrey and Schmitz (2000, 2002) have made between different types of governance in a global value chain. Humphrey and Schmitz (2000: 4) define governance as 'coordination of economic activities through non-market relationships', and they see the risk that buyers face as the key determinant of governance. Three different types of governance are being distinguished: first, 'network relations' based on cooperation between 'equals'; second, 'quasi-hierarchy', combining cooperation with asymmetrical power relationships in which buyers dominate over suppliers; and third, 'hierarchy', associated with vertical integration, in which the buyer takes direct ownership of the operations (Halder 2002; Humphrey and Schmitz 2000; Palpacuer 2000). In case buyer and supplier do not need to collaborate in product definition, because either the product is standard, or the supplier defines it without reference to particular customers, the term 'arm's-length market relations' is used, which is often considered a fourth type of governance. The increasing risks that buyers face may result in a shift from arm's-length relations to more active forms of cooperation between buyers and suppliers, such as network and quasi-hierarchical relations (Humphrey and Schmitz 2000).

To determine the implications of these shifts in governance we need to establish how power is distributed in agricultural chains. Gereffi (1994: 97) uses the concept of 'global chain governance' to link global value chain analysis with power relations, which he defined as 'the authority and power relationships that determine how financial, material, and human resources are allocated and flow within the chain'. This concept is helpful in an analysis of the impact of a shift from arm's-length relations to quasi-hierarchical relations, in a situation where international buyers are still determining the flow of resources within the chain. It also enables us to look more closely at the role and power of other actors.

The cocoa sector in transition: experiences in West Africa

Cocoa is an internationally traded commodity, with a total production of around 3 million tons, and a value of around $6 billion (Gresser and Tickell 2002). Approximately 14 million workers worldwide are involved in cocoa production, some 10 million workers of which are in Africa (ICCO 1999). Originally the cocoa tree comes from tropical rainforests in the Amazon and Mexico, but once established in Ghana cocoa production expanded rapidly and by the mid-1920s Africa became the main producer. Nowadays, West Africa is responsible for over 70 per cent of the worldwide production of cocoa, with the world's largest producer Côte d'Ivoire providing 40 per cent of global supply, followed by Ghana, and then Nigeria, Cameroon and Togo.

Before market reforms in West Africa took place, cocoa in this region was produced and marketed under state-controlled systems. Different marketing and pricing systems operated in the different cocoa producing countries. Anglophone countries produced under the marketing board system while Francophone countries made use of the stabilisation fund. The low cocoa prices in the mid-1980s were the incentive for liberalisation; the general notion was that reforms would enable an increase in the producer price by reducing the costs of inefficient marketing and pricing systems and by improving efficiency of related cocoa activities. As the World Bank expected major advantages of such market reforms they were imposed on countries in West Africa through SAPs. Table 14.1 presents the World Bank view on the differences between a free market system, the stabilisation fund and the marketing board system with respect to cocoa-marketing and cocoa-pricing systems (Akiyama *et al.* 2001). All West African cocoa-producing countries undertook some reforms: Cameroon, Nigeria and Togo initiated drastic reforms, while Côte d'Ivoire and Ghana chose a more gradual approach to liberalisation.

Before looking into the gradual reforms that have taken place in Ghana, I will briefly discuss the effects of the reforms of other cocoa-producing countries in West Africa. With the marketing reforms in the different cocoa-producing countries in West Africa competition was introduced among buyers of cocoa. The removal of restrictions on who could engage in cocoa trading caused the entering of a large number of new (foreign) traders and middlemen. These newcomers were often inexperienced. Local buyers, who feared that they might start to take over their market share and exploit their market power, looked upon the increased number of foreign buyers with apprehension. In Côte d'Ivoire this fear has become a reality, given that 'by 2000, 85 per cent of all Ivorian exports were in the hands of foreign firms' (Kaplinsky 2004: 24).

As planned the reforms in the cocoa sector reduced the marketing costs and resulted in higher producer prices, as farmers received a higher share of the FoB price. However, due to the decline in world cocoa prices the absolute price increase was considerably lower. In Côte d'Ivoire the producer price initially even fell below the price as set prior to liberalisation. It is only recently that the world cocoa prices have gone up again. Even though this

Table 14.1 The World Bank view on differences in cocoa marketing and pricing systems

	Free market	*Stabilisation fund*	*Marketing board*
Legal ownership of crop	Traders, exporters	Traders, exporters	Marketing board
Physical handling of crop	Traders, exporters	Licensed private agents	Marketing board
Domestic price setting	Market forces	Stabilisation fund	Marketing board and government institutions
Price stabilisation	None	Yes	Yes, but not explicit
Taxation	Absent or very low	Mainly explicit	Implicit
Producer prices	High	Medium to low	Low

Source: Adapted from Akiyama *et al.* (2001: 41).

improved the position of farmers and helped to recover the general economy of the country, cocoa farmers in Côte d'Ivoire are still poorly paid (Akiyama *et al.* 2001). Also in Nigeria prices are currently unstable and unfavourable. In Nigeria the percentage of the FoB value increased substantially, which boosted cocoa production and exports (Akiyama *et al.* 2001; LMC International and University of Ghana 2000), but the expected raise in income was limited as a result of a sharp decline of the exchange rate of the local currency (naira) in 2001. Togo was more successful, as the share of the FoB price expanded from below 60 to 80 per cent, which compensated for the fall in world price. Since the reforms meant that price guarantees were no longer given, in all countries the fluctuating prices have posed new risks for producers, who have seen their income become less secure.

After the reforms cocoa was purchased with little regard for quality, and much was exported before it had been fully fermented and dried. Especially in countries where the process of liberalisation took place almost overnight, as Nigeria, the quality of the cocoa beans deteriorated. This meant a loss of the premium on the world market and a decline in demand for Nigerian cocoa, which ultimately resulted in a loss of income for the farmers as well as for the state. Warnings against quality deterioration by international buyers as well as governments of cocoa-producing countries have been frequent for the poor-quality cocoa caused a loss of $18 million annually (Cocoa Producers' Alliance 1998; LMC International and University of Ghana 2000). The deterioration in quality, however, is not only the result of liberalisation. In Nigeria it was also due to a deficiency in the foreign exchange sector, whereas in Côte d'Ivoire the quality of cocoa may always have been mediocre. Besides, the production of high-quality cocoa is not necessarily in the interest of farmers (cf. Gibbon 2003) as producing premium quality cocoa involves high costs for them.

Due to the institutional reforms in the cocoa sector production costs went up. Prior to privatisation inputs were in general free or heavily subsidised, but privatisation of input distribution caused enormous production cost increases in Nigeria and in Côte d'Ivoire. This situation was exacerbated because of a reduced availability of labour and land, increasing the costs of production and the demand for credit (Cocoa Forum 2004). Yet in most cocoa-producing countries, as a result of the reforms, the position of local banks weakened. In Côte d'Ivoire the consolidation of foreign buyers made it more difficult for local financiers to spread their risk (ICCO 2003). In Cameroon credit facilities generally diminished, and while well-developed arrangements for the export sector existed, there were only a few credit facilities for the farmers, rendering it utterly impossible to pay for the higher costs of production (Cocoa Producers' Alliance 1998). In Nigeria the lack (and irregularity) of credit facilities for investment in the productivity of farm operations, together with the lack of accessible land for expansion of cocoa production has resulted in poor maintenance of farms.[4] Also with liberalisation the subsidies on extension services fell, and consequently the quality of services declined. The private sector took over part of these responsibilities. Although this development has received support in for example Nigeria, scholars such as Gilbert (2000) argue that the provision (or subsidising) of extension should remain a priority of the government as the private (and/or civil) sector is often unable to undertake effective extension. In general it is concluded that cocoa extension services are under-funded and that institutional support for extension is lacking (Amezah 2004). Weak extension services render it more difficult to bring new knowledge and technology to the farmers, affecting their ability to upgrade their product and production process and to anticipate on market changes.

Contrary to the intention of the reforms, overall a less enabling environment for farmers has been the result. The World Bank view on the different characteristics of cocoa-marketing and -pricing system as presented in Table 14.1 proves to be incomplete and exaggerates the advantages of a free market system. By focusing on the differences in producer price it neglects the development of the world price, its volatility and the increase in costs of production, which resulted in a decline in farmer income. It also fails to integrate the effect of the transfer in financial risk of cocoa production from the state to the farmer. Still, the reforms did have certain positive effects. As a result of the introduced competition among local buyers of cocoa, buyers started to make sure that they paid promptly and began to provide additional services to cocoa farmers. For example in Nigeria local buyers started to provide pesticides on a credit basis, and in Côte d'Ivoire buyers sought collaboration with farmer-based organisations (Amezah 2004).

Considering institutional reforms at the level of the farmers, most cocoa-producing countries tried to strengthen their cooperative structure. Organised farmers have been better able to negotiate for prices and services, but the farmers' response to the reforms has not helped them to sufficiently overcome the increase in production costs and the reduced availability of services. There are still many farmer groups that are not operational, often because they do not have enough members and/or lack equipment and funds, and many cooperatives are still very weak and require institutional support. In Côte d'Ivoire the (international) cocoa industry is involved in the strengthening of cooperatives and searches for alliances with organised suppliers, partly because of the increased risks for supplier failure.[5] Another factor is the growing interest of consumers of cocoa products in sustainable production methods, which is partly a response to the recent tumult about the cases of child labour on cocoa plantations in West Africa (cf. IITA 2002). International buyers want to gain more control over the supply side of the chain and increase its transparency. The Sustainable Tree Crop Programme (STCP), which is a public–private partnership, offers a platform for buyers to deal with these kinds of issues in the region.

The need for buyers to gain more control on the supply chain has also been a reason for international processors to increase their grinding activities in cocoa-producing countries. Prior to the SAPs the state-owned marketing boards (or the stabilisation funds) were the dominant drivers of the chain. The state fulfilled the role as intermediary, which made it possible for international buyers to buy cocoa without any direct relation with their suppliers. After liberalisation, instead of the state, international grinders and, to a lesser extent, chocolate manufacturers became the main drivers of the cocoa production chain (Kaplinsky 2004: 24). Local buyers took over the role of the state as intermediary and have increasingly become involved in the provision of marketing channels and services, credit and input.

Liberalisation of the cocoa sector in Ghana

Cocoa has dominated the political economy of Ghana since 1920. Local farmers and their families who responded very successfully to the world demand for a new cash crop created the cocoa industry. According to Dennis Austin (in Anin 2003: 56): 'Cocoa built the roads, harbours, railways, schools, hospitals, and universities; it capitalised domestic trade and its local markets; it gave impetus to the nationalist movement . . . it has continued to finance the state and its civilian and military rulers'. In the early 1970s Ghana was the world's leading cocoa producer. However, due to a drastic fall in the world market price, together with droughts and bush fires, Ghana lost its leading position to Côte d'Ivoire. Currently Ghana produces around 18 per cent of the world's cocoa production, which makes it the world's second largest producer of cocoa (World Cocoa Foundation 2005). Cocoa provides around 30 per cent of Ghana's export revenue and is still considered to be the economic backbone of the country. An estimated 3.2 million Ghanaians are involved in cocoa production in Ghana (ICCO 1999), from a total population of almost 19 million people.

Prior to liberalisation the organisation of the cocoa sector was rather straightforward. The Cocoa Marketing Board (Cocobod) was in control of external and internal marketing and there was only one (state-owned) buying company, the Produce Buying Company (PBC). Different subsidiaries of Cocobod provided support and services for the farmers. The Cocoa Marketing Company (CMC) of Cocobod sold all cocoa beans to buyers overseas, which were responsible for roasting, grinding, the making of cocoa products and the branding and marketing of these products (see Figure 14.1).

Liberalisation of the cocoa sector in Ghana is, just like in other countries, not a new phenomenon. Until the 1940 establishment of the West African Cocoa Control Board, which was replaced in 1942 by the wider West African Produce Control Board (WAPCB), the cocoa sector in Ghana had been operating under a free market system. In 1947 Cocobod was established and (resulting from wartime regulations) it was decided that through Cocobod the British Ministry of Food was to be the only seller of the cocoa produced in Ghana, while the existing (mainly expatriate) cocoa-buying companies were appointed agents of the WAPCB and continued to have responsibility for buying (Anin 2003: 15). In 1953 the United Ghana

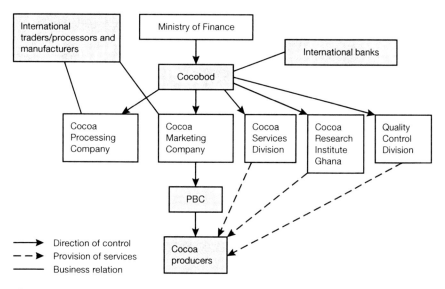

Figure 14.1 The cocoa sector in Ghana prior to liberalisation

Farmers' Cooperative Council was founded as 'a general farmers organisation with political objectives', and it became the so-called farmers' wing of
the Convention People's Party (CPP) led by President Nkrumah (Beckman
1976: 11). The Farmers' Council was given sole responsibility for cooperative development and it became the head of the movement. In 1961 the
Farmers' Council took over the cocoa trade and became the monopoly
buyer of Ghana's cocoa. This nationalisation of the local cocoa was a turning
point from fairly liberal economic policies to a more state-controlled
economy. When in 1966 the Nkrumah government was overthrown by a
military coup, the Farmers' Council was dissolved and banned (Beckman
1976: 11–17; Dadson 1988). However, the monopoly by the government
on external as well as internal marketing prevailed: PBC remained the sole
local buyer of cocoa until liberalisation in 1992, and CMC is still the sole
exporter of cocoa beans.

Reforms in Ghana already started in 1981. As part of the Economic
Recovery Programme reforms in the cocoa sector were implemented through
the Cocoa Rehabilitation Project and the Agricultural Sector Adjustment
Programme. The Cocoa Rehabilitation Project put emphasis on reform of
the cocoa sector and liberalisation of Cocobod and its subsidiaries, attempting
to stop its declining production trend at the time (Fold 2002; Ministry of
Finance 1999), but the reforms did not significantly alter the organisation
of the cocoa sector. Officially Cocobod (still) functions under the mandate
of the Ministry of Finance, although its staff level decreased drastically. In
the early 1980s there were approximately 100,000 people employed by

Cocobod while in 2003 this number was only 5,140. Many former employers of Cocobod are still involved in the cocoa sector, as private consultants, providers of extension services and/or as buyers of cocoa. Cocobod continues to determine the producer price of cocoa and is still the sole exporter of cocoa beans. Through a system of forward sales Cocobod manages to pre-finance the cocoa and it is responsible for regulation of the internal marketing of cocoa. In short, despite the reforms Cocobod still governs the cocoa production chain and holds a central position in the national cocoa cluster as the provider of marketing channels and services.

Liberalisation of internal marketing

The liberalisation of internal marketing started in 1992. The objective was to improve its operational and financial performance in order to enable higher competitive producer prices. The price set by the government would function as the administrative/floor price. Until 1992 PBC had been the only buyer of cocoa, but with the liberalisation of internal marketing also private licensed buying companies (LBCs) entered the cocoa sector. In order to avoid a monopolistic position of one of the buyers, anti-monopoly regu-lation was put in place to check speculative mergers and takeovers. At the community level LBCs hire so-called purchasing clerks, who buy the cocoa directly from the farmers and/or their caretakers.

Recently PBC itself has been partly privatised and its shares are traded on the stock market, with the government being the company's major share-holder (39 per cent). PBC remains the largest buyer of cocoa in Ghana and holds around 35 per cent of the market share, but other companies seem to be catching up. In 2003 there were around 20 LBCs registered; however, their number fluctuates over time, as does their active involvement in cocoa buying. The number of (local) foreign buyers is still limited to two: Armajaro and Olam, owned by their parent companies in the UK and Indonesia respectively. LBCs receive a yearly fixed 'buyers-margin' set by the govern-ment, and all buyers, including PBC, have to keep to this percentage. Unfortunately, since the introduction of competition in internal marketing the quality of Ghanaian cocoa has declined. Whatever the exact cause, the result has been that international buyers have rejected Ghanaian beans, and this has (temporarily) damaged the good reputation of Ghana as producer of premium quality cocoa.[6]

As the reforms in other West African countries have had an overall nega-tive effect on the quality of their cocoa, most stakeholders agree that a process of further liberalisation in Ghana should be approached with due caution. With all the reforms for both internal and external marketing on the table, one major recommendation is that the final quality control should remain in the hands of the Quality Control Division (Ministry of Finance 1999: 70), even if this means that the costs for (maintaining) the production of premium quality cocoa will be high. According to Fold (2002: 232), even though on paper all the key actors support the maintenance of the quality control system, a shift towards a more flexible system seems inevitable.

In all West African countries the liberalisation of internal marketing has changed the composition of the cocoa chain and affected the power relations within this chain. For instance in Nigeria, with the introduction of competition in internal marketing, private buyers started to offer additional services to cocoa farmers, such as providing pesticides on credit. In Côte d'Ivoire, in response to the perceived risks, buyers have started to seek collaboration with cooperatives. It is evident that competition between buying companies has changed the situation for producers of cocoa as they now can choose whom to sell their cocoa to (although farmers in more remote communities usually only have a choice of one or two LBCs). While the introduction of price differentiation was one of the main goals of liberalisation of internal marketing, it has turned out that LBCs do not compete with regard to the price they pay to the farmers as they all pay the floor price as set by the government. Buying companies have found other ways to ensure that farmers sell (only) to them, ranging from prompt payment to selecting their purchasing clerks with the help of community representatives, social involvement with the farmer communities (e.g. by attending funerals) and/or the provision of services or subsidised input (Farmers Surverys (FS) 2003, 2005).[7]

If buying companies are unable to pay promptly, farmers can decide to sell their cocoa to another buyer. For farmers this is a significant improvement. Yet, our research seems to show that the introduction of competition between buyers has generated more opportunities for farmers than are currently utilised. In 2003, more than 65 per cent of the farmers interviewed indicated that they did not receive any help from the buying companies, which can be partly explained by the lack of organisation among farmers. Organisation of farmers into farmer groups could help them in, for example, bargaining with LBCs for services, input or the provision of credit (FS 2003).

Liberalisation of external marketing

Following the introduction of competition in the internal marketing of cocoa the government decided to also allow qualified licensed cocoa-buying companies to export part of their cocoa purchases as of October 2000. It was decided to start the liberalisation of external marketing with a 70:30 split between CMC and the LBCs. Officially, LBCs are allowed to export 30 per cent of their domestic purchases if they meet the conditions set by the Ministry of Finance. A period of transition would allow the LBCs to become familiar with external marketing and to acquire the necessary techniques. At the same time it would allow CMC to continue with forward selling in order to maintain the fixed producer prices. One of the lessons learned from the experiences of other cocoa-producing countries was that a lack of professionalism among buyers created considerable losses in quality. The transition period was planned to end in the season of 2002–3, at which point a decision was to be taken on whether full liberalisation of the external market would indeed be the best strategy to follow. However, a formal decision has not yet been taken, and from interviews with representatives of the Ghanaian government and Cocobod it can be concluded that they are in no rush to implement further reforms.

Despite the formal changes, in practice none of the LBCs is currently exporting cocoa directly to international buyers, which means that CMC continues to handle all external marketing of cocoa beans, cocoa liquor and cocoa butter. The high volumes traded by CMC enable offshore borrowing to finance local purchases. Due to the reliable marketing system Cocobod and CMC enjoy a high reputation for contract and quality fulfilment, for which they receive a cocoa premium on the international market. Because the price is still determined before the crop is harvested, farmers are guaranteed reliable income (even if the price of cocoa in the world market falls in the course of the purchasing period), and the government is similarly assured its revenues from cocoa (Ministry of Finance 1999: 83).

Representatives of the government and Cocobod have been stressing the incapability of buying companies to take over the role of CMC (Laven 2005). They claim that the buying companies are not ready to export and/or are not interested in exporting directly. However, in interviews LBC representatives argue that although some local private buyers do meet the requirements Cocobod is deliberately hindering their involvement in export activities. Yet most LBCs do not complain about these practices as they depend on Cocobod for their licence to buy cocoa.[8]

In reality, then, LBCs operate under the restrictions of CMC. Fold (2002: 232) argues that

> the extent of these restrictions depends on the balance of forces between, on one hand, the World Bank and bilateral donors' pressure for full scale price competition throughout the chain and, on the other hand, alliances between domestic and foreign pressure groups to maintain or change only slightly the present system.

Currently the balance of forces is in favour of alliances between domestic and foreign pressure groups, which predominantly consist of representatives of Cocobod and the Ghanaian government and international processors and manufacturers of chocolate. Ghana is considered a 'safe haven' for the cocoa industry, because the country produces consistent quantities of good quality cocoa for which the international buyers have to put in relatively little effort (besides the paying of a premium). It is obvious therefore that the vested interest, of both the Ghanaian government and international buyers, in the cocoa sector and the way it is currently organised is high. Ghana's recent achievements in terms of attaining an increased producer price (up to more than 70 per cent of the FoB) as well as a boost in the production of cocoa beans (from 409,000 tons in 1997–8 to 625,000 tons in 2003–4), together with the negative experiences in other cocoa-producing countries that have liberalised the cocoa sector, seem to have convinced the World Bank that for now further reforms are not a priority in Ghana.[9]

In Ghana, despite reforms, the government's control over the private sector thus remains high, and competition among buying companies remains limited due to their restricted resources. This rather repressive regime does not favour the development of a strong and active private sector that is able to take over tasks of the public sector. In the long term, if full liberalisation is indeed considered the end-goal, the current situation is not beneficial for the sector as a whole. If LBCs are expected to be 'main movers in restructuring the domestic part of the chain', as suggested by Fold (2002: 232), they should to be trained and supported instead of slowed down. Unprofessional buyers are no real competition for foreign buyers, and, consequently, in the future foreign buyers may take over the market share of local buyers and exploit their market power.

For farmers the result of the current situation is that buying companies are less motivated to invest money in the provision of services to them. A great deal of the promises made by LBCs has not been fulfilled (FS 2003). In addition, purchasing clerks, who are key figures in the cocoa supply chain because they are in direct contact with the farmers, have not been sufficiently trained. As a consequence, these clerks not only cheat the farmers with wrongly adjusted scales, but they are also accused of buying cocoa that is not yet thoroughly fermented and/or dried (FS 2003, 2005). This has resulted in the rejection of Ghanaian cocoa on the world market, with the effect that cocoa farmers have not been paid for their produce.

Institutional reforms and shifts in governance

As already argued, liberalisation has not gone hand in hand with institutional reforms that could have enabled farmers to set up their own buying company and to participate as a real entrepreneur in the chain. According to Tiffen,

> the concepts underpinning the liberalisation process ignored the institutional framework in Ghana and the severely disadvantaged position of farmers which made them vulnerable and therefore likely 'losers' in the process. From the institutional perspective small-scale farmers appear to have been invisible to the designers and implementers of Structural Adjustment Programs in Ghana.
>
> (Tiffen n.d.)

Tiffen rightly poses the question why 'in the vacuum created by the abolition of the state marketing boards, . . . weren't new forms of institution, for example farmers co-operatives, considered, given the context of a rural-based activity like commodity crop production?'

Cooperative enterprise in Ghana was introduced in the cocoa industry around 1928 as the government wanted farmers to become organised into groups in order to teach them improved ways of fermenting cocoa for higher-quality beans. This set-up was successful and stimulated a fast expansion of cooperatives in cocoa and other crops. In addition to product upgrading, cooperation among farmers also improved input and credit facilities. By 1937, there were over 400 cooperative societies (Dadson 1988: 173). The cooperative movement became an economic and political force under the socialist model of the Nkrumah government, but in the 1980s it was this political involvement that caused the collapse of the cooperative movement. Currently there is only one cocoa cooperative registered by the Department of Cooperatives, the Ghana Marketing Cooperative Association, but due to mismanagement it is no longer operational. Whereas most farmers recognise the benefits that can result from cooperation, 44 per cent of the farmers interviewed in 2003 declared that they did not work together in any way (FS 2003).[10]

Not officially registered as a cooperative, but often referred to as Ghana's only major cocoa cooperative, is the Kuapa Kokoo Union (KKU), which is both a farmers' union and a buying company. KKU was established in 1993 with the support of the SNV Netherlands Development Organisation and the English non-governmental organisation (NGO) Twin Trading, and is also supported by the UK Department for International Cooperation. KKU has approximately 45,000 members, and these farmers are the owners of the company. The mission of KKU is to 'empower farmers in their efforts to gain a dignified livelihood, to increase women's participation in all of its activities, and to develop environmentally friendly cultivation' (Kuapa Kokoo Limited 2002).[11] In general there seems to be agreement about the positive achievements of KKU (Mayoux n.d.; Tiffen n.d.), and KKU is frequently asked to become involved as a partner in projects that concern the sustainable production of cocoa. Nevertheless, research among several Kuapa Kokoo societies shows that KKU (just like any other buying company) depends to a high extent on the benevolence of the purchasing clerk who buys the cocoa from the farmer. While in principal KKU is supposed to be owned and controlled by farmers, in reality some of the participating farmers are unaware of KKU's semi-cooperative status and consider it just as any other buying company (FS 2003).[12]

The changes in institutions that (used to) provide services to Ghanaian farmers have resulted in a less enabling environment. Experiences in other countries, where liberalisation negatively affected the quality control systems, have made Cocobod insist on maintaining the control of production of good quality cocoa. According to representatives of Cocobod the recent problems with quality are directly related to the recent involvement of private buying companies in quality control on the society level. The Cocoa Services Division used to have the monopoly on the procurement and distribution of inputs, but in 1995 the Ghana Cocoa, Coffee and Sheanut Farmers Association took over this responsibility. The objective of this privatisation of input supply was to increase competition, which would (hopefully) lead to the availability of the right quantity of inputs at the right time, and moreover effect a reduction in the price paid for the inputs. The real outcome of privatisation, however, was different: the removal of subsidies, depreciation of the local currency (cedis) and high interest rates resulted in an enormous rise in the price paid for inputs, which directly affected the rate at which these inputs were being used. Private input suppliers have entered the market, some of which are foreign-owned, though Ghanaians own the majority.

In addition to its role as input provider, the Cocoa Services Division used to be responsible for Cocoa Extension Services, which consisted of advising farmers in cocoa and coffee production, the production and distribution of planting materials and the control of pests and diseases (Amezah 2004: 1). In 1999, the extension services of the division were merged with that of the Ministry of Finance to reduce the costs and staff of Cocobod so as to create more cost effective agricultural extension services to farmers. The new idea was that since most cocoa farmers also cultivate other crops (and some of them keep livestock), they should be considered as 'general farmers' and receive a unified extension system (Ministry of Finance 1999). In practice, this new policy of a unified extension system has been problematic and is heavily criticised (and currently reviewed by the government).

The lack of adequate extension services has resulted in experiments with farmer-based extension in the so-called farmer field schools, based on local level cooperation between farmers and supported by public institutions and (international) NGOs. Supposedly these schools are a cost effective means to get technical assistance to farmers, relying on farmers themselves and a 'learning by doing' approach in which farmers share newly acquired knowledge with other farmers (CI (n.d.)). Inadequate extension on the part of the government has also been a reason for the private sector to become involved in providing these services. For example Wienco, one of the major input providers, is active in educating farmers on effective use of input and the importance of good farm practices. Finally, there is also an initiative by the World Bank to link research more explicitly to extension services.

Liberalisation of input distribution and the reform of extension services have thus resulted in shifts in responsibilities and in the introduction of new actors in the cocoa chain. Farmers who participated in farmer field schools are in general most satisfied with the received support. Also Wienco has managed to reach a considerable number of farmers and to establish a relation of trust with them. However, as these new initiatives cannot reach all the farmers many of them are worse off because input has become more expensive and extension services are not working effectively. Simultaneously, on average the need for the use of input has increased, due to the migration of farmers to the Western region, where the soil is less suitable for cocoa production and due to the rehabilitation of old cocoa farms in the Eastern region (Nyanteng 2005 in Laven 2005). Farmers thus increasingly need support and access to credit.

With respect to credit facilities, the situation in Ghana shows a growing involvement of the LBCs. It is increasingly common practice that in order to get a loan from a local bank farmers need a guarantee of an LBC. The main reason for this is that rural banks have had bad experience with providing credit to farmers in the past. For LBCs the provision of credit can be a way of committing farmers to sell their cocoa to them.[13] Although the involvement of buying companies in the provision of credit has increased, these companies are just like banks, that is, overall they remain reluctant to lend money to farmers, as farmers often fail to pay back their loans. The recent collapse of buying company Cashpro, which went bankrupt because of standing debts of farmers, has contributed to this unwillingness.

Still, farmers do not solely rely on LBCs for access to credit. They may acquire a loan through the bank if they have a savings account. However, most farmers do not earn enough to be able to save money, and banks charge between 28 and 36 per cent interest per year and demand collateral, in the form of land or a farm. In many communities in Ghana there is no 'bank–farmer' relationship because farmers tend to mistrust banks and prefer to keep their money in the house, whereas banks are often too far away and at times have no cash available. Other options are the private moneylenders who lend money at a 50 to 100 per cent interest rate, or borrowing money through credit unions. Following the withdrawal of subsidies, between 1990 and 1993 Cocobod, the Cocoa Services Division and PBC put in place a credit scheme to assist farmers to purchase inputs for farm maintenance. The credit was interest free, given in kind, and channelled through farmer societies. Recently both the government and the Agricultural Development Bank re-introduced a comparable initiative by providing fertiliser on credit (the so-called high-tech programme). The government has taken measures to ensure that the LBCs guarantee the payback of the loans.

In general, though, the credit facilities for farmers in Ghana are inefficient and insufficient. The issue of large distances and consequent high transaction costs could be solved through strengthening so-called non-bank financial intermediaries such as credit unions and informal lending systems. The setting up of cheque cashing centres (closer to the farmers) or mobile bank facilities has also been explored (Ministry of Finance 1999). In addition, new experiments have been taking place with providing loans to groups of farmers, who are then collectively responsible for the payback. Although in the past similar experiments have often failed, it is widely recognised that farmers' need for credit is very high, which is why some banks, with the involvement of other partners such as LBCs and input providers, are willing to try it again.

In most cocoa-producing countries liberalisation has altered the way the cocoa chain is being governed, and instead of the state, international grinders and chocolate manufacturers have become the main drivers of the cocoa production chain. Even in the exceptional case of Ghana foreign grinders are coming onto the scene. This is partly the result of the political insta- bility of Côte d'Ivoire, and partly caused by domestic policies that aim at adding local value to the cocoa beans. Currently four processing factories are operational. The Cocoa Processing Company Limited at Tema used to be a subsidiary of Cocobod, but now has been privatised with Cocobod as its major shareholder. Two other processing factories in Takoradi are run by the West African Mills Company (WAMCO), which is a joint venture between Cocobod and a small German processor. A fourth processing company has recently been installed in Tema, namely the Swiss 'giant' Barry Callebaut. Together these processors use around 18 to 22 per cent of the total bean production (Ministry of Finance 1999).

The increasing presence of the foreign private sector is not limited to marketing activities and grinding, but is also observed in the provision of services and the strengthening of farmer-based organisations. This has to do with the increased risks of supplier failure perceived by (international) buyers of cocoa. Some processors and manufacturers have chosen to keep an office in the country. The recent commotion about cases of child labour on cocoa plantations in West Africa has increased the need for more control on the supply chain. In Ghana it is difficult for the chocolate industry to deal directly with farmers and their local buyers, as Cocobod is still standing in between, but also there are the industry attempts to establish more direct relations with their suppliers.[11]

Taken together, the increased presence of international buyers in Ghana has contributed to an imbalance in the cocoa chain, as they have become stronger entities in a chain where local suppliers (and local buyers) have not been able to strengthen their position. However, the involvement of inter- national buyers in the supply chain also creates opportunities. As we have seen, some of these buyers even use their power to improve the position of farmers, and reverse some of the existing imbalance in the cocoa value chain.

Conclusion

The experience with liberalisation in other major cocoa-producing coun- tries (in terms of a decline in the produced quality of cocoa beans, a fall in farmers' income and a less enabling environment for farmers) gives reason to be sceptical about the benefits from further reforms in Ghana. The gradual scale of the reforms that have taken place in Ghana make it possible for the government to continue with guaranteeing a minimum price for cocoa and secure the export of premium cocoa, which tempers the growing imbal- ance between buyers and suppliers. Furthermore, the Ghanaian government is still in a position to intervene in domestic cocoa production. They have recently realised a remarkable increase in the producer price paid to the farmers and have contributed to a boost in national cocoa production. Foreign pressure groups, consisting mainly of international buyers, share the interest of the Ghanaian government to maintain or only slightly change the present system. They fear that further liberalisation will affect the quality and the consistent supply of Ghanaian cocoa.

The alliance between the government of Ghana and international buyers has created a rather static regime in which little attention is paid to the imperfections of the cocoa sector, to new opportunities, and to how the system can be improved. In Ghana, then, a situation has occurred where the government hinders, instead of enables, local private buying companies in optimising their operations, thereby jeopardising their future ability to compete with foreign buyers. As a result farmers are also worse off, as they receive little support from buying companies that are not motivated (nor able) to invest in a better position for producers of cocoa. In this sense, the government in Ghana contributes to the imbalance in the chain between local suppliers and international buyers, rather than opposing it. The government has also failed to facilitate the formation of new forms of institutions that would (continue to) support (the organisation of) farmers, as the services of Cocobod's subsidiaries diminished due to the gradual reforms and the costs for cocoa production increased.

This less enabling environment has made it difficult for Ghana's cocoa farmers to operate as real entrepreneurs. The private sector, which has taken over the state's role as intermediary, is not (yet) capable of fulfilling the institutional vacuum that resulted from the gradual reforms. Given the increased asymmetry in the value chain, there is urgent need for the producers of cocoa to find ways of strengthening their position in the cocoa chain. This could be accomplished through farmers organising themselves, and Ghanaian farmers are aware of the importance of working together, but consensus, trust and resources are lacking. They stress that others should facilitate a process of organisation and support the farmers with expertise and money. So far, little has been achieved in Ghana.

Based on the experiences in other cocoa-producing countries in West Africa it can be concluded that Ghana should be cautious with further liberalisation of the cocoa sector. However, such caution should not be confused with bringing the process of liberalisation to a standstill. The current status quo is too risky for farmers and local buyers, as well as the state. Although the alliance between buyers and the state is strong, its existence depends mainly on the buyers. Currently, international buyers prefer Ghana because of its consistent supply of high volumes of good-quality cocoa, despite the higher prices. However, as soon as a cheaper alternative becomes available they will most likely move away from Ghana. Instead of leaning heavily on this temporary alliance with international buyers, the state should strengthen farmers and local buyers of cocoa, and enable them to survive in a future of a fully liberalised cocoa sector.

Notes

1 Apart from the mentioned references, the following websites have been consulted for (background) information: www.cocobod.gh , www.divinechocolate.com/kuapa. htm, www.eftafairtrade.org , www.ghana.co.uk, www.fairventures.nl/cocoa.html, www.finance.gov.gh, www.icco.org, www.nipc-nigeria.org, www.ghana-youth. com, www.southcentre.org.
2 Interview with Mr E. Dwumfour, World Bank Ghana, 2005; see also IFAD (2001).
3 Personal communication with Mr T. Terheijden, Cargill, 2005.
4 In Nigeria, only 5 per cent of the total volume of loans from formal sources goes to small-scale farmers (*www.nipc-nigeria.org*).
5 Cocoa production is highly concentrated in Côte d'Ivoire and Ghana: together they produce almost 60 per cent of world's supply. In 1999 a *coup d'état* caused a political crisis in Côte d'Ivoire, which threatened the trade in cocoa.
6 LBCs, which are nowadays responsible for the initial quality checks, are suspected of pressurising farmers to sell their beans before adequate fermenting and/or drying have taken place (Asenso-Okeyere 1997: 117). It is generally believed that because certain LBCs do not encourage farmers to continue their traditional good farm practices high percentages of so-called purple beans have come onto the market. In interviews, farmers and representatives of LBCs do not confirm this practice. They claim that there are other causes for the purple bean, such as smuggling from Côte d'Ivoire, the increased volume of cocoa and the planting of hybrid trees.
7 Based on interviews with LBCs, and on Farmers Surveys (FS) done during fieldwork research in 2003 and 2005. In one of the surveys among farmers we asked the farmers how they selected the LBC they wanted to do business with. Prompt payment was put forward most frequently as the decisive selection criterion, followed by a social relation with the purchasing clerks.
8 Most LBCs as well as other stakeholders in the chain emphasised during the interviews that the stake of the Ghanaian government in cocoa is very high and that for this reason their representatives are reluctant to let the private sector become involved in direct export of cocoa. It has also been suggested that in addition to unwillingness the government itself is 'not ready' because of its weak tax collecting system.
9 Interview with Mr E. Dwumfour, World Bank, Ghana, 2005.
10 These farmers only work with their family and occasionally with seasonal workers, yet as much as 96 per cent of the farmers who were not members of a cooperative expressed a desire to become members. During group discussions (FS 2003, 2005) cocoa farmers gave various reasons for this difference between desire and practice, in particular: the absence of cooperatives; a lack of trust; a lack of consensus among farmers; and a lack of support. If we look at other countries we see that external donors and other agents play a role in facilitating farmer organisations, but in this regard little has been achieved in Ghana.
11 KKU produces a small part of its cocoa as fair trade cocoa for the Max Havelaar Foundation. The farmers who are members of KKU receive a small extra bonus for each bag of cocoa. Another benefit for the farmers is that there are two credit schemes where farmers can save money and apply for a loan. In addition to its activities in cocoa production and internal marketing, KKU is an official shareholder of the Day Chocolate Company, which produces Divine fair trade milk chocolate in the UK.
12 Interview with Nana Osafo-Ansong, Senior Advisor SNV, 2003.
13 Also on the informal level LBCs, via purchasing clerks, are at times involved in providing (small) credit to trustworthy farmers.

14 In 2003, the STCP started an office in Ghana, and has been experimenting with the provision of extension through the set-up of farmer field schools. Chocolate manufacturers (e.g. Mars) who are active partners in STCP expect that these schools provide a structure among farmers that contributes to the traceability of the chain.

Bibliography

Akiyama, Takamasa, John Baffes, Donald Larson and Panos Varangis (2001) 'Market reforms: lessons from country and commodity experiences', in Akyiama *et al.*, *Commodity Market Reforms, Lessons of Two Decades*, Washington, DC: The International Bank for Reconstruction and Development/The World Bank.

Amezah, Kwame A. (2004) *Draft: The Impact of Reforms (Privatization of Cocoa Purchases and CSD/MOFA Merger) on Cocoa Extension Delivery*, Ministry of Food and Agriculture, Directorate of Agric. Extension Services, Accra, Ghana.

Anin, Theophilus Ernest (2003) *An Economic Blueprint for Ghana*, Accra: Woeli Publishing Services.

Asenso-Okeyere, Kwadwo (1997) 'Transforming agricultural production and productivity for sustained rapid growth and development', in Institute of Statistical, Social & Economic Research (ISSER), *ISSER Ghana in the 21st Century, ISSER Millennium Seminar Series*, Accra: University of Ghana.

Beckman, Björn (1976) *Organising the Farmers, Cocoa Politics and National Development in Ghana*, Uppsala: Scandinavian Institute of African Studies.

CEC (Commission of the European Communities) (2004) *Communication from the Commission to the Council and the European Parliament, Agricultural Commodity Chains, Dependence and Poverty – A Proposal for an EU Action Plan*, COM(2004) 89 final, Brussels.

CI (Conservation International) (no date) *Conservation Cocoa in Ghana, Purpose and Progress*.

Cocoa Forum (2004), see www.businessdayonline.com/index.php?fArticleId=2681 (accessed 15 July 2004).

Cocoa Producers' Alliance (1998) 'Problems arising from the liberalisation of cocoa trade in Nigeria and ways on how these problems can be resolved', in paper presented during Workshop on the Liberalisation of the Cocoa Trade, Lomé (Togo), 26–8 October.

Dadson, J.A. (1988) 'The need for cooperative reorientation – the Ghanaian case', in Hans Hedlund (ed.), *Cooperatives Revisited*, Scandinavian Institute of African Studies, Seminar Proceedings 21, Stockholm, pp. 173–80.

Duursen, John van, and Derk-Jaap Norde (2003) *Identifying and Assessing Convergences of Interest for Stakeholders in the Ghanaian Cocoa Chain, in Order to Attain Increased Farm Income and Wider Sustainable Production*, EPCEM internship at AGIDS, University of Amsterdam.

Fold, Niels (2002) 'Lead firms and competition in "bi-polar" commodity chains: grinders and branders in the global cocoa-chocolate industry', *Journal of Agrarian Change*, 2 (2): 228–47.

GCMA (Ghana Co-operative Marketing Association Limited) (2002) *3-Year Strategic Plan 2003–2005* (First farmer-based organization in Ghana), Accra: GCMA.

Gereffi, Gary (1994) 'The organization of buyer-driven global commodity chains: how US retailers shape overseas production networks', in G. Gereffi and M. Korzeniewicz (eds), *Commodity Chains and Global Capitalism*, Westport, CT: Praeger.

Gibbon, Peter (2003) *Commodities, Donors, Value Chains Analysis and Upgrading*, Copenhagen: Danish Institute for International Studies.

Gilbert, Christopher L. (2000) 'Commodity production and marketing in a competitive world', *UNCTAD X Presentation*, Bangkok.

Gresser, Charis, and Sophia Tickell (2002) *Mugged, Poverty in your Coffee Cup*, Oxfam, Make Trade Fair.

Grobler, Carmen (no date). Available from www.knet.co.za/cgchocolate/origin.htm.

Halder, Gerhard (2002) *How does Globalization Affect Local Production and Knowledge Systems: The Surgical Instrument Cluster of Tuttlingen*, Heft 57/2002, Duisberg: Gerhard-Meractor-Universität Duisburg.

Humphrey, John, and Hubert Schmitz (2000) *Governance and Upgrading: Linking Industrial Cluster and Global Value Chain Research*, IDS Working Paper 120, Institute of Development Studies, University of Sussex and Institute for Development and Peace of the University of Duisburg.

—— (2002) 'Developing country firms in the world economy: governance and upgrading in global value chains', in IDS-INEF project, The interaction of global and local governance: implications for industrial upgrading, Heft 61/2002.

ICCO (1999) 'How many smallholders are there worldwide producing cocoa? What proportion of cocoa worldwide is produced by smallholders?', www.icco.org/questions/smallholders.htm.

—— (2003) 'Information on the effects of liberalisation on Ivory Coast's cocoa market', www.icco.org/questions/ivory.htm.

—— (2004) 'Daily prices of cocoa beans', www.icco.org/prices/pricesave.htm.

IFAD (2001) 'Rural Poverty Report 2001 – The challenge of ending rural poverty', www.ifad.org/poverty/chapter2.pdf.

IITA (2002) *Child Labour in the Cocoa Sector of West Africa, A Synthesis of Findings in Cameroon, Côte d'Ivoire, Ghana and Nigeria*, under the auspices of USAID/USDOL/ILO, Sustainable Tree Crops Program, International Institute of Tropical Agriculture.

Kaplinsky, Raphael (2004) *Competitions Policy and the Global Coffee and Cocoa Value Chains*, Institute of Development Studies, University of Sussex, and Centre for Research in Innovation Management, University of Brighton.

Kuapa Kokoo Limited (2002) *2001–2002 Annual Report*, Ghana: Kumasi.

Laven, Anna (2005) *Towards a Sustainable Cocoa Chain, A Ghanaian Perspective*. Report of a workshop held at the British Council, 31 of March 2005, in collaboration with Professor V.K. Nyanteng and SNV Netherlands Development Organisation, Accra, Ghana.

LMC International and University of Ghana (2000) *Liberalization of External Marketing of Cocoa in Ghana*, Accra: Cocoa Sector Reform Secretariat and School of Administration, University of Ghana.

Mayoux, Linda (no date) *Case Study: Kuapa Kokoo, Ghana*, Enterprise Development Impact Assessment Information System (EDIAIS): Institute for Development Policy and Management (IDPM) of Manchester University; Women In Sustainable Enterprise Development Ltd (WISE Development); and DFID. Available from www.enterprise-impact.org.uk/informationresources/casestudies.shtml.

Ministry of Finance (1999) *Ghana Cocoa Sector Development Strategy*, Accra: Ministry of Finance.

Oxfam (2004) *The Commodity Challenge, Towards an EU Action Plan, A Submission by Oxfam to the European Commission*, Oxfam, January.

Palpacuer, Florence (2000) *Preparatory Note, Characterizing Governance in Value Chain Analysis*, IDS/Rockefeller Foundation Meeting on Global Value Chains, Bellagio, Italy, 25 September–2 October, Montpellier: CREGO, University of Montpellier II.

Tiffen, Pauline (no date) 'The creation of Kuapa Kokoo', www.divinechocolate.com.

UNCTAD (2003) *Economic Development in Africa, Trade Performance and Commodity Dependence*, New York and Geneva: United Nations.

Vingerhoets, Jan (1997) *The World Cocoa Economy: Perspectives on a Global Level*, Head of Economics and Statistics Division, International Cocoa Organization: London, www.cacao.sian.info.ve/memorias/pdf/01.pdf.

World Cocoa Foundation (2005) *Partnership Meeting*, Renaissance Brussels Hotel, 3–4 May.

Part IV

Central and
Eastern Europe

15 The Kremlin and the oligarchs

Clashing economic interests in Russia

André Mommen with Vasiliy Valuev and Serghei Golunov[1]

The Russian financial crisis of 1998 marked the beginning of the end of President Yeltsin's regime. After Putin's election in 2000 the oligarchs monopolising the media, the banking sector and the exporting industries were losing their foothold. Backed by the security forces Putin was opting for a strong and centralised Russian state financed out of export revenues. He does not regret the fall of communism, but the loss of centralised control that ensured political and military stability. Putin has no intention of reversing the privatisations of the early 1990s; he prefers to create a working relationship between state and enterprises in order to achieve the declared goals of sustained economic growth, financial stability and military strength. In the meantime, Putin launched a war on the oligarchs controlling Russia's exporting industries in the sector of oil, gas and metals. Tight control on export gains has to generate financial reserves to be used for a comprehensive industrial modernisation project that has to strengthen Russia's position as an important economic power and as a major player in the Eurasian region.

Putin's war on the oligarchs and his re-centralisation policy have concentrated much more power into the hands of the Kremlin administration than under his predecessor Yeltsin. This was at the expense of local power brokers and oligarchs who had acquired vested interests in Russia's regions. What is clear is that Putin's concept of modernisation is based on two mutually dependent approaches: the first one is recreation of national capital, and the second one is Bonapartist corporatism. In Putin's corporatist model a group of well-performing export-oriented companies has to become the backbone of a strong and centralised state monitoring accumulation of capital. Therefore, Putin explicitly wants to cope with mismanagement of Western technical and financial assistance programmes; to make the Russian transforming industry competitive and to give it access to foreign markets; and to use a part of Russia's huge oil and gas revenues for the funding of a modern welfare state. The question whether Putin is aiming to make Russia independent from pressures coming from the West is rather hypothetical now that the Kremlin has acquired a solid position in the Europe–Asia region and has extended its control over the country.

In this chapter several aspects of Russia's politics and economic policy-making will be studied. Much attention will be paid to the position of industrial conglomerates dominating the export sector and active in the mining and oil and gas sector. Furthermore, two major industrial regions, Nizhny Novgorod and Volgograd, will be analysed. Both regions are known as important industrial centres dominated by conglomerates belonging to the military-industrial complex and by industries suffering from the post-communist economic downturn.

The Russian privatisation game

Much has changed since President Yeltsin's resignation on 31 December 1999. The neoliberal ideologues have lost their influence in politics. Putin's presidential party could gain an impressive majority in the State Duma. The Russian economy is recovering from a deep crisis wherein it had sunk at the end of the Soviet empire (Bogomolov 1992), but transition from socialism to capitalism proved to be extremely painful. According to Joseph Stiglitz all calamities Russia has experienced during the long transition period were caused by *external* pressures exercised by the International Monetary Fund (IMF) and US Treasury Department on Russian shock-therapists and economists whose faith in the market was unmatched by an appreciation of the subtleties of its underpinnings, that is, 'of the conditions required for it to work effectively' (Stiglitz 2000: 5). These ultra-liberal reformers, however, completely failed to move Russia towards a real market economy as they paid little attention to the institutional infrastructure that would allow a market economy to flourish. The shock-therapists not only believed in their quick reforms, but also speculated on the creation of a group of people – later to be known as the oligarchs – with vested interests in capitalism in order to prevent a reversion to communism. The result was a lost decade in which most people lost any confidence in neoliberalism and Western-style capitalism.

Super-privatiser Anatoly Chubais, who as deputy prime minister and head of the privatisation organisation Goskominushchestvo (GKI) was one of the main architects of the introduction of Western-style capitalist reforms, believed that Russian enterprises had to sever their links with the state and the political machinery. Therefore the Russian parliament passed on 11 June 1992 a law on privatisation. Vouchers worth 10,000 roubles each to every Russian citizen were issued. The vouchers could be exchanged for shares in enterprises (Boycko *et al.* 1996: 69–95). A quarter of the shares were directly given to the employees and these employees could purchase another 15 per cent at a discounted price. However, the mighty lobby of industrialists pressed for a second option whereby 51 per cent of the shares were sold to the workers and 49 per cent were auctioned. Finally, a third option allowed a management buyout by a group that promised to restructure the firm. In the end 73 per cent of the privatised Russian enterprises chose the second option, and in 1994 15,000 large and medium-sized enterprises had been privatised.

The voucher privatisations were a source of massive corruption, because they permitted special deals (Blash *et al.* 1997). Managers discovered opportunities to buy vouchers and shares with funds borrowed from their company. Auctions were manipulated. Some young investors were better informed and could get control over the best enterprises. Most oil, gas, diamond, gold and other metal producers were privatised 'privately' because they were hard-currency earners and competitive on the world market. In this privatisation game, the government under Prime Minister Viktor Chernomyrdin played a crucial role. Chernomyrdin was known as the co-founder of Gazprom, an oil and gas company employing 300,000 people, controlling 25 per cent of world's gas production and still being good for 25 per cent of total fiscal revenues (*Le Monde* 1 June 2001). In the case of Gazprom only individual investors were admitted, excluding foreign and professional buyers.

In 1995 a new stage in Russia's economic and political history was reached (Brady 1999). With the presidential elections in the offing and president Yeltsin's low popularity, the Russian state was nearby bankrupt due to heavy subsidies to failing industries and poor tax collection. Oligarch Vladimir Potanin of Uneximbank had a luminous idea: he proposed to the government that a group of bankers should loan funds to the cash-strapped government, with repayment secured by the government's majority stake in key strategic, but lucrative metals, oil and other industries excluded from voucher privatisation. The loans-for-shares was a deal Yeltsin could use in 1996 when he was in need of financial and political support from the oligarchs controlling the media and the banks in order to bar the communist Gennadi Zyuganov the path to the Kremlin. According to former Finance Minister Boris Fyodorov, this loans-for-shares privatisation gave shares as security to the Moscow-based banks of the oligarchs 'splitting up companies among old friends' (Rousso 2001: 9). The right to manage the auctions was parcelled out among the major banks that succeeded in acquiring the firms with bids at or just above the minimum. The biddings were rigged by having affiliates of the banks organising the auctions and by excluding for 'technical reasons' competing bids.

'Auction' became a euphemism for a selling off at knock-down prices. Uneximbank handled the selling of a 38 per cent stake in Norilsk Nickel, but submitted itself the winning bid of $170 million, only $100,000 over the government's minimum price. Refinery corporation Sidanko was auctioned off for $130 million to an affiliate of Vladimir Potanin's Uneximbank, which was also organising the auction. The winner paid the equivalent of 2 cents a barrel for Sidanko's known reserves, when the going rate for international reserves was $4–5 per barrel. Two years later British Petroleum Amoco (BP) paid four times that amount for a 10 per cent stake in the company (primarily for a share in the Kovykta gas field in eastern Siberia from which it planned to pipe gas into China). Surgut with an annual oil output of $88 million a year acquired a 40 per cent stake in Surgutneftegaz, which was the size of France's TotalFina. Lukoil affiliates bought 5 per cent of Lukoil for $250.01 million, only $10,000 over the minimum bid. Auction organiser Bank Menatep bought 78 per cent of Yukos, Russia's second largest oil company, with a bid of $309.1 million, only $9 million over the minimum. A consortium led by Boris Berezovsky won 51 per cent of Sibneft, Russia's seventh largest oil company, for $100.3 million, some $3 million over the minimum bid (Rousso 2001: 10).[2]

After the privatisation drive no financial information was made available to outsiders and most companies refused external audits. Outsiders were denied a seat on the board of directors although they owned a minority of the firm's capital. Managers issued new shares in order to dilute holdings of the other shareowners at a low price. In 1994 a Securities Commission was created, but the authorities showed that they were not interested in taking steps to ensure effective corporate governance. At the regional level governments protected insiders and officials allowed tax breaks in an attempt to protect local employment and to prevent takeovers or, eventually, re-nationalisation (Rousso 2001: 9). In addition, privatisation set a premium on perpetuating inefficiencies and corruption, which 'undermined confidence in government, in democracy, and in reform' (Stiglitz 2002: 159).

At that time, no one knew how concentrated the Russian economy was or who the real owners of the new industrial conglomerates were. It took the Kremlin many years to investigate the privatised firms dominating the national economy. Finally, in July 2004 the Russian Audit Chamber acknowledged a fundamental survey of the results of Russian privatisation that took place in the 1990s. Over an eight-year period the auditors checked 140 enterprises to find out whether they were legally privatised and whether the Russian state incurred any losses in the process. Auditor Vladislav Ignatov stated that in 56 out of the 140 cases serious violations were committed, and that as a result of the privatisation of these 56 enterprises the Russian state incurred 45 billion roubles ($1.5 billion) worth of losses. Of the discovered violations 89 per cent were made by state authorities, and only 11 per cent of the violations concerned the actions of new members of state property. The Audit Chamber called the privatisation a socially ill-conceived and economically ineffective project. According to Aleksander Semikolennykh, the deputy chairman of the Chamber, 'the sale of state property did not create a class of private property owners who would be oriented at the social development of the state' (MosNews.com 2 July 2004).

War on the oligarchs?

When Putin took over in 2000 there were signs that the Kremlin was ushering in a form of 'state capitalism' (Sobell 2001; Sakwa 2004). In August 2000, the Kasyanov government established a council for entrepreneurial activities and an investment commission. In his State of the Union address Putin said he would eliminate the 'oligarchs-as-a-class' (*The Economist* 13 May 2000). He warned the oligarchs that their days of running the country were over. In January 2001, when meeting the oligarchs, he denied them the right to control Russia. Obviously, Putin was thinking about exercising a tighter control over the oil and gas exports and making the oligarchs 'observe the rules of the game' (*Izvestiya* 14 July 2000). After all, Russia is the world's biggest exporter of crude after Saudi Arabia. Re-nationalisation of the Russian oil business would give the Kremlin the strategic leverage in oil that it already enjoys in gas, which the state-controlled monopoly Gazprom sells to the former Soviet republics and most EU countries. On several occasions, Putin called for a reconsideration of the oligarchs' accumulated wealth and influence on politics, and clashes between the Kremlin and some individual oligarchs revealed a profound contradiction between the Kremlin centralisers and the *liberal* oligarchs. More important than the conflict in 2000 between Berezovsky and Gusinsky on the one hand,[3] and the Kremlin on the other hand, was the clash that occurred in 2003 between Mikhail Khodorkovsky and the Kremlin about the control over oil giant Yukos, which pumps 2 per cent of world oil production.

When in 1995 Khodorkovsky and his partners bought Yukos from the state in one of the highly controversial privatisation auctions of that period, they acquired an oil-rich company burdened with massive debts, but with a bright future. Khodorkovsky pushed out minority US shareholder Kenneth Dart, and later cold-shouldered Western banks that had sought a sizable share in Yukos after Khodorkovsky's Bank Menatep defaulted on loans during the 1998 financial crisis. Within a few years Khodorkovsky had Yukos transformed into Russia's largest oil company, bringing its production costs per barrel down from $12 to $1.5, the lowest level for the Russian oil industry. Yukos took the lead in introducing Western governance practices and opened its ownership to foreign investors. Khodorkovsky received honours at home and abroad as Russia's most *enlightened* capitalist, funding a literary prize, setting up children camps and schools, financing non-governmental organisations (NGOs) and backing charity projects.

In 2003, Khodorkovsky moved further into the limelight. He criticised Putin's opposition to the war in Iraq, defied the government on the sensitive project of prospective export oil pipelines, and supported anti-Putin liberals in the State Duma. There were speculations about his political and electoral ambitions gained from Yukos' growing economic weight and power. Its acquisition of another leading Russian oil company, Sibneft, was to create the world's fourth largest oil company. Khodorkovsky reportedly discussed selling a part of his stock to a major US oil company, which angered the Kremlin. During a meeting between Putin and the nation's business leaders in February 2003, Khodorkovsky chided the government for laxness in combating graft. Putin responded harshly, questioning the origins of Yukos' wealth and tying it to official corruption. In July 2003, Platon Lebedev, the head of Yukos holding company Group Menatep, was arrested. In October 2003, Khodorkovsky was jailed on tax charges after he threw his billions behind political opponents of Putin.[4] Yukos' assets were frozen and the Tax Ministry put forward a hefty claim. Putin distanced himself from the probe, depicting it as a part of his anti-corruption efforts, but observers argued that Putin wanted to expropriate his rival. In the end, besieged for a year and a half, Yukos was finally and irrevocably eviscerated, while Khodorkovsky remained in prison waiting for his trial. Through a forced auction Yukos' Yuganskneftegaz, which accounted for 60 per cent of Yukos' oil production capacity, was sold by the government for $9.5 billion, ostensibly to pay some of Yukos' huge tax bill.[5]

Khodorkovsky's arrest was meant in part as a warning to the other oligarchs not to fund opposition parties. As it created uncertainty for foreign investors, it also led to a new surge in capital flight. Its legitimate aim, however, was to clamp down on tax evasion – a move that has been reinforced by Putin's appointment of members of the Kremlin administration to the board of the remaining state-owned enterprises. The Khodorkovsky affair clearly showed that tax claims could threaten the oligarchs' survival 'as a class' now that better tax collection had become Putin's most important objective. In 2003, the timing of new tax proposals had attracted attention because of the clash between Putin and Yukos, executives of which have been charged with tax evasion and other crimes. Ministers loyal to Putin, including Finance Minister Alexei Kudrin and Economic Development and Trade Minister German Gref, proposed that the major oil and mineral-producing companies should be subject to new and higher levels of tax. An attempt by the Finance Ministry to raise the tax take from the two Russian aluminium producers, Russian Aluminium (RusAl) and Siberian Ural Aluminium (SUAL), by cancelling tax-free tolling, was abandoned after intense industry lobbying. Another proposal was that mineral producers would no longer be taxed at only 8 per cent (on the domestic price of the metals they produce) and to bring these taxes in line with crude oil taxes (based on the international price, calculated each quarter for Urals blend, the Russian export benchmark for crude oil). In April 2004 the law on a higher rate for the extraction tax for oil and higher crude oil export tariffs was approved by the Russian Federation Council, imposing a 45 per cent crude oil export tariff if oil prices average $20 to $25 a barrel, and if oil prices are higher than the $25 per barrel benchmark, crude oil export tariffs will be 65 per cent. These tax amendments will result in higher budget revenues.[6]

After his clash with Khodorkovsky and after his successful tax reform, Putin launched a new offensive against the oligarchs. On July 1, 2004 he met again with the country's most influential businessmen in the Kremlin. Again, he used the meeting to preach on his usual themes of paying taxes, showing social responsibility and overcoming poverty. The 21 assembled

businessmen learned of the new tax claim against Yukos. Putin told them
that he expected businesses to abandon tax optimisation schemes and indicated that this was only fair given the lowering of taxes such as the unified
social tax and the value added tax (VAT). He expected that all the freed-
up funds should go into the real economy or that they should be invested
in production and in raising wages.

Russian media speculated that Oleg Deripaska would be the next in line
for investigations of his business practice by the Kremlin. But, unlike most
of his fellow oligarchs, Deripaska has no interest in leaving his country.[7] As
an outspoken opponent of Russia's entry into the World Trade Organization
(WTO), he clashed with US ambassador to Russia Alexander Vershbow.
Deripaska's ally in business Roman Abramovich owes his success to Boris
Berezovsky and the latter's friendly relations with then-president Boris
Yeltsin. The two tycoons amassed a fortune, among other things, by
privatising in 1995 the oil giant Sibneft at a fraction of its market value.
Abramovich also bought considerable stock in Aeroflot[8] and RusAl. He was
the first oligarch to conglomerate all of his assets into a single company,
Millhouse Capital, registered abroad. Although he acquired the post of
governor in Chukotka Autonomous Okrug in 2000, he never was in the
focus of the Kremlin's recent crackdowns on oligarchs (which was also a
factor in Sibneft's cancellation of the merger deal with Yukos). Like other
oligarchs, however, he had come under fire when accusations concerning
the origin of his wealth surfaced. When Berezovsky fled Russia in 2000 to
escape fraud charges, Abramovich bought out his stake in Sibneft and the
ORT television network.

It is, of course, no secret that a handful of oligarchs dominate the Russian
economy, but until recently no one knew all the names in the oligarchy,
exactly what they own, how many industries they dominate or to what effect.
Are oligarchs leading the modernisation of Russia, as they claim, or are
they crippling progress? Answers have been hidden behind the thicket of
shell companies that still obscure Russian accounting. The World Bank
dispatched dozens of researchers to cut through the murk and produce the
first clear view of just who controls Russia. In 2003 it released the surprising
finding that the 23 biggest oligarchs control 35 per cent of industrial
sales, high by European standards but less than the 50 per cent claimed by
earlier estimates. The oligarchs dominate, at any rate, the key sectors of the
Russian economy – including oil, gas, metals, autos and banks – but not
much else. In addition, they have only a tiny 2 per cent share of the fast-
growing service sector.

Still, the oligarchs may be a bigger threat than even some pessimists
thought. They undermine small businesses, bargain tax breaks, monopolise
scarce resources, promote corrupt politicians, and export profits. The World
Bank studied regions in which local government had been 'captured,'
meaning that one business won more than half of all preferential legislation
– tax breaks and the like – between 1996 and 2002. The robber barons

did so at the expense of competitors, who saw sharp drops in profit and productivity. Where smaller businesses or foreign companies received preferential treatment, rivals did not suffer – or in some cases actually gained. Why is this? Local legislatures normally weigh the special pleading of businessmen against other interests, but it is hard to resist big tycoons who can threaten to throw thousands out of work if they do not get their way. An oligarch like Abramovich went into local politics in order to influence policy-making.

Another good example is aluminium tycoon Deripaska. In the 1990s, Deripaska belonged to the Yeltsin clan. He is married to Polina Yumashev, the daughter of Yeltsin's former chief of staff, who himself married Yeltsin's daughter. Deripaska's political influence was felt in Moscow, where he supported politicians of the (far) right. One of Deripaska's deputies at RusAl was running in the December 2003 Duma elections on a ticket of the Liberal Democratic Party of Russia. Meanwhile, Deripaska's economic weight has increased as RusAl has $4 billion in annual sales and is the world's second largest aluminium producer. His other businesses include power stations, Russia's largest car and commercial vehicle manufacturer (Gorky Automobile Plant – GAZ), several bus builders, paper and pulp interests, and the country's largest insurance company (Ingosstrakh Insurance). In 1999 and 2000 Deripaska 'captured' the government of the Krasnoyarsk region of Siberia. Thereupon, Deripaska won tax breaks, discounted rail-freight and electricity rates. Local business groups protested that they paid far higher electricity bills than Deripaska's plants, but such firms are no match for oligarchs like Derispaska with a far-reaching influence at the national level.

The upshot of all this is that Putin has to launch a broader campaign to restrain all the oligarchs and to restructure their conglomerates. Critics such as the World Bank and others say Russia needs to encourage both the downsizing of its oversized factories and the consolidation of its undersized companies. They recommend opening the economy to more foreign competition, and encouraging mergers and acquisitions in hope of transforming the oligarchs' holding companies into Russian versions of General Electric (GE) or Siemens. At the same time, they claim Russia needs an aggressive trust-busting agency to break up the monopolies run by the oligarchs, much as the United States did with its own robber barons in the early twentieth century. Russian oligarchs are seen as an obstacle to the highly needed technological modernisation of basic industries. Oligarchs cannot boast about their accomplishments in major industrial projects, the construction of large new plants and investment in high-tech breakthroughs promoting important productivity gains. The Russian oil industry is one of the most advanced sectors, yet its level of production is not impressive: productivity in this branch, with all its technological innovations, declined by 22 per cent from 1985 to 2001. Many Russian conglomerates practise a kind of slash-and-burn strategy; they may buy a coal mine, for instance, and exploit it for short-term profits, then declare bankruptcy without being concerned about the legal implications. In addition, Russian oligarchs have demonstrated the brevity of their time horizons by supporting Western, rather than Russian projects.[9] The conglomerates are headed by investment firms with footholds in tax heavens abroad. Corporate transparency is kept as low as possible in order to avoid taxes and to export profits (Volkov 2002; Gustafson 1999).

The *siloviki*

Putin's war on the oligarchs was fought by his staff and confidants he recruited from the security forces and appointed on strategic political and economic positions. These new men – also called the *siloviki* – do not want to create a new set of oligarchs. Persons originally tipped to be future oligarchs, such as two bankers, Vladimir Kogan and Sergey Pugachev, have continued to prosper, but they have not become extremely wealthy. Officials with suspected business operations are rather small fishes. The most notable ones, Leonid Reiman, the communications minister, and Mikhail Lesin, the former press minister and now presidential adviser, even predate Putin. There are incipient potential oligarchs, such as Alexei Mordashov of Severstal, a steel firm, one of whose executives is now minister of transport. But the main new power-brokers are not oligarchs but executives: people such as Rosneft's Igor Sechin, Kremlin boss Dmitry Medvedev of Gazprom and other advisers to Putin with control over state firms. They all are defending the state's economic interests.

According to Olga Khryshtanovskaya (*The Economist* 7–13 August 2004) the *siloviki* and their allies are – like Putin – second-rate ex-KGB officers who do not want more liberalising reforms in a cash-rich Russia. They want to tighten their grip on the commanding heights of the economy and their power reflects a pattern of rising Kremlin control at all levels of society, including corporate appointments. Igor Sechin, a long-time Putin confident was appointed deputy chairman of the state-owned oil company Rosneft.[10] Another representative of Putin's inner circle, Vladislav Surkov, was appointed to the board of directors of state-owned oil company Transnefte-produkt. Behind it all lies the issue of the world price of oil, which has given Russia high nominal growth. The Kremlin fears a drop in oil prices. When President Bush invaded Iraq in 2003, foreign minister Igor Ivanov feared that oil prices would sink (*The Guardian* 10 September 2004). Since then, Putin has taken direct command of Russia's oil output. In September 2004, he reassured other European leaders that all Russia's – ostensibly privately owned – oil companies 'without exception' would 'continue to increase the extraction of oil and they will increase their deliveries to the global market' (*The Times* 10 September 2004). Meanwhile, the Kremlin was continuing negotiations with Chinese state officials over the potential disposal of Yuganskneftegaz, a division of Yukos that accounts for 60 per cent of its oil production. Apparently, the Kremlin is interested in building an alliance with Peking in order to control this part of Russian oil and gas reserves.

The members of the economic elite demonstrate their readiness to support any twist in the policy of President Putin. For instance, Anatoly Chubais, the supposedly liberal head of the gigantic state electricity company UES, in order to please the president, invented the concept of 'liberal empire'. Another liberal, Alfred Koch,[11] in order to demonstrate his loyalty to the regime, proposed the idea of seizing by military means the Crimea, which is now a part of the Ukraine. In yet another case, the Prosecutor General Vladimir Ustinov, known for his anti-oligarchic views, was ready to ignore the crimes of oligarchs such as Abramovich who were being protected by the president.

The attacks on the oligarchs are also inspired by political factors (Rutland 2003). Perception is that oligarchs try to enrich themselves as much as possible and that they are neglecting the interests of the country. Therefore, the remaining oligarchs may foresee the future with great uncertainty and pessimism. They may fear the major changes in the political system, property rights and economic relations Putin is working out. This explains why they make decisions based on their short-term interests. But not all industrialists tend to ignore the interests of their country. The Russian Union of Industrialists and Entrepreneurs (RSPP) seems to be willing to contribute to the creation of a national programme to fight poverty. Nonetheless, the RSPP is popularly dubbed as a tycoons' trade union. However, RSPP Vice President Oleg Kiselev thought that his organisation should distance itself from the Yukos affair and abstain from criticising courts' rulings on the case. Its president, Arkady Volsky, is preparing a number of social projects, to cover areas such as medicine, agriculture and education, which will be aimed at raising the living standards of the least advantaged groups (*RIA Novosti* 5 August 2004).

When Economic Development and Trade Minister Herman Gref said that the government would decide on a mode of selling off Svyazinvest while retaining its control over 'natural monopolies', Volsky said that Svyazinvest should not have been included in the list of companies slated for privatisation in 2005 and 2006, because public companies of strategic importance could not normally put up for sale in developed countries. But in the minister's opinion, government regulation of conventional communications operators (Svyazinvest holds a controlling block of shares in such companies) makes them less successful in competing with operators providing mobile communication services (*RIA Novosti* 5 August 2004).

Internationalisation

After the financial crisis of 1998 Russian industrial conglomerates started internationalising their businesses and attracting foreign direct investment (FDI). Most Russian conglomerates needed foreign partners in order to solve acute cash problems and to collect investment funds. Norilsk Nickel tried to attract foreign investors to develop the Sukhoi Log gold deposit. Others are mobilising funds out of their commercial activities abroad. OAO Lukoil, Russia's second largest oil producer, expanded throughout the US Mid-Atlantic and the Northeast in these regions where its subsidiary Lukoil Co. owns 2,074 gas stations. Then Lukoil acquired Getty and Mobil stations on the East Coast.[12] Lukoil produces 19 per cent of Russia's oil and 2 per cent of the world's oil. In the United States, most of Lukoil's strength is in the New York area, where it opened its first station in May 2003. President Putin later visited the location to boost the company's efforts. Today, Lukoil gas stations receive their supply mostly from Canadian and domestic sources, but OAO Lukoil's global expansion is aimed at using its new facilities in the Leningrad region (the Vysotsk terminal) to export petroleum products to the United States. For purely *strategic* reasons, Russian mineral conglomerates also established ties with mining corporations in mineral-rich Africa.[13]

In January 2003, Russia's second largest aluminium producer SUAL launched with London-based Fleming Family & Partners SUAL International as its international arm. Its management company is OAO SUAL-Holding (Russia). SUAL International is a vertically integrated aluminium company that will be transformed into a diversified company with assets in the ferro-nickel, tantalum and coal sectors. The SUAL Group, mining about 90 per cent of Russia's bauxites and producing 60 per cent of its alumina and 25 per cent of its primary aluminium, has an integrated aluminium operation, mining bauxite, refining alumina, smelting aluminium and producing semi-finished and some finished aluminium products.[14] The owner of SUAL, Viktor Vekselberg, failed to attract either assets or investors to hit the $3 billion in capital targeted at the time of the launch of his vehicle in 2000. Vekselberg allied with Anglo American and Lonmin. Like other Russian oligarchs he seeks international protection for his Russian assets and dividend income. He visited South Africa where he set up a branch of one of his companies, Renova, in an effort to develop black empowerment deals and secure support in Pretoria. According to the international practices of corporate management, SUAL actively involved highly skilled managers having international experience.

Aluminium giant RusAl's strategy does not differ from that of SUAL. Since 2000, when RusAl was jointly created on a 50:50 base by Deripaska and Abramovich after a merger of a number of the largest smelters and aluminium producers, Russia's biggest aluminium producer with a 75 per cent of all aluminium produced in the country (10 per cent worldwide) acquired a foothold in Ukraine, Jamaica, Armenia and Guinea.[15] In 2003, Russia's largest and the world's third largest aluminium corporation employed 60,000 people in seven Russian regions and nine foreign countries, and had an aluminium output of 2.6 million tonnes and annual sales of more than $4.5 billion. RusAl is planning to set up a multinational corporation with headquarters in Russia (MosNews.com 9 September 2004) in order to maintain its current share of international production while achieving full self-sufficiency in raw materials. Deripaska's international strategy was criticised when he wanted to sell Russia's largest aluminium rolling mill at Samara, plus the smaller Belaya Kalitva plant in Rostov for about $220 million to Alcoa, the US global aluminium leader. Since the Ministry of Economic Development and Trade must give its permission, Deripaska's autonomy has waned. RusAl schemes to buy or build expensive new mines, refineries and smelters abroad have been proposed, but most are still up in the air, awaiting Kremlin judgement.

FDI in Russia's oil and mining sector was frustrated because of particular post-communist business practices. BP-Amoco, which had taken a 10 per cent share for $484 million in Sidanko, saw the controlling shareholders selling its refineries. Vladimir Potanin, president of the Interros Holding, which owned 44 per cent in Sidanko, was hard hit by Russia's financial crisis of 1998. His Uneximbank could not pay interest on a $50 million international bond. Meanwhile, the Fuel and Energy Ministry had restricted Sidanko's access to export pipelines for failing to produce in time proof of debt repayment to the budget and of supplies to local refineries. Then BP was thinking of pulling out of Russia. Tyumen Oil Company (TNK), taking advantage of loopholes in the Russian legislation, acquired Sidanko's producing units Kondpetroleum and Chernogoneft. This prompted BP to launch a fierce anti-TNK campaign in the US, as a result of which the US administration punished TNK by blocking Uneximbank guarantees for a $500 million loan the Russian firm had been due to receive. Chernogorneft was returned to Sidanko. In 2002, TNK sold another 15 per cent of Sidanko to BP for $375 million. By 2004, a pooling of the three companies' assets was announced with BP contributing $6.75 billion to a new holding company to be established jointly with TNK and Sidanko. The partners admitted that their project had the blessing of top officials in Russia and Britain (*Moscow News* 8 October 2004).[16]

After the deal Alfa Bank head Mikhail Fridman philosophised about alliances with foreign investors:

> The agreement between BP, TNK and Sidanko to set up an oil holding company marks a major breakthrough toward Russia's integration into the world economy. We hope it is the first among a large number of future global projects involving Russian and foreign companies. The agreement signifies the international community's recognition of Russia's growing political stability and sustained economic development. It would not have been possible for the three partners to clinch the deal without strong support from the Russian political leadership.
>
> (*Moscow News* 8 October 2004)

The Kremlin's natural resources policy

The Kremlin is well aware of the offshore strategies the oligarchs are developing in close collaboration with foreign companies. Therefore, the Kremlin is exercising a tighter control over mining activities, and tries to extort funding from foreign companies. In March 2004, freshly appointed Minister of Natural Resources Yury Trutnev proposed a set of new measures for adoption by the State Duma. The first was a limitation on the rights of foreign mining companies to bid for Russian mineral deposits. The second was the takeover by the federal government of the two-key system for licensing mineral and oil deposits, eliminating the role of the regional governments. A new territorial limit of no more than 100 square kilometres for exploration permits for mineral deposits, and territorial restrictions for onshore and off-shore oil tracts were also proposed. Trutnev's proposals stopped short, however, of banning foreign companies from certain mineral or oil fields. Thereupon, Trutnev pretended that there were situations when the state should protect the national interests in the sphere of natural resources usage. The small print of Trutnev's proposal would allow foreign miners to bid for Sukhoi Log, so long as they register Russian subsidiaries to do so.[17]

In the meantime, Kremlin adviser on mining policies Vladimir Litvinenko[18] argued that Sukhoi Log, Russia's largest unmined goldfield in the Irkutsk region, was a considerable deposit with a complicated geological structure, and that only in the absence of domestic contenders should foreign investors be invited on the same conditions as the Russian contenders. Litvinenko is hostile to the oligarchs. Calling for the adoption of a mineral and mining code on the model of developed countries with a market economy, he prefers limiting foreign investment to the processing segment of the resource sector. As for mining, he wants a system of privileges and preferences for the domestic firms to a system with foreign investors controlling Russian mining enterprises. Shares can be sold outside Russia, but control should be vested in a 'golden share' held by the Russian state. According to Litvinenko, applying this limit on divestment by the Russian oligarchs was urgent in the cases of Gazprom, UES, Norilsk Nickel, some important oil companies, and several other companies (*Russia Journal* 5 August 2004).

Corporate resistance to any changes into the existing mining legislation proved to be tenacious. When in 2002 Dmitry Kozak, then a senior staff member in the Kremlin forwarded a paper to the government in order to apply South African mining legislation, immediate opposition from the oil businessmen rose. They claimed that a concession scheme is a form of political blackmail. Within weeks the oilmen forced Kozak to retract his proposal. The oil and mining companies think that Putin, in contradiction to Article 9 of the Constitution and other laws, wants to replace the licensing mechanism with concessions and to introduce state ownership of not only subsoil, but also of the natural resources that are extracted. According to Sergey Aleksashenko, vice president of Interros (the controlling shareholder of Norilsk Nickel), it would be

extremely difficult to implement such a law . . . I doubt very much that the state would gain anything from replacing licenses with concession agreements. Adoption of such a law will have disastrous consequences for the Russian stock market and will make the future of [mining and extraction] companies absolutely uncertain. I don't think the state will be able to increase its revenues from rent payments for the use of subsoil in such a way either.

(Russia Journal, 2 November 2003)

The oligarchs have lost much ground since Khodorkovsky's imprisonment in October 2003. That month Aleksander Voloshin lost his job as head of the presidential administration. Apparently, some important policy changes had been prepared, because since then Dmitry Kozak could rise in the Kremlin hierarchy to the post of deputy to the new chief of staff, Dmitry Medvedev. In addition, the presidential administration planned to exercise much more control than before over the exploitation of Russia's minerals. As a part of this move, it proposed to remove licensing powers from the regions, which will increase economic centralisation, reduce regional influence and force companies to concentrate their lobbying efforts on the Federal Ministry of Natural Resources in Moscow. Meanwhile, Minister Yuri Trutnev started actively checking up on the use companies have made of subsoil licences (*Oxford Analytica* 4 August 2004).

In addition, the presidential administration succeeded in gaining tighter control over Russia's gas monopoly. Alexei Miller managed his aim of establishing full control over all key financial flows of Gazprom. Managers from St Petersburg took almost all the important posts in the company. Only the head of Gazexport, the gas company's operator on foreign markets, went to Aleksander Medvedev. By 2001, the state had lost formal control over the monopoly, as some stock was sold to foreign investors and some was distributed among Gazprom's subsidiaries, which were not under the control of top management. Now the state directly owns 39 per cent of the stock and Gazprom subsidiaries under full control hold at least 12 per cent. By using a bankruptcy procedure, Miller kept Sibur assets from slipping out of Gazprom's hands. Sibur owns Russia's largest natural gas-processing plants. Several gas companies, including Severneftegazprom and Zapsibgazprom, as well as oil and gas company Stimul were returned to the Gazprom fold. Gazprom regained control over a number of small but profitable assets, in particular natural gas-filling stations. Control over the agrochemical corporation Azot and gas company Vostokgazprom is being restored. However, Gazprom lost control over two ferrous metallurgy firms. To prevent assets withdrawal, Gazprom approved standard bylaws of associated companies, under which deals in stock require approval of the parent company's board of directors.

Gazprom had been inadequately protected from the beginning, when it was created by rustlers such as Viktor Chernomyrdin, Rem Vyakhirev, and his family. Alexei Miller's appointment by President Putin had to bring Gazprom back into the orbit of the Kremlin. Gazprom managed to restore its control over part of its export supplies, which had floated into the hands of Itera, Sibur and other intermediaries, or had been siphoned off by former Vyakhirev associates such as Alisher Usmanov. Usmanov had been in charge of converting Gazprom receivables and debt into assets and revenue streams managed through Gazprom investment holdings.[19] In order to stop this bleeding, Miller's top management decided to set up a number of large subsidiaries responsible for the company's main areas of activity and their cash flows. Finally, Miller's team managed to cope with the problem of the company's debt and to improve the structure of its portfolio debt. Like the other oil companies he is looking abroad for expansion. In September 2003 he obtained access to terminals of Chevron Texaco in exchange for the share in LN gas projects (*Russia Journal* 23 September 2003, 6 October 2003). Earlier, Gazprom in tandem with Rosneft entered into the similar framework agreement with Norwegian Statoil where it was seeking to access Statoil terminals in North America. In exchange, Statoil was offered a share in the first stage of Shtokmanovsky gas condensate production project, which sets forth construction of the liquefied natural (LN) gas works.

In September 2004 Gazprom merged with Rosneft forming a giant oil and gas company. The centralised holding Rosneft with a unified industrial and financial policy was the only entirely state-owned oil company performing a complete production cycle from geologic prospecting and producing hydrocarbons to sales of the end-user products. Rosneft was engaged in projects in virtually all principal oil and gas regions of the country – in Western Siberia, on Sakhalin, in the Timan and Pechora province, in the south of Russia as well as in a number of foreign countries, including Kazakhstan, Algeria and Colombia.[20] Both Russian and foreign media expressed their doubts about the effectiveness of corporate management of the new monopoly. They started speaking about the 'gazpromisation' and 'yukosisation' of the Russian economy, seeing the Gazprom–Rosneft merger as a political event now that Putin was trying to increase the Kremlin's influence on the oil and gas sector. Prime Minister Mikhail Fradkov said the merger allows the government to obtain a controlling stake in this large company of international significance and solve the problem of liberalising the company's share market. In addition, he said, the merger will boost the competitiveness and effectiveness of the Russian company on foreign markets. According to Gazprom CEO Alexei Miller the company is interested in increasing the percentage of exports in its oil business (*Russia Journal*, 15 September 2004).[21]

Gazprom may be on its way to the creation of a vertically integrated energy giant. Such energy conglomerates are not unique in the world. Evidently, a vertically integrated Gazprom controlling its own outlets and downstream activities will be of crucial importance to Putin's foreign policy to the 'near abroad' and most European countries. The new giant is estimated to control some 177 billion barrels of oil or five times as large as the amount of reserves owned by Exxon Mobil. The merger will allow foreigners to invest in the Russian oil industry with fewer restrictions. However, under Russian law, Gazprom holds sole rights to export natural gas from Russia to other countries.

Bonapartism

After a decade of unlimited kleptocratic capitalism (Gustafson 1999) Putin could reverse Russia's economic and political fortune. During his first term Putin managed to stabilise Russia's economy after many years of decline (Sokoloff 2003: 527–39). For the first time after the fall of communism Russia's economic growth exceeded expectations and the country is now placed on the path of sustainable regeneration. Economic stabilisation went hand in hand with political centralisation in favour of the Kremlin and the security forces in which Putin was placing his trust. At the domestic economic level, the 1998 devaluation and the ensuing strengthening of oil prices have certainly helped the Kremlin to keep capital flight under control (Buiter and Szegvari 2002). In 2001 private capital flight from Russia came to $14.8 billion (*Pravda* 29 October 2002), and decreased to $8.1 billion in 2002. In 2003, $9.6 billion was brought into the country by the banking sector (against $2.5 billion in 2002), while non-financial corporations accounted for capital flight of $12.5 billion, leaving overall capital flight at $2.9 billion. On 18 December 2003, while speaking in a live interview with the Russian people, Putin said the best way of avoiding capital flight is to create better conditions for investing in the Russian economy. However, despite continuing capital flight (especially during the Yukos affair in 2004), Russia has shown its ability to pay debts as long as oil and gas prices are high and there are no technical problems preventing the pipelines from functioning at full capacity.[22]

At the domestic *political* level Putin succeeded in establishing a Bonapartist 'controlled democracy' after a decade of severe upheavals. These factors easily explain Putin's extraordinary popularity and the origins of the actual one-dimensional party-political structure that emerged after the last parliamentary elections of December 2003. The dominant division between the forces pushing for change and those opposing capitalism had to be overcome by a strong presidency uniting all supporters of change. In the tradition of Bonapartist rulers Putin succeeded in superseding this standard left–right divide by isolating the traditional forces of the left embodied by the Communist Party of the Russian Federation (KPRF) and its allies and by marginalising the so-called 'liberal' parties, such as Yabloko and the Union of Right Forces (SPS). This terminal blow to the 'threat' of communism was eased by the fact that the KPRF had no credible economic alternative. Moreover, the party had become infiltrated by business interests and local pressure groups, leaving the pursuit of market reforms under the aegis of Putin as the only option.

The December 2003 Duma elections were memorable for the defeat of the political parties defending Parliamentarism (or Democratism) against Presidentialism (or Bonapartism). The presence in the Duma of the long-standing liberal parties Yabloko and SPS collapsed. The KPRF was reduced from 113 to 53 seats. The communist protest vote was severely eroded chiefly by the newly formed party Rodina led by the economist Sergei Glazyev and foreign affairs expert Dmitry Rogozhin (9 per cent of the vote and 37 Duma seats). Resurgent nationalism was also responsible for the comeback of the Liberal Democratic Party of Vladimir Zhirinovsky. But Rodina's success prevented the latter from collecting an important share of the protest votes.[23]

Rodina's Glazyev is not an oligarch-basher, but a 'moderniser' pleading for a systematic increase of taxation of what he calls the 'super-profits' generated by the windfall of strong global energy prices and the rising value of oil companies' assets. The increased flows to the state budget would be channelled to neglected sectors such as social security, health, education and research and development. He wants to marry a robust capitalist system with a state taking responsibility for social security and he presented a credible, distinctly social-democratic alternative to 'Putinism'. It is for his emphasis on the management of Russia's recent success and a more rational and equitable distribution of its fruits, rather than on the protests at the transition to capitalism, that he could entice a part of the left vote. The focus of Glazyev's programme on the energy sector cut right into the heart of the social-democratic and middle-class electorate: Rodina performed very well in Moscow and St Petersburg, the traditional bastions of the Yabloko and the other liberal political forces. Finally, the landslide victory of the Presidential Party in December 2003 obliged the long-standing opposition leaders to boycott the presidential elections, passing their candidatures to lesser-known figures (Sobell 2004).

During his first term Putin was confronted with the unsolved crisis of the Russian welfare state, poor tax collection, a large shadow economy and pervasive corruption of state bureaucracy, wage arrears, a poorly designed social safety net, and a growing number of welfare claimants. His reforms were too timid and too incremental. At the end of his first term Putin was confronted with numerous bottlenecks and constraints the still vast Russian bureaucracy had failed to tackle with success. Especially welfare provisions and old-age pensions are insufficiently developed. Numerous federal social programmes are supplemented by even more numerous ones at the regional and local levels, or by new kinds of non-monetary assistance. The neoliberalisation of the Russian welfare state and the growth of private pension plans reappeared on the political agenda. A big concern is the lax regulation of Russia's newly created funded pension system. Most pension investment decisions are made by employers, often members of the pervasive business oligarchy. The operation of existing voluntary pension plans reveals that they are run by employers such as Lukoil and Gazprom investing their pension money almost exclusively in company assets.

With his large majority in the State Duma Putin was able to pass consti-tutional reforms such as the end of the system of direct popular election of Russia's governors, and to have the State Duma elected on the basis of slates chosen by national party leaders he mostly controls.[24] Putin's United Russia has enrolled a large number of small parties, power brokers and local bosses by merging them in a large faction occupying 222 Duma seats. Together with the votes of 75 independents Putin can hold a firm grip on the legislative process. The presidential administration intends to push more bills through this compliant parliament, Prime Minister Kasyanov said at the opening of the newly elected State Duma. Among the priorities for the new Duma Kasyanov listed social security reform (compulsory health insur-ance, a safety net for those who lose their jobs), tax reform (individual property tax, taxation on inheritance and gifts, and water and land taxes), reform of the natural gas sector (reform of Gazprom), and banking reforms. The government should have little trouble getting its bills considered or passed: Putin's United Russia is heading all 29 Duma committees and Duma deputies of United Russia will not be allowed to talk to journalists directly (*Moscow Times* 19 January 2004). The communists are still in parliament, but they are now little more than a Duma decoration. The two liberal parties Yabloko and SPS obtained four and two seats respectively and they are both looking like forces of the past. SPS's Anatoly Chubais, who as deputy prime minister in the mid-1990s oversaw the privatisations that made the oligarchs rich, symbolises that past.

Well before his re-election on 14 March 2004 Putin fired his prime minister, Mikhail Kasyanov, and the entire government. Apparently, this decision had been inspired by the desire once again to set out his position on the course of the country's development after the election and to show to the surviving oligarchs that he was firmly in control of the situation. Kasyanov, who was the last remnant from Yeltsin's administration, and also the oligarchs' friend, had been the most public critic of the arrest of Yukos' boss Mikhail Khodorkovsk, who had used his financial clout to win polit-ical influence. Putin chose Mikhail Fradkov as Kasyanov's successor. Together with Fradkov the *siloviki* occupy all levels of power in the Kremlin's presidential staff and in some key ministries. They now can start extracting more revenues from the natural resources firms still owned by the oligarchs. The radically restructured government under Fradkov has only 17 minis-ters instead of the previous 30. Several groups of ministries were grouped to streamline work on the main policy areas, such as transport, railways and communications; energy, atomic energy, industry and construction; and economic development and trade. Several former ministers such as German Gref, Alexei Kudrin (finance) and Alexander Zhukov (deputy prime minister and economic policy) returned to office. Dmitry Kozak is in charge of carrying out Putin's plans for slimming the bureaucracy as his chief of staff.

Viktor Khristenko, responsible for energy, has to tackle the Gazprom monopoly.[25] The *siloviki* do not feature in this group. They run the 'power ministries', such as defence, foreign affairs, home affairs and justice.

Financial-industrial groups in the Nizhny Novgorod Oblast

Nizhny Novgorod Oblast (NNO) is a region in the centre of the European part of Russia – a few hundred kilometres east of Moscow – with 3.7 million inhabitants of whom 1.3 million live in the city of Nizhny Novgorod. In its development after the Soviet Union collapse NNO has undergone three major periods in terms of regional governance. During the first period regional authorities were the dominant actors, and initiatives on regional economic and political development lay with NNO governor Boris Nemtsov. The central government was too concerned to retain the democratic changes in the country (and power in its hands) to interfere in local politics. Moscow had just started its liberal economic reforms, but as mechanisms to conduct them were elaborated just for the national level, regions were left free to have their own peculiarities. Therefore, NNO as most other regions enjoyed considerable freedom. Moreover, the oblast declared itself a pioneer of democratic and liberal reforms and received Moscow's support and encouragement. Unlike regions rich in natural resources, NNO did not see the rise of oligarchs. Most of its economy was focused on the defence needs (the city of Nizhny Novgorod was even closed to foreigners until 1991). After the drastic fall in contracts with the Defence Ministry lacking in money, most big enterprises found themselves on the eve of bankruptcy and high dependence on the conversion programmes Nizhny Novgorod authorities developed.

During the second period, the initiative on regional development was taken by President Putin, and particularly by the presidential envoy in the Volga Federal District (VFD), Sergei Kirienko, an ex-prime minister who drove the country through the financial crisis in 1998. Central government filled in the vacuum of regional leadership that emerged after Boris Nemtsov had gone to the Moscow Kremlin. Putin's administrative reform in 2000 when seven federal districts were created had a significant effect on NNO, as Nizhny Novgorod became the capital of the VFD and the presidential envoy and district governmental bodies reside in the city. Moreover, this status meant almost automatic support by Nizhny Novgorod of all presidential initiatives.

However, this system of regional governance started to erode after the first Russian financial-industrial groups (FIGs), owned by oligarchs, started penetrating the region (see Table 15.1). This paved the way for a start of a new period, during which state authorities (regional officials and the presidential envoy) have faced the necessity to reshape the relationship with business in the face of oligarchs entering NNO.

Table 15.1 Some Nizhny Novgorod Oblast companies belonging to Russian groups

Nizhny Novgorod Oblast companies	Owning Russian groups
Gorky Automobile Plant (GAZ), Pavlovsky Automobile Plant (PAZ), Arzamas Machine-building plant, and other companies	Sibirsky Aluminium (Sibal; renamed Base Element): ranks among the world's top 10 aluminium producers; includes some of Russia's leading aluminium plants; produces a broad array of aluminium products and alloys, including parts and components for aeronautics, space, cars and shipbuilding
Vyksa Steel Works pipe mill	The United Metallurgical Company (UMC): specialises in manufacturing pipes of diversified destination as well as railroad wheels, motor-car springs, high precision steel strip, and rolled products
Hydromash Facility (supplies components and hydraulics to Airbus), Sokol Aircraft Manufacturing Facility, and other companies	The Kaskol Group: focuses on the aerospace industry, including aircraft design and manufacturing, high-tech engineering and information technology, and aircraft cargo operations
Krasnoe Sormovo shipyard, Lazurit (R&D) Nizhegorodsky Teplokhod	OMZ (Uralmash-Izhora Group): is a leading Russian company in knowledge-intensive equipment and machinery for the nuclear energy and mining industries, and a wide range of heavy industrial equipment and specialty steel
Zavolzhsky Engine Plant (ZMZ), Kulebaksky Steel Plant	Severstal (generated from Cherepovets Iron and Steel Complex)
Lukoil – Volganefteproduct, Lukoil – Nizhegorodnefteorgsintez (formerly Norsi-Oil)	Lukoil: Russia's second largest oil company

Sources: *Delovaya Nedelya* (no. 8, 2004) and companies' websites.

An interesting fact of Russian FIGs active in NNO is that they hold just a few enterprises in NNO, but that these are the biggest. Among about the 90 largest NNO companies, 29 remain state-owned, 31 belong to NNO entrepreneurs, 3 are controlled by international companies, and (only) 25 are possessed by Russian national companies. However, in 2003, out of the over RUR38 billion NNO received as taxes, most came from NNO companies owned by Russian FIGs: GAZ – RUR3.4 billion, Lukoil-Nizhegorodnefteorgsintez – over RUR2 billion, Vyksunsky Metal Plant – RUR1.3 billion, Pavlovsky Autobus – RUR900 million. In contrast, Nizhegorodsky Maslozhirovoi Kombinat, the greatest enterprise owned by NNO entrepreneurs, paid only RUR250 million taxes.[26] The taxes from the Russian enterprises constitute most regional budget incomes, and each of these enterprises is the greatest taxpayer of the territory (city, town) it is located in. For example,

25 per cent of Nizhny Novgorod city budget revenues come from GAZ, and if local enterprises dependent on cooperation with GAZ are taken in consideration, this figure reaches 45 to 47 per cent.[27]

NNO enterprises owned by Russian FIGs are not only the greatest taxpayers but they are also the greatest employers. Each of these enterprises is the major employer for local residents, even in the case of the city of Nizhny Novgorod where, for example, one of its seven municipal districts evolves around GAZ and another around Krasnoe Sormovo. In addition, the Russian FIGs are the major social welfare burden carriers. Since the Soviet times great enterprises traditionally finance or subsidise a number of social facilities such as dormitories, kindergartens, schools, hospitals, summer camps, training centres and cinemas.[28] Usually these social facilities are located in the territory where an enterprise is situated and all residents are supposed to be somehow connected to this enterprise: they either used to work at this enterprise, or any of their parents is working there, or they are expected to be a prospective employee.

NNO authorities and Russian FIGs often clash. A first source of conflict is that state authorities pretend to control the entrance of any FIG and seek to have the 'admission' right. Any large Russian company swallowing up a local enterprise with no prior consultation with regional authorities is treated as a 'seizure'. Norsi-Oil (oil-refinery) Company President Vadim Vorobyov stated that he was thankful to NNO governor Ivan Sklyarov who did not pose obstacles for Norsi-oil bankruptcy for subsequent sale to an oil-extracting company[29] (Lukoil turned out to be the only purchaser). By contrast, when Uralmash-Izhora Group (OMZ) decided to boost its stake at military-industrial enterprise Krasnoe Sormovo to over 50 per cent with no regional authorities' agreement, it faced strong opposition from authorities and had to overcome many obstacles. Sergei Kirienko, presidential envoy in the VFD, even managed to persuade the Russian Federal Property Fund to 'freeze' its share of 8 per cent and not to sell it for two years, whereas those shares were for urgent sale. At that time, the measure was supposed to be a key obstacle for Kahka Bendukidze to take over Krasnoe Sormovo, as enterprise management owned 13 per cent of shares, and the State Property Ministry 26 per cent (not for sale as it is a strategic military-industrial enterprise). Kahka Bendukidze possessed only 37 per cent and had to deal with a great number of minor shareholders who possessed the rest. Moreover, enterprise management also started acquiring shares, and the NNO governor was said to have arranged with some shareholders not to sell their stake to Bendukidze. Nevertheless, by January 2001 Kakha Bendukidze had managed to accumulate over 50 per cent of the shares. As soon as this news reached information agencies, the 'seizure' discourse was developed by news agencies loyal to the authorities. Sergei Obozov, NNO chief federal inspector, said that Bendukidze's deals to acquire shares he needed to control the enterprise seemed dubious and an investigation into these dealings would be made.[30]

Second, clashes occur when state authorities seek more transparency and information about the final goals of up and coming FIGs. As head of the NNO government, Sergei Obozov noted that he did not have clear information about the final goals of new great investors. For example, there was great uncertainty over the reconstruction of GAZ started by the new management, which was appointed by new shareholder Sibirsky Aluminium Group (Sibal). An often heard (popular) view was that this was done by Sibal to resell GAZ at a higher price, and this gloomy assessment was shared by some state officials. According to Sergei Obozov, vice VFD presidential envoy, none of the new owners of the greatest machine-building NNO enterprises has brought big investments, which means that Russian FIGs are still uncertain about their strategic goals in NNO and do not rule out the resale of NNO companies.[31]

A third issue causing clashes is state authorities encouraging the new owners of NNO enterprises to behave with more responsibility towards their local employees. There are two major reasons for state authorities' concern. First, newcomers seek to increase effectiveness of their new possessions and try to get rid of the social welfare burden. While FIGs do not want to waste money on funding local social infrastructure, to local authorities social expenditures are big burden. Second, the new holders started reconstruction of the NNO enterprises. They aspired to decrease the number of employees (about 10 per cent of the personnel was retired), but to increase the salary of the remaining employees to get from them more motivation and accountability. The new owners of GAZ also started reshaping the company's relations with its suppliers and dealers. Because of corruption at GAZ, most of its supplies had been provided at prices higher than the market price, and GAZ production had been sold to dealers incomparably cheaper. GAZ broke up those corruptive practices that resulted in diminishing the number of 'parasites'. However, all these reconstruction measures led to social tensions.

Finally, clashes occur as authorities seek more accountability of Russian groups. State officials have often used the discourse of tax evasion by NNO enterprises held by Russian FIGs. The major comment by Vice Governor Vladimir Bulanov to OMZ boosting its share of Krasnoe Sormovo over 50 per cent was that the task of the city and the oblast was to reach arrangement with OMZ not to direct taxes to other regions and to retain Krasnoe Sormovo as one of the greatest NNO taxpayers. In the same way authorities developed an attack of panic when taxes from GAZ decreased sharply after Sibal became the owner. After officials had accused Sibal of transferring taxable value from NNO other regions, GAZ management tried hard to convince the authorities that the taxes fall was temporary and due to reconstruction. However, according to a tax official, almost all NNO companies that are part of FIGs move taxes away from NNO to other regions. In some cases, this practice is seen as a 'punishment measures' by FIGs towards NNO authorities. Lukoil, for example, is said to have directed taxes worth RUR1 billion away from NNO.[32]

With oligarchs entering NNO, regional enterprises have become integrated into industrial chains of Russian FIGs. For most of the region's enterprises this was either the only way to survive, or a good promotion to increase their competitiveness and enter new markets. Let us here review a few cases (see also Table 15.1). Prior to being purchased by Lukoil, oil-refinery factory Norsi-Oil faced severe oil shortages and economic losses. The oil shortages could result in stopping the refinery process, which would require huge investments in restarting the technological process later (replacing some equipment and infrastructure). In this regard, Lukoil purchasing Norsi-Oil guaranteed the latter's oil supply. The purchase of Krasnoe Sormovo by OMZ (of Kakha Bendukidze) was driven by OMZ's aim to provide all equipment for oil-extracting in the Caspian Sea. The Krasnoe Sormovo shipyard was to produce the most important parts of crafts, which would be transported to Astrakhan for crafts to be assembled there. Besides this promotion to the international market, Krasnoe Sormovo found a stable consumer market for its production within the holding. In the case of GAZ that was acquired by the Sibal group of Oleg Deripaska, Sibal wanted to expand its business from metal production and its export to investing in some of its metal consumers. In turn, Sibal brought new ideas and investments to GAZ, and GAZ benefited from getting a good lobbying supporter in the Russian government. A last example is that of Sokol, taken over by the Kaskol group (of Sergei Nedoroslev), which unites a number of enterprises specialised in aircraft building and technologies. Sokol could benefit from Kaskol's international projects, such as the Mooney International consortium (set up with the US Mooney Airplane Company and the British BAE Systems).[33]

NNO enterprises have also become embedded in oligarchs' ambitious plans and arrangements. For instance, in 2000–1 the Russian conglomerates Severstal and Sibal simultaneously decided to expand their business into the automobile-building industry, and while Sibal acquired Pavlovsky Automobile Plant (PAZ) and GAZ, Severstal became the new owner of Ulyanovsky Automobile Plant (UAZ). NNO companies Zavolzhsky Engine Plant (ZMZ) and GAZ are highly interdependent: ZMZ is the major national producer of engines applicable to GAZ manufactured automobiles. As about 80 per cent of ZMZ production goes to Sibal's GAZ and PAZ, Sibal group expected that it could control ZMZ without purchasing it. Inevitably, Sibal's reshaping of its relationship with its suppliers and new tough requirements touched ZMZ as well. However, as soon as Severstal became the greatest shareholder of ZMZ, the latter took a more independent position in negotiations with GAZ and increased prices for its engines. President of GAZ Nikolai Pugin states that Severstal had already negatively influenced GAZ: GAZ obtained metal from Cherepovets Metal Factory, which belongs to Severstal, and when in 1998 Severstal sharply raised prices this made GAZ less profitable by 11 per cent. Therefore, Pugin had very gloomy expectations of Severstal's purchase of ZMZ (for both GAZ and NNO). However, as GAZ already belonged to Sibal it could oppose to the new prices. As a response to Severstal policy, Sibal became the greatest shareholder of Volzhskie Motory (the key supplier of engines for UAZ-made automobiles), which in turn belonged to Severstal. Therefore, each oligarch possessed an automobile plant and the engine factory of the other's automobile plant. As a result, both ZMZ and GAZ became secured in the face of the offensive policies of each other.[34]

By accumulating a significant share of economic resources Russian oligarchs could foster their monopoly in NNO. Lukoil is a case in point. Lukoil already had a network of petroleum-stations before purchasing Norsi-Oil refinery and its petroleum-stations. Despite anti-monopoly legislation Lukoil has expanded its petroleum-stations network in the region. According to Gennady Gudkov, head of the Nizhny Novgorod branch of the Anti-monopoly Policy Ministry, there is a weak competition in NNO and, as a result, the petrol price is very high. Hardly any of the few competitors of Lukoil petroleum-stations dare to set their petrol price lower than Lukoil.[35]

As mentioned above, Russian FIGs acquired the largest NNO enterprises. Traditionally, the directorate (in the Soviet times) or management of these enterprises was always involved in regional politics. First, as the main employers and taxpayers large enterprises heavily influence regional economic, social and political developments, and their managers are always named among the top influential people in NNO ratings. Evidently, regional authorities have a great interest in maintaining good relations with the enterprise's directorate/management, and the entrance of FIGs hardly changed the situation: the names of the new owners were simply added to the top of the ratings. The practice worth noting that regional authorities (in NNO as well as in the rest of the country) started developing towards newcomers was signing agreements with them. While authorities pledge to develop a good investment climate and provide some tax liberties, the enterprises in return promise to provide employment and support social welfare at their new enterprises. The agreement is just a political document, a memorandum of wishes by which the sides have no real obligations.

Another type of political involvement of Russian economic groups in NNO is in elections. As their NNO enterprises employ thousands of people election candidates aim to mobilise these employees to vote for them. In addition, with whole municipal districts of the city of Nizhny Novgorod evolving around these enterprises, most of their residents depended on them, and the enterprise directorate could use its administrative resources and affect its employees' and their families' voting. The entry of oligarchs and their enterprise reconstruction has clearly been employed as one more tool to influence people's voting. During the last Nizhny Novgorod mayoral elections, for instance, voting took place under the fear of enterprise policies of 'retirement for personnel optimisation'.

Finally there is a strong tendency of oligarchs influencing politics by nominating enterprise candidates to elected governmental bodies. Enterprises seek to obtain seats in legislative bodies, namely the NNO Regional Assembly and Nizhny Novgorod municipal legislature. This practice is used by most enterprises (e.g. GAZ, Krasnoe Sormovo, Sokol and Gidromash). More rarely enterprises aim at the federal level and nominate their own candidates to the State Duma (half of which is elected under partisan slates, and half under the majority system in special territorial districts that Russia is divided into) as in the case of GAZ. Enterprises also participate in the executive branch elections at the regional level. For instance, Lukoil is expected to partake in 2005 gubernatorial elections. Its NNO top-manager Vladimir Vorobyov is named as a prospective nominee, but his nomination depends on the presidential envoy's approval. Sibal is to support ex-NNO Vice Governor and present State Duma Energy, Transport and Communications Committee Deputy Head Yury Senturin.[36] However, oligarchs holding NNO enterprises stay 'above' regional politics in the sense that they do not become politicians themselves.

Political-economic relations in the Volgograd Oblast

Volgograd Oblast is a subject of the Russian Federation, located in the southeast of the European part of Russia, more than 1,000 kilometres from Moscow. Although representing less than 1 per cent of the territory of the Russian Federation, Volgograd Oblast's high industrial and agricultural potential already in the Soviet period made the region one of the economic leaders within the USSR. Because of the key importance of the heavy and military industry as well as of unstable (arid zone) conditions for agriculture the development of this potential could be achieved only with permanent and large-scale state support. As a result, the social crisis after the collapse of the Soviet Union proved to be more painful for Volgograd Oblast than for the neighbouring provinces. No wonder that after 1996 Volgograd Oblast temporarily found itself in the so-called 'Red Belt' of provinces that supported communists during national and regional elections.

The deep socioeconomic and political transformations caused dramatic changes in regional policies as well as in the alignment of forces that influence provincial politics. These forces include administrative elites, leaders of big industrial and agricultural enterprises of the region, financial and industrial structures on a national scale, and a number of regional political organisations. The interaction between these forces, which in some cases goes beyond conventional ideas about political and economic logic, can have various consequences on the politics of the regional government, the federal centre, and the public opinion of the region. Here we will review the alignment of the most politically influential economic elites.

An interesting analysis of the relations between regional elites is made by the Russian political scientist Vladimir Gelman (2000). He explains that in the Soviet period the most influential forces in the mentioned elites were the agrarian, industrial and urban groups (the latter representing the interests of the regional centre). Within the top party echelons (the regional committee of the Communist Party of the Soviet Union (CPSU)), which essentially governed the region, the agrarian group was dominant, while the industrial group (which was not united in its interests) had an extraterritorial status, representing enterprises of ministerial, rather than regional administrative hierarchy. In Gelman's view, the interaction between the regional committee and the industrial group mainly took place within the system of coordination between the ministerial and regional party leadership, and did not lead to the creation of stable informal connections (Gelman 2000: 116–17).

The curtailment of the federal centre's support to the industrial group provided the preferred position to the agrarian elite, and the first governor of Volgograd Oblast was Ivan Shabunin who was formerly the leader of the region's agro-industrial complex. He counted on the agricultural sector but could not overcome the deep economic crisis due to cheap foreign imports. Moreover, the Volgograd Agro-Industrial Financial Corporation (made by the regional authorities the monopolist in distribution of corresponding budget funds and in the centralised purchases of agricultural products) was accused of numerous and large-scale financial abuses. Gelman (2000) explains that as a consequence a considerable part of the agrarian elite turned their eyes to the communists as potential promoters of their interests in the sphere of fighting the financial abuses in the distribution of aid, and also in defending local manufacturers. The victory of KPRF member Nikolai Maksiuta in the gubernatorial elections of 1996 was achieved due to the support of the electorate of rural areas and regional cities.

For the period since the mid-1990s, however, it has become complicated to use the same analytical approach as Gelman applied effectively for studying the Soviet realities and the early 1990s. Since then the branchwise 'solidarity' has weakened while property relations have surged. In many cases high-ranking regional officials are directly or indirectly involved in such property relations, but as a rule they are not advertised publicly. It would be, for example, a simplification to consider Nikolai Maksiuta as a protégé of the agrarian group. Formally representing the industrial elite (he came into politics after directing a shipbuilding factory), the new governor much more than his predecessor had to deal with different forces: an agro-industrial complex requiring large subsidies (as the rural electorate had brought Maksiuta his victories in 1996 and 2000), FIGs increasingly conquering the key economic positions in the region, various (by ideology and interests) informal groups within the regional branch of KPRF, and even more diverse groups of the United Russia.

The most important political-economical phenomenon of the second half of the 1990s was the control that the region's biggest enterprises established through financial-industrial structures, such as the oligarchic groups, did on the national scale. This has increased the level of independence of such enterprises from the regional and municipal leadership. As a result, the oblast and especially Volgograd city often receive a relatively insignificant share of tax revenue in the territory in which the enterprises were located. These changes have decreased the effectiveness of an important lever of influence over the respective structures, and have narrowed the financial base of the local budgets. Meanwhile, the strengthening of FIGs in different spheres of regional economics was eroding the power balance determined not so much by branch-wise interests as by the interests of definite 'oligarchic groups'.

At present, the most influential company representing the industrial lobby in the region is Lukoil with its subsidiaries Lukoil-Volgogradnizhnevolvzhskneft (specialising in oil extraction) and Lukoil-Volgogradneftpererabotka (petroleum refining). Lukoil is not only the actual monopolist in fields of extraction and processing of oil, sales of gasoline and other petroleum products, but is also the biggest creditor of the region, and one of the main sources of agricultural subsidies. Over the years of its work in the region, Lukoil has managed to concentrate in its hands the control over the most powerful and dynamic sector of the industry, represented by the fuel and petrochemical enterprises (producing about 30 produce of the gross regional product). As such, it has obtained a significant tax concession and established gasoline prices 5 to 12 per cent higher than in the neighbouring regions.[37]

Lukoil has also taken control over the agro-industrial complex strongly depending on fuel supplies and subsidies that not always can be repaid by agricultural producers. This took place at the end of 2002 when the regional government was unable to pay off debts of more than $33 million to Lukoil and other creditors and found itself on the verge of bankruptcy and political crisis. This was avoided by huge efforts at the cost of losing control (as a result of suits against the provincial government) over some profitable property objects, back-payments and constriction of Volgograd's municipal budget. The agro-industrial group thus lost a significant part of its former influence despite the fact that some of its representatives have continued to occupy high positions in the administrative structures at the provincial and especially district level. One of such representatives, deputy of the State Duma Vladimir Plotnikov (whose election campaigns since 1993 have been supported by Lukoil[38]), has even become the leader of the Agrarian Party of the Russian Federation.

After Maksiuta came to power in 1996, Lukoil established close relations with the new provincial government, becoming the most influential undercover political actor in the region. The oil giant provided support for Maksiuta's successful electoral campaign in 2000 whereas several protégés of Lukoil were placed in high positions. Yuri Sizov, a former director of the Lukoil insurance company, is currently responsible for the government's informational policy and public organisations. Anatoly Khodyrev, a former director of the company Lukoil-Volgogradneftepererabotka, became responsible for the fuel and energy complex, and in 2004 he was replaced by Igor Stefanenko, who had also been an employee of that company. Both of Volgograd Oblast's representatives in the Federation Council who were appointed in 2004 are also indirectly related to Lukoil: Vadim Artiukhov (32 years old, formerly an advisor of Prime Minister Mikhail Kassianov, and the son of former Minister of Natural Resources Vitaly Artiukhov) and Dmitry Skarga (34 years old, formerly director of oil-tanker company Sovkomflot). The careers of the two young senators were made outside the region, and the dominant pro-governmental party United Russia supported their election by the regional parliament. These examples, as well as the employment in Lukoil of Maksiuta's son, daughter and a son-in-law, clearly demonstrate coalescence between the regional power and the leading FIG.

Thus, the situation since the mid-1990s can hardly be considered an example of 'unstable bi-centrism' (according to the terminology of Vladimir Gelman). The 'one-and-half polar system', within which one actor has evident advantage over the others, seems to be a more suitable concept for this case. Nevertheless, the advancing of new financial-industrial structures taking control over major plants, factories and other enterprises can lead to some changes within the 'shadow political-economic structure of power relations'. The economic crisis of 1998, which seriously damaged regional industry and especially financial-credit system, facilitated this process. Among the mightiest economic structures establishing or strengthening their influence in the region at the end of 1990s and beginning of 2000s were: Sibur, a subsidiary of Gazprom that in 2000 took control over several chemical industry enterprises and tyre factory Voltair; Siberian-Ural Aluminium Company or SUAL, controlling Volgograd Aluminium Plant; Russian Chemical Group NIKOS, possessing chemical factories Kaustik and Plastcard; Midland Resources Holding Ltd company, which owns metallurgical plant Krasnyi Oktyabr; Promyshlennye Investory (Industrial Investors, owned by former Minister of Fuel and Energy Complex Serghei Generalov), possessing Volgograd Tractor Plant; and some structures controlled by the well-known Russian oligarch Roman Abramovich, especially the bank Moskovskii Delovoy Mir (MDM) (Moscow Business World), acquiring among other things Volzhsky Pipe Plant. Purchasing enterprises use financial-industrial structures such as offshore companies; in 1999 the largest volume of regional export fell on the Virgin Islands.[39] At the same time some Volgograd-originated business still hold key positions as they control major enterprises such as Konfil (confectionery), Khimprom (chemical industry), Silicate Plant, Pivovar (brewing) and Sady Pridonya (juices).[40]

The majority of the new FIGs are capable of lobbying for their interests through both executive and legislative powers. For example, the representatives of the structures related to Gazprom, SUAL and MDM are currently represented in the regional parliament (Oblast Duma). The campaign of the 'struggle against oligarchs' (inspired by Moscow) may weaken some of these structures and change some actors for other ones, but it cannot fundamentally change the system. As a rule, the FIGs use their political influence in order to defend their particular interests but without challenging the dominant positions of Lukoil. In 1999, however, some forces related to Roman Abramovich and partially to the Yukos oil company attempted to change the political balance. Having acquired two big enterprises in Volzhsky city (Volzhsky Bearing and Volzhsky Pipe plants), MDM bank supported its candidates in running for the position of mayor of Volgograd. Former board member of the bank and Deputy of the State Duma Yevgeny Ischenko (representing the Liberal Democratic Party of Russia) was a candidate for this position. Oleg Savchenko, who had been director of the Chukotka Development Foundation and was director of the Volzhsky bearing plant (since 1999, after the control packet of shares was transferred to MDM-related mediator companies[11]) opted for the position of governor of the Volgograd region.

In the course of Savchenko's election campaign his image-makers put their bets on their candidate in his struggle against Lukoil's baneful monopolisation of the regional economy with the acting head of the administration as its protégé. During the campaign Savchenko proposed to revise the results of the key Lukoil enterprises' privatisation.[12] Similarly, the electoral campaign of the leader of the Centre of Economic Strategy of the Volgograd region, Anatoly Popov, was backed by Lukoil's competitor, namely the petroleum company Yukos. In turn, Maksiuta's spin doctors emphasised Lukoil's favourable influence in the region wherever possible, while portraying Savchenko as a protégé of the well-known oligarchs Boris Berezovsky and Roman Abramovich, who were allegedly eager to usurp their control over the province and sell its resources abroad.

Although in both cases the leaders of the 'party of power' Yuri Chekhov and Maksiuta scored a victory, Ischenko and Savchenko continued to be influential political figures. The former was re-elected deputy of the State Duma, and the latter, having lost the election, announced his intention of becoming the main opposition leader against the existing government. In order to achieve their political purposes Ischenko and Savchenko decided to join the regional branch of the party United Russia, and supported President Vladimir Putin and his policy.[13] Originally, in its struggle against the communists United Russia staked just on the well-advertised figures of Ischenko and Savchenko. In the spring of 2003 Savchenko was elected the head of the party's Volgograd regional branch forcing to the background other political leaders including Chekhov. After the latter's resignation from the mayor's position in June of 2003, Savchenko firmly supported Ischenko's candidature for the September election. As a result, Ischenko gained a convincing victory over his main competitor Vladimir Goriunov. The ex-mayor and some members of his team have taken control over some major profitable enterprises in the city, such as Volgograd Wholesale Grocery Market and Hotel Volgograd.

The new Volgograd city administration has been formed by experienced managers and businessmen. This team tried to improve the uneasy economic situation, sometimes using dubious methods such as forcing (by indirect administrative pressure) Volgograd businessmen to transfer money to special funds for the city's development.[14] The events after the mayoral elections showed that in the long run the centre had not made its choice in favour of the alliance between Ischenko and Savchenko.[45] This can be explained both by their incapacity to consolidate the variegated regional branch of United Russia and by the (Moscow) campaign of 'the struggle against oligarchs', including the structures controlled by Boris Berezovsky, Mikhail Khodorkovsky and partially Roman Abramovich. Trying to provide electoral success for United Russia and Vladimir Putin, the centre preferred to rely on the provincial authorities with Nikolai Maksiuta (who had withdrawn from KPRF) at the top. Nevertheless, United Russia could not achieve convincing success at both national (28 per cent) and regional (37 per cent) parliamentary elections.

The influence of Ischenko and Savchenko decreased when in March 2004 the latter was removed from his leading position in the regional branch of United Russia because of the mayor's intrigue. He was replaced by Vladimir Goriunov, who has headed football club Rotor and related commercial structures enjoying the significant support (financial help and tax remissions) of regional authorities. Ischenko, Savchenko and Maksiuta became the main candidates for the governor's position in the elections of December 2004. Maksiuta was the favourite; he was supported by Lukoil and had the strongest position among the rural electorate. Savchenko had lost not only the support of official Moscow but also a significant part of the financial resources for his electoral campaign. Meanwhile the manager's image of Goriunov (officially supported by United Russia) was seriously damaged by Rotor's last place in the Russian football championship. As a result, the elections were won by Maksiuta.

In sum, the case of Volgograd region demonstrates that there is a complex system of relations between political and economic elites, which are closely tied to one another. The existing ('one-and-half polar') system is dominated by Lukoil. Other similar forces, among which the share of external FIGs increases steadily, as a rule desist from direct confrontation with this petroleum giant, and engage in re-distribution of property and lobbying of their interests outside the economic leader's sphere of influence. Of course, the main actor within the regional political system is not Lukoil but the federal centre with related administrative and political structures. Having very powerful instruments to change the current balance of forces, the centre has not (yet) made a final choice in favour of any elite, and still desists from the evident interference. It seems that such intervention presently can weaken or strengthen any of the mentioned actors, but it cannot radically change the entire system of these actors' relations with the regional authorities, which is defined by unmatched priorities as the necessity to subsidise unstably developing agriculture, the demands of industrial giants, and the infrastructure problems of Volgograd city.

Final remarks

Although some tycoons still have an overwhelming hold on Russia's economy, the Moscow Kremlin is gaining a dominant influence in the oil and gas sector and the export of raw materials. As long as the economy will stay afloat thanks to the oil and gas exports Putin's authority will remain unshaken. His re-election in March 2004 with more than 71 per cent of the popular vote proved that his popularity is overwhelming and his authority unshaken. For the Kremlin, maintaining macroeconomic stability is indispensable. Although high oil and metal prices in combination with the rouble devaluation in 1998 have helped Russia regain some international footing, the country's economic future is uncertain (US Congress 2001; Sokoloff 2003: 595–605).[46]

Russia's recent economic history illustrates how privatisation without the necessary institutional infrastructure leads to asset stripping and the creation of a class of immensely rich tycoons. A return to a strong executive authority in line with Russia's past (Vichnevski 2000) is congruent with Putin dominating the State Duma, with mainstream liberals banished from power, with mainstream technocrats now posting up as Putin's advisers, and with governors standing guard in towns and provinces. The Putin administration believes that under globalisation no nation will be able to develop successfully in isolation. Therefore Putin is pushing for thoroughgoing institutional reforms and centralisation.

Notes

1 The largest part of this chapter is written by André Mommen and deals with President Putin's economic and political agenda towards Russia's oligarchs. Vasiliy Valuev is the author of the section about the FIGs in the NNO. Serghei Golunov has written the section on political-economic relations in the Volgagrad Oblast.

2 Under Putin, the selling of companies at knock-down prices has continued, such as the control package of Slavneft that was sold at a low price in 2002.

3 Berezovsky was not allowed to add the aluminium industry to his financial empire. He resigned from the State Duma and fled to the West. Gusinsky (of Media-MOST) was forced to sell his shares in Gazprom and to cede his television station NTV. He also emigrated to the West.

4 Yukos was the only serious financing group of Yabloko. After Khodorkovsky's arrest the party was left without money. The Union of Right Forces was sponsored by RAO Unified Energy Systems headed by Anatoly Chubais, Alfa-Bank, Surgutneftegaz and ALROSA.

5 The sale was not to Gazprom, but to a mystery shell company named Baikal Finance Group in Tver. Later on the state-owned oil company Rosneft revealed that it had bought Baikal for an undisclosed sum. The chairman of Rosneft, Igor Sechin, is a close confidant of Putin. Putin, however, claimed that the auction had adhered to the best market standards.

6 Taxes and duties totalling $98 billion were collected over January to August 2004, which is 22 per cent more than the sum of taxes collected in January to August 2003.

7 In late 2000, a competitor filed a civil suit for racketeering against him and his company in a New York court, including charges of bribery, judicial corruption and armed force. Deripaska was barred from travel to the United States and from entrance to the Davos economic summit in Switzerland.

8 However, Putin appointed Viktor Ivanov, a former KGB and FSB agent, as chairman of the soon to be privatised main air carrier of Russia.

9 The most famous achievements of Russian oligarchs in the last few years include the purchase of the English football club Chelsea by Abramovich, and the purchase of Fabergé eggs by Viktor Vekselberg. Vladimir Potanin gave a lot of money to the Guggenheim Museum in New York, while Friedman made a big donation to the Jewish Museum in the same city. Before his arrest, Khodorkovsky had generously supported the Carnegie Endowment for International Peace, the American Enterprise Institute, the Library of Congress and other non-profit projects. Moreover, Russia's oligarchs want to show their wealth by purchasing property in the West and by buying real estate, mostly in Moscow or at the outskirts of the city.

10 According to the daily *Vedomosti*, this former head of the presidential administration had called for the Yukos group to be broken up and sold when in July 2003 charges of tax evasion and involvement in contract killings had initiated the Yukos case (*Transitions Online* 20 September 2004).

11 Alfred Koch started his career in St Petersburg as a protégé of Chubais. He became head of the State Property Committee of the Russian Federation, but lost his job in 1997 after a financial scandal. He became CEO of the managing company ZAO Montes Auri. In 2000 he was appointed general director of OAO Gazprom Media.

12 In 2000, Lukoil acquired for $71 million some 1,300 stations from Getty Petroleum Marketing Inc. To further expose its brand, Lukoil in January 2004 bought 773 Mobil stations with supply contracts from ConocoPhillips Co. for roughly $269 million. On 29 September 2004, ConocoPhillips bought the Russian government's 7.4 per cent stake in Lukoil for almost $2 billion.

13 In 2004, Vladimir Potanin's Norilsk Nickel purchased a 20 per cent stake of Gold Fields, but the Kremlin started an investigation on whether to approve or veto Potanin's $1.16 billion purchase (after Putin had already warned Potanin that his company was paying too little tax). Then, the South African shareholders of Gold Fields decided to merge with the Canadian miner IAMGold, thereby diluting Potanin's share value.

14 The integrated Timan Bauxite Mine is located in the remote Komi Republic. The project here entails the expansion of the mine from the existing 1 million tonnes of bauxite per annum to produce up to 6 million tonnes per annum and to start the construction of an associated alumina refinery.

15 RusAl was an amalgamation of aluminium smelters and alumina refineries owned and operated by core shareholders in Sibirsky Aluminium (since renamed Base Element) and Sibneft. In 2001 RusAl began managing production at Bauxite. In October 2003 Deripaska's holding Base Element acquired an additional 25 per cent stake of RusAl for an estimated $3 billion from fellow oligarch Abramovich.

16 The new company will have oil reserves of one billion tonnes and an annual output of 60 million tonnes of crude. It will own five oil refineries with an aggregate capacity of 50 million tonnes of oil products a year, and also filling-station chains in Russia and Ukraine totalling 2,100 outlets. It will be accorded exclusive rights to carry out the oil projects of BP, Access/Renova and the Alfa Group in Russia and Ukraine.

17 Trutnev's position favours Highland Gold (a London-registered goldminer) and Trans Siberian Gold (another London-listed junior), but Trutnev's would also favour the oligarchs Potanin and Vekselberg, who have established links to foreign multinationals (Gold Fields and Lonmin).

18 Litvinenko, rector of the St Petersburg Mining Institute, in the past supervised Putin's research for a doctoral dissertation on mining resources.

19 Usmanov is the owner of the Oskol steel plant, Urals Steel (formerly the Nosta steel plant) and the Lebedinsky iron-ore mine. Through a Cyprus registered firm called Gallagher Holdings he became an 11 per cent minority shareholder of the Anglo-Dutch steelmaker Corus until in 2004 he suddenly sold his stake in Corus (*Russian Journal* 18 March 2004).

20 Since 2001 NK Rosneft participates in a project for exploration in Western Kazakhstan. In 2002, Rosneft was authorised to be engaged in the development of the Kurmangazy oil and gas bloc of the Caspian shelf. Rosneft and Strojtransgaz signed a contract in 2001 for exploration, development and production of hydrocarbons with Sonatrak, the Algerian state-owned oil and gas company. And together with two Colombian companies Rosneft formed a consortium with the aim of taking part in a tender for development of fields in Suroriente; Rosneft America Inc. was formed.

21 Analysts believe that Gazprom is also interested in buying Yukos' main production subsidiary OAO Yuganskneftegaz and that the acquisition of Rosneft by Gazprom is the first step towards the creation of a state-owned industrial and raw material conglomerate, after which the state could capture the electricity sector too.

22 In October 2003 Russia paid about $238.5 million to the IMF (*International Investment Projects*, Moscow, 26 October 2003).

23 Rodina's launch had reportedly been sanctioned by the Kremlin as a ploy to weaken the communists. Glazyev had participated in Gaidar's reformist government in 1992, but he left the government a year later for patriotic activities in the orbit of the KPRF. In 2003 he jumped at the opportunity to abandon the communists for Rodina. Glazyev argued that Putin's government has been drifting along the 'status quo', failing to speed up structural changes so needed for freeing the Russian economy from its current excessive dependence on the energy and raw materials sector.

24 These reforms were announced in Putin's speech on 13 September 2004. Since 2000, Putin has been strengthening the Kremlin's control over governors by removing them from the Federation Council, appointing presidential envoys to watch over them, and centralising the appointments of regional police chiefs, prosecutors and security-agency heads.

25 After his re-election Putin broke his silence on the restructuring of the state gas monopoly, Gazprom, proposing to scrap the ban on foreigners owning domestically traded shares, create an internal gas market, and give other Russian producers access to Gazprom's pipelines. But he did not mention more radical steps, such as breaking the company into separate production and distribution parts, or scrapping the two-tier system of domestic and export gas prices that is one of the European Union's main demands before Russia can join the WTO.

26 *Delovaya Nedelya* No. 8 (044), April 2004: 11.

27 www.nizhny.ru/?HCID=report&article=19119&folder=73789.

28 For example, GAZ is estimated to spend about RUR500 billion on the social infrastructure annually. www.nizhny.ru/?HCID=report&article=19119&folder=73789.

29 Interview with Vadim Vorobyov, 15 May 2000, http://www.infonet.nnov.ru/nta/arch/print.phtml?mess_id=20970.

30 *Ekonomicheskaya Zhizn* No. 1 (300), 18–24 January 2001: 3; www.nizhny.ru/?HCID=report&article=19511&folder=73789.

31 See Sergei Obozov, 'Comments to new investors entrance to NNO' (www.hotcom.ru/main/?id=11174); statements of some officials, e.g. www.regions.ru/article/any/id/573230.html or http://www.hotcom.ru/main/?id=11174; *Delovaya Nedelya* No. 8 (044), April 2004: 13.

32 *Gorod I Gorozhane* No. 3, 16 January 2001: 6; www.regions.ru/article/any/id/550995.html; www.regions.ru/article/any/id/554299.html; *Delovaya Nedelya* No. 8 (044), April 2004.

33 4 February 2004, www.abm.r52.ru/index.phtml?rid=13&fid=78&sid=4&nid=198.

34 'Igra na operezhenie', *Nezavisimaya Gazeta* 20 February 2001 (www.politeconomy.ng.ru/corp/2001–02–20/3_game.html); interview with Nickolay Pugin, 15 February 2001 (www.nizhny.ru/?HCID=report&article=21463&folder=73789).

35 Interview with Gennady Gudkov in *Delovaya Nedelya* No. 8 (044), April 2004.

36 www.abm.r52.ru/index.phtml?rid=10&fid=26&sid=10&nid=2206.

37 Galina Beloussova, 'Gubernator pomog tem . . . chto otkazal v pomoschi' (The Governor Helped by . . . that He Refused to Help), *Gorodskiye vesti* 11 October 2004.

38 *'Gorod Geroyev' Informational Agency*, 'Gusevskii mentalitet', (www.gorodgeroev.ru/fact.php?id=1718).

39 'Vneshneekonomicheskie sviazi Volgogradskoi oblasti v 1999 godu. Informatsionnyi obzor' (Foreign Economic Relations of Volgograd Region in 1999. An Information Review), Volgograd: Departament mezhdunarodnogo sotrudnichestva Administratsii Volgogradskoi Oblasti, s.a., 2.

40 See in Natalya Shabunina, 'Hochesh' uspeha – ne smotri na rodoslovnuyu' (Want Success – Don't Look at a Lineage), *Delovoye Povolzhye* 28 February 2001.

41 See in Grigory Punanov, 'Abramovichu do vostrebovaniya' (Poste Restant for Abramovich), *Izvestiya* 2 August 2001.

42 This privatisation concerned the companies Nizhnevolzhskneft and Volggorad-n'eftepererabotka. See Viktor Serov, 'Novyi' peredel sobstvennosti nachinayetsya s Volgograda' (The New Property Repartition Starts from Volgograd), *Novaya Gazeta* 7 December 2000.

43 The party had a lack of outstanding political figures able to challenge seriously the pro-communist regional government; therefore it counted on affiliating almost all loyal influential politicians. As a result, United Russia was joined by political rivals: the mayor of Volgograd Yuri Chekhov, Deputy of the State Duma Vassily Galushkin, the president of the football club Rotor, Vladimir Goriunov, and, of course, Yevgeny Ischenko and Oleg Savchenko. The rivalry between them did not end but only took on the intra-system character.

44 *Kommersant – Nizhnee Povolzhye*, 'Volgogradskiye predprinimateli vystupili protiv dobrovol'no prinuditel'nogo sponsorstva' (Volgograd Businessmen Raised Their Voices against the Voluntary-forced Sponsorship), 16 November 2004.

45 Yevgeny Ischenko considered the mayor's position as a stepping stone before the governor elections of 2004, but in November of that year his candidature was cancelled because he had submitted inauthentic information to the Regional Election Committee.

46 High commodity prices contributed to Russia's post-1998 economic and financial stability (*Moscow News* 10–16 January 2001). Total foreign debt declined from $158 billion in January 2000 to $146 billion in January 2002. In 2002, debt servicing still devoured $14.2 billion, including $6.8 billion for net debt repayments (Abalkin 2002: 872–3).

Bibliography

Abalkin, Leonid (2002) 'Some notes on current problems of foreign economic relations of Russia', *The World Economy*, 25 (6): 869–74.

Blash, Joseph R., Maya Kroumova and Douglas Kruse (1997) *Kremlin Capitalism: Privatizing the Russian Economy*, Ithaca, NY and London: Cornell University Press.

Bogomolov, Oleg T. (1992) 'The collapse of the communist empire: an avenue to European civilization', in Michael Keren and Gur Ofer (eds), *Trials of Transition: Economic Reform in the Former Communist Bloc*, Boulder, CO: Westview Press.

Boycko, Maxim, Andrei Shleifer and Robert Vishny (1996) *Privatizing Russia*, Cambridge, MA: MIT Press.

Brady, Rose (1999) *Kapitalizm: Russia's Struggle To Free its Economy*, New Haven, CT and London: Yale University Press.

Buiter, Willem H. and Ivan Szegvari (2002) 'Capital flight and capital outflows from Russia: symptom, cause and cure', Working Paper no. 73, European Bank for Reconstruction and Development.

Gelman, Vladimir (2000) 'Demokratizatsiia, strukturnyi pliuralizm i neustoi'chivyi bitsentrizm: Volgogradskaia oblast' (Democratization, structural pluralism and unstable bicentrism: Volgograd oblast), *Polis*, no. 2.

Gustafson, Thane (1999) *Capitalism Russian Style*, Cambridge: Cambridge University Press.

McFaul, Michael (2001) *Russia's Unfinished Revolution. Political Change from Gorbachev to Putin*, Ithaca, NY and London: Cornell University Press.

Rousso, Alan (2001) 'Privatisation and corruption in Russia', paper delivered at the Tenth International Anti-Corruption Conference, Prague.

Rutland, Peter (2003) 'Putin and the oligarchs', in Dale R. Herspring (ed.), *Putin's Russia. Past Imperfect. Future Uncertain*, Lanham, MD: Rowman & Littlefield.

Sakwa, Richard (2004) *Putin. Russia's Choice*, London and New York: Routledge.

Sobell, Vlad (2004) 'The origins and future of Putin's managed democracy', Daiwa Institute of Research, Daiwa Securities America Inc. (DSA) and Daiwa Institute of Research Europe (DIREL), New York.

Sokoloff, Georges (2003) *Métamorphose de la Russie 1984–2004*, Paris: Fayard.

Stiglitz, Joseph (2000) 'The insider: what I learned at the world economic crisis', *The New Republic*, 17 April.

—— (2002) *Globalization and Its Discontents*, London: Allen Lane/Penguin Books.

US Congress (2001) *Russia's Uncertain Economic Future*, Joint Economic Committee, 107th Congress, 1st Session, Washington, DC: Government Printing Office.

Vichnevski, Anatoly (2000) *La faucille et le rouble. La modernisation conservatrice en URSS*, Paris: Gallimard.

Volkov, Vadim (2002) *Violent Entrepreneurs. The Use of Force in the Making of Russian Capitalism*, Ithaca, NY and London: Cornell University Press.

16 The rise of conglomerates in Ukraine

The Donetsk case

Hans van Zon

In the change from a centrally planned economy, two private conglomerates emerged in Donetsk that today control the larger part of the regional economy, especially the steel and coal industries. The Industrial Union of Donbass (IUD) and System Capital Management (SCM) did not emerge in a context of free competition but in a clan economy in which the assets of the regions were divided among the strongest players, while competitors were pushed aside with unfair and often criminal methods. Access to and control over public authorities was crucial in this process. The merging of political and economic power led to a situation in which the prices and allocation of main products were manipulated by the Donetsk clan structures, which constituted a quasi-monopoly. The way business was done was very much reminiscent of Soviet times, with parliamentary democracy until recently a façade for a non-competitive authoritarian regime that differs from those in most other Ukrainian provinces. The question is to what extent the Orange Revolution and the regime change that followed can change the situation in Donetsk. The influence of Donetsk in Kyiv has diminished drastically, and it seems that the cohesiveness of the Donetsk clan has been undermined through the new power configuration in Kyiv. Expansion is now sought through the acquisition of assets, mainly steel enterprises, abroad.

This chapter traces the origins of the IUD and SCM, the two most powerful conglomerates in the Ukraine. They are both based in the industrial town of Donetsk (in eastern Ukraine) and control the regional economy of the province of Donetsk. This chapter aims to explain the modus operandi and strategy of these conglomerates and the conditions for their continued expansion. It is thereby as much the story of a region as the biography of the tycoons who are heading the conglomerates. It also involves the history of a business model. The Donetsk model became associated with Viktor Yanukovitch, the former prime minister and former governor of Donetsk, who lost the presidential elections of 2004 during the Orange Revolution (which unseated a corrupt regime that had committed massive electoral fraud).

One of the puzzles of independent Ukraine is how conglomerates built on 'industries of the past', that is, coal and steel, could become the most successful.[1] It will be argued that their success is to a large extent related to the merging of politics and economics, which means growing at the expense of state property and thanks to state subsidies. The success of the conglomerates of Donetsk is also a result of the relative success of the Donetsk model, once characterised as quasi-decentralised central planning. The model gave some stability to the regional economy of Donetsk and seemed to fit very well in the traditions of the Donbass.

Ukraine and the rising Donetsk clan

The primary context of Donetsk is Ukraine, which became independent in 1991. Since then Ukraine has known an economic and social implosion as a result of the abolishment of the centrally planned economy and communism, and the dissolution of the Soviet Union. Rather than a transition towards market economy and parliamentary democracy Ukrainians saw a transition towards a neo-patrimonial society and kleptocracy. Real income of Ukrainian households contracted by 44 per cent from 1992 to 2000. Often, Ukrainians were not paid for months and usually their jobs did not provide enough income for survival. They had to take second or even third jobs in order to survive. Often their private plots provided the means for survival. Per capita gross domestic product (based on purchasing power parity) fell to $2,000 in 1998, somewhere between that of China and India, and only half that of Russia.

The difference with Russia can be explained by the fact that Russia is an oil and gas exporter, while Ukraine imports most of its consumed energy. Moreover, Russia took over the central Soviet state bureaucracy that had ample governing experience while the Ukrainian elite was inexperienced in running a country, let alone building state institutions almost from scratch.[2] Ukrainian leaders preferred a slow path of reform. While privatisation of large enterprises took place in Russia during the mid-1990s, in Ukraine it only started in the late 1990s. Therefore, oligarchs appeared on the political scene later than in Russia.

Authoritarian rule in the Ukraine was softer than in Russia, partly because of the diversity in regional cultures that had to be accommodated. Some western Ukrainian provinces had (historic) experience with pluralistic power structures under Polish or Austrian rule, and the strength of the democratic and nationalist movement was traditionally much stronger than in eastern Ukraine. Despite increasingly authoritarian rule under President Leonid Kuchma (1994–2004), the opposition managed to strengthen with Viktor Yushchenko, who was prime minister during 2000–1, as its undisputed leader. It was, above all, the spread of corruption that angered the population. Despite the economic growth since 2000, dissatisfaction spread as the overwhelming majority of the population had very little share in it. In November 2004 fraudulent elections led to massive demonstrations that finally forced a rerun of the presidential election: the outcome was that Yushchenko won and Viktor Yanukovitch, former governor of Donetsk, was defeated. Many Yushchenko voters feared that with Yanukovitch as president, Ukraine would follow the Donetsk model of governance, which is a non-competitive form of authoritarian rule, with closer relations with, and even submission to, Russia.

Although Donetsk had always been part of the Ukraine it felt traditionally closer to Moscow. Most inhabitants of Donetsk are Russian speakers and many are ethnic Russians.[3] Even more than other Ukrainian regions, Donetsk had been integrated in the Soviet economy. Even in Soviet and Tsarist times the Donbass (Donetsk province is together with neighbouring Luhansk part of the Donbass region) was a region with a pronounced character. The population came from all parts of the vast country in order to work in the coal mines and steel mills that started to emerge in the nineteenth century. These workers were frequently peasants who sought to escape slavery, and a spirit of freedom characterised the new industrial region.[4] The Soviet Union gave a major boost to the region, which in turn became a showcase for Soviet industrialisation. A cohesive territorial production complex emerged around heavy industries. Even nowadays one-fifth of all employed work in coal mining, and heavy industry still accounts for more than half of industrial production. Coal and steel workers were well paid and constituted the elite of the workforce. However, a relative decline of the Donbass coal industry started in the 1970s and a process of disinvestment began.

Although the Donbass was a model region it also suffered more than its share of Stalinist repression. Nevertheless, a spirit of combativeness remained alive and the Donetsk clan dared to start a conflict with the centre in Moscow that culminated in a miners' strike in 1989, initiated by Yefim Zviahilsky, director of the Zasiadko mine, the biggest mine in the Soviet Union. The reason behind the strike was the intensification of mining and also a shift in investments from Donbass to Kuzbass. It was the first big miners' strike in Soviet history and shook the Soviet establishment.

The end of Soviet rule saw the emergence of clan networks in Donetsk that operated partly legally and partly 'in the shadows'. The reforms under Mikhail Gorbachev, especially the creation of private cooperatives, gave opportunities for the upper echelons of the party-state, notably the Komsomol (communist youth organisation) leaders, to enrich themselves by profiting from scarcities in many fields.[5] They established construction companies and real estate business and became active in show business. Above all, trade activities were profitable. Satellite companies were formed around large state enterprises while trading with them. Even before the collapse of the Soviet Union, fortunes had been made by squeezing state-owned companies. The bureaucracy gradually started to appropriate state assets more openly.

In Donetsk the myriad of commercial firms that emerged around large state enterprises were connected to these enterprises through close personal links. Often, the commercial firms that provided services to these state-owned companies or purchased their products were headed by close relatives of the directors of the state-owned companies; and sometimes the directors of the state-owned companies themselves headed the commercial companies. The squeezing of state-owned enterprises was overseen by the local and provincial public authorities. They were complicit in this state-managed economy and profited directly from the plunder of state-owned companies. Often, state functionaries were involved in the commercial firms and without the approval of state functionaries, the squeezing of state-owned enterprises would not have been possible. Therefore, the primary accumulation of capital in Donetsk was based on the plunder of state-owned companies with the complicity of public authorities.

After the independence of the Ukraine, during the period of hyperinflation (1992–5) that followed, the commercial firms boomed as prices were freed and opportunities for speculation widened. Especially with energy trade and steel exports huge fortunes have been made, while in contrast the population lost its savings and purchasing power. In Donetsk the origins of many fortunes lay in state-owned coal mining. A very popular business was supplying steel, equipment, conveyor belts and other materials to coal mines in exchange for coal (especially coke coal) with its further supply to coke-chemical plants, metallurgical enterprises and power plants. Although coal mining was a loss-making sector and dependent upon massive state subsidies, commercial groups were price setters and created big profit margins in trading coal. Through their influence upon public authorities in Donetsk they arranged that they were appointed as the sole coal suppliers for enterprises. This also happened with the gas and electricity trades.

Part of the profits of these commercial firms disappeared into offshore accounts; other parts were used for buying up other firms. In the waves of privatisation commercial firms acquired a broad range of enterprises. Privatisation started with, for example, local football clubs, hotels, cafés and restaurants. Then the large strategic enterprises that are dominating the economy of Donetsk were privatised from the late 1990s onwards.

With this so-called transition, former communist leaders stayed in power, gradually supplemented by representatives of the new commercial groups and criminal elements. Elections were manipulated and the popular voice was barely represented in the polity of Donetsk. Starting in 1992, hired killers assassinated many leaders of the criminal gangs that terrorised the Donbass, and by 1994 practically all gang leaders of the 'old generation' had been assassinated. In 1994 and 1995 all attempts of gangs led by Georgians, Armenians and Dagestanians to take over control were thwarted and Akhmet Bragin (Alik the Greek), a man of 'great authority' in underworld circles, took over control over the local market.

In 1993 local leaders decided to influence decision-making in Kyiv and organised a wave of coal miners' strikes that brought Yefim Zviahilsky as deputy prime minister and later prime minister to Kyiv. At the same time the Donetsk clan began to reconquer what the Dnipropetrovsk clan (headed by Kuchma, prime minister duting 1993–3) had taken away from them.

With the appointment of prominent clan member Vladimir Shcherban as head of the provincial council (in July 1994), the clan was also at the top of the political hierarchy in Donetsk. After Kuchma had been elected as president in 1994 he decided to prosecute Zviahilsky for the embezzlement of $20 million. Zviahilsky fled to Israel, following which Bragin and Yevhen Shcherban were able to establish themselves as undisputed leaders. The new clan leaders kept the old generation of leaders at bay.

In 1995 the IUD was founded with Sergey Taruta as acting director. However, Bragin and Yevhen Shcherban were the real power behind the IUD. The initial purpose of the IUD was to make money by supplying gas to enterprises in the region and by asset stripping the companies they acquired or started to control during the early phase of transition. In the mid-1990s, clashes between competing clans about control over energy supplies became very violent. Bragin, at that time owner of the football club Shakhtyer and mentor of Rinat Akhmetov, the present most powerful tycoon in Donetsk, was blown up with six of his bodyguards during a football match. Later Yevhen Shcherban was gunned down, and two other leading Donetsk businessmen were assassinated. As a result of all this in 1996 Vladimir Shcherban was removed as head of the provincial council.

Outsiders from other Ukrainian regions were also involved in these violent clashes in Donetsk. Prime Minister Pavel Lazarenko (1996–7), from a clan based in Dnipropretovsk, amassed a fortune by buying and selling natural gas from Russia. He sought to expand his business empire by taking control of steel enterprises in Donetsk, and wanted his United Energy Systems to control the emerging chain of gas–metal–gas pipes (Lyakh 2001: 9). Lazarenko also wanted to prevent the emergence of a united Donbass clan that could outgrow all other Ukrainian clans. To this end according to the general prosecutor of Ukraine, he ordered, the killing of several leaders of the Donetsk clan, including Bragin and Yevgeny Shcherban. The Donetsk groups lost the conflict and concentrated afterwards on seizing control over steel enterprises in Donetsk.

Between 1995 and 1997 the unification of fragmented elite groups started under the banner of regional autonomy. Politicians from Donetsk wanted regional autonomy in order to take control of local energy resources and to maintain the freedom to develop economic relations with Russia. Also groups that were previously involved in the shadow economy became active in legal business. This period was marked by a further criminalisation of the political sphere. In May 1997, after ten months being governor of Donetsk, the Lazarenko protégé Sergey Poliakov was forced to resign after Donetsk tycoon Akhmetov, who had inherited the business empire of Bragin, waged a campaign against him. Viktor Yanukovitch, a close associate of Akhmetov with a background of convictions for robbery and assault and two jail terms, replaced him. Vitali Gaiduk, also from IUD, became his first deputy. Yanukovitch's appointment was a compromise between Donetsk and the authorities in Kyiv. A co-founder of IUD, he had business interests in Donetsk and was close to Akhmetov, but at the same time he supported President Kuchma. Yanukovitch, Akhmetov and Boris Kolesnikov (Akhmetov's associate and close friend) put an end to uncontrolled criminal activities and restored order. Restoring order, however, did not mean restoring rule of law; in Donetsk the law of the strongest reigned.

Monopolisation and quasi-decentralised central planning

The new businessmen (the 'merchants') clearly stayed aloof from the red directors (or 'strong bosses') that made their fortunes in the first phase of transition, such as Yefim Zviahilsky, Vladimir Rybak (former mayor of Donetsk) and Vladimir Boyko (director of Illich steel mill), and they gradually overshadowed them. After the coal mines and coke factories, the major commercial groups took control over the steel enterprises (most of which were privatised from 1998 onwards) and transformed themselves into financial-industrial groups (FIGs). The FIGs were so powerful, financially and politically, and so well organised, having eliminated hundreds of small commercial competitors while forging unity among the few remaining holding companies, that the takeover of the large enterprises in Donetsk was an easy task. Corruption and extortion was used in the process. They focused first on controlling the supply of raw materials to local businesses, starting with coal and gas, and later iron ore.

In 2000, the privatisation of machine-building enterprises started and local FIGs obtained controlling stakes in most of these enterprises. The IUD and the related ARS group created Ukruglemash, which unified six local enterprises producing equipment for mining and steel manufacturing. One year later Donbassenergo, the largest energy distributor in Ukraine and owner of several thermal power generating stations, also came under the control of IUD after a shadow privatisation. As was the case for all regional energy distributors, Donbassenergo was heavily indebted. A commercial company linked to steel mills and under the control of the IUD filed a lawsuit against Donbassenergo related to a debt of $50 million, and the court in Donetsk declared Donbassenergo bankrupt. Donbassenergo's assets were assessed by a company that valued its property at approximately 20 per cent of its market value (although the amount owed to Donbassenergo was valued at more than $285 million, while payables were $415 million). With the auction of Donbassenergo the IUD gained control over by far the largest power supplier in Donbass. The government and President Kuchma protested but were unable to annul the court verdict.

In short, the whole energy sector (basic industries plus the larger part of machine-building) in Donetsk has come under the control of the Donetsk FIGs, who were closely cooperating with each other.[6] Energy deliveries to all enterprises in Donetsk are now controlled by the Donetsk clan. The FIGs have integrated production in Donetsk both horizontally and vertically.

Vertical integration has the advantage of avoiding value added tax in the production chain.

Until 2000 the Donetsk clan tried to consolidate its position in Donetsk while keeping firms from other regions and countries out. The clan hardly ventured beyond the region, apart from some attempts to acquire enterprises in Dnipropretrovsk and Crimea. This changed from 2000 onwards.

Privatisation was meant, according to the Ukrainian government, to create more efficient economic structures and competition. Instead, in Donetsk, privatisation created a quasi-monopoly that controlled the whole regional economy. The Donetsk clan managed to get a monopoly on most of the inputs for the steel industry, which then allowed them to squeeze competitors out of the market. For example, in 2004 Akhmetov came to control the iron ore production in the Ukraine. In December of that year, in the midst of presidential elections, the iron ore producers raised prices from 20 to 34 per cent while pointing to shortages, forcing some of Ukraine's major steel mills that did not belong to the Donetsk clan to a halt. However, the rest of the year all steel mills had been fully supplied with ore and the ministry had even made efforts to cut the import of ore. Also, when the state still owned the iron ore production, steel producers never complained of shortages. A further problem nowadays is the super-profits made by intermediaries who trade the ore (*The Day* 15 February 2005).[7] A similar problem exists for the supply of coking coal that is largely controlled by Akhmetov's enterprises. Ukrainian producers that are not part of the clan structures had to pay 30 to 80 per cent more than a market-based price for coke and iron ore, according to President Yushchenko (*Ukrayinska Pravda* 10 February 2005). Domestic consumers paid 10–15 per cent more than foreign consumers for the same Ukrainian steel.

Another example is the privatisation of Pavlogradvuhilla coal mine, which was very profitable. First public authorities closed the coal mine with the argument that it was not profitable, showing Western donors that they were serious about restructuring the coal industry. Subsequently, in July 2004, the coal mine was sold to Akhmetov for 2.4 million hryvna (the currency of the Ukraine) although the mine had been valued at ten times more (*Ukrayinska Pravda* 2 February 2005). These are all examples of how the expansion of the Donetsk conglomerates is not the result of raising productivity and product quality but of abusing monopoly positions and privileged access to state resources.

The monopolisation of the regional economy of Donetsk led to what some analysts describe as quasi-decentralised central planning. No enterprise can do business in Donetsk without the permission of the ruling clans. Markets are highly regulated by price manipulation and tax evasion. In addition, the state subsidises the Donetsk clan through corrupt schemes. For example, 2 billion hryvna a year has been spent recently to subsidise the coal industry that is mainly state-owned yet controlled by the Donetsk clan, including the profitable coke sector that delivers to the steel industry. According to

President Yushchenko, all the resources that are being invested into the coal sector are being siphoned off to the shadow sector and are therefore not yielding any results (*Ukrainian News Agency* 19 May 2005). Among the major problems of the coal industry identified by the World Bank are asset stripping, inappropriate mixture of commercial and public interests, and murky ownership structures (World Bank 2003: 10).[8]

The steel industry is very energy intensive, especially in the Ukraine. During the mid-1990s, energy accounted for 60 per cent of the production costs of cast iron whereas this was only 18 to 25 per cent in the Organization for Economic Co-operation and Development (OECD) area (*Zerkalo Nedeli* 5 January 2002). Ukrainian steel enterprises thus use up to 60 per cent more energy than their foreign competitors. However, Ukrainian steel enterprises can remain competitive through tax preferences, cheap inputs and the absence of environmental protection. Of mine equipment production in the Ukraine, 90 per cent is owned by IUD which can therefore dictate prices. From 2000 to 2005, mine equipment became 200 per cent more expensive, coking coal 53 per cent and energy coal 49 per cent.[9] Meanwhile banks only served enterprises of the Donetsk clan and they were also used to launder money.

Donetsk contributes only 7.7 per cent to the national budget whereas it has 9.9 per cent of the Ukrainian population and represents 12.4 per cent of the nation's gross value added.[10] This can be explained, among other things, by subsidies for coal mines, tax preferences for steel enterprises and enterprises in Free Economic Zones, created in 1999. Moreover, non-payment for energy is, in Donetsk, more frequent than in Ukraine as a whole. In 2004 only 78 per cent of energy deliveries were paid and in January 2005 only 66 per cent, the lowest percentages for the Ukraine. Approximately two-thirds of the regional economy of Donetsk is 'in the shadows', while in the Ukraine as a whole it is 55 per cent, according to President Yushchenko (*Ukrayinska Pravda* 10 February 2005). It is an indicator of the level of criminalisation of the Donetsk economy. Due to this criminalisation foreign investors are afraid to invest in Donetsk. In 2003 the inflow of foreign direct investment in Donetsk province was $90.2 million, which was only 2.7 per cent of the foreign direct investment inflow into the Ukraine that year (Statistitshnii Tshoritsnik Ukraini 2003: 279)

The way in which the Ukranian local and provincial authorities operate nowadays are very reminiscent of Soviet methods. For example, in 2000 local transport was faced with a crisis as a result of dwindling allocations from the ministry and many workers could not reach their place of work. The mayor of Donetsk called local enterprises to a meeting and asked them to provide scrap metal for free, so that local steel enterprises could process it and the receipts used to buy buses. Student brigades were also created to assist in improving the public transport infrastructure (*Zerkalo Nedeli* 3 July 2001). Provincial Governor Yanukovitch was well known for this hands-on style of management, which closely resembled problem-solving methods in communist times. As journalist Vladimir Belov wrote:

> The new wave of young Donetsk representatives was consistent with
> talented and sober-minded people. They realised that the constant
> robbery of the region could cause a social outburst that would destroy
> everything and, first of all, themselves. That is why, in the first run, in
> 1998 Yanukovitch covered the pension debts, and a year after he
> managed to repay the wage debts to the employees of budget subsidised
> organisations. This eased the tensions in the region and secured the
> teachers' and doctors' loyalty to the local authorities, which essentially
> simplified the control over the election process.
>
> (*Donetskiye Novosti* 19 December 2002)

Like the communist rulers before them, the leaders of Donetsk realised that
even they, while dividing the region's assets among themselves, needed a
certain level of legitimacy. When interviewed during the last presidential
campaign, supporters of Yanukovitch in Donetsk often referred to his support
for coal mines while Yushchenko, when prime minister, was determined to
close them. They also referred to the more regular payment of pensions
and salaries under Prime Minister Yanukovitch.

The account given above shows the development of the regional economy
and polity. Informal ways of doing business are very much rooted in the
way things were done in Soviet times. Also the way authorities and tycoons
have dealt with dissent in reminiscent of Soviet times. Critical journalists
are systematically harassed and sometimes killed.[11] News media that come
into the hands of local tycoons immediately lose any editorial scope for
manoeuvre. For instance, when the newspaper *Segodnya* was taken over by
Akhmetov, the editor resigned because of growing censorship. When opposition candidate Yushchenko tried to organise a meeting of his party in
Donetsk in 2003, local authorities prevented him from doing so and depicted
him as a fascist. The result was that by late 2004 almost no dissident voices
could be heard in Donetsk.

Soviet-style methods of running the economy and society did not, however,
prevent an economic revival of the region from 1999 onwards. After economic growth proved sustainable, investment picked up and the machinery
industry started to boom after a decade of sharp decline. Economic
dynamism, in terms of gross domestic product (GDP) growth, was even more
pronounced in Donetsk than in the Ukraine as a whole. Donetsk accounted
in 2004 for 25.4 per cent of Ukrainian exports (21.5 per cent in 2003 and
18.2 per cent in 2001) although it held only 9.9 per cent of the Ukrainian
population. Therefore many in Kyiv and other provincial capitals looked
with interest to the way the Donetsk clan was managing the regional economy
of Donetsk.

The biography of Rinat Akhmetov, nowadays by far the richest man in the
Ukraine, is illustrative of the history of the Donetsk clan and the regional economy of Donetsk. Rinat Leonidovich Akhmetov was born in 1966 in a family
of coal miners (of Tatar origin) in the city of Donetsk. He graduated from the

Economics Department of the Donetsk State University in the early 1990s. As early as 1986 Rinat and his brother Igor were involved in criminal activities. Igor was caught in Gorlovka, a small town in Donetsk, shortly after a robbery where three people had been killed, however no criminal proceedings against the brothers Akhmetov were started. According to an anonymous former policeman (*Grani Plus* 7 July 2005), part of the police and secret service protected criminal groupings even in those times. At that time Akhmetov was active in the gambling business, but shortly afterwards he became involved in illegal cloth trading as an assistant of Bragin. The vice procurer, Gennady Vasileev, who would later become general prosecutor of the Ukraine, helped Bragin in obtaining property. And in the early 1990s Akhmetov started acquiring property through extortion, helped, among others, by Vladimir Malitsev, then general of the secret service in Donetsk province, and later to become head of security of SCM, owned by Akhmetov.

Akhmetov founded the Donetsk City Bank in 1995. At the time he was less influential than the other clan members, but in 1995 and 1996 the series of assassinations of powerful men in Donetsk described earlier (including Bragin and Yevhen Shcherban) changed the situation and Akhmetov emerged as the *primus inter parus*. He inherited a vast financial empire from Bragin.[12] Until 2003 Akhmetov did not officially interfere in politics. He was a well-known figure in Donetsk, pouring a lot of money into football club Shakhtyer, which he owned, and doing charity work. By 2004 Akhmetov's enterprises employed 300,000 people and he had assets worth $2.4 billion.[13]

Economic and political expansion

In the period of 2001 to 2003 a redistribution of assets took place in order to streamline the portfolio of activities of the major groupings. Rinat Akhmetov founded SCM and the IUD became the second most important group, led by Sergey Taruta. In this restructuring of assets the Donetsk clan lost some of the cohesiveness that had made it so strong in Kyiv. On the other hand, the redistribution of assets made the core FIGs more efficient and freed finances to expand further beyond the borders of Donetsk. This expansion first took place in the bordering provinces of Zaporizhzhya, Dnipropetrovsk, Luhansk and Crimea, and later in Kyiv. And the FIGs started to enter other regions and other countries.

By 2004 SCM was the twelfth largest steel producer in the world with 15.4 million tonnes a year (*Financial Times* 31 May 2005). Apart from large steel mills (such as Azov steel, and Krivorizstal until mid-2005), coal mines, iron ore producers and coke factories, SCM owns also several bakeries and breweries in Donetsk as well as several hotels, the Segodnya publishing group (Kyiv), the Ukraine TV and radio company, and a local mobile phone company. It also has majority shares in the Donetsk City Bank, the First Ukrainian International Bank and ASKA insurance company. Recently SCM acquired the Italian steel mill Ferriera Valsider, made a bid for the

Czech steel mill in Vitkovice (together with IUD but lost to Eurasia Holding
from Russia), and tried to acquire a Turkish steel mill for about $1 billion
(*Zerkalo Nedeli* 7 May 2005; *Ukrayinska Pravda* 16 June 2005). Of SCM assets
80 per cent is in the steel industry. There is a strategic alliance with Leman
Commodities in Switzerland. A new development is that SCM is working
with Western banks to finance its operations. Investment plans for the coming
five years amount to $3 billion and the plan is to borrow 70 per cent of
this amount (*Zerkalo Nedeli* 7 May 2005).

The most important assets of IUD are the Alchevsk metallurgical plant,
the Dnipropetrovsk tube plant, the Dnipropetrovsk steel mill, the Dunaferr
steel mill (Hungary), DAM steel (Hungary), the Alchevsk coke plant,
Duzhkovsky ceramic works and a range of machine-building plants. In 2004
IUD had a turnover of 12 billion hryvna and a net profit of 2 billion hryvna
(*Ukrayinska Pravda* 11 March 2005). IUD is more internationally orientated
than SCM and has more machine-building plants than SCM. It also has a
strong presence in the local agro-business. While SCM owns the football
club Shakhtyer Donetsk, IUD owns the local rival Metallurg.[14] IUD has
started to use the services of international banks and secured a loan of $250
million from a European consortium (*Financial Times* 31 May 2005). From
2003 to 2005 IUD bought two steel enterprises in Hungary, obtained a 39
per cent stake in the Uzbek Uzneftegazstroi, acquired a steel plant in
Czestochowa (Poland) and showed interest in a Polish shipyard (*Zerkalo Nedeli*
20 February 2004; *Financial Times* 31 May 2005). These initiatives fit into
the strategy of controlling whole production cycles. However, the purchase
of Huta Czestochowa was initially blocked by the Polish government and
the mill was granted to the Indian steel tycoon Mittal, based in London.
The Polish minister Sharavarski said that 'Poland will rather deal with an
enterprise from the first-class industrial league than with some odd investors'.
According to the Polish Agency for Internal Security, IUD represented
capital from an unclear origin, a non-transparent corporate structure and
possible money laundering (*Polish News Bulletin* 4 March 2004). However, in
January 2005 a Polish court decided that the privatisation was illegal and
that the tender had to be organised again; in July 2005 IUD bought the
steel plant.

After the violent clashes in 1995 and 1996, the Donetsk clans built up
their empires in silence without openly challenging state power in Kyiv. A
compromise emerged between President Kuchma and Donetsk in 1998:
Donetsk organised support for the president, guaranteeing a majority for
him during the presidential elections of 1999 in Donbass, and in return the
government in Kyiv let the Donetsk clan manage its own affairs without
asking awkward questions about how they had accumulated their fortunes.
The device was 'politics is done in Kyiv and business in the Donbass'.
It meant that the Donetsk clan could constitute its own fiefdom, with its
own rules, which differ from those in Kyiv, under a condition of loyalty to
President Kuchma. Indeed, in 1999 Donetsk organised a majority for

President Kuchma against his contender, the communist Petro Symonenko, despite the fact that Donetsk was the bastion of Symonenko.[15] Again, in 2002 during the parliamentary elections, the Donetsk clan delivered the vote for pro-presidential political parties. Actually, Donetsk was the only province where pro-presidential parties, united under 'For a United Ukraine', acquired a majority.

An innovation in Donetsk was the creation of Free Economic Zones. President Kuchma supported this idea in 1999 in exchange for election victory in Donetsk during the presidential elections. However, in the virtual world of Donetsk everything is different from how it appears. Free Economic Zones were not intended to attract foreign direct investment through tax holidays but to enable tax evasion by enterprises of the Donetsk clan.[16]

President Kuchma ruled by balancing the interests of the Ukraine's dominant clans. When Minister of Energy Yulia Timoshenko wanted to reform the coal mining industry (in 2000), thereby touching upon vital interests of the Donetsk clan, she was sacked and then jailed (for a short time), after the Donetsk clan had lobbied for her dismissal. In 2001 Prime Minister Yushchenko was sacked and replaced by the less reform-minded Anatoly Kinakh, while oligarch Viktor Medvedchuk, who orchestrated the fall of Yushchenko in parliament, rose to prominence after becoming the head of the presidential administration, so becoming the second most influential man in the Ukraine.[17] He even managed to get the president to sign a decree that the government had to obey all orders from the presidential administration. As Medvedchuk became too powerful in the eyes of the president, the Donetsk clan was allowed to 'deliver' the prime minister in November 2002 when the governor of Donetsk, Viktor Yanukovitch, accepted the post. It was also a reward for delivering the vote in the elections of 1999 and 2002. Many from the Donetsk clan moved to Kyiv with Yanukovitch in order to occupy key posts. This meant that coal mining, with its complicated barter schemes (with which coal mines were squeezed and state subsidies for coal mines were used for supporting the expanding conglomerates), was not reformed.[18]

In Kyiv, the Donetsk clan not only started to control the energy ministry (after Yulia Timoshenko left the post in January 2001), but also Mykola Azarov, who had led the Party of the Regions (represented the interests of the Donetsk clan), came to head the tax office, thereby making sure that the Donetsk clan would not pay too many taxes. And in March 2003 Medvedchuk's man in the state property fund was replaced by a man from Donetsk (*Russia and Eurasia Review* 30 April 2003). Moreover, Henadiy Vasylyev, former prosecutor in Donetsk Oblast, who was in office during the gang wars in the province without managing to capture a single one of the assassins of the dozens of politicians and gang masters, managed to become general prosecutor. Even in his new post he harassed journalists who tried to publish about his dealings with organised crime (*BBC Monitoring Service* 22 December 2003).

Yanukovitch gained greater autonomy with respect to the presidential administration, unlike his predecessor Prime Minister Anatoly Kinakh, who had to accept daily interference from the presidential administration in the running of his government. In March 2003 the president decreed that executive bodies would no longer be legally obliged to obey orders from the presidential administration (*Russia and Eurasia Review* 30 April 2003). However, the president interfered personally in the work of government and, for example, overruled the government decision not to raise tariffs for rail transport of coal in 2003.

The advance of the Donetsk clan in Kyiv greatly helped their business interests, and they acquired many enterprises extremely cheaply. The most spectacular deal was the sale of the steel mill Krivorozstal for $800 million to Rinat Akhmetov and Kuchma's son-in-law Viktor Pinchuk while their competitors had bid $2.5 billion. The terms of the tender were such that only Akhmetov and Pinchuk could qualify. In 2004 SCM also acquired the ore enrichment works Skhidenerho, the Donetsk power plant and distributor Servis-Interest, Pavlohradvuhilya (Ukraine's largest coal producer), Dokuchayevsk Flux and Dolomite Combine, Novotriyitske Rudoupravlinnya company and Ktyvbaspidryvprom enterprise.

However, the poor manners of the Donetsk clan (unable to leave behind the ways of the criminal milieux from which many originated) and the way they ignored the interests of other clans created opposition. Especially the bare knuckles approach to governance of Prime Minister Yanukovitch raised eyebrows. Also, within the Donetsk clan, animosity increased, in particular once it became clear that Yanukovitch would lose the presidential elections.[19] Although most Ukrainian oligarchs supported the nomination of Yanukovitch as successor to Leonid Kuchma in the presidential elections of 2004, many did not do so wholeheartedly because he represented one clan too many. He was too weak a politician and too much an instrument of the powers that stood behind him. Also, the turning away of Ukrainian foreign policy from European integration towards submission to Russia alarmed many (in 2003 the Ukrainian government signed a treaty for a CIS Economic Space that would indicate further submission to Russia). Even among the richest oligarchs, there were those who were not happy with Yanukovitch becoming president, and a significant part of the security establishment sided with opposition candidate Yushchenko.

The Orange Revolution in 2004, which led to the rerun of the fraudulent presidential election, can also be seen as an end of the attempt to supplant the Donetsk model – a merging of political and economic power with total suppression of dissent and unbridled corruption – to the national level. It remains to be seen whether the Donetsk model, which is very much an extension of Soviet civilisation, is sustainable in Donetsk and the neighbouring provinces of eastern and southern Ukraine. In Donetsk, by the end of May 2005, three vice governors and seven heads of district administration had still not been replaced, according to the head of the presidential administration Alexander Zinchenko. He commented that the backbone of corruption and the shadow economy had not been smashed yet, and that democracy and media freedom still did not exist (*Ukrainskaya Pravda* 26 May 2005). According to President Yushchenko in early June 2005, the eastern province of Zaporizhzhya, bordering Donetsk, is still ruled in a feudal way by a clan of three families (*BBC Monitoring Service* 4 June 2005).

The Donetsk conglomerates in the new Ukraine

How should the economic success of the Donetsk conglomerates be measured? Has the economic growth in Donetsk mainly come from the take up of unused capacities in the enterprises bought by the Donetsk clan, opening up new markets? Or is the economic dynamism also related to new management practices, increased productivity and innovation in the enterprises managed by the Donetsk clan? In the case of SCM, the purchased companies became more profitable, which might be related to better marketing strategies and the streamlining of enterprises. Akhmetov has been keen to appoint younger and better-qualified managers, but some say that his inclination to micro-manage his enterprises neutralised this management potential. Akhmetov is very good at asset manipulation yet less so at management. So far Akhmetov has not appeared to be a genuine captain of industry. It seems that in the case of SCM enterprises, as in most Ukrainian enterprises, it is still the *khozhain* (master) who runs the place, exhibiting an obsessive control over all aspects of the enterprise, and not a modern manager. These enterprises also have estate-like qualities, governing many aspects of the worker's life, including housing and leisure activities. However, McKinsey has been hired recently to improve management (*Zerkalo Nedeli* 7 May 2005).

   Growth might be to a large extent export driven and related to the dynamism of the world steel market, as there are no signs that steel mills in Donetsk have been fundamentally restructured. It is still the case that 64 per cent of steel is produced in open-hearth furnaces (Martin ovens), which were abandoned several decades ago in the Western world.[20] Steel production increased mainly through the exploitation of previously unused capacities rather than through investing in new capacities, although more recently there have been substantial investments.[21] Steel output in the Ukraine, two-thirds of which originates from Donetsk, increased in dollar terms by 150 per cent from 2001 to 2004, and in 2004 steel accounted for 40 per cent of Ukrainian exports and 27 per cent of Ukrainian industrial output. However, output in tonnes only increased by 15 per cent: from 33 to 38 million tonnes (*Financial Times* 31 May 2005). In the coal sector production recently has gone up, but working circumstances remain archaic: 69 per cent of the mines have not been reconstructed for the past 20 years; two-thirds of machinery needs urgent replacement; and almost 60 per cent of coal is extracted manually, with hammers.[22] President Yushchenko maintains that most state subsidies for the coal industry disappear in the pockets of intermediaries who operate 'in the shadows' (*Ukrayinska Pravda* 20 May 2005).

392   *Hans van Zon*

The present economic structure of Donetsk is very unfavourable and biased towards heavy industry. In 2003 investments were only 38 per cent of the 1990 level (Statistitshnii Tshoritsnik Ukraini 2003: 219), and while the Ukraine has little investment in comparison with other Central European countries, investment in Donetsk has been even more limited than in the Ukraine as a whole.[23] Ferrous metals accounted for 39 per cent of industrial production in Donetsk, coal mining 17 per cent and electric power generation 13 per cent (in 2002). The industrial structure of Donetsk deteriorated rapidly during the 1990s. In 2000, the basic industries accounted for 81 per cent of all industrial output while in 1990 this had been 59 per cent. The share of light industry in industrial output was decimated from 7 per cent in 1990 to 0.3 per cent in 2000 and the share of food processing decreased from 7.9 to 5.3 per cent in the same period. Only since 1999 have the non-basic industries started to grow faster than the basic industries. Machine-building suffered most during the 1990s. The share in industrial output decreased from 17 per cent in 1990 to 9 per cent in 2000, which should be seen in the context of a fall in industrial output of 48 per cent in the 1990s. It is conspicuous that high value industries, in which one might expect that Donetsk might have a competitive advantage, have seen the sharpest decline.

This concentration of economic activity into basic (heavy) industry is matched with economic concentration into a small number of large enterprises. Recent growth in Donetsk has been secured by two dozen large enterprises. In 2000 almost two-thirds of regional industrial sales were provided by only 17 enterprises, 8 of which were steel plants. Only 2 enterprises out of these 17 do not belong to heavy industry, showing that recent industrial growth is based on sectors with a bleak future. Finally, export performance is fragile since 70 per cent of Donetsk exports consist of steel and steel products (Lyakh 2001: 4).

The economic success of the Donetsk clan is related, apart from its concentration in one region, to the fact that it tried to control whole production chains while squeezing monopoly profits and seizing state assets on the cheap. Oligarchs from other regions often created very diverse portfolios or concentrated on acquiring media assets. An advantage for the oligarchs from Donetsk is that they were not very prominent in politics. Both Sergei Taruta, the director of IUD, and Rinat Akhmetov shunned the media, and it was only in 2003 that Akhmetov started to give interviews about politics, and relying wholeheartedly on the success of his candidate Yanukovitch in the 2004 presidential elections. Taruta, the third richest man in Ukraine, with an estimated fortune of $1 billion, maintained good relations with both presidential candidates although officially supporting Yanukovitch. Another strength of the Donetsk clan is the cohesiveness of Donetsk province and the Donbass. Donetsk has a strong regional identity, and is proud of its legacy as an old industrial region, while its regional economy shows a high degree of cohesiveness with closed production circles (Zimmer 2002). Although massive fraud occurred in Donetsk during the presidential election in 2004, during the rerun of the elections 96 per cent of voters voted for 'their' candidate Viktor Yanukovitch (exit polls showed a similar result).[24] It points to the high level of support for the ex-governor of Donetsk as well as the level of consensus in Donetsk as far as politics is concerned.

A weakness, however, is the fact that the Donetsk clan's way of doing business is not accepted in many other parts of the Ukraine. (A rapprochement might be possible if the Donetsk clan's methods become more civilised.) Another weakness is the fact that the Donetsk clan possesses little in the way of all-Ukrainian media outlets. If the government of Yulia Timoshenko follows up its promises of cleaning up the coal mining industry and abolishing privileges for the oligarchs, the steel and coal businesses of the Donetsk clan will suffer greatly. Similarly, re-privatisation is likely to target dubious acquisitions of the Donetsk clan. However, Timoshenko stressed the strategic importance of coal mining for the Ukraine and has also promised low prices for energy and raw materials for the steel industry (*Ukrayinska Pravda* 6 May 2005, 16 June 2005). Despite this, tax preferences in the Free Economic Zones framework (which were concentrated in Donetsk) have been abolished gas prices and rail tariffs for coal transport have gone up.

Recently there have been signs of a split occurring in the cohesive Donetsk clan. In March 2005 IUD director Sergei Taruta accompanied the new President Yushchenko on his visit to Germany and proclaimed that he always had supported Yushchenko. It should be recalled that Akhmetov profited most from Yanukovitch being prime minister: during the latter's reign SCM's assets doubled in size (*Ukrayinska Pravda* 14 March 2005). After the presidential elections of 2004 Akhmetov did not immediately side with Yushchenko, and subsequently Boris Kolesnikov, a close partner of Akhmetov and head of the regional council, was arrested. Only in April 2005, after having spent some weeks abroad, did Akhmetov make some moves towards the new government in Kyiv and meet with President Yushchenko.

In September 2005 the president sacked Prime Minister Timoshenko and her government against the background of a conflict about policy orientation: Timoshenko was a proponent of the re-privatisation of many enterprises and of greater government interference in the economy, while the presidential administration favoured an opening to the world market and liberal economic policies. Subsequently the president signed a memorandum of understanding with his former opponent Yanukovitch in which, among other things, they agreed to grant local and provincial representatives immunity for prosecution and to stop re-privatisation (September 2005). This memorandum marked the division of the Orange camp and the re-entering of the Party of the Regions from Donetsk into mainstream politics. It did not prevent the re-privatisation of Krivorizstal, which was sold to Mittal for five times the amount it was sold for to Akhmetov and Pinchuk in 2004.

It seems that Yushchenko's main aim is to normalise the situation in Donetsk and to make the regional budget and regional authorities accountable to the state and not to the Donetsk clan, as the journalist Pukish-Yunko suggested

(*Vysokyy Zamok* 24 May 2005). The government of Timoshenko was addressing corruption in the Donetsk region. Among others, a gang based in Zaporizhzhya but headed by criminals from Donetsk was arrested for tax evasion amounting to hundreds of millions of hryvnas a year. It has also become known that, in 2004, companies from Donetsk paid 415 million hryvna in value added tax (VAT) but received 625 million hryvna of reimbursed VAT payments. In addition, tax evasion schemes of the iron ore companies of Akhmetov have been revealed (*Zerkali Nedeli* 21 May 2005; *Intellinews* 6 June 2005; *Ukrayinska Pravda* 16 May 2005). Nonetheless, after the sacking of Prime Minister Timoshenko no high-profile corruption cases were uncovered in Donetsk.

It should be recalled that Donetsk, and more broadly eastern Ukraine, is the economic powerhouse of the Ukraine. Donetsk province alone accounts for one-quarter of Ukrainian exports while the southeastern provinces of Donetsk, Luhansk, Dnipropetrovsk and Zaporizhzhya, where Kuchmist civil servants and tycoons are still in charge, account for 55 per cent of Ukrainian exports (2004) and 27 per cent of the population. Here the most powerful clans of the Ukraine are based – and they have many means to sabotage economic and political reforms.

Many in Donetsk feel humiliated and marginalised after the defeat in the presidential elections. After being over-represented in government during the premiership of Yanukovitch, there was not a single representative of Donetsk in the Timoshenko government. In Soviet times Donbass was a model region for the whole of the Soviet Union, situated in the heart of the country. Currently though, many in Donetsk feel as though they are in a marginalised region, far from Kyiv and far from Europe. Twice the Donetsk clan managed to supply a successful candidate for prime minister and occupy the leading political positions in Ukraine, and subsequently it has failed twice, defeated by forces outside Donetsk. In the period from 2002 to 2004 the possibility emerged of the Ukraine adopting the Donetsk model: semi-feudal oligarchic capitalism with a command-and-control approach to governance in which no dissent is tolerated. Late in 2005, it seems that the Donetsk clan has become less cohesive but it still retains enormous assets, inside and outside the region. Leverage in Kyiv is at a low, which means fewer subsidies and tax preferences from the centre. Another weak point is that the fortunes of the Donetsk clan are dependent on the world steel market. It remains to be seen to what extent the Donetsk conglomerates will shift from an asset-stripping strategy towards substantial investment and innovation in the enterprises of Donetsk. Will the IUD and SCM be able to transform their strategies in such a way as to lead Donetsk towards economic recovery?

Notes

1 This phenomenon can also be observed in Russia where, in 2004, the ten fastest growing fortunes were all held by metal industry tycoons (*AFP* 13 February 2005).

2 For a detailed comparative analysis of the Ukraine and Russia see van Zon (2000).
3 Ethnic Russians comprise 38 per cent of the population of Donetsk province (2001 census).
4 See Kuromiya (1998).
5 Already in December 1985 Alexander Yakovlev, the chief ideologue of the Communist Party, recommended in a letter to Secretary-General Michael Gorbachev the restoration of a market economy, i.e. the introduction of a capital market, and an end of the monopoly of the Communist Party (according to his memoirs, as quoted by J.-M. Chauvier in *Le Monde Diplomatique* of June 2005).
6 The Donetsk clan controls the three most important production chains in Donetsk: coking, coal-coke-steel; energy, coal-electricity-steel, and gas-steel-gas pipes.
7 Other authors point to the opportunity of selling iron ore abroad related to price rises on world markets: in 2004 Ukrainian ore exports soared as did imports by those companies who could not afford Ukrainian ore (*Zerkalo Nedeli* 21 May 2005).
8 The output of some coke mines has been pushed to more than 200 per cent of the original design capacity with the result, among other things, of a growing accident rate (World Bank 2003: 14).
9 According to Minister of Energy Ivan Plastjkov (in *Zerkalo Nedeli* 14 May 2005).
10 The figure of 7.7 per cent is from President Yushchenko as cited by BBC Monitoring Service (10 February 2005). The other figures are from Statistitshnii Tshoritsnik Ukraini (2003). According to Yushchenko, 24 per cent of all electricity debts are in Donetsk, additionally the energy debts in Donetsk increased in 2004 by 30 per cent to attain 4 billion hryvna. These figures run counter to popular beliefs nurtured by authorities according to which eastern Ukraine, including Donetsk, is massively subsidising western Ukraine.
11 A well-known case is that of journalist Ihor Aleksandrov who reported criminal activities, and was subsequently killed in 2002.
12 In 1997, Prime Minister Lazarenko admitted that Akhmetov was the only person in the Ukraine that he could be on equal terms with (this was before Lazarenko's flight to the United States).
13 This information is based on the listing of billionaires by *Forbes* magazine, according to which, in 2005, Akhmetov was number 258 of the world's richest people (www.forbes.com).
14 According to a local anecdote only two things in life are certain: one is that we are all mortal, the other is that Shakhtyer will beat the town's second club Metallurg (since 1991 Metallurg has never beaten its local rival nor has it even taken a point off them).
15 During the first round of the presidential election Leonid Kuchma had 32 per cent of the votes in Donetsk province, while the communist Symonenko had 39 per cent, and other left-wing candidates Vitrenko and Moroz respectively 12 and 6 per cent. In the second round, with only Kuchma and Symonenko, Kuchma got 52 per cent against Symonenko's 41 per cent. The turnout increased from 66 to 78 per cent.
16 Foreign enterprises were not really welcome as the Donetsk clan did not want to share the assets of Donetsk. In the words of former President Kuchma, the Free Economic Zones have become semi-criminal zones that barely attracted foreign direct investment (*Kyiv Post* 6 February 2003). The Donetsk attitude reminds one very much of the situation in Russia where, as a rule, local rulers are playing the political-economic game among themselves and consciously strategise to prevent newcomers from entering it. They keep much of the information about local affairs to themselves and have established an exclusionary system of elite politics (Mendras 1999: 304–6).

17 Twice the Ukrainian government tried to introduce genuine competition in the coal market. The first time was by the government of Prime Minister Fokin in 1992; shortly after Fokin made a speech about freeing coal prices he was forced to leave office. The second time was in 2001, when Prime Minister Yushchenko wanted to initiate reforms that would especially deprive the steel industry of cheap coal, and (after the director general of Illich steel plant reminded Yushchenko of Fokin's fate) had to leave office a few months later. At that time also the vice prime minister responsible for energy, Yulia Timoshenko, was sacked and put in jail for a short time after lobbying by the Donetsk clan (*BBC Summary of World Broadcast* 26 January 2001, 27 September 2001).

18 According to 69 per cent of the respondents in a survey, embezzlement and corruption are the major causes of the crisis in the Ukraine's coal mining industry (*The Day* 30 September 2003).

19 When Akhmetov visited Kyiv and was welcomed at the airport by Yanukovitch, the latter was slapped in the face by Akhmetov saying 'so much hay was invested in you, and you are not yet President', after which Akhmetov boarded the plane again (according to www.maidan.org.ua 9 December 2004).

20 No other country in the world has such a high share of steel production by Martin ovens; in 2003 Russia was second on the list with 23.7 per cent of steel production in Martin ovens (International Iron and Steel Institute 2004).

21 For example, in July 2004 an international consortium decided to lend $100 million to Azovstal steel mill in order to modernise the plant.

22 According to Ivan Plastjkov, Ministry for Energy, in *Zerkalo Nedeli* (14 May 2005).

23 In the first quarter of 2002 the investment level in Donetsk related to industrial output was 10.2 per cent, compared with 14.7 per cent in the Ukraine (*Ukrainian Economic Trends* March 2002). In 2001, the province of Donetsk accounted for only 11 per cent of total capital assets put into operation in the Ukraine, while Donetsk accounted for about 20 per cent of industrial production. Here it should be taken into account that in the Ukraine investment as a share of GDP (19 per cent) is rather low if compared to Central European countries (e.g. 28 per cent in Czech Republic, 24 per cent in Hungary, 20 per cent in Russia and 19 per cent in Poland; see World Bank 2005).

24 In Donetsk fraud mainly occurred through adding extra votes for Viktor Yanukovitch. In Donetsk the turnout at every third polling station was more than 100 per cent. In several polling stations in Donetsk up to 99 per cent of voters picked Yanukovitch.

Bibliography

International Iron and Steel Institute (2004) *2003, World Steel in Figures*.

Kovaleva, E. (2001) 'Regional politics in Ukraine's transition: Donetsk elites', contribution to the Conference Confronting Change: North East England and East European Coalfields, Newcastle, 12–13 November.

Kuromiya, Hiroaki (1998) *Freedom and Terror in the Donbas: A Ukrainian–Russian Borderland, 1870s–1990s*, Cambridge Russian, Soviet and Post-Soviet Studies, no. 104, New York: Cambridge University Press.

Lyakh, A. (2001) 'Economic restructuring and investing in the Donetsk region: internal factors and an international perspective', contribution to the Conference Confronting Change: North East England and East European Coalfields, Newcastle, 12–13 November.

Mendras, M. (1999) 'How regional elites preserve their power', *Post-Soviet Affairs*, 15 (October–December): 295–312.

Statistitshnii Tshoritsnik Ukraini (2003) (Statistical report), Kyiv.

World Bank (2003) *The Coal Sector and Mining Communities of Ukraine: Advancing Restructuring to the Benefit of All*, September, Washington, DC.

—— (2005) *World Development Indicators*, Washington, DC.

Zimmer, K. (2002) 'Einheit, Eintracht und Wiedergeburt', *Zur Rolle und Relevanz des Donezker Clans. Der politische Einfluß von Wirtschaftseliten in der Ukraine. Nationale und regionale Oligarchen*, Arbeitspapiere und Materialien, Bremen: Forschungsstelle Osteuropa.

van Zon, Hans (2000) *The Political Economy of Independent Ukraine*, Basingstoke: Palgrave Macmillan.

17 The impact of multinational investment in Central and Eastern Europe

Wioletta Niemiec and Mariusz Niemiec

Foreign capital flowing into the economy of a country in the form of foreign direct investment (FDI) leads to a number of changes, both economic and social. By building new production facilities or taking over the existing ones, foreign companies affect domestic and foreign firms, the economy as a whole as well as its segments, sectors, branches and particular markets. This impact can be both positive and negative. The positive consequences of foreign investors' influence include the transfer of modern production technologies, management methods and techniques; the introduction of new products and services, and higher quality and environmental standards; the creation of new jobs, the improvement of workforce qualifications; and better balance of payments. On the other hand, there are such negative effects of foreign investors' involvement as the risk of increased unemployment (due to the elimination of unprofitable domestic competitors from the market or restructuring of acquired companies), worsening trade balance (due to excessive import) or the inflow of so-called 'dirty technologies'.

Each country accepting foreign investors tries to influence the investors' actions in such a way that they will bring more profit than loss and satisfy the expectations of local communities. This is especially evident in Central and Eastern European (CEE) countries, which try to attract the capital they need so much to carry out their economic transformation, but are simultaneously forced to respond when foreign capital focuses only on its own objectives that do not always match these countries' needs. This study aims at assessing the significance of foreign investors for the development of these economies, particularly by pointing out positive and negative consequences of FDI.

Inflow of FDI to CEE

Foreign investors became more interested in CEE in the early 1990s, when countries of that region began market reforms that led to restructuring and modernisation of their economies and opened them to the world and foreign capital. As a result, between 1990 and 2004 these countries were able to attract increasing flows of FDI, totalling around $260 billion (see Figure 17.1).

Although in the first half of the 1990s the scale of investments was still relatively small, the situation improved considerably over the next few years. Since 1998 the annual volume of FDI inflows has not fallen below $20 billion. In 2002, investments in CEE reached a record level of $31 billion, equalling 4.6 per cent of the world's FDI (see Figure 17.2).

The upward trend in FDI inflow was halted in 2003 when CEE countries attracted less than $21 billion (3.7 per cent of the total FDIs in the world). Yet not all of the economies in the region saw FDI decrease. In fact, 10 out of the 19 CEE countries attracted more foreign investments in 2003 than a year before, while in the remaining 9 countries the inflow fell, with the biggest falls witnessed by the Czech Republic (from $8.4 billion in

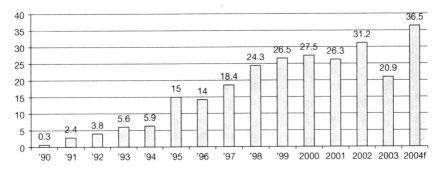

Figure 17.1 Inflow of FDI to CEE countries, 1990–2004 (US$ billion)

Note: 2004f = forecast for 2004.

Source: Compiled by the authors from UNCTAD (2004).

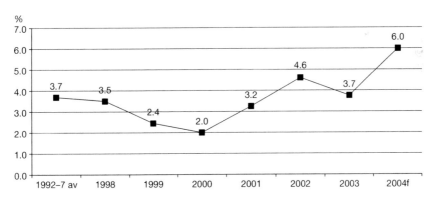

Figure 17.2 CEE's share in global FDI, 1992–2004 (percentages)

Note: 1992–7av = annual average from 1992 to 1997; 2004f = forecast for 2004.

Source: Compiled by the authors from UNCTAD (2004).

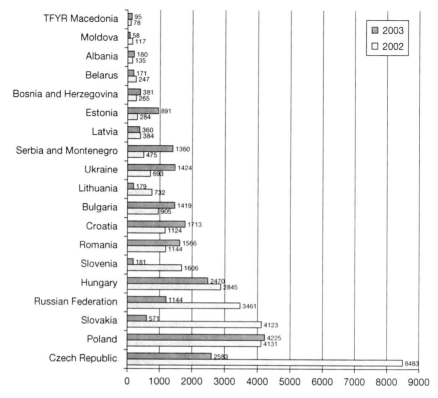

Figure 17.3 Inflow of FDI to CEE countries, 2002–3 (US$ billion)
Source: Compiled by the authors from UNCTAD (2004).

2002 to $2.5 billion in 2003) and Slovakia (from $4.1 billion in 2002 to $0.5 billion in 2003), mainly because of the fact the more important privatisation processes had been completed in that period (see Figure 17.3).

It has to be noted, however, that according to preliminary estimates of FDI in the world economy in 2004, CEE countries attracted in total over $36.5 billion, which amounts to 6.0 per cent of the $612 billion of investments in the world. If these forecasts are confirmed, this will mean that in that year CEE attracted the largest amount of capital of the last 15 years.

Major recipients of FDI in CEE

Countries in CEE differ substantially with respect to the amount of direct investments. There are five undisputed leaders in this group. The economies that so far have managed to attract the greatest number of FDIs are Poland, the Czech Republic, Hungary, Russia and Slovakia (see Table 17.1).

Table 17.1 Inflow of FDI to CEE countries, 1992–2003 (US$ billion)

Country / region	1992–7 (average)	1998	1999	2000	2001	2002	2003
CEE	11,533	24,305	26,518	27,508	26,371	31,232	20,970
Poland	2,889	6,365	7,270	9,341	5,713	4,131	4,225
Hungary	2,924	3,828	3,312	2,764	3,936	2,845	2,470
Czech Republic	1,304	3,700	6,310	4,984	5,639	8,483	2,583
Total	7,117	13,893	16,892	17,089	15,288	15,459	9,278
Share (%)	61.7%	57.2%	63.7%	62.1%	58.0%	49.5%	44.2%
Estonia	180	581	305	387	542	284	891
Latvia	229	357	347	411	163	384	360
Lithuania	108	926	486	379	446	732	179
Slovakia	235	707	428	1,925	1,584	4,123	571
Slovenia	166	218	106	137	369	1,606	181
Total	918	2,789	1,672	3,239	3,104	7,129	2,182
Share (%)	8.0%	11.5%	6.3%	11.8%	11.8%	22.8%	10.4%
Remaining countries	3,498	7,623	7,954	7,180	7,979	8,644	9,510
Share (%)	30.3%	31.4%	30.0%	26.1%	30.3%	27.7%	45.4%

Source: Compiled by the authors from UNCTAD (2004).

Three countries have been the region's main FDI beneficiaries: Poland, the Czech Republic and Hungary. Between 1998 and 2003 they together attracted $87.9 billion, which is about 56 per cent of the $159.9 billion invested in CEE in total. An analysis of the volume of FDI in particular countries reveals that the biggest number of investments went to Poland, which received over $37 billion, equalling 24 per cent of all investments in CEE between 1998 and 2003. The second country is the Czech Republic with investments amounting to $31.7 billion (20 per cent), and the third is Hungary with almost $19.2 billion (12 per cent). Such a great interest of foreign investors in the economies of Poland, the Czech Republic and Hungary results mainly from the fact that these countries, unlike others in the region, are characterised by highly advanced market reforms, relative economic, social, political and legal stability, and advanced privatisation processes. Another factor not to be overlooked is the geographic and cultural proximity to Western Europe.

Although Poland, the Czech Republic and Hungary have been the main recipients of FDI in CEE, their share in the total amount of investments coming to this region decreases every year. By 2001 their share hovered around 60 per cent (from 63.7 per cent in 1999 to 58 per cent in 2001), but in 2003 it dropped to around 44 per cent, and the preliminary data for 2004 show that the share of those three countries in the total amount of investments in CEE may be only slightly over 33 per cent.

As the share of Poland, the Czech Republic and Hungary in FDI directed to CEE decreased, other economies in the region grew in significance. At the turn of 1999 and 2000 Estonia, Lithuania, Latvia, Slovakia and Slovenia almost doubled their share of FDI in the region. We should look for reasons in, among other things, successful market reforms carried out in those countries, competent policy of attracting foreign investors, and also in growing integration of those countries with the European Union. Although over the last few years there have been significant changes in the share of countries in FDI directed to CEE, together these eight countries – all EU members since 1 May 2004 – have invariably attracted around 70 per cent of investments in the region. The year 2003 was different in this respect, as other countries of the region received around $9.5 billion of investments, which means a rise of 17.7 percentage points in comparison with the previous year. On the one hand, this is an effect of decreasing privatisation reserves in the economies of the new EU members. On the other hand there is a growing interest of foreign investors in such countries as Bulgaria, Croatia, Romania, Serbia and Montenegro, and the Ukraine, which began to reform their economies and expressed their wish to strengthen their integration with Western Europe.

Participation of foreign investors in privatisations

In the early 1990s countries in CEE began to transform their economies from the centrally planned system to the market system. A lack of domestic capital necessary for restructuring and modernisation made those countries take actions to attract as many foreign investors as possible. Since privatisation was one of the first stages of transformation, a vast majority of direct investments were realised through taking over the control of already existing companies. Between 1990 and 2003 the share of mergers and acquisitions (M&A) in the total FDI in the region increased (see Figure 17.4). In 1993,

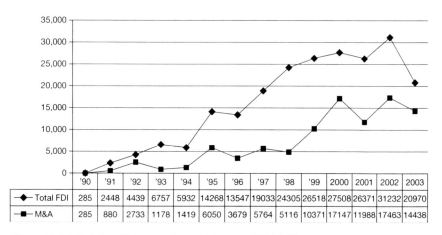

Figure 17.4 M&A in CEE countries, 1990–2003 (US$ billion)

Source: Compiled by the authors from UNCTAD (1996, 2001, 2002, 2003, 2004).

2

M&A accounted for 17 per cent ($1.2 billion of $6.7 billion) of all FDI; in 2003 this figure had risen to 70 per cent ($14.4 billion of $21 billion). The different levels of M&A in various years are a consequence of gradual privatisation in those economies, with respect to both the number of companies and also the industries and sectors included in the process.

The share of M&A in total FDI also differed geographically. In the initial period the main privatisation base was constituted by the economies of the Czech Republic, Hungary and Poland. These countries led economic transformation in CEE and, at the same, were the biggest beneficiaries of FDI. As Table 17.2 shows, in 1995 over 90 per cent of the $6 billion of M&A investments in CEE went to those three countries; the share of this type of investments was also very high (70–80 per cent) in 1990 (when the transformations began), 1996 and 2000.

Although this indicator usually exceeded 50 per cent, in 1997 it barely went over 30 per cent, which was the first sign of the investors' growing interest in other markets that had started reforms and, as a result, increased their privatisation offer, becoming a more attractive place for investments. In Russia, for example, in 1997 the value of M&A soared to $2.6 billion. Another equally significant decrease of the leaders' share in attracted privatisation acquisitions came in 2003 when the indicator reached the level of just over 25 per cent. In this case, however, it was a consequence of two factors working at the same time. First, next to Russia, which attracted 54 per cent of the total M&A in that year, new recipients of this form of investment appeared. Bulgaria, Croatia, Romania, the Ukraine, and Serbia and

Table 17.2 Share of Czech Republic, Poland and Hungary in M&A in CEE, 1990–2003 (US$ billion)

	1990	1991	1992	1993	1994	1995	1996
Total mergers and acquisitions in CEE	285	880	2,733	1,178	1,419	6,050	3,679
Czech Republic	–	–	–	226	408	2,366	507
Hungary	226	267	392	382	139	2,106	1,594
Poland	-	74	1,396	197	357	983	993
Total	226	341	1,788	805	904	5,455	3,094
Share (%)	79.3%	38.8%	65.4%	68.3%	63.7%	90.2%	84.1%

	1997	1998	1999	2000	2001	2002	2003
Total mergers and acquisitions in CEE	5,764	5,116	10,371	17,147	11,988	17,463	14,438
Czech Republic	671	362	2,402	1,924	1,968	5,204	1,756
Hungary	298	612	537	1,117	1,370	1,278	1,109
Poland	808	1,789	3,707	9,316	3,493	3,131	802
Total	1,777	2,763	6,646	12,357	6,831	9,613	3,667
Share (%)	30.8%	54.0%	64.1%	72.1%	57.0%	55.0%	25.4%

Source: Compiled by the authors from UNCTAD (2004).

Montenegro together attracted almost 20 per cent of the region's M&A. Second, this shift in the investors' interest resulted from the fact that important privatisation processes had been completed in such countries as the Czech Republic (from $5.2 billion in 2002 to $1.7 billion in 2003), Poland (from $3.1 billion in 2002 to $0.8 billion in 2003), Slovakia (from $3.3 billion in 2002 to $0.2 billion in 2003), and Slovenia (from $1.5 billion in 2002 to $0.01 billion in 2003) as Figure 17.5 shows.

When analysing the above-mentioned figures related to M&A in various years, one should remember that they depend to a large extent on the privatisation offer at a given time. It may happen that in a given year an attractive industry, sector or company is being privatised in one country, a fact that increases the inflow of capital to that country at the expense of reduced investments in other countries. Privatisation in Poland serves as an example of this. Between 1991 and 2004 over 50 per cent of income from privatisation came from transactions involving foreign investors (see Table 17.3).

Although the average ratio of foreign investors' share in Polish privatisation in that period was 51.94 per cent, there were years when it hovered around 15 per cent, as well as years when it exceeded 70 per cent (1999, 2001 and 2002). A record-breaking year came in 2000 when over $5 billion out of $6.2 billion of privatisation income came from foreign entities, and when nearly a half of all foreign investments were in the form of M&A. As can be seen in Table 17.4, such a large share of foreign investors in the Polish privatisation process between 1999 and 2002 was a consequence of the sale of very attractive companies, including Telekomunikacja Polska SA (telecommunications), Pekao SA (banking) or PZU SA (insurance). In contrast, in 2004 the share of foreign investors in privatisation income did not exceed 10 per cent, which is a result of the fact that over 97 per cent

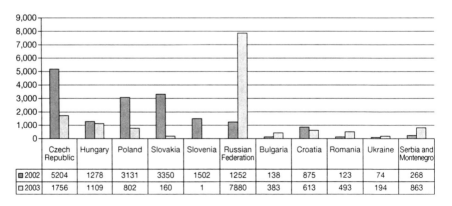

	Czech Republic	Hungary	Poland	Slovakia	Slovenia	Russian Federation	Bulgaria	Croatia	Romania	Ukraine	Serbia and Montenegro
2002	5204	1278	3131	3350	1502	1252	138	875	123	74	268
2003	1756	1109	802	160	1	7880	383	613	493	194	863

Figure 17.5 M&A in selected CEE countries, 2002–3 (US$ million)

Source: Compiled by the authors from UNCTAD (2004).

Table 17.3 Foreign share in privatisation revenues in Poland, 1991–2004
(US$ million)

Year	Privatisation revenues	Foreign investors share in privatisation revenues	3:2 (in %)	Total FDI	3:5 (in %)
1	2	3	4	5	6
1991	170.9	95.4	55.8	–	–
1992	372.7	214.7	57.6	–	–
1993	433.6	190.2	43.9	2.830	6.7
1994	724.9	107.0	14.8	1.491	7.2
1995	1,100.6	540.7	49.1	2.510	21.5
1996	1,442.2	395.3	27.4	5.197	7.6
1997	2,043.0	505.6	24.6	5.678	8.9
1998	2,079.0	322.0	15.5	9.574	3.4
1999	3,422.4	2,648.9	77.4	7.891	33.6
2000	6,263.1	5,114.1	81.7	10.601	48.5
2001	1,666.0	1,288.1	77.3	7.147	18.0
2002	702.6	498.8	71.0	6.064	8.1
2003	1,065.2	432.4	40.6	6.420	13.2
2004	2,806.2	261.8	9.3	–	–
Total	24,292.5	12,617.3	51.9	–	–

Sources: Compiled by the authors from *Privatisation Quarterly* (January–December 2004); MSP (2005).

of privatisation transactions went through public offering, addressed first of all at individual and not institutional investors.

An increased inflow of M&A investments in a given year does not mean that the tendency will be maintained in subsequent years – privatisation reserves diminish with time and this is why it is so important for countries to be prepared early enough to attract green-field investments that could alleviate the decreased inflow of privatisation investments and could counteract the fall in the total number of investments attracted by a given country. This is a problem that countries such as the Czech Republic and Slovakia are facing at the moment. They have attracted important investors from the automotive industry (Toyota-PSA in the Czech Republic and Hyundai-Kia in Slovakia), but the first effects of those investments will be felt only after a few years when the plants now being built will start operating.

The fact that privatisation reserves are drying up almost simultaneously also in other countries of the region (e.g. in Poland and Hungary) leads to a situation in which these countries start competing against each other to attract green-field investments. In 2004, for instance, Poland and Slovakia competed for the French Peugeot-Citroen and the Korean Hyundai-Kia. As a result, investors receive increasingly favourable conditions for their

Table 17.4 Largest privatisations in Poland involving foreign investors (US$ billion)

Year	Company	Investors	Country of origin	Value of transaction	Sector of investment
2000	Telekomunikacja Polska SA	France Telecom Kulczyk Holding	France Poland	4,290.35	Telecommunications
1999	Pekao SA	Uni Creadito Italiano/ Alianz	Italy	1,087.20	Banking
2001	Telekomunikacja Polska SA	France Telecom Kulczyk Holding	France Poland	894.58	Telecommunications
1999	PZU SA	Eureko BV Big Bank Gdański SA	Holland Poland	773.85	Insurance
1999	Bank Zachodni SA	AIB European Investments	Ireland	584.62	Banking
2004	PKO BP SA	Inwestorzy instytucjonalni	Inter- national	562.10	Banking
2002	Stoen SA	RWE Plus AG	Germany	370.16	Energy
1998	Polfa Poznań SA	GlaxoGroup Limited	Great Britain	226.57	Pharmaceutical
1996	Zakłady Przemysłu Tytoniowego SA	Philip Morris Holland BV	Holland	222.98	Tobacco

Source: Compiled by the authors from MSP (2005).

businesses in the form of financial incentives (including cash incentives), tax relief, local tax exemptions, adaptation of the infrastructure to their needs or the most attractive locations for their investments. The scale of these incentives can be seen in the competition between Poland and Slovakia for the $1.5 billion investment of the Korean company. In order to attract this investor, the Polish side offered to: place the investment in Kobierzyce a town located on the A4 expressway and not far from Poland–Germany and Poland–Czech Republic border crossings; build a special railway and a siding on the plot offered to the investor as well as a new section of road connecting it with the A4 expressway; exempt the investment from income tax under the special economic zone rule; provide a financial grant (for purposes including creation of new jobs) of around €140 million, €80 million of which were cash incentives; exempt the investment from property and local tax; provide around €5 million from local authorities for personnel training; and finally, provide formal and legal assistance during the implementation of the project (including preparation of the geological report already for the negotiation stage, preparation of meteorological report, a report on the development of the automotive sector in Poland, a report on the capability of absorbing EU funds and a report on the Polish trade unions).

Role and significance of foreign privatisation acquisitions

In every economy privatisation of state-owned enterprises carries with it a number of consequences, economic as well as social, political and environmental. The consequences can be both positive and negative, and their character and scope do not depend solely on the foreign investor (its strategy for entering a particular market; strategy for functioning in this market, investment plans for the acquired company; ways and rules of including this company in the system of capital, trade or service structures within the corporation; or the product offered), but also on the state selling the company (the country's ability to attract this particular investor, its management of financial resources obtained from privatisation, its ability to negotiate favourable provisions in the privatisation agreement with respect to investment, social, employee or environmental commitments, and then its ability to enforce those provisions).

When analysed from the point of view of the investors who chose M&A as their investment strategy to enter the CEE market, privatisation of key industries and sectors of the economy (such as banking, insurance, energy, oil, telecommunications), including, in particular, the biggest, the most important flagship companies, creates an opportunity for entering the given market that is relatively quick and less risky than it is in the case of greenfield investments, though on the other hand, it is in most cases also relatively capital-intensive. By taking over a company through privatisation acquisition, the foreign company takes over all its strengths, such as a well-known brand name, years of tradition, a ready market for its products, its customers with their devotion and loyalty, the distribution network, and sub-suppliers and buyers. Therefore, it does not have to build all this potential from scratch, risking at the same time that its idea for a business in a new market governed by its own rules (still little known despite the application of the investor's capital and experiences up to that point) will not work. That investors take these elements into account is confirmed by the results of a study carried out in Poland on the participation of foreign investors in privatisation of state-owned enterprises. The results show very clearly that foreign entities are interested mainly in large companies operating in the same or similar sectors, located in big urban areas, and with relatively stable domestic and eastern markets for their products (MSP 2004).

Another argument in favour of such a strategy of winning CEE markets is the fact privatisation reserves are running out in those countries, and the fact that in some sectors with a monopolistic or oligopolistic competition structure (such as the telecommunications, fuel and energy sectors) the offering is limited to one or a few companies. If the foreign investor does not accept the offer at the particular moment, this will mean that the investor, if, of course, still interested in that particular market, will have to penetrate it by using other forms of internationalisation (such as export or sale of licences) or by building the company from scratch. On the other hand, adapting an existing company to the investor's needs, a company with all its production infrastructure, existing distribution and supply systems, and employed personnel, requires the new owner to restructure and modernise it, which often not only consumes a lot of capital and time, but also requires unpopular decisions that meet with opposition in the local community, decisions including job cuts. What is more, privatisation very often involves the adoption by the foreign investor of a so-called social package, such as a package that guarantees a level of employment for a specific period (even up to ten years), introduces compensations for people who will be laid off, maintains the current system of salaries, guarantees one-off bonuses (the so-called privatisation bonuses), and offers a suitable system of training and qualifications improvement (see Table 17.5). Starting a business operation from scratch allows the investor to avoid these and other costs, but at the same time it limits the benefits mentioned above.

Table 17.5 Elements of the social package in selected privatisation processes in Poland

Privatisation date	Polish company	Foreign investor	Social package
2000	Elektrownia Połaniec SA	Electrabel	Employment guaranteed for at least 10 years after the signing of the agreement
2001	Elektrownia Rybnik SA	Electricité de France International Energie Baden-Württemberg AG	Employment guaranteed for 6 years after the signing of the agreement
1995	Firma Oponiarska Dębica SA	The Goodyear Tire & Rubber Company	Pay guarantees, payment of privatisation bonus, training and retraining of personnel
1998	Polfa Poznań	Glaxo Wellcome	Employment guaranteed for 4 years after the signing of the agreement
2000	Górnośląski Zakład Elektronergetyczny	Vattenfall	Employment and pay guarantees, social and health care guarantees, payment of privatisation bonus

Source: Compiled by the authors from MSP (2005).

Foreign investors bring various benefits to companies in whose privatisation they take part. This is mainly due to restructuring and modernisation consistently carried out in those companies. In privatisation agreements foreign investors commit themselves to increasing the capital of the company, earmarking specific sums for investments, including investments in environmental protection, new technologies, licences and modernisation of the machine stock, which were neglected areas during the period of the centrally planned economy. The aim of these and other investors' actions is to modernise privatised companies and raise their competitiveness and attractiveness. Taking into account the fact that no company operates in isolation, the positive changes taking place in companies privatised with the participation of foreign investors will also trigger off changes both in the companies with which they compete and in those with which they cooperate. In the case of cooperating entities the influence of investors leads to a situation when the suppliers, if they want to continue the cooperation, are willing to change the conditions of their production or provision of services, in order to meet the expectations of their customers as best as possible, expectations related to specific quality standards, the use of specific materials, and the delivery of specific components or semi-finished products within a strictly specified time limit.

What is decisive in the case of competing companies is the so-called competition effect. Usually the foreign investor can offer a product of higher quality and usefulness at a similar price. Thus it threatens the existence of domestic companies, which are forced to improve and modernise their products in order to withstand growing competition and remain on the market. What is more, such a strong competitive pressure on the part of the investors makes domestic firms merge with other entities (as equal partners or through the takeover of one company by another). Such a strategy is based on the conviction that the potential of a single entity is not enough to compete successfully with large transnational corporations.

What is also important when it comes to investors influencing domestic companies is the so-called demonstration effect – regardless of how much the foreign investor will try to protect its technology, know-how or other competitive advantages, in the end it will always want to present its product and place it on the market. Domestic producers get a clear signal that such a product exists, they have an opportunity to see its features and, what is more, they receive information on the demand for this product on the market. This effect is also closely connected to another phenomenon, referred to as *learning by watching*, when the foreign investors' knowledge and technological experience is imitated by domestic producers (Hildebrandt 2003: 34–5).

Restructuring and modernisation of privatised companies that extend additionally to rival and cooperating companies can therefore lead to modernisation and development of whole industries or sectors, and contribute to the development of not only the cities in which the companies are located, but also – through the spill-over effect described earlier – whole regions. The changes in various sectors and regions of particular countries will in turn contribute to the improvement of the competitiveness of the economy of the host country as a whole. Yet the spill-over of the foreign investor's influence onto neighbouring regions may have negative consequences as well, especially when there are marked differences between those regions (i.e. the region where the investor operates and the neighbouring region) with respect to the level of development. A more dynamic development of a company supported by foreign capital may cause the most valuable capital, material and human resources 'sucked out' of the weaker region. If this process lasts relatively long, its very likely consequence will be a further deepening of the disparities between regions and their eradication may with time turn out to be extremely difficult (Nowicki 2003: 21).

This problem is highlighted especially in CEE countries, in which there are considerable differences in the level of development between the regions of one country. In Poland this is referred to as 'Poland A', which is the western part of the country characterised by high level of urbanisation and industrialisation, and 'Poland B', which is the eastern regions mainly agricultural in their character. This is in a way a legacy of the centrally planned economy, in which the location of enterprises was not decided by market conditions (such as proximity to the supply sources and markets, suitable infrastructure, labour costs, qualified personnel, and communication availability), but by the government's political will. Currently, all CEE countries make a great effort to eliminate existing differences, by actions including attracting investors for weaker regions or creating special economic zones, in which investors (foreign and domestic) in exchange for starting their operations, measured by investment outlays and the number of new jobs, receive reliefs and preferential treatment (mainly fiscal). Joining the European Union in 2004 made some CEE countries eligible for funding from structural funds earmarked for the development of underdeveloped regions.

The investors' activity also affects the functioning of the local community. Companies that manage, through changes they have introduced, to function effectively on the market also support actions that, although not directly connected with their activity, are important for the local community. Thus they sponsor various sporting and cultural events, assist sports clubs, fund scholarships for talented youth and children who would otherwise be unable to study, or cooperate very closely with scientific and academic centres. Together with universities offering courses in subjects relevant to the company's activity, the investors organise traineeships for students, assist students in writing their theses (often inviting the best of them to take part in the company's logistic, technological or quality management projects), and they take part in research carried out by post-graduate students and young scientists. It is usually foreign capital that initiates the implementation of new systems in companies, research into new fields, and the promotion of new technological and technical solutions.

Obviously, the involvement of a foreign investor in the privatisation of a specific company does not mean an automatic improvement of its financial and economic standing, and an increase of its development potential. The development of a given company requires the difficult process of restructuring, which is connected with increased demands towards personnel, necessity for some employees to change their qualifications or improve their professional qualifications, or even with job cuts. According to the latest estimates, the number of jobs in some Polish companies privatised with the participation of foreign investors has fallen as much as four times (see Figure 17.6).

Jobs are not always cut after the social package inscribed in the privatisation agreement expires. In the majority of companies, redundancies take place within programmes of voluntary leave, which prepare the employees who leave for new jobs and guarantee them substantial financial compensation that the investor would not have to pay after the social package expired. An example of such an approach is the Polish company GlaxoSmith Kline Pharmaceuticals SA where shortly before the social package expired (it was in effect from 1998 to 2002) over 300 employees were laid off (for a comparison, in 2004 the company employed around 700 people in total) and were paid financial compensation that amounted to 15–17 monthly salaries (MSP 2004). In the case of Elektrownia Połaniec (Połaniec Power Plant) over 800 employees (out of 2,400) took advantage of a voluntary leave programme, with each of them receiving on average around PLN100,000 or around €25,000 (Świderek 2005). And although laid off workers receive substantial financial compensation (the average Polish salary in the sector was around PLN2,400 or around €600), such actions have a negative impact on the local job market and the local community as families thus lose one (often even the only one) source of income.

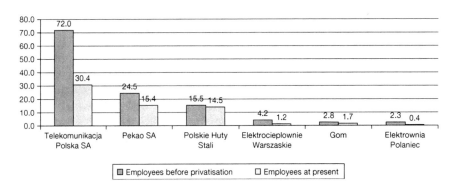

Figure 17.6 Job cuts in selected Polish companies privatised with the involvement of foreign investors (thousands of people)

Source: Świderek (2005).

Companies' market position and economies' technological potential

Privatisation of state-owned companies, including privatisation in which foreign investors take part, may be of crucial importance for the company. Thanks to this type of process the use of all of the company's assets is rationalised, the economic potential is better used, and the company gets a chance of further development. A well-prepared privatisation consistently carried out may have a significant impact on the company's position on the market. In the case of foreign investors who decide to acquire another company and include it in their added value chain, this strengthening can be not only national (i.e. related to the domestic market of the privatised company), but also international or even transnational.

This is was happened with the privatisation of a Polish tyre manufacturer, Stomil Dębica SA, when over 30 per cent of its shares were bought by Goodyear Tire & Rubber Company in December 1995 for $55.1 billion. The company is now functioning as Tyre Company Dębica SA and the foreign investor has a stake of over 50 per cent in it. Attracting one of the biggest companies in the industry as an investor meant not only financial resources necessary for the company's development, and access to modern technologies and research and development (R&D) centres, but also the necessity of implementing thorough changes in order to adapt the plant to the standards binding in the whole concern. The changes covered almost all areas of the company's activity, beginning with the organisational structure, through finances, trade, and ending with investments in launching the production of new types of tyres. At present, TC Dębica SA is the biggest of Goodyear's 15 companies in Europe and the third largest factory among the 85 all over the world. It is the leader on the Polish market in the production of tyres for delivery vans and cars, producing tyres not only under its own brand name, but also under Goodyear, Dunlop or Fulda. Such a dynamic growth of output and product range was also reflected in a growth of exports: in 2003 around 80 per cent of tyres produced in Dębica were exported (MSP 2004). TC Dębica SA's achievements have been recognised in numerous competitions and the company has received many awards related both to the quality of its products (five-time winner of the Gold Medal of the Poznań International Fairs between 1996 and 2000), and directly to its position on the market: the title 'Best Firm of the Year' (1996), 'Outstanding Polish Exporter' (1997), 'Golden Yen' prize for innovativeness (1998).

Equally dynamic was the growth of the Czech car company Skoda. In April 1991, this company with over a century-old tradition of car manufacturing (the first car was produced in 1905 although the beginnings of the company go further back to 1895) became the fourth part of the international Volkswagen Group, after Volkswagen, Audi and SEAT. Such a strong partner made it possible for Skoda to introduce all the necessary changes to enable rationalisation and general restructuring of the company.

The main goals at the time were the quality improvement, broadening of the product range, creation of distribution network and rebuilding of the Skoda brand's image. After a few years Skoda Auto won a strong position not only on the domestic market (it is the biggest Czech exporter with over 7 per cent market share), but also on the international market. It has four branches (in Slovakia, Germany, Poland and India), operates actively on nearly 90 markets all over the world, and generates around 85 per cent of its sales profits from transitions outside its native Czech Republic. Western Europe has the biggest share in the sale of Skoda cars, receiving over 50 per cent of the company output (Germany is Skoda Auto's biggest export market), followed by Central European countries with almost 20 per cent, around 7 per cent to Eastern Europe (mainly Russia and the Ukraine), and the remaining markets, mainly Asia with India and Turkey being the biggest customers (Skoda Auto 2004).

These examples of privatisation acquisitions show that from the point of view of the country receiving a foreign direct investor and of the company that is the subject of the acquisition, the most desirable are pro-export investments, that is those in which the acquired company becomes not only a supplier for the domestic market, but also part of the foreign investor's international distribution network. In order for this to happen, the products the company offers have to be adapted to the requirements of the global market. That is why the period of export expansion is always preceded by thorough transformations of production organisation, its quality and product range. If complete success is to be achieved, the markets of highly developed countries have to have a relatively bigger share in the sales, because then the product will have to meet standards higher than those for less demanding markets. Investments of this type have a positive impact also on the country's economy as a whole – their pro-export character contributes to the growth of the country's export sales. Foreign investors do make purchases for the needs of the production outside the country in which the investment is located (for example, this is a result of centralisation of purchases made for the needs of the whole concern, or various functions performed by various companies within a group), yet this process is not as detrimental as it is in the case of foreign investors producing only for the needs of the local market, importing subassemblies, semi-finished products and components.

When analysing FDIs in CEE countries in the form of privatisation acquisitions, also the impact of those investments on the technological potential of the investigated economies should be assessed. In the case of Poland, there is interesting information on production technologies used by foreign investors in Polish production plants (i.e. plants they acquired through privatisation) in a study carried out in 2001 by Joanna Kotowicz-Jawor and others of the Instytut Nauk Ekonomicznych Polskiej Akademii Nauk (Institute of Economic Sciences of the Polish Academy of Sciences). The report, entitled 'Influence of foreign direct investments on structural changes within companies', shows that following the acquisition of the companies in question by foreign capital, there was an improvement in their innovativeness, but, as the authors emphasise, only 'some improvement' because new production technologies were introduced in only little over a half of the studied companies (56.7 per cent). In over one-third of those companies (36.7 per cent) no new technologies were introduced, and the production was continued on the basis of the already existing machines and facilities.

In addition to implementing innovative projects, an equally important element in the company's development strategy is planning investment projects, including those that lead to the improvement of the production technology. In the analysed cases the researchers note that for 2001, apart from classic innovative actions, such as computerisation of production processes or technological and construction changes in those processes, the companies also planned pro-environmental actions, including the improvement of the energy-saving index, and the purchase of facilities for utilisation of waste products. Whether those initiatives will be implemented and what their effects will be is difficult to say, but a positive element of such companies' activities in Poland lies in the fact that these companies, or at least a vast majority of them, do take into account environmental issues. It is all the more important because such strategies – based on the idea of environmentally friendly development – are alien to many Polish enterprises.

Another significant conclusion of the report is that for the vast majority of the analysed companies (73.3 per cent), acquisition by a foreign investor increased their access to state-of-the-art technologies, and thus, at least potentially, access to much more innovative production methods and techniques. According to interviewees, this is manifest on two levels: first in increased capability of financing purchase of technologies, and second, in the use of knowledge and experiences of parent corporations in production processes. Conversely, the hypothesis that international corporations with production plants in this part of Europe provide them with old production technologies was difficult to verify. While there is not a vast majority of foreign investors following such practices, nor is it true that most of them do not do it, and the truth seems to be lying somewhere in the middle. In nearly 50 per cent of the companies foreign machines and equipment used in production are 'second-hand' (mostly machines previously used in other plants of the same international corporation). It does not, however, mean that they are all technologically obsolete, depending on the age of machines and the degree of their innovativeness. While many technologies brought to CEE countries are past their prime, in most cases they are still more modern than the production methods used in those companies before. We can conclude, therefore, that although previously used machines and equipment are indeed transferred to CEE, the statement that all are outdated production technologies is a simplification of the problem. It would be better to say that among the 'older' technologies imported to the CEE countries there are technologies whose level of innovativeness is very low. However, this is not – as some people suggest – the rule.

Still, within privatisation processes we may encounter situations in which the foreign investor is not interested in the development of the acquired company, but will want to limit its operation, and in some cases even wind it up completely. This usually happens when the investor takes part in the privatisation of rival companies, or when they decide to acquire a stake in a company whose profile does not correspond to the profile of the whole concern, but which has other assets, such as an attractive location or close contacts with the scientific community and universities that make it possible to launch research in an area that the investor is interested in.

Green-field investments

The gradual drying up of privatisation reserves in the CEE countries – one of the major motives of FDI inflow – increasingly makes these countries undertake actions to attract investors willing to build companies from scratch and provide them with the necessary material and human capital. A particularly dynamic growth in this type of investment could be witnessed in the 1990s when over a period of eight years (1991–8) the value of investments launched each year increased 12 times, from $1.5 billion to nearly $20 billion. After this period green-field investments fell by almost half (in 2000 they amounted to just over $10 billion). This was a result of the FDI market domination by M&A investments as in that period countries of this region privatised important sectors and industries (see Figure 17.7).

In comparison with privatisation acquisitions, green-field investments enable the investor to create a company fully adapted to its needs and expectations, beginning with the choice of location, through the size of the facility, installation of processing and production lines, storage systems, and ending

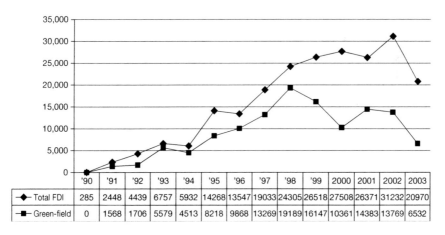

	'90	'91	'92	'93	'94	'95	'96	'97	'98	'99	2000	2001	2002	2003
Total FDI	285	2448	4439	6757	5932	14268	13547	19033	24305	26518	27508	26371	31232	20970
Green-field	0	1568	1706	5579	4513	8218	9868	13269	19189	16147	10361	14383	13769	6532

Figure 17.7 Green-field investment in CEE, 1990–2003 (US$ million)

Source: Compiled by authors from UNCTAD (2004).

with the choice of personnel without the necessity to guarantee any social packages. Such an investment strategy is characteristic for, among others, Japanese corporations that recently have decided to enter CEE markets (mainly Poland, the Czech Republic and Hungary). Actually, it would be hard to point out privatisation processes in which Japanese companies were taking part, not to mention the finalisation of such transactions. This is mainly a result of their unfamiliarity with the market, especially with enterprises on sale, with their brands, products, potential, development perspectives, and with a different management and organisational culture. According to the Japanese, a much better and, first of all, much more effective solution is to create a completely new organisation of work on the basis of their own, proven management techniques – even if it means taking a huge risk – rather than trying to rebuild an already existing structure. In addition, in order to optimise operating costs, including labour costs, Japanese companies never allow the salaries in their overseas investments to exceed the level of the average salary in a given country. Thus, by opting for green-field investments, they avoid taking on commitments related to maintaining or even raising the level of pay, as is the case in privatisation acquisitions.

On the other hand, these advantages may just as well become major barriers in the investment process. Usually, attractive locations in the vicinity of transport routes, supply sources and ready markets are extremely expensive and not always possible to acquire. What is more, this type of investment involves the necessity to fulfil all administrative requirements, including various kinds of construction permits, which may be an important problem if the investor has limited or no knowledge of provisions existing in a given country. It may also happen that an attractive location is in a region that lacks all the other elements, such as a properly qualified workforce, and proximity to suppliers and customers.

Building a company from scratch also means typically market-related problems. What is necessary is the time for creating the company not only in its material dimension (buildings, machines and facilities, access roads, etc.), but also in its organisational dimension: placing the product on the market; creating a suitable distribution (and supply) network; building up the product's brand; creating the company's image; and presenting it to all market stakeholders (customers, but also potential partners and suppliers). All this requires the investor to be very familiar with the market conditions in the country and to be able to function on this particular market. This is extremely important because although we are living in the age of globalisation, national markets still differ in certain areas, which may have a strategic value from the point of view of a particular investment. Linguistic blunders illustrate this. When a product receives a name used globally in the investor's corporation – a name that may not have any particular meaning in the investor's mother tongue and other foreign markets – it may have a pejorative meaning in the host country, reducing the customers' interest in the product, as happened with the Osram light bulbs in Poland.

The creation of the distribution network can be of crucial importance for the region in which the foreign investor's company functions. If the foreign investor decides to include domestic suppliers in its network, then it is highly probable that positive elements of the investment will be transferred to these domestic entities through the spillover effect. What is more, by attracting such a significant partner, the domestic companies, which are usually smaller, may get a great chance to develop and expand economically. This in turn leads to the creation of new jobs, investments in fixed assets, revenue for the state budget, etc. In the majority of cases, however, the investors use their own suppliers and not the domestic suppliers. On the one hand, this may be a consequence of the corporation's strategy and the division of functions among various organisational units, one of which is the global (or regional) supply centre from which materials, components and semi-finished products are delivered to various plants all over the world. For the host country this means not only losses related to lack of growth of domestic companies, but also negative impact on foreign trade turnover. On the other hand, such an approach may result from the trust in and loyalty to current suppliers that follow their clients (i.e. the investors), with the positive effect of one investment attracting another.

Organisation of the supply and distribution networks is directly linked to the problem of the foreign investors' impact on the host country's trade balance. If their import activity (supplies from outside the host country) is on a large scale and, additionally, exceeds exports (which in extreme cases may not exist at all), then the investors will contribute to trade deficit, which has an adverse impact also on the internal balance. An assessment of the impact of the foreign investors on the trade balance cannot be distorted by the fact that most of them are significant exporters from the point of view of the host country; for instance, exports of Opel, Audi and Suzuki constitute 17 per cent of Hungary's total exports. However, in order to get the full picture of the importance of these companies to the Hungarian economy, we would have to compare those figures with the companies' imports.

Green-field investments and technology

A key element of every green-field investment process is the provision of a broadly defined technological capital (machines, equipment, the knowledge necessary to operate them, patent, brands) to the newly created company. In the majority of cases newly installed production lines are modern and use state-of-the-art technical knowledge. This modernity may, however, have two dimensions. First, the machines and equipment may be highly innovative in comparison with those used in the given corporation or even industry as a whole. The activities of the Volvo Group in Poland serve as an example here. Between 1996 and 2000 the management decided to spend around

$50 million to locate in this part of Europe the biggest and at the same time the most advanced plant for the production of buses. To this end, the plant was equipped with state-of-the-art technical and technological solutions that were the results of R&D work carried out in research centres in Sweden. In addition, within its organisational structure, a Product Development Department and a Product Engineering Department were created, apart from such traditional departments as production, supply or sales. As a result, the Wrocław plant produces today (on the basis of five production lines over an area of around 40,000 km^2) some of the most modern buses in the world, offering them not only to the domestic but also to foreign customers – over 85 per cent of the production goes to Western European markets, including Sweden, Germany, Austria, France and Switzerland, markets that are very demanding with respect to both quality and environmental standards. A measure of modernity, and thus technological innovativeness, of the buses offered by Volvo Polska is the fact that the buses are equipped with Euro 3 diesel engines, which meet the strictest environmental standards when it comes to exhaust gas emission (at the moment work is under way on the implementation of the Euro 4 standards), and natural gas engines (Volvo 7000 CNG model). In addition, the production of these buses is based on the same TX-type platform that is the most advanced achievement of the Volvo Group, enabling it to generate numerous benefits on the level of production and the market.

Second, technologies introduced by the foreign investor may be more advanced than those used in domestic companies of the host country, but not than those used in other plants belonging to the investor, a situation that arises when one plant is wound up and the production is transferred to another country (for various reasons) together with the plant's machine stock. Countries undergoing transformation are interested in attracting investment that will guarantee the use of state-of-the-art technologies, yet it has to be emphasised that even when modern but not the most advanced solutions are used, green-field investments do contribute to the technological development of those economies.

An investment of this type does not, however, always mean transfer of new technologies. Guided by various considerations (e.g. lower environmental standards, less demanding market, lower quality of products offered, placing a new version of the product on the parent market and at the same time transferring of older products to less demanding markets) the investor may decide to transfer technologies that are not innovative at all, and, in extreme cases, can even be outdated. Such an approach was characteristic for some car manufacturers who invested in CEE in the early 1990s. While most developed countries had already banned the production and sale of cars without catalytic converters, in CEE those companies still produced and sold cars that did not meet such standards. This shows that in the period analysed here, this part of Europe had more liberal conditions in the production and sale of cars. This problem was particularly relevant with respect to environmental protection. Some even talked about a kind of environmental neocolonialism: the transfer of so-called dirty technologies because of lower environmental standards.

The problem of technology transfer to the host country is closely connected with the issue of the creation of R&D units in those companies. Obviously, the most desirable investments are those within which local R&D centres are established for the needs of the newly created production plant. The strategy of creating a company together with an R&D centre has a positive impact not only on the plant itself, which can directly absorb the results of research and influence the direction and scope of the research according to its needs, but also on the plant's environment. This applies first of all to local R&D centres that become involved in the research, and to local universities whose graduates find work in those centres, as illustrated by the investments of the French company Valeo in the Czech Republic. Valeo specialises in the design, manufacturing and sale of parts and modules for cars and trucks of such companies as Renault, Peugeot, Citroen, General Motors, and many others. An important element of this investment was the creation of an R&D centre in Prague that employed local personnel (highly qualified graduates of technical universities) and to which Valeo transferred some of its research. What is more, not only do Valeo plants in the Czech Republic use the results of this centre's work, but also so do the plants in Western Europe.

Some positive elements of the work of local R&D centres working for foreign investors can also be found in their contacts with key suppliers, who become acquainted with research projects or their parts that directly apply to them (such as the use of new materials in the production of semi-finished products and subassemblies, novel construction and design solutions). Competitors with whom these suppliers cooperate or may potentially cooperate, however, do not often practise this, because of the necessity of protecting intellectual property against illegal use.

From the point of view of the host economy, a definite advantage that green-field investments have over privatisation acquisitions is the creation of new jobs. While in privatisation acquisitions the investor employs the personnel of the acquired company, in the case of green-field investments the investor employs new workers, including people who have been unemployed up to that moment. What is more, acquisitions are often accompanied by considerable job cuts, which have a negative impact on local job markets, a feature that does not characterise green-field investments. This is especially important for the CEE countries, which cope with high unemployment rates. However, the role and significance of green-field investments in the activation of local job markets should not be overestimated. The newly created plants are highly modern and, consequently, the production processes are to a large extent automated. As a result, few people are employed in the new plants in comparison to the number of those that seek jobs. Also, people employed in the new plants frequently come from outside the investment location, which means that the investment has absolutely no impact on the local community. This phenomenon is all the more negative given the fact that regions that want to attract investors are mainly the least prosperous ones, and the regional authorities see investments as chances for their region's development. They offer potential employers numerous concessions and preferences, and the region that benefits from the investment is not theirs, but the one from which new employees come. This problem has been highlighted by, for instance, special economic zones in Poland. Local authorities in those areas openly accuse foreign investors of not fulfilling the obligations related to the number of jobs and of attracting new employees from outside the host region.

Conclusion

This review of the impact of FDIs on the economies of the countries in CEE clearly shows that virtually every element can be either positive or negative and it is difficult to make any generalisations in this respect. Even similar investments, with similar financial outlays, similar profiles, or a similar degree of innovativeness can influence local environment in a variety of ways. Whether they are green-field or an M&A investment does not matter. Assessments should thus be made on the level of an individual company and its direct and indirect influence on the job market, domestic firms, the volume of foreign trade, and the transfer of technologies.

The scale of the positive or negative impact of foreign investors depends to a large extent on the ability of local and national governments to direct the investors' operations in such a way that they will not ignore the needs and expectations of the local community when carrying out their own objectives and plans. This problem affects the CEE countries in particular, as they are very determined to attract investors, especially those that represent modern production centres. When it comes to such investors, these countries are willing to make substantial concessions, without receiving, in return, any guarantees that all investment promises will be fulfilled, such as promises related both to investment outlays and to employment.

Summing up, if we take into account the needs of the CEE countries related to transformation of their economies, these countries should try to attract investors that are willing to use state-of-the-art technologies; conduct extensive research; establish contacts with local companies; create distribution networks; keep the current jobs and create new ones; support initiatives that are important for local communities; and contribute to a growth of exports of the host country. Investments that fulfil all these requirements would be optimal for these countries, though in practice they are very rare. It seems that pro-export green-field investments are closest to this model.

Bibliography

Hildebrandt, Anna (2003) *Profil wrażliwości gospodarki regionalnej na integrację z Unią Europejską. Województwo dolnośląskie*, Gdańsk: Instytut Badań nad Gospodarką Rynkową.

Kotowicz-Jawor, Joanna (2001) 'Inwestycje, innowacje i majątek trwały', *Gospodarka Narodowa*, 5–6.

MSP (2004) 'Wybrane procesy prywatyzacje z udziałem inwestorów zagranicznych', Ministry of the Treasury, Republic of Poland, Department of European Integration and Foreign Relations, Warsaw, www.msp.gov.pl.

—— (2005) *Privatisation Quarterly*, January–December 2004, Ministry of the Treasury, Republic of Poland, Department of European Integration and Foreign Relations, Warsaw, www.msp.gov.pl.

Nowicki Marcin (2003) *Jak integracja z Unią Europejską wpłynie na polskie regiony?*, Gdańsk: Instytut Badań nad Gospodarką Rynkową.

Skoda Auto (2004) *Annual Report*, www.skoda-auto.com.

Świderek Tomasz (2005) 'Redukują zatrudnieni, by obniżyć koszty', *Rzeczpospolita*, 29 January 2005.

UNCTAD (1996) *World Investment Report 1996: Investment, Trade and International Policy Arrangements*, New York and Geneva: United Nations.

—— (2001) *World Investment Report 2001: Promoting Linkages*, New York and Geneva: United Nations.

—— (2002) *World Investment Report 2002: Transnational Corporations and Export Competitiveness*, New York and Geneva: United Nations.

—— (2003) *World Investment Report 2003: FDI Policies for Development: National and International Perspectives*, New York and Geneva: United Nations.

—— (2004) *World Investment Report 2004: The Shift Towards Services*, New York and Geneva: United Nations.

Index

References to relevant figures and tables are in *italic* type. References to notes follow the page number and the letter 'n', e.g. 26n2.